Fourth Edition

ACCOUNTING THEORY

Eldon S. Hendriksen
Professor of Business Administration
University of Santa Clara

1982  RICHARD D. IRWIN, INC.
Homewood, Illinois   60430

ISBN 0-256-02588-6

Library of Congress Catalog Card No. 81–84837

Printed in the United States of America

3 4 5 6 7 8 9 0 MP 9 8 7 6 5 4

PREFACE

This fourth edition is designed to provide a frame of reference for junior, senior, and graduate courses in financial accounting and financial accounting theory; seminars on financial accounting standards and issues; and seminars on the theory of income and asset valuation. Those who wish to obtain a good understanding of financial accounting standards or want a general survey of financial accounting theory and those who wish to study for the theory section of the Uniform CPA Examination should find this book useful. The assumption is made that the reader has a knowledge of the basic structure of accounting. Experience has shown, however, that mature students who have not studied accounting can understand the subject matter with concurrent additional formal or independent study of this basic structure. A background in finance or economics can also lead into this book.

A general frame of reference has been continued to evaluate the many areas of financial accounting theory and practice. The frame of reference includes a number of theories that are not necessarily consistent with each other and that may lead to different conclusions. Evaluations are made at three basic levels: (1) the structural level, including the relationships between and within procedural systems and financial reports; (2) the semantic interpretation level—the relationships of descriptions and measurements to real-world phenomena; and (3) the behavioral level—the reactions of all individuals affected by accounting reports, including users (individually and in capital markets) and producers of accounting information. Emphasis is placed on the inductive-deductive and the capital markets approaches in the evaluations, although other approaches are discussed where appropriate. In some cases, the several viewpoints resulting from the different approaches are criticized without attempting to suggest a solution or the best alternative. In other cases, the author has expressed his view and presented supporting evidence based on a priori logic and empirical findings where available. In all cases, suggested solutions are tentative and subject to change as new evidence becomes available.

The first five chapters of this edition present the general background for the development of accounting theories. These include a chapter on methodology, a chapter on the development of accounting theory, and three chapters on three significant approaches—the inductive-deductive approach, capital markets theories, and individual decision processes. These are followed by a chapter on accounting policy with an emphasis on the setting of financial accounting standards. The next six chapters present the basic framework of accounting theory relating to income determination, cash and funds flows, and the problems of asset measurement and classification. A chapter on the reporting for price changes emphasizes the effect on income determination, but also discusses the problems of asset measurement under conditions of changing prices, including the use of current costs. The fourth section contains six chapters that discuss the applications of accounting theory to the reporting problems of specific asset and liability groups. The final three chapters cover the basic problems of ownership equities and the disclosure of relevant information to investors, creditors, and other interested readers of financial statements.

This edition has as one of its objectives the extension of the discussions to include the many new ideas in accounting theory set forth since the publication of the third edition. Among the basic changes in this edition are (1) two new chapters on capital market theories and individual decision processes, (2) a new chapter on accounting policy, (3) a separate section in Chapter 9 on current costs replacing discussions in several chapters, (4) an evaluation of the FASB conceptual framework project both in general and as it relates to specific concepts and elements, (5) critical evaluations of recent pronouncements of the FASB, (6) an increased emphasis on the history of accounting thought and the development of financial accounting standards, with a reduction of the material on the history of accounting, and (7) the elimination of a few topics of little interest to accomodate new material.

At the close of each chapter is a list of selected readings on specific parts of the chapter. These articles and sections of books have been selected on the basis of their quality, availability, and their ability to present the several sides of current controversial topics. Because of the rapid expansion of the literature relevant to these topics, the selections represent only a sample of those available. Students are encouraged to make use of the many readings available, including those that will become available after the publication of this book. This is particularly true for the capital market theories. Since the material covered in Chapter 4 is extremely brief, students are particularly encouraged to study the basic literature on that topic. There is no substitute for wide reading in the area of accounting theory to obtain an understanding and balanced evaluation of the many different points of view found in the literature.

At the end of the book is a group of questions classified by chapter topics selected from the theory section of the Uniform CPA Examination of recent years and adapted for greater relevancy for use with this book. I wish to express my appreciation to the officers of the American Institute of Certified Public Accountants for their kind permission to reprint these questions.

I wish to express appreciation also to the many students and colleagues who have made comments on the third edition of this book. These have all been most helpful, although for special reasons I may not have incorporated all of the ideas suggested. I am particularly indebted to Robert N. Anthony for general comments on the third edition and for specific comments on the three new chapters of the fourth edition, and to David C. Burns for comments on the new chapters. Most of all, I am indebted to my wife, Kathleen, for her patience and support.

Eldon S. Hendriksen

CONTENTS

CHAPTER 1

INTRODUCTION AND METHODOLOGY OF ACCOUNTING THEORY

Probably the most relevant definition of *theory* as it applies to accounting is that theory represents ". . . the coherent set of hypothetical, conceptual, and pragmatic principles forming the general frame of reference for a field of inquiry."[1] Thus, *accounting theory* may be defined as logical reasoning in the form of a set of broad principles that (1) provide a general frame of reference by which accounting practice can be evaluated and (2) guide the development of new practices and procedures. Accounting theory may also be used to explain existing practices to obtain a better understanding of them. But the most important goal of accounting theory should be to provide a coherent set of logical principles that form the general frame of reference for the evaluation and development of sound accounting practices.

A single general theory of accounting may be desirable, but accounting as a logical and empirical science is still in too primitive a stage for such a development. The best that can be accomplished in this developmental stage is a set of theories (models) and subtheories that may be complementary or competing. By definition, each theory consists of a set of statements or propositions connected by rules of logic or inferential reasoning. The statements must include testable hypotheses or premises and a conclusion, although one or more of the premises may be based on explicit value judgments. The primary test of a theory, however, is its ability to explain or predict. But explanations in the abstract are seldom useful by themselves; they may be used to predict a past or current event, and the verification of that prediction (explanation) serves as at least a partial test of the ability of the theory to predict future events or conditions.

All theories are subject to modification or abandonment with the development of new information or new theories that permit better predictions. The general notion that "what goes up must come down" was drastically modified when objects were shot into space never to return, al-

---

[1] *Webster's Third New International Dictionary, Unabridged* (Springfield, Mass.: G. & C. Merriam, 1961), p. 2371.

1

though the refined theories of gravitational pull had long before predicted such an event. Thus, *predictability* is always a relative term, being improved gradually with the development of better theories and the development of better methods of applying the theories operationally. But the reliability of predictions is frequently difficult to measure because of the behavioral implications of the prediction itself. The prediction of an economic depression may cause the state to take actions to avert the depression, or it may cause individuals to take actions that may actually create or deepen a depression (such as hoarding or panic selling of securities). A theory that could lead to the prediction of business failure could actually bring about such a failure if people believed the prediction. By denying funds to a firm having difficulties, investors and creditors could cause the firm to go into bankruptcy. Accountants are not unaware of this possibility with traditional accounting procedures, and more accurate predictions could even multiply these concerns. Therefore, the ability to predict is not the only consideration in the development of theories in accounting. In most situations, an additional consideration is the ability of the theory to measure risk, or the probability of the prediction being an accurate statement of future events.

LEVELS OF ACCOUNTING THEORY

Although there are several ways of classifying accounting theories, a useful frame of reference is to classify theories according to prediction levels. Three main levels of theory are as follows:

1.   Theories that attempt to explain current accounting practices and predict how accountants would react to certain situations or how they would report specific events. These theories relate to the *structure* of the data collection process and financial reporting (syntactical theories).

2.   Theories that concentrate on the relationship between a phenomenon (object or event) and the term or symbol representing it. These can be referred to as *interpretational* (semantical) theories.

3.   Theories that emphasize the behavioral or decision-oriented effects of accounting reports and statements. These are referred to as *behavioral* (pragmatic) theories.

Theories relating to the accounting structure

Two excellent discussions of the theoretical framework of traditional accounting practice are those of Ijiri[2] and Sterling.[3] Ijiri's model is an at-

---

[2] Yuji Ijiri, *The Foundations of Accounting Measurement: A Mathematical, Economic and Behavioral Inquiry* (Englewood Cliffs, N.J.: Prentice-Hall, 1967).

[3] Robert R. Sterling, "Elements of Pure Accounting Theory," *Accounting Review,* January 1967, pp. 62–73, and Robert R. Sterling and Richard E. Flaherty, "The Role of Liquidity in Exchange Valuation," *Accounting Review,* July 1971, pp. 441–56.

tempt to explain traditional accounting practice; however, he does place emphasis on the historical cost system. Certain deviations, such as the lower of cost or market, are considered anomalies and are not explained by the theory. Sterling attempts to explain "what accountants do when they account," but again most of the discussion is limited to the historical cost system.

Other descriptions of accounting practice include those of Grady,[4] Goldberg;[5] Sanders, Hatfield, and Moore;[6] and Paton and Littleton;[7] however, the last of these was more prescriptive than descriptive at the time of its writing. Grady's study, like that of Sanders, Hatfield, and Moore, is a description of accounting practices thought to be generally accepted. Neither of these can be called a theory of existing practice because they lack the necessary connectives among the premises and statements.

Theories explaining traditional accounting practice are desirable to obtain greater insight into current practice, permit a more precise evaluation of traditional theory, and permit an evaluation of existing practices that do not correspond to traditional theory. Such theories relating to the structure of accounting can be tested for internal logical consistency, or they can be tested to see whether or not they actually can predict what accountants do. A test of the latter type was provided by Sterling, Tollefson, and Flaherty.[8] Their study indicated that, although conventional theory is incomplete, they had identified the relevant variables.

Other theories cannot be tested except to determine whether or not accountants follow precise rules. That is, the rules can be tested, but the concepts cannot because the concepts have no correspondence to the activity of accountants, but rather are reifications of abstract concepts.[9] For example, the term *cost* is treated as if it were a material object in such phrases as "cost flows" and "costs attach."

The effect on reported income or balance sheet amounts, however, can be determined by following through the pattern of the system. For example, the following statement can be tested within the system: "In periods of rising prices, LIFO will tend to result in a lower reported income than FIFO." This can be tested within the system as follows: Except in very unusual circumstances, when prices are rising, inventory computed by

---

[4] Paul Grady, "Inventory of Generally Accepted Accounting Principles for Business Enterprises," *Accounting Research Study No. 7* (AICPA, 1965).

[5] Louis Goldberg, *An Inquiry into the Nature of Accounting*, American Accounting Association Monograph No. 7 (AAA, 1965).

[6] Thomas Henry Sanders, Henry Rand Hatfield, and Underhill Moore, *A Statement of Accounting Principles* (New York: American Institute of Accountants, 1938).

[7] W. A. Paton and A. C. Littleton, *An Introduction to Corporate Accounting Standards*, American Accounting Association Monograph No. 3 (AAA, 1940).

[8] Robert R. Sterling, John O. Tollefson, and Richard E. Flaherty, "Exchange Valuation: An Empirical Test," *Accounting Review*, October 1972, pp. 709–21.

[9] I am indebted to Loyd Heath for the suggestion that the term *reification* is the historical successor to *personification* as a means of explaining accounting procedures. *Reification* refers to the use of concepts as if they were real objects.

the LIFO procedure will be lower than if FIFO is used. Cost of goods sold is computed by subtracting the amount of the ending inventory from the cost of goods available. Income is a product of the system and is computed by subtracting cost of goods sold and other expenses from revenues. Therefore, if the ending inventory is smaller, cost of goods sold is larger and income is smaller. Note, however, that this says nothing about the "truth" value of income, nor the effects of reporting a lower income figure (except possibly for the income tax effects).

Interpretational theories

Particularly by borrowing from economics, accountants have long attempted to find a correspondence between accounting measurements and economic or physical concepts of real-world phenomena. This search has been necessary in order to give some meaning to accounting theory and accounting practice. An accounting structure, although logically formulated, does not convey meaningful interpretations unless the symbols and words representing descriptions or measurements are related empirically to real-world phenomena. Without this relationship, the accounting structure becomes an exercise in circularity without empirical meaning. Particular care must be made to assure that the interpretations of concepts by accountants are the same interpretations made by the users of accounting reports. Therefore, theories relating to interpretations (semantics) are necessary to provide meaning to accounting propositions.

Examples of attempts to interpret accounting concepts in terms of economic concepts and empirical observations can be found in Canning,[10] Sprouse and Moonitz,[11] and Edwards and Bell.[12] Although Canning's emphasis was on providing carefully stated definitions, he did give economic interpretations to his definitions. Sprouse and Moonitz suggest that the best interpretation of asset valuation is that it represents the value of future services. Alternative procedures are then judged with respect to how well they measure this concept. Edwards and Bell give economic interpretations to the concepts of value and profit and suggest how these can be measured operationally. Subsequent to these studies, several empirical research studies have been conducted to show the correspondence between the economic interpretations and measurements obtained from actual data.[13]

In general, accounting concepts are uninterpreted and have no meaning other than as a result of following specific accounting procedures.

---

[10] John B. Canning, *The Economics of Accountancy* (New York: Ronald Press, 1929).

[11] Robert T. Sprouse and Maurice Moonitz, "A Tentative Set of Broad Accounting Principles for Business Enterprises," *Accounting Research Study No. 3* (AICPA, 1962).

[12] Edgar O. Edwards and Philip W. Bell, *The Theory and Measurement of Business Income* (Berkeley and Los Angeles: University of California Press, 1961).

[13] See, for example, Carl R. Beidleman, "Valuation of Used Capital Assets," *Studies in Accounting Research No. 7* (AAA, 1973).

Asset valuation, for example, is generally a figure resulting from the application of such specific accounting procedures as first-in, first-out or the application of straight-line depreciation to historical costs. Accounting income is an artificial concept representing the excess of revenues over expenses after following specific rules for the measurement of these revenues and expenses. It is the realm of accounting theory to give meaningful interpretations to these concepts and evaluate alternative accounting procedures in terms of these interpretations. General concepts, however, frequently cannot be interpreted and are given different meaning by different researchers. *Value,* for example, has no specific interpretation. If we specify *current value,* we are in closer agreement; however, even in this case we must move to subconcepts before we can provide specific rules for interpretation so there is a clear agreement on the interpretation. The concepts of present value of future services, discounted cash flows, current market price, and net realizable value are all subconcepts of current values, and each can then be given specific rules of interpretation.

An example of the application of interpretive theory is as follows: Let us assume that we wish to measure the current value of inventories. The first step is to provide a subconcept to which we can apply specific rules of interpretation. If we choose current buying price, we can define *current value* as the exchange price for an item in the buying market at the balance sheet date. If market quotations are not available, or if it is not considered feasible to use them, an alternative is to evaluate other available accounting procedures in terms of this interpretation. We may, therefore, conclude that first-in, first-out is the best alternative because it results in the closest approximation of the current value of inventories. However, we can assume only a relative approximation in this case, not an absolute one. How well the FIFO results approximate current value is dependent upon several factors, including the average period the inventory is held and the rate of price changes.

Verification of interpretational theories can be obtained from research studies made to determine whether users of accounting information understand the information producers' intended meaning, consistent with the theory. Accounting numbers and classifications do vary with respect to the degree of interpretation that can be inferred by the reader of accounting reports. For example, the item *cash* in the statement of financial condition is fairly well understood to mean what accountants intend it to mean. On the other hand, the classification *deferred charges* and the balance of the account classified as *intangibles* do not have any specific interpretation apart from the structural processes that give rise to these amounts. Most items reported in financial statements fall between permitting good interpretation and losing interpretation because of the emphasis on the structural process. The role of theories that emphasize interpretation is to find ways to improve the ability of accounting information to be interpreted in terms of human observations and experience.

Behavioral theories

A more recent emphasis in the development of accounting theories has been the acceptance of a communication-decision orientation. The focus is on the relevance of information being communicated to decision makers and the behavior of different individuals or groups as a result of the presentation of accounting information. The most important users of accounting reports presented to those outside the firm are generally considered to include stockholders, other investors, creditors, and government authorities. However, behavioral theories can also take into consideration the effect of external reports on the decisions of management and the feedback effect on the actions of accountants and auditors. Thus, behavioral theories attempt to measure and evaluate the economic, psychological, and sociological effects of alternative accounting procedures and reporting media.

The behavioral approach to accounting theory is still in its infancy, but it does appear to provide one of the best promises for the development of theories that will guide accounting toward more useful ends. This approach has already stimulated a search among both academic and practicing accountants for basic objectives of accounting and for answers to the following questions: Who are the users of published financial statements? What is the nature of the specific information wanted by the several user groups? Can common needs be found for the presentation of general purpose statements or should specific needs be met?[14] How do investors, creditors, and managers react to different accounting procedures and presentations?

Attempts to derive normative investment decision models have not been successful because of the inability to test the models. Decision processes are subjective for each individual and are unique to each decision maker. Therefore, aggregations and generalizations regarding investor decision processes are difficult, if not impossible, with current research technology. In addition, individuals are not able to describe their own decision processes except in very general terms. An alternative is to study the effect of new information on security market prices. Thus, the usefulness of accounting information can be implied from the behavior of the market.

Recent studies in the area of human information processing have begun to discover behavioral relationships relevant to individual decision making in an accounting context. For example, individuals have been found to be limited in their abilities to process information in a complex setting. To overcome the complexity, they will attempt to simplify the information and reduce the uncertainty as they perceive it. Also, the presence of extraneous information increases the complexity, and the repetition of information causes an individual to give undue weight to that item.

---

[14] Technically, no information is *needed* to make a decision, but information is generally *wanted* because of uncertainties. The term *needs* is used here because of common usage.

Other behavioral research topics include the feedback effects of accounting information on managerial decisions, the economic and social consequences of alternative accounting procedures, and the interaction among accounting, organizations, and society. The implications for accounting of capital markets theories, human information processing, and economic and social consequences are discussed in later chapters.

DEDUCTIVE AND INDUCTIVE REASONING

Regardless of the level of theory selected for study, all formal theories that can be tested and verified must include some elements of both deductive and inductive reasoning. At least some of the propositions or premises in a deductive theory must be inductively conceived, and any theory that is primarily inductively oriented must contain some deductive reasoning or follow interconnective rules of logic.

Deductive reasoning

The deductive method of reasoning in accounting is the process of starting with objectives and postulates and, from these, deriving logical principles that provide the bases for concrete or practical applications. Thus, the practical applications and rules are derived from the logical reasoning; the postulates and logically derived principles should not merely support or attempt to explain accounting conventions or currently accepted practice.

The structure of the deductive process should include the following: (1) the formulation of general or specific objectives of financial reporting; (2) a statement of the postulates of accounting concerning the economic, political, and sociological environment in which accounting must operate; (3) a set of constraints to guide the reasoning process; (4) a structure, set of symbols, or framework in which ideas can be expressed and summarized; (5) the development of a set of definitions; (6) the formulation of principles or generalized statements of policy derived by the process of logic; and finally (7) the application of the principles to specific situations and the establishment of procedural methods and rules.

In the deductive process, the formulation of objectives is most important because different objectives might require entirely different structures and result in different principles. This is one of the main reasons why rules for determining taxable income are different in many respects from the generally accepted practice for the determination of financial income. Whereas there may be many advantages in applying the same income concepts to both tax and financial accounting, the basic objectives are different, and it is not likely that the same principles and procedures will meet the different objectives equally well. The frequent proposal for a single all-pervasive concept of income also has many advantages, but it does assume that such a concept could serve all accounting objectives equally well. Although this is not true, it would not be desirable to set up an entirely different set of principles for every purpose served by accounting. Some compromises must be made, but there should also be some freedom to serve different objectives as well as possible. Thus, accounting theory should be flexible enough to provide the needs of different objectives, but rigid enough to provide for some uniformity and consistency in financial reports to stockholders and the general public.

The objectives, postulates, constraints, and structural framework will be discussed at greater length in Chapter 3. However, they are all essential to the deductive process. The postulates are not necessarily numerous or complicated; they may even seem trivial or obvious. But it is desirable to make them explicit to provide a framework for subsequent logical reasoning. The constraints are restrictions to the development of principles derived from the objectives and postulates. These restrictions are necessary because of certain limitations of the environment, particularly those caused by uncertainty regarding the future and changes in the environment, such as fluctuations in the value of the measuring unit—money.

Symbols and a general working structure are necessary to provide a means of communication of ideas. In accounting, the structure may be the accounting equation and the several derived financial statements. In this structure the statements articulate with each other in order to provide internal consistency, although articulation is not necessary in alternative structures.

A more precise method of formulating the symbols, structure, and constraints is found in the axiomatic or mathematical approach to accounting theory. In this method, mathematical symbols are given to certain ideas and concepts. The framework is provided in the form of mathematical models utilizing matrix algebra or symbolic logic. Constraints can be applied in the form of mathematical expressions. Therefore, starting with basic postulates and rules of logical inference, theorems can be formulated and tested through mathematical operations. Thus, the axiomatic method can provide a very rigorous application of the deductive method.

Basic properties of the axiomatic method are that (1) propositions are selected and stated with the basis for acceptance being explicit and with at least some of the propositions capable of being verified empirically; (2) the relationships *among* the propositions are clearly stated and can be examined separately from the specific assertions *in* the propositions. The basic relationships among the propositions include the concepts negation (*not*), conjunction (*and*), disjunction (*either . . . or*) and implication (*if . . . then*). Examples of the use of the axiomatic method are found in the writings of Mattessich[15] and Chambers.[16]

---

[15] Richard Mattessich, *Accounting and Analytical Methods* (Homewood, Ill.: Richard D. Irwin, 1964). © 1964 by Richard D. Irwin, Inc.

[16] Raymond J. Chambers, *Accounting, Evaluation and Economic Behavior* (Englewood Cliffs, N.J.: Prentice-Hall, 1966).

One of the main disadvantages of the deductive method is that if any of the postulates and premises are false, the conclusions may also be false. Also, it is thought to be too far removed from reality to be able to derive realistic and workable principles or to provide the basis for practical rules. But these criticisms generally stem from a misunderstanding of the purpose and meaning of theory. It is not necessary that theory be entirely practical in order to be useful in establishing workable procedures. The main purpose of theory is to provide a framework for the development of new ideas and new procedures and to help in the making of choices among alternative procedures. If these objectives are met, it is not necessary that theory be based completely on practical concepts or that it be restricted to the development of procedures that are completely workable and practical in terms of current known technology. In fact, many of the currently accepted principles and procedures are general guides to action rather than specific rules that can be followed precisely in every applicable case.[17]

The inductive approach

The process of induction consists of drawing generalized conclusions from detailed observations and measurements. However, it is not possible to divorce the inductive from the deductive approach because the latter provides a guide to the selection of the data to be studied. But only after a few observations, properly selected, can generalizations be made regarding the entire universe or a group of similar situations. These generalizations, however, are subject to later confirmation or refutation after further experimentation and observation. All principles inductively derived are, therefore, conceptually falsifiable. Thus, through the inductive process, Newton was able to observe the characteristics of motion and from these observations and measurements derive generalizations, or laws of motion.

In accounting, the inductive process involves the making of observations of financial data regarding business enterprises. If recurring relationships can be found, generalizations and principles can be formulated. Thus new ideas and principles can be derived, particularly if the observers do not let themselves be influenced by current principles and practices. For example, by observations of a number of firms, it may be found that a historical trend of past sales may be a better predictor of cash to be received from customers in the future than the actual record of cash received in the past because of leads and lags in the collection process. Although this may always be subject to later refutation, a generalized conclusion may be reached from this that revenue reported for several prior years is relevant in the reporting process.

---

[17] For example, the criteria for the capitalization of long-term leases provide a general guide that cannot necessarily be followed with precision in every case, particularly if the lease contract includes the purchase of services acquired jointly with the use of property. The criteria presented in *FASB Statement No. 13* may be inadequate.

Just because the observers look only at raw data does not mean, however, that they do not need some initial postulates and concepts. By the mere making of a choice regarding what to observe they are reflecting preconceived notions of what might be relevant. By restricting themselves to the financial data of a firm, for example, they are drawing on certain postulates regarding the environment of accounting. Furthermore, if they restrict themselves to observing only financial transactions, they may only confirm existing practice.

The advantage of the inductive approach is that it is not necessarily constrained by a preconceived model or structure. The researchers are free to make any observations they may deem relevant. But once generalizations or principles are formulated, they should be confirmed by the logical process of the deductive approach and verification of the conclusions. However, the main disadvantage of the inductive process is that observers are likely to be influenced by subconscious ideas of what the relevant relationships are and what data should be observed.

Another difficulty with the inductive approach is that, in accounting, the raw data are likely to be different for each firm. Relationships may also be different, making it difficult to draw generalizations and basic principles. For example, the relationship between total revenues and costs of goods sold may be a constant over time for some firms, but this does not necessarily mean that the historical gross margin concept is necessarily a good measurement for the prediction of the future operations of a firm in all cases.

Both inductive and deductive theories may be descriptive (positive) or normative. Descriptive theories attempt to set forth and explain what and how financial information is presented and communicated to users of accounting data. Normative theories attempt to prescribe what data ought to be communicated and how they ought to be presented; that is, they attempt to explain what *should* be rather than what *is*. Inductive theories, by their nature, are usually descriptive; but it does not follow that deductive theories are necessarily normative. In generalizing from specific observations by the inductive process, the descriptive conclusions should not be confused with a normative standard. That is, what exists is not necessarily what should be. Normative conclusions can be drawn from theories that contain inductive propositions and deductive reasoning or drawn from theories that contain normative or value judgment propositions and deductive reasoning. When normative propositions are included in a theory, however, the basis upon which they might be acceptable should be clearly stated. Others may then reject the normative conclusions by refusing to accept the normative propositions, but the basis of disagreement is then well defined. An example of a descriptive theory based on both inductive propositions and on deductive reasoning is *The Foundation of Accounting Measurement* by Yuji Ijiri.[18] *Accounting, Eval-*

---

[18] Ijiri, *Accounting Measurement.*

uation and Economic Behavior by Raymond J. Chambers is an example of a normative theory employing both inductive propositions and deductive reasoning.[19]

ALTERNATIVE BEHAVIORAL APPROACHES

One of the first steps in the development of accounting theories is a clear statement of the behavioral objectives. In descriptive statistics, a summarized description of a population cannot be made unless the statistician first understands the type of information that is wanted. A description of the height and weight of the individuals in a given country may be of little value to a person who is interested in their economic well-being. Similarly, the type of information useful to management in the making of decisions is not necessarily the same as the type of information needed by stockholders and prospective investors of the firm.

Managers seek information that will help them predict the effect of current decisions on future cash flows. Stockholders who have an effective control of management need information to be able to judge the relative efficiency of management. Stockholders, prospective investors, and creditors need information that will help them predict the future course of the firm and the probability of future financial success that will permit repayments and cash distributions. While these objectives may lead to a single set of accounting principles, different sets of principles may be required to meet the several possible goals of accounting. The major emphasis in this book is on the development of financial accounting theories based on reporting to stockholders, investors, creditors, and other outside interests, although the objectives of reporting to management are taken into consideration in specific instances. Consideration is also given to meeting the objectives of general social and economic interests of a nation or geographic area.

Some of the alternative behavioral approaches include the following: (1) theories of investment valuation, (2) human information processing, (3) predictive indicators, (4) the events approach, (5) the ethical approach, (6) the use of communication theory, (7) emphasis on sociological factors, (8) a macroeconomic approach, (9) the pragmatic approach, and (10) nonspecific behavioral objectives. These behavioral approaches, however, are not independent of each other. Generally more than one must be used either explicitly or implicitly in the development of accounting principles. The discussions of theories relating to specific policies or procedures in the following chapters are eclectic in nature, drawing upon several of these approaches at various points.

---

[19] Chambers, *Accounting, Evaluation.*

Theories of investment valuation

Most writers in the area of financial accounting assume either explicitly or implicitly that the primary objective of financial accounting reports is to present information to stockholders and potential stockholders in order to assist them in making buy-sell-hold decisions regarding the firm's common stock. Because well-formulated investment decision models have not been developed for use in accounting theory, several models have been borrowed from time to time from the finance literature. These include the "intrinsic value" theories, the efficient markets hypotheses, and the theory of portfolio management.

"Intrinsic value" theories.   Because of uncertainties regarding future economic conditions and the success or failure of any specific firm, investors have different expectations regarding the financial consequences of owning a firm's stock. An investor will purchase a security when he or she believes that the "intrinsic value" of the security is greater than its market price. The intrinsic value is what the investor considers to be the real value of the security and the value that will be reflected in its market price when other investors reach the same conclusions. Two basic approaches to intrinsic value are the discounted dividends approach and the discounted earnings approach, although several modifications of each are presented in the literature. Miller and Modigliani have demonstrated that, properly understood, the two approaches are identical.[20]

Although the intrinsic value approach may have merit in explaining security prices, it has little to add to the development of accounting theories. It is not sufficient to know that expected dividends are important to investors. A rigorous and tested model showing how investors determine their expectations regarding future dividend flows or how they should determine such flows is not available. This is an important research area for accounting theory. On the other hand, the earnings approach is even less helpful for accounting theory because income is a product of the accounting model, and little if any meaningful interpretation can be drawn from it. Investors are accustomed to working with financial statements prepared according to current practice; little is known regarding how they would react to accounting information prepared under different concepts and alternative procedures.

The efficient markets hypothesis.   The efficient markets hypothesis states that the market for securities is efficient if security prices reflect fully and promptly all available information. Three forms are generally recognized: (1) the weak form—security prices fully reflect information implied by the historical sequence of prices; (2) the semistrong form—security prices fully reflect all publicly available information about the

---

[20] Merton H. Miller and Franco Modigliani, "Dividend Policy, Growth, and the Valuation of Shares," *Journal of Business,* October 1961, pp. 411–33.

firm; and (3) the strong form—security prices fully reflect even privileged information.

The relevance of particularly the semistrong form is that it can be assumed that the information content of accounting data can be evaluated on the basis of market reactions to this information. Although this association does provide a basis for research regarding the relevance of accounting data, several qualifications should be considered. First, it should be recognized that this association does not imply that the accounting procedures used result in information that is optimal for the investment decision process. Second, this association does not tell us anything about the expected benefit to society, including the optimal allocation of resources. Third, the association does not take into account necessarily the costs of providing accounting information compared with alternative sources of the same information.[21] Accounting research may, however, be expanded to take these factors into consideration.

Portfolio theory.   Briefly, portfolio theory states that rational investors will prefer to hold portfolios that maximize the expected rate of return for a given degree of risk or minimize the degree of risk for a given expected rate of return. Such portfolios are referred to as efficient. Therefore, the relevant level of concern for the decision maker is the expected impact on the portfolio, not the expected performance of the specific security. Thus, the measurement of risk that is relevant is not the total variability of the individual security, but rather its covariability with the other securities in the portfolio. That is, the riskiness of two securities may be high, but the total risk may be reduced if the variability of the two securities is inverse to each other. Portfolio theory is normative in that it depicts how investors should react; the capital asset pricing model describes the market relationships that would result in equilibrium if investors did follow portfolio theory.

The importance of portfolio theory is that it points out a need for a distinction between systematic risk (variability associated with general market movements) and nonsystematic risk (variability of the rate of return of a security that is not correlated with rates of return for the market as a whole). Since the latter form of risk can be eliminated through diversification, only the former is relevant in portfolio selection. Accounting theory that focuses only on the individual security without considering the portfolio context might, therefore, be in error. However, this does not imply that measurements of nonsystematic risk may not be important for some investors who choose not to diversify or who may be unable to do so, although the market will not reward investors for the nonsystematic risks they may wish to carry.

---

[21] See Robert G. May and Gary L. Sundem, "Cost of Information and Security Prices: Market Association Tests for Accounting Policy Decisions," *Accounting Review,* January 1973, pp. 80–94.

Human information processing

Several psychological research techniques have been applied to the area of accounting in order to learn more about the decision process of individuals. The objectives of these studies are (1) to improve the ability of financial information to portray accurately the real events or objects (the predictive significance of the information set), (2) to obtain an understanding of how the amount, type and format of financial accounting information affect the judgments or predictions of users (cue usage), (3) to obtain an understanding of the ability of the decision maker to respond accurately to a perception of the environment (response accuracy), and (4) to obtain an understanding of how individuals deal with complexity in decision making. These are discussed at greater length in Chapter 5.

Predictive indicators

A concept derived from the investment valuation models is that of predictive ability. If accounting data are to be relevant for the making of decisions by investors, they must provide input into the decision models of the investors. And since only expectations of future objects and events are relevant for these decision models, it follows that if accounting data are to be relevant, they must provide or permit predictions of future objects or events. However, the emphasis on prediction leaves several questions unanswered: (1) What objects or events are or should be included in investors' decision models? (2) What relationships should be assumed or sought between accounting data and the inputs into decision models? (3) What alternative sets of accounting data and what alternative accounting procedures best meet the predictive ability criterion?

Before the predictive ability test can be applied, there must be some knowledge of what decision models are in use or what decision models investors should be using. The former can be studied through descriptive theories of investors and market reactions to accounting data. The main difficulty with using descriptive models is that investors are limited by the information made available to them. Therefore, it is difficult to evaluate the effect of alternative accounting data or procedures. The normative approach has the advantage of permitting freedom to select alternative accounting procedures and accounting data not previously reported. Normative theories, however, are always difficult to evaluate and must always be subject to change as new information is obtained. A normative approach was selected by Revsine in his study of the predictive nature of replacement cost accounting.[22]

As suggested by the 1969–71 American Accounting Association Committee on Corporate Financial Reporting, there are at least four

---

[22] Lawrence Revsine, *Replacement Cost Accounting* (Englewood Cliffs, N.J.: Prentice-Hall, 1973).

ways by which accounting data can be related to the inputs of decision models.[23]

1.　Direct prediction can be made by accountants or by managements in the form of forecasts, which may be evaluated by independent accountants. Historically, accountants have been reluctant to have anything to do with forecasts because of their potential misuse and the potential liability in the case of inaccurate forecasts.

2.　Indirect prediction is the most common concept applied to the predictive ability of accounting data. Past data are assumed to have predictive ability if they can be used to forecast future objects or events by the extrapolation or projection of the past into the future. This assumes that there is a high correlation between past events and future events, although changes in the environment and external factors may be used to alter the form of the extrapolation.

3.　The use of lead indicators would emphasize the ability of accounting data to predict turning points, rather than a mere extrapolation of past data into the future. That is, accountants should search for data whose movements precede the movements in the objects or events being predicted. An increase in the debt-equity ratio, for example, might precede a deterioration in the cash flows to the firm available for dividends.

4.　Corroborating information may also be used as predictive indicators. That is, specific accounting data may not be useful alone in the making of predictions, but they may be relevant along with other information in evaluating future prospects of the firm. For example, the ratio of costs of goods sold to average inventory and gross profit margins may be helpful in evaluating managerial efficiency and thus help in the prediction of future operating cash flows and the ability of the firm to pay dividends in the future.

The predictive ability concept has considerable potential for future development of relevant financial reporting. However, several major obstacles stand in the way at present. A major obstacle is the lack of tested normative (or even descriptive) investor decisions models with a sufficient description of the model inputs. A second obstacle is the lack of understanding of the relationship between accounting data and relevant objects or events that may be inputs into decision models. It is improper to assume that a given concept of income, for example, is a relevant predictor just because it permits a prediction of future values of itself. Accounting income is an artifact derived from the formal accounting structure and is relevant for prediction purposes only if it is also a good substitute (surrogate) for a relevant input into the decision models. At the present time, the complexities of the business environment, the lack of understanding of the relationships of past and future measurements of objects and

---

[23] American Accounting Association, "Report of the Committee on Corporate Financial Reporting," *Accounting Review*, supplement to vol. 47 (1972), pp. 526–27.

events, and the inability to formulate reliable normative or descriptive decision models make the predictive ability test a difficult one.

The events approach

Three basic conflicts in the development of accounting theory are: (1) Should financial statements be directed to specific users and their needs or to a wide variety of users with unspecified needs? (2) How much detail regarding specific types of accounting information should be presented? (3) What types of information should be selected for presentation? Although these questions are interrelated, they are discussed separately with respect to the events theory.

While not limited to the events theory, a basic premise of this approach is that the users of financial statements are many and varied and that accountants should not attempt to direct the major published financial reports to specific assumed users. Furthermore, it is assumed that decision models cannot be formulated either descriptively or normatively with sufficient precision to dictate the types of accounting information relevant as inputs into these decision models. However, Sorter argues that, even when more is known about users' decision models, it is possible that such models may be more consistent with the events approach than with the value approach.[24] That is, investors may wish to use accounting data to predict specific events (such as sales by product lines) and use their own predictions of these events to formulate the more specific inputs into their decision models. Thus, less need be known about users' decision models to determine what accounting data may be relevant to investors.

If accounting data are to be relevant for a wide range of decision models and if the objective is to provide a wide range of information assumed to be relevant for specific predictions, it follows that there must be an expansion of the accounting data presented in financial reports. That is, more detail and less aggregation are assumed to be appropriate. Some normative decision models may also require disaggregated data, but the events approach requires more detail because it is assumed that the user should be able to select the desired information from a broader list and also to decide the amount of aggregation. A user can generally aggregate accounting data with sufficient detail, but cannot disaggregate data without the detail.

An event is an occurrence, phenomenon, or transaction that is assumed to be observable and have better semantic interpretation than value measurements of assets and liabilities. However, only certain characteristics of events can be measured and reported; in the events approach to accounting, exchange prices are assumed to be observable, verifiable, and relevant. As a consequence, the balance sheet is viewed as an aggregation

---

[24] George H. Sorter, "An 'Events' Approach to Basic Accounting Theory," *Accounting Review,* January 1969, pp. 12–19.

of events that have occurred in the past. The importance of the income statement is in the presentation of operating activities of the firm; the final figure of net income has little if any meaning. The funds statement also focuses on the activities of the firm rather than on the change in working capital.

The disadvantages of the events approach are the following: (1) The criterion for selecting what information should be presented is very vague, and therefore it does not lead to a fully developed theory of accounting. (2) The expansion of data may result in an information overload on users. Evidence from human information processing studies indicates, for example, that there is a limit to the amount of information an individual can efficiently handle at one time. (3) Evidence is lacking that the measurement of events is necessarily more verifiable than the measurement of objects or that presentation of event characteristics necessarily leads to better predictions than the presentation of selected events and objects.

The ethical approach

As indicated above, the several approaches to accounting theory are not independent of each other. This is particularly true of the ethical approach; defining it as a separate approach does not necessarily imply that other approaches do not have ethical content, nor does it imply that ethical theories necessarily ignore all other concepts. Pattillo, for example, stressed the ethical concept as primary, but stated that in his approach its basic standard is an ethical one, its method is logical and coherent, and the ultimate test of the formulations lies in its application to the real world.[25]

The ethical approach to accounting theory places emphasis on the concepts of justice, truth, and fairness. D R Scott suggested that the basis for the determination of accounting practice reaches back to the principles underlying social organizations. His basic concepts were (1) accounting procedures must provide *equitable* treatment to all interested parties; (2) financial reports should present a *true* and *accurate* statement without misrepresentation; and (3) accounting data should be *fair, unbiased,* and *impartial,* without serving special interests. To these basic concepts he added the requirements that accounting principles should be subject to continual revision as necessary to allow for changing conditions and that accounting principles should be applied consistently whenever possible.[26]

Fairness, justice, and impartiality refer to judgments that accounting reports and statements are not subject to undue influence or bias. They should not be prepared with the objective of serving any particular indi-

---

[25] James W. Pattillo, *The Foundation of Financial Accounting* (Baton Rouge: Louisiana State University Press, 1965), p. 11.

[26] D R Scott, "The Basis for Accounting Principles," *Accounting Review,* December 1941, pp. 341–49.

vidual or group to the detriment of others. The interests of all parties should be taken into consideration in proper balance, particularly without any preference for the rights of the management or owners of the firm, who may have greater influence over the choice of accounting procedures. *Justice* frequently refers to a conformity to a standard established formally or informally as a guide to equitable treatment.

Truth, as it relates to accounting, is probably more difficult to define and apply. Many seem to use the term to mean "in accordance with the facts." However, not all who refer to truth in accounting have in mind the same definition of *facts*. Some refer to accounting facts as data that are objective and verifiable. Thus, historical costs may represent accounting facts. On the other hand, the term *truth* is used to refer to the valuation of assets and expenses in current economic terms. For example, MacNeal stated that financial statements display the truth only when they disclose the current value of assets and the profits and losses accruing from changes in values, although the increases in values should be designated as realized or unrealized.[27]

Truth is also used to refer to propositions or statements that are generally considered to be established principles. For example, the recognition of a gain at the time of the sale of an asset is generally considered to be a reporting of true conditions, while the reporting of an appraisal increase in the value of an asset prior to sale as ordinary income is generally thought to lack truthfulness. Thus, the established rule regarding revenue realization is the guide. But the truthfulness of the financial reports depends on the fundamental validity of the accepted rules and principles on which the statements are based. Established rules and procedures provide an inadequate foundation for measuring truthfulness.

Probably the greatest disadvantage of a primary reliance on the ethical approach to accounting theory is that it fails to provide a sound basis for the development of accounting principles or for the evaluation of currently accepted principles. Principles must be evaluated on the basis of subjective judgments; or, as generally occurs, currently accepted practices become accepted without evaluation because it is expedient to do so.

Corporate social accounting approach

Traditional accounting theory approaches focus on the view of the enterprise as an economic entity with its main activities affecting the economy through its operations in markets—markets for capital and factors of production and markets for its products or services. In the traditional view, it is assumed that the firm should maximize its profits for, by so doing, it is thought to be making a maximum contribution to society.

With the modern complexities of societies and international politics,

---

[27] Kenneth MacNeal, *Truth in Accounting* (Philadelphia: University of Pennsylvania Press, 1939), p. 203.

and the expansion of multinational economic organizations, the traditional view does not necessarily meet the demands or priorities of society. Environmental pollution, unemployment, unhealthful working conditions and other social problems are not normally reported by a firm, except to the extent that their costs can be borne directly by the firm through taxation or regulation. The purpose of social accounting is to provide information to permit an evaluation of the effect of a firm's activities on society.

A theory of social accounting requires a statement of objectives, a set of relevant social concepts and measurement methods, and a structure for reporting and communicating the information to interested parties.[28] Objectives should include the reporting of the net social contribution of the firm, which includes both costs and benefits internal to the firm and costs and benefits affecting only society (externalities). Other objectives might include (1) making a comparison of corporate goals and activities with social priorities and (2) providing for public accountability for contributions to social goals. The information reported should include both market and nonmarket data and social effects that cannot be measured directly in money terms.

Since social accounting theories are primitive at the present time, it is difficult to obtain agreement on the concepts or the measurement methods. As additional studies are made, these obstacles may be overcome.

Macroeconomic approach

A macroeconomic approach is similar to the social accounting approach in that it may be either descriptive or normative. As a descriptive approach, it would attempt to explain the effect of alternative reporting procedures on economic measurements and economic activities. For example, the widespread shift from FIFO to LIFO for inventory valuation purposes in 1974 had the effect of reducing the measured gross national product. Although the effect of inflation on inventory profits is removed by the inventory valuation adjustment, the adjustment did not allow for this shift. Some economists were concerned that this artificial reduction of reported GNP would have the effect of reducing consumer demand if it led consumers to anticipate a more severe recession than they otherwise might expect. As a normative approach, one of the objectives of accounting could be to direct the behavior of firms and individuals toward the implementation of specific national economic policies. For example, national economic objectives might require accounting reports that will permit and even encourage higher dividends and larger capital expenditures during slack economic periods and discourage investments during periods of inflation. While most countries implement such a policy

---

[28] See, for example, Kavasseri V. Ramanathan, "Toward a Theory of Corporate Social Accounting," *Accounting Review,* July 1976, pp. 516–28.

through monetary and fiscal policies and direct controls, some countries, notably Sweden, do attempt to base accounting concepts and practices on macroeconomic goals.[29] One of the main aspects of this policy is the objective of reporting stable earnings from year to year. Thus, the use of reserves and flexible depreciation policies are examples of the legitimate smoothing of income.

In the United States, macroeconomic policy has had little influence on accounting. However, the influence of government administrators was partially responsible for the deferral of an *Opinion* of the Accounting Principles Board of the AICPA in 1967. The *Opinion* would have made cost reduction and deferred recognition of the investment tax credit the preferred method, as opposed to the flow-through method. Both methods were subsequently accepted. The main reason for the governmental opposition was the fear that the *Opinion* would have an adverse effect on government economic policy.

VERIFICATION OF ACCOUNTING THEORIES

If accounting theories are to be at all persuasive in the development of an understanding of accounting or in influencing accounting practice, they must be subject to verification or confirmation. Such confirmation, however, must be acceptable at several levels: (1) Premises regarding the real world should be based on a correspondence between the statement and observable phenomena. (2) The interrelationship of the several statements in the theory should be tested for logical consistency. (3) If any of the premises are based on value judgments or inconclusive empirical verification, the conclusions of the theory or the hypothesis being tested should be subject to independent empirical verification.

But the question still remains as to when a premise or hypothesis is confirmed. Space does not permit a full discussion of this topic here, but one method is to measure the empirical truth value of the premise or hypothesis under given levels of statistical significance. The level of significance selected, however, introduces a normative quality to the verification process. It should be noted that an important characteristic of empirically confirmed premises or hypotheses is that they are always subject to subsequent refutation. This is not only true because conditions change over time in the social sciences, but also because it is impossible to capture in any study all of the relevant variables. Sampling and other statistical errors may also creep in. In spite of the necessity for empirical verification, however, relevant hypotheses can be formulated through the process of logical inquiry.

---

[29] See Gerhard G. Mueller, *International Accounting* (New York: Macmillan, 1967), pp.

CONTROVERSY IN THE DEVELOPMENT
OF ACCOUNTING PRINCIPLES
AND PROCEDURES

The critical analysis of accounting principles and procedures presented in the following chapters is based on an eclectic concept of accounting theory. Each of the several approaches to accounting theory has some merit in helping to establish and evaluate accounting principles and procedures. Inductive reasoning permits a better understanding of data that provide the foundation for accounting. Theories of investment value and the concept of predictive indicators help set the stage for determining the objectives of accounting and for selecting what data should be reported. The ethical approach can also be applied in a general way as a basic objective in establishing logical accounting principles and procedures. No one has proposed that accounting statements should reflect information and relationships that are not true, just, or fair. The social accounting and macroeconomic approaches add to the controversies of theory development and application. Although none of the several approaches to accounting theory is adequate by itself, any complete theory formulation must be accompanied by some deductive reasoning. Therefore, the accounting theory developed and applied throughout this book attempts to place all approaches to theory in proper perspective with special emphasis on the deductive process with discussion of empirical verification where research findings are relevant.

The controversy in the development of accounting principles and procedures does not stop with the verification of accounting theories. Some method must be devised to permit the results of theory research to influence the choice of accounting alternatives in practice. This is not an easy task as theoreticians are accused of talking only to each other, and practicing accountants prefer to avoid change because change causes stress and the life of an accountant is anything but free of stress. Nevertheless, change is inevitable and conflicts require resolution.

The laissez-faire approach, permitting accountants or clients to do as they wish, is not the answer because it results either in a proliferation of alternatives or, through Gresham's Law, in the selection of the weakest of several alternatives. A second method is that of voting either directly or indirectly by accountants or by users of accounting reports. When the Accounting Principles Board relied only on the general acceptance of its pronouncements, this was in essence a method of voting by accountants. Abdel-khalik suggested a method by which voting by users can result in the reporting of the most preferred value-measurement method.[30] Although this model is worth considering, it does have specific weaknesses, particularly in the impoundment of new concepts and procedures sug-

---

[30] A. Rashad Abdel-khalik, "User Preference Ordering Value: A Model," *Accounting Review,* July 1971, pp. 457–71.

gested by newly developed theories and empirical studies. Users are likely to prefer the customary and understood to the unknown. But the voting process itself, whether by accountants or users, does have specific disadvantages, which may or may not be compelling.[31] The imposition of accounting procedures by an official body seems to be the direction in which most countries are moving, particularly the United States, with the Financial Accounting Standards Board. The role of the FASB in establishing accounting policies is discussed in Chapter 6.

The following chapter presents the historical development of accounting theories. Accounting theories have not always been made explicit when used as support for specific procedures, nor have accounting procedures always been logically conceived. However, a historical perspective permits a better understanding of the several theories currently proposed and why accounting is what it is today.

One of the first steps in evaluating the normative deductive approach to accounting theory is to examine the basic postulates, standards, and hypotheses on which it is based. A discussion of these postulates, standards, and hypotheses is presented in Chapter 3. Postulates should include the objective of accounting, the basic assumptions regarding the economic and political environment of accounting, and the constraints required because of the limitations of measurement, uncertainty, or other pragmatic reasons.

Alternative theories are discussed in Chapter 4 and 5. Chapter 4 presents a discussion of capital markets theories and their relationship to accounting information, and Chapter 5 presents a discussion of theories relating to the individual decision process including theories and research relating to human information processing. Empirical research findings are presented and discussed in later chapters relating to the specific topics.

SELECTED ADDITIONAL READING

General methodology

American Accounting Association. Report of the Committee on Foundations of Accounting Measurement." *Accounting Review.* Supplement to vol. 46 (1971), pp. 37–45.

American Accounting Association. "Report of the Committee on Accounting Theory Construction and Verification." *Accounting Review.* Supplement to vol. 46 (1971), pp. 53–63.

American Accounting Association, Committee on Concepts and Standards for External Financial Reports. *Statement on Accounting Theory and Theory Acceptance* (1977).

Beams, Floyd A. "Indications of Pragmatism and Empiricism in Accounting Thought." *Accounting Review* 44, no. 2 (April 1969): 382–88.

---

[31] See Joel S. Demski, "Choice among Financial Reporting Alternatives," *Accounting Review,* April 1974, pp. 227–32.

Devine, Carl Thomas. *Essays in Accounting Theory*. Vol. 3. Tallahassee, Fla.: privately published, 1971, pp. 1–80.

Kam, Vernon. "Judgment and the Scientific Trend in Accounting." *Journal of Accountancy*, February 1973, pp. 52–57.

Kuhn, T. S. *The Structure of Scientific Revolutions*. 2nd ed. Chicago: University of Chicago Press, 1970.

McDonald, Daniel L. *Comparative Accounting Theory*. Reading, Mass.: Addison-Wesley Publishing, 1972.

Mattessich, Richard. "Methodological Preconditions and Problems of a General Theory of Accounting." *Accounting Review*, July 1972, pp. 469–87.

Sterling, Robert R. "An Explication and Analysis of the Structure of Accounting, Part One." *Abacus*, December 1971, pp. 137–52; and "Part Two," *Abacus*, December 1972, pp. 145–62.

———, and Richard E. Flaherty. "The Role of Liquidity in Exchange Valuation." *Accounting Review*, July 1971, pp. 441–56.

Yu, S. C. *The Structure of Accounting Theory*. Gainesville, Fla.: University of Florida Press, 1976.

Behavioral theories

Demski, Joel S. "Choice among Financial Reporting Alternatives." *Accounting Review*, April 1974, pp. 221–32.

Hawkins, David F. "Behavioral Implications of Generally Accepted Accounting Principles." *California Management Review*, Winter 1969, pp. 13–21.

Hofstedt, Thomas R. "Some Behavioral Parameters of Financial Accounting." *Accounting Review*, October 1972, pp. 679–92.

———. "The Processing of Accounting Information: Perceptual Biases." In *Behavioral Experiments in Accounting*, edited by Thomas J. Burns. Columbus: College of Administrative Science, The Ohio State University, 1972, pp. 285–315.

See also Chapter 5, Selected Additional Reading.

Normative deductive theories

Bedford, Norton M. "The Impact of A Priori Theory and Research on Accounting Practice." In *The Impact of Accounting Research on Practice and Disclosure*, A. Rashad Abdel-khalik and Thomas F. Keller. Durham, N.C.: Duke University Press, 1978, pp. 2–31.

Langenderfer, Harold Q. "A Conceptual Framework for Financial Reporting." *Journal of Accountancy*, July 1973, pp. 46–55.

Pellicelli, Georgio. "The Axiomatic Method in Business Economics: A First Approach." *Abacus*, December 1969, pp. 119–31.

Tippet, Mark. "The Axions of Accounting Measurement." *Accounting and Business Research*, Autumn 1978, pp. 266–78.

Normative theories

Demski, Joel S. "The General Impossibility of Normative Accounting Standards." *Accounting Review*, October 1973, pp. 718–23.

Hakansson, Nils H. "Normative Accounting Theory and the Theory of Decision." *International Journal of Accounting Education and Research,* Spring 1969, pp. 33–47.

Theories of investment valuation

See Chapter 4, Selected Additional Reading.

Predictive ability

American Accounting Association. "Report of the Committee on Corporate Financial Reporting." *Accounting Review.* Supplement to vol. 47 (1972), pp. 525–28.

Ashton, Robert H. "The Predictive-Ability Criterion and User Prediction Models". *Accounting Review,* October 1974, pp. 719–32.

Beaver, William H.; John W. Kennelly; and **William M. Voss.** "Predictive Ability as a Criterion for the Evaluation of Accounting Data." *Accounting Review,* October 1968, pp. 675–83.

Greenball, M. N. "The Predictive-Ability Criterion: Its Relevance in Evaluating Accounting Data." *Abacus,* June 1971, pp. 1–7.

Libby, R. "Accounting Ratios and the Prediction of Failure." *Journal of Accounting Research,* Spring 1975, pp. 150–61.

Louderback, Joseph G., III. "Projectability as a Criterion for Income Determination Methods." *Accounting Review,* April 1971, pp. 298–305.

Revsine, Lawrence. "Predictive Ability, Market Prices, and Operating Flows." *Accounting Review,* July 1971, pp. 480–89.

————. *Replacement Cost Accounting.* Englewood Cliffs, N.J.: Prentice-Hall, 1973, chaps. 4 and 5, pp. 86–138.

The events approach

Benbasat, Izak, and **Albert S. Dexter.** "Value and Events Approaches to Accounting: An Experimental Evaluation." *Accounting Review,* October 1979, pp. 735–49.

Johnson, Orace. "Toward an 'Events' Theory of Accounting." *Accounting Review,* October 1970, pp. 641–53.

Lieberman, Arthur Z., and **Andrew B. Whinston.** "A Structuring of an Events-Accounting Information System." *Accounting Review,* April 1975, pp. 246–58.

Revsine, Lawrence. "Data Expansion and Conceptual Structure." *Accounting Review,* October 1970, pp. 704–11.

Sorter, George H. "Events Approach to Basic Accounting Theory." *Accounting Review,* January 1969, pp. 12–19.

Ethical approaches

Arnett, Harold E. "The Concept of Fairness." *Accounting Review* 13, (April 1967): 291–97.

Burton, John C., ed. *Corporate Financial Reporting: Ethical and Other Problems.* New York: American Institute of Certified Public Accountants, 1972, esp. pp. 17–27, 73–86, and 107–32.

Pattillo, James W. *The Foundations of Financial Accounting,* particularly chap. 3, "The Accounting Standard: Fairness to All Parties." Baton Rouge: Louisiana State University Press, 1965.

Spacek, Leonard. *A Search for Fairness in Financial Reporting to the Public.* Chicago: Arthur Andersen & Co., 1969, particularly pp. 27–38 and 349–56.

Corporate social accounting approach

American Accounting Association. "Report of the Committee on Accounting for Social Performance." *Accounting Review.* Supplement to vol. 51 (1976), pp. 38–69.

American Institute of Certified Public Accountants. *The Measurement of Corporate Social Performance* (1977).

Anderson, John E., and Alan W. Frankle. "Voluntary Social Reporting: An Iso-Beta Portfolio Analysis." *Accounting Review,* July 1980, pp. 467–79.

Burton, Eric James, and Manuel A. Tipgos. "Toward a Theory of Corporate Social Accounting: A Comment." *Accounting Review,* October 1977, pp. 971–83 and "Reply," pp. 977–83.

Dierkes, Meinolf, and Raymond A. Bauer, eds. *Corporate Social Accounting.* New York: Praeger Publishers, 1973.

Estes, Ralph. *Corporate Social Accounting.* New York: John Wiley & Sons, 1976.

Ingram, Robert W. "An Investigation of the Information Content of (Certain) Social Responsibility Disclosures." *Journal of Accounting Research,* Autumn 1978, pp. 270–85.

Jensen, Robert E. *Phantasmagoric Accounting: Research and Analysis of Economic, Social, and Environmental Impact of Corporate Business.* AAA Studies in Accounting Research, no. 14 (1976).

Ramanathan, Kavasseri V. "Toward a Theory of Corporate Social Accounting." *Accounting Review,* July 1976, pp. 516–28.

Spicer, Barry H. "Investors, Corporate Social Performance and Information Disclosure: An Empirical Study." *Accounting Review,* January 1978, pp. 94–111.

Macroeconomic approach

Enthoven, Adolf J. H. *Accountancy and Economic Development Policy.* New York: American Elsevier Publishing, 1973.

Mueller, Gerhard G. "Accounting Within a Macroeconomic Framework." *International Accounting.* New York: Macmillan, 1967, chap. 1.

Verification of accounting theories

American Accounting Association. "Report of the Committee on Accounting Theory Construction and Verification." *Accounting Review.* Supplement to vol. 46 (1971), pp. 53–79.

Gonedes, Nicholas J. "Perception Estimation and Verifiability." *International Journal of Accounting Education and Research,* Spring 1969, pp. 63–73.

Schrader, William J., and **Robert E. Malcolm.** "A Note on Accounting Theory Construction and Verification." *Abacus,* June 1973, pp. 93–98.

Sterling, Robert R. "On Theory Construction and Verification." *Accounting Review,* July 1970, pp. 444–57.

Williams, Thomas H., and **Charles H. Griffin.** "On the Nature of Empirical Verification in Accounting." *Abacus,* December 1969, pp. 143–78.

CHAPTER 2

THE DEVELOPMENT OF ACCOUNTING THEORY

Accounting theory has progressed through a major revolution, particularly during the late 1960s, the 1970s, and continuing into the 1980s. During this same period and going back about 50 years, accounting thought has also developed by an evolutionary process. A need for a study of the history of accounting thought stems from this relationship with the past.

Accounting theory, however, is closely related to accounting practice whether it be an evaluation of practice and its effects, an explanation of practice, or the development of a framework for the guidance of changes in accounting practice and its adaptation to new environments. Before 1930, accounting theory as a well-defined body of logical reasoning did not usually precede accounting practice, if indeed it can be said to do so today. Accounting developed historically as the needs arose, and changes occurred gradually in accounting techniques and concepts. But new accounting practices have been necessary to keep pace with changing economic institutions and relationships and the changing objectives of accounting. However, many techniques and concepts continue in use long after the conditions requiring them have ceased.

THE DEVELOPMENT OF ACCOUNTING THOUGHT AND PRACTICE BEFORE 1930

The development of accounting practice has been subjected to two major periods of turmoil in recent years—the early 1930s and the 1960s—and an almost revolutionary change in accounting practice with the adoption of inflation accounting as supplemental information in 1979. In 1930 as in 1960, considerable pressure came from individuals and groups outside the accounting profession accompanied by dissatisfaction by practicing accountants and academicians. As a result of the pressures building up in 1930, the American Institute of Accountants[1] appointed a committee for the purpose of cooperating with the New York Stock Exchange in matters

---

[1] In 1957 the name was changed to the American Institute of Certified Public Accountants.

relating to the common interest of investors, exchanges, and accountants. Also in 1930 the Institute appointed its first standing committee to consider problems of accounting procedure and to make pronouncements that might carry weight in the profession. Earlier, questions of accounting procedure had been disposed of through the work of special committees created specifically to study the particular questions. Another important development in 1930 was the first ruling of the New York Stock Exchange relating specifically to accounting practice—that stock dividends of a subsidiary should not be taken into the income of the parent corporation in an amount greater than that charged against the earnings or earned surplus (retained earnings) of the subsidiary.

In the United Kingdom, the Companies Act of 1929 had required sweeping reforms in the financial reporting of limited companies, including the requirement of a profit and loss account for the first time.

These events of the 1930s, however, were indicative of a desire to improve accounting practice rather than accounting theory as such. Furthermore, most of the accounting pronouncements and innovations of the 1930s were the result of developments in accounting thought of 10 to 20 years earlier. But it cannot be denied that the development of accounting theory was stimulated by the discussions that came out of these events of the early 1930s. In a round-table discussion of "Developments in Accounting Theory and Practice Since 1929" at the 50th Anniversary Celebration of the American Institute of Accountants in 1937, the consensus was that there had been no developments in theory since 1929, only in practice. However, in these discussions, it was apparent that the disagreement on basic principles and the stimulation of accounting thought had done much to develop theory.

The most important shift in basic accounting thought coming out of the writings and discussions of the late 1920s and early 1930s was the change in the objective of accounting from that of presenting information to management and creditors to that of providing financial information for investors and stockholders. The pressure for this change in objective came from the financial sectors and stock exchanges rather than from accountants. The rapid growth in the widespread ownership of corporations, particularly during the several years following World War I, created new needs for accounting information. The average number of shares listed on the New York Stock Exchange in 1900 was about 60 million shares, compared with 180 million in 1917 and 1,212 million in 1930 (unadjusted for stock splits).[2]

Two men, William Z. Ripley and J. M. B. Hoxsey, were particularly influential in stating the case for an improvement in accounting standards for reporting to stockholders and investors. Ripley, professor of economics at Harvard, made an attack on the accounting practices of the

---

[2] *New York Stock Exchange Fact Book* (1959) p. 38.

railroads in 1915[3] and criticized severely the paucity of information available to stockholders of industrial corporations in 1926.[4] Hoxsey, executive assistant to the Committee on Stock List of the New York Stock Exchange, in an address before the annual convention of the American Institute of Accountants in 1930, made a specific plea for providing adequate, understandable information in financial statements presented to stockholders. He argued that this information should avoid misleading the stockholders in any respect and should aid them in determining the true value of their investments.[5]

The change in the objective of financial statements led to the following changes in accounting thought: (1) a deemphasis of the balance sheet as a statement of values, by adhering more closely to the going-concern concept as opposed to liquidation, and by looking at the balance sheet as the link between two income statements rather than the reverse; (2) the consequent increased emphasis on the income statement and a uniform concept of *income*; (3) the need for full disclosure of relevant financial information, by presenting more complete financial statements and increasing the use of footnotes; and (4) an emphasis on consistency in reporting, particularly with respect to the income statement. These changes are evident in the literature and in the pronouncements of several interested organizations before and after 1930. It is interesting to note that these changes in accounting thought were not the direct result of the stock market crash of 1929 nor the depression of the 1930s, but rather they were the result of institutional changes that had begun much earlier and to which accountants had not as yet adapted themselves. They were, of course, made more urgent by the events of the period.

One of the most significant of these changes was the shift in emphasis from the balance sheet to the income statement occurring in the United States and in Europe during the period from about World War I to the late 1930s. As early as 1908, Schmalenbach in Germany had pointed out that annual accounts should provide information about the operations of a business as well as about the state of its capital.[6] During the 1920s in the United States and in Great Britain, an increasing number of firms were providing information regarding their income accounts. The effect of this was, as we shall see from the writings and pronouncements of the 1920s and 1930s, to focus attention on the nature of allocations and accruals and their consequent effect on income. There is also evidence of an increasing arbitrary use during this period of deferrals of losses and income items to

---

[3] William Z. Ripley, *Railroads, Finance and Organization* (New York: Longmans, Green & Co., 1915).

[4] William Z. Ripley, "Stop, Look, Listen!" *Atlantic Monthly,* September 1926, included in *Main Street and Wall Street* (Boston: Little, Brown, 1927).

[5] J. M. B. Hoxsey, "Accounting for Investors," *Journal of Accountancy,* October 1930, pp. 251–84.

[6] Eugen Schmalenbach, *Dynamic Accounting* (London: Gee & Co., 1959), p. 3.

permit a smoothing of income from one year to the next. This led to the attempts in the 1930s to establish better standards for the presentation of the income statement.

THE DEVELOPMENT OF STANDARDS
BEFORE 1930

As early as 1894, the American Association of Public Accountants (predecessor to the American Institute of Accountants and the AICPA) adopted a resolution recommending that the order of presentation in the balance sheet should be from the quickest realization to the least, indicating clearly an emphasis on providing information for creditors. A second step was taken in 1920 when a committee of the Association was appointed to formulate definitions of technical accounting terms in order to give uniformity to their meaning. Subsequent pronouncements were intended to standardize audit procedures and to facilitate the presentation of financial statements useful to bankers.

The presentation of financial statements

In 1917, the Federal Reserve Board and the Federal Trade Commission recognized a need for standardization in the preparation of financial statements submitted to bankers for credit purposes. Accordingly, the Federal Trade Commission requested the American Institute of Accountants (AICPA) to prepare a memorandum on standardized procedures. After this memorandum was approved by the council of the Institute and the Federal Trade Commission, it was presented to the Federal Reserve Board for consideration. The Federal Reserve Board gave it tentative endorsement and submitted it to bankers and banking associations throughout the country for their consideration and criticism. The memorandum was published in the April 1917 issue of the *Federal Reserve Bulletin* and reprinted (with minor changes) in 1917 in pamphlet form under the title *Uniform Accounting* and again in 1918 under the title *Approved Methods for the Preparation of Balance Sheet Statements.*[7] A revised edition entitled *Verification of Financial Statements* was published by the Federal Reserve Board in 1929.

The 1929 edition, like the 1918 edition, set forth suggestions for the verification and preparation of statements specifically for credit purposes. It stated, however: "A more condensed form of balance sheet is usually prepared for general distribution, but in no case should any essential feature be omitted."[8] The instructions contained in this bulletin were

---

[7] "Uniform Accounting" also appeared in the June 1919 issue of *Journal of Accountancy*, pp. 401–33, and in *Canadian Chartered Accountant,* July 1917, pp. 5–33.

[8] *Verification of Financial Statements,* rev., A Method of Procedure submitted by the Federal Reserve Board for the Consideration of Bankers, Merchants, Manufacturers, Auditors, and Accountants (Washington, D.C.: U.S. Government Printing Office, 1929), p. v. See also *Journal of Accountancy,* May 1929, pp. 321–54.

submitted for use by auditors; however, the reporting procedures as well as the auditing procedures were given, and these were believed to represent the best modern practice of the profession.

The following general observations on the content of the 1929 edition and the suggested procedures regarding the balance sheet reflect some of the accounting thought of the 1920s, but stem largely from the credit objective of the statements: (1) Most of the instructions relate to the audit and presentation of balance sheet accounts, particularly current assets and current liabilities. (2) Inventories are to be stated at cost or market price, whichever is lower. (3) In regard to the audit and presentation of fixed assets, emphasis was on the changes during the period and a classification of the items included. Departures from the cost basis were permitted if disclosure was made regarding the basis of the appraisal.

The following observations relating to the profit and loss statement were suggested in the 1929 bulletin: (1) Depreciation is included under the caption "deductions from income" along with interest and taxes. (2) A distinction is made between "net income for the period" and "profit and loss for the period." The profit and loss for the period is the result of adding special credits to and deducting special charges from net income for the period. (3) Adjustments of prior periods are treated as additions to or subtractions from surplus. (4) The combined form of profit and loss and surplus statement is suggested.

The 1936 revision of the bulletin was prepared and published by the American Institute of Accountants and entitled *Examination of Financial Statements by Independent Public Accountants*. This bulletin serves as an interesting contrast to the 1929 edition. The preface to this edition states:

> Developments of accounting practice during recent years have been in the direction of increased emphasis on accounting principles and consistency in their application, and of fuller disclosure of the basis on which the accounts are stated. . . . The suggestions contained in this bulletin are intended to apply to examinations by independent public accountants of financial statements prepared for credit purposes or for *annual reports to stockholders.* [9]

The following observations and quotations from the 1936 revision indicate some of the changes in accounting thought during the seven intervening years since the 1929 edition was published:

1. The general objective of accounting statements is changed:

> Financial statements are prepared for the purpose of presenting a periodical review or report on progress by the management and deal with the status of the investment in the business and the results achieved during the period under review.

---

[9] American Institute of Accountants, *Examination of Financial Statements by Independent Public Accountants* (New York: January 1936), p. v. (Italics added for emphasis.)

2.   An increased emphasis on the cost basis and the going-concern concept is specifically stated:

> One of the important accounting conventions is that the balance sheet of a going concern shall be prepared on the assumption that the concern will continue in business. Plant assets, permanent investments and intangibles are usually stated at cost or on some other historical basis without regard to present realizable or replacement value.[10]

3.   With the increased emphasis on the cost basis, the writers of the 1936 bulletin recognized the need for greater consistency in the application of procedures.

4.   Reflecting the need for better information for investors, the need for an improvement in the reporting of income and the recognition of the earning power concept of income are stated in the bulletin:

> From an investor's point of view, it is generally recognized today that earning capacity is of vital importance and that the income account is at least as important as the balance sheet.[11]

5.   The emphasis on the income statement is then reflected in the general approach to the balance sheet—recognizing changes in the balance sheet from year to year, rather than placing significance in a single statement.

6.   The suggested profit and loss statement is more concise than that recommended in 1929. Nonoperating or extraordinary charges and credits are included in the "other income" and "other charges" captions. The item "net income for the period" is then eliminated, and the final figure is called "net profit (loss) for period carried to surplus."

One of the important characteristics of the 1936 *Bulletin* was the elimination of all references to the balance sheet audit, the term "examination of financial statements" being substituted therefor. The balance sheet audit was first heard of about 1910 and achieved widespread popularity by 1917. The desire on the part of clients to save audit expenses and the fact that its special conservatism was acceptable to bankers appear to have been the main factors responsible for the popularity of the balance sheet audit. Its popularity was very important to the development of accounting theory because it temporarily counteracted those forces that normally would have shifted the emphasis from the balance sheet to the income statement much sooner. The development and growth of the large corporation, the rapid development of cost accounting methods, and the income tax laws all tended to emphasize the profit and loss viewpoint.[12]

---

[10] Ibid., p. 2.

[11] Ibid., p. 4.

[12] Stephen Gilman, *Accounting Concepts of Profit* (New York: Ronald Press, 1939), pp. 35–37.

DEVELOPMENT OF ACCOUNTING PRINCIPLES BY THE AMERICAN INSTITUTE OF CERTIFIED PUBLIC ACCOUNTANTS

What have become known in the United States as "generally accepted accounting principles" (GAAP) have been influenced considerably by the pronouncements of the AICPA, particularly before the formation of the Financial Accounting Standards Board in 1973. Since the 1930s, this influence was the result of reports of special committees, *Accounting Research Bulletins* issued by the Committee on Accounting Procedure, *Accounting Terminology Bulletins* issued by the Committee on Terminology, *Research Studies* of the Accounting Research Division, and *Opinions* and *Statements* of the Accounting Principles Board.

The special committees

Before the formation of the continuing Committee on Accounting Procedure in 1938, special committees of the AIA (AICPA) had made material contributions toward the development of accounting standards. For example, a special committee worked from 1927 to 1930 on the development of the definition of *earned surplus*. Another special committee reported in 1929 on asset valuations in the balance sheet. Other committees studied such topics as terminology and accounting principles in foreign exchange.

In the early 1930s the New York Stock Exchange attempted to improve the reporting of firms listed with it by seeking the assistance of corporate officials, the Controllers Institute (now the Financial Executives Institute), and the AIA. As a result, a Special Committee (of the AIA) on Cooperation with the Stock Exchanges was appointed to set forth some general objectives for the improvement of accounting standards. In a letter dated September 22, 1932, addressed to the Committee on Stock List of the New York Stock Exchange, the AIA committee made the observation that with the growing complexity of business units, the measurement of firm progress from year to year by annual valuations had become increasingly impracticable. As an alternative, the committee recommended the earning capacity of the enterprise as the real value of any large business. It also recommended the universal acceptance by listed corporations of certain broad principles of accounting that had won general acceptance and that no attempt should be made to restrict the right of corporations to select their own accounting methods within these broad principles.[13]

The Institute's special committee recommended five rules to the New York Stock Exchange in 1933. These rules are summarized as follows: (1)

---

[13] AIA, *Audits of Corporate Accounts*, 1933. Reprinted in G. O. May, *Twenty-Five Years of Accounting Responsibility, 1911–1936* (AIA, 1936), pp. 119–20.

Unrealized profit should not be credited to the income account either directly or indirectly. Profit is deemed to be realized when a sale in the ordinary course of business is effected except under special circumstances. (2) Capital surplus should not be used to relieve the income account of any year except upon reorganization or quasi reorganization. (3) "Earned surplus of a subsidiary company created prior to acquisition does not form a part of the consolidated earned surplus of the parent company and subsidiaries; nor can any dividend declared out of such surplus properly be credited to the income account of the parent company." (4) Dividends on treasury stock should not be credited to income. (5) Notes or accounts receivable due from officers, employees, or affiliated companies must be shown separately. They also recommended the first standard form of auditors' report, which included the term "accepted principles of accounting" later changed to "generally accepted accounting principles."

These five rules, plus a sixth rule regarding donated capital stock and asset valuation, were adopted by the Special Committee on Development of Accounting Principles and by the membership of the Institute in 1934. These six rules, together with the report of the Committee on Accounting Procedure to the Executive Committee in 1938, dealing with profits or losses on treasury stock, were published as *Accounting Research Bulletin No. 1* in September 1939 and reprinted in chapter 1 of *Accounting Research Bulletin No. 43*.

The Committee on Accounting Procedure

From 1933 to 1936, a Special Committee on Development of Accounting Principles was comprised of seven members, each of whom was the chairman of a designated Institute committee. From 1936 to 1938 a similarly constituted committee had the title of Committee on Accounting Procedure. And from 1938 until 1959, the Committee on Accounting Procedure was comprised of 21 members. The decision of the Institute Council to expand the committee in 1938 and to authorize it to issue pronouncements on matters of accounting principle and procedure was based on the belief that this was necessary to establish practices that would become generally accepted by corporations.

As evidenced by the topics of the special committees and the *Accounting Research Bulletins* published by the Committee on Accounting Procedure before 1960, the AICPA devoted its attention almost entirely to resolving specific accounting problems and topics rather than developing general accounting principles. Because of the urgency of solving specific problems, it was necessary to use the limited resources of the Institute in putting out fires, rather than in developing fire prevention.

The *Accounting Research Bulletins*.   Before publication, the *Accounting Research Bulletins* were to be examined by the Technical Services Department and the Director of Research of the Institute and be approved by at least two thirds of the members of the Committee on Accounting Procedure. These bulletins, however, were not directives to the members of the Institute, but received their authority only upon their general acceptance by the profession. In 1964, however, the Council of the Institute adopted recommendations that departures from effective *Bulletins* (as well as *Opinions* of the Accounting Principles Board) should be disclosed in financial statements or in audit reports of members of the Institute.

Of the first 42 bulletins, 8 were reports of the Committee on Terminology and were published separately in 1953 as *Accounting Terminology Bulletin No. 1,* "Review and Resume." Of the remaining 34 bulletins, 31 were consolidated and rewritten as *Accounting Research Bulletin No. 43,* and between 1953 and 1959 *Bulletins No. 44* through *51* were published. Several bulletins have been superseded by statements of the Accounting Principles Board and the Financial Accounting Standards Board.

Although the bulletins dealt with specific topics requiring greater uniformity of treatment or clarification of accepted standards, several general principles or standards are specifically stated or implied throughout. These are summarized as follows:

1. With respect to the determination of income, the current operating concept of income for material items was presented as the basic standard in Chapter 8 of *Accounting Research Bulletin No. 43.* Supporting this general recommendation, the combined statement of income and earned surplus was suggested in chapter 2(B).

2. The concept of revenue realization at the time of sale was implied in the recommendations regarding inventory pricing (chapter 4). Exceptions were permitted in the case of precious metals (chapter 4), cost-plus-fixed-fee contracts (chapter 11A), and in the case of long-term construction-type contracts when estimates of costs to complete and the extent of progress are reasonably dependable (*Bulletin No. 45*). Exceptions were also permitted in the cases where uncertainty was high, as in the case of foreign operations (chapter 12).

3. The proper recognition of expenses when benefits are received and the distinction between expenses and losses were discussed under several topics. These include the amortization of intangible costs (chapter 5); the handling of real and personal property taxes and income taxes (chapter 10); the treatment of pension costs and employee stock options (chapter 13 and *Bulletin No. 47*); the treatment of unamortized discount, issue cost, and redemption premium on bonds refunded (chapter 15); and the acceptance of the declining-balance method of depreciation for accounting purposes and the adjustment of income taxes when the declining-balance method is used only for tax purposes (*Bulletin No. 44*).

4. The general acceptance of the cost basis of accounting is reflected in the discussions of inventory pricing (chapter 4), accounting for depreciation during period of high costs (chapter 9A), and in the preparation of consolidated statements (chapter 12 and *Bulletin No. 51*).

5. Proper disclosure and classification of balance sheet and income

statement items were presented in several places. Disclosure was discussed in relationship to the presentation of comparative statements (chapter 2A), the proper use of contingency reserves (chapter 6 and *Bulletin No. 50*), the disclosure of long-term leases (chapter 14), the dating of earned surplus (*Bulletin No. 46*), and the presentation of earnings per share (*Bulletin No. 49*). Proper classification was discussed in the presentation of current assets and current liabilities (chapter 3) and in the proper distinction between capital and income accounts (chapter 7 and *Bulletin No. 48*).

The *Terminology Bulletins*.   While a Committee on Terminology had been constituted as early as 1920, the terminology bulletins summarized in *Accounting Terminology Bulletin No. 1,* and the three bulletins published from 1955 to 1959 reflect the opinions of the Committees on Terminology from 1939 to 1959. As the members of this committee were chosen primarily from the membership of the Committee on Accounting Procedure, it is not surprising that general principles and standards implied in the stated definitions do not differ significantly from the general principles and standards implied in the *Accounting Research Bulletins*. These are summarized as follows:

1.   The importance of the income statement is reflected in the definition of the *balance sheet* as a summary of balances carried forward—a step between two income statements (paragraphs 10 and 21 of *Bulletin No. 1*).
2.   The emphasis on the cost basis is reflected in the definition of *value* (paragraph 36) and in the definition of *depreciation* (paragraph 56).
3.   The general standard of revenue realization at the time of sale is implied in the definition of *revenue* in *Accounting Terminology Bulletin No. 2*.

The Accounting Principles Board

Particularly during the 1950s, the Committee on Accounting Procedure of the Institute was criticized for moving too slowly in the preparation of the written expression of generally accepted accounting principles. It also found itself unable to cope with major institutional changes in business practice because of a lack of research facilities. Recognizing the problem, Alvin R. Jennings, the president of the Institute, proposed in October 1957 a new research organization to examine basic accounting assumptions, identify "best" principles, and devise new methods to guide industry and the accounting profession.[14] As a result of Jennings' speech, the Special Committee on Research Program was appointed in December 1957.

_____

[14] Alvin R. Jennings, "Present-Day Challenges in Financial Reporting," *Journal of Accountancy,* January 1958, pp. 28–34.

Its report of December 1958 recommended the formation of the Accounting Principles Board and an accounting research staff.

As a result of the reorganization of 1959, the Accounting Principles Board was formed to supersede the Committee on Accounting Principles, with increased authority and responsibilities. The objectives of the Board were to advance the written expression of generally accepted accounting principles, narrow the areas of difference in appropriate practice, and lead in discussions of unsettled and controversial issues. Its official pronouncements were intended to be based primarily on the extensive studies of the Accounting Research Division; its conclusions were to be supported by reasoning; and the opinions were to include minority dissents by members of the Board. The composition of the Board was 18 to 21 members selected primarily from the accounting profession, but also including members representing industry, the academic community, and government (all members of the Institute, however).

The *Opinions* of the Accounting Principles Board and effective *Accounting Research Bulletins* of the former Committee on Accounting Procedure were enforced primarily through the prestige of the Institute and the APB. In 1964, the Council of the Institute adopted recommendations that after 1965 all departures from *APB Opinions* and effective *Accounting Research Bulletins* should be disclosed in footnotes to financial statements or in audit reports of members. That is, all *Opinions* of the APB were considered to constitute substantial authoritative support for generally accepted accounting principles. And while the Institute recognized that there might be other sources of authoritative support, the decision in these cases rested with the reporting member. A member who decided that the principle or procedure did not have substantial authoritative support was required to handle the situation in accordance with the Code of Professional Ethics of the Institute (Rule 203). If the principle did have support outside the official pronouncements of the APB, the member was required to disclose such departure if material. A failure to disclose was considered to be substandard reporting and was referred to the Practice Review Committee of the Institute. The activities of this committee were concerned with educating the reporting member and encouraging compliance with the above recommendations. The committee also published bulletins periodically to encourage self-discipline among Institute members through education.

During the 14 years of the life of the APB, it published 31 *Opinions* and four *Statements*. These *Opinions* can be classified roughly as (1) Interpretive opinions and amendments and clarifications of prior statements of the APB or the previous Committee on Accounting Procedure; (2) *Opinions* relating primarily to disclosure of information not presented formally in the financial statements; (3) *Opinions* relating primarily to the form of the financial statements or to classifications within the statements; and (4) *Opinions* attempting to narrow the alternatives for the valuation of assets and liabilities and the amount of reported net income.

How does this record compare with the stated objectives of the APB at its inception? Did it advance the written expression of generally accepted accounting principles, narrow the areas of difference in practice, and lead in discussions of unsettled and controversial issues? According to Moonitz, the Board found ready acceptance of the *Opinions* relating to the form of financial statements and the classification of items within statements.[15] However, topics relating to the amount of net income and the valuation of assets and liabilities were much more difficult in finding agreement among the members of the Board as well as obtaining acceptance by the profession, the financial executives, the Securities and Exchange Commission, and others. As a result, exposure drafts were rewritten extensively before the final *Opinion* was published in many cases and in several cases, subsequent opinions were issued to amend or change extensively the recommendations of earlier opinions.

One of the best-known controversies was that regarding the investment tax credit. *Opinion No. 2* recommended that the investment credit be handled in effect as a deferral of the tax saving. Since this *Opinion* was issued with a considerable minority dissent, it is not surprising to find that it was not well-received by professional accountants. Because of this difference of opinion, the SEC accepted both the deferral method and the flow-through method in reports filed with it. The confusion that resulted forced the APB to reconsider its position and release an amendment (*Opinion No. 4*) permitting several alternatives, including the immediate reduction of income tax expense. This failure of the APB to establish uniformity in this matter was one of the basic causes for the recommendation, mentioned above, that disclosures of departures from *APB Opinions* be made mandatory. A sequel to this conflict was an attempt to reinstate only one method for handling the investment credit in *Opinion No. 11, "Income Taxes."* General opposition, and specific opposition from the Internal Revenue Service in this case, caused the APB to withdraw this recommendation before the final draft in order to restudy the case. These situations serve to point out the difficulty in resolving conflict in accounting arising from diverse objectives and diverse origins of concepts accepted as valid accounting theory. Another example is the fact that even after four *Opinions* on the subject of leasing, this topic was placed high on the agenda for study and resolution by the Financial Accounting Standards Board.

The APB used two other methods of communicating recommendations on reporting problems. The first was a series of four *Statements*. The first of these was merely a report on the receipt of *Accounting Research Studies Nos. 1 and 3* from the Accounting Research Division without taking further action on them. *Statement No. 2* was an interim recommendation on the "Disclosure of Supplemental Financial Information by Diversified

---

[15] Maurice Moonitz, "Obtaining Agreement on Standards in the Accounting Profession," *Studies in Accounting Research No. 8* (AAA, 1974), pp. 23–24.

Companies" in advance of research and study by the Board. *Statement No. 3* was a detailed recommendation for the supplemental presentation of general price-level restatements without making them mandatory. *Statement No. 4* was an attempt to carry out their charge to devote its attention to the broad fundamentals as well as to specific accounting problems. This *Statement* is discussed more fully below. The second method was a series of *Accounting Interpretations* relating to the application of the *Opinions*. Although the interpretations required only the approval of the executive vice president of the Institute and the chairman of the APB, they were considered to be authoritative pronouncements because they expressed what the APB intended in the *Opinions*.

The Accounting Research Division

Attempts to prepare a comprehensive statement of accounting principles that would be all-inclusive were made and abandoned by the Institute in 1939 and in 1949–50. But in 1959, acting on the recommendations of the Special Committee on Research Program, the Institute was reorganized to permit the advancement of "the written expression of what constitutes generally accepted accounting principles for the guidance of its members and of others."[16] One of the objectives of the reorganization was to be able to attack the broad problems of financial accounting at four levels: (1) the establishment of basic postulates; (2) the establishment of broad principles; (3) the setting up of rules or other guides for the application of principles in specific situations; and (4) research. Accordingly, a permanent accounting research staff was organized to carry out the research program.

Research studies were made by independent investigators or by members of the research staff under the advisement of the director of accounting research and a project advisory committee. Upon completion of a research project, the results of the investigation and the conclusions were published to stimulate interest and discussion before the Accounting Principles Board made a pronouncement on the subject. The *Research Studies,* therefore, were not official pronouncements of the Institute but were published under the authority of the director of accounting research.

The major differences between this approach to accounting research and the development of accounting principles and the earlier approach of the Institute are as follows: (1) The approach of the Accounting Research Division was intended to be broader in scope and to rely more heavily on the deductive method in the development of accounting principles and their application to accounting practice. (2) The Research Division cooperated with the Accounting Principles Board, but it was intended to be a more independent division than was the Accounting Research Depart-

---

[16] "Report to Council of the Special Committee on Research Program," *Journal of Accountancy,* 106 (December 1958): p. 62.

ment in its relationships to the Committee on Accounting Principles before 1960. (3) The *Research Studies* were given wide publicity to stimulate discussion before being acted upon by the Accounting Principles Board. (4) The *Research Studies* were intended to provide a detailed discussion of the problems with a complete reasoning leading to the conclusions.

Accounting Research Study No. 1, entitled "The Basic Postulates of Accounting," and *ARS No. 3*, entitled "A Tentative Set of Broad Accounting Principles for Business Enterprises," resulted from the directive in the Report of the Special Committee on Research Program and in the Charter Rules of the Accounting Principles Board, which stated,

> As soon as possible after its organization the Division shall undertake a study of the basic postulates underlying accounting principles generally . . . [and] undertake a study of the broad principles of accounting, and the preparation of a reasonably condensed statement thereof. The results of these, as adopted by the [Accounting Principles] Board, shall serve as the foundation for the entire body of subsequent pronouncements by the Institute on accounting matters, to which each new release shall be related.[17]

With the release of these two basic *Research Studies,* the Accounting Principles Board reacted promptly with a statement to the effect that they were too radically different from generally accepted practice for the Board to consider their acceptance at that time, while they recognized the contribution of the studies to accounting thought.

As a result of the rejection of *ARS Nos. 1* and *3,* on the grounds that they did not represent statements of what accounting principles were at that time, a new study was commissioned to review existing accounting principles. Thus, *ARS No. 7* was published under the title "Inventory of Generally Accepted Accounting Principles for Business Enterprises." The purposes of this study were to discuss the basic concepts of accepted accounting principles, to summarize accepted principles and practices, and to summarize the pronouncements of the Accounting Principles Board and its predecessor committee. One major difference between this study and *ARS Nos. 1* and *3* was the emphasis on inductive and pragmatic methods and the practical applications of accounting, instead of the deductive method. Accounting is thought to attain its validity through the test of experience, although a few alternative new methods are suggested as worthy of experimentation. Diversity in accounting was proposed as a basic concept, in recognition of diversity in business life. While this study had greater acceptance by the accounting profession than did *ARS Nos. 1* and *3,* it did not lead to a statement of broad principles of accounting. Accordingly, *Accounting Research Studies* continued to be ad hoc studies without a common foundation supporting them. Each study was based on

---

[17] Ibid.

the researcher's basic fundamental concepts and findings in the specific area.

Including these 3 *Studies,* 15 were published during the life of the Accounting Principles Board. How well did they meet the original intent that they be thorough-going independent studies upon which pronouncements of the Board would rest? According to Thomas Burns, only a little more than a third of the *Opinions* could be linked even casually with prior research studies.[18] The recommendations of the *Research Studies* were not followed in the *Opinions* for several reasons: (1) Independent reasoning and preconceived notions of Board members led to different conclusions. (2) The research and argumentation of the *Studies* were not always thorough or convincing. (3) Pressure came from certain groups or bodies who had a vested interest in the specific procedures or results. (4) Practitioners resisted rapid change because of the disturbance and confusion it might cause. (5) Traditionally, new methods have been brought into practice as an addition to existing procedures, but the pressure to reduce the number of alternatives requires that a choice be made; therefore, the new ideas of the studies were deferred. (6) The completion of *Research Studies* was a slow process, and new problems arose demanding solutions faster than the research studies could be produced. Accordingly, particularly during the last six years of the life of the APB, there appeared to be no attempt to rely on assistance from research studies. According to Zeff, the APB was then ". . . working in very much the manner of its predecessor, the Committee on Accounting Procedure."[19]

APB Statement No. 4

As indicated above, the Charter Rules of the Accounting Principles Board directed the Accounting Research Division to study the basic postulates and broad principles of accounting to serve as the foundation for subsequent pronouncements after being adopted by the Board.[20] *ARS Nos. 1* and *3* were rejected by the APB; although *ARS No. 7* was received more politely, it was also not accepted by the APB as the statement referred to in its Charter. Subsequently, a Special Committee (of the AICPA) on Opinions of the Accounting Principles Board recommended that at the earliest possible time, the Board should, among other things, set forth the objectives of accounting, enumerate and describe basic concepts and accounting principles, and define words and phrases used in accounting including the term "generally accepted accounting principles."[21] As a response to this directive, the Board published *APB Statement No. 4,* "Basic

---

[18] From a quotation in Moonitz, "Obtaining Agreement," p. 27.

[19] Stephen A. Zeff, *Forging Accounting Principles in Five Countries: A History and an Analysis of Trends,* Accounting Lectures 1971. (Champaign, Ill.: Stipes Publishing, 1972.

[20] "Report to Council of the Special Committee on Research Program," p. 62.

[21] "Summary of the Report of the Special Committee on Opinions of the Accounting Principles Board," *Journal of Accountancy,* June 1965, pp. 12, 14, 16.

Concepts and Accounting Principles Underlying Financial Statements of Business Enterprises."[22]

In accordance with the above directive, the stated purpose of the *Statement* was to provide a basis for an understanding of the broad fundamentals of accounting and to provide a basis for its future development. How well did the *Statement* meet these two objectives? First, it should be emphasized that by its own admission, the *Statement* is primarily descriptive, not prescriptive. This fact, alone, limits its ability to provide a basis for the development of financial accounting. As stated in George Catlett's dissent to the *Statement,* by granting authoritative support to and providing a conceptual basis for generally accepted accounting principles not studied by the APB, the *Statement* may impede the development of new ideas and new approaches. Granted, the Board stated explicitly that the publication of the *Statement* does not mean the approval by the Board of current practices not covered in *APB Opinions.* But, approval for publication as an *APB Statement* by the Board with only one dissent did give it considerable authority in the accounting profession.

One basic feature of the *Statement,* however, does have prescriptive implications. In the section on users of financial accounting information, it states that "improving financial accounting requires continuing research on the nature of user needs, on the decision processes of users, and on the information that most effectively serves user needs."[23] The section on users and common and special needs of users is an advancement in the official publications of the AICPA. However, the presumption that general-purpose information can provide common needs but not satisfy the specialized needs of individual users is not supported by evidence. The only way to find out what information might be common to the needs of many user groups would be to start with the specialized needs of individual users and then determine what information might be common to the needs of many user groups. *Statement No. 4* makes the assumption without evidence that traditional financial accounting statements satisfy the common needs of many user groups.

Although *Statement No. 4* is intended to provide a basis for an understanding of the broad fundamentals of financial accounting, it is deficient as a theory of accounting for several reasons. First, although the section on the environment of financial accounting presents interpretive (semantic) descriptions of such concepts as economic resources and economic obligations, these are not related to the terms used in describing financial accounting. Since the accounting terms do not have interpretive content, the statement does not go beyond the structure or procedural content of accounting. For example, *assets* is defined as "economic resources (and certain deferred charges that are not resources) of an enterprise that are recognized and measured in conformity with generally accepted account-

---

[22] *Accounting Principles Board Statement No. 4,* "Basic Concepts and Accounting Principles Underlying Financial Statements of Business Enterprises" (AICPA, 1970).

[23] *APB Statement No. 4,* p. 20.

ing principles." Thus, the definitions are not expressed in terms of real-world objects or events.

Second, there is not a clear relationship between the objectives, the basic elements of financial accounting, and the pervasive and detailed principles. Thus, as a theory of existing practice, it is incomplete. For example, no evidence or logic is presented to show that the pervasive principle that "assets and liabilities are measured by the exchange prices at which the transfers take place" (p. 57) follows from the primary qualitative objective of relevance (p. 36). Nor is there any logical relationship between the broad operating principle that "costs of some assets are charged to expense immediately on accquisition" (p. 85) is derived from the pervasive principle that assets are measured at cost.

Third, a complete theory should contain descriptive statements that are verified empirically or at least are verifiable. When normative statements are made, the basis for the judgment should be given. Neither of these conditions is found in *Statement No. 4*. While it is conceded that generally accepted accounting principles "become generally accepted by agreement rather than by formal derivation from a set of postulates or basic concepts" (p. 55), the *Statement* does not indicate the basis for establishing when agreement exists. What percentage of disagreement would deny a specific practice the right to be included among GAAP? Apparently, the authors of the *Statement* were in doubt themselves, since many of the principles of financial statement presentation are stated in normative terms without presenting the basis for the judgment in each case.

In summary, *Statement No. 4* is neither a theory of current accounting practice, nor a clear statement of generally accepted accounting principles. In the words of Staubus, the *Statement* is "a fine set of objectives of financial accounting juxtaposed against a set of principles that clearly fall short of what is needed to meet the objectives."[24] But the APB should not be criticized too severely for attempting to do what was impossible. Accounting theory had not arrived at a stage where a grand theory could have been formulated.

THE FINANCIAL ACCOUNTING STANDARDS BOARD

Even during its first five years of life, the Accounting Principles Board came under attack from several directions for its inability to fulfill its mission to narrow the areas of difference and inconsistency in accounting practice and advance financial reporting in new problem areas. Much of this initial attack came from the accounting profession itself.[25] But

---

[24] George J. Staubus, "An Analysis of *APB Statement No. 4*," *Journal of Accountancy,* February 1972, p. 43.

[25] For example, see *A Search for Fairness in Financial Reporting to the Public,* selected addresses by Leonard Spacek (Chicago: Arthur Andersen & Co., 1969).

pressures also came from the Securities and Exchange Commission and other government agencies. It became common to predict that if the APB did not accelerate its progress in establishing accounting principles, the SEC would take the initiative in doing so.[26]

As a result of these basic criticisms of the Accounting Principles Board, the rapid change in financial institutions, and the many abuses of financial accounting reporting during the 1960s, a seven-member group was appointed by the Board of Directors of the Institute in March 1971 to study the establishment of accounting standards. The report of the Wheat Study Group was submitted to the AICPA in March 1972 and adopted by the AICPA Council in June.[27] Its recommendations included the following: (1) The establishment of a Financial Accounting Foundation (FAF) to be separate from all other professional bodies with principal duties to appoint the members of the Financial Accounting Standards Board and to raise the funds for its operations. (2) The formation of a Financial Accounting Standards Board consisting of seven full-time members appointed by the Board of Trustees of the FAF. The Board's function was to be establishing standards for financial reporting and necessary interpretations. (3) The formation of a Financial Accounting Standards Advisory Council of approximately 20 members appointed by the Board of Trustees of the Foundation (41 members in 1981). Serving without compensation, (except for the Chairman and Executive Director in 1981) the members of the Council were to assist the Standards Board in maintaining contact with business and the accounting profession. (4) The organization of an accounting research staff closely associated with the Standards Board.

What were the major causes of this crisis that brought down the APB and led to the formation of the FASB? First, the decade of the 1960s was a period of rapid change in business and financial institutions and methods. Corporate mergers and acquisitions, particularly by the so-called conglomerates, seemed to be the easiest way to give the appearance of rapid growth in assets, profits, and earnings per share. By selecting from among alternative accounting practices that were generally accepted, these firms were able to report earnings per share figures that gave the appearance of high rates of growth. A large number of new issues of exotic securities created new accounting problems to be solved. The investment tax credit and other new tax laws created larger differences between reported income and taxable income and thus a greater significance to the question of tax allocation. Other financial reporting problems arose in the greatly expanded franchising industries, in the land development businesses, and in the reporting of many new types of lease transactions. The writings of Briloff during this period had a considerable impact in bringing to the

---

[26] See, for example, Robert N. Anthony, "Showdown on Accounting Principles," *Harvard Business Review,* May-June 1963, pp. 99–106.

[27] "Establishing Financial Accounting Standards: Report of the Study on Establishment of Accounting Principles" (AICPA, 1972).

attention of the financial community the abuses of financial reporting in these several areas.[28]

A second major area of disturbance was the disclosure of a number of fraud cases wherein unqualified audited financial reports were subsequently found to be misleading because of a failure to disclose relevant information or because of a failure in the interpretation and application of generally accepted accounting principles. Equity Funding, Student Marketing, Penn Central, and Investors Overseas Services are among the names that will be long remembered in financial circles as situations where fraud and misrepresentations in financial reporting went hand in hand.

A third major area causing distrust in the ability of the APB to operate effectively was its inability to establish basic fundamentals to serve as a guide in the establishment of principles and the failure to integrate basic research into the official pronouncements. As a result, the Board was unable to obtain general acceptance for many of its proposals. In some cases *Opinions* were issued to modify previous *Opinions,* and in other cases exposure drafts were changed significantly to permit alternative methods rather than narrowing the number of alternatives. Among others, disagreements continued in the areas of the investment tax credit, income tax allocation, purchase and pooling accounting, earnings per share, and the equity method of reporting nonconsolidated subsidiaries. As a result, the APB was accused of an inability to solve major reporting problems, a failure to take prompt action when required, and a failure to take into consideration the views of all interested parties.

How well can the FASB overcome these obstacles and meet new problems as they arise? The current status of the FASB and problems in the development of accounting policy are discussed in Chapter 6.

The conceptual Framework Project

The conceptual Framework Project of the FASB can be considered to reflect a revolution in accounting thought. Some of the changes have evolved gradually since the publication of the Paton and Littleton Monograph in 1940.[29] Other changes have obtained general acceptance since the publication of *APB Statement No. 4* in 1970. Some of these changes in accounting thought are: (1) an emphasis on a broad social objective of accounting; (2) a recognition of the decision-usefulness approach and the perceived importance of cash flows in decision processes; (3) a basic change in approach from the matching concept of income to an emphasis on the measurements in the balance sheet with income measured by

---

[28] See Abraham J. Briloff, *Unaccountable Accounting* (New York: Harper & Row, 1972) and his several articles in *Barron's* and *Forbes Magazine* and in several accounting journals during the 1960s.

[29] W. A. Paton and A. C. Littleton, *An Introduction to Corporate Accounting Standards,* American Accounting Association Monograph No. 3 (AAA, 1940).

balance sheet changes; and (4) an emphasis on the semantic interpretation of the elements of financial statements, rather than on the former
reliance on procedural definitions.

The broad social objective in *Statement of Financial Accounting Concepts No. 1* (*SFAC 1*) is that financial reporting should enhance the effectiveness of securities and money markets in allocating scarce resources
among competing uses. This is assumed to be attained if financial reporting provides information useful to those that make investment and loan
decisions. But the recognition of a broad social objective is not new. Paton
and Littleton, for example, stated that "there is another way in which
accounting is important from the social point of view. Capital should flow
into those industries which serve the public interest, and within an industry into those enterprises in which the management is capable of using
capital effectively."[30] Paton and Littleton, however, did not link this to
accounting, but *SFAC 1* attempts to do so.

The role of accounting in the aggregate working of the economy is
vague. However, *SFAC 1* assumes that this objective leads to the selection
of investors and creditors as the prime potential users of accounting information. Although a case could be made for a broader group of users,
there is a general consensus that accounting reports should be useful for
at least these individuals.

The assumption that investors and creditors *are* interested in cash
flows has not been verified. Although it may be relatively easy to agree
with this premise (on a priori grounds), it is more difficult to take the next
step that assumes that the "interest in an enterprise's future cash flows
and its ability to generate favorable cash flows leads primarily to an
interest in information about its earnings rather than information directly about its cash flows."[31] This statement may be true if either (1)
accrual accounting provides a better prediction of future cash flows than a
record of past cash flows or (2) accrual accounting provides information
that can be used in conjunction with other information to make cash flow
predictions. With respect to the former, there appears to be some truth in
the statement regarding accruals, but not for deferrals. The second alternative is more difficult to evaluate because little is known about the
decision processes of individuals, particularly with respect to the ability
to combine different sources and types of information.

The change from an income-oriented approach in the Paton-Littleton
model to a balance sheet approach is potentially more significant than the
changes in objectives. It represents a different approach than that taken
in previous pronouncements, even in *APB Statement No. 4*. In the Paton-
Littleton model, income is the result of matching revenues and expenses,
and the balance sheet represents the unallocated debits and credits carried forward plus the monetary claims and obligations. In the conceptual

---

[30] Ibid., p. 3.
[31] *AICPA Professional Standards,* para. 1210.43.

framework model, the assets and liabilities in the balance sheet are assumed to be measured independently of the income computation. Comprehensive income represents the total change in net assets during a period, except for those arising from transactions with stockholders.

Another very significant change is the adoption of the qualitative characteristic of representational faithfulness (semantic interpretation). This is not unrelated to the balance sheet approach because if the balance sheet is the focal point in the accounting model, the individual items must have interpretative significance. Together, the two concepts could result in a framework for the reporting of resources and obligations and a measure of comprehensive income that may have greater information content than reported income as currently computed.

If these two basic concepts (the balance sheet approach and representational faithfulness) are interpreted fairly strictly, the conceptual framework could be considered to be revolutionary. However, if they had been interpreted narrowly, they probably would not have been adopted by the Board, and there would have been opposition to them. Because the Board did not wish to foreclose the use of current practices, a broad interpretation is given to the definitions of assets and liabilities and to the interpretation of representational faithfulness. As a result, the conceptual framework project has done little more than rule out the deferral of losses, which has not been condoned in recent years.

The current status and problems in the development of accounting policy by the FASB and the SEC are discussed in Chapter 6.

THE DEVELOPMENT OF ALTERNATIVE
THEORY APPROACHES

Most of the development of accounting thought has come from the research and writings of individuals or teams in the academic community and from a few authors and researchers in the accounting profession. Accounting literature relating to accounting theories can be classified as follows: (1) discussions critical of specific areas of accounting theory or practice and pointing out specific anomalies, (2) articles and books advocating new theories or partial theories and approaches, (3) attempts to formulate a general theory of accounting, (4) the adaptation of theories from other disciplines to accounting, and (5) empirical tests of theories or partial theories. The following is a brief description of some of the writings that have led to current theories and proposals.

Accounting literature in the 1920s and 1930s

The accounting thought expressed in some of the texts and journals published in the 1920s and 1930s was more advanced than accounting practice of that time. Hatfield, for example, discussed the current value concept in his 1909 and 1927 editions.[32] In his 1909 edition, however, he was more favorable to the valuation of inventories at the present value to the holders as a "going concern," while in his 1927 edition he favored the cost basis for fixed assets, despite a subsequent decline in their value. For circulating assets, he considered current values as the most relevant, but questioned their acceptance when they exceeded the original cost. With respect to income, Hatfield discussed in his 1909 edition what were later to be called the all-inclusive and current operating concepts of income.

Canning made a valuable contribution to accounting theory in *The Economics of Accountancy,* published in 1929.[33] The subtitle, "A Critical Analysis of Accounting Theory," helps explain this contribution. Canning drew from the writings of Cole, Hatfield, McKinsey, Montgomery, Paton, Stevenson, and Sprague; he also compared the current accounting thought with economic theory, particularly with that set forth by Irving Fisher. The two most important areas discussed by Canning were the valuation problems and concepts and the measurement and concepts of net income.

Two significant publications of the mid-1930s treating specific areas of accounting theory are Perry Mason's *Principles of Public-Utility Depreciation*[34] and Henry Sweeney's *Stabilized Accounting.*[35] In addition to presenting a set of general principles for the treatment of depreciation by public utility commissions, Mason discussed the basic concepts of depreciation and provided a framework for a clearer understanding of the depreciation process. Sweeney's contribution was a presentation of the first complete discussion of the adjustment of financial statements for the effect of price-level changes. His major contribution to accounting theory was the criticism of the general acceptance of the monetary measurement as representing a stable purchasing power over time. His recommendations for the adjustment of financial statements by the use of a single conversion purchasing power index are discussed more fully in a later chapter.

Much of the writing of the early 1930s is summarized in a paper presented by Gilbert R. Byrne at the Fiftieth Anniversary Celebration of the American Institute of Accountants in 1937. His illustrative principles include the following:

1. Accounting is essentially the allocation of historical costs and revenues to the current and succeeding fiscal periods.
2. The investment in an industrial plant should be charged against the operations over the useful life of the plant.
3. In computing the net income (available for dividends) for a period, all forms of expense incurred in the production of such net income must be provided for.

---

[32] Henry Rand Hatfield, *Modern Accounting* (New York: Appleton-Century-Crofts, 1909) and *Accounting, Its Principles and Problems* (1927).

[33] John B. Canning, *The Economics of Accountancy* (New York: Ronald Press, 1929).

[34] Perry Mason, *Principles of Public-Utility Depreciation,* American Accounting Association Monograph No. 1 (AAA, 1937).

[35] Henry W. Sweeney, *Stabilized Accounting* (New York: Harper & Row, 1936).

4. The income shall include only realized profits in the period during which realized; profit is deemed to be realized when a sale in the ordinary course of business is effected, unless the circumstances are such that collection of the sale price is not reasonably assured.
5. Losses, if probable, even though not actually incurred, should be provided for in arriving at net income.
6. Capital-stock and capital-surplus accounts, taken together should represent the net contribution of the proprietors to the business enterprise.
7. Earned surplus should represent the accumulated earnings of the business from transactions with the public, less distributions of such earnings to the stockholders.
8. While it is not in many cases of great importance which of several alternative accounting rules is applied in a given situation, it is essential that, once having adopted a certain procedure, it be consistently adhered to in preparing the accounts over a period of time.[36]

Many of these principles may seem trite or axiomatic to the student who is accustomed to being concerned with the more complex problems of accounting. But in the early 1930s, these were the basic principles necessary for an improvement in accounting theory and practice. Item 1 emphasized the cost basis of accounting and with item 3 states the necessity for a proper matching of revenues and expenses. Item 2, in effect, states that depreciation should be taken; the method of depreciation was of less concern when many firms were still omitting depreciation entirely. Item 4 states the realization postulate, item 5 the doctrine of conservatism, and item 8 the necessity for consistency in accounting.

In 1938, at the request of the Haskins & Sells Foundation, Sanders, Hatfield, and Moore published *A Statement of Accounting Principles.*[37] In the "Letter of Transmittal" to the monograph, the authors stated:

> In the preparation of its statement the committee has attempted to set forth the principles and rules of accounting which dictate what should appear in a balance-sheet and an income statement and in the accounts from which they are compiled.

However, the content of the monograph reveals that the authors were more concerned with accepted practice than with presenting the most advanced ideas of accounting theory. The "accounting principles" were obtained by personal interviews and correspondence with competent persons, by a review of accounting literature, by giving proper consideration to statutes and decisions referring to accounting, and by an examination of current corporation reports. Thus, the monograph probably does represent the best accepted accounting practices of the 1930s.

In summary, the points of major emphasis in the monograph include

---

[36] American Institute of Accountants, *Fiftieth Anniversary Celebration, 1937,* p. 249.

[37] Thomas Henry Sanders, Henry Rand Hatfield, and Underhill Moore, *A Statement of Accounting Principles* (New York: American Institute of Accountants, 1938).

the following: (1) a careful distinction between transactions relating to capital and those relating to revenue; (2) consistent application of accounting procedures; (3) the need for a conservative treatment of items to which judgment must be applied; (4) the application of the current operating concept of income; (5) the application of the cost or market rule with respect to current assets; and (6) in reporting deferred charges, the need for giving particular care to the distinction between charges inuring to the benefit of future periods and losses actually sustained.

In the second monograph published by the American Accounting Association in 1939, Daniels presented an evaluation of these accounting principles as they were reflected in financial statements.[38] He also compared the application of accounting principles with corporate published financial statements, noting considerable improvement since his review of published statements five years earlier.[39]

Also in 1939 Gilman published his *Accounting Concepts of Profit.*[40] This was the first comprehensive discussion of accounting theory since the shift in emphasis from the balance sheet to the income statement point of view. Gilman was particularly interested in the application of the entity theory, the effect of valuation on income determination, and the assignment of income to periods.

Accounting literature from 1940 to the 1960s

Probably the most significant contribution to the development of the historical inductive-deductive cost approach to accounting theory during this period was *An Introduction to Corporate Accounting Standards* by Paton and Littleton published in 1940 as *Monograph No. 3* of the American Accounting Association.[41] The authors were members of the original Executive Committee of the American Accounting Association, which prepared "A Tentative Statement of Accounting Principles Underlying Corporate Financial Statements," published in 1936. *Monograph No. 3* was an attempt to present the basic theory underlying the "Tentative Statement." The intention was to present a framework of accounting theory conceived to be a coherent, coordinated, and consistent body of doctrine from which accounting standards could be formed based on current practice of the time. The objective was to present the financial condition and operations of a firm without taking into consideration the usefulness of the information for users, although owners and creditors as well as management are implicit users. Because of the emphasis on the computa-

---

[38] Mortimer B. Daniels, *Financial Statements,* American Accounting Association Monograph No. 2 (AAA, 1939).

[39] Mortimer B. Daniels, *Corporation Financial Statements* (Ann Arbor: University of Michigan, 1934).

[40] Stephen Gilman, *Accounting Concepts of Profit* (New York: Ronald Press, 1939).

[41] W. A. Paton and A. C. Littleton, *An Introduction to Corporate Accounting Standards,* American Accounting Association Monograph No. 3 (AAA, 1940).

tion of income and the introduction of the matching concept, this has become known as the general purpose income statement approach.

Preceding the income statement approach and continuing to the present are theorists who emphasize the measurement of net assets or economic wealth as a major objective of accounting, leading to the conclusion that income represents a change in wealth. Although this school generally focused on the statement of financial condition in its traditional form as a starting point, many writers proposed the use of market prices as a substitute for historical costs. For example, Edwards and Bell suggested a detailed model for the use of replacement cost in the measurement of subjective value and subjective profit.[42] About the same time, Sprouse and Moonitz proposed the use of discounted present values, sales market prices, and replacement costs in an attempt to measure changes in enterprise wealth.[43]

The 1977 Committee on Concepts and Standards for External Financial Reports of the American Accounting Association classified the major approaches during this period as either true income or inductive approaches.[44] To the extent that income and wealth were considered to be measurements independent of the nature of the use of the measurements, several approaches can be said to be advocates of true measurements. Other works (of which Ijiri's has been the most fully developed in its approach and logic) have been largely inductive and have emphasized the explanation of extant practice.[45] However, most of the research and writing of this period was a combination of inductive approaches, and to the extent that they offered normative prescriptions, they were generally explicitly or implicitly based on either the procedural income approach or the economic wealth approach.

The user-orientation approach

Before the 1960s, a number of writers recognized the importance of accounting information to specific types of users without specifying a decision model or how the information would be used. Alexander, for example, proposed different measures of income for different users.[46] Starting about the late 1950s and the 1960s, a number of writers were concerned with the development of implicit or explicit decision models, both descriptive and

---

[42] E. O. Edwards and P. W. Bell, *The Theory and Measurement of Business Income* (Berkeley: University of California Press, 1961).

[43] Robert T. Sprouse and Maurice Moonitz, "A Tentative Set of Broad Accounting Principles for Business Enterprises," *Accounting Research Study No. 3* (AICPA, 1962).

[44] American Accounting Association Committee on Concepts and Standards, "Statement on Accounting Theory and Theory Acceptance," (AAA, 1977).

[45] Yuji Ijiri, *The Foundations of Accounting Measurement* (Englewood Cliffs, N.J.: Prentice-Hall, 1967).

[46] Sidney S. Alexander, "Income Measurement in a Dynamic Economy," *Five Monographs on Business Income* (New York: The Study Group on Business Income (AICPA, 1950). Reprinted by Scholars Book, Lawrence, Kans., 1973.

normative, of investors and creditors. Several of these writings emphasized the need for cash flow information and other information that were assumed to be of assistance to the investor and creditor in predicting the amount, timing, and probabilities of future cash payments by the enterprise for interest, dividends, or repayment of debt. Staubus, for example, emphasized the "value to investors in judging their future cash receipts from the investment relation" and "the factors upon which the investor's future cash receipts depend."[47] Subsequently, the AAA Committee on External Reporting attempted to use a normative decision model with cash flows as a basic part of the model leading to recommendations regarding the significance of cash flow information as relevant information to be included in financial accounting reports.[48] The explicit assumption that investors wish to predict cash flows from the firm in making investment decisions is found in the report of the AICPA Study Group on the Objectives of Financial Statements[49] and also in *FASB Statement of Financial Accounting Standards No. 1.*[50] However, these two documents state that although the investor is primarily interested in future cash flows, information about the earnings of an enterprise is more relevant than information directly about the cash flows of the firm.

Other major contributions to the user-orientation approach include the 1966 AAA Committee to Prepare a Statement of Basic Accounting Theory[51] and the works of Chambers and Sterling relating to the relevance of exit price information to the decision processes of users of financial accounting reports.[52]

THE FRONTIERS OF RESEARCH IN ACCOUNTING THEORY

The revolution in accounting research and thought during the 1970s and 1980s has come about largely because of the rapid increase in the number of accounting researchers qualified in statistical and other quantitative research techniques and the availability of the computer. Through more refined research technology, researchers have been able to study more

---

[47] George J. Staubus, *A Theory of Accounting to Investors* (Berkeley: University of California Press, 1961), p. 15.

[48] American Accounting Association Committee on External Reporting, "An Evaluation of External Reporting Practices," *Accounting Review,* supplement to vol. 44, 1969, pp. 80–83. See also Lawrence Revsine, *Replacement Cost Accounting* (Englewood Cliffs, N.J.: Prentice-Hall, 1973), chap. 2, for the use of a normative cash flow model.

[49] American Institute of Certified Public Accountants, *Report of the Study Group on the Objectives of Financial Statements* (New York: AICPA, 1973).

[50] *AICPA Professional Standards—Accounting,* vol. 3, particularly paras. 1210.24 and 1210.43.

[51] AAA, *A Statement of Basic Accounting Theory* (1966).

[52] Raymond J. Chambers, *Accounting, Evaluation and Economic Behavior* (Englewood Cliffs, N.J.: Prentice-Hall, 1966); and Robert R. Sterling, *Theory of the Measurement of Enterprise Income* (Lawrence, Kans.: The University of Kansas Press, 1970).

readily the nature of accounting information, test extant theories, and derive new theories through the experimental method. Of the several research techniques in use, empirical research and the use of quantitative methods have become common because of the important logical rigor they add to basic research.

No basic trend can be discerned at the present time, but some of the major areas of research conducted in the 1970s and 1980s are summarized briefly as follows: (1) attempts to construct fully integrated structures of accounting theory upon which standards may be based; (2) the extension of empirical research into the nature of accounting numbers; (3) research into the decision-making process of the individual, particularly with reference to the using of accounting information; (4) research into the implications of Efficient Capital Markets theories for accounting; (5) research regarding the economic and political consequences of accounting standards; (6) research regarding the impact of changes in the sociological and economic environment upon accounting theory and practice; and (7) explorations into the international aspects of accounting and accounting theory.

The search for fully integrated structures of accounting theory upon which all accounting standards can be based has not been very fruitful. Since the publication of two attempts by Mattessich and Chambers in the 1960s,[53,54] little has been done in this area except for the FASB series of *Statements of Financial Accounting Concepts*. These *Statements* are intended to provide a conceptual framework that can be used as a guide in the formulation of consistent accounting standards. The major deficiencies of the conceptual framework project are its lack of rigor and the gaps in logic. However, given the continuing disagreements among accounting theorists and the need for continuity in accounting practice, the conceptual foundation project does provide a useful attempt to obtain consistency in the development of standards.

Basic research in the 1970s and 1980s has been directed toward the formulation or verification of partial theories or subtheories, such as the relationship between security prices and accounting information. Empirical research in accounting theory involves primarily the testing of meaningful hypotheses. Hypotheses can be stated and tested for the logic and acceptance of their premises, but the real test comes in the application of the hypothesis to the real world. Thus, many statistical or behavioral studies have been made to find whether or not assumed relationships and behavior patterns actually exist. That is, are assumed measurements and relationships good predictors of future activities and events, and do the presentation and analysis of accounting information permit adequate decisions by those relying on accounting reports? Partial answers to these

---

[53] Richard Mattessich, *Accounting and Analytical Methods, Measurement and Projection of Income and Wealth in the Micro- and Macro-Economy* (Homewood, Ill.: Richard D. Irwin, 1964). © 1964 by Richard D. Irwin, Inc.

[54] Chambers, *Accounting Evaluation.*

questions may be found by studying past and current behavior, or by the simulation of the real world by the use of statistical techniques and by the use of computers to speed the simulation process.

In summary, recent developments in accounting theory are proceeding in several directions at the same time. Many of these developments are necessary to keep up with the changing economic institutions and to meet the new economic and sociological situations. But many of the changes challenge the fundamental basis of traditional accounting thought. Although a wholesale rejection of "received" accounting theories may not occur rapidly, accountants should be receptive to new ideas and recognize that accounting theory is not, and probably never will be, completely stable.

SELECTED ADDITIONAL READING

History of accounting thought

Chatfield, Michael. *A History of Accounting Thought.* Rev. ed. New York: Robert E. Krieger Publishing, 1977.

De Roover, Raymond. "New Perspectives on the History of Accounting." *Accounting Review* 30 (July 1955): 405–20.

Littleton, A. C., and V. K. Zimmerman. *Accounting Theory: Continuity and Change.* Englewood Cliffs, N.J.: Prentice-Hall, 1962.

Peloubet, Maurice E. "The Historical Background of Accounting." In *Modern Accounting Theory,* edited by Morton Backer. Englewood Cliffs, N.J.: Prentice-Hall, 1966, pp. 5–27.

The historical development of accounting standards

Carey, John L. *The Rise of the Accounting Profession.* Vols. 1 and 2. AICPA, 1969 and 1970.

Moonitz, Maurice. "Obtaining Agreement on Standards in the Accounting Profession." *Studies in Accounting Research No. 8.* AAA, 1974.

Storey, Reed K. *The Search for Accounting Principles—Today's Problems in Perspective.* AICPA, 1964.

Zeff, Stephen A. *Forging Accounting Principles in Five Countries: A History and an Analysis of Trends.* Accounting Lectures 1971. Champaign, Ill.: Stipes Publishing, 1972.

APB Statement No. 4

Ijiri, Yuji. "Critique of the *APB Fundamentals Statement." Journal of Accountancy,* November 1971, pp. 43–50.

Schattke, R. W. "An Analysis of *Accounting Principles Board Statement No. 4." Accounting Review,* April 1972, pp. 233–44.

Staubus, George J. "An Analysis of *APB Statement No. 4." Journal of Accountancy,* February 1972, pp. 36–43.

Securities and Exchange Commission

Blough, Carman. "Development of Accounting Principles in the United States." *Berkeley Symposium on the Foundations of Financial Accounting.* Berkeley: Schools of Business Administration, University of California, 1967, pp. 1–14.

Burton, John C. "Some General and Specific Thoughts on the Accounting Environment." *Journal of Accountancy,* October 1973, pp. 40–46.

Kapnick, Harvey. "Accounting Principles—Concern or Crisis?" *Financial Executive,* October 1974, pp. 23–25, 64.

Pines, J. Arnold. "The Securities and Exchange Commission and Accounting Principles." *Law and Contemporary Problems* Uniformity in Financial Accounting, Autumn 1965, pp. 727–51.

Rappaport, Louis H. *SEC Accounting Practice and Procedure.* 2d. ed. New York: Ronald Press, 1963, chaps. 2 and 3.

Development of alternative theory approaches

American Accounting Association Committee on Concepts and Standards for External Financial Reports. "Statement on Accounting Theory and Theory Acceptance" (1977).

Chambers, Raymond J. "Canning's *The Economics of Accountancy*—After 50 Years." *Accounting Review,* October 1979, pp. 764–75.

Danos, Paul. "A Revolution in Accounting Thought? A Comment." *Accounting Review,* July 1977, pp. 746–47.

Hakansson, Nils H. "Where We Are in Accounting. A Review of 'Statement on Accounting Theory and Theory Acceptance.'" *Accounting Review,* July 1978, pp. 717–25.

Mattessich, Richard. "On the Evolution of Theory Construction in Accounting: A Personal Account," *Accounting and Business Research,* no. 37A, Special Accounting History Issue, 1980, pp. 158–73.

Wells, M. C. "A Revolution in Accounting Thought?" *Accounting Review,* July 1976, pp. 471–82.

————. "A Revolution in Accounting Thought? A Reply." *Accounting Review,* July 1977, pp. 748–50.

Whittington, Geoffrey. "Pioneers of Income Measurement and Price-Level Accounting: A Review Article." *Accounting and Business Research,* Spring 1980, pp. 232–40.

CHAPTER 3

THE NORMATIVE DEDUCTIVE APPROACH—CONCEPTS, MEASUREMENTS, AND STRUCTURE

Current accounting policies have developed over the years in a framework that applies implicitly or explicitly the normative deductive or the inductive-deductive approach. Many of the arguments for specific procedures or measurement methods were prescriptive and thus normative. They also started from an observation of existing procedures or of business practices. The deductive logic followed from a few implicit or explicit assumptions. Frequently, the basic difference between alternative proposed theories was in the assumptions or premises. But since the assumptions are generally subjective in nature, general agreement on conclusions could not be obtained. Furthermore, the theories were partial and intended to support conclusions regarding specific procedures only.

Historically, little was done until recently to develop integrated formal structures for the formulation of accounting principles and theory. However, in 1922 William Paton stated and examined some of the basic premises and postulates implicit in accounting thought of that time.[1]

In the search for accounting principles during the 1930s and in an attempt to improve financial reporting, neither the American Institute of Accountants (AICPA) nor the American Accounting Association made specific attempts to develop complete logical structures, either to develop new accounting practices or to evaluate or justify current practice. In directing its efforts to the solution of specific problems, the Institute presented and discussed specific rules and recommendations as isolated problems in the context of an implicit structure of postulates and basic principles. The American Accounting Association in its statements of 1936, 1941, and 1948 attempted to set forth some of the bases upon which financial statements rest, but it attempted to present neither basic postulates of accounting nor a formal structure of accounting thought. Only in

---

[1] William Andrew Paton, *Accounting Theory* (New York: Ronald Press, 1922), chap. 20, pp. 471–99.

the 1957 revision of the AAA statements was an attempt made to discuss basic concepts underlying the conventions of accounting.

The need to develop a framework of accounting theory to encourage the logical development of accounting principles and practices and to assess current practices has long been felt. The current interest in this area was sparked by the recommendations in 1958 of the AICPA Special Committee on Research Program, which suggested that research studies should be undertaken by the AICPA to set forth the basic postulates and principles of accounting.[2] As a result of this recommendation, *AICPA Accounting Research Study No. 1* was prepared by Maurice Moonitz,[3] and *Accounting Research Study No. 3* was prepared by Robert T. Sprouse and Maurice Moonitz.[4] Subsequent studies have been published by a Study Group at the University of Illinois, Richard Mattessich, Raymond J. Chambers, and Louis Goldberg.[5] Other studies discussed in Chapters 1 and 2 include those by Yuji Ijiri and Robert Sterling, *APB Statement No. 4*, and the FASB Conceptual Accounting Framework.

THE FRAMEWORK OF ACCOUNTING THEORY

The type of framework used to house a theory of accounting may be formal, as in the axiomatic approach to theory; or it may be informal or implicit, as in the pragmatic and ethical approaches. Using the inductive approach, Littleton suggested a framework whereby rules of action can be converted into accounting principles.[6] Starting with accounting conventions and rules that are thought to be relevant to assumed accounting objectives, accounting principles can be derived as justifying reasons. Postulates appear to be omitted from this framework, but they are implicit in the formulation of the conventions and rules. That is, the conventions and rules are inductively derived from accounting and its environment. How-

---

[2] "Report to Council of Special Committee on Research Program," *Journal of Accountancy* 106 (December 1958): pp. 62–68. For a discussion of the roles of others, including Mattessich and Chambers, see Richard Mattessich, "On the Evolution of Theory Construction: a Personal Account," *Accounting and Business Research,* Special Accounting History Issue, 1980, pp. 158–73.

[3] Maurice Moonitz, "The Basic Postulates of Accounting," *Accounting Research Study No. 1* (AICPA, 1961).

[4] Robert T. Sprouse and Maurice Moonitz, "A Tentative Set of Broad Accounting Principles for Business Enterprises," *Accounting Research Study No. 3* (AICPA, 1962).

[5] Study Group at the University of Illinois, "A Statement of Basic Accounting Postulates and Principles" (Urbana: Center for International Education and Research in Accounting, University of Illinois, 1964); Richard Mattessich, *Accounting and Analytical Methods* (Homewood, Ill.: Richard D. Irwin, Inc. 1964); Raymond J. Chambers, *Accounting, Evaluation and Economic Behavior* (Englewood Cliffs, N.J.: Prentice-Hall, 1966); Louis Goldberg, *An Inquiry into the Nature of Accounting,* American Accounting Association Monograph No. 7 (AAA, 1965).

[6] A. C. Littleton, *Structure of Accounting Theory,* American Accounting Association Monograph No. 5 (AAA, 1953), esp. pp. 186–87.

ever, the implicit postulates need to be examined to determine the soundness of the system.

In the deductive approach to accounting theory, the framework for logical reasoning should be fairly formal in order to obtain general agreement on the argumentative method and to discover the point or points in the reasoning where disagreement may exist. The framework is also necessary to point out the generally agreed assumptions behind the propositions and to indicate which propositions are more basic than others and which can be verified empirically; that is, a distinction should be made between the major and the minor premises and verifiable and nonverifiable premises. If the premises are relevant and generally assumed to be true or can be derived logically from other premises that may be assumed to be true, the derived principles should be sound. However, it is possible that certain practical difficulties in carrying out these principles may act as constraints to the basic principles. Therefore, the accounting principles and the rules derived from them may have to be modified to make them operational. Finally, accounting theory can be made operational only in a framework that can meet the objectives of accounting. This requires a set of definitions, methods of classification and measurement, and methods of presentation of financial data in summarized forms.

A theoretical framework for accounting can focus on any one of the three levels of accounting theory: (1) theories relating to the formal structure of the accounting process, including the rules and procedures and the interrelationship of these with formal financial statements; (2) theories that concentrate on the relationships between objects and events and the terms or symbols representing them (interpretational or semantic theories); (3) theories that emphasize the needs of users of accounting information and the behavioral or decision-oriented effects of accounting reports and statements. A complete framework of accounting theory should include all three levels, and regardless of the starting point, a logically derived theoretical framework for the development of sound accounting practices should include the following considerations:

1. A statement of postulates regarding the nature of the accounting entity and its environment.
2. A statement of the basic objectives of financial accounting.
3. An evaluation of the user's needs and the constraints regarding the user's ability to understand, interpret, and analyze the information presented.
4. The selection of what should be reported. This should include a selection of the objects and activities of the entity or its environment and the specific attributes that are relevant to the objectives of accounting.
5. An evaluation of the possible measurement and descriptive processes for communicating information regarding the firm and its environment.

6. An evaluation of constraints regarding the measurement and description of the entity and its environment.
7. The development of principles or general propositions that can be used as guidelines in the formulation of procedures and rules.
8. The formulation of a structure and format for the gathering and processing of data and for summarizing and reporting the relevant information.

Regardless of the starting point in the development or evaluation of sound accounting practices, all of the above factors should be given adequate consideration. If we wish to evaluate current reporting practices, it may be necessary to start with the format, procedures, and rules and attempt to establish from these presuppositions or assumed objectives and postulates. The soundness of the reporting practices rests, then, upon the validity of the objectives and postulates and an evaluation of the measurement processes. If the presuppositions regarding the objectives and postulates are not acceptable, or if the measurement procedures are invalid, the current practices can be assumed to be inadequate or misleading, at least until other presuppositions can be found to support the validity of the accepted practices. In the development of new practices, the theory structure should follow the above steps. However, upon completion, all assumptions should be reexamined for their validity, and the logic should be reexamined for its internal consistency.

THE NATURE OF ACCOUNTING POSTULATES

According to *Webster's Third New International Dictionary,* the most relevant definitions of *postulates* appear to be (1) "a proposition advanced with the claim that it be taken for granted or as axiomatic" and (2) "an underlying hypothesis or assumption."[7] The first of these definitions refers to statements that are assumed to be generally accepted, but the validity of which is necessary for the acceptance of other postulates or general principles, standards, or procedures. Even though such a postulate is generally accepted, however, it may be falsifiable upon further investigation or found to be irrelevant to further development of accounting thought. The second definition of *postulate* refers to a hypothesis that is as yet unproven and may, in fact, not require proof if it leads to relevant ideas and a logical development of thought and useful conclusions.

In general, propositions that are advanced with the claim that they may be taken for granted relate to observations or experiences that are not likely to be refuted or they are propositions that can be verified or are likely to be validated by research. These are usually descriptive state-

---

[7] *Webster's Third New International Dictionary, Unabridged* (Springfield, Mass.: G.&C. Merriam, 1961), p. 1773.

ments; that is, statements regarding the nature of things or what *is* as opposed to what *ought* to be. Examples of descriptive statements would include one proposed by Moonitz, which states, "Most of the goods and services that are produced are distributed through exchange and are not directly consumed by the producers."[8] A postulate proposed by Chambers states, "In respect of all properties attributed to persons, individuals differ."[9] Both of these statements are descriptive of the nature of things and are not likely to be challenged. For this reason and because their relationship to accounting propositions is quite remote, many critics have called them trivial and unnecessary. To the extent that they are not controversial and because they do not necessarily serve as a basis for other controversial propositions, it is not important that they be stated. Furthermore, since there may be such a large number of propositions descriptive of the environment of accounting, it is uneconomical to make an encyclopedic listing, and incomplete to list only a few. Therefore, descriptive statements regarding the environment of accounting may be omitted if they do not directly support propositions necessary to the logic or if other statements provide more basic support for the propositions.

A second type of descriptive proposition that may be true but that may not lead to a logical development of accounting theory is one that tries to explain what accountants do. For example, Moonitz stated, "The results of the accounting process are expressed in a set of fundamentally related financial statements which articulate with each other and rest upon the same underlying data."[10] This is a true statement, but the danger of stating it as a postulate is that it may be interpreted as a normative statement; that is, that it *should* be true. As a normative statement, it is subject to research and debate. This does not mean, however, that such descriptive statements should not be made. On the contrary, any evaluation of current accounting practice should set forth propositions regarding what accountants do as well as the presuppositions regarding why it is done. Only by such a process can an evaluation of current practice be made sufficiently convincing to gain general acceptance.

Postulates that are normative in formulation (those prescribing what accounting should do or how it should be done) should be stated explicitly, rather than assumed by general consent or agreement. Furthermore, they require the greatest amount of support to establish their validity. Their explicit statement in any proposed logical development stems from the fact that if they are not adequately supported, the conclusions derived from them can only be tentative. It is also important that they be stated so that areas of disagreement can be located and argued at the proper level. Examples of normative propositions would include the imperative postulates set forth by Moonitz in *Accounting Research Study No. 1*. One of

---

[8] Moonitz, "The Basic Postulates."

[9] Chambers, *Accounting Evaluation*, p. 75.

[10] Moonitz, "The Basic Postulates."

these imperatives states that "the procedures used in accounting for a given entity . . . should be followed consistently from period to period."[11] This may be a desirable goal but, nevertheless, it may be subject to debate and rejection. Such statements, however, are more in the nature of hypotheses to be tested than postulates that can be assumed to require no proof for their validity.

In summary, therefore, postulates are basic assumptions or fundamental propositions concerning the economic, political, and sociological environment in which accounting must operate. The basic criteria are that (1) they must be relevant to the development of accounting logic; that is, they must serve as a foundation for the logical derivation of further propositions; and (2) they must be accepted as valid by the participants in the discussion as either being true or providing a useful starting point as an assumption in the development of accounting logic. It is not necessary that the postulates be true or even realistic. For example, the assumption in economics of a perfectly competitive society has never been true, but it has provided useful insights into the working of the economic system. On the other hand, an assumption of a monopolistic society leads to different conclusions that may also be useful in an evaluation of the economy. The assumptions that provide the greatest degree of prediction may be more useful than those that are most realistic.

One of the major criticisms of the postulation approach is that if postulates are stated broadly enough to secure general agreement, they can likely serve as a basis for many further propositions, and thus they do not necessarily support a single set of logical propositions. On the other hand, if they are stated specifically, so as to lead to specific propositions, they are likely to fail in gaining general agreement. And since most postulates of this type cannot be tested, there is no way of testing alternative sets of propositions by testing the validity of the postulates. Furthermore, it can be argued that postulates are frequently formulated with the objective of *supporting* preconceived propositions, rather than using the postulates to *derive* the further propositions. However, the order in deriving postulates and principles is not important so long as the final argumentative structure is based on internally consistent logic and provides a basis for prediction. To this extent, we may find that several different logical structures support each other, rather than reach the conclusion that one structure is right and the others wrong.

Many of the postulates and assumptions set forth by Moonitz, Chambers, Mattessich, and others include propositions regarding the objectives of accounting and measurement in accounting. Since these are special areas requiring specific investigation, they are discussed separately below.

As indicated above, an agreement on postulates is the first step in the logical development of accounting theory. However, this does not mean

---

[11] Ibid.

that postulates should be developed without consideration of the other steps in the logic. On the contrary, the selection of postulates may be interrelated with the objectives of accounting and the measurement and descriptive processes.

ENVIRONMENTAL POSTULATES

The environment of accounting has a direct bearing on the objectives of accounting and on the logical derivation of principles and rules. But not all aspects of society are relevant to accounting. Some are clearly irrelevant, others are only indirectly relevant, and many economic, social, and political aspects are directly relevant. What may be relevant at one period of time may be irrelevant at another and vice versa. For example, the development of the railroads and the proximity of a plant to a railroad may have been much more important to some firms before the construction of high-speed highways. On the other hand, international trade and the international balance of payments may be more significant for many firms today than in an earlier period. However, the relevance of environmental conditions may also be different geographically, that is, among the various nations of the world. For example, governmental economic policy is more important in some countries than in others. Even in those areas where certain aspects of society are relevant to accounting, there may be conflicting situations or a variety of institutions that may affect accounting differently. The objective of stating environmental postulates is to point out what aspects of society are relevant to accounting and to decide which of conflicting situations or of several institutions are more significant for providing a framework for broad generalizations.

Most statements of environmental postulates include an assumption that exchanges in the economy take place in markets and that market prices have significance for accounting. However, there is not agreement regarding which prices are relevant. Moonitz, for example, states that "accounting data are based on prices generated by past, present or future exchanges which have actually taken place or are expected to."[12] Chambers, on the other hand, states as a postulate that "the domain of accounting is the range of retrospective and contemporary measurements and calculations."[13] Thus, Chambers rejects expected prices, and Moonitz would include them. This difference arises from the different objectives of the two authors and their assumptions regarding measurement concepts. However, if it were not for certain measurement constraints, Chambers' postulates and objectives could lead to the presentation of expectations in financial reports because of the importance he places on expectations in informed action.

---

[12] Ibid., p. 37.
[13] Chambers, *Accounting Evaluation,* p. 102.

FASB Statement of Financial Accounting Concepts No. 1 (SFAC No. 1) discusses a number of environmental postulates, including an assumption of a highly developed exchange economy with business enterprises raising capital by issuing equity and debt securities that are traded in highly developed securities markets.[14] It also makes the assumption that the function of accounting is to provide information to investors and creditors.

Other environmental postulates relate to assumptions, regarding the behavior of the users of accounting information. Chambers, for example, states a number of postulates relating to the behavior and beliefs of individuals.[15] In other works, Prince states several motivational postulates regarding the firm.[16] Pattillo postulates certain broad social responsibilities of the business enterprise.[17]

Other frequently stated postulates relate to the accounting entity, the measurement process, or objectives of accounting. The postulates regarding the accounting entity are discussed in the following section. The objectives of accounting and the measurement process are discussed separately because of their basic nature and because they cannot be classified as postulates in the same way as the environmental postulates.

The accounting entity

Most sets of postulates and concepts include assumptions regarding the nature of the accounting entity. The main reason for the significance of this concept is that it defines the area of interest and thus narrows the possible objects and activities and their attributes that may be selected for inclusion in financial reports. Furthermore, postulates regarding the *nature* of the entity may also further narrow the selection of what to include in reports and aid in determining how best to present information regarding the entity. Thus relevant features may be disclosed, and irrelevant features that cloud the basic information may be omitted.

One approach to the definition of the accounting entity is to determine the economic unit that has control over resources, accepts responsibilities for making and carrying out commitments, and conducts economic activity. Such an accounting entity may be either an individual, a partnership, or a legal corporation or consolidated group engaged in carrying out either profit-seeking or not-for-profit activity. This is the basic view of Moonitz in *Accounting Research Study No. 1* and of *FASB SFAC No. 1*.[18]

An alternative approach is to define the entity in terms of the area of

---

[14] *AICPA Professional Standards,* para. 1210.34.

[15] Chambers, *Accounting Evaluation,* pp. 35–39.

[16] Thomas R. Prince, *Extension of the Boundaries of Accounting Theory* (Cincinnati: South-Western Publishing, 1963), p. 175.

[17] James W. Pattillo, *The Foundation of Financial Accounting* (Baton Rouge: Louisiana State University, 1965), chap. 2.

[18] Moonitz, "The Basic Postulates," p. 22.

economic interest of particular individuals, groups, or institutions. This definition is that selected by the AAA 1964 Concepts and Standards Research Study Committee on the Business Entity Concept.[19] It states, for example, that "the boundaries of such an economic entity are identifiable (1) by determining the interested individual or group and (2) by determining the nature of that individual's or that group's interest."[20] Thus, this approach is oriented to the interests of the users of financial reports.

Both approaches may lead to the same conclusions, but the user-oriented approach may lead to a selection of different information than the economic activity approach; and it may extend the boundaries of the entity to include some environmental activity, such as attempts to improve sociological relations within the enterprise or the community and information regarding the social responsibilities of the enterprise.

The concept of the accounting entity may include the legal enterprise, a division of the enterprise, or a superenterprise, such as a consolidation of several interrelated firms. The choice of the appropriate entity and the determination of its boundaries depends upon the objectives of the reports and the interests of the users of the reported information. The nature of the entity and the interests in the entity may be classified according to proprietary, entity, funds, or enterprise theories. These theories are discussed in Chapter 19.

Continuity.   A further observation generally made regarding the nature of the relevant accounting entity is that most economic units are organized for operation over an indefinite period of time. Therefore, it is frequently argued that it is a logical step to recognize that the entity should be viewed as remaining in operation indefinitely under normal circumstances (the traditional going-concern postulate). Moonitz included this postulate among the classification of imperatives, apparently because accounting practice does not generally recognize this assumption throughout the entire accounting process. But if continuity is a generally accepted proposition and if it is necessary to support subsequent propositions, it should be considered an environmental postulate.

As generally applied, the continuity postulate assumes that the accounting entity will continue in operation long enough to carry out its existing commitments. Sterling argues, however, that since commitments are of varying time periods, new commitments will have to be made continually into the future to carry out all commitments, thus in effect making the continuity assumption one of indefinite life.[21] If there is evidence that it will not continue in existence long enough (for example, where there are large and persistent losses or where it appears unlikely that the firm can continue at a profitable level), general accounting prin-

---

[19] "The Entity Concept," *Accounting Review*, April 1965, pp. 358–67.

[20] Ibid., p. 358.

[21] Robert R. Sterling, "The Going Concern: An Examination," *Accounting Review*, July 1968, pp. 481–502.

ciples would not apply, and the accountant has the responsibility of informing the reader accordingly. The reason for including the continuity postulate is generally to support the benefit theory of valuation, or in some cases to support the use of historical costs as opposed to liquidation values.

Not all theorists agree, however, with this interpretation of the continuity postulate, and several do not include it among the relevant postulates. Chambers, for example, states that a going concern is a firm that adapts itself by the sale of its assets in the ordinary course of its business, that is, in orderly liquidation as opposed to forced liquidation.[22] This assumption, then, supports his proposition regarding the relevancy of current cash equivalents. On the other hand, Mattessich assumes a set of hypotheses regarding the expected life of the entity without necessarily assuming that it will be indefinite.[23] This would include an expected life of zero. Ijiri and Sterling do not include a postulate regarding continuity, either because they feel it is not necessary or because it is not desirable to do so, or both.[24,25] Vatter, however, states that "the continuity concept is not an assumption, but a condition—one that is at least to a large extent a verifiable attribute of the business system."[26] He contends that it is a status quo assumption that is really an extension of the measurement process.

In opposing the necessity and desirability of including continuity as a postulate, Sterling contends that as a status quo assumption it is falsifiable and misleading.[27] Rather than making continuity an assumption, it should be a prediction. Furthermore, the mere fact that we assume that a firm will not be forced into liquidation does not justify valuations based on historical cost; other valuations may be more relevant. As indicated earlier, postulates should be accepted on the basis of their ability to permit predictions. Information regarding a specific firm should be presented in such a way that users of financial reports can make their own assessments regarding the future of the enterprise. Therefore, in this author's opinion, the continuity postulate should not be interpreted to be either a status quo assumption or a justification for historical cost (or even the benefit concept) in the valuation of assets. However, it is a relevant postulate, leading to the presentation of information regarding resources and commitments and operational activity (such as the sales of goods and services over several years, or even for one year) on the ground that such informa-

---

[22] Chambers, *Accounting Evaluation*, p. 218.

[23] Mattessich, *Analytical Methods*, pp. 44–45.

[24] Yuji Ijiri, "Axioms and Structures of Conventional Accounting Measurement," *Accounting Review*, January 1965, pp. 36–53.

[25] Robert R. Sterling, "Elements of Pure Accounting Theory," *Accounting Review*, January 1967, pp. 62–73.

[26] William J. Vatter, "Postulates and Principles," *Journal of Accounting Research* 1 (Autumn 1963): 189.

[27] Sterling, "The Going Concern."

tion may aid in the prediction of future operational activity. Continuity assumes some connection between the past and the future, although not necessarily that the future will be a repetition of the past. In the case of a discontinuity, such as a forced liquidation, the usual accounting procedures would not apply, and the accountant should disclose the nature of the discontinuity.

THE OBJECTIVES OF ACCOUNTING

The starting point for any field of study is to set forth its boundaries and determine its objectives. In the field of accounting, the objectives can be considered part of the postulates in the formal structure, or they can be viewed as a set of propositions above or at the same level as the postulates. But it cannot be denied that some agreement on objectives is necessary to determine what postulates are relevant to accounting and to evaluate the principles and rules based on the postulates in order to determine whether or not they fulfill the requirements of the system. That is, the principles and rules should be logically derived from the postulates and meet the test of squaring with the basic objectives of accounting.

In addition to the emphasis on the specific needs of users of financial statements, discussions of accounting objectives frequently focus on one of the three levels of accounting theory (syntactical, semantical, and behavioral).[28] Those who focus on one of the first two levels generally assume that financial statements are prepared for a set of unknown users with multiple objectives. The objective of financial reporting, then, is assumed to provide information regarding a firm's transactions and resources that should be relevant for the making of economic decisions by many persons or organizations outside the reporting enterprise or entity.

Objectives relating to the first level of theory are stated under the assumption that conventional historical cost accounting is useful because it is used and that conventional financial statements, therefore, must be relevant. According to this line of reasoning, the primary objective of financial reporting is the computation and presentation of net income resulting from specific realization and matching rules and a balance sheet that relates the current period to future periods. Accordingly, emphasis is on the data collection process and the format of financial statements. Examples of this viewpoint are expressed in the following quotations:

> The reliance of business on conventional accounting is no accident. Alternatives to it have been advanced before, some very much like those proposed today, but a pragmatic consideration of the possibilities has always found historical cost, in spite of its acknowledged limitations, to be superior.[29]

---

[28] See Chap. 1 for a discussion of these three levels.

[29] Ernst & Ernst, "Additional Views on Accounting Objectives: An Expansion of the Views Previously Expressed to the AICPA Accounting Objectives Study Group," May 1972, p. 18.

. . . the primary objective of financial statements should be to communicate reliable financial information concerning an enterprise's business transactions—including (*a*) the resulting assets, liabilities, and ownership equities and (*b*) indications of profit or loss therefrom (derived by deducting costs and expenses from related revenues). . . .[30]

The main difficulty with an emphasis on the accounting process and the conventional reporting structure is that the accounting terms and measurements have little or no interpretational significance to real-world phenomena. They are the artifacts of accountants, and although it is possible for such artifacts to be useful in making predictions of real-world phenomena, the evidence does not support the validity of making the structure of accounting its basic objective.

Those who focus on objectives at the second level of accounting theory emphasize the need to measure and report wealth and changes in wealth as well as specific claims against the enterprise. These terms still leave open the possibility of varying interpretations, but they do not depend on accounting procedures for that interpretation as do the terms *income, asset,* and *equity.* Implicit in these objectives is also the assumption that financial statements are prepared for a set of unknown users. But the emphasis in this case is on the measurement of objects and events that have real-world referents. Moonitz, for example, in *Accounting Research Study No. 1,* restricted the accounting description of the enterprise and its activities to information regarding wealth, changes in wealth, and claims to wealth. In his definition of accounting, he stated:

> The function of accounting is (1) to measure the resources held by specific entities; (2) to reflect the claims against and the interests in those entities; (3) to measure the changes in those resources, claims, and interests; (4) to assign the changes to specifiable periods of time; and (5) to express the foregoing in terms of money as a common denominator.[31]

This definition served as a basis for the emphasis in *Accounting Research Study No. 3* on the balance sheet and the income statement as measurements of wealth and changes in wealth.[32]

APB Statement No. 4 stated as a general objective of financial reporting the providing of reliable financial information about economic resources and obligations of a business enterprise.[33]

In similar fashion, Arthur Andersen & Co. stated that . . . the overall purpose of financial statements is to communicate information concerning the nature and value of the economic resources of a business enterprise,

---

[30] Arthur Young & Company, "The Objective of Financial Statements: Responding to Investors' Needs: Comments to the Study Group on the Objectives of Financial Statements," May 1972, p. 7. However, in this paper and in their comments to the FASB, Arthur Young & Company did state a need for better understanding of the decision-making process of investors.

[31] Moonitz, "The Basic Postulates," p. 23.

[32] Sprouse and Moonitz, "A Tentative Set," p. 53.

[33] *APB Statement No. 4,* "Basic Concepts and Accounting Principles Underlying Financial Statements of Business Enterprises" (AICPA, 1970), p. 33.

the interests of creditors and the equity of owners in the economic resources, and the changes in the nature and value of those resources from
period to period.[34]

A basic difficulty with the application of objectives at the second level
of theory is that the postulates, principles, and procedures applied to these
objectives can be quite different. The objectives are not defined clearly
enough to permit agreement on either an appropriate selection of the
items to be included in financial reports or their measurement. The solution has been to include as much information as possible that accountants
can justify on the basis of verification and measurement standards.

At the third level of accounting theory (the behavioral level), emphasis
is placed on the needs of users of financial statements. Users could include
employees, customers, and the public, but the main interested parties are
generally assumed to be stockholders, other investors, and creditors.

Applying this level of theory, *SFAC No. 1* states:

> The objectives stem primarily from the informational needs of external
> users who lack the authority to prescribe the financial information they
> want from an enterprise. . .[35]
>
> The information should be comprehensible to those who have a reason-
> able understanding of business and economic activities and are willing to
> study the information with reasonable diligence.[36]

By specifying the information needs of users, the FASB has implicitly
assumed that the investors using financial statements would apply the
intrinsic value investment theories and would possibly find predictive
indicators useful. The efficient markets hypothesis, however, assumes
that the stock market prices are established by actions of sophisticated
investors. If this is the case, the objective of financial reporting should not
be to provide information for the investor with limited authority and
ability, but rather to make publicly available information that might
otherwise be used to earn monopoly returns by those who have access to
private or inside information.

This approach to the presentation of information in financial reports on
the basis of the needs of specific users of accounting statements is in
accord with the definition of *accounting* specified by the Committee to
Prepare a Statement of Basic Accounting Theory of the American Accounting Association (ASOBAT). The committee stated that accounting is
"the process of identifying, measuring, and communicating economic information to permit informed judgments and decisions by users of the
information."[37] This definition leads to the identification of users of exter-

---

[34] Arthur Andersen & Co., *Accounting Standards for Business Enterprises Throughout the World* (Chicago: Arthur Andersen & Co., 1974), p. 13.

[35] *AICPA Professional Standards,* para. 1210.28.

[36] Ibid., para. 1210.34.

[37] Committee to Prepare a Statement of Basic Accounting Theory, *A Statement of Basic Accounting Theory* (AAA, 1966), p. 1.

nal financial reports and the selection of the information needed for the predictions required in their decisions and judgments regarding the firm. Notice that the selection of reported information is based on known or presumed decision models, but the reported information is intended only to aid the users in making predictions. No attempt should be made to *make* the predictions, except where the errors of measurement and prediction can be estimated and reported.

One difficulty in applying this approach is in the selection of the information relevant to the various prediction and decision models of the users. However, initially, these models can be established on a normative basis and improved by empirical research. It may be possible to establish the decision models by finding out how the users actually make the decisions and what information they want, but this procedure may not lead to the best results because users are limited by the accounting information now available or because they may not be using the best models based on information that might be made available to them. The accounting process should be educational as well as informative with respect to user preferences.

A second difficulty is that this selection procedure either leads to different reports for different users or requires the presentation of a considerable amount of information, much of which will be irrelevant to any specific user. Thus, if a single set of reports is prepared, the process of selection and summarization will be left to the user, making the financial reports less useful to any single set of users.

Relevance

The approach to accounting objectives that assumes a set of unknown users of financial reports has also assumed that information regarding wealth and/or economic transactions of an enterprise is relevant for the many data needs of the users. That is, if information regarding income and financial position is adequately described and presented in financial statements, it is assumed that this information will be useful without attempting to explain what information is intended to be used for which purposes. A well-informed reader of financial statements is assumed to be able to select the wanted information and make adequate decisions from the information presented.

Recently, this general assumption of usefulness has been challenged on the grounds that accountants need to know more about what information is preferred by specific users of financial statements, as well as more about who these users are and what their objectives are in using the accounting information. This changing emphasis toward the communication of information intended for specific users and for specific purposes has led to a greater refinement of the concept of relevance. The Committee to Prepare a Statement of Basic Accounting Theory defined *accounting* in such a way that relevance became their primary standard:

Relevance . . . requires that the information must bear upon or be use-
fully associated with actions it is designed to facilitate or results desired
to be produced.[38]

The above concept of relevance is that of decision relevance; that is,
emphasis is placed on accounting information that can be useful in either
normative or descriptive decision models. An alternative concept of relevance might relate to the achievement of the goals of the users of the
financial statements—goal relevance. This might be the best concept of
relevance for evaluating financial information, but it is the most difficult
to measure. Although normative or generalized goals might be specified,
it is more difficult to determine when these goals are met as a result of
accounting information than it is to verify the predictive nature of accounting numbers. Furthermore, in reality, goals are subjective in nature, particularly with respect to the trade-off between risk and the
maximization of wealth or cash flows. Semantic relevance has less significance for the evaluation of accounting information than either decision
relevance or goal relevance, but at this juncture in the development of
accounting theory it is generally the best that can be accomplished.
Semantic relevance is attained if the receiver of the information understands the intended meaning of the information reported. It is unlikely
that information will be decision relevant or goal relevant if it is not at
least semantic relevant.

APB Statement No. 4 states "The emphasis in financial accounting on
general-purpose information is based on the presumption that a significant number of users need similar information. General-purpose information is not intended to satisfy specialized needs of individual users."[39]

This is also a basic assumption of *SFAC No. 1*. However, further research may identify the specific needs of different classes of users of financial statements. When this occurs, it will be necessary to omit some relevant information to many users if such information is not also relevant to
other groups. Since it will not be possible to maximize the amount of
relevant information to any specific group of users without the preparation of specific reports, the selection of reported information will be one of
satisfying the needs of the largest number of users possible. It is conceiv-
able, however, to imagine future accounting as a data bank of information
from which users can retrieve at computer terminals only the information
relevant to their specific uses.

Empirical tests of accounting numbers under the assumptions of the
efficient market hypothesis have been used to measure the effect of accounting numbers on market share prices. If the effect is positive, it can
be assumed that the accounting numbers provide information to the market and, therefore, are decision relevant. To the extent that conventional
reports are found to be relevant, there is danger in then concluding that

---

[38] Committee to Prepare a Statement of Basic Accounting Theory, p. 7.
[39] *APB Statement No. 4*, p. 20.

untried concepts and procedures should not be adopted because they might be less relevant. Also, alternative procedures not in use cannot be tested.

Information and data.   A general distinction relevant for accounting is made between information and data. *Data* can be defined as measurements or descriptions of objects or events. If these data are already known or are of no concern to the person to whom they are communicated, they cannot be information. *Information* can be defined as data that have a surprise effect on the receiver. Furthermore, information should reduce uncertainty, communicate a message to the decision maker that has a value greater than its cost, and potentially evoke a response in the decision maker.[40] The body of literature regarding information theory should be investigated, but it is sufficient at this point to recognize that a starting point in the selection of data for presentation is to assure that they are at least information; otherwise they cannot be relevant.

When accounting data included in financial statements have already been obtained by the users from other sources, they do not contain surprise characteristics and, therefore, are not information (for example, dividend announcement dates or information relating to economic conditions published in the financial press). If this is the case and if there is any cost to their inclusion, such data could be omitted from the financial statements. Furthermore, some information may be obtainable from alternative sources at a lower total social cost (including the cost to the user of obtaining the information separately). When this is the case, consideration should be given to excluding such information from accounting reports and permitting the alternative source to provide the information. However, data that confirm expectations without changing them would be relevant.

USER CONSTRAINTS

The environmental postulates and the objectives of financial reporting provide a general framework for the development of accounting principles. However, limitations of the users of external financial reports place restrictions on the logical derivations of principles from these postulates and objectives alone. Principles could be derived logically from these postulates and objectives; but without specific qualifications, the principles might not find ready acceptance, and therefore they might not fulfill the needs of the users of the reports. These restrictions or constraints should, therefore, be made explicit and taken into consideration in the development of principles. But the constraints should not determine the principles; they only require modifications of basic principles.

---

[40] Errol R. Iselin, "The Objectives of Accounting in an Accounting Theory Based on Deductive Methodology," University of Queensland Papers, vol. 2, no. 1 (St. Lucia, Australia: University of Queensland Press, 1971), p. 22.

The major constraints arise because the accountants have very little control over the ability of the users to handle large masses of data or to interpret summarized data in making their predictions, regardless of the refinement of the accounting statements and the presentation of all necessary information to permit the predictions necessary for decisions based on them. Although the "standard" reader can be assumed to be one who has an adequate acquaintance with accounting reports, the statements should be prepared only after taking into consideration the amount of detail that the reader can assimilate (the relative materiality of detailed information), the consistency of the reports of a firm from one year to the next to permit intertemporal comparisons and predictions based on trends, and the uniformity or comparability of information presented for different firms.

Materiality

The concept of materiality in accounting is very similar to the concept of relevance in many respects. As indicated above, the concept of relevance implies that all information should be presented that may aid in the prediction of the types of information required in the decision processes or that may aid directly in the making of decisions. But materiality has also been used in a positive sense to determine what should be disclosed for general undefined uses. That is, information may be considered to be material (and thus disclosure is necessary) if the knowledge of this information may be significant to the users of accounting reports. According to *SFAC No. 2,* the basic feature of materiality is that " . . . it is probable that the judgment of a reasonable person relying upon the report would have been changed or influenced by the inclusion or correction of the item.[41]

On the other hand, materiality may be looked upon as a constraint determined by the inability of the specific users to handle large masses of detail. Financial information that may be relevant for investment and other decisions can generally be made available in considerable detail, particularly with the widespread use of computers and other communication devices. One of the responsibilities of the accountant in financial reporting is to summarize this mass of data in such a way that it will be meaningful to the users of the reports. Too much data can be just as misleading as too little. If too much information is presented, the relevant items are buried, and the reader must base decisions on inadequate data, in which case the decisions are not likely to be sound. Just as too little information does not promote good predictions and decisions, information that is replete with insignificant details may also detract from good prediction and decision making. Thus materiality places a restriction on what should be disclosed.

---

[41] *AICPA Professional Standards,* para. 1220.132.

Materiality may relate to the significance of value changes, to corrections of errors in prior reports, or to the several means of disclosure of quantified data and relevant descriptions or qualifications of this data. These changes, corrections, and descriptions should be considered to be material if they are large enough or significant enough to influence the decisions of the users of financial reports.

The types of items where materiality may be involved in the decision to disclose or not include the following: (1) quantitative data, such as items affecting net income and asset valuation; (2) the extent of aggregation or itemization of quantitative data in the formal statements; (3) quantitative data that cannot be estimated accurately enough to be included in the statements; (4) quantitative features that must be disclosed by descriptive phrases or sentences; (5) special relationships between the firm and particular individuals or groups affecting the rights and interests of other individuals or groups; and (6) relevant plans and expectations of management. Materiality regarding the measurement of accounting data is implied throughout most of the remainder of this book.

Consistency

The doctrine of consistency has been a basic tenet in accounting for many years. *Consistency* has been used to *refer* to the use of the same accounting procedures by a single firm or accounting entity from period to period, the use of similar measurement concepts and procedures for related items within the statements of a firm for a single period, and the use of the same procedures by different firms. This latter meaning of the term is discussed below in the discussion of uniformity, and the term *consistency* will be applied only to the first two meanings.

Consistency in the use of accounting procedures over time is a user constraint required because of the difficulty in making predictions based on time series data that are not measured and classified in the same way over time. If different measurement procedures are used, it is difficult to project trends or discern the effects on the firm from period to period caused by external factors (changes in economic conditions, actions of competitors, etc.) If different methods are used from period to period, the user will have difficulty in separating the fluctuations caused by internal and external economic factors. If assets are valued at cost in some periods and at replacement cost in others, both the fluctuations from period to period and the trend may be distorted, especially if price changes are significant over time.

The consistency constraint is valid, however, only when there is a choice among two or more equally relevant and valid procedures. The general argument that consistency within a single firm over time overcomes the practice of diversity in the use of procedures among different firms cannot be supported on theoretical grounds because these comparisons are of a different nature.[42] The argument for consistency also loses its force on the ground that if all relevant information is presented each period, with adequate disclosures of measurement concepts and procedures being used, consistency will be implicit to the extent that it is necessary or relevant for the making of predictions for user decisions regarding the firm. Also, the constraint does not hold when a change can be made to a method that provides more accurate or more useful information for predictions or decision making. When a change is made, however, the objective of disclosure would require that the effect of the change be stated clearly so that the users of the data can take the change into account in their decisions. Of course, disclosure is not necessary if the change would not affect any of the decisions likely to be based on the accounting data.

Consistency within a given set of statements of a firm at a specific date and for a specific time period also is not necessary as a specific constraint if emphasis is placed on the presentation of all relevant information necessary for the making of the predictions by the users. Examples of inconsistency within the statements would be (1) the presentation of plant and equipment at cost and the related depreciation on the basis of replacement cost or (2) the aggregation of several inventory amounts, some based on FIFO and some on LIFO. If the aggregated amounts and the relationships are relevant, consistency in the use of measurement concepts and procedures might be necessary for the presentation of the appropriate data.

According to *APB Opinion No. 20,* an accounting change includes a change in an accounting principle, in an accounting estimate, or in the reporting entity. It states further that an accounting principle once adopted should not be changed unless the new method can be justified as being preferable. Changes should be disclosed in the period in which the change is made. Only a few types of changes should be reported by restating the financial statements of prior years.[43]

Timeliness

It is not only necessary that users have financial information that is relevant to their predictions and decisions; the information should also be current in nature, rather than relating only to prior periods. That is, the information used by investors and creditors should be current at the time of making the predictions and decisions. This, of course, is included in the concept of relevance, but it should be stressed as an important constraint on the publication of financial statements. The accumulation and sum-

---

[42] However, for an empirical support for consistency, see Andrew M. McCosh, "Accounting Consistency—Key to Stockholder Information," *Accounting Review,* October 1967, pp. 693–700.

[43] *APB Opinion No. 20,* "Accounting Changes" (AICPA, 1971). Also in *AICPA Professional Standards,* section 1051.

marization of accounting information and its publication should be as rapid as possible to assure the availability of current information in the hands of the users. This also implies that financial statements should be presented at frequent intervals so as to reveal changes in the firm's situation that may in turn affect the user's predictions and decisions.

MEASUREMENT IN ACCOUNTING

The first step in the presentation of information to external users of financial statements is to select objects and activities or events and their attributes relating to the firm that are relevant to the needs of specific or general users. Examples of objects would include receivables, plant and equipment, and long-term debt; examples of activities would include sales of goods and services and dividend payments. Before measurement can take place, however, the specific attribute to be measured must be selected. In the case of receivables, the selected attributes might include the number of dollars to be received and the expected date of collection. Attributes of plant and equipment might include physical capacity to produce, resource outlay at the time of acquisition, or resources necessary to replace the assets currently. The selected attributes may be considered relevant to user's needs if they aid the user in predictions and decision making. It should be recognized that most attributes are relevant only because they can be used to represent something else; that is, they represent a surrogate of the real attribute desired. For example, historical cost under certain circumstances may be relevant as a surrogate for the current value of an asset, which in turn may aid in the prediction of future values.

Measurement in accounting has traditionally meant the assignment of numerical values to objects or events related to an enterprise and obtained in such a way that they are suitable for aggregation (such as the total valuation of assets) or disaggregation as required for specific situations. However, measurement also involves a process of classification and identification, and accountants have recognized the need for many years for the presentation of information that is nonquantifiable in nature, such as disclosures frequently placed in footnotes or elsewhere in the statements. An emphasis on quantitative measurement is found in the postulates of Moonitz in *Accounting Research Study No. 1,* as one of the basic standards of *A Statement of Basic Accounting Theory*, in the assumptions of Chambers[44] and Mattessich,[45] and in the *Statements of Financial Accounting Concepts*.

These attempts to set forth a general framework for accounting theory also emphasize the importance of a market system in an exchange econ-

[44] Chambers, *Accounting Evaluation*, pp. 101–2.
[45] Mattessich, *Analytical Methods*, p. 52.

omy as a valuable source of quantitative data. Since goods and services are generally exchanged in terms of money, a monetary measurement of economic data can be assumed to be useful in decision making, particularly for those decisions relating to wealth and changes in wealth and the production of goods and services. Following from the assumption of an exchange economy, it is logical that exchange prices (market prices) would be relevant to external reporting. And it also follows that since economic decisions can affect only current and future outcomes, current and future exchange prices are more relevant than past exchange prices. However, certain constraints discussed below, particularly the existence of uncertainty and the need for objectivity and verifiability, may make current market prices more reliable than future prices, and in many cases, past exchange prices more reliable than current prices.

Traditionally, accounting has looked to the transactions or exchanges directly affecting the accounting entity itself for its monetary measurements. However, many recent proposals have suggested that market prices determined by exchanges between other entities may be relevant for the measurement of goods and services for a specific accounting entity. For example, current costs and appraisal values may be relevant in certain circumstances as suggested in the Trueblood Report.[46]

It cannot be denied that many types of monetary data may be relevant in external reporting, but it is also possible that nonmonetary data, such as productive capacity in tons or numbers of employees, may be found relevant for certain predictions and decision making. Accountants should also search for improved alternative methods of measuring and presenting both monetary and nonmonetary data. For example, it might be possible to present data showing probability intervals and ranges (in probabilistic form) as well as single-valued data (in deterministic form). Also, it may be desirable to present multiple values representing different attributes of objects and activities if they are all found to be relevant. In addition, consideration should be given to the presentation of budget data as evidence of management's plans and expectations.

MEASUREMENT CONSTRAINTS

As indicated above, measurement in accounting should be directed toward providing information relevant for specified uses. However, limitations of available data and certain characteristics of the environment place restrictions on the accuracy and reliability of measurements. These restrictions or constraints should, therefore, be made explicit and be taken into consideration in the development of accounting principles and procedures. But the constraints should not determine the principles; they only require modifications of basic principles. Nevertheless, since the con-

---

[46] Study Group on the Objectives of Financial Statements, "Objectives of Financial Statements" (AICPA, October 1973), p. 36.

straints cannot be removed by accountants, either because they are caused by the nature of the environment or because of a lack of adequate measurement tools, they should enter directly into the selection of measurement concepts and procedures. Insofar as they can be removed, the restrictions are not basic constraints of accounting measurement.

The major measurement constraints arise because economic data are presented on the assumption that they have some relevance for a prediction of the future. Since the relationship between the present and the future is generally highly uncertain, it is generally difficult to determine the relevant measurements for this purpose. But the inability to make reliable measurements of specific attributes that are thought to be relevant is due to the lack of reliable measurement techniques and the inability to find measurement procedures that adequately describe the attributes being measured. Thus constraints are caused by uncertainty, the lack of objectivity and verifiability in measurements, and the lack of a stable monetary unit. Conservatism acts as a constraint on accounting measurement because it is so highly ingrained in the minds of management and accountants, but it should be removed as a constraint by appropriate educational methods.

Uncertainty

Uncertainty in accounting arises from two main sources: (1) Accounting information generally relates to entities that are expected to have continuity of existence into the future; since allocations are frequently made between past and future periods, assumptions must be made regarding the logic of these allocations and on the basis of expectations regarding the future. Although some of these assumptions and expectations regarding allocations may be validated in later periods, many allocations can never be verified completely. (2) Accounting measurements are frequently assumed to represent monetary expressions of wealth that require estimates of uncertain future amounts. The reliability of these estimates may vary considerably, and no monetary quantification of wealth can be known with certainty. Thus, any measurement based on estimates can only be tentative. However, this does not mean that estimates and predictions should not be made as accurately as possible if they are relevant. But it does imply that measurements based on past estimates should be scrutinized closely and adjusted as new and more reliable estimates become possible.

Objectivity and verifiability

In order that accounting measurements can be as reliable as possible in presenting information relevant for predictions and decision making of investors and other users of financial reports, accountants must decide what attribute is being measured and then select a measurement procedure that is likely to describe accurately the attribute. In this attempt to produce reliability, accountants have turned to the concept of objectivity to either justify current practice or to claim superiority of certain principles and procedures over others. However, objectivity has meant different things to different writers. Several of these meanings are: (1) measurements that are impersonal or existing outside the mind of the person making the measurement, (2) measurements based on verifiable evidence, (3) measurements based on a consensus of qualified experts, and (4) the narrowness of the statistical dispersion of the measurements of an attribute when made by different measurers.

The first meaning of objectivity implies that the measurement has an existence separate from the person making the measurement. Thus, an absence of subjective valuation and personal bias is assumed. For example, the reporting of revenue at the time of sale is said to be objective because it can be measured from the results of an external transaction. However, particularly in accounting, an important question is whether or not a measurement independent of the measurer can exist. Even though the accountant may look at specific external evidence, it is impossible to obtain this measurement without going through the mental process of determining what it is. Although an external transaction may exist, the accountant must determine the value of what is given up and the value of what is received.

In the second definition (a measurement based on verifiable evidence) the emphasis is on the evidence, rather than on the measurement itself. For example, Paton and Littleton place considerable emphasis on verifiable, objective *evidence* as a test of the accuracy of a statement.[47] The evidence provides the means whereby the measurement itself can be verified. For example, revenue is accepted as realized on the basis of the sales as the evidence. As another example, cost has traditionally been accepted as objective evidence of the value of an asset. The difficulty with this approach is that although the evidence may be verifiable, the selection of the evidence to be used as a basis for the measurement desired may be subject to personal bias. If historical cost has been selected as evidence of the current value of an asset, the evidence (cost) may be objective, but its selection as the current value of the asset may reflect personal bias. Accountants traditionally reflect this type of bias when they report historical costs in financial statements, but move to a current market price when this is lower than cost.

The third meaning of objectivity has greater significance for measurement theory in accounting. Measurements can be said to be objective if they can be verified by intersubjective consensus of qualified experts. Moonitz, for example, states that *objective* "means . . . unbiased; subject to verification by another competent investigator."[48] This meaning is

---

[47] W. A. Paton and A. C. Littleton, *An Introduction to Corporate Accounting Standards* (AAA, 1955), pp. 18–21.

[48] Moonitz, "The Basic Postulates," p. 42.

similar to the standard of verifiability proposed by the Committee to Prepare a Statement of Basic Accounting Theory. The committee defined verifiability as

> that attribute of information which allows qualified individuals working independently of one another to develop essentially similar measures or conclusions from an examination of the same evidence.[49]

If several investigators use the same or similar methods of measurement of an attribute based on similar evidence, the several resulting measurements will most likely provide a range of values. If the measurements are free from personal bias, it is probable although not necessary that a frequency distribution of these measurements will produce a symmetrical curve. For any given number of observations or measurements, the degree of objectivity or verifiability depends upon the dispersion of the measurement values around a mean or average figure. This is demonstrated by the following two measurement procedures, which result in the same average value:

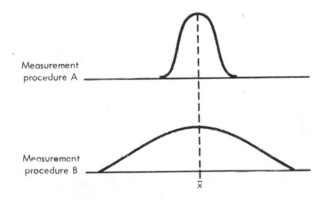

Measurement procedure A is more verifiable than procedure B, since any measurement value x_i has a greater probability of being close to the mean value $\bar{x}$ by using procedure A than by using procedure B. Thus, verifiability is a relative concept. Very few procedures will result in values upon which many accountants would have complete agreement. Although objectivity or verifiability cannot be obtained unless the measurements are relatively free from personal bias, measurement errors and differences in interpretation may also result in the loss of verifiability. Note, however, that the relative degree of objectivity or verifiability alone does not determine the reliability of the measurement procedure to describe accurately the attribute under consideration. Even the mean value $\bar{x}$ may fail to measure accurately the attribute.

---

[49] Committee to Prepare a Statement of Basic Accounting Theory, p. 10. See also *FASB Statement of Financial Accounting Concepts No. 2; AICPA Professional Standards— Accounting,* vol. 3, paras. 1220.081–.089.

Freedom from bias

The term *freedom from bias* has been used to mean that the information presented is characterized by neutrality and fairness.[50] Under this standard of neutrality, "freedom from bias" then represents the ability of the measurement procedure to provide an accurate description of the attribute under consideration.

Bias inherent in the measurement procedure can be demonstrated by the following diagrams:

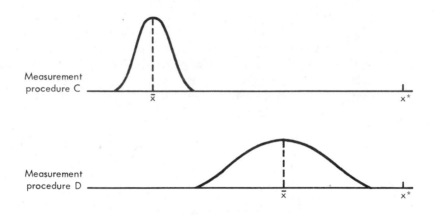

Bias is determined by the relative deviation of the mean value x̄ determined by the measurement procedure and the alleged or "true" value x^* of the attribute. Therefore, measurement procedure C is more verifiable than D, and procedure D is less biased than C because the mean value produced lies closer to the alleged value x^*. Since a true value for an attribute cannot be determined, the difference between the mean value x and the alleged value x^* must be based upon expert judgment, taking into consideration the logical relationship between the measurement procedure and the attribute being measured.[51] For example, historical cost is not likely to be free from bias in measuring the current market value of an asset if prices have changed radically since the date of acquisition. On the other hand, a procedure that adjusts historical cost for changes in the specific prices of that class of asset may be less verifiable, but result in less bias.

Reliability is defined by Ijiri and Jaedicke as the degree of objectivity or verifiability plus the bias factor. For a statistical measure of reliability,

---

[50] Study Group on the Objectives of Financial Statements, p. 58.

[51] The AAA Committee on Accounting Valuation Bases suggested that since the true value cannot be known, an alternative is to measure the displacement (bias) of the present measure from the next best measure that can be regarded as the challenger. Committee on Accounting Valuation Bases, "Report of the Committee on Accounting Valuation Bases," *Accounting Review*, supplement to vol. 47 (1972), p. 563.

they suggest the use of the mean-square-error.[52] However, such a computation would be difficult because of the unknown nature of the true or alleged value x^*. It might be better to judge verifiability and bias separately and then valuate the trade-offs, taking into consideration the nature of the information and its relevance for prediction of the several elements required in the decision models of users.

Limitations of the monetary unit

Although accounting data are not limited to measurement in terms of a monetary unit, accounting reports have traditionally included primarily financial information. And in many cases, the monetary unit provides the best measurement unit, particularly where aggregation is necessary or desirable. However, the monetary unit has its limitations as a method of communicating information. The most serious limitation or constraint is due to the fact that the value of the monetary unit is not stable over time. Since many predictions and decisions must rely on valid comparisons of accounting data over time, the lack of a stable monetary unit means that accounting data based on past exchange prices must be restated to be comparable with current and future exchange prices in order to be relevant and reliable for the making of appropriate predictions and decisions. In other words, the measurement constraint of instability of the measuring unit requires some modification in the use of exchange prices of different time periods expressed in terms of money. The problems resulting from this instability and the effect on the derivation of accounting principles are discussed at greater length in Chapter 9.

Conservatism

The general constraint of uncertainty has served as a basis for the traditional accounting concept of conservatism. As it is generally stated, the concept of conservatism is not a postulate of accounting, nor should it be one of the constraints. But in its operational form, it serves as a constraint to the presentation of data that may otherwise be reliable and relevant. To understand conservatism in accounting, we should try to understand the conditions that give rise to it and point out the element of truth in the constraint, if indeed there is any.

The term *conservatism* is generally used to mean that accountants should report the lowest of several possible values for assets and revenues and the highest of several possible values for liabilities and expenses. It

---

[52] Yuji Ijiri and Robert K. Jaedicke, "Reliability and Objectivity of Accounting Measurements," *Accounting Review* 41 (July 1966), pp. 480–83. Also included in Yuji Ijiri, *The Foundations of Accounting Measurement* (Englewood Cliffs, N.J.: Prentice-Hall, 1967), pp. 142–45.

also implies that expenses should be recognized sooner rather than later and that revenues should be recognized later than sooner. Therefore, net assets are more likely to be valued below current exchange prices than above them, and the computation of income is likely to result in the lowest of several alternative amounts. Thus, pessimism is assumed to be better than optimism in financial reporting.

One of the arguments for conservatism is that the tendency toward pessimism is assumed to be necessary to offset the overoptimism of managers and owners. Entrepreneurs are naturally optimistic about their own enterprises, and it is assumed that this optimism tends to be reflected in both the selection and emphasis in accounting reports. Through the pressure of creditors and other users of financial reports, the accountants of the 19th century were continually under pressure to refrain from reflecting this optimism in their reports. Thus, many of the traditional tenets in accounting were supported by conservatism, and many of these concepts permeate accounting practice today. In this context, conservatism has no place in accounting theory. Deliberate understatements may lead to poor decisions just as frequently as do overstatements.

A second argument for conservatism is that overstatement of profit and valuations is more dangerous for the business and its owners than understatement. That is, it is assumed that the consequences of loss or bankruptcy are much more serious than the consequences of a gain. Therefore, it is argued that there is no reason why the measurement and recognition rules for losses should be the same as for gains when the consequences are different.[53] The objection to this argument is that the accountant is in a better position to evaluate risk than is the investor or creditor. However, the evaluation of risk and the preference or aversion for risk are subjective judgments, which cannot be assumed by the accountant. Instead of applying conservatism, the objective of financial reports should be to provide adequate information to permit the users to make their own evaluations of risk.

A third argument for conservatism is based upon the assumption that the accountant has access to much more information than can be communicated to investors and creditors and that the accountant is faced with two types of risk. On the one hand, there is the risk that what is reported may turn out subsequently to be untrue. On the other hand, there is the risk that what is not reported may subsequently turn out to be true. This is similar to the *alpha* and *beta* risks of statistics. The *alpha* risk involves the acceptance of a hypothesis that is in fact unacceptable, and the *beta* risk involves the rejection of a hypothesis that is in fact acceptable. With respect to favorable items, the support for the rejection of that which might be true is greater than the support for the acceptance

---

[53] See Eugen Schmalenbach, *Dynamic Accounting,* English trans. (London: Gee & Co., 1959), pp. 81–82.

of that which might be untrue, and vice versa for unfavorable items.[54] The objection to this practice is that there is no basic evidence that the consequence of the one risk is so much greater than the consequence of the other to justify this bias in accounting reports. The accountant should attempt to balance these risks as much as possible and provide information for a proper evaluation of the risk whenever possible.

Conservatism is, at best, a very poor method of treating the existence of uncertainty in valuation and income. At its worst, it results in a complete distortion of accounting data. Its main danger is that, because it is a very crude method, its effects are capricious. Therefore, conservatively reported data are not subject to proper interpretation even by the most informed readers. It should be noted also that conservatism conflicts with the objective to disclose all relevant information, and with consistency to the extent to which that is a relevant constraint; and it can lead to a lack of comparability because there can be no uniform standards for its implementation.

THE FRAMEWORK OF ACCOUNTING THEORY

The general framework of accounting theory requires for its implementation a set of symbols and a structure in which ideas and data can be expressed and summarized. The traditional structure that has served accounting well for many years includes double entry, with the concepts of accounts, ledgers, and trial balances, and the presentation of accounting data in the form of financial statements that articulate with each other. *Accounting Research Study No. 1* confirmed the utility of this structure by stating that "the results of the accounting process are expressed in a set of fundamentally related financial statements which articulate with each other and rest upon the same underlying data."[55] Some type of structure is necessary, but the selection of any particular set of symbols and reports should not be included among the postulates. *ARS No. 1* did not necessarily limit the structure to conventional types of financial statements, but it did state that they should articulate with each other and rest on the same underlying data. These restrictions may be desirable, but they should be evaluated on the basis of their usefulness as a structure, rather than as a postulate.

The characteristics of a desirable framework, however, can be derived from the objectives of accounting, the environmental postulates, the measurement concepts, and the constraints. Articulation has been thought to

---

[54] See Arthur L. Thomas, *Revenue Recognition* (Ann Arbor: University of Michigan Press, 1966), pp. 53–54; and Carl Thomas Devine, "The Rule of Conservatism Reexamined," *Journal of Accounting Research* 1 (Autumn 1963): pp. 137–38.

[55] Moonitz, "The Basic Postulates," p. 52.

be desirable in order to make the information more understandable and more useful for decision making, because of the availability of consistent and comparable summaries. It has been thought that if the statements are related and based on the same underlying data, the entire structure can be made more formal, resulting in greater logic, better consistency, and a greater degree of uniformity. However, articulation and the rigid application of double entry have resulted in the presentation of meaningless or misleading information in one statement as a result of an attempt to improve reported information in another. The application of the LIFO procedure for inventory evaluation is an example. There is also little evidence that retained earnings or total stockholders' equity is meaningful for predictions or decision making or that the articulation of the income statement with the funds statement provides relevant information. Nevertheless, articulation is likely to continue so long as accountants and users of financial reports believe that it provides some assurance that some relevant information is not omitted or some assurance that management is not manipulating the information released for its own benefit. In fact, articulation provides no assurance that either of these is true.

The types of financial statements presented in formal reports should meet the objectives of potential users of the reports in accordance with the measurement standards and in light of realistic constraints. Before the 1930s, the balance sheet was thought to be the most useful form, primarily because it provided information to creditors. Subsequently, the income statement came to be considered the most relevant statement, on the ground that it provided better information for investors and stockholders. More recently, the funds statement and experiments in the development of statements that adjust for changes in the level of prices have been added to the reports considered relevant for external users. Future developments in the accounting framework and the reporting structure are imperative to permit the optimum amount of relevant information to be presented in external reports. The external reports should probably include at least information regarding resources and commitments and also regarding funds and resource flows, both historically and as plans for the future. In the interests of economy, a single data base should probably be devised upon which reports for both internal and external uses can be built.

SELECTED ADDITIONAL READING

Postulates

Deinzer, Harvey T. *Development of Accounting Thought.* New York: Holt, Rinehart & Winston, 1965, chaps. 8 and 9.

Lambert, Samuel Joseph, III. "Basic Assumptions in Accounting Theory Construction." *Journal of Accountancy,* February 1974, pp. 41–48.

Mautz, R. K. "The Place of Postulates in Accounting." *Journal of Accountancy,* January 1965, pp. 46–49.
Metcalf, Richard W. "The Basic Postulates in Perspective." *Accounting Review* 39 (January 1964), pp. 16–21.
Popoff, Boris. "Postulates, Principles and Rules." *Accounting and Business Research,* Summer 1972, pp. 182–93.

Continuity

Devine, Carl Thomas. "Entity, Continuity, Discount, and Exit Values." *Essays in Accounting Theory* 3 (1971), pp. 111–35.
Fremgren, James M. "The Going Concern Assumption: A Critical Appraisal." *Accounting Review* 43 (October 1968), pp. 649–56.
Sterling, Robert R. "The Going Concern: An Examination." *Accounting Review,* July 1968, pp. 481–502.
Yu, S. C. "A Reexamination of the Going Concern Postulate." *International Journal of Accounting, Education and Research,* Spring 1971, pp. 37–58.

Objectives

Anton, H. R. "Objectives of Financial Accounting: Review and Analysis." *Journal of Accountancy,* January 1976, pp. 40–51.
Beaver, William H., and Joel S. Demski. "The Nature of Financial Accounting Objectives: A Summary and Synthesis." *Studies on Financial Accounting Objectives: 1974.* Supplement to vol. 12 of the *Journal of Accounting Research,* pp. 170–87.
FASB. *Statement of Financial Accounting Concepts No. 1,* "Objectives of Financial Reporting by Business Enterprises." AICPA, *Professional Standards — Accounting,* vol. 3, Section 1210.
Goetz, B. E., and J. G. Birnberg. "A Comment on the Trueblood Report." *Management Accounting,* April 1976.
Kenley, W. John, and George J. Staubus. "Objectives and Concepts of Financial Statements." *Accounting Research Study No. 3* Melbourne: Accountancy Research Foundation, 1972.
Sterling, Robert R. "Decision-Oriented Financial Accounting." *Accounting and Business Research,* Summer 1972, pp. 198–208.
Williams, Jan Robert. "Differing Opinions on Accounting Objectives." *CPA Journal,* August 1973, pp. 651–56.

Relevance

Chambers, R. J. "Usefulness—The Vanishing Premise in Accounting Standard Setting." *Abacus,* December 1979, pp. 71–92.
Martin, Alvin. "An Empirical Test of the Relevance of Accounting Information for Investment Decisions." *Empirical Research in Accounting: Selected Studies, 1971* pp. 1–31.
Shwayder, Keith. "Relevance." *Journal of Accounting Research* 6 (Spring 1968), pp. 86–97.

Materiality

Barlev, Benzion. "On the Measurement of Materiality." *Accounting and Business Research,* Summer 1972, pp. 194–97.

Bernstein, Leopold A. "The Concept of Materiality." *Accounting Review* 42 (January 1967): 86–95.

Frishkoff, Paul. "An Empirical Investigation of the Concept of Materiality in Accounting." *Empirical Research in Accounting: Selected Studies,* 1970, pp. 116–29.

Rose, J.; W. Beaver; S. Becker; and **G. Sorter.** "Toward an Empirical Measure of Materiality." *Empirical Research in Accounting: Selected Studies,* 1971, pp. 138–53.

Timeliness

Courtis, J. K. "Relationships between Timeliness in Corporate Reporting and Corporate Attributes." *Accounting and Business Research,* Winter 1976, pp. 45–56.

Gilling, Donald M. "Timeliness in Corporate Reporting: Some Further Comment." *Accounting and Business Research,* Winter 1977, pp. 34–36.

Accounting measurement

Ashton, Robert H. Objectivity of Accounting Measures: A Multirule-Multimeasurer Approach. *Accounting Review,* July 1977, pp. 567–575.

Dewhirst, John F. "Dealing with Uncertainty." *Canadian Chartered Accountant,* August 1971, pp. 139–46.

Ijiri, Yuji. *The Foundations of Accounting Measurement.* Englewood Cliffs, N.J.: Prentice-Hall, 1967.

"Report of the Committee on Foundations of Accounting Measurements." *Accounting Review,* supplement to vol. 46 (1971), pp. 3–48.

"Report of the Committee on Accounting Valuation Bases." *Accounting Review,* supplement to vol. 47 (1972), esp. pp. 556–68.

CHAPTER 4

EFFICIENT CAPITAL MARKETS

The inductive-deductive approach to accounting theory has some serious deficiencies as discussed in the previous chapter. Probably, the most important of these deficiencies is the inability to test the theories empirically. Even though a theory may be logically consistent, it may not agree with real-world observations because of erroneous premises, insufficient observations, or incorrect objectives. But a real-world test is extremely difficult if not impossible if the objective is to predict what accounting information may be most useful to individual investors. Because usefulness of information to individual investors is largely a matter of individual decision-making processes, even if measurements of subjective personal utilities were made, aggregation for even specific classes of investors would be difficult.

Observations of market reactions to accounting information provide a means of testing theories that do not depend upon assumptions regarding individual investors' subjective utilities. Instead, assumptions regarding personal utilities can be derived from the observations of market reactions, although the reactions reflect aggregate, rather than individual, utilities. Therefore, a study of market reactions to accounting information provides an excellent alternative to the inductive-deductive theories with their emphasis on the decision process of the individual investor.

A second deficiency of the inductive-deductive approach is that it focuses on the welfare of the individual investor rather than the welfare of society. The intrinsic value theories assume that an objective of accounting is to provide information to help the investor find securities that are underpriced in the market—that is, where the intrinsic value is greater than current market price. If this does occur, the result of a securities transaction would be a transfer of wealth from one individual to another. That is, the investor purchasing the undervalued security would gain, and the investor selling the security would lose. There would not necessarily be an increase in wealth to society.

The alternative market approach focuses on the welfare of society rather than of the individual. Although it is the aggregation of individual decisions that determines market behavior, it is an error of composition to assume that optimum market behavior can be attained by focusing on individual behavior. It is the role of a securities market to provide the funds for those who make productive investment decisions in the economy and to provide a means whereby security investors can alter their consumption-wealth patterns over time.

A focus on the securities market rather than on the individual investor results in a different objective for accounting information. First, information is necessary to permit an optimum allocation of resources among producers. An optimum allocation will occur when producers are able to obtain capital funds in order to attain a maximum gross national product with a given amount of resources. This definition of *optimum allocation* must be qualified in order to include social welfare and other goals. In any case, information to a securities market is important in the allocation of resources.

Second, information is necessary to permit investors to hold security portfolios that are optimum with respect to the risk-return preferences of the investors within the framework of the security prices existing in the market. That is, information is necessary for the establishment of security prices that reflect risk and return relationships and for individual investors to obtain portfolios that reflect their own preferences in obtaining a maximum rate of return with a given degree of risk.

THE EFFICIENT MARKET HYPOTHESIS

The Efficient Market Hypothesis (EMH) is based on the assumption of a competitive securities market. That is, the prices of securities are free to move in such a way that they will reach equilibrium when the supply and demand for each security are equal. Whenever new relevant information regarding a specific security becomes available, it is likely to alter the expectation of investors such that the relative price of the security will change until a new equilibrium is reached. It should be kept in mind that it is the *relative* prices that will change with new information regarding specific securities. The *level* of securities prices is a result of a number of general economic factors, including the prevailing rate of interest, the rate of inflation, and expectations regarding general economic conditions—although individual securities may be affected differently by each of these factors.

A securities market is considered to be efficient when the prices of the securities fully reflect all available information. No relevant information is ignored by the market. In its theoretical form, the sufficient conditions for an efficient market are:

1. There are no transaction costs in the trading of securities.
2. All available information is equally available to all traders without cost.
3. All traders have homogeneous expectations regarding the implications of available information.

These conditions are sufficient for the theoretical model, but they are not necessary in order to obtain an approximation of an efficient market in the real world. All that is really necessary for market efficiency is that all available information be impounded in security prices immediately or with a minimum of delay and in an unbiased manner.

The weak form of the EMH

The weak form of the EMH states that security prices fully reflect information implied by the historical sequence of prices. Sufficient research has been conducted that this hypothesis is now generally accepted as being confirmed. Earlier studies of what was known as the random walk theory found that security price changes are random with respect to the information available before the change. That is, excess gains cannot be obtained merely by a knowledge of past security prices.

The importance of this form of the EMH for accounting is that it implies that new information is impounded immediately in security prices. If the new information were reflected in prices gradually over time, one price change would be an indication of the size and direction of the next price change. Only if the market adjustment to new information is instantaneous, would the price changes be independent, which has been proven to be the case. Since this form of the EMH does not have further relevance for accounting, we must look further at studies relating information to securities markets.

The semistrong form of the EMH

The semistrong form of the EMH states that security prices reflect all *publicly available* information. This would include, of course, information regarding current and previous securities prices. If the market is efficient in the semistrong form, new information publicly available will be impounded in stock prices instantaneously and in an unbiased manner. A number of research studies have supported the EMH in the semistrong form so that it is now fairly generally accepted for the securities markets in the United States and in several other countries.[1]

Market efficiency in the semistrong form does not imply that all investors will understand and take into account immediately all new information. It is sufficient that there be enough informed or professional analysts and investors to react to new information quickly. If the information is incorrectly interpreted, there will be investors available to take advan-

---

[1] For a discussion of supporting evidence and some evidence that questions efficiency, see Thomas R. Dyckman, David H. Downes, and Robert P. Magee, *Efficient Capital Markets and Accounting: A Critical Analysis* (Englewood Cliffs, N.J.: Prentice-Hall, 1975), chaps. 2 and 3.

tage of the situation, and potential excess earnings will disappear quickly if not immediately. That is, when new information becomes available, both buyers and sellers of securities will adjust their expectations accordingly, and transactions will take place at the new equilibrium price. The investor who, through lack of knowledge or because of deliberate action, does not take the new information into account does not gain or lose by buying or selling at the market price. However, the market will be efficient only if a sufficient number of investors use the new information in an attempt to earn superior returns. That is, they must react as if the market were not efficient.

The semistrong form of EMH has some important implications for accounting. It should be made clear, however, that accounting is only one source (and possibly not the major source) of publicly available information regarding firms and their securities sold in the market. Industry-wide and general economic information may have special implications for a specific firm. News reports and articles in financial journals may also provide insights into a firm. Other sources include corporate press releases and interviews of corporate officials by financial analysts, major investors, or representatives of public groups. However, most information relating directly to the specific firm will come originally from the firm itself, and much of this will come from the accounting department, although it may not first be made public through accounting reports.

The result may be that by the time accounting financial reports are published, the information contained in the reports will already have become public information or have been anticipated. For example, revenue and earnings amounts are frequently published by the press before the publication of financial statements. In other cases partial information, such as production or employment data, may become available from time to time, thus permitting financial analysts to forecast fairly accurately the earnings and earnings per share numbers before they are fully computed. The result is that security prices will react to the information as soon as it becomes public or is anticipated, and no further adjustment may be necessary at the time the financial statements are published.

If the securities markets do not react to financial accounting reports at the time they are published, it may still be possible that the reports are relevant. Financial reports may at least confirm information published by other sources and confirm or refute forecasts made on the basis of other information. This permits financial analysts and investors to evaluate the reliability of other sources and forecasts. However, financial accounting may also be relevant to individual investors if we relax the assumption of homogeneous expectations. If investors form different expectations regarding the relative riskiness of different securities, they may use accounting information to aid in forming their own expectations in order to obtain optimum portfolios, even though they are unable to earn excess returns based on the market's expectations. (This is discussed at greater length in a later section.)

The strong form of the EMH

The strong form of the EMH states that all *available* relevant information is reflected in security prices. That is, security prices fully reflect privileged (insider) information as well as all publicly available information. However, the evidence to date has not shown this hypothesis to be true. Therefore, it may be assumed that the market is inefficient with respect to insider information and that excess earnings could be obtained by trading on the basis of such information. This assumption is difficult to prove, however, for several reasons. First, there are laws in the United States prohibiting certain individuals, (such as financial analysts and corporate officers) and firms from trading on the basis of privileged insider information. But even the laws are not clear regarding what can be considered insider information and what is public information. Second, by definition insider information is not available to the public and is therefore difficult to observe and study. Third, it is not clear how insider information could be fully reflected in security prices, since it is available to only a small segment of the market participants.

On a priori grounds, insider information could become impounded in security prices in at least two ways:

1. If those obtaining insider information trade on the basis of such information, the additional demand alone for the security would increase the price until the information became public or no longer became relevant. But if those trading on such information had limited resources, the effect on the market price would be minimal. As the number of individuals using such information increases, the information can at some point be considered to be public. So it is difficult to assess on either a priori grounds or empirically the effect of insider information on security prices.

2. A second way that insider information could affect security prices is really associated with the first way. If those known to possess or likely to possess insider information increase the volume of their trades in that security significantly, other participants in the market will assume that there is positive or negative information available to those individuals thought to possess such information; thus, the other participants will react to the information without knowing precisely what it is. In this way, at least the implications of the insider information become public and are impounded in the market. The difficulty is that those using the insider information will already have obtained a competitive advantage and were at least temporarily able to earn excess (monopoly) returns.

The implications of the strong form of the EMH for accounting are that if accounting is to serve a social function, it should attempt to make relevant financial information available publicly as soon as possible in order to minimize the possibility for the use of insider information. When insider information is used to the advantage of specific individuals, other participants in the market lose. The effect is a transfer of wealth from some investors to others. And since prices do not reflect this information immediately, the allocation of resources is less than optimum. Furthermore, individual investors are not able to evaluate securities properly in order to obtain optimum portfolios.

SOME MISCONCEPTIONS ABOUT THE EFFICIENT MARKET HYPOTHESIS

In the field of economics, it is dangerous to take observations of an individual's behavior and apply them to the economy as a whole. This general statement applies to an understanding of the efficient market hypothesis. What the individual investor does or is thought to do does not necessarily apply to the securities markets.

One area that needs clarification is the nature of market efficiency. It should not be confused with efficient portfolios, productive efficiency, or the efficient allocation of resources. A certain amount of information is necessary and assumed for these other concepts of efficiency. However, market efficiency (in the semistrong form) assumes only that all publicly available information is impounded in the security prices. If there were no published financial reports and no accounting information available, the market could still be efficient. Public information available from other sources could not be used to gain abnormal returns. However, the securities market structure of prices and possibly the variability of prices would be different than they now exist.

An efficient securities market does not react differently to alternative sources of the same information. We cannot assume that just because the information is included in published financial statements, the information somehow has a different impact on security prices. There may be a difference, however, in the cost and effort incurred by the investor in obtaining and using the information. If the cost to investors is greater than the benefit they expect from the information, such information will not be used. But relevant information included in published financial reports would be taken into consideration. However, this does not mean that information published in financial reports is necessarily provided at a lower social cost than the cost would be in an alternative source.

A third misconception is that by observing market reactions to alternative accounting procedures, it is possible to assess the desirability of one as opposed to other procedures. Stated differently, do changes in security prices provide evidence regarding the preferences of investors for alternative accounting procedures? Gonedes and Dopuch examined this question extensively and concluded that capital market efficiency alone cannot be used to make judgments regarding the desirability of alternative accounting procedures.[2] Very briefly, the reason that security prices cannot be

---

[2] Nicholas J. Gonedes and Nicholas Dopuch, "Capital Market Equilibrium, Information Production, and Selecting Accounting Techniques: Theoretical Framework and Review of Empirical Work," *Studies on Financial Accounting Objectives: 1974,* supplement to vol. 12 of the *Journal of Accounting Research,* pp. 48–120.

used alone in assessing alternative accounting procedures is that the value of the information is not included in the security prices. Because the information is publicly available at no cost to the investors, no one would be willing to pay for the information (the free-rider concept). This is not to say, however, that the *effects* of alternative accounting procedures cannot be assessed by using security prices in an efficient market setting.

Another misconception is that the market can be fooled by accounting gimmicks or tricks. The *functional fixation principle* is that investors associate the value of securities with certain accounting numbers, such as earnings per share, regardless of how the numbers are computed or the informational content of the numbers. That is, investors are functionally fixed to the numbers rather than to the information, and thus they may make incorrect evaluations of security return and risk. But this principle is inconsistent with an efficient market, although it may be consistent with the intrinsic value theory. With an efficient market, it is the publicly available information that is impounded in the security price, not the accounting number itself. A sufficient number of investors will see through the accounting numbers, and the security prices will be based on the best information for evaluating return and risk. It follows from the above discussion that accounting procedures based on arbitrary allocations and changes in accounting procedures that do not reflect the amount, timing, or probability of future cash flows to or from the firm would not provide information to securities market and thus would not affect security prices. The market will react only to information that will affect expectations regarding return and risk. In other words, an efficient market will utilize only information that has semantic interpretation.

CAPITAL ASSET PRICING THEORY

The efficient market hypothesis explains the effect of relevant information on security prices. However, in order to test for market efficiency or test for the relevancy of information, a theoretical model is needed to explain what factors or parameters determine security prices in equilibrium. Such a model could have a very large number of parameters because a large number of factors could affect security prices. There is considerable merit, however, in a model that has a few number of parameters and still has a high degree of predictability.

One of the models developed—the Capital Asset Pricing Model—has the characteristics of having only two parameters—risk and return—and a high degree of predictability. Before describing the model, it is important to look at portfolio theory, upon which the model is based.

Portfolio theory

Portfolio theory is based upon two basic assumptions regarding investment decisions under uncertainty:

1. Investors are risk-averse and prefer a greater return for a given level of risk or a lower risk for a given level of return.
2. Security returns are normally distributed.

The second assumption is important because it implies that security returns can be measured by the *mean* of their distribution and that risk can be measured by their *variance*. These assumptions represent a simplification of the actual decision process; however, they are a fairly accurate representation of reality and have the added advantage of avoiding complex relationships.

Since every investor can invest in several securities, it is the portfolio risk and return that are important, rather than the risk and return of the individual securities. The portfolio return is the mean of the returns of the individual securities; but the variance (measure of risk) of the portfolio is not the same as the mean of the variances of the individual securities. This is so because of the covariance of the individual securities in the portfolio. Through diversification, an individual investor can obtain a lower level of risk for the same return. Since diversification is readily available to all investors, the market will not pay a price for the risk borne by those investors who do not (by choice or otherwise) diversify. The remaining risk, which cannot be eliminated through diversification, is called the systematic risk. The systematic risk of an individual security is the effect that security has on the riskiness of a well-diversified portfolio. This is demonstrated in Figure 1. An investor with portfolio B can reduce

FIGURE 1:   The efficient portfolio curve

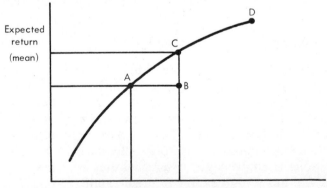

1. the amount of risk by the amount AB and still maintain the same return. As an alternative, he/she could invest in such a way as to increase the return to C with the same risk as at B. The curve ACD represents the highest expected return for a given level of risk or the lowest risk for a given level of return. This is referred to as the efficient frontier, and any portfolio on the curve is an efficient portfolio. A portfolio under the curve

is less preferable than a portfolio on the curve. Portfolios A, C, and D, however, are valued equally by the market. That is, the market is indifferent regarding the combinations of risk and return represented by portfolios on the curve. An individual investor, however, may have a preference for a specific risk and return combination, and other investors will have other preferences depending on their personal degree of aversion to risk and their income and wealth situation.

The market model

Before it is possible to test for the effects of new information in securities markets, it is necessary to develop a model of the market itself. The return and risk of an individual security are affected by many factors, some of which affect the market as a whole as well as the individual security and others that affect only the individual security. The latter must be isolated in order to evaluate the effect of information on the structure of security prices. Certain types of information, such as that which affects expectations regarding inflation, interest rates, and general economic conditions, are reflected in all prices in the market to some extent. Therefore, these general price movements must be neutralized by measuring the covariability of individual security prices with the market as a whole.

The market as a whole can be thought of as a portfolio of securities expanded until it includes all securities weighted by the value of each security priced in equilibrium. This is known as the market portfolio. With the concept of a market portfolio, the capital asset pricing model (CAPM) takes the assumption of the efficient market hypothesis that the securities market is complete and perfectly competitive with zero transaction costs. It also takes the assumptions of portfolio theory that investors are risk-averse and that security returns are normally distributed. In addition, the CAPM assumes that (1) all investors are able to borrow and lend at a riskless rate and (2) that all investors have common investment horizons and identical beliefs about the means, variances, and covariances of securities in the future. These assumptions will be relaxed in later discussions, but they are important for the development of the theory.

The CAPM model is demonstrated in Figure 2. The riskless rate (R) is shown at the left side of the chart. From this point to the right, any increase in return is associated with an increase in risk. For individual portfolios of securities, the curve AB (the efficient portfolio frontier) is concave from below because of diminishing marginal returns with increases in risk. The line RC represents a linear relationship between the risk and return for the market portfolio and the riskless rate. The portfolio efficient frontier will be tangent to this line at M, because this is where the risk/return relationship for the market portfolio and for an individual portfolio are the same. With the assumption that investors can

FIGURE 2: The capital asset pricing model

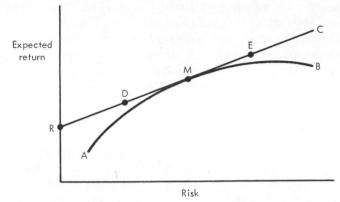

borrow and lend unlimited amounts at the riskless rate, they can move from any point on the efficient frontier by holding the portfolio with the same variance as the market portfolio and then borrowing or lending at the riskless rate to move unto the line RC. For example, an investor who is highly risk-averse can invest in a portfolio with risk at M and lend a sufficient amount at the riskless rate to reduce the overall risk to D. An investor who prefers risk will invest in a portfolio with risk at M and borrow a sufficient amount at the riskless rate, investing this amount at risk M, so that the overall risk of the net investment will be at E.

Within the context of the above discussion, the expected return for an individual security is equal to the return on a riskless asset plus the relative risk (referred to as beta) of the security times the excess of the expected market portfolio return over the return on a riskless asset. This is expressed in the following formula:

$$E(\tilde{R}_i) = R_r + \beta_i[E(\tilde{R}_m) - R_r]$$

where:

$E(\tilde{R}_i)$ = the expected return on security i
R_r = the return on a riskless asset
$E(\tilde{R}_m)$ = the expected return on the market portfolio
β_i = the relative risk of the security i as measured by the covariance of the security returns with the market portfolio returns.

The relative risk of an individual security (beta) is measured by the covariance of the security returns with the market portfolio returns. It is a measure of the sensitivity of the returns of an individual security or portfolio to the variability of returns of the market portfolio. That is, the beta for the market portfolio is one, since the covariance of any distribution with itself is unity. Any security with a risk (measured by the covariance) greater than that of the market portfolio would have a beta greater than one; conversely, any security with risk less than that of the market portfolio would have a beta less than one.

The capital asset pricing model predicts that the only difference between the return on an individual asset or portfolio and the market portfolio is due to the covariance of the individual return with the market portfolio return and that there is a positive linear relationship between the expected return of a security and its beta. Empirical tests have concluded that these relationships hold fairly accurately in most large securities markets.

Implications of the capital asset pricing model

The efficient markets hypothesis and the capital asset pricing model imply that relevant new information will have an immediate effect on the price of a security by either altering expectations regarding the average return on the security or altering the expectations regarding the security's beta. If all investors' expectations are homogeneous, a change in the price of the security relative to the prices of all securities in the market is an indication that the new information has an effect on market expectations. Therefore, one of the important implications of the CAPM is that it provides a means of testing the effect of making new information publicly available.

Within the restrictive assumptions of the CAPM, an individual investor should hold a portfolio with a beta risk of one (the market portfolio beta) and borrow or lend at the riskless rate in order to attain the appropriate risk level in accordance with his/her preference or aversion for risk. If we relax the assumption that the investor has an unlimited ability to borrow and lend at the riskless rate, the best that one could do would be to move to the efficient portfolio frontier through diversification. The beta for each security must be known in order to establish the beta for the portfolio and adjust the portfolio appropriately for personal risk preferences.

One of the difficulties with an interpretation of the implications of the CAPM is that the risk and return concepts are *ex ante* or expectations and risk is associated with the uncertainty of future returns. However, most measurements of the mean return and beta are *ex post* computed from a past period of 60 months in many cases. There is some evidence that future values of beta can be estimated on the basis of past long-term measurements of beta; however, it is the expected values of returns and beta that determine the relative prices of securities. If we relax the assumption that all investors have the same expectations regarding the mean and distribution of future returns, information that will aid individual investors in making their personal expectations is just as important as information directed toward the market as a whole. There is some evidence that some of the traditional accounting partial measures of risk, such as financial leverage (debt to equity ratios), operating leverage (the ratio of fixed to variable expenses), and liquidity, are associated with the market measures of beta and thus with future expectations of beta.[3]

One of the main advantages of the capital asset pricing model and the supporting efficient market hypothesis and portfolio theory is that it is empirically testable. However, the validity of the tests and the conclusions that can be reached are limited by the assumptions and the statistical techniques used. Both of these are being improved in current accounting research. However, it should be recognized that research on the effect of accounting on capital markets can only provide a partial answer to questions regarding the validity of accounting measures, the degree of relevance of accounting information, and the choice of alternative accounting procedures. Policy-making decisions should include many other factors, including the political preferences of certain groups, social implications, and the relative costs and benefits of presenting information in financial reports.

THE ECONOMICS OF
ACCOUNTING INFORMATION

Capital markets theory and the efficient market hypothesis permit the assessment of the effects of reporting different information or alternative accounting procedures. A knowledge of effects can be very important in the setting of accounting standards or in the establishment of accounting policy for a specific firm. However, a number of other factors must be considered in the establishment of a social policy regarding accounting information. One of these factors is the relationship between the costs and benefits of the published information.

If no financial information were made publicly available by either accountants, firms, or the government, it is likely that a market for this information would be established through other sources. Investors would be willing to pay for information if they could receive it before it is made publicly available and thus earn monopolistic returns from the private information. Once, the information has become publicly available through several investors receiving and acting upon it, the monopolistic returns would disappear. However, even after the monopolistic returns have disappeared, investors would pay some amount for information to permit them to move to efficient portfolios. That is, even though an investor could not improve the returns from each security, the returns of a portfolio could be increased within any risk class through diversification and the selection of appropriate securities with different values of beta.

Keeping in mind that the social objectives of accounting should be to

---

[3] See, for example, John S. Bildersee, "The Association between a Market-Determined Measure of Risk and Alternative Measures of Risk," *The Accounting Review,* January 1975, pp. 81–98.

permit optimum allocations of resources among producers and optimum portfolios held by investors, it is very difficult to measure the benefits of accounting information. From a social point of view, these benefits should not include the excess monopolistic returns that might be available to a select few who might be able to gain by trading on the basis of the information before it became publicly available. The benefits stem from providing the securities markets with all information relevant for investment decisions. Relevance can be assumed if information has an effect upon security prices or the volume of security sales. Thus, the market determines the relevance, and it can be assumed that an optimum amount of information would facilitate reaching an optimum allocation of resources through the appropriate pricing of securities. It should be clearly understood, however, that market efficiency alone does not necessarily result in an optimum allocation of resources. Furthermore, the relative degrees of association between accounting information and security prices cannot be used as a method of determining the relative benefit to society from providing the information.

Without a method of evaluating directly the benefits of accounting information, the focus of attention can turn toward the cost side. Several types of costs should be considered: (1) the direct costs of producing and publishing the information, (2) the costs of producing and publishing the information by alternative sources, (3) the costs of interpreting and evaluating the information incurred by investors and other decision makers, (4) the costs that would be incurred by investors if they had to search for the information for themselves, and (5) such indirect costs as the adverse effects of published information on the efficient operation of the firm.[4]

Published accounting information is produced and distributed at a cost to the firm (and indirectly to stockholders and possibly others) and is received without charge by the investor (with a few exceptions, such as financial libraries and special financial services). A reduction of the costs to the firm would provide a social benefit if the published information is irrelevant, if it is not used by any investors or the market, or if the information is provided more timely and at no additional cost by some other source. That is, accounting information produced and published at a material additional cost should be eliminated if no benefit for the information can be found or even assumed to exist.

Financial reports and other published financial information derived from accounting data may be the most economical way to provide such information to securities markets. However, alternative sources do exist, and the relative cost of these sources should be considered in establishing accounting policy. Professional financial analysts and managers of institutional and mutual funds obtain information directly by interviews with the executives or employees of the corporations or through man-

---

[4] The economic consequences of publishing information is discussed in Chapter 6.

agement's press releases. Pressures to transfer the disclosure of much of this information may only result in the transfer of the information-gathering costs from the financial analysts to the firms and their stockholders. On the other hand, information relevant to all investors for the establishment of efficient portfolios may be produced at a lower cost by the firm than the cost to investors of obtaining the information indirectly by purchasing it from brokers, investment analysts, or investment advisors.

In summary, it can be assumed that the allocation of resources will be improved by any increase in the amount of information impounded in market prices. But this does not mean that it is possible to state a preference for one set of accounting procedures over another on the basis of the association with market prices. Several other factors must be considered in evaluating accounting policy, including the costs of producing and distributing the information, the costs of alternative sources, and the costs of analyzing the information by investors and analysts.

SELECTED ADDITIONAL READING

Efficient capital markets

Anderson, James A., and **Stephen L. Meyers.** "Some Limitations of Efficient Markets Research for the Determination of Financial Reporting Standards." *Abacus,* June 1975, pp. 18–36.

Beaver, William H. "The Behavior of Security Prices and Its Implications for Accounting Research (Methods)." In American Accounting Association, "Report of the Committee on Research Methodology in Accounting." *Accounting Review.* Supplement to vol. 47 (1972), pp. 407–37. Also in *Research Methodology in Accounting,* edited by Robert R. Sterling. Lawrence, Kans.: Scholars Book, 1972, pp. 9–37.

—————. "Implications of Security Price Research for Accounting: A Reply to Bierman." *Accounting Review,* July 1974, pp. 563–71.

Bierman, Harold, Jr. "The Implications to Accounting of Efficient Markets and the Capital Asset Pricing Model." *Accounting Review,* July 1974, pp. 557–62.

Davis, Darrel W.; James R. Boatsman; and **Elba Baskin.** "On Generalizing Stock Market Research to a Broader Class of Markets." *Accounting Review,* January 1978, pp. 1–10.

Dyckman, Thomas R.; David H. Downes; and **Robert Magee.** *Efficient Capital Markets and Accounting: A Critical Analysis.* Englewood Cliffs, N.J.: Prentice-Hall, 1975.

Gonedes, N. J., and **N. Dopuch.** "Capital Market Equilibrium Information Production and Selecting Accounting Techniques: Theoretical Framework and Review of Empirical Work." *Journal of Accounting Research,* Supplement, 1974, pp. 48–129.

Lev, B. *Financial Statement Analysis: A New Approach.* Englewood Cliffs, N.J.: Prentice-Hall, 1974, chaps. 12–16.

Mayer-Sommer, Alan P. "Understanding and Acceptance of the Efficient Markets Hypothesis and its Accounting Implications." *Accounting Review,* January 1979, pp. 88–106.

Ronen, J. "The Need for Accounting Objectives in an Efficient Market." *Objectives of Financial Statements. Vol. 2, Selected Papers.* New York: AICPA, 1974, pp. 36–52.

Sterling, R., and W. Harrison. "Discussion of Capital Market Equilibrium, Information Production, and Selecting Accounting Techniques: Theoretical Framework and Review of Empirical Work." *Journal of Accounting Research,* supplement 1974, pp. 142–57.

Weston, J. Fred. "Investment Decisions Using the Capital Asset Pricing Model." *Financial Management,* 2, no. 1, (Spring 1973) pp. 25–33.

Portfolio theory

Keane, Simon M. "Portfolio Theory, Corporate Objectives, and the Disclosure of Accounting Data." *Accounting and Business Research,* Summer 1974, pp. 210–19.

Insider information

Ronen, Joshua. "The Effect of Insider Trading Rules on Information Generation and Disclosure by Corporations." *Accounting Review,* April 1977, pp. 438–49.

Systematic risk

Beaver, W. H.; P. Kettler; and M. Scholes. "The Association between Market-Determined and Accounting-Determined Risk Measures." *Accounting Review,* October 1970, pp. 654–82.

Beaver, W. H., and J. Manegold. "The Association between Market-Determined and Accounting-Determined Measures of Systematic Risk: Some Further Evidence." *Journal of Finance and Quantitative Analysis,* June 1975, pp. 321–84.

Bildersee, John S. "The Association between a Market-Determined Measure of Risk and Alternative Measures of Risk." *Accounting Review,* January 1975, pp. 81–98.

Hamada, Robert S. "The Effect of the Firm's Capital Structure on the Systematic Risk of Common Stocks." *Journal of Finance,* 27, no. 2 (May 1972), pp. 425–52.

Economics of accounting information

May, Robert G., and Sundem, Gary L. "Cost of Information and Security Prices: Market Association Tests for Accounting Policy Decisions." *Accounting Review,* January 1973, pp. 80–94.

CHAPTER 5

USE OF ACCOUNTING BY INDIVIDUALS AND HUMAN INFORMATION PROCESSING

The semistrong form of the efficient markets hypothesis assumes that all publicly available information will be impounded immediately and in an unbiased manner in security prices. Individual preferences and decisions are reflected in the market through the prices of securities. It is not necessary that we know either how individuals make their investment decisions, nor how information is used in the decision processes of individual investors. In fact, we cannot know directly how decisions are made because individuals cannot generally describe how they go about making decisions. Furthermore, it is impossible to obtain generalized decision models from individual decision processes because of the problem of aggregating subjective utilities. Each person may place a different weight on each piece of information taken into consideration in the decision process.

In spite of the difficulties of studying individual decision processes that can guide accounting policy, there are several reasons for learning as much as possible about individual decision making in an accounting context. These include the possibility of improving the quality of individual decisions and decreasing the cost of processing information by both accountants and investors. It may also be possible to improve the set of information available to the individual and to the market, although the relationship to the market is unclear at this time. These objectives may improve the allocation of resources in the economy as well as improve the welfare of individuals. As a first approximation, improving the welfare of individuals is desirable if in so doing the welfare of no one else is decreased (*Pareto optimality*). Three methods of reaching these goals are discussed in the following paragraphs.

1. Research on individual decision processes may provide clues regarding what information should be included in financial reports. There may be no limit to the amount of information that can be utilized by the market as a whole, but individuals do have limitations; therefore, it may prove desirable to publish different statements for different groups of

investors. The capital asset pricing model can be used to test the effect on security prices of certain information, but there must be some means of determining which information to publish before the market test can be made. Making a random selection of potentially relevant information would be an expensive way to proceed. Therefore, a knowledge of individual decision processes would permit improvements in the set of information provided to decision makers. Although the market may be efficient with the existing set of information (or with any set), an alternative set may provide an improvement in the allocation of resources and minimize the possibility of monopoly returns through the use of insider information.

2.   The capital asset pricing model assumes a given state of technology in the use of information. That is, the ability of decision makers to use information is assumed to be constant. Research on the individual decision-making process might improve this ability. By improving the quality of investment decisions, resource allocation would also be improved, and investors would be better off because they would be holding portfolios closer to the optimum. The education of investors in the new technology would take time, but the market would react to the new methods quickly because some investors would attempt to exploit the new opportunities immediately. However, there is evidence that learning is not efficient, which raises a question regarding the ability of the market to utilize new technology.[1]

3.   A third method of improving the quality of investment decisions and reducing the cost of processing the information is the possibility of constructing investment decision models that would take the available information and process it as the investor would do. This could lead to lower processing costs for the investor and to greater consistency in the quality of the decisions. However, many problems now prevent these models from becoming reality. Much more research is needed before models can be constructed to fit different individuals and to account for changes over time in the variables and their weights that are taken into consideration by the individual investor.

NORMATIVE INVESTMENT
DECISION MODELS

Particularly during the decades of the 1950s and 1960s, normative investment decision models were developed and refined (based primarily on economic theories) in an attempt to learn more about the decision processes of individual investors and from these to derive inferences regarding what financial information might be relevant to include in financial reports. With this knowledge, it was hoped that accountants would be

---

[1] Einhorn, Hillel J., "A Synthesis: Accounting and Behavioral Science," *Journal of Accounting Research,* Supplement, 1976, p. 197.

able to determine the financial information needed by investors and creditors. Since that time, more emphasis has been placed on the concept of cost-benefits, instead of relevance, and on user preferences, rather than needs. More recently, research on individual decision making by users of accounting information has been based on previous studies in psychology, rather than on economics. However, it is important to review these decision models not only from a historical point of view, but also because most of the extant financial accounting standards are still based on the deductive logic from these decision models. For example, *FASB Statement of Financial Accounting Concept No. 1* stated that the objectives of financial reporting are based on "the informational needs of external users who lack the authority to prescribe the financial information they want from an enterprise."[2] In addition, it stated that

> Cost benefit considerations may indicate that information understood or used by only a few should not be provided. Conversely, financial reporting should not exclude relevant information merely because it is difficult for some to understand or because some investors or creditors choose not to use it.[3]

These quotations imply that it is the individual investor or creditor to whom published financial information should be directed, rather than the market or a broader group in society. As a result *FASB Statement of Financial Accounting Concepts No. 1* (p. 7822, par. 25) gives expected cash flows a major position in an implicit decision model of potential users of financial information.[4] The model is then modified to emphasize enterprise earnings and its components as a better indication of enterprise performance than the firm's cash flows as desired information for predicting the cash flows to investors and creditors. (p. 7828, par. 38, and *FASB/SAC No. 3,* par. 5).

In the professional literature of finance in the 1960s, valuation models using both dividends and earnings became popular.[5] Basically, the value of a security in these models was the discounted present value of the expected dividend or earnings adjusted for growth. Risk was taken into consideration by adjusting the interest rate to a required rate for a given level of risk or by adjusting the expected dividend stream and using instead a certainty equivalent (the amount the investor would be willing to take with certainty instead of the expected value).

---

[2] *FASB Statement of Financial Accounting Concepts No. 1,* "Objectives of Financial Reporting by Business Enterprises," *AICPA Professional Standards,* p. 7824, para. 28.

[3] Ibid., p. 7827, para. 36.

[4] See also *FASB Statement of Financial Accounting Concepts No. 3,* "Elements of Financial Statements of Business Enterprises," December 28, 1979, p. 2, para. 5.

[5] See, for example, Alexander A. Robichek and Stewart C. Myers, *Optimal Financing Decisions* (Prentice-Hall: Englewood Cliffs, N.J., 1965), chap. 6; and Eugene M. Lerner and William T. Carleton, *A Theory of Financial Analysis* (New York: Harcourt Brace Jovanovich, 1966), chap. 7.

Several normative investment decision models have also been proposed in the accounting literature.[6]

One of these models reduces available alternatives to a common denominator by computing the utility-adjusted present value of the expected gain or loss from acquiring and holding a security for a given period of time. This basic model states that the net subjective gain or loss to be obtained from a specific investment in stock or bonds is the sum of the present values of the expected cash distributions to the investor less the current price of the security. Since the cash distributions (particularly for dividends) in any one year can be represented by a probability distribution, an expected value for each year must be selected and adjusted by a certainty equivalent factor determined by the investor's personal utility preference for risk. Both the expected cash flow for each year and the expected opportunity discount factor should also be adjusted for marginal tax effect.[7]

UNCERTAINTY IN THE INVESTMENT DECISION PROCESS

Published financial accounting information has traditionally been reported in terms of single-valued measurements (point estimates). However, these measurements are surrogates for descriptions of events that occur with some degree of probability. For example, sales volume for a particular period depends upon the probability of certain events occurring and the method of revenue recognition selected for accounting purposes. To the extent that investors use this accounting information in their decision processes, they must explicitly or implicitly take into consideration the factor of uncertainty of the accounting measurement system.

Of additional importance is an understanding of the way individuals process information in arriving at predictions and decisions relating to

---

[6] See, for example, Lawrence Revsine, *Replacement Cost Accounting* (Englewood Cliffs, N.J.: Prentice-Hall, 1973), chap. 2, for the use of a normative model for the evaluation of replacement cost accounting.

[7] This basic investment valuation model as suggested by the American Accounting Association Committee on External Reporting can be expressed as follows:

$$P_{0k} = \sum_{i=1}^{n_k} \left(\frac{(\infty_{ik})(D_{ik})(1 - T_{ik})}{[1 + r(1 - T_{ik})]^i} \right) - I_o$$

P_{ok} = The subjective present value of the gain or loss to be obtained by an investor (k) for a specific investment at time period (0).
n_k = The time horizon used by the investor (k).
D_{ik} = The expected value of each cash distribution to the investor in year (i).
∞_{ik} = The adjustment for the investor's utility preference for risk.
T_{ik} = The expected marginal tax rate for each cash flow.
r = The before tax opportunity rate for a riskless investment.
I_o = The investment price at the time of decision.

From: Committee on External Reporting, "An Evaluation of External Reporting Practices," *Accounting Review*, supplement to vol. 44 (1969), pp. 80–83.

uncertain future events. Although research in the area of human information processing and the way individuals handle uncertainty in decision making has only recently been applied to the field of financial accounting, several conclusions have direct relevance for accounting theories and for the development of accounting policy.

The major difficulty with an attempt to understand the decision-making process is that it is impossible with current technology to study the operation of the mind directly. Indirect means must be found. However, if we study only the information inputs or availability and the decision outcomes, it is likely that false conclusions might be obtained. Indirect methods including the lens model approach, the Bayesian approach, and cognitive style are discussed in a later section.

Most of the studies relating to an understanding of the decision process are based on an assumption that individuals make decisions rationally within the limits of available information. A rational decision is defined as one that is optimal for the decision maker or the beneficiary of the decision (the investor if the decision is made by a fund manager or trustee) within the constraints of the available information and individual preferences, including preferences for risk or an attempt to minimize such investment costs as the time required to manage a portfolio. It is not uncommon for individuals to invest their entire savings in the stock of one company, either for family reasons or in order to hold a stock that pays a steady dividend and requires little or no attention on the part of the investor, such as AT&T. In this case, the investor is willing to forego a higher return by incurring the nonspecific risk arising from the failure to diversify because of a desire to minimize the time and costs of managing a portfolio.

Early studies in decision strategy were made by mathematicians in the form of game theory. The simplest form of game theory is in the two-party game wherein the optimum strategy is referred to as the maximin (the maximation of the minimum gain) or the minimax (the minimization of the maximum loss). Under conditions of free rational decisions, equilibrium occurs when the maximin of one party is the minimax (or maximin) of the other. Although it is possible to apply game theory to some investment decisions, it is difficult to apply to accounting situations.

Probability in decision making

Individuals are limited in their abilities to process information in a complex environment with uncertain probabilities regarding future events. Because of these limitations, it is natural that persons should wish to simplify the complexity of the situation as they perceive it and reduce the uncertainty. Some of the methods for achieving this are as follows:

1. An individual prefers a limited amount of information on which to make a decision. Thus, some information may be omitted as being insignificant or irrelevant, and other information may be used in an aggre-

gated form. This accounts, in part, for the popularity of indexes, such as stock price indexes and earnings and earnings per share figures.

2. If there is a choice, a person will normally prefer a situation in which the probabilities are well specified, rather than a situation in which they are ambiguous. For example, a person who is attempting to predict the color of a marble drawn from a bowl would usually prefer a bowl with a known number of red and blue marbles, rather than a bowl where the number of each color is unknown.

3. In earlier studies of decision making, it was thought that individuals used subjective probabilities and drew from these an Expected Value or Certainty Equivalent (the mean or mode of the distribution). The Expected Value was then used in the decision process or as the object to be maximized. However, subsequent studies have revealed that people who rely on subjective statistical procedures act in a biased manner. For example, studies have shown that individuals attribute greater certainty to unreliable information than is warranted.[8] Also, individuals tend to base estimates and predictions on recent or available observations, even though these may neither be representative of long-run conditions nor reflect objective probabilities.

4. Functional fixation is the process of focusing on numbers or indexes as though they have the same meaning regardless of how they are computed.

5. Anchoring is the process of using a known figure or amount as a starting point and then adjusting for available information.

Individual judgment

If we wish to know how individuals use accounting information, it is important to understand how they make judgments regarding future probable events. Two of the theories originating in the literature of psychology and applied to accounting are functional fixation and anchoring.

Functional Fixation. The functional fixation theory states that individuals use symbols, aggregations or surrogates in making judgments regarding the future in such a way that they are assumed to maintain the same meaning and relevance over time, regardless of changes in what they represent or in the way they are computed. In accounting, this implies that investors use accounting numbers (such as earnings per share) consistently over time without making full adjustments for changes in accounting techniques. For example, if the firm changes from capitalization of R&D expenses to current expensing, functional fixation on the reported earnings would result in an incorrect judgment, since the change

---

[8] Ian R. C. Eggleton, "Patterns, Prototypes, and Predictions: An Exploratory Study," Studies on Human Information Processing in Accounting, *Journal of Accounting Research,* Supplement, 1976.

in reported earnings resulting from the accounting change would not reflect fundamental economic changes (assuming no income tax effect).

In a carefully designed study of judgments of financial analysts with the presence of a change in inventory valuation method from FIFO to LIFO, Abdel-khalik and Keller concluded that functional fixation was present, even though the analysts understood the accounting change on reported income, cash flows, and taxes.[9] Although investors do adapt to the changes in accounting procedures over time, they do not readily change the way they interpret the meaning and importance of the earnings figure in making a judgment regarding the value of the firm.

These findings are significant for financial reporting because they imply that consistency in the use of accounting procedures is important and that when material changes in procedures are made, figures computed under both methods should probably be reported during the adaptation period. There is also an implication that accounting classifications and aggregations should permit as much semantic interpretation as possible. A third implication is that decomposition of financial data may be desirable in order to avoid functional fixation on aggregate figures, which may fail to disclose fundamental economic relationships.

A disturbing characteristic of functional fixation is that it is inconsistent with the efficient markets hypothesis. According to the EMH, the market does not react to accounting changes that have no substantive economic implications. If individuals do react to these accounting changes, we can assume that either the market is not efficient or that there are a sufficient number of investors who are not affected by functional fixation.

Anchoring. As discussed previously, when individuals are faced with the necessity to make predictions and decisions in complex settings, there is a desire to simplify the information to be used. One method of simplification is anchoring. The individual selects a particular piece of information as a starting point and using other available information makes an adjustment to form a prediction. For example, an investor might use the prior period's earnings or earnings per share for an anchor, add to it current information about specific economic conditions for the firm, and then make a prediction of the current year's earnings. As a second example, a couple attempting to place a value on their home might use the original cost as an anchor and then make adjustments for changes in building costs and selling prices of homes in the neighborhood.

The difficulty with the anchoring process is that individuals generally fail to fully adjust for the new information. If an upward adjustment is required in light of new information, the estimate or prediction is likely to be lower than is realistically warranted. On the other hand, if the new

---

[9] A. Rashad Abdel-khalik and Thomas F. Keller, *Studies in Accounting Research No. 16,* "Earnings or Cash Flows: An Experiment on Functional Fixation and the Valuation of the Firm," (AAA, 1979), p. 50.

information indicates a downward adjustment, the prediction is likely to be too high. This concept is important for accounting because, generally, individuals are not aware of this bias, and most persons do not know that they are using an anchoring process.

Findings regarding anchoring are not necessarily inconsistent with the Efficient Market Hypothesis. They are descriptions of biases in the individual investment decision process; however, the selection of an anchor and the adjustment process are unique to the individual. There is no current way to know how these biases work out in the aggregate to affect a market price. It is possible that the biases are offsetting in the aggregate so that the market does reflect fundamental economic relationships. This does not imply that the anchoring bias is unimportant for accounting. The biases do affect individual welfare and permit a less than optimum distribution of securities among investors.

What then can be done in publishing financial reports to reduce the anchoring bias? First, it is important that the accounting numbers available for anchoring have semantic interpretation. If the economic events measured by the accounting numbers are correctly understood by investors, there should be less opportunity for anchoring bias. Second, this appears to provide an argument for the use of current market prices as much as possible instead of historical costs. The older the information that may be used as an anchor, the greater the adjustment process and, therefore, the greater the likelihood of bias. These suggestions are made with considerable caution, however, since there has not been sufficient research on the anchoring bias in accounting to actually know how it can be eliminated or even reduced.

Information set characteristics

Many of the studies of human information processing in general and in accounting specifically focus on the information set or cue set and how the selection and presentation of the information affect the judgment, prediction, or decision of the investor. Characteristics of particular interest in accounting include the following:[10]

1. Scaling characteristics, such as ordinal, discrete, and probabilistic.
2. Statistical properties, such as number and interrelationship of informational cues.
3. Predictive significance of information, such as bias, reliability, and relationship to the criterion.
4. Method of presentation, such as the format and degree of aggregation.
5. The context in which the information is used.

---

[10] From Robert Libby and Barry L. Lewis, "Human Information Processing Research in Accounting: The State of the Art," *Accounting, Organizations and Society* 2, no. 3 (1977): 247.

Research on the affect of the information set on decision making has provided several findings important for accounting.[11]

1. If irrelevant information is added to an information set, such as financial accounting reports, the performance of the decision making tends to decrease.
2. There is a tendency for decision makers to overweight highly correlated information (for example, the number of automobiles sold by Ford Motor Company and the total dollar sales volume of the Company).
3. Increasing the amount of information tends to inhibit learning.
4. Decision makers generally overestimate the importance they place on minor cues. That is, they believe that they give greater weights to minor information than they actually do.
5. Decision makers rely more heavily on a few major variables than they believe that they do.

RESEARCH APPROACHES TO HUMAN INFORMATION PROCESSING

Three approaches to human information processing have received sufficient attention in the accounting literature to merit a brief discussion here. These are the lens model, the probabilistic judgment (Bayesian) approach and the cognitive complexity/cognitive style approach. Readers interested in a more precise understanding of these approaches are referred to the additional reading references at the end of this chapter.

The lens model

The lens model is used by researchers to study the relationship between the environmental criteria (states of the world) and the information set, between the information set and subject responses, and between subject responses and the environmental criteria. This model is of particular importance to accounting because of the emphasis on the information set. Of particular significance is the ability to study the impact of the information set on such variables as the predictability of the information, the accuracy of the subject response, and the effect of the information set on the decision process.

The basic framework of the lens model is demonstrated in Figure 1. Regression equations and correlation coefficients are used to describe the associations. *Predictive significance* of the information set is measured by the relationship between the environmental criteria and the information set. Standardized estimates of the environmental data are derived from

---

[11] See ibid., p. 246 and Paul Slovic, "Psychological Study of Human Judgment: Implications for Investment Decision Making," *The Journal of Finance,* September 1972, p. 787.

FIGURE 1

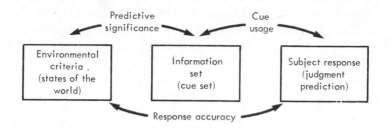

linear equations or equations obtained by multiple regression analysis. The estimated multiple correlation coefficient describes the relationship between the predictions of the environmental criteria and the actual criteria. The cue weights in the equations provide an indication of the relative importance of the information sets in predicting the environment.[12] The degree of relevance in the environment is measured by the correlation between the environmental model and the information set. The *response accuracy* of the subjects is measured by the relationship between the judgments or predictions and the environmental criterion (or the environmental model). The degree of relevance of the cue for the subject's response is measured by the correlation of the response and the information set (a measure of *cue usage*). A number of other relationships are obtained by using regression equations, correlation statistics, or analysis of variance.

Probabilistic Judgment (Bayesian)

In studies of probabilistic judgment, information is evaluated in a sequential process, whereas in the lens model the information set is available at one time. That is, each cue is evaluated in terms of how a subject revises the perceived probabilities of future events. The most common technique used in studies in the accounting literature is the Bayesian approach.

In the Bayesian approach, subjects are requested to generate a probability distribution for each of a given number of variables. This distribution is based on all of the information available to the subject at this time (including all previously known information). The subjects are then given new information and requested to provide revised subjective probability distributions. These revised (posterior) subjective probabilities are then compared with the optimum probability distributions generated with the normative model of Bayes' theorem.

The objective of the Bayesian approach is similar to that of the lens

---

[12] For a presentation of the statistical relationships and a more precise description of the process, see American Accounting Association, "Report of the 1976–77 Committee on Human Information Processing" (AAA, 1977) and other readings listed at the end of this chapter.

approach. It is used in research to study the actual judgments or predictions of decision makers with particular emphasis on the impact of the information set. In accounting research, characteristics of the information set, such as level of aggregation and the use of alternative procedures, have been studied along with characteristics of the decision maker and the decision rule. Like the lens model, the Bayesian model has been used to study cue usage and predictive significance.

Some of the significant studies in the accounting literature using the Bayesian approach include research on materiality, the effect of aggregation compared with disaggregated data, the effect of presenting alternative information systems compared with presenting both alternatives, and research on the consistency of subjective probability assessments.

Cognitive complexity/cognitive style

Both cognitive complexity and cognitive style approaches are used in studies of the relationships between the subject response or human information processing and the decision or action taken based upon a given information set. This relationship is shown in Figure 2.

FIGURE 2

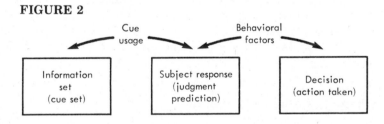

Cognitive complexity deals with the relationship of the decision process to differing levels of environmental complexity reflected in the information set. Research on cognitive complexity in accounting has primarily focused on information load—the quantity of information available in the information set and the amount of information used by the decision makers. Since some decision makers consistently use more information than others, an objective of cognitive complexity studies is to determine the format and amount of information to be presented in multipurpose financial statements and the degree to which different formats and amounts of information should be available to different groups of investors or other users of financial reports.

Cognitive style refers to the study of the decision rules and approaches or style in information processing preferred by different decision makers. For example, studies of cognitive style have divided decision approaches into two types of approach—heuristic and analytic. The heuristic approach refers to an intuitive manner of arriving at a decision and is characterized by a trial-and-error method and a satisficing goal, rather than an optimizing one. The analytic approach is a systematic approach to the problem and is characterized by the use of mathematical analysis and an optimizing goal. In one study of the difference in performance using each of these methods, the analytics significantly outperformed those using the heuristic approach (in terms of profit and cost, but with greater decision time). However, learning was affected neither by the decision approach nor by the information structure.[13] In other studies, it has been found that the quantity and type of information requested (or purchased) and used varied depending on the cognitive style of the decision maker.[14]

One of the objectives of cognitive style research is to help design information systems and financial reporting formats that are most useful for the different styles of decision making. One of the problems of relating this to external financial reporting, however, is that not much is known at this time regarding the decision styles of investors and creditors as classes and that the cost of presenting information for several decision styles may be greater than the benefits.

SUMMARY

Some of the objectives of studying individual decision making in an accounting context include: (1) a possible improvement in the ability of financial information to portray accurately the real events or objects (the predictive significance of the information set); (2) an understanding of how the amount, type, and format of financial accounting information affect the judgments or predictions of the investor or analyst (cue usage); (3) an understanding of the ability of the decision maker to respond accurately to a perception of the environment (response accuracy); and (4) an understanding of how individuals deal with complexity in decision making and an understanding of the effect of the different styles of decision making on how information is used (the behavioral factors).

A number of studies on how individuals handle uncertainty have concluded that individuals are poor intuitive statisticians. That is, when faced with a complex environment with uncertain probabilities, individuals tend to be biased in their estimates and judgments and use simplifying rules (heuristics) that make the task less difficult, but the results less accurate. Examples include the concepts of anchoring and functional fixation.

Research approaches to human information processing that have re-

---

[13] Theodore J. Mock, Teviah L. Estrin, and Miklos A. Vasarhelyi, "Learning Patterns, Decision Approach, and Value of Information, *Journal of Accounting Research,* Spring 1972, pp. 129–53.

[14] See, for example, Michael J. Driver and Theodore J. Mock, "Human Information Processing, Decisions Style Theory and Accounting Information Systems," *Accounting Review,* July 1975, pp. 490–508.

ceived attention in accounting literature include the lens model, the probabilistic judgment (Bayesian) approach and the cognitive complexity /cognitive style approach. These research methods have their origin in the literature of psychology and related fields, and the capital market theories have been based upon studies in economics and finance. Both directions of research have proven to be significant for an understanding of financial accounting, including its production and final use and for aiding in the development of accounting policy and the establishment of standards. However, research in the area of human information processing is still in its infancy, and much has to be done before definitive conclusions can be reached.

One of the basic problems yet to be solved is what is the direct relationship between capital market theories and individual decision making. The former suggests that the market is efficient and that in equilibrium securities prices are in an optimum relationship to each other within the limits of available public information. Research on individual behavior suggest that all individual decisions are suboptimal. How can aggregate decisions be optimal if all of the individual decisions are suboptimal? The answer to this question lies in future research. We can only speculate that either the market is not as efficient as it has been thought to be, or a sufficient number of individual decisions are optimal or have been made optimal with the aid of sophisticated models or unbiased heuristics.

SELECTED ADDITIONAL READING

Human information processing

American Accounting Association. "Report of the 1976–77 Committee on Human Information Processing," *Committee Reports,* Volume 1978–2. AAA, August 1977.

Libby, Robert, and **Barry L. Lewis.** "Human Information Processing Research in Accounting: The State of the Art," *Accounting, Organizations, and Society* 2, no. 3 (1977): 245–68.

Slovic, Paul. "Psychological Study of Human Judgment: Implications for Investment Decision Making." *The Journal of Finance,* September 1977, pp. 779–97.

Uncertainty in decision making

Eggleton, Ian R. "Patterns, Prototypes, and Predictions: An Exploratory Study," *Journal of Accounting Research: Studies on Human Information Processing in Accounting,* Supplement 1976, pp. 68–131.

Swieringa, Robert; Michael Gibbins; Lars Larson; and **Janet Lawson Sweeney.** "Experiments in the Heuristics of Human Information Processing," *Journal of Accounting Research: Studies on Human Information Processing in Accounting,* Supplement 1976, pp. 68–131.

Functional fixation

Ashton, Robert H. "Cognitive Changes Induced by Accounting Changes: Experimental Evidence on the Functional Fixation Hypothesis." *Journal of Accounting Research: Studies on Human Information Processing in Accounting,* Supplement 1976, pp. 1–24.

Abdel-khalik, A. Rashad, and **Thomas F. Keller.** "Earnings or Cash Flows: An Experiment on Functional Fixation and the Valuation of the Firm." *American Accounting Association Studies in Accounting Research No. 16* (AAA, 1979).

Lens and Bayesian approaches

Ashton, Robert H. "The Predictive-Ability Criterion and User Prediction Models," *Accounting Review,* October 1974, pp. 719–32.

Libby, Robert. "The Use of Simulated Decision Makers in Information Evaluation," *Accounting Review,* July 1975, pp. 475–89.

Wright, William F. "Analysis and Comparison of the Lens and Bayesian Information Processing Paradigms," *Stanford Research Paper No. 407,* November 1977.

Cognitive complexity/cognitive style

Driver, Michael J., and **Theodore J. Mock.** "Human Information Processing, Decision Style Theory and Accounting Information Systems," *Accounting Review,* July 1975, pp. 490–508.

CHAPTER 6
ACCOUNTING POLICY

Accounting policy is the process of selection of specific alternative reporting methods, measurement systems, and disclosure techniques from among all that might be available for financial reporting by business enterprises. Some choices are made by specific firms within the alternatives available to them, and descriptions of these are required to be included in the financial statements if they are significant.[1] However, in a broader sense, accounting policy refers to the accounting standards, opinions, interpretations, rules and regulations established by government or private bodies with the authority to establish policies that are enforceable by several means. The most relevant bodies in the United States are the Financial Accounting Standards Board (FASB) and the Securities and Exchange Commission (SEC), although such other bodies as the former Cost Accounting Standards Board (CASB) and Congress (e.g., through the Internal Revenue Code and other acts) have determined policies affecting accounting and financial reporting.

The accounting policies in other countries, such as Great Britain and The Netherlands, are neither as highly structured nor as detailed as in the United States, and the process of developing accounting policy in these countries is less formal. On the other hand, accounting policies are being established on an international level through the International Accounting Standards Committee (IASC), although compliance with its standards is limited to the acceptance of the standards by the representing professional accounting societies and by other organizations and governmental agencies within represented countries.

The purpose of national accounting policies is to narrow the areas of differences among firms in the disclosure, measurements, and method of presentation of financial information in financial statements and financial reports and to change the quantity and quality of information in published financial reports. The effect of accounting policies established by the FASB, SEC, or other bodies is, therefore, to limit the number of choices and the amount of discretion available to individual firms in their financial statements and reports.

The process of establishing accounting policy is difficult because of the

---

[1] APB Opinion No. 22, "Disclosure of Accounting Policies," AICPA Professional Standards—Accounting, vol. 3, Section 2045.08.

complexities in the economic and social environment in which it must operate. Accounting theories and their verification through research do provide some guidelines. However, no accounting theories or research methods have been able to provide conclusive evidence that a single alternative is socially superior to all others. In addition to accounting theories, policy makers must take into consideration the social, economic, and political consequences of their decisions. Accounting theories and accounting research, therefore, can contribute to policy making, but only as one of many economic and social considerations.

WHY REGULATE ACCOUNTING POLICY?

It is possible that the establishment of accounting policies could be left entirely to the decisions of individual firms. In fact, freedom of choice in the United States was complete before 1918[2] and almost complete before the 1930s.[3] Since 1938 pronouncements on accounting policy have become increasingly more specific and written in greater detail. The more important pronouncements include the *Accounting Research Bulletins* of the Committee on Accounting Procedure of the AICPA from 1938 to 1959, the *Opinions* of the Accounting Principles Board, and the *Statements* and *Interpretations* of the Financial Accounting Standards Board since 1973, as well as *Accounting Series Releases* and other pronouncements of the Securities and Exchange Commission since 1934.

The nature of accounting information

A basic characteristic of accounting information is that it is publicly available at little or no cost to those who wish to obtain and use the information. The costs of production and publication are borne by the firms. The publication of financial information, however, is not without benefit to the firms, since it is to their advantage to have an orderly capital market in which to obtain capital funds, and it is to the advantage of the stockholders to see that there is a market for their shares. Therefore, even without regulation, the firms would be willing to incur costs in order to publish financial information as they did before the 1930s. The difficulty was that the financial reports were in many cases very brief and infrequent. As a result, the speculative boom in the stock market during 1928 and 1929 was based on inadequate information, and many share prices rose to many times any realistic expectation of return. The stock

---

[2] The primary exception was in the regulation of public service companies. Government regulation of the railroads began in the 19th century, and regulation of public utilities by state commissions began about 1907.

[3] In 1917, under the request of the Federal Trade Commission, the American Institute of Accountants (AICPA) prepared a memorandum on standardized procedures (*Uniform Accounting*) setting forth suggestions for the verification and preparation of financial statements.

market bust of October 1929 created additional pressure for regulation to assure a more orderly market for capital.

As indicated in previous chapters, the amount and quality of publicly available information affects both the allocation of resources in the economy and the selection of a portfolio by individual investors. Accounting information, therefore, has significant social and economic consequences. Regulation of accounting policy cannot be adequately considered without a discussion of these consequences.

The objectives of accounting policy

The establishment of accounting policy requires the setting of goals. The prescribing of measurement methods, disclosure rules, and forms of presentation is not sufficient in itself as a goal, since there are economic and social consequences relating to alternative decisions. The several theories of accounting can focus on specific objectives, such as the preferences of management, accountants, individuals, or the market or the interests of other groups in society. However, a national accounting policy should take into consideration the broader social welfare, as well as the preferences of specific groups in society.

The inductive-deductive approach to accounting focuses primarily on the preferences of the users of accounting information, particularly investors and creditors. However, focus can also be placed on the consistency in the application of accounting rules (the syntactical level) or on the measurement of resources and resource claims (the semantical level). These are basic objectives of the FASB as stated in *FASB Statement of Financial Accounting Concepts, No. 1*.[4] For example, "the objectives begin with a broad focus on information that is useful in investment and credit decisions. . . .[5] The focus is then narrowed to the assumed interest of investors and creditors in the prospective cash flows from the firm and finally to the measurement of resources, resource claims, and enterprise performance.

The market theories focus on a descriptive process of the impact of accounting information on the price and sales volume of securities in organized markets and the role of the markets in resource allocation and portfolio selection. The FASB does not specifically state how the market theories should affect accounting policy, but it does recognize the importance of securities markets and the place of accounting information in the operation of those markets. For example, *FASB Statement of Financial Accounting Concepts No. 1* states that "well-developed securities markets tend to allocate scarce resources to enterprises that use them efficiently and away from inefficient enterprises."[6] And further: "The effectiveness of

---

[4] Also the basic objectives of *APB Statement, No. 4,* "Fundamentals of Financial Accounting."

[5] *AICPA Professional Standards,* vol. 3, par. 1210.32.

[6] *AICPA Professional Standards—Accounting,* vol. 3, para. 1210.13.

individuals, enterprises, markets, and government in allocating scarce resources among competing uses is enhanced if those who make economic decisions have information that reflects the relative standing and performance of business enterprises to assist them in evaluating alternative courses of action and the expected returns, costs, and risks of each."[7]

Additional factors that should be considred in the framing of accounting policy include the recognition that accounting information is only one source of financial information for individuals and markets. Decisions regarding accounting policy should take these alternative sources into account and permit nonaccounting sources to provide the information where it can be made available more efficiently and at a lower cost to the firm and the investors combined.

In addition, a policy-making body should also take into consideration the costs and benefits of the information. The costs include the direct costs of production and publication of the information by the firm and also the costs associated with adverse consequences of accounting policy to the enterprises or other individuals or groups. The benefits include not only the relevance of the information to decision making, but also the potential positive consequences resulting from reactions of the firm or others because of the publication of the information.

In summary, the objectives of accounting policy could focus on the preferences of both the producers and the users of financial information. However, this is possible in only a general manner by using partial solutions from inductive deductive theories or from research studies in the area of information processing of individuals. A major difficulty is that individual, firm, and group preferences cannot be combined to form unique total preferences. An alternative is to focus the objective of accounting policy on the economic and social consequences. This includes the possible improvement in resource allocation and portfolio selection. But it should also take into consideration the favorable and unfavorable consequences to the firm and specific individuals and groups. The appropriate balancing of these favorable and unfavorable consequences is not an easy matter, but at least it establishes an appropriate objective for the establishment of accounting policy.

The main difficulty with the setting of broad goals for the establishment of accounting policy is that they are difficult to implement on the basis of sound research or positive evidence. The result is that the process of setting accounting policy tends to be simplified by falling back on procedural goals, such as being consistent with traditional accounting procedures or with narrowly defined objectives. One of the frequently stated goals has been the narrowing of available alternatives. This has been supported by the many criticisms of accounting that the availability of many alternatives permits firms to report their financial performance in the best light by using what is referred to as creative accounting, or

---

[7] Ibid., para. 1210.16.

frequently creative bookkeeping.[8] A general consensus has been that unless the policy-making bodies meet these criticisms by establishing greater uniformity, there will be a loss of credibility of accounting information in the eyes of the investors and general public and that the policy-making process will be moved entirely into the government sector.

Uniformity and comparability

Uniformity among firms in their financial reporting is frequently thought to represent a desirable goal for its own sake. That is, the goal of uniformity frequently implies the presentation of financial statements by different firms using the same accounting procedures, measurement concepts, classifications, and methods of disclosure, as well as a similar basic format in the statements. As used in this context, the concept is rightfully criticized. The objective should be comparability, not strict uniformity. The primary objective of comparability should be to facilitate the making of predictions and financial decisions by creditors, investors, and others. It may be defined as the quality or state of having enough like characteristics to make comparison appropriate.

The main opposition to uniformity is based on the claims that (1) it would infringe on the basic rights and freedoms of management; (2) it would place accounting in a straitjacket of rules and procedures that would make financial statements less comparable; and (3) it would stifle progress and prevent desirable changes. On the other hand, the arguments for some degree of uniformity are that (1) the wide variety of acceptable practices makes comparability among different firms impossible or at least difficult; (2) the freedom of management to choose their own methods may introduce the possibility of bias, through manipulation of reported information to suit the purposes of those who control the reports; and (3) if the private sector does not take steps to achieve greater uniformity, it may be imposed by the Securities and Exchange Commission or some other governmental agency.

In determining how much uniformity is desirable, the basic preferences of the users of financial reports should be considered. Comparability may be an important concept if it is assumed that users rely upon comparisons of detailed aspects of the firms, rather than evaluating the firms as a whole. For example, such specific ratios as the current ratio or the debt-equity ratio may be used as surrogates for an evaluation of the risk inherent in being a creditor of each of several firms; or the rate of return on stockholders' investment may be used as a substitute for present values of the expected dividends of several firms. In these cases, it is desirable that these ratios be as comparable as possible and that they be based upon information computed by uniform procedures in those cases in which

---

[8] See, for example, "Paper Profits: Slick Accounting Ploys Help Many Companies Improve Their Income—By Proper or Improper Means They 'Manage' Earnings for the Desired Effect," *The Wall Street Journal,* June 20, 1980, p. 1.

there is no evidence that one procedure is better than another. Differences in procedures used by the various firms within an industry would be permissible only if conditions in the several firms were not alike. Therefore, in each case, the procedure providing the most accurate or most reliable data would be in use, and where there is little differences in the various procedures, a uniform procedure would be adopted.

On the other hand, it may be argued that all relevant information for each firm should be presented to permit the investors and creditors to make predictions regarding each specific firm. The investors and creditors should then use these predictions to make subjective estimates of the present value of the firm and to evaluate the risk inherent in each firm. Comparisons should then be made for decision making only at the aggregated level. That is, the estimated subjective present values and subjective evaluations of risk should be used in making the final comparisons, rather than relying on comparisons of detailed information regarding the firms. Therefore, accountants should be concerned with presenting relevant information for each firm, rather than being concerned with presenting comparable detailed data. However, it is still important that predictions regarding several firms be made based on equally reliable data. In the absence of specific guidelines for determining what information is relevant for specific firms, some general standards are necessary regarding the choice of information to be presented, the degree of detail to be presented, and the selection of measurement concepts and procedures relevant for specific users in their making of predictions and decisions. However, uniformity of disclosure is more important than uniformity of procedures if the goal is to improve the information available to efficient capital markets.

Narrowing the areas of difference in financial reporting among firms may be desirable as an objective of accounting policy; however, it can only be one of the means of achieving the basic goals of moving toward an optimum level of social and economic welfare. If diverse procedures or methods of disclosure are found to provide greater benefits or even equal benefits, the firms are likely to choose the methods that are least costly or that have the more favorable economic consequences for themselves. Since it is impossible to anticipate all of the possible economic consequences, there is some merit in permitting each firm to make some choices so long as investors and creditors are not harmed by so doing.

SOCIAL AND ECONOMIC CONSEQUENCES

All decisions regarding accounting policy should have economic consequences. If there were no economic consequences, there would be no reason for the policy decision. The desired consequences include an improvement in the information available to investors and other users with the result of permitting sounder economic decisions or a reduction in the information-gathering costs for users. Through the securities markets, better decisions should result in an allocation of resources closer to the optimum and an opportunity for an improvement in portfolio selections. If decisions are not altered and if information costs to users are not reduced, this is evidence that the policy decision was not desirable.

Not all consequences, however, can be anticipated, and not all are necessarily desirable. To the extent that undesirable consequences can be anticipated or demonstrated to exist because of existing policies, they should be taken into consideration in policy decisions. But it is difficult to prove that undesirable consequences do exist or may exist, and even if they are known to exist, it is difficult to know what weight to give them in policy decisions. As a result, it has been suggested that accounting policy should be based primarily on technical considerations. By so doing, accounting is said to be evenhanded with respect to interested parties. That is, if information regarding risk and return are present in an unbiased manner, all parties affected would be treated fairly.[9] For example, the decision to prohibit so-called self-insurance reserves (*FASB Statement No. 5*) is consistent with accounting concepts, even though it is claimed that some firms would be forced to purchase insurance that would not have been obtained otherwise, thus incurring uneconomical costs. The argument for the current policy either denies that adverse consequences exist or that the smoothing of income as an objective is not consistent with presenting information regarding the risks and returns of the enterprise.

In addition to the decisions of investors and creditors, many other types of decisions are affected by accounting policies. Some of these decisions may alter the economic wealth or cash flows of the firms directly, for example, the decisions of corporate management or governmental regulatory bodies. Other more subtle and less direct consequences affect the behavior toward the enterprise of individuals, including customers, employees, and the general public. Policies that are perceived to affect national goals may come under direct attack by Congress or administrative agencies. Only some of the possible consequences can be considered here because there is inadequate evidence regarding the validity of many of the claims regarding economic consequences.

Investors and creditors

As discussed in previous chapters, investors and creditors are considered by the FASB to be the most important users of external financial information. Therefore, an intended economic impact of accounting policy is to assist them in their financial decisions, which in turn should help them achieve more efficient portfolios and through the market mechanism af-

---

[9] See, for example, Oscar S. Gellein, "The Task of the Standard Setter," *Journal of Accountancy,* December 1978, pp. 75–79.

fect the allocation of resources in the economy. However, there are some less obvious consequences affecting investors and creditors.

One effect is the cost of gathering and analyzing financial information. How much of the burden should be placed on the enterprise and how much on investors and creditors? Regarding financial information of the firm itself, the firm has a comparative advantage in information production. Therefore, total welfare is increased if accounting policy requires the disclosure of a certain amount of information that will be used in investment and credit decisions.

A less obvious effect results from the fact that many contracts, equity relationships, and legal covenants of credit arrangements are frequently expressed in terms of accounting numbers or financial statement ratios. If accounting policy changes affect the meaning of these numbers and ratios, the economic relationships are changed from what was originally intended. For example, the capitalization of long-term leases may affect the debt-equity ratio and thus affect relationships that are tied to this ratio. It can be argued that the contracts and financial arrangements can be adjusted to take into consideration the new meanings of the accounting numbers and ratios. However, this cannot be accomplished quickly, so the effect may be significant for a long time.

The corporation

It is generally accepted in most western countries that corporations should incur the costs of producing and publishing information considered to be in the public interest. But the question is how much information should be required and are the costs less than the benefits of making additional information publicly available? In some cases, the costs may be minimal if the firm produces the information for internal use in the absence of regulation. However, many changes in accounting policy require significant sums for both start-up costs and for annual maintenance costs. For example, the initiation of both line-of-business reporting and accounting for the effects of inflation required significant costs to generate information that was not available previously even within the firm.

Capital costs. One of the common arguments against new accounting policies or the elimination of current practices is that the change would lower the market price of corporate stocks or bonds. Generally, corporate executives prefer procedures that tend to smooth reported income because, they assert, the more volatile the reported income, the greater will be the investors' perception of risk and the lower the price of the securities. For example, some financial executives opposed the required expensing of research and development costs because of the effect on reported income and the potential effect on security prices. However, a number of research studies have concluded that the securities markets are efficient and that they cannot be fooled by changing accounting procedures. But some studies have provided evidence that some accounting policies have had a negative effect on security prices. For example, Lev concluded that the *FASB Exposure Draft* eliminating the full costing method for oil and gas companies did result in lower security prices, particularly for those firms using full costing.[10] According to capital market theories, there should have been no effect on security prices. These unexpected conclusions can possibly be explained by the fact that there may have been a real effect on the firms' financial operations. For example, outstanding contracts and debt covenants may have been adversely affected, or it may have been expected that the reduced reported earnings would result in lower dividends. But it is also possible that investors did react to the change even though there was no economic effect on the firms.

Management. Managers' preferences for specific accounting policies may result from the way they perceive the effect of the policies on their own interests. Management compensation and bonuses are frequently based on reported accounting numbers, such as corporate net income before extraordinary gains and losses. If a new policy is likely to reduce their own compensation, they are likely to oppose the change. The otherwise desirable policy change may have the side effect of causing an unanticipated change in compensation and thus an unanticipated transfer of wealth. But even if compensation is not affected, managers may oppose a policy that reduces reported earnings because such a decrease might reflect on their abilities and threaten their security.

Information inductance. Information that is published has an intended effect on the behavior of the receiver, but it may also have an effect on the decisions and actions of the sender. This feedback effect is known as information inductance.[11] Measurement and disclosure requirements may cause management to take certain actions to offset the perceived or anticipated effect of the information requirement, even though the actions may not be in the interests of either management or the firm. For example, it was claimed that the required reporting of foreign currency gains and losses would cause multinational firms to engage in uneconomical hedging transactions. It was also claimed that the required elimination of self-insurance reserves would result in the purchase of insurance that was not in the best interests of the firm.

In most of these cases, it can be argued that the managements should not change their methods because of an accounting policy. However, if the firms do, in fact, react to the information requirements, there is a question regarding whether or not this should enter into the accounting policy-making decision. There is insufficient evidence at this time to suggest that information inductance should enter into the policy-making decision.

---

[10] Baruch Lev, "The Impact of Accounting Regulation on the Stock Market: The Case of Oil and Gas Companies," *Accounting Review,* July 1979, pp. 485–503.

[11] See Prem Prakash and Alfred R. Rappaport, "Information Inductance and Its Significance for Accounting," *Accounting, Organizations and Society* 2, no. 1 (1977): 29–38.

National goals

Accounting policy has its greatest influence in achieving national goals by providing information for securities markets and for other governmental and private uses. Traditionally, the market system is expected to permit an efficient allocation of resources in the nation with only a minimum amount of governmental regulation. However, political and social interests are increasingly brought into governmental processes in order to assist the market system meet specific economic goals or achieve noneconomic social goals.

If it is true that accounting policy has unexpected economic consequences, particularly with respect to the actions of business enterprises, the achievement of national goals may be affected. One of the early accounting controversies that was influenced by public policy concerns was the investment tax credit. When the investment tax credit was first established in the United States, the Accounting Principles Board agreed on an *Opinion (APB Opinion No. 2, 1961)* requiring the investment credit to be deferred and allocated over the useful life of the depreciable asset. Opposition from both the commerce and treasury departments and corporate officials was sufficient to convince the SEC to overrule the APB and permit both of the two methods (deferral and flow-through). As a result, the APB was forced to reverse its opinion and permit both procedures (*APB Opinion No. 4*). When the investment tax credit was revived in 1971 after a lapse of two years, the APB again attempted to restrict the reporting of the credit to the deferral method. However, opposition from the Treasury Department and from industry was strong enough to convince Congress to pass a bill permitting taxpayers to use whichever method they wished in accounting for the tax credit.[12]

The basic national policy question was regarding the effect of the choice of accounting procedure on the amount of investment by corporations. The argument for permitting the flow-through method (the immediate offset of the tax credit against tax expense) was that the purpose of the tax credit was to encourage investment in order to aid economic recovery. Because of the immediate impact of the flow-through method on reported earnings, it was thought to have the greatest effect as an investment incentive.

Another accounting policy that was thought to have national policy implications was the requirement that the successful-efforts method, rather than the full-costing method be used for oil and gas exploration costs. (*FASB Statement No. 19*, December 1977). Opposition from an important segment of industry, the Justice Department and the Federal Trade Commission and the SEC required a reversal by the FASB in 1979, permitting both methods (*FASB Statement No. 25*).[13]

The claims of economic consequences from requiring the successful

---

[12] Stephen A. Zeff, *Forging Accounting Principles in Five Countries: A History and an Analysis of Trends* (Champaign, Ill.: Stipes Publishing, 1972), p. 221.

[13] Lev, "Impact on the Stock Market," p. 487.

efforts method were many. From a national policy point of view, they centered on the possible effects on competition, since it was mostly the smaller oil and gas producers that were using the full-costing method. It was claimed that the restriction on using the full-costing method would have an adverse effect on the ability of these firms to raise capital and compete with the larger firms. Another argument was that it was a disincentive in risk-taking in the exploration for oil and gas.

Whether or not accounting policies have economic and social consequences affecting national goals is difficult to prove in most cases. But the strength of the lobbies and the force of governmental action are sufficient to have an impact on the establishment of accounting policies. However, this does not mean that the FASB or other policy making body should consider the national goals in each decision. The problem is usually too complex and the results not conclusive enough to require a consideration of national goals in most cases.

Other economic consequences

The number of possible economic consequences of accounting policies are too many and varied to discuss fully here. They include the possible effects on the policies of regulatory commissions for, through the regulation of prices, product quality, and production processes, the revenues and expenses of the firms may be directly affected.

Profits and other financial information published in newspapers or reported by radio or television frequently create a public reaction against specific corporations or industries. Customers may refuse to purchase the products of companies reported to be in financial difficulty. Special taxes (such as the excess profits tax and state surtaxes on oil companies) have been imposed or proposed as a result of news coverage given to the reported profits of specific firms or in certain industries.

One of the more important consequences of accounting policy is credibility. If investors and the general public believe that published financial reports lack credibility, they lose confidence in the corporations, and possibly in the capitalistic system itself. A complete freedom in the choice of accounting methods with only disclosure rules might provide all of the information desired by investors in an efficient market. But such freedom gives some investors and the general public the impression that firms use this choice only to present the enterprise in the best light or to conceal high profits or whatever they do not want to be known. Therefore, some degree of uniformity may be necessary in order to give credibility to accounting reports and to the private enterprise system.

The impact of politics on accounting policy

Should the establishment of accounting policy be influenced by a political process? The answer to this is not clear cut. The selection of accounting policies does have economic and social consequences, some of which are real and some of which are only perceived to be real. In either case, some individuals believe themselves to be better off and others believe themselves to be worse off because of accounting policy. As a result, some individuals will attempt to achieve or maintain favorable policies, and others will oppose those policies that seem unfavorable to them or with which they feel threatened. Governmental agencies or Congress may also consider accounting policies to be consistent or inconsistent with national goals or with the specific goals of the agencies. These many forces are the causes of political intervention into the establishment of accounting policy.

When Congress takes action through the legal process, the political impact cannot, of course, be ignored. In other cases, the FASB has attempted to use persuasion or mediation with governmental agencies. The interests of investors and corporations are taken into consideration through the members of the FASB who are also members of the Financial Analysts Association or the Financial Executives Institute and through the oral and written comments received by the Board before issuance of statements.

The setting of accounting policies, however, is primarily a technical matter. The primary focus should be on obtaining representational accuracy and the dislosure of relevant information. An attempt should be made to be neutral with respect to the economic consequences, unless it can be shown that certain policies cause adverse consequences including economic costs without sufficient offsetting benefits.

Establishing accounting policy is not significantly different from the policies regarding the computation of some economic statistics, such as the consumer price index and the rate of unemployment. The methods of computing these indexes are subject to controversy because they have considerable economic and social consequences with respect to many contracts, laws, and national policies. But this does not mean that the methods of constructing the indexes should be continually changed for political reasons, although this has been suggested from time to time.

Lobbying by corporations and other interested groups or individuals is evidence of attempts to make accounting policymaking a political process. Whenever the economic consequences to a corporation (including the effect on regulation of revenues and the costs of compliance) exceed the costs of lobbying, corporations may be expected to carry out lobbying activities with the FASB, the SEC, or Congress. Large firms that come under governmental or public attack because of high reported profits are likely to be in favor of an accounting policy that would reduce reported earnings. In spite of increased costs of compliance, most very large firms favored general price level accounting because of the potential decrease in reported earnings (decrease in operating earnings for regulated firms).[14]

---

[14] Ross L. Watts and Jerold L. Zimmerman, "Towards a Positive Theory of the Determination of Accounting Standards," *Accounting Review,* January 1978, pp. 112–34.

The existence of lobbying activities or occasional interference by government, however, does not make the selection of accounting policies a political process. Technical considerations at the three levels (syntactical, semantical, and behavioral) are still of greatest importance in each of theory, research, and practical applications. This does not mean that social and economic consequences should not be considered, only that they should not be the most important consideration.

THE FINANCIAL ACCOUNTING STANDARDS BOARD

In 1973 the Financial Accounting Standards Board (FASB) was organized as the successor to the Accounting Principles Board (APB) as the organization in the private sector for establishing accounting policy. FASB pronouncements are officially recognized as authoritative by the Securities and Exchange Commission[15] and by the American Institute of Certified Public Accountants (AICPA).[16]

The seven members of the FASB have diverse backgrounds, including professional accounting, industry, finance, law, government, and academia. The Board members are appointed by the Financial Accounting Foundation, an independent organization that also finances the activities of the FASB through contributions from industry, the financial community, and the public accounting profession. The work of the Board is aided by the Financial Accounting Standards Advisory Council primarily through consultation.

The FASB was formed as a result of the basic criticisms of the APB, the rapid change in financial institutions, and the many abuses of financial accounting reporting during the 1960s. One of the difficulties with the APB was that it was composed only of members of the AICPA (including industry and academic members) and was appointed and financed by the institute. The change to a semi-independent organization with a broader base of support and full-time members has overcome some of these difficulties, but many problems persist. If the FASB is to succeed, it must maintain the support of many groups, including the accounting profession, industry, financial analysts, and government.

Many of the controversies regarding accounting policy relate to a basic philosophy of the Board that reported earnings should highlight differences in risk, rather than obscure them through allocations or averaging, and that similar situations should be reported in similar ways. Industry has frequently opposed this policy and lobbied against exposure drafts and statements in oral and written presentations to the Board and to Congress and federal agencies in a number of cases. The adverse conse-

---

[15] By *SEC Accounting Series Release No. 150,* December 1973.
[16] Under AICPA Rules of Conduct, Rule 203 as amended, May 1973 and May 1979).

quences perceived by corporate executives include perceived increases in the cost of capital resulting from a greater fluctuation in reported earnings. As a result of this opposition, the FASB has changed its position on several exposure drafts and reversed itself on a few *Statements.*[17]

One of the early and continuing projects of the FASB is the development of a series of Statements of Financial Accounting Concepts known as the conceptual framework project. The first *Statement,* "Objectives of Financial Reporting by Business Enterprises," was based on the report of the Trueblood Committee of the AICPA.[18]

Other *Statements* include "Qualitative Characteristics," "Elements of Financial Statements and Their Measurement," "Objectives of Financial Reporting by Nonbusiness Organizations," "Reported Earnings." Projects in process include "Accounting Recognition Criteria," "Funds Flows and Liquidity," and "Financial Statements and Financial Reporting." Many of the topics discussed in the published material relating to this project were also discussed in *APB Statement No. 4.*[19]

The technical aspects of this project are discussed in the relevant sections elsewhere in this book. The main questions of concern here are why the conceptual framework statements are necessary or desirable and whether or not they will be able to assist in the development of accounting policy.

The purpose of the conceptual framework project as stated by the FASB is to establish objectives and concepts to be used in the development of accounting standards, aid in the preparation of financial statements (particularly in cases for which there are no specific published standards), and increase the user's understanding and confidence in financial statements. The objective of establishing a conceptual foundation framework is a noble one. It could operate as a constitution setting forth broad goals and policies that would find general agreement among almost all interested parties. These broad goals and policies would then serve as a foundation for the establishment of a cohesive set of accounting standards. However, the establishment of a conceptual framework has not proven to be an easy task. Previous attempts have been either rejected or ignored in the setting of standards (e.g., *AICPA Accounting Research Studies No. 1* and *3* and *APB Statement No. 4*). With respect to the current project, there is no evidence that it can serve directly as a guide to provide solutions to difficult problems where there are differences of opinion.[20]

---

[17] For example, see FASB Exposure Draft, "Financial Reporting in Units of General Purchasing Power" of December 31, 1974; Exposure Draft "Constant Dollar Accounting" of March 2, 1979; and *FASB Statement No. 33,* "Financial Reporting and Changing Prices" of September 1979.

[18] Report of the Study Group on the Objectives of Financial Statements, "Objectives of Financial Statements" (AICPA, October 1973).

[19] *Accounting Principles Board Statement No. 4,* "Basic Concepts and Accounting Principles Underlying Financial Statements of Business Enterprises" (AICPA, 1970).

[20] See Nicholas Dopuch and Shyam Sunder, "FASB's Statement on Objectives and Elements of Financial Accounting: A Review," *Accounting Review,* January 1980, pp. 1–21.

One of the major difficulties with the conceptual framework project is that it is based on the immediate objective of providing information, and not on the more basic objective of social and economic consequences. A second difficulty is that it is discussed in terms of the traditional accounting concepts, many of which do not have clear semantic interpretation. But these difficulties are to be expected if there is to be any general acceptance. Tradition in an established profession cannot be overthrown easily. Only gradual changes will obtain general acceptance.[21]

Establishing accounting standards

Considering the difficulties facing the FASB, how should accounting policy be established in consideration of both theoretical and practical issues? The use of inductive-deductive theories of which the conceptual framework is a partial example is the most practical starting point at the present time, in large part because there is not sufficient empirical research evidence to do otherwise. But controversies arise because the alternative solutions cannot be confirmed and because the inductive-deductive process leads to a number of competing theories. In fact, Watts and Zimmerman demonstrated that there is a demand for normative accounting theories, which are used as excuses for political action.[22] That is, specific theories are used to support the position of a specific group, and the theories are useful justifications for a preferred position, even though it is impossible to verify the theory. But if other theories cannot be verified either, the controversy cannot be settled on the basis of the inductive-deductive theories alone. Many other factors must be considered.

The recent revolution in accounting research, however, has provided some relief. The capital market approach and human information processing research have been able to provide some evidence regarding social and economic consequences, particularly when the research is confirmed by additional studies and replication. But in all cases to date, the conclusions of research projects can provide only partial answers. No general theory or research study is possible that could encompass all relevant variables in accounting policy decisions. A main policy guideline should be that the general social and economic welfare should be the most important objective whenever possible, and the social and economic consequences affecting specific individuals or groups should be taken into consideration only when the granting of individual or group preferences would not decrease social and economic welfare. But these generalities are not easy to put into practice because of the enormous complexity of the accounting environment.

---

[21] For example, *Accounting Research Studies No. 1* and *3* were rejected by the APB because they were too radically different from generally accepted practice.

[22] Ross L. Watts and Jerold L. Zimmerman, "The Demand for and Supply of Accounting Theories: The Market for Excuses," *Accounting Review*, April 1979, pp. 273–305.

THE SECURITIES AND
EXCHANGE COMMISSION

The Securities and Exchange Commission (SEC) was created by an act of Congress setting up an independent regulatory agency of the United States government to administer the Securities Act of 1933, the Securities Exchange Act of 1934, and several other acts. The Securities Act of 1933 (originally administered by the Federal Trade Commission) provides for the registration of securities with the SEC before they may be sold to the public (with certain exemptions). The act provides for the disclosure of specific financial and other information by means of a registration statement and a prospectus, both of which are available for inspection by the public. Among several other major provisions, the Securities Exchange Act of 1934 provides for the filing of an application for registration by any company that desires to have its securities registered and listed for trading on a national securities exchange. This filing requires the disclosure of information similar to that required under the Securities Act. In addition, however, the information available to the public must be kept up to date by periodic reports filed by the company.

Under the several acts administered by the SEC, the Commission has broad powers to prescribe accounting procedures and the form of accounting statements filed with it. During the years from 1936 to 1938, the Commission engaged in heated controversy regarding whether or not it should promulgate a set of accounting principles to be followed by all firms filing reports with it. Due in large part to the persuasiveness of the chief accountant, the Commission decided in 1938 to permit the profession to lead the way in the formulation of accounting principles. This policy was issued in the form of *Accounting Series Release No. 4,* which stated that the Commission would accept only financial statements prepared in accordance with accounting principles that have substantial authoritative support or in accordance with rules, regulations, or other official pronouncements of the Commission or the chief accountant. Thus was established the policy of relying on generally accepted principles and practices as developed in the accounting profession. However, since 1937 the SEC has put pressure on the AICPA, the APB, and the FASB to reduce the areas of differences in accounting practice with the threat that if the Institute did not do so, the SEC would.

The influence of the SEC has been primarily through its comments on drafts of *APB Opinions* and *FASB Statements* and the concurrences with drafts of *Opinions* and *Statements* before their publication. However, it has also had a direct influence through the publication of *Regulation S-X, Accounting Series Releases* of the Commission or the Chief Accountant, and official decisions. In a few cases, the SEC has in effect overruled an *APB Opinion* or acted when the APB or FASB did not do so. For example, in *Accounting Series Release No. 96,* the SEC gave acceptance to several methods of handling the investment credit, although *APB Opinion No. 2* had previously recommended only those methods resulting in deferral of the effect on income. In another case, the APB had considered expressing an opinion regarding the classification of deferred income taxes relating to installment receivables, but decided not to require uniform classification in this case. Upon the petition of a national public accounting firm, the Commission issued *Accounting Series Release No. 102,* specifying that the deferred income taxes should be classified consistent with the classification of the related accounts receivable.

The relationship between the SEC and the FASB was clarified somewhat in 1973 by *SEC Accounting Series Release No. 150,* which stated that "principles, standards and practices promulgated by the FASB will be considered by the Commission as having substantial authoritative support, and those contrary to such FASB promulgations will be considered to have no such support." Although this does indicate that the SEC intends to look to the FASB for private sector leadership in the development of financial reporting standards, the *Release* also stated that "the Commission will continue to identify areas where investor information needs exist and will determine the appropriate methods of disclosure to meet these needs." This endorsement of the FASB by the SEC has some reservations, but at least government regulation in the United States has not placed rigid controls on the presentation of general financial statements or on the variety of accounting procedures in use. Rigid controls would have stifled the development of accounting theory and the progress in accounting practice stemming from new ideas in theory.

The SEC has, however, overridden the FASB pronouncements on certain occasions and taken the initiative on others. For example, in 1978 the SEC issued *Accounting Series Releases Nos. 253* and *258,* prescribing a form of full-cost accounting for oil and gas producers as an acceptable alternative to the successful-efforts method. Previously, the FASB had required the use of the successful efforts method (*Statement No. 19*). But, as a result of the action of the SEC, the FASB issued *Statement No. 25* in 1979, which suspended the required use of successful-efforts accounting.

Evidence of cooperation with the FASB, however, was demonstrated when the SEC took the initiative in 1976 in requiring the disclosure of certain replacement cost information (*ASR No. 190*) and deleted this requirement in 1979 (*ASR No. 271*) when the FASB issued *Statement No. 33,* "Financial Reporting and Changing Prices."

Another indication that the SEC has been innovative and cooperative in the 1970s and 1980s is the trend toward the requirement for so-called soft data (information that cannot be audited in the traditional manner), such as current cost information, information regarding oil and gas reserves, interim information data, and proposals for forecast information, but with safe-harbor provisions for accountants as demonstrated in *ASR No. 203* relating to current cost information required by *ASR No. 190.*[23]

---

[23] For a fuller discussion of changes in SEC policies over the years, see John Gary Previts "The SEC and Its Chief Accountants: Historical Impressions," *Journal of Accountancy,* August 1978, pp. 83–91.

SUMMARY

The establishment of accounting policies determining the amount and type of information disclosure, measurement rules and procedures, and the form of presentation of financial statements and financial reporting is a complex process. The main responsibility for accounting policy was granted to the SEC by Congress in 1934 for corporations whose securities are publicly traded. The FASB was formed as an independent agency in the private sector to establish accounting policy enforced by the AICPA on its members. But the support of the FASB by the SEC has given it considerably greater authority. Even with regulation, however, accounting policies must still be formulated by the AICPA,[24] professional accounting firms, and the reporting enterprises.

Traditionally, accounting policy has been based on generally accepted practice and inductive-deductive logic in an attempt to narrow the areas of differences. Research, particularly in the areas of capital markets and human information processing, does provide some assistance in meeting the objectives of accounting policy to improve social and economic welfare. Other social and economic consequences should also be considered in accounting policy decisions in relationship to the costs and benefits of the policies. Economic consequences that affect specific industries, individuals, or corporations must be placed in this broader context. However, because of these economic consequences, there is an attempt through lobbying and other means to place the establishment of accounting policy in the political arena. These political pressures cannot be ignored, and individuals and corporations should have an opportunity to be heard; but accounting policy should not be established by the political process alone. Technical considerations including the results of theory and research should be of primary importance with the objective of producing the greatest benefit to society.

SELECTED ADDITIONAL READING

Accounting policy—standard setting

Bromwich, Michael. "The Possibility of Partial Accounting Standards." *Accounting Review,* April 1980, pp. 288–300.

Demski, Joel. "Choice among Financial Reporting Alternatives." *Accounting Review,* April 1974, pp. 221–32.

May, Robert G., and **Gary L. Sundem.** "Research for Accounting Policy: An Overview." *Accounting Review,* October 1976, pp. 747–63.

Moonitz, Maurice. "Obtaining Agreement on Standards in the Accounting Profession." *Studies in Accounting Research No. 8.* AAA, 1974.

---

[24] The FASB in *Statement No. 32* declared the specialized accounting and reporting principles contained in AICPA *Statements of Position* (*SOP*s) and *Guides* on Accounting and Auditing Matters to be preferable accounting principles for purposes of justifying a change in accounting principles (under *APB Opinion No. 20*).

Uniformity and comparability

Hendriksen, Eldon S. "Toward Greater Comparability through Uniformity of Accounting Principles." *New York Certified Public Accountant,* now *CPA Journal,* February 1967, pp. 105–15.

Merino, Barbara D. and **Teddy L. Coe.** "Uniformity in Accounting: A Historical Perspective." *Journal of Accountancy,* August 1978, pp. 62–69.

Miller, Paul B. W. "A New View of Comparability." *Journal of Accountancy,* August 1978, pp. 70–77.

Revsine, Lawrence. "Towards Greater Comparability in Accounting Reports." *Financial Analysts Journal,* January-February 1975, pp. 45–51.

Simmons, John K. "A Concept of Comparability in Financial Reporting." *Accounting Review* 42, October 1967, 680–92.

Sterling, Robert R. "A Test of the Uniformity Hypothesis." *Abacus,* September 1969, pp. 37–47.

"Uniformity in Financial Accounting." *Law and Contemporary Problems* 30 (Autumn 1965).

Economic consequences of accounting policy

American Accounting Association. *Report of the Committee on The Social Consequences of Accounting Information. AAA Committee Reports, vol. 1978–4.*

Benston, George J. "The Economic Consequences of Financial Accounting Statements," in *FASB Economic Consequences of Financial Statements,* Selected Papers, July 1978, pp. 161–252.

Dhaliwal, Dan S. "The Effect of the Firm's Capital Structure on the Choice of Accounting Methods." *Accounting Review,* January 1980, pp. 78–84.

Lev, Baruch. "The Impact of Accounting Regulation on the Stock Market: The Case of Oil and Gas Companies." *Accounting Review,* July 1979, pp. 485–503.

Rappaport, Alfred. "The Economic Impact of Financial Accounting Standards—Implications for the FASB." *1976 Accounting Research Convocation: Emerging Issues.* University of Alabama, 1977, pp. 113–28. Also, see *Journal of Accountancy,* May 1977, pp. 89–98.

Wyatt, Arthur R. "The Economic Impact of Financial Accounting Standards." *1976 Accounting Research Convocation: Emerging Issues.* University of Alabama, 1977, pp. 129–38. Also, see *Journal of Accountancy,* October 1977, pp. 92–94.

Zeff, Stephen. "The Rise of Economic Consequences." *Journal of Accountancy,* December 1978, pp. 56–63.

The impact of politics on accounting policy

Gerboth, Dale L. "Research, Intuition, and Politics in Accounting Inquiry." *Accounting Review,* July 1973, pp. 475–82.

Horngren, Charles T. "The Marketing of Accounting Standards." *Journal of Accountancy,* October 1973, pp. 61–66.

Solomons, David. "The Politicization of Accounting: The Impact of Politics on Accounting Standards." *Journal of Accountancy,* November 1978, pp. 65–72.

Watts, Ross L., and Jerold L. Zimmerman, "Toward a Positive Theory of Determination of Accounting Standards." *Accounting Review,* January 1978, pp. 112–34.

———. "The Demand for and Supply of Accounting Theories: The Market for Excuses." *Accounting Review,* April 1979, pp. 273–305.

Financial Accounting Standards Board

Beaver, William H. "What Should Be the FASB's Objectives?" *Journal of Accountancy,* August 1973, pp. 49–56.

Dopuch, Nicholas, and Shyam Sunder. "FASB's Statements on Objectives and Elements of Financial Accounting: A Review." *Accounting Review,* January 1980, pp. 1–21.

Moonitz, Maurice. *Studies in Accounting Research No. 8.* "Obtaining Agreement on Standards in the Accounting Profession." AAA, 1974, pp. 80–87.

Securities and Exchange Commission

Benston, George J. "Required Disclosure and the Stock Market: An Evaluation of the Securities Act of 1934." *American Economic Review,* March 1973.

Blough, Carman. "Development of Accounting Principles in the United States." *Berkeley Symposium on the Foundations of Financial Accounting.* Berkeley: Schools of Business Administration, University of California, 1967, pp. 1–14.

Pines, J. Arnold. "The Securities and Exchange Commission and Accounting Principles." *Law and Contemporary Problems.* Uniformity in Financial Accounting. Autumn 1965, pp. 727–51.

Previts, Gary John. "The SEC and Its Chief Accountants: Historical Impressions." *Journal of Accountancy,* August 1978, pp. 83–91.

Rappaport, Louis H. *SEC Accounting Practice and Procedure.* 3d ed. New York: Ronald Press, 1972.

CHAPTER 7

INCOME CONCEPTS FOR FINANCIAL REPORTING

The accrual concept of income continues to come under challenge as a fundamental measurement; however, from an informational perspective, it does describe accounting activity.[1] On the basis of efficient capital market assumptions, empirical research supports the view that accounting income does have informational content.[2] Whether it is from a desire for a single measurement of income or from the recognition of the information included in the computation of accounting income, practicing accountants continue to emphasize the role of income measurement, and financial analysts continue to demand its measurement and publication. For example, *FASB Statement of Financial Accounting Concepts No. 1* states that "the primary focus of financial reporting is information about an enterprise's performance provided by measures of earnings and its components."[3] This demand for income measurement is also supported by the preliminary findings of a laboratory experiment by Pankoff and Virgil, which concluded that there was rather close agreement among analysts that earnings per share and sales were the most important of normally available information items.[4] However, they also concluded that earnings per share had very little, if any, general impact on the expectations of all but a few analysts.[5] This chapter examines the several concepts of income at the structural (syntactical), interpretive (semantic), and behavioral levels in order to evaluate the theoretical difficulties and attempt to explain the divergence between theory and practice with respect to the concept of accounting income.

---

[1] See, for example, William H. Beaver and Joel S. Demski, "The Nature of Income Measurement," *Accounting Review* 54 (January 1979): 38–46.

[2] See R. Ball and P. Brown, "An Empirical Evaluation of Accounting Income Numbers," *Journal of Accounting Research,* Autumn 1968, pp. 159–78.

[3] *AICPA Professional Standards,* vol. 3, *FASB Statement of Financial Accounting Concepts No. 1,* "Objectives of Financial Reporting by Business Enterprises," para. 1210.43.

[4] Lyn D. Pankoff and Robert L. Virgil, "Some Preliminary Findings from a Laboratory Experiment on the Usefulness of Financial Accounting Information to Security Analysts," *Journal of Accounting Research* (Empirical Research in Accounting: Selected Studies, 1970), p. 22.

[5] Ibid., p. 23.

The following are some of the criticisms of accounting income in its traditional form:

1. The concept of accounting income has not yet been clearly formulated.
2. There is no long-run theoretical basis for the computation and presentation of accounting income.
3. Generally accepted accounting practices permit inconsistencies in the measurement of periodic income of different firms and even between different years for the same firm.
4. Price-level changes have modified the meaning of income measured in terms of historical dollars.
5. Other information may prove more useful to investors and stockholders for the making of investment decisions.

Recognizing that the measurement of income has considerable conceptual and practical problems, several suggestions have been made to provide solutions. The following five major positions are probably representative of the suggestions regarding the problem of income measurement:

1. Much of the discussion today centers on an attempt to improve the reporting of what may be called accounting income by focusing on transaction data and the accrual process.
2. Others support a single operational concept of income that can be used as an indication of the firm's ability to pay dividends.
3. One belief is that future progress in accounting theory depends upon agreement on a single concept of income that will conform more closely to what is referred to as economic income.
4. Some writers subscribe to the idea that several concepts of income should be measured and reported for different purposes.
5. More recently, several suggestions have been made to the effect that all measurements of income are deficient and that they should be superseded by other measures of economic activity.

The concepts of income on the structural, interpretative, and behavioral levels are discussed in this chapter following a discussion of the objectives of income reporting. The theory and measurement of the several elements making up accounting income are discussed in the following chapter, and suggestions for the substitution of alternative measures of economic activity are discussed in Chapters 10 and 21.

THE OBJECTIVES OF NET INCOME REPORTING

A knowledge of different measurements of a firm's net income may be useful for different purposes, but there is thought to be an advantage in the general acceptance of one all-pervasive concept of net income for external reporting purposes. However, a close analysis of the various concepts and objectives of net income indicates clearly that a single concept cannot serve all purposes equally well if, indeed, it can serve any purpose well. At least two choices are possible—a single concept that meets most of the objectives fairly well or several net income figures clearly labeled to serve the several objectives. Disadvantages and difficulties in both of these choices are discernible in the following discussion.

The primary objective of income reporting, of course, is to provide useful information to those who are most interested in financial reports. But more specific objectives must be spelled out in order to obtain a clearer understanding of income reporting. One of the basic objectives assumed to be most important for all users of financial reports is the need to distinguish between invested capital and income—between the stocks and flows—as a part of the descriptive process of accounting. More specific objectives include the use of income as a measurement of the efficiency of management, the use of historical income figures to aid in predicting the future course of the business or future dividend distributions, and the use of income as a measurement of accomplishment and as a guide to future managerial decisions. Each of these objectives is discussed at greater length in the following paragraphs. Other objectives not discussed include the use of income as a base for taxation, the use of income as a means of regulating firms vested with a public interest, and the use of income figures by economists in evaluating the allocation of resources.

INCOME CONCEPTS AT THE STRUCTURAL LEVEL

Although accountants give lip service to the real-world interpretation of accounting income (generally economic income) or its behavioral impact (either its predictive ability or its general relevance in decision processes), they generally base principles and rules on premises that may not be related to real-world phenomena or behavioral effects. For example, the Study Group on the Objectives of Financial Statements said that "earnings . . . are based on conventions and rules that should be logical and internally consistent, even though they may not mesh with economists' notions of income."[6] The conventions and rules are made logical and consistent by being based on premises and concepts that have been developed from existing practice. However, such concepts as realization, matching, accrual basis, and cost allocations must also be defined in terms of precise rules because they do not have real-world counterparts.

Accountants have used these terms so often and for so long that we tend to accept them as having interpretation in the real world. It is difficult to accept the fact that they have no significance outside of their

---

[6] American Institute of Certified Public Accountants, *Report of the Study Group on the Objectives of Financial Statements,* "Objectives of Financial Statements" (October 1973), p. 22.

limited role in the logic of the accounting structure. This may be one reason why many students have difficulty grasping the meaning of accounting concepts; they try to give interpretive significance to concepts that have no relationship to real objects and events. This does not mean to imply, however, that all accounting concepts lack interpretive significance. Many concepts, such as product sales, are based on external transactions or other observable events. But accounting income is the summation of many positive and negative items, many of which do not have interpretive content; if any one or more of these items lack interpretive significance and are material, the resulting net income will also lack interpretive significance, even though it may contain information for capital markets.

FASB Statement of Accounting Concepts No. 1 assumed that accounting income is a good measure of a firm's performance and that accounting income can be used in the prediction of future cash flows. Other writers assume that accounting income is relevant in a general way for the decision models of investors and creditors. However, these assumptions have not been proven to have empirical validity. Bedford, on the other hand, contends that readers of income reports should realize that the meaning of accounting income can be understood only by knowing how the income was measured (operationalism). That is, the readers should understand the operations used by the accountant to produce the income amount.[7]

The transactions approach to income measurement

The transactions approach to income measurement is the more conventional approach used by accountants. It involves the recording of changes in asset and liability valuations only as these are the result of transactions. The term *transactions* is used in the broad sense to include both internal and external transactions. External transactions arise from dealing with outsiders and the transfer of assets or liabilities to or from the firm. Internal transactions arise from the use or conversion of assets within the firm. Changes in values are excluded if they arise from changes in market valuations or changes in expectations alone. To the extent that asset valuations are adjusted at the end of the period to take these changes into consideration, there is a deviation from the pure transactions approach; this adjustment represents an application of the annual inventory method implicit in the capital maintenance approach.

To the extent that new market valuations replace the input (cost) valuations when an external transaction takes place, income is recognized when the external transaction occurs. Internal transactions could lead to valuation changes, but only those that result from the use or conversion of

---

[7] Norton Bedford, "The Income Concept Complex: Expansion or Decline," in *Asset Valuation,* ed. Robert Sterling (Lawrence, Kans.: Scholars Book, 1971), p. 142.

assets are usually recorded. When conversions take place, the value of the old asset is usually transferred to the new asset. Therefore, the transactions approach lends itself readily to the concept of realization at the time of sale or exchange and to the cost convention in accounting.

The main advantages of the transactions approach are these:

1. The components of net income can be classified in several ways, such as by product or class of customer, in order to obtain more useful information for management.
2. The incomes arising from the various sources such as from operations and from external causes can be reported separately to the extent that they can be measured.
3. It provides a basis for the determination of the types and quantities of assets and liabilities existing at the end of the period. Other valuation methods can then be applied more easily to this inventory.
4. Business efficiency requires the recording of external transactions for other reasons.
5. The various statements can be made to articulate with each other, which is assumed to permit greater understanding of the underlying data.

The general procedure is to record revenues and expenses as they arise from external transactions. The problems of timing and valuation are present in the recording of each transaction, but the main problem is focused upon the proper matching of expenses with the related revenue reported during the specific period. These problems are discussed in the next chapter. As we shall see in our later discussion, the several concepts of net income computed by the several methods of determining capital maintenance can be incorporated into the transactions approach by making adjustments to revenues and expenses at the time of recording each transaction and by making adjustments to asset valuations at the end of each period. Thus, current accounting practice is a combination of capital maintenance concepts of income, operational concepts, and the transactions-based approach to income measurement.

The activities approach to income measurement

The activities approach to income differs from the transactions approach in that it focuses on a description of the activities of a firm rather than on the reporting of transactions. That is, income is assumed to arise when certain activities or events take place, rather than only as a result of specific transactions. For example, activity income would be recorded during the planning, purchasing, production, and sale processes, as well as possibly during the the collection process. In its application, it is merely an expansion of the transactions approach, since it starts with the transaction as a basis for measurement. The main difference is that the transactions approach is based on the reporting process that measures an external event—the transaction; the activities approach is based on the real-world concept of activity or event in a broader sense. Both approaches, however, fail to reflect reality in the measurement of income because they both are dependent upon the same structural relationships and concepts that have no real-world counterpart.

One of the assumed advantages of the activities approach is that it permits the measurement of several different concepts of income, which can be used for different purposes. Income arising from the production and sale of merchandise involves different types of evaluations and predictions than does the income arising from buying and selling securities or from holding assets for expected capital gains. The efficiency of management can be measured better if the components of income are classified according to the different types of operations or activities that are subject to more or less control by management. Furthermore, the classification of income components by types of operations permits better predictions because of the different behavioral patterns of the different types of activities.

INTERPRETIVE CONCEPTS OF INCOME

Accountants frequently refer to two economic concepts based on real-world observations as logical starting points for a definition of a concept of accounting income. These two economic concepts are the change in well-being and the maximization of profit under specified conditions of market structure, product demand, and input costs. These concepts have been recognized by the FASB in its assertion that "Comprehensive income is the change in equity (net assets) of an entity during a period . . . "[8] and "The test of success (or failure) of the operations of an enterprise is the extent to which the cash returned exceeds (or is less than) the cash spent (invested) over the long run."[9] The former is the concept of capital maintenance, and the latter is another form of the profit maximization concept or measurement of efficiency. Economists have attempted to refine these concepts as saying something about real-world observations, even though they disagree among themselves regarding their significance. However, economists have not been very helpful in solving the measurement problems surrounding these concepts. As a result, accountants have chosen to apply precise rules for income measurement regardless of how close they may come to measuring the economists concepts. This section explores these interpretive concepts of income and alternative methods suggested for their measurement. Practical and conceptual limitations are also presented.

[8] *FASB Statement of Financial Accounting Concepts No. 3,* "Elements of Financial Statements of Business Enterprises," *AICPA Professional Standards,* para. 1230.56.

[9] *FASB Statement of Financial Concepts No. 1,* "Objectives of Financial Reporting by Business Enterprises," *AICPA Professional Standards—Accounting,* vol. 3, para. 1210.39.

Capital versus income

In the terms of the economist Irving Fisher, *capital* is a *stock* of wealth at an instant of time.[10] *Income* is a *flow* of services through time. *Capital* is the embodiment of future services, and *income* is the enjoyment of these services over a specific period of time. With these definitions, it does not seem possible to confuse the two terms. The one relates to the amount in the reservoir at any one time, and the other refers to the amount flowing out of the reservoir during a period of time.

When these terms are related to a business enterprise, however, they take on slightly different meanings. In the above definition, income is the enjoyment from the use of capital; however, a business enterprise does not exist for the purpose of enjoyment. Its purpose is to provide a flow of wealth for the benefit of its owners or beneficiaries—the equity holders. Whereas, capital is still the *stock* of wealth that can provide future services, income is thought of as the *flow* of wealth or services in excess of that necessary to maintain a constant capital. Although a firm may be thought of as relatively permanent in nature, it is not the responsibility of the accountant to see that the invested capital is preserved. This is the responsibility of management, or possibly the decision of the owners or equity holders. The accountant's responsibility is to report the amounts that have been made available to the beneficiaries for their enjoyment or reinvestment and the change in the capital of the enterprise. Thus, there is an important distinction between the flows to beneficiaries that represent amounts that can be enjoyed without impairing the future cash flows and those flows that represent reductions in wealth. In accounting terms, this is the distinction between income and a return of capital.

Why is it important to distinguish between enterprise income and a return of capital? The answer is twofold. First, changes in the capital of the enterprise may affect the amount of future flows to residual equity holders (the holders of common stock) and thus the value of their equity at any point in time. Second, changes in enterprise capital may affect the relationships among the various equity holders, including the holders of debt and preferred stock.

The residual equity holders are interested not only in how much they can expect to receive from the enterprise during the following period, but also in the net changes in the ability of the enterprise to provide future flows. Current investor interest is focused not only on the ability of the firm to maintain dividends, but in many cases on its growth potential. The knowledge of these changes is even more important when the ownership rights to these future flows are transferred frequently during the life of the enterprise. During the early period of the railroad industry in the United States, it was not uncommon for promoters to pay huge dividends

---

[10] Irving Fisher, *The Nature of Capital and Income* (New York: Macmillan, 1906), p. 52.

out of capital during the early life of the firm. Investors, believing this to be the true income of the firm, paid high prices for the stock, only to find later that the ability to pay dividends in the future was being eroded because of these huge early dividends. Equity requires that both buyers and sellers of common stock have adequate information to make expectations regarding the current and future dividends of the firm.

With the separation of ownership and control in most large corporations, accounting also has the responsibility to report on the stewardship of the management group entrusted with the proper use of the invested capital. A proper distinction between income and changes in capital is one of the means of determining the extent to which management has carried out the function of operating the enterprise for the benefit of the owners.

The concept of wealth maintenance is also important to bondholders, preferred stockholders, and the providers of short-term credit. All of these equity holders are interested in the probability of repayment at some future date. The prospect of repayment is greater if the total invested capital of the enterprise is maintained at a constant level or permitted to increase. The prospect of repayment is less if the capital is diminished either through losses or by the payment of dividends in excess of earnings. The creditors cannot always be protected against losses, but if they are properly notified, they may be able to protect their position before it is too late. To a certain extent, creditors are protected legally and often contractually from the impairment of invested capital by the payment of dividends in excess of earnings.

The various classes of equity holders are also interested in the return on their investment, whether it be contractual (as interest on debt) or dependent on earnings (as dividends on preferred and common stock). Since invested capital reflects, in part, the ability of the firm to continue the payment of a return to equity holders in the future, changes in the amount of invested capital are vital in decisions regarding the future flow of this return to any class of equity holders.

The concepts of capital and income, however, are not clearly formulated. *Capital* can be defined in terms of the current monetary unit or a monetary unit of constant value; in physical terms; in terms of capacity to produce goods and services; or in terms of the future expectations regarding future flows to stockholders. The measurement difficulties in separating capital and income are even greater. These conceptual and measurement difficulties are discussed in the following section.

The wealth maintenance concepts of income

Among economists, Adam Smith was the first to define *income* as that amount that can be consumed without encroaching upon capital, including both fixed and circulating capital. Hicks elaborated upon this by saying that income is the amount that a person can consume during a period of time and be as well off at the end of that time as at the beginning.[11] However, there is no clear understanding or agreement as to the precise meaning of *well-offness*. Several approaches to this concept are discussed in the following paragraphs, but the measurement of well-offness during periods of price-level changes is discussed in Chapter 9. In the following discussion, we assume for argument's sake that the general value of money remains constant over time and that meaningful measurements of wealth can be obtained and expressed in money terms.

The concept of wealth maintenance implies an overall view of the capital invested in the firm. Once the concepts are developed, we shall see that they can be applied to the analysis of specific transactions; but, in the following discussion, income is computed by placing a valuation on the net assets of the firm at the end of the period and comparing this with the valuation at the beginning of the period. For example, if the net assets of the firm were $80,000 at the end of the period and $76,000 at the beginning, the net income would be $4,000 in the absence of capital transactions and the payment of dividends. If additional capital stock in the amount of $11,000 had been sold and if dividends in the amount of $8,000 had been paid during the period, the net income would have been $1,000.

The greatest difficulty with this approach is in the measurement of the net assets at the beginning and end of the period. Several methods of valuation include (1) capitalization of the expected future net stream of cash or services to be received over the life of the firm, (2) the aggregation of the selling prices of the several assets of the firm less the summation of the liabilities, (3) valuation of the firm on the basis of the current stock market prices applied to the total stock outstanding, and (4) valuation of the firm by using input values (either historical or current cost) for nonmonetary assets and adding the present cash value of monetary assets and subtracting liabilities.

Capitalization. One of the suggested concepts for measuring the net assets at the beginning and end of the year is the capitalization of all expected future cash distributions by the firm to stockholders. *Capitalized value* can be defined as the present discounted value of the expected cash distributions to stockholders by the firm during the remaining life of the enterprise, including the final amount expected to be paid at liquidation. In computing this capitalized value, three factors must be estimated—the amount of the net cash distributions expected to be paid each year, the number of years of remaining life, and the appropriate discount factor. This relationship can be expressed by the following formula:

$$P_0 = R_1(1 + i)^{-1} + R_2(1 + i)^{-2} + R_3(1 + i)^{-3} \ldots R_n(1 + i)^{-n} \quad (1)$$

---

[11] J. R. Hicks, *Value and Capital* (Oxford: Clarendon Press, 1946), p. 172.

or as:

$$P_0 = \sum_{t=1}^{n} \frac{R_t}{(1+i)^t} \tag{2}$$

where:

$P_0 =$ The present value or capitalized value at time 0.
$R_t =$ The net cash distribution to stockholders expected in period t.
$i =$ The appropriate discount factor.
$n =$ The number of years of expected life.

Income can be computed for the first year by the following formula:

$$I_1 = P_1 - P_0 + R_1 \tag{3}$$

where the value of P_1 is as follows:

$$P_1 = \sum_{t=2}^{n} \frac{R_t}{(1+i)^{t-1}} \tag{4}$$

As an example, let us assume certainty and the following cash distributions during a life of five years for a firm:

Year	Cash flow (net)
1	$100
2	300
3	200
4	400
5	500

In the case of certainty, the appropriate discount rate would be the opportunity cost to the owners (assumed to be 5 percent in this case) and the present value of the firm would be $1,261.[12] At the end of the first year

---

[12] These present values are computed as follows:

Beginning of First Year

$100 \times 0.9524 \left[\left(\frac{1}{1.05} \right) \right] = \$\ 95$

$300 \times 0.9070 \left[\left(\frac{1}{1.05} \right)^2 \right] = 272$

$200 \times 0.8638 \left[\left(\frac{1}{1.05} \right)^3 \right] = 173$

$400 \times 0.8227 \left[\left(\frac{1}{1.05} \right)^4 \right] = 329$

$500 \times 0.7835 \left[\left(\frac{1}{1.05} \right)^5 \right] = 392$

$\$1,261$

End of First Year

$300 \times 0.9524 \left[\left(\frac{1}{1.05} \right) \right] = \$\ 286$

$200 \times 0.9070 \left[\left(\frac{1}{1.05} \right)^2 \right] = 181$

$400 \times 0.8638 \left[\left(\frac{1}{1.05} \right)^3 \right] = 346$

$500 \times 0.8227 \left[\left(\frac{1}{1.05} \right)^4 \right] = 411$

$\$1,224$

the capitalized value of the remaining cash distributions would be $1,224 and the net income for the first year would be computed as follows:

Cash distributed at the end of the first year	$ 100
Capitalized value at the end of the first year of the cash flows for the remaining years	1,224
Total value of the firm at the end of the first year assuming no distributions to stockholders	1,324
Less: Capitalized value at the beginning of the year	1,261
Income for year	$ 63

Since this income of $63 represents the increase in the total value of the firm during the year, it also represents 5 percent of the initial capitalized value of $1,261. It represents, in effect, interest on the capital invested. If the cash distribution each year is greater than the income (interest), the income would decline each year. In the case cited, the incomes for each of the five years would be $63, $61, $42, and $24. Note that this has no direct relationship to the cash distributions in each year. However, if the initial income of $63 were distributed to stockholders and the remaining amount of available cash were reinvested by the firm in projects that will yield 5 percent, both the income and the capitalized value of the firm would remain constant into the future.

In the absence of certainty, the future cash payments represent expected values of probability distributions. For example, if the subjective estimates of the cash dividend for the first year are either $120 with a probability of 0.6 or $70 with a probability of 0.4, the expected value would be $100.[13] The number of probable values could be few or many, including all possible values of the monetary unit. Each value would be assigned a probability value such that the sum of all probabilities is one. Note that the expected value is subjective because of the necessity of estimating the possible values and because of the assignment of subjective probability values to these.

The appropriate discount rate in the case of certainty is the opportunity rate that could be earned on a riskless security. In the case of uncertainty, most authors define the appropriate rate as the subjective required rate for investments of equal risk or the target rate of return. While there are some theoretical difficulties in including the adjustments for risk in the interest factor, this will be discussed in Chapter 11, and a subjective rate will be assumed at this point in order to focus on the income concepts. Therefore, in the absence of changes in expectations and if the actual cash distribution the first year is equal to the expected cash payment, income as computed in the above example is equal to the subjective rate of return multiplied by the beginning (or average) capitalized value. Edwards and

---

[13] The expected value of the cash flow would be computed as follows:

$$\begin{aligned} \$120 \times 0.6 &= \$ 72 \\ 70 \times 0.4 &= \underline{28} \\ &\ \$100 \end{aligned}$$

Bell call this the subjective profit, because it is defined as the interest at the target rate on the subjective value of the firm's assets at the beginning of the period.[14]

But if the anticipations at the end of the period have changed since the beginning of the period, the actual subjective profit for this period will differ from the anticipated subjective profit. While the anticipated subjective profit is based on the subjective value of the firm's assets at the beginning of the period, the actual or *ex post* subjective profit includes changes in the subjective value of the assets at the end of the period. For example, if the cash flow during the first period is $100 as anticipated, but at the end of the period the cash flows for the following four periods are now expected to be $400 a year instead of $300, $200, $400, and $500, the income for the first year would be computed as follows:

Cash distributed at the end of the first year	$ 100
Capitalized value at the end of the year of remaining expected cash flows of $400 a year for four years	1,418
Total value of the firm at the end of the year	1,518
Less: Capitalized value at the beginning of the year	1,261
Income for year	$ 257

This income of $257 is made up of the following:

Anticipated subjective profit	$ 63
Increase in subjective value of the firm	194
Total income	$257

There is some question as to whether the increase in subjective value of the firm of $194 is really income. One contention is that this change in expectations is really an adjustment of the original value of the firm, which was in error at the beginning of the year. In fact, one argument is that with the current expectations at the end of the year, the value at the beginning of the year should have been $1,446 instead of $1,261. Therefore, the net change in capitalized value can be analyzed as follows:

Subjective profit or interest (5% × $1,446)	$ 72
Adjustment of original subjective value ($1,446 less $1,261)	185
Total increase in capitalized value	$257

If, on the other hand, the expectations regarding future cash flows do not change, but the cash receipt for the first year is $130 instead of $100 as anticipated, the income for the period would be as follows:

Cash distributed at the end of the first year	$ 130
Capitalized value at the end of the year of remaining expected cash flows (unchanged)	1,224
Total value of the firm at the end of the year (before dividend payment)	1,354
Less: Capitalized value at the beginning of the year	1,261
Income for year	$ 93

[14] Edgar O. Edwards and Philip W. Bell, *The Theory and Measurement of Business Income* (Berkeley and Los Angeles: University of California Press, 1961), pp. 38–44.

This income of $93 is made up of the following:

Anticipated subjective profit (interest)	$63
Increase in the cash distributed over that expected	30
Total income	$93

What does this concept of income include and what does it mean? (1) The main part of the income is the subjective interest on the capitalized value of the firm. Note that this is a function of only time, the interest rate, and the expected cash flows in the future. The expected cash flows, however, may be due to either current or future production and sales efforts. (2) The changes in expectations regarding future cash flows arise because of changes either in the appraisal of management's efficiencies or deficiencies, or in expectations regarding economic conditions (such as changes in tastes). They may also be due to general optimism or pessimism. (3) The difference between the actual cash available for distribution and that expected may be due to windfall gains and losses from external causes or miscalculations in original expectations.

Conventional accounting practice recognizes some of these concepts, but rejects them most of the time. In a few cases, such as the recognition of interest on investments, the accrual concept requires the reporting of income on the basis of time alone. Actual cash receipts in excess of the expected amount are traditionally included in ordinary income or classified as extraordinary losses. However, accounting practice does not require the actual receipt of the cash for this recognition; changes in anticipated cash flows may be recorded when they become fairly certain and the amount is verifiable, such as when an asset is sold under a contract requiring payment at a later date. Other changes in expectations, however, are generally denied recognition.

While the capitalization concept has merit as an economic concept of income, it has some specific conceptual and practical disadvantages for accounting purposes. The practical disadvantages arise primarily from the subjective nature of the expectations. Even an accountant independent in judgments is likely to be overly optimistic or overly pessimistic in the eyes of management, stockholders, or other users of the financial reports. The ideal would be to provide adequate information to permit each user of accounting statements to apply his/her own judgment regarding expectations of future cash flows and the selection of an appropriate discount factor.

But the capitalization concept is also deficient conceptually for the following reasons:

1.   Expectations regarding future cash flows cannot be converted into single values or certainty equivalents without knowing the risk preferences of the users of the information; the adjustment for risk by including it in the subjective discount rate is conceptually inappropriate.

2.   Emphasis is placed upon the time factor and expected cash flows; all other economic events and activities are ignored.

3.   The income measurement does not disclose whether it is due to commendable actions of management or only to fortuitous circumstances; that is, it does not provide information useful for measuring management efficiency.

4.   The value of the firm is determined by discounting all expected cash flows indefinitely into the future, many of which have no relationship to current or past activity.

5.   One of the main deficiencies is that it places the cart before the horse. Net cash flows of future periods must be predicted accurately in order to compute current income. In a world of certainty, there would be no reason to compute periodic income, as this would be known in advance; and under conditions of uncertainty, expected cash flows are used to determine current income. However, one of the objectives of measuring current income is thought to be to permit the users of financial reports to make reliable predictions of future cash flows. Since predictions must be based at least in part on current and past economic activity, the users of financial data should be given some measurements of past activity in order to make their own predictions or evaluate the predictions of others.

6.   Finally, in a world of uncertainty, expectations are dependent at least in part on the state of optimism or pessimism existing at the time. A consistent treatment of uncertainty from one period to another would be difficult to accomplish.[15]

Market valuation of the firm.   As an alternative to the capitalization of future cash flows, it may be possible to determine what investors may be willing to pay for the entire firm. Thus, the expectations of others are substituted for the expectations of the accountant. However, even if such valuations were obtainable, it would be difficult to separate the income based on the subjective rate of return from the change in value arising from changes in expectations. The burden of subjective determination is passed to persons other than the accountants; otherwise, it has all of the difficulties of the capitalization method.

An alternative is to measure the value of the firm by multiplying the number of shares outstanding by the market price of the stock as determined by exchange markets. The advantage of this procedure is that a verifiable valuation can be obtained that is based on the market's evaluation of future cash flows to stockholders. This is different from the capitalization method because the opportunity rate of return and the adjustment for risk in the market may be different than the accountant's subjective discount rate. Another major difference is that the quoted market price represents the price of a few shares, but does not imply that all shares could be purchased at that price. Thus, this method has many of the disadvantages associated with the capitalization process except for its

---

[15] For a further discussion of valuation on the basis of discounted expected cash flows, see Chapter 11.

verifiability. But verifiability may be offset by a lack of freedom from bias, particularly since stock prices are affected by external and capricious factors.

Current cash equivalent. As another alternative to the capitalization of a firm, the firm's capital can be defined as the sum of the money or cash equivalent of all assets less the sum of the money equivalent of the liabilities. The current cash equivalent can be defined as the market selling price or realizable price of the assets held by the firm.[16] By computing the net assets of the firm at the end of the period and subtracting the net assets computed in a similar fashion at the beginning of the period, and adjusting for capital transactions, the income for the period can be determined.[17]

The value of the firm determined by the summation of market prices is assumed to be more objective or verifiable than the capitalized value of the firm, because these prices depend upon the expectations of others outside the firm. Note that these are opportunity cost values. They represent values for which the existing assets could be exchanged in the market. The capitalized value of the firm would normally be greater than the sum of the market prices of the specific assets, because if it were not, the firm would be better off by selling its assets in the market. This difference is due, in part, to the exclusion of goodwill and other intangibles that do not have market prices separate from the summation of asset prices. However, it may also be due to the evaluations of expectations, the selections of discount factors, and the adjustments for risk, as well as costs involved in the sale and transfer of specific assets.

In addition to the increased verifiability by the use of cash equivalents, the computation of income by comparing changes in the market prices of assets and liabilities has the advantage of providing a better basis for judging the alternatives open to management. But it provides a limited basis for the prediction of future changes because it does not disclose the nature of the changes arising in prior periods.

A major disadvantage of using market valuations is the lack of a ready market for many of the assets owned by a firm. For many items of plant and equipment, the only market prices available would probably represent liquidation or forced-sale values rather than the price that could be obtained in organized markets. As a result, the income would be similar to the income that would be obtained if the firm were liquidated at the end of each period and then started over with the liquidation valuations for the next period.

Historical input prices. An assumed concept of wealth maintenance similar to that accepted in practice is the use of input prices either in

---

[16] See Raymond J. Chambers, *Accounting, Evaluation and Economic Behavior* (Englewood Cliffs, N.J.: Prentice-Hall, 1966), p. 92.

[17] Ibid., pp. 112–14.

terms of historical costs or current costs (less depreciation where necessary). It should be emphasized that although this appears to have the structure of the other capital maintenance concepts, it is not subject to real-world interpretation because of the reliance on depreciation allocations and a concept of realization.[18] The resulting income computation is based on structural rules rather than reality. It is discussed here because it is frequently discussed as financial capital maintenance with income representing the difference between beginning and ending valuations.

In the absence of price changes, real invested capital is assumed to be maintained if the assets at the end of the period, expressed in terms of input prices (costs), are equal to the total input prices of the assets at the beginning of the period. Income is reflected in an increase in these values adjusted for capital transactions and dividend payments. This income results from the conversion of input prices into market values by the process of sale and exchange. Cash and receivables are received in exchange for the assets valued at cost. Therefore, some of the asset values at the end of the period as well as some at the beginning (the monetary assets) are expressed in terms of market values (output prices).

The computation of income by the comparison of net asset values at the end of the period with those at the beginning of the period results in a concept of income that is all-inclusive. No classification of income by source can be made. Some of the net income will be the result of normal operations, and a part will arise from abnormal transactions and from capital gains resulting from unexpected value changes. If assets are expressed in terms of historical costs, however, only so-called realized capital gains and losses will be included.

Current input prices. When the inputs are expressed in terms of current values, the computation of income is the same as with historical costs, but the income resulting includes holding gains and losses arising from price changes—whether or not these holding gains and losses have been realized through sale or exchange. That is, the income will include gains and losses from the holding of assets as well as the normal operating profit.[19] By expressing the asset values at the beginning of the period in terms of end-of-period input costs, some of these gains and losses can be eliminated; but unless adjustments are made for changes in input values of costs incurred during the period, capital gains and losses will still be included.

Maintenance of constant purchasing power. One of the arguments of economists is that income should be measured in real terms, rather than in terms of maintaining monetary values. When changes in the general level of prices occur, the measurement of income by comparing

---

[18] See Chapters 8 and 15 for further discussion of the lack of real-world interpretation of these concepts.

[19] See *AICPA Professional Standards,* para. 1072.100.

capital values at different times in terms of the monetary unit at each time results in measurements that do not represent changes in real capital. Therefore, many suggestions have been made for the adjustment of capital values so that income can be measured in terms of a constant purchasing power or in terms of a constant value of the monetary unit. These suggestions and the problems involved in making adjustments for changes in the purchasing power of money are discussed at greater length in Chapter 9.

Summary.   All of the wealth maintenance concepts of income require an evaluation of total or specific assets and liabilities at the beginning and end of each period. The measurement of capital is based on expectations regarding future cash flows or on market prices as substitutes for subjective expectations. A part of current accounting practice is devised and defended on the basis of the capital maintenance concepts. However, aside from some of the theoretical difficulties with the capital maintenance concepts, a practical disadvantage is their inability to provide adequate information regarding the specific operational activities of the firm.

Income as a measurement of efficiency

The efficient operation of an enterprise affects both the current dividend stream and the use of the invested capital for providing a future dividend stream. Therefore, all equity holders, but particularly the common stockholders, are interested in the efficiency of management. The present equity holders can take the necessary steps to obtain a new management if the present management is not operating efficiently, or they may provide for incentives or bonuses to efficient managements. Prospective stockholders will attempt to evaluate the efficiency of management before investing or placing a value on the stock of the firm. In either case, a measurement of the efficiency of the firm provides a basis for decisions. This objective of measuring the efficiency of a firm is reflected in *FASB Statement of Financing Accounting Concepts No. 1*. It states that "Financial Reporting should provide information about an enterprise's financial performance during a period."[20]

Efficiency has a real-world referent at least in concept. One of its interpretations is that it represents the relative ability to obtain the maximum output with a given amount of resources, a constant output with the use of a minimum amount of resources, or an optimum combination of resources together with a given demand for the product (and therefore price) to permit a maximum return to owners. However, with this concept of income as a goal, how could a measurement of past income provide a basis for determining the efficiency of a firm? *Efficiency* is a relative term and has meaning only when compared with an ideal or some other base. It also depends on whether the goal of the firm is to maximize income or to

---

[20] *AICPA Professional Standards,* para. 1210.42.

provide a fair or reasonable return on investment. If the capital employed by the firm is constant from year to year, the income figure itself may be useful as a measure of the efficiency of the firm. The income of the current year can then be compared with prior years, and some judgment would have to be made whether the income of any year has reached, exceeded, or fallen short of the proper goal. However, if the capital invested changes from year to year, the income must be compared with some changing magnitude, such as invested capital or total revenue.

When net income is divided by invested capital, the result is called the rate of return on investment. This can be computed by dividing the net income to stockholders by the stockholders' equity—the rate of return on stockholders' investment—or by dividing the net income plus interest (net of taxes) by the total capitalization of the firm, including long-term debt and stockholder equity—the rate of return on total equity. In either case, a measurement of the efficient utilization of the capital employed in the enterprise is thought to be obtained. But, again, the criterion of efficiency depends upon the standard used. The rate of return for prior years, the rate of return earned by other firms, an arbitrary rate, or a market-determined rate can be used as the standard. One important aspect of the rate of return as a measure of efficiency should be noted. Its validity depends upon not only the proper measurement of income, but also the proper measurement of capital employed in the business.

Another base for comparing income is the total revenue of the period. Although the total revenue of the period can be measured more accurately than the capital invested, using total revenue as a base has some definite disadvantages. A comparison of the net income to sales for several years is valid only if capacity utilization is the same each year or if the failure to utilize capacity is considered a part of the inefficiency of management. Comparisons with other firms are even more difficult to make. Only if the capital turnover (sales divided by capital) is the same for several firms, would the ratio of income to sales be comparable. As this is not likely, this ratio is not valid for interfirm comparisons.

BEHAVIORAL CONCEPTS OF INCOME

Behavioral concepts of income relate to the decision processes of investors and creditors, the reactions of securities prices in organized markets to income reporting, the capital expenditure decisions of management, and the feedback reactions of management and accountants. It should be kept in mind that all theories should in the long run be based on concepts that have interpretive significance; behavioral theories of income cannot be valid in the long run without a real-world concept of income and a verification of the behavioral implications. In 1938, a radio program depicted a landing in New Jersey of men from Mars. Many people who had not heard the beginning of the program thought it was real, and the result was near panic. Theories of handling a panic could be applied immediately, but the long-run solution was to convince people that the Martians were fictitious. If income reporting is based on fiction, the behavioral theories cannot prove their significance in the long run. But let us look at some of the behavioral implications of income as reported in the literature.

Income as a predictive device

FASB Statement of Financial Concepts No. 1 states that investors, creditors, and others are concerned with assessing the prospects for enterprise net cash inflows, but that they often use earnings to help them evaluate earning power, predict future earnings, or assess the risk of investing in or lending to the enterprise.[21] Thus, there is an assumed relationship between reported income and cash flows, including cash distributed to owners.

The current value of a firm and the value of a share of stock in the firm are dependent upon the expected future stream of distributions to stockholders. Based on these expectations, a current stockholder may decide either to sell the shares or continue to hold them. An investor who is not currently a stockholder may decide either to purchase shares in the firm or to invest the capital elsewhere. Thus, expectations regarding future distributions are paramount in these investment decisions. If there is a relationship between reported income and dividend distributions, investors may focus their attention on their expectations regarding future incomes of the firm. For many firms, income predictions are assumed to be more relevant in predicting the future market price of stock than are predictions of short-term dividend distributions; and long-term distributions are assumed to be dependent upon retained income and growth factors. Therefore, expectations of future incomes are used by many investors as a main factor in predicting future dividend distributions, and expected dividends are an important factor in placing a current value on shares of stock or on the entire firm.

Bondholders and short-term creditors are also interested in the future income. The greater the expectation of income for the firm, the greater the expectation that the creditors will receive their annual return and also the greater the expectation that they will receive repayment of the principal when the debt matures.

Can a knowledge of past incomes aid in the prediction of future incomes and thus in the current value of the firm? A recent study concluded that past values of accounting income computed on the basis of historical costs provide a better predictor of future values of the same series than do past values of income computed on the basis of current costs. Both models were shown to be superior to general price-level adjusted income.[22] How-

---

[21] *AICPA Professional Standards*, paras. 1210.43 and 1210.46.

[22] Dale Buckmaster, Ronald M. Copeland, and Paul E. Dascher, "The Relative Predictive Ability of Three Accounting Income Models," *Accounting and Business Research,* Summer 1977, pp. 177–86.

ever, the study suggests that both concepts of income can be useful in predicting future values of the same series, particularly on an industry basis. However, projection assumes either that the future values being predicted are good surrogates for a meaningful concept of income that has real-world significance or that the projected accounting concept of income is relevant in the decision processes of investors. There is no evidence that either of these conditions prevails. However, since many investors believe that a prediction of future reported incomes is relevant to an evaluation of a firm's stock in buy-sell decisions, many writers suggest that there is some validity in the presentation of a measurement of income that will permit projections of future income. It is this concept of predictive ability that has led to arguments for the smoothing of periodic income.[23] Whereas smoothing is advocated as appropriate also for internal measurement and control, its defense for external reporting purposes rests on the assumption that income is an indicator of future cash flows and that capital asset values are related to the expected stream of future cash flows including a future sale price of the security. In the author's opinion, smoothing hides more information than it discloses. Information regarding variability of activity from year to year is relevant in an evaluation of risk and therefore in the decision process.

Other behavioral concepts

A number of theories proposed in recent years have behavioral implications. Because of space limitations, it is impossible to give adequate discussions to each of these or even provide a complete list of the many approaches suggested in the literature. The following is a summary of a few of these theories.

1. **Managerial decision making.** The formal financial statements are directed primarily to the external users of accounting data, but accountants must also furnish management with the tools and raw material required for control and rendering good decisions. Just as the investor is interested primarily in future dividend flows, so also is management interested primarily in what will happen in the future. Decisions can affect only future events. But management is not so interested in predicting future dividends as it is in making decisions to meet its goals regarding current and future cash flows.

To the extent that income is used by managements for decision and control purposes, care should be taken to assure that the arbitrariness of allocations and matching are minimized or made neutral. Neutrality is achieved only if the decisions are not affected by the allocations and matching procedures applied in the measurement of income. If this can-

---

[23] See, for example, Carl R. Beidleman, "Income Smoothing: The Role of Management," *Accounting Review,* October 1973, p. 653. *Smoothing* can be defined as the use of alternative procedures and measurements to minimize variability of accounting income.

not be avoided, income should not be used as a basis for managerial decisions.

Managements do, however, react to what they consider the behavior of investors and creditors to reported income. Even though the reported income is based only on the accounting structure, the feedback phenomenon will affect the choice of accounting methods by management. For example, many firms believe that the price of their shares will be maximized if the reported net income grows at a constant rate each year. Consequently, they choose available accounting policies and procedures to report income that meets this goal or report earnings per share figures that will create the greatest demand for their stock.[24] The smoothing of reported income figures over time is frequently a goal based on the premise that investors will pay more for stock if the reported income deviates very little over time from a constant or growth trend than if the reported income varies widely from year to year.

2. Estimation theory.[25]   Although estimation theory appears to have some similarity to the capitalization theory of income, its emphasis is on the presentation of reported income that will permit investors to predict the internal rate of return for the firm as a whole and thus predict future cash flows and the firm's present value. Note that it differs from the capitalization approach in that the internal rate of return is used, rather than an opportunity rate. Depreciation and other allocations are computed in such a way that the overall internal rate of return is constant for the firm as a whole. Therefore, the reported ratio of income to book value is also constant, since this reflects the internal rate of return.

The advantage of estimation theory is that because it does not require a severe break from traditional accounting income, a transition to its use should be easier than proposals for severe reformulations of accounting statements. It also has the advantage that it avoids most of the interaction problems relating to the reporting of revenues and expenses because income is computed from aggregate revenue and expense data only. But this also appears as a disadvantage to those who are accustomed to income computations based on individual revenue and expense allocations. It also has its limitations in that the accountants' forecasts of future cash flows are needed to estimate the internal rate of return. This is then coded in the statements with the hope that investors will be able to decode the information without significant information loss. Would it not be easier for accountants to report their forecasts directly?[26]

---

[24] For many examples of the misuse of accounting to influence and even deceive investors, see Abraham J. Briloff, *Unaccountable Accounting* (New York: Harper & Row, 1972), and Anthony Sampson, *The Sovereign State of ITT* (New York: Stein and Day, 1973), p. 142.

[25] See, for example, Richard P. Brief and Joel Owen, "A Reformation of the Estimation Problem," *Journal of Accounting Research,* Spring 1973, pp. 1–15.

[26] Arthur L. Thomas, "The Allocation Problem: Part Two," *Studies in Accounting Research No. 9* (AAA, 1974), p. 107.

3. User-orientation approaches. Direct and indirect observations suggest that reported earnings per share and projected earnings per share have a direct impact on the market price of common shares and are in demand by individual investors even though the efficient markets hypothesis implies that individuals cannot gain by a knowledge of this information. However, in the semistrong form of the efficient markets hypothesis (security prices fully reflect all publicly available information about the firm), the use of the information content of reported income is assumed on the basis of market reactions to this information. Several empirical studies have suggested that reported earnings per share or projected earnings per share do have a direct impact on the market price of common shares.[27]

Another user-oriented approach is the theory that accounting reports should present the information demanded by users comparable to the concept of consumer sovereignty in economics. Even though accounting income may have no semantic interpretation, users may want this information for several reasons. (*a*) Reported accounting income has become a basis for many legal and contractual relationships in society; to this extent, it has behavioral implications even though it may not have semantic interpretation. (*b*) Investors, rightly or wrongly, perceive a relationship between changes in accounting income and the firm's cash flows including the payment of dividends. (*c*) Investors may demand income information if only because they believe that other investors use that information in decision models or that other investors believe that there is semantic relevance in income numbers.

WHAT SHOULD BE INCLUDED IN INCOME?

The computation of income by an annual valuation of the firm raises important questions regarding the proper valuation methods that provide the most meaningful measurement of net income. A more important limitation of the annual valuation procedure is the inability to reveal the nature and composition of income necessary in meeting the objective of predictability discussed earlier in this chapter. The transactions approach, on the other hand, makes it possible to record changes when specific events occur and to summarize these changes in financial statements according to the nature of the firm's activities.

One of the major objectives of business enterprise is the maximization of the dividend flow to stockholders over the entire life of the enterprise, or the maximization of the liquidation value or market value of the enterprise at the end of its life, or at intermediate points, or some combination of these. All economic changes are relevant for an evaluation of the over-

---

[27] See, for example, Ray Ball and Philip Brown, "An Empirical Evaluation of Accounting Income Numbers," *Journal of Accounting Research,* Autumn 1968, pp. 159–78.

all success or failure of the enterprise over its lifetime. But the more common objectives of income measurement require a measurement of income for shorter periods of time in order to provide a means of control and a basis for decisions of stockholders, creditors, and management on a continuing or periodic basis. The overall measurement of income for the entire life of the enterprise does not provide the information when it is most useful, nor does it describe the causes of success or failure. Success may be the result of good fortune or efficient management. The sources or causes of income are thus important in a proper evaluation of the progress of the firm. But some accountants have held that the figure called "net income for the period" should include all recorded economic events and that income arising from specific sources should be labeled properly. This controversy has led to two basic concepts of income—the current operating concept and the all-inclusive concept of income—and an intermediate position required in *Accounting Principles Board Opinion No. 30* and *FASB Statement No. 16*.

The current operating concept of income.   The current operating concept of income focuses on the measurement of the efficiency of the business enterprise. The term *efficiency* relates to the effective utilization of the firm's resources in operating the business and earning a profit. In the broad economic sense, it relates to the proper combination of the factors of production—land, labor, capital, and management. An evaluation of relative efficiency, however, requires a comparison with a given standard or ideal. This necessarily requires some subjective evaluation, but as a starting point, comparisons can be made with the results of previous periods and with the incomes of other firms or industries.

In the computation of income, particular emphasis is placed on the terms *current* and *operating*. Only those value changes and events that are controllable by management and that result from decisions of the *current* period should be included. However, this statement must be qualified to include the use of factors acquired in a prior period but used in the current period. Each period is not a separate economic experience. Most of the capital equipment and even the services of most of the workers will have been obtained or contracted for in prior periods. The decisions of the current period involve the proper use and combination of these factors. The changes that should be excluded are those that actually arose in prior periods but were not recognized or recorded previously. For example, equipment that is discovered to be obsolete in the current period may have become obsolete in prior periods. The decision to abandon its use in the current period may be the result of efficient management and, therefore, this is not an operating event of the current period. Likewise, recognition of an error in the computation of a prior period's income is not a reflection on the efficiency of management in the current period. But one note of caution—errors in the computation of income for prior periods do affect the evaluation of the efficiency of management in those prior periods.

The second aspect of this concept is that the relevant changes arise only from *normal* operations. A better comparison can be made with other years and with other firms if the net income relates only to the regular operations. Also, it is here that the relative efficiency of management shows up best. While nonoperating activities may also be affected by managerial efficiency, it is more difficult to obtain a standard with which to measure the period results. At least, a different standard must be used, and this requires a separation of the results of the operating and nonoperating activities. It is also frequently suggested that nonoperating activities should be reported separately because they are nonrecurring. This is really a different reason for separate classification, and it is discussed more fully below. If nonrecurring items arise from normal operations, the current operating performance concept of income should include them to provide a good measure of the firm's earning power and a means of projecting and evaluating income trends.

Proponents of the current operating concept suggest that the resulting reported net income is more meaningful for interperiod and interfirm comparisons and for making predictions. They also suggest that although classification of operating and nonoperating items may be difficult, the trained accountant is in a better position to make this classification than outsiders or nonaccountants. There should be full disclosure of noncurrent and nonoperating items, but financial analysts and other users of accounting data frequently emphasize one figure for the net income for the year. Thus, it is proposed that if only one figure is quoted, the current operating net income is more useful as a measure of current operating performance.

The all-inclusive concept of income (comprehensive income).   The all-inclusive concept of income is defined as the total change in proprietorship recognized by the recording of transactions or the revaluation of the firm during a specific period, except for dividend distributions and capital transactions. All changes in the retained earnings section of the stockholders' equity should arise from either net income, dividend distributions, appropriations of net income, or the return of appropriations to "free" retained earnings. If a classification of operating and nonoperating or recurring and nonrecurring items is desirable, it should be made in the income statement before arriving at the figure labeled "net income for the period."

Proponents of the all-inclusive concept of income claim the following reasons for this measurement of income:

1.   The annual reported net incomes, when added together for the life of the enterprise, should be equal to the total net income of the enterprise. It is claimed that the charges resulting from extraordinary events and from corrections of prior periods tend to exceed the credits, resulting in an overstatement of the net income for a series of years if these are omitted.

2.   The omission of certain charges and credits from the computation of net income lends itself to possible manipulation or smoothing of the

annual earnings figures. This fear has been well-founded in recent years.[28]

3.   An income statement that includes all income charges and credits recognized during the year is said to be easier to prepare and more easily understood by the readers. It is not subject to the personal judgments of management or the accountants preparing the statement. This is based on the assumption that accounting statements should be as verifiable as possible; several accountants working independently on the same figures should be able to arrive at similar results.

4.   With full disclosure of the nature of income changes during the year, the reader of the statements is assumed to be more capable of making appropriate classifications to arrive at an appropriate measurement of income than are the accountants and management, who cannot anticipate the specific needs of the users.

5.   The distinction between operating and nonoperating charges and credits is not clear-cut. Transactions classified as operating by one firm may be classified as nonoperating by another firm. Furthermore, items classified as nonoperating in one year may be classified as operating by the same firm in a subsequent year. This, in itself, leads to inconsistencies in making comparisons among different firms or over several periods for the same firm. But the definition of operating income becomes even more clouded when we look beyond the trees and see that some extraordinary events are really ordinary and expected over a longer period of time and that the frequent occurrence of "nonoperating" events may be normal to business operations. The family can budget its entire income for the normal family requirements, such as food, housing, clothing, and entertainment; special items such as medical bills, car repairs, and semiannual payments for property taxes are not normal expenditure items in any one single month. If the budget, however, does not include provisions for these extraordinary items, the family may soon be in financial difficulties. Each item may be extraordinary for any single month, but as a group, the extraordinary items become normal.

A major difference between the current operating and the all-inclusive concepts of income is in the assumed objective for reporting net income. While the current operating net income emphasizes the current operating performance or efficiency of the firm and the possible use of this figure for predicting the future performance and earning power, the proponents of the all-inclusive net income claim that both the operating efficiency and the prediction of future performance can be improved if they are based on the entire historical experience of the firm over a series of years. Because the useful lives of assets usually extend over many periods and because income-producing transactions are not at uniform stages of completion at the end of each period, the net income of a single period is, at best, an estimate based on good judgment. Because of this necessarily subjective

---

[28] See Briloff, *Unaccountable Accounting,* pp. 178 and 194–95.

nature of accounting, the net income of a single period is tentative and always subject to verification at later dates.

Recurring and nonrecurring income. The proponents of the current operating performance concept of income frequently claim that operating items are generally defined as recurrent features of business operations and that nonoperating items are generally considered to be irregular and unpredictable. However, this is not necessarily true. Many items may be operating in nature, but not necessarily recurring. The necessity to pay overtime labor rates during a rush period and the acquisition of raw materials under extremely fortunate circumstances are both operating events, but are possibly nonrecurring. On the other hand, some nonoperating events are recurring in nature. Annual floods in unavoidably hazardous areas may result in nonoperating charges, but they are recurring in nature.

A net income figure based on recurring events is generally more useful to investors in predicting possible future income and dividend flows. Recurring nonoperating events are just as important as those recurring events that are the result of normal operations. The distinction between operating and nonoperating, however, is more useful for measuring management efficiency. The assumption upon which this statement is based is that operating events tend to be more controllable than nonoperating events. This, of course, may also be disputed in many instances.

The advantage of classifying income charges and credits as recurring or nonrecurring is based upon the improved usefulness of the resulting net income figure in the making of predictions by investors. It is probably more difficult for outsiders to distinguish between recurring and nonrecurring events than it is for them to distinguish between operating and nonoperating items.

The disadvantages of the classification and reporting of recurring income are similar to the disadvantages of the current operating concept of income. These disadvantages can be readily recognized in the above discussion of the all-inclusive concept of income.

Prior period adjustments. The FASB has come very close to the adoption of the all-inclusive concept of income for annual reporting purposes in *Statement No. 16,* which states that, with only two exceptions, all items of profit and loss recognized during an annual period shall be included in the computation of the annual earnings.[29] The main exception is the correction of an error in the financial statements of a prior period. An *error* is defined as a mathematical mistake, a mistake in the application of accounting principles, or oversight or misuse of facts that existed when the financial statements were prepared.

The FASB apparently attempted to leave little room for judgment re-

---

[29] *AICPA Professional Standards,* para. 2014.10. Special exceptions are made for prior interim periods of the current year.

garding classification as a prior period adjustment. Thus, the emphasis is on objectivity and verifiability of the reported net income, rather than on its predictability. That is, reported earnings computations are not based on the current operating performance concept. Corrections of estimations and measurements of prior periods are included in the reported income of the current period. Therefore, there appears to be no reason why corrections of errors should not also be included in the computation of reported income. It might be better to follow an all-inclusive concept completely, rather than follow it for some items and exclude others on the basis of the current operating concept.

Following the implications of the efficient markets hypothesis, disclosure of prior period corrections is sufficient to impound the information in the market prices. It does not really matter whether the items are disclosed in the income statement or in the statement of retained earnings. However, it can be argued that the income statement is a primary statement and that disclosure within that statement is more prominent than disclosure within the retained earnings statement. On the other hand, it can be argued that, because of possible functional fixation on the net income figure, noncurrent items should be excluded if it can be done objectively without permitting manipulation of reported income.

Extraordinary items. *APB Opinion No. 30* defined an extraordinary item as including events and transactions that are both infrequent (or nonrecurring) and unusual (or not related to normal operations). Both criteria must be met in the classification of extraordinary items. The objective apparently was to restrict the use of this classification to unusual items that may affect predictability but will not permit the use of management discretion in determining the computation of net income before extraordinary items.

However, the theoretical reason for this separate classification is not clear. Since unusual items that do recur are included in the computation of net income before extraordinary items, this partitioning of net income does not reflect current operating income. Furthermore, since items that are nonrecurring but of a normal nature are not separately disclosed, the ability to meet the predictability objective is weakened. For example, a significant nonrecurring increase in an operating item would be included in the results of normal operations. Therefore, the separation of extraordinary items from other income statement items does not result in a separation of recurring and nonrecurring items, nor a separation of operating from nonoperating activities. However, an emphasis on behavioral characteristics of at least some items is a step in the right direction. Nevertheless, a movement toward a greater recognition of the separate disclosure of recurring and nonrecurring items is apparent.[30] The purpose

---

[30] See, for example, *FASB Discussion Memorandum* "Reported Earnings," July 31, 1979 and *FASB Statement of Financial Accounting Concepts No. 3,* "Elements of Financial Statements of Business Enterprises," *AICPA, Professional Standards,* para. 1230.152.

would be to permit greater evaluation of the components of net income, rather than an emphasis on the bottom-line amount. This is consistent with the efficient market thesis and also might minimize the effect of functional fixation.

Net income to whom?

Stemming from the proprietary approach to accounting, net income has usually been assumed to mean net earnings or net profits accruing to current stockholders or owners of the business. However, there may be valid reasons for the presentation of a net income figure that represents net earnings to a narrower or broader group of recipients.

The value-added concept of income.   Broadly speaking, it is possible to view the enterprise as having a large group of claimants or interested parties, including not only owners and other investors, but also employees and landlords of rented property. This is the value-added approach.[31] In economic terms, value added is the market price of the output of an enterprise less the price of the goods and services acquired by transfer from other firms. Thus, all employees, owners, creditors, and governments (through taxation) are recipients of the enterprise income. This is the total pie that can be divided among the various contributors of factor inputs to the enterprise in the production of goods and services. How this pie is divided is usually subject to contractual agreements and bargaining.

This concept becomes most meaningful when it is applied to the very large corporations that affect the lives of thousands of individuals and have a general social and economic significance beyond the narrow interests of the owners or stockholders. The value-added income would include wages, rent, interest, taxes, dividends paid to stockholders, and undistributed earnings of the corporation. A question arises regarding the nature of retained earnings in this concept. It does not necessarily accrue to the owners alone, but also to all of the other recipients or claimants of corporate value added. Only in the case of liquidation do common stockholders have the residual claims. In the long run, the retention of earnings provides for a growth in the firm's capital, which through increased productivity may provide increased flows of income to all recipients. If the corporation is assumed to have perpetual or indefinite life, the stockholders may never receive the direct and sole benefit from the retention of earnings in the business.

Enterprise net income.   According to the 1957 statement of the American Accounting Association, " . . . interest charges, income taxes, and true profit-sharing distributions are not determinants of enterprise net

---

[31] Michael F. Morley, *The Value-Added Statement: A Review of Its Use in Corporate Reports* (London: Gee & Co., 1978).

income.[32] The conclusion follows, then, that these items are distributions of net income, rather than deductions before arriving at net income. It also follows that stockholders, holders of long-term debt, and governments are beneficiaries of the corporation.

This concept of net income has an advantage from the point of view of separating the financial aspects of the corporation from the operating. The net income to the enterprise is an operating concept of net income. Interest to debt holders and earnings to stockholders are financial in nature. Income taxes are neither financial nor strictly operating; and their exclusion from the computation of enterprise net income has some merit because they do not represent controllable input costs. But the treatment of governments as beneficiaries of the corporation when employees and other groups are excluded is of dubious merit from a logical point of view.

Net income to investors.   In accordance with the entity concept of the business enterprise, both stockholders and holders of long-term debt are considered equally as investors of permanent capital. With the separation of ownership and control in the large corporation, the differences between stockholders and debt holders are no longer as important as they once were. The main differences arise in the priorities of claims against income and against assets in liquidation. With the emphasis on the observed indefinite life of most large corporations, the claims in liquidation become less important. When we observe the claims against income more closely, we find that the differences between many bond issues and some preferred stock issues are quite fuzzy. Holders of income bonds, for example, may have less security in their claim against income than some holders of cumulative preferred stock, and holders of convertible bonds may obtain rights in undistributed earnings by converting their interests to common stockholder claims.

In the entity concept, income to investors includes the interest on debt, dividends to preferred and common stockholders, and the undivided remainder. This concept of income has considerable merit for several purposes: (1) The decisions regarding the sources of long-term capital are financial rather than operating matters. Therefore, the net income to investors reflects more clearly the results of operations. (2) Because of differing financial structures, comparisons among firms can be made more readily by using this concept of income. (3) The rate of return on total investment computed from this concept of income portrays the relative efficiency of invested capital better than does the rate of return to stockholders.

In the computation of net income to investors, income taxes are treated as expenses. This is the treatment recommended by the APB and adopted

---

[32] Committee on Accounting Concepts and Standards, *Accounting and Reporting Standards for Corporate Financial Statements and Preceding Statements and Supplements* (AAA, 1957), p. 5.

by the FASB.[33] It is the author's opinion that this is the realistic position. The government is not a beneficiary of the corporation in the same way that investors are. The corporation does receive direct benefit from the government, although not in direct proportion to the amount of the tax. The right to operate in a viable economy and to obtain the protection of the courts and obtain protection from external force and violence are only a few of these benefits. Furthermore, corporate income *after* taxes is much more stable—by industries—than income before taxes; income taxes seem to be "passed on" much as other expenses.[34] Also, both investors and managers seem to make most of their decisions on the basis of income after taxes.

Net income to stockholders.   The most traditional and accepted viewpoint of net income is that it represents the return to the owners of the business. Although this concept has its firm foundation in the proprietary approach, many authors apply it to the entity approach and consider the accounting profit of the entity to be a liability to the owners.[35] Implicit in the *Statements* of the FASB is the concept that net income accrues to all stockholders. *FASB Statement of Financial Accounting Concepts No. 1* emphasized the predictive nature of reported earnings. It states, for example, that in addition to being used to evaluate management's performance, reported earnings may be used to predict future earnings, to predict the long-term earning ability of the enterprise, or to evaluate the risks of investing in or lending to the enterprise.[36]

The concept of net income to shareholders also has its support in the field of economics. Although the definition of *economic profits* is different from that of *accounting profits,* economists usually treat accounting profits statistically as the total return to the entrepreneurs in their various roles as managers, investors of capital, risk takers, and rentiers. It may or may not be desirable, but it is a realistic fact that the users of accounting statements usually interpret net income to mean the return to shareholders.

Net income to residual equity holders.   In financial statements presented primarily for stockholders and investors, the net income available for distribution to common stockholders is usually thought to be the most important single figure in the statements. Net income per share of common stock and dividends per share are the most commonly quoted figures

---

[33] *AICPA Professional Standards,* p. 8795, sec. 4091 13.

[34] See Marian Krzyzaniak and Richard A. Musgrave, *The Shifting of the Corporation Income Tax* (Baltimore: Johns Hopkins Press, 1963), pp. 65–66.

[35] See, for example, Stephen Gilman, *Accounting Concepts of Profit* (New York: Ronald Press, 1939), p. 598.

[36] *AICPA Professional Standards,* vol. 3, para. 1210.47.

in financial news, along with the market price per share. Therefore, there is pragmatic support for presenting statements from which the net income to residual equity holders can readily be obtained.

In a profitable enterprise with indefinite life, the residual equity holder would be the common stockholder or an investor who can become a common stockholder through conversion or exercise of other rights. But there is always the possibility that through reorganization, or because of default in the payment of preferred claims, one of the other groups of investors—preferred stockholders or bondholders—might become the residual equity holders. Therefore, the priorities in the claims to income are important to all groups. The residual net income indicates the degree of security of the priority claims as well as the amount available for distribution to the residual claimants.

The holders of common stock and the prospective buyers of common stock are interested primarily in the future flow of dividends. Normally, only a part of the residual net income is distributed as dividends, but the knowledge of the net income available and the financial policy of the corporation may provide useful information to common stockholders in their evaluation of the firm and in their prediction of the total amount of annual dividend distributions in the future. However, in order to predict the amount of dividends he may receive in the future, an investor must also predict the number of shares that will be outstanding in each period. To the extent that there are outstanding senior stock or debt securities convertible into common shares or stock options, warrants, or agreements for the sale of common stock at less than market prices, a potential dilution of earnings per share and dividends per share exists. *APB Opinion No. 15* recognized this potential dilution and recommended that supplementary pro forma computations of earnings per share should be presented, showing what the earnings per share would have been if the conversions or options had been executed. The computation of earnings per share when potential dilution is present is discussed at greater length in Chapter 20.

Thus, although it is possible to view current net income as the return to current outstanding stockholders, potential residual equity holders must be taken into consideration in predictions regarding future earnings and dividends per share. Furthermore, if current net income is not distributed to current stockholders, the amount added to retained earnings may be shared by these potential holders of common stock.

Summary of net income classification by income recipients. The following tabulation summarizes the several concepts of corporate income classified by the income recipients. Note that the value-added concept requires the recognition of income during production, as all product values are expressed in terms of selling prices. The other concepts are more liberal in their acceptance of the several methods of income recognition.

Income concept	Income included	Income recipients
Value added.	Selling price of firm's product less cost of goods and services acquired by transfer.	All employees, owners, creditors, and governments.
Enterprise net income.	Excess of revenues over expenses; all gains and losses. Expenses do not include interest charges, income taxes, and true profit-sharing distributions.	Stockholders, bondholders, and governments.
Net income to investors.	Same as enterprise net income, but after deducting income taxes.	Stockholders and holders of long-term debt.
Net income to shareholders.	Net income to investors less interest charges and profit-sharing distributions.	Stockholders (preferred and common).
Net income to residual equity holders.	Net income to shareholders less preferred dividends.	Current and potential common stockholders unless priority payments cannot be met.

SUMMARY OF CONCEPTS OF ENTERPRISE INCOME

The concept of income most appropriate for reporting financial operations of business enterprises is determined largely by the objectives of the intended recipients of the summarized accounting data and the interpretive content of the reported amount. A concept useful for one group of individuals or for one purpose may not be the best choice for another. The main questions regarding the choice of an appropriate concept of income are: (1) What are the major objectives of income reporting? (2) What are the basic elements of each of the several income concepts, and how well do they meet the objectives? (3) What types of changes should be included in or excluded from the computation of net income? (4) Who are the major income recipients? This last question is, of course, related to the objectives of income reporting.

A common objective of income reporting is that it should be the result of rules and procedures that are logical and internally consistent. It is assumed that if users of financial statements understand these rules, they will be able to interpret the meaning of income. Since accounting income is based on such concepts as revenue realization and the matching of expenses with revenues, it is generally assumed that the major activities of the firm can be measured and reported as well as aggregate firm activity.

A necessary long-run objective of an income concept is that it should be related to real-world observations. Two basic interpretive concepts are as follows: (1) The wealth maintenance concepts are assumed by many to be most basic because they derive their support from economic theory. Changes in the capitalized value of expected cash receipts serve as the foundation of this concept; however, current market prices and similar alternatives are frequently justified on the basis that they represent surrogates (reasonably acceptable substitutes) for current value. (2) Net income and its components are frequently used as measures of the efficiency of management. Efficiency has interpretive meaning in the economic sense of the optimum utilization of limited resources.

As a third major objective, income should be evaluated on the basis of behavioral dimensions. One behavioral characteristic is predictive ability. The net incomes of several periods may be useful in the making of predictions regarding the future operations of a firm if proper care is taken to include other relevant factors. Investors may be interested in predicting future incomes or future dividends and share prices. Other groups may wish to make predictions regarding the solvency or other characteristics relevant to decisions regarding relationships with the firm. A similar characteristic is the assumption that income should be closely tied to cash or funds flows. Cash flow activity is considered more relevant in the investment decisions than attempts to measure value changes directly. This concept will be discussed at greater length in Chapter 10. Other behavioral characteristics include managerial decision making, the relationship of income changes to market prices, and the demand for income figures by investors regardless of their lack of interpretive content.

A final argument is that all concepts of income are both theoretically and practically unsound in the presentation of relevant information to investors and others. That is, they either lack the necessary real-world interpretation or they are not relevant because they lack the necessary behavioral characteristics. Alternative information systems are suggested that may permit the readers of statements to select the relevant data and make their own predictions regarding the value of the firm and other evaluations necessary in their decision making.

What should be included in the computation of net income is dependent upon which of the several objectives are considered to be the most relevant. Income based on the maintenance of capital requires the inclusion of all changes during the period. A report on stewardship should emphasize those changes that are controllable by management. For predictive purposes, changes that are recurring and changes with distinct behavioral characteristics should be disclosed along with these characteristics. The separation of extraordinary items and the exclusion of certain corrections of prior periods suggested in *APB Opinion No. 30* are steps in this direction, but they are inadequate to fulfill this objective. Management is interested primarily in those operating changes that are variable or controllable and are thus relevant for managerial planning and decisions. Because of these several uses for reported income and income components and the different types of information needed for each use, suggestions have been made that several concepts of income should be reported. A single concept of income may serve several purposes at least partially, but it is not likely to serve all objectives equally well.

From a broad social and economic point of view, all income generated by the firm should be reported as income. But the division of this income among the income recipients should be reported as well as the total generated. More complete information can probably be presented if the residual net income is restricted to a few income recipients. In any case, the report of net income should state to whom the income accrues. If a broad classification, such as net income to the enterprise, is used, the division of this income should also be presented. Furthermore, when a dilution of income per share is likely because of outstanding convertible securities, warrants, or grants, the probable effect of such a dilution should also be presented.

Conventional accounting practice has tended to emphasize a single net income to stockholders or to the entity. But the computation of this net income has been based on an eclectic approach. One of the major difficulties with discussions regarding alternative accounting procedures is that the writers do not usually indicate the basic concepts of income that they have in mind; therefore, many arguments are fruitless, since the opposing statements are based on different premises without a clear indication of these premises, nor a clear discussion of the basic concepts upon which the arguments rest. A critical analysis of conventional accounting practices regarding valuation procedures and in terms of the various concepts of income will be found in the following chapters.

SELECTED ADDITIONAL READING

Accounting concepts of income

Barlev, Benzion, and Haim Levy. "On the Variability of Accounting Income Numbers." *Journal of Accounting Research,* Autumn 1979, pp. 305–15.

Beaver, William H., and Joel S. Demski. "The Nature of Income Measurement." *Accounting Review,* January 1979, pp. 38–46.

Bedford, Norton M. "Income Concept Complex: Expansion or Decline." In *Asset Valuation and Income Determination,* edited by Robert R. Sterling. Lawrence, Kans.: Scholars Book, 1971, pp. 135–44.

———. *Income Determination Theory: An Accounting Framework.* Reading, Mass.: Addison-Wesley, 1965.

Sprouse, Robert T. "The Importance of Earnings in the Conceptual Framework." *Journal of Accountancy,* January 1978, pp. 64–71.

Economic concepts of income

Alexander, Sidney S. "Income Measurement in a Dynamic Economy." Revised by David Solomons and reprinted in W. T. Baxter and Sidney Davidson, *Studies in Accounting Theory*. Homewood, Ill.: Richard D. Irwin, 1962, pp. 126–200.

Barton, A. D. Expectations and Achievements in Income Theory." *Accounting Review,* October 1974, pp. 664–81.

Lee, T. A. *Income and Value Measurement: Theory and Practice.* Baltimore, Md.: University Park Press, 1975.

Shwayder, Keith. "A Critique of Economic Income as an Accounting Concept." *Abacus,* August 1967, pp. 23–35.

————. "The Capital Maintenance Rule and the Net Asset Valuation Rule." *Accounting Review,* April 1969, pp. 304–16.

Solomons, David. "Economic and Accounting Concepts of Income." *Accounting Review,* July 1961, pp. 374–83.

Income as a measure of efficiency

Amey, L. R. *The Efficiency of Business Enterprises.* New York: Augustus M. Kelley, 1970.

Glautier, W. E. "Theoretical Considerations of Accounting Profit with Particular Reference to the Assessment of Operating Efficiency." *Journal of Business Finance,* Summer 1972, pp. 5–14.

Predictive ability

Foster, George. "Quarterly Accounting Data: Time-Series Properties and Prediction—Ability Results." *Accounting Review,* January 1977, pp. 1–21.

Lorek, Kenneth. "Predicting Annual Net Earnings with Quarterly Earnings Time-Series Models." *Journal of Accounting Research,* Spring 1970, pp. 190–204.

Louderback, Joseph G. III. "Projectability as a Criterion for Income Determination Methods." *Accounting Review,* April 1971, pp. 298–305.

Income and capital market theories

Basu, S. "The Effect of Earnings Yield on Assessment of the Association between Annual Accounting Income Numbers and Security Prices." *Accounting Review,* July 1978, pp. 599–625.

Beaver, W. "An Information Content of Annual Earnings Announcements." *Journal of Accounting Research,* Empirical Research in Accounting: Selected Studies, 1968, pp. 67–92.

Firth, M. "Impact of Earnings Announcement on the Share Price Behavior of Similar-Type Firms." *Economic Journal,* June 1976, pp. 296–306.

Extraordinary items

Barnea, Amir; Joshua Ronen; and **Simcha Sadan.** "The Implementation of Accounting Objectives: An Application to Extraordinary Items." *Accounting Review,* January 1975, pp. 58–68.

————. "Classificatory Smoothing of Income with Extraordinary Items." *Accounting Review,* January 1976, pp. 110–22.

Bernstein, Leopold A. "Extraordinary Gains and Losses—Their Significance to the Financial Analyst." *Financial Analysts Journal,* November-December 1972, pp. 49–52, 88–90.

————. *Accounting for Extraordinary Gains and Losses.* New York: Ronald Press, 1967, esp. chaps. 1, 2, 3 and app. B.

Estimation theory

Brief, Richard P., and Joel Owen. "A Reformulation of the Estimation Problem." *Journal of Accounting Research,* Spring 1973, pp. 1–15.

————. "Present Value Models and the Multi-Asset Problem." *Accounting Review,* October 1973, pp. 690–95.

Jarrett, Jeffrey E. "Notes on the Estimation Problem in Financial Accounting." *Journal of Accounting Research,* Spring 1972, pp. 108–12.

CHAPTER 8

REVENUES AND EXPENSES, GAINS, AND LOSSES

As discussed in previous chapters, accounting concepts can be evaluated at three basic levels—the structural, interpretive, and behavioral levels. Accounting income has been developed fairly well at the structural or procedural level, but fails to meet basic objectives at the interpretive and behavioral levels. This is, at least in part, the result of the fact that revenues, expenses, gains and losses have been defined and measured on the basis of the normative deductive approach. However, it is possible that some of the components of accounting income may be relevant at the interpretive and behavioral levels as well as at the structural level. This chapter attempts to present an evaluation of the traditional components of income, specifically the concepts of revenues, expenses, gains, and losses, and some of the connecting linkages. Some of the alternative forms of these concepts may reflect real-world observations and may permit evaluations or predictions of the activities and future cash distributions of the firm.

The main emphasis in the activities approach to income is the recognition and classification of favorable and unfavorable changes during the accounting period. Favorable changes are classified as revenues or gains, and unfavorable changes as either expenses or losses. The main problems of recording these changes during an accounting period include problems of classification, timing, and valuation. Each of the several favorable and unfavorable changes will be discussed separately in relationship to these problems.

REVENUES

The concept of revenue is difficult to define because it is generally associated with specific accounting procedures, certain types of value changes, and assumed or implicit rules for determining when revenue should be reported. The measurement and timing of revenue are interesting problems of accounting theory, but they should be approached with an open mind; they should not be restricted by a narrow definition of revenue.

Conversely, revenue should be defined separately from the valuation and timing problems. Therefore, revenue is discussed here from the following specific points of view: (1) the nature of revenue, (2) what should be included in revenue, (3) the measurement of revenue, and (4) the timing of revenue (the period in which revenue is recorded).

The nature of revenue

The concept of revenue has not generally been clearly defined in accounting literature, primarily because it has usually been discussed in relationship to its measurement and timing and usually in the context of the double-entry system. However, the basic nature of revenue activity and its relevant attributes should be explored before we tackle the measurement and timing problems. Two approaches to the concept of revenue can be found in the literature, one focusing on the inflow of assets resulting from the operational activities of the firm and the other focusing on the creation of goods and services by the enterprise and the transfer of these to consumers or other producers. That is, revenue is considered to be either an inflow of net assets or an outflow of goods and services.[1]

The more traditional definition of *revenue* is that it represents an inflow of assets or net assets into the firm as a result of sales of goods or services. This was the approach of the FASB in *Statement of Financial Accounting Concepts No. 3 (SFAC 3)*.[2] However, this confuses the *measurement* and *timing* of the revenue with the revenue *process*. Assets are generally increased or liabilities liquidated at the time of sale or delivery of goods or services, and the amount of the revenue is traditionally determined by the monetary measurement of the assets received. This definition is, therefore, in accord with traditional practice, but it does not permit a broader perspective of the measuring and timing processes. The inflow approach also requires a careful statement of which inflows should be considered revenues and which should not. Assets may increase and liabilities decrease for many reasons, of which revenue is only one. Also, if revenue is defined in this way, the exceptions must be clearly stated. For example, in a few cases revenue is reported prior to sale and before there is an actual inflow of assets.

Revenue is also frequently defined in terms of its effect on stockholders' equity. The revenue account has a credit balance and is closed at the end of the accounting period to retained earnings through the revenue and expense summary account. Therefore, it has the effect of increasing the stockholders' equity. But many offsets (expenses) are directly associated

---

[1] See George J. Staubus, "Revenue and Revenue Accounts," *Accounting Research* 7 (July 1956): 284–94. Reprinted in Sidney Davidson, David Green, Jr., Charles T. Horngren, and George H. Sorter, *An Income Approach to Accounting Theory: Readings and Questions* (Englewood Cliffs, N.J.: Prentice-Hall, 1964), pp. 78–88.

[2] *APB Statement No. 4.* Also in *AICPA Professional Standards* (Chicago: Commerce Clearing House, 1975), p. 7248.

with the revenue before there can be a net change in stockholders' equity. Also, there are several reasons for increases in stockholders' equity not associated with revenue. This definition also has the disadvantage of relating revenue to the double-entry system, rather than to its basic nature.

The basic concept of revenue is that it is a flow process—the creation of goods or services by an enterprise during a specific interval of time. Paton and Littleton called it the product of the enterprise.[3] Notice that this definition does not dictate either the amount or the timing of the revenue, but is neutral with respect to these aspects. Generally, revenue is expressed in monetary terms, although the measurement of revenue under this concept is open for discussion without changing the nature of the item being measured.

Several similar definitions also state that the revenue is the product of the enterprise, but they imply that the product must leave the firm (an outflow concept). For example, the Committee on Accounting Concepts and Standards of the American Accounting Association defined revenue in the 1957 statement as follows:

> Revenue . . . is the monetary expression of the aggregate of products or services transferred by an enterprise to its customers during a period of time.[4]

The FASB, in *SFAC No. 3,* defined *revenue* initially as an inflow of net assets; however, it stated further that revenue is derived from delivering or producing goods, rendering services, or other major activities of the firm[5] (an outflow concept).

In the opinion of the author, the definition of revenue as the product of the enterprise is superior to the outflow concept, and the outflow concept is superior to the inflow concept. The product concept is neutral with respect to both timing and measurement, and the inflow concept as it is generally proposed avoids neither.

What should be included in revenue?

The definition of *revenue* as the product of the enterprise seems clear enough, but the several attempts to describe revenue or the nature and content of income do not agree on what should be included in the revenue concept. On the one hand, it is suggested that all changes in the net assets of a firm other than capital transactions reported during a period should be considered revenue. On the other hand, other proposals suggest that a distinction should be made between the revenue-producing activities of a

---

[3] W. A. Paton and A. C. Littleton, *An Introduction to Corporate Accounting Standards,* American Accounting Association Monograph No. 3 (AAA, 1940), p. 46.

[4] AAA Committee on Accounting Concepts and Standards, *Accounting and Reporting Standards for Corporate Financial Statements and Preceding Statements and Supplements* (AAA, 1957), p. 5.

[5] *AICPA Professional Standards,* para. 1230.063.

firm and other gains or losses. Most discussions of income, however, are not clear with respect to a classification of revenue as distinct from gains. Although such a classification may, at times, appear artificial, the view expressed in this book is that a better understanding of accounting may be obtained by making a distinction between the wealth-producing activities of the firm and unexpected transfers of wealth arising from gifts or windfalls.

Among those who take a comprehensive view of revenue is the APB in *Statement No. 4.* In addition to sales and services, it included in revenue the sale of resources other than products, such as plant and equipment and investments.[6]

The more narrow definition of *revenue* as the products or services of the enterprise was expressed in *FASB SFAC No. 3* as follows: "Revenues . . . result [from] the enterprise's ongoing major or central operations during the period."[7] Thus, *revenue* does not include gains in this definition. Paton and Littleton also expressed this view by recognizing the flow of accomplishment as the primary source of revenue.[8] But they were careful to include in revenue the entire range of goods and services furnished by the enterprise regardless of the relative amount of a particular item.

In the following discussion, the term *revenue* will be used in the latter, narrower sense. Gains will be treated separately. Note, however, that the product of the enterprise refers to all types of services, including rentals and interest-bearing loans. Thus, revenue may be operating or nonoperating, recurring or nonrecurring. But revenue in this sense does have real-world interpretation.

The measurement of revenue

Revenue is best measured by the exchange value of the product or service of the enterprise. This exchange value represents the cash equivalent or the present discounted value of the money claims to be received eventually from the revenue transaction. In many cases, this may be equivalent to the price established in the transaction with the customer. But appropriate allowance must be made for the necessity to wait for final collection. A cash sale for $100 produces $100 of revenue, but a similar sale permitting the same payment a year later produces less than $100 of revenue because of the necessity to discount the latter amount. When the waiting period is short, the discount may be ignored for three pragmatic reasons: (1) At low rates of discount the amount of the discount is small and does not materially affect the total revenue valuation. For example, if the claim is to be paid in 60 days, the amount of the discount at a rate of 10 percent per year would be less than 2 percent of the revenue. (2)

---

[6] *AICPA Professional Standards,* para. 1026.12.

[7] *AICPA Professional Standards,* para. 1230.064.

[8] Paton and Littleton, *Corporate Accounting Standards,* p. 47.

Because interest is classified as a part of total revenue, the main effect is that of timing. Interest should be recorded subsequent to the recording of the revenue from the initial transaction. But if the interest is not material in amount, including it in the sales revenue would have little effect on total revenue for the period. (3) The classification of revenue arising from waiting (interest) would be lost and included in the classification of revenue arising from the sale of the product or service. Again, if the implicit interest is not material in amount, little useful information is lost by the failure to classify it separately.[9]

The above criterion for the measurement of revenue refers to the present value of the money or money equivalent finally to be received as a result of the production process or the revenue transaction. From this criterion it is clear that all returns, trade discounts, and other reductions of the billed prices should be deducted from the revenue resulting from the specific transactions. The treatment of cash discounts and losses resulting from uncollectible accounts may not be quite so clear. However, these are also reductions from billed prices, even though unintentional, as in the case of the bad debt losses.

Cash discounts are granted, in part, to equate the value of the money received within the discount period with the present discounted value of the money that would be received under the granted credit terms. But one of the main purposes of the cash discounts is to reduce the bad debt losses. If the cash discount rates were set rationally, sellers would be indifferent whether they received the net discounted price or the gross price less a normal expectation of bad debt losses. In many cases, sellers may be able to obtain the same results with a lower cash discount rate than the maximum they would be willing to grant. Cash discounts and expected bad debt losses are, therefore, similar in nature.

In a world of certainty, the actual amount to be received finally in cash, discounted appropriately for the necessity of waiting, should be recorded as the revenue from the transaction. With uncertainty, the principle remains the same, but the cash discounts expected to be taken and the expected bad debt losses must be estimated. These items are, therefore, deductions in computing revenue. Their traditional treatment as expenses does not result in a different amount of reported income, but it should be recognized that they do not have the basic characteristics of expenses as discussed later in this chapter.[10] If the degree of homogeneity

---

[9] Receivables arising from revenue transactions are exempt from the discounting requirements of *APB Opinion No. 21* if they are due within one year.

[10] Those who claim that cash discounts and bad debt losses are true expenses argue that they represent alternatives to other expenses, such as collection expense and interest expense. There is an element of truth in this approach, but it is the opinion of the author that the concepts of revenue and expense are made clearer if these items are treated as revenue deductions. Also, it does not seem logical to classify any item on the basis of an alternative action. There are many cases in which revenues are reduced as an alternative to increasing expenses.

is increased, total revenue will be a better representation of real-world observations.

The timing of revenue reporting

In our definition of *revenue* as the product of the enterprise as measured by an exchange value or cash equivalent, we still have the problem of deciding the point or points in time when we should measure and report the revenue. From an economic point of view, the value added by productive activity is a continuous process. The product of the enterprise appears gradually as raw materials are assembled and changed in form or processed by the application of labor and capital equipment. The transportation of raw materials to the plant and the finished product to the market are also part of the production process in an economic sense. Likewise, storage, either as a part of the production process or as a necessary requirement of meeting market demand, is also a part of the service provided by a firm. As indicated in the previous chapter, value added by the firm is the excess of the exchange value of the firm's products over the value added by other firms or individuals. Product exchange price, therefore, represents the distributions to all factors of production, including the contribution (a positive or negative residual) by the firm itself—the return to the several equity holders.

Revenue reporting entails not only the acknowledgment that the firm has produced economic value in the form of goods or services, but also the measurement of that value. As indicated in the previous section, the product or service can be measured best by the money or money equivalent expected to be received for the product at some time in the future. It is the uncertainty of this expected receipt and the search for verifiable measurements that have led accountants to the adoption of specific rules for the timing of revenue.

Sprouse and Moonitz stated that

> revenues should be identified with the period during which the major economic activities necessary to the creation and disposition of goods and services have been accomplished, provided objective measurements of the results of those activities are available. These two conditions, i.e., accomplishment of major economic activity and objectivity of measurement, are fulfilled at different stages of activity in different cases, sometimes as late as time of delivery of product or the performance of a service, in other cases, at an earlier point of time.[11]

The author is in general agreement with this view that revenue should be acknowledged and reported at the time of the accomplishment of the major economic activity if its measurement is verifiable and free from bias.

---

[11] Sprouse and Moonitz, "Broad Accounting Principles," p. 47.

An alternative to the reporting of revenue at the time of accomplishing the major economic activity is the *critical event* (or crucial event) concept of revenue reporting.[12] In most cases, the value added by the firm (reported as the net income) is jointly associated with the entire process of planning, producing, providing the goods or services for customers, and the final collection of cash and, in some cases, the providing of services (such as repairs under warranties) beyond the collection process. Because of the jointness of this value added over time, it is impossible to make a logical allocation to the several processes. Therefore, an expedient alternative is to report the value added by the firm at a single point in time. The critical event concept suggests that the most appropriate moment of time is when the most critical decision is made or when the most difficult task is performed. This could be at the point when the contract is signed, the time when the services are performed, when the cash is collected, or at some other time.

The 1964 AAA committee that reported on *The Realization Concept* proposed the crucial event concept, but it suggested that some of the revenue should be recognized later if additional economic functions or activities are to take place subsequently. The committee rejected the reporting of income on the basis of costs incurred, but it implied that the value added by the firm should be allocated to more than one point in time. Even if the value added by the firm is reported at a single point in time, the amount of revenue represented by the value added by other economic factors should be reported at a later time if, in fact, the services provided by these factors follow the main point of recognition. This is the net realizable value concept—the final cash sales price less additional costs to produce and sell.

The term *revenue realization* is used in a technical sense by accountants to establish specific rules for the timing of revenue reporting under circumstances where no single solution is necessarily superior to others in the above context of revenue. The realization concept has, therefore, become a pragmatic test for the timing of revenue. Although many attempts have been made to give it theoretical content, it continues to lack analytical precision. However, many writers in the area suggest that the realization concept enriches accounting terminology and reporting.[13]

One of the main difficulties with the realization concept is that *realization* means different things to different people. In a broad sense, the term has been used to mean simply the recognition (reporting) of revenue. Many writers who use the term in this sense have in mind specific rules applying to the reporting of transactions, and others would include all value increases, regardless of their type or source. The general view,

---

[12] See John H. Myers, "The Critical Event and Recognition of Net Profit," *Accounting Review* 34 (October 1959): 528–32; and the 1964 Concepts and Standards Research Study Committee, "The Realization Concept," *Accounting Review* 40 (April 1965): 316.

[13] For example, see Charles T. Horngren, "How Should We Interpret the Realization Concept?" *Accounting Review* (April 1965): 325.

however, is that realization represents the reporting of revenue when an exchange or severance has occurred. That is, goods or services must have been transferred to a customer or client, giving rise to either the receipt of cash or a claim to cash or other assets. In this view, realization cannot take place by the holding of assets or as a result of the production process alone. Thus, the term *realization* has come generally to mean the reporting of revenue when it has been validated by sale.[14] The reporting of revenue before or after the point of sale is generally considered an exception to the realization rule.

The 1973–74 AAA Committee on Concepts and Standards—External Reporting stated that "income should be reported as soon as the level of uncertainty has been reduced to a tolerable level." Recognizing that realization cannot predate the critical events giving rise to income, the Committee defined *realization* as follows:

> Realization is not a determinant in the concept of income; it only serves as a guide in deciding when events otherwise resolved as being within the concept of income, can be entered in the accounting records in objective terms; that is, when the uncertainty has been reduced to an acceptable level.[15]

This definition has the advantage of being broadly stated, with emphasis on the necessity for objectivity as a means of dealing with uncertainty. As recognized by the Committee, however, the realization concept is primarily a procedural guide for the reporting of revenues.

In view of the confusion, emotionalism, and even mysticism that have surrounded the realization concept, this author suggests that accountants abandon the term. In its place, emphasis should be placed on the reporting of valuation changes of all types, although the nature of the change and the reliability of the measurement should also be disclosed. Furthermore, accountants may be able to provide more relevant information to users of external reports if less emphasis is placed on the relationship of revenue to net income and more emphasis on the informational content of the several measurements of revenue. For example, it is likely that several attributes of revenue—such as sales price of goods produced, goods and services sold, and the final amount of cash received for goods and services rendered—may be relevant to external users. Acceptance of one attribute should not necessarily exclude disclosure of other attributes.

The reporting of revenue during production. The traditional accrual basis of accounting recognizes revenue as earned if there is a simultaneous increase in the claim against the customer or client. This is the

---

[14] Paton and Littleton, however, stated that the dominant view was that realization includes the test of ". . . validation through the acquisition of liquid assets." Paton and Littleton, *Corporate Accounting Standards,* p. 49.

[15] AAA Committee on Concepts and Standards—External Reporting, "Report of the 1973–74 Committee on Concepts and Standards—External Reporting," *Accounting Review,* supplement to vol. 40 (1974), p. 209.

general practice with respect to services. The product of the enterprise emerges as the services are provided. The amount of the claim is usually determined by prior agreement or contract, or often by established trade prices, even though the client or tenant may not be required to make payment until a later date or at least until a determinable amount of service has been provided.

Examples of the accrual basis of revenue recognition are rent, interest, commissions, and personal services performed on a time basis. In each of these examples the basic criteria for revenue reporting are met. The services are usually performed on a time basis and the performing of services may be assumed to be crucial. The amount of the revenue has been established by prior contract or agreement. Related expenses are usually determinable simultaneously with the revenue. In addition, a valid claim arises against the customer, client, or tenant even though the amount is not billed and payment is not required until a later date.

Long-term contracts.   A second accepted application of the reporting of revenue during production is the recognition of revenue on long-term contracts. The general acceptance in this case is based on pragmatic grounds and supported by theory. An individual or firm would usually object to publication of financial statements showing no income for a year during which the firm had spent considerable effort in obtaining partial completion of a contract that would have permitted a reasonable profit with a fair degree of certainty. If contracts are completed at irregular intervals, the reporting of income only when the contracts are completed could result in a hardship or injustice to stockholders who wish to sell their interests before the completion of major contracts because of a lack of relevant information. The annual income statement might have less meaning also from either a managerial or a financial point of view.

What conditions support the recognition of revenue during production in this case? The most important consideration is that the total price of the contract is determined in advance or is determinable. Uncertainty regarding the selling price is minimized, and uncertainty regarding collection is usually not very great, particularly if the buyer is a governmental unit or a large established corporation. Two areas of uncertainty remain, however: (1) At any particular point, it may be difficult to determine the sale price of the product produced to date. (2) The total costs of the project may be difficult to estimate with accuracy. If the actual costs of completion differ from the estimated costs, the net income of each period will have been affected.

The percentage of completion is usually computed by comparing the costs incurred in a specific accounting period with the total estimated costs for the project. The expected profit on the contract is then allocated to each period on the basis of these costs. This procedure has two main difficulties: (1) It assumes that the firm's profit is earned as costs are incurred. But an important part of the firm's contribution may come from the planning stage, before large costs are incurred. Furthermore, many of the costs involve work performed by subcontractors and are not the result of the firm's contribution. An alternative might be to include only those costs included in the concept of value added. But the assumption that each dollar of cost produces the same amount of revenue implies that the value added by the firm is related to the use of other economic factors, an assumption that is conceptually unacceptable. (2) A second difficulty arises because the percentage is computed by using total costs as the denominator. As noted above, total costs also may be uncertain, particularly where excavation and weather conditions may present unknown hazards.

The second area of general uncertainty is the estimation of expected net income. Although the total contract price may be fixed, the costs are uncertain; so it becomes difficult to allocate this uncertain income to periods. In the case of cost-plus-fixed-fee contracts, the total income is determined in advance, and only the precentage of completion may be uncertain. Uncertainty, however, should not be a cause for the failure to report revenue when the value increase can be measured. Reasonable estimates based on contract prices and expert judgment regarding costs may provide better information regarding the progress of the firm than can the holding to the narrow realization concept. The precentage-of-completion method is accepted in the United States for revenue recognition.[16] However, the allocation procedures applied do not result in measurements that reflect real-world observations.

Accretion.   Related to the reporting of revenue during production is the recognition of increased values arising from natural growth or an aging process. This natural growth or aging over time is just as much as part of the production process from an economic point of view as the process of changing the form of commodities. In an economic sense, then, accretion gives rise to revenue. Examples include growing timber, nursery stock, and livestock, and the aging of certain liquors and wines.

The revenues or income from accretion can only be recognized through the process of making comparative inventory valuations. This recognition is not the result of transactions. Therefore, it does differ from the cases of revenue reporting during production discussed so far. But this does not affect the logic of reporting the increases in asset measurement. The limitations are primarily from a practical standpoint. The present discounted value is difficult to determine because it depends upon expectations regarding future market prices and expectations regarding future costs of providing for growth and future costs of harvesting and getting the product ready for market. In some cases, such as nursery stock and livestock, because the product has a market price at the various stages of growth, the valuation process is simplified. But these measurements, even though verifiable, are also only approximations of the discounted net fu-

---

[16] *AICPA Professional Standards,* para. 4031.04.

ture values. If the product is held for future sale, it may be presumed that the owner considers, at least subjectively the present value to be greater than the current market price; otherwise the owner would sell the product in the current market. So the current market price less costs of harvesting is probably a conservative estimate of the present discounted value.

The argument that accretion is not income because it cannot be available for dividends is the wrong criterion for the recognition of revenue. Current accounting practice recognizes many situations wherein income results in liquid assets, but for several reasons, prudent financial management may preclude the payment of dividends. The important criterion is the certainty regarding the final sales price of the product and the additional costs required to permit optimum growth and preparation for sale. If a reasonable market is not assured, or if additional costs are highly uncertain, the reporting of revenue from accretion may be highly improper. The wide range of probable outcomes may prohibit objective verification or even the valid estimation of a single-valued amount of revenue or income.

The reporting of revenue at the completion of production. When a product is completed, one of the former uncertainties—the cost of production—can now be computed with a fair degree of accuracy. The selling price and the additional costs of selling and delivering may still remain uncertain. But when these can be estimated reliably, there is good justification for reporting the revenue at this time. In many industries, the production process may be a crucial part of the firm's operations. From an economic point of view, value is added in all of the necessary economic activities of the firm, including production.

The reporting of the revenue at the completion of production, however, is dependent upon the degree of certainty with which the selling price and the additional costs can be estimated. When there is a firm contract for the production and delivery of a given product, the selling price is known, and the costs of selling have already been incurred. The remaining uncertainties include the possibility of failure to collect the selling price and the additional expenses of delivery. These, however, can usually be estimated fairly accurately, and accountants have generally expressed approval of reporting revenue on this basis.

In a few cases, the reporting of revenue at the completion of production is permitted even though the products are not manufactured under contract. The main criteria are (1) the existence of a determinable selling price or stable market price, (2) no substantial cost of marketing, and (3) interchangeability of units. Some question can be raised as to whether interchangeability is really necessary if the first criterion is met. Prices in a ready market are relevant only if they apply to the specific commodity in question, which implies some interchangeability. Gold and silver are common examples that meet these criteria. Other commodities, such as other precious metals and agricultural commodities, may also meet the above criteria if there is a ready market for the commodity with a determinable market price. In these cases, technical production rather than selling activity is the major activity of the firm. In many cases, however, market prices fluctuate widely, and considerable uncertainty exists regarding the price at which the product will be sold.

According to *APB Statement No. 4,* revenue may be reported at the completion of production under the above criteria only for "precious metals that have a fixed selling price and insignificant marketing costs."[17] Similar treatment is acceptable for agricultural, mineral, and other products only if the firm is unable to determine appropriate approximate costs. In all cases, however, the sales prices should be reduced by the estimated costs of disposal. Note that the lack of cost measurement is not a basic standard for using market prices; rather it is an extenuating circumstance under which market prices are permitted.

The inability to determine costs is not a logical reason for recognizing revenue at the completion of production. The main consideration should be the ability to obtain verifiable measurements of revenue and additional costs which are reliable. For most commodities, the lack of a stable market price is a major stumbling block for the general acceptance of the recognition of revenue at the completion of production.

The reporting of revenue at the time of sale. For many years the time of sale has been the general rule for the reporting of revenue. This rule is supported on several grounds: (1) The price of the product is now established rather definitely. (2) The product has left the firm and a new asset has taken its place—an exchange has occurred. (3) For most concerns, the sale is assumed to be the most significant financial event in the economic activity of the firm. (4) Most of the costs relating to the manufacture or acquisition of the product and the costs of disposal have now been incurred or are now readily determinable.

The uncertainties regarding the final measurement of revenue are minimal at the time of sale, but they are not eliminated. Accepted business practice may permit the return of all or a part of the merchandise, thus canceling the sales contract. Failure to collect the sale price is often a possibility, the likelihood of which may depend upon the credit rating of the customer. Also, additional expenses may arise, many of which are unexpected. These would include abnormal collection charges and expenses of meeting express or implied customer warranties. However, usually the uncollectible accounts and the additional expenses may be estimated from past experience.

When does a sale take place? From a legal point of view, the sale occurs when title passes and a claim for payment arises. Because of the technicality of the passing of title, accountants generally recognize the sale as occurring when delivery of the merchandise is made to the customer or to

---

[17] *AICPA Professional Standards,* para. 1027.10.

a common carrier. But the sale is also assumed to occur when merchandise is physically segregated or marked for the customer after the customer has indicated a desire to purchase. As with all rules, however, exceptions are not uncommon. In many cases, the fact of delivery or segregation is not sufficient. The intent on the part of both parties to consummate a sale must also be present. For example, the delivery of merchandise on consignment does not generally carry with it the intent to bring about an exchange between the consignor and the consignee. A delivery on approval may carry a similar intent, as the customer has not indicated a direct intention to buy. Evidence of a completed transaction is lacking. To say that the sale should be recorded when an invoice is presented to the customer is a weak criterion for the timing of revenue, but nevertheless it has some merits. The burden of deciding when the evidence is strong enough to record a sale is transferred to the sales department, and the accountant accepts this decision. This is merely another way of saying that revenue should be reported at the time of sale; no basic criterion is established.

A more precise set of criteria for the recognition of a sale would include (1) the appearance of definite evidence that the buyer intends to buy and that the seller intends to sell, (2) the identification of the specific completed merchandise in question, and (3) an agreement between the buyer and seller regarding the price or a formula for establishing the price.

The AAA Committee on Concepts and Standards—External Financial Reporting suggested that the sales point is an appropriate point for revenue recognition only when the criteria for reporting are not met earlier.[18] Also, revenue should be recognized beyond the sales point in some cases. Particularly in the land development and franchising industries, revenue has been reported when the buyer and seller entered into a contract for sale even though the seller's responsibilities under the contract had not been discharged. This resulted in inflated reported profits in these industries during the 1960s and early 1970s.[19]

The reporting of revenue subsequent to sale. Cash receipts or anticipated cash receipts are significant in the measurement of revenue, but they are not generally crucial in the operational process giving rise to the increase in net assets of the firm. Thus, while the expected cash receipts to be received subsequent to sale provide a verifiable measurement of revenue, there is little theoretical justification for delaying the reporting of revenue beyond the time when a valid claim against customers arises and the basic activity regarding such sale of products or services has been accomplished. However, delaying the reporting of revenue beyond the time of sale may be justified if one of the two following criteria is met: (1)

---

[18] AAA Committee on Concepts and Standards—External Financial Reporting, "Report of the 1973–74 Committee," p. 213.

[19] See Abraham J. Briloff, *Accountable Accounting* (New York: Harper & Row, 1972), chap. 7 and pp. 108–14. Such practices are now prohibited for land development firms.

if it is impossible to measure the assets received in the exchange with a fair degree of accuracy, or (2) if additional material expenses directly associated with the transaction are likely and if these cannot be estimated with a fair degree of accuracy.

With respect to the valuation of the assets received in the exchange, two types of situations may lead to the deferral of revenue reporting. *First,* a tangible asset or other nonmonetary asset may be received. If the asset does not have a recognized market value and if appraisal is difficult or impossible, the reporting of revenue may have little meaning. Only when the valuation of the asset can be measured by sale or by other verifiable means will the measurement of the revenue be meaningful. These cases, however, should be the exception. Such transactions are not common in business practice, and when they do occur a valuation can usually be placed on the assets received. In those rare cases where a valuation cannot be placed on the assets received, there is justification for transferring the input price of the goods sold to the new asset received so that revenue is not recorded. *Second,* the claim against the customer may be of dubious collection. In general this can be handled by estimating the probable amount of uncollectible accounts. Only rarely is this impossible, and therefore only very few situations justify the deferral of revenue recognition on the ground that collection is too doubtful to establish a reasonable current valuation of the receivables.

The AICPA Accounting Standards Division has recommended that when a seller is exposed to the risks of ownership through return of the property, the revenue should not be recognized currently unless future returns can be reasonably predicted. If this and other specific conditions are met, the transaction can be reported as revenue if immediate provision is made for any costs or losses that may be expected relating to possible future returns.[20]

The most often quoted example of justifiable deferral of revenue reporting is the case of installment sales. Collection is said to be doubtful because the customers who enter into these installment contracts often overextend themselves and therefore are poor risks. Billing and collection expenses subsequent to the time of sale are usually large, and warranty expenses may also enter into the picture. These arguments are usually quite weak, however. Even though uncollectible accounts may be large, they can usually be estimated on the basis of past experience of the specific firm or of other firms in the industry. Furthermore, the accounts are usually protected by the fact that title to the goods does not usually pass to the customer until the claim is fully paid. Billing and collection expenses can also be estimated fairly accurately, and warranty expenses should be very little different from those cases following open account or cash sales.

---

[20] AICPA Accounting Standards Division Statement of Position (SOP 75–1), *Revenue Recognition When Right of Return Exists* (1975).

In a few cases where a venture is highly speculative, there may be justification for the deferral of revenue reporting. The final net income from a project may depend on the sale of a minimum quantity of the product, or the existence of joint costs may result in period income determination that is highly tentative. In these unusual circumstances, an alternative may be to consider the life of the venture the relevant period for income determination. A resort to the cash basis does not necessarily render the reporting of period net income more accurate; the result may often be the reverse with uniform time periods.

A modification of the installment basis has often been suggested for highly speculative ventures where cash collections are received in installments and where the collection of the final installments may be doubtful. Under these circumstances, the final net income or loss cannot be determined until all collections have been received. Accordingly, the first installments are considered to be a return of invested costs, and income is recorded only after all costs have been recovered. After all costs have been recovered, all additional installments are treated as income. A good example is where a bond is in default and payments of principal and interest are made as cash becomes available through liquidation of the mortgaged property or through other means. Because of the uncertainty regarding future payments under the bond contract, all collections, whether considered payments of principal or interest by the trustee, are treated as a return of the bond investment until such investment has been fully recovered.

The position of the Accounting Principles Board in *Opinion No. 10* was that " . . . revenues should ordinarily be accounted for at the time a transaction is completed, with appropriate provision for uncollectible accounts"; and in the absence of circumstances where the sale price is not reasonably assured, it concluded that the installment method of recognizing revenue is not acceptable. A footnote, however, weakened this position by recognizing exceptional cases in which there may be no reasonable basis for estimating the degree of collectibility. In the author's opinion, this exception is not warranted because installment sales probably would not be made under such conditions.

Summary of revenue reporting.   The recording of revenue in accounting statements should be based on the following criteria: (1) Economic value must have been added by the firm to its product. (2) The amount of the revenue must be capable of measurement. (3) The measurement must be verifiable and relatively free from bias. (4) Related expenses must be capable of being estimated with a fair degree of accuracy.

In general, accounting statements are improved if revenue is reported at the earliest possible point after the value increase can be measured. However, probabilistic measurements of revenue would be an improvement over the reporting of single-valued amounts representing certainty equivalents.[21] The following tabulation summarizes the several periods and the conditions under which reporting may be appropriate:

Time of Reporting	Criteria	Examples
During production.	Establishment of a firm price based on contract or general business terms or existence of market prices at various stages of production.	Accruals; long-term contracts; accretion.
At completion of production.	Existence of a determinable selling price or stable market price. No substantial cost of marketing.	Precious metals; agricultural products; services.
At time of sale.	Established price for the product. Reasonable method for estimating amount collectible. Estimation of all material related expenses.	Most merchandise sales.
At time of cash collection.	Impossible to value assets received with fair degree of accuracy. Additional material expenses are likely, and these cannot be estimated with a fair degree of accuracy at the time of sale.	Installment sales; exchange for fixed asset without verifiably determined value.

EXPENSES

Like the term *revenue,* the term *expense* is also a flow concept, representing the unfavorable changes in the resources of the firm. But not all unfavorable changes are expenses. More precisely defined, expenses are the using or consuming of goods and services in the process of obtaining revenues. They are the expirations of factor services related either directly or indirectly to the producing and selling of the product of the enterprise. The values of these factor services expire when they leave the enterprise by final consumption or by the transfer of the product to customers; they represent expirations of factor services associated with new measurements of the value of the product of the enterprise when revenue is reported before sale. When service expirations result in a product still held by the enterprise, but on which revenue has not been reported, the measurement of the goods and services used is assumed to become embodied in the measurement of the product (a transformation of the service value), and there is no final expiration or transfer out of the firm.

The unfavorable aspect of revenue operations (expenses) has a tendency to reduce the stockholders' equity in the firm. Expenses are often defined in this context. But it is not meaningful to emphasize the unfavorable aspects without also referring to the favorable (revenues). Both

---

[21] See, for example, the suggested probabilistic reporting suggested by the AAA Committee on Concepts and Standards—External Financial Reporting, "Report of the 1973–74 Committee," pp. 219–22.

determine net operating income, under both the accounting and the net increase in wealth concepts of income. Because of the relationship to revenues and because expenses do not include all of the unfavorable changes in equities, expenses should not be defined solely in terms of their effect on stockholders' equity.

Frequently expenses are defined in terms of cost expirations or cost allocations. However, these terms are descriptions of the structural model for the measurement of accounting income. They do not reflect real-world observations. The valuation of expenses is a problem distinct from the definition of *expense*. Expenses are measured by the valuation of the goods or services used or consumed, but this measurement does not define the expense. The reader should be careful to distinguish between the measurement of an expense based on cost and the definition of an expense as an activity or process. Emphasis on the latter has the advantage of leaving the measurement of expense open for futher discussion.

The questions arising with respect to the term *expense* are similar to the questions asked regarding revenue. They are: (1) What should be included in the term *expense?* (2) How should expenses be measured? (3) When are expenses incurred and when should they be reported for accounting purposes?

What should be included in expenses?

In the above definition of expenses, only those unfavorable changes incurred in the process of obtaining revenue are included. The converse of this is that asset expirations or asset reductions not related to the process of providing goods or services to customers or clients should be classified as losses rather than as expenses. This does not deny their rightful place in the income statement under certain circumstances. Losses and expenses may both be relevant changes in the computation of net income to stockholders or to the enterprise; but only expenses can be matched with revenues of the period in the computation of "net operating income" under the structural approach to income.

Several authorities, however, define *expenses* broadly to include the expiration of both operating and nonoperating costs. For example, the 1948 statement of the American Accounting Association defined *expenses* as consisting of both operating costs and losses. On the other hand, *FASB SFAC No. 3* clearly distinguished between expenses and losses. Only expenses relate to the major or central operations of the firm. Losses result from transactions or events that are peripheral or incidental to the operations of the enterprise. This distinction will be carried into the following discussions in order to maintain clarity of exposition.

The controversy between the all-inclusive and the current operating concepts of income discussed in the previous chapter is relevant in the necessity to classify unfavorable changes as either expenses or losses; but it does not alter the nature of these changes. The all-inclusive concept of income includes all expenses and losses recognized during the current period; there is no need to differentiate between the two in the computation of net income. On the other hand, the current operating concept excludes from the computation of net income those expenses actually incurred in a prior period but not recognized until the current period and all losses. This is a problem, however, of choosing a meaningful concept of net income, rather than a problem of defining expenses. Extraordinary items (deductions) are not the same as losses, as will be discussed later.

In the proper delineation of expenses, care should be taken to distinguish between those unfavorable changes that are expenses and those that are offsets to revenue or valuations of revenue. Sales returns and allowances are normally treated as revenue offsets, and rightly so. On the other hand, sales discounts and bad debt losses have been treated conventionally as expenses. In the opinion of the author, however, it is more logical to classify them as offsets to revenue than as expenses.[22] Sales discounts do not represent the use of goods or services. A small part of such discounts may represent the monetary discount or interest equal to the cost of waiting in the absence of uncertainty. But if the discount is taken, the net price represents the price of the goods; the discount is a reduction of the revenue and not a cost of borrowing funds. Likewise, bad debt losses do not represent expirations of goods or services, but rather reductions of the amount to be received in exchange for the product.

A careful distinction should also be made between expenses and offsets to capital or stockholders' equity. Asset expirations and obligations incurred in relation to capital transactions should not be classified as expenses, but shown as reductions of capital or one of its components. Costs incurred in the sale of capital stock, for example, are not expenses, but reductions of the amount of capital received by the corporation. Likewise, the write-off of capital stock discount has no place in the income statement. Thus we see that the use of goods and services is not a sufficient definition of *expenses*. The objective of obtaining revenue must also be present, although the relationship to revenue might be quite indirect, as in the case of expenditures necessary to service debt.

The classification of expenses as "selling," "administrative," or "cost of goods sold" may be useful for analytical purposes within the firm, such as establishing functional responsibilities. However, for external reporting purposes, it serves no particular useful function. The reader of financial reports is neither better able to make predictions by using this classification nor able to evaluate the contributions of the several functions. Although each classification may represent the use of goods or services at different times in the enterprise operating process, they are all expenses. The "cost of goods sold" is an expense just as much as sales representatives' salaries. Care should be taken to avoid the assignment of priorities to expenses; all are equal in the determination of income. Expenses are

---

[22] See note 10 above.

not recovered in preferential order. There can be no meaningful income measurement until all expenses have been subtracted from the total revenues.

A classification of expenses that might be useful to investors and others in making predictions and in evaluating current management decisions would be one that describes the behavioral nature of the expenses. That is, expenses should be classified and described according to whether they are variable or fixed in nature with respect to production or sales volume, or whether they vary with respect to some other factor. There may also be an advantage in describing their relationship to cash flows. Items that result from cash expenditures of a prior period have a different effect upon the firm than expenses resulting from current or future cash outflows.

How should expenses be measured?

Measurement of the goods and services used in the operations of the enterprise does not have a simple solution. This is so because the objectives for such measurement are not clearly defined, and the measurement found acceptable is determined in large part by the income concept applied. Many of the controversial discussions regarding the appropriate measurement do not lead to solutions, primarily because the proponents of the different viewpoints have in mind different objectives or different income concepts, which are not generally clearly stated.

According to those who define expenses as decreases in the net assets of the firm, a logical measurement is the value of the goods and services at the time they are used in the operations of the enterprise. These are the unfavorable aspects of revenue operations and represent the economic sacrifice required to obtain the revenue. The term *value* has many meanings, but it is usually used in this context to represent the exchange price of the goods or services or their opportunity cost. On the other hand, those who emphasize the reporting of cash flows of the enterprise usually suggest that expenses should be measured in terms of transactions to which the firm is a party and measured by the past, current, or future cash expenditures. In either view of income, the purpose is to measure the amounts assignable to the current period and to defer to future periods those amounts that represent transformations of goods or services to be used in future periods. The most common measurements of expense are (1) historical cost, (2) current measurements, such as replacement cost, and (3) opportunity costs or current cash equivalents.

Historical cost.   The conventional method of measuring expenses is in terms of the historical cost to the enterprise. The main reason for adhering to historical costs is that they are assumed to be verifiable, since they represent cash outlays by the firm. But it is also claimed that they represent the exchange value of the goods and services at the time they were acquired by the enterprise. An essential feature of this argument is that management considered the value of the goods and services to be at least as great as the cost at the time of acquisition or they would not have been acquired. Also, there is no real evidence that the firm would have acquired the goods and services if it had had to pay a higher price for them. Thus, the best evidence available indicates that they were worth just what they cost the firm, no more or less.[23] If the goods and services turn out to be worth more than the historical cost, the excess represents a gain to the firm, which will be included in aggregate income at the time revenue is reported if the expense is then reported at historical cost. The opposite is the case if the goods and services are subsequently worth less than cost. The main disadvantages of historical cost are that it frequently does not represent a relevant measurement of the goods and services used in attempting to meet the objectives of the external users of financial reports, and that it does not permit a separation of operating activity from gains and losses arising from fortuitous purchases or unpredictable price changes. The measurement and timing of these gains and losses are discussed later in this chapter.

What is meant by *cost* and what should be included in the term? Basically, cost is measured by the current value of the economic resources given up or to be given up in obtaining the goods and services to be used in operations; this is the value in exchange. When cash is paid or agreed to be paid for merchandise, supplies, and personal services, the measurement of cost is fairly definite. The cash paid or agreed to be paid represent the exchange value determined by the market price or by agreement between the buyer and seller. The cash represents the monetary value of claims to economic resources given up by the buyer.

When economic resources other than cash or claims to cash are given up in the exchange, however, the problem of valuation still remains. A possible solution can be found in the market price of the goods and services acquired, or in the market prices of the goods given up in the exchange. If the goods or services given up were acquired previously for cash or its equivalent, this original cost may now be assumed to be the cost of the newly acquired goods and services. Because this latter cost is considered more verifiable than the current market price of either the goods received or the goods given up, it would usually be preferred by accountants, but its relevance is suspect. Suppose, for example, that a plot of land is exchanged for a piece of equipment to be used in the business. The original cost of the land would be considered the basis for valuing the expense of using the equipment, but such cost may have little relevance to current conditions or objectives.

The complexities of cost determination will be discussed more fully in the following chapters. But the following situations suggest some of the

---

[23] For an additional discussion of cost, see Chapter 11.

problems that are relevant in the measurement of expenses in terms of cost: (1) The total agreed price may be payable at a deferred date, in which case the discounted price may be the appropriate measurement of the expense. (2) The appearance of joint costs may permit no adequate solution to the measurement of the several types of expenses. (3) Cost prices that are not the result of arm's-length transactions may be less valid than other methods of measurement. (4) The aggregate cost price should include all of the costs necessary to acquire the goods or services, not only the invoice or quoted price.

Current prices.   As revenue is usually measured in terms of the current prices received for the product, it is frequently argued that the expenses matched against this revenue should also be measured in terms of the current prices of the goods or services used or consumed. Income resulting from the sale transaction is the excess of the cash or claims received over the amount of the resources used. Thus, the measurement of expenses in terms of current prices has the advantage of distinguishing between (1) the income arising from the transaction, and (2) the gains or losses arising from the holding of assets prior to use. The holding of assets for a period prior to use (or allocation to expense) may result from a deliberate decision to speculate or from the necessity to acquire goods and services prior to use. The gains and losses occurring prior to use may arise from price changes, from deterioration, or from obsolescence or other factors. When the acquisition of goods or services prior to use is necessary and the loss or deterioration is also necessary and can be anticipated, this reduction in value should be included in the measurement of the expense; it is a necessary part of the revenue operations of the firm.

Current prices can be obtained to represent either a current liquidation (sale) price or a replacement cost. A current liquidation price or current cash equivalent may be relevant in the measurement of expense because it represents the opportunity cost to the firm in using the specific asset. Furthermore, this measurement of the expense does not require speculation regarding the future possibility of replacement. If there is a good market in which the item can be purchased and sold with little loss, the liquidation price may be particularly relevant. On the other hand, the current replacement cost represents the acquisition price at the time of use, and therefore it may permit a better prediction of the results of future firm activity if there is likely to be continuity of the past into the future. One of the difficulties with the use of a replacement cost is that there may not be a current price available for the same type of goods or services previously acquired or there may be no verifiable measurement of such a price.

Many expenses are contracted for or obtained currently, so that cost is not far removed from the current price. Those cases where the costs may be materially different from the current prices comprise primarily the valuation of inventories and fixed assets. These problems are discussed more fully in Chapter 9 and in the later chapters on inventories and fixed assets. In the following discussion of the timing of expenses, reference will be made primarily to costs, but it should be recognized that the term *current prices* could be substituted for *costs* at any point.

The timing of expenses

By definition, an expense is incurred when goods or services are consumed or used in the process of obtaining revenue. The timing or reporting of expense is brought about by recording this activity in the accounts or including it in financial reports. The reporting of the expense may coincide with the activity of using the goods or services; or it may follow the activity; or, in unusual circumstances, it may precede the activity.

When expenses should be reported is, in part, determined by the approach to income being proposed either explicitly or implicitly. The definition of *income* as changes in values generally suggests that expenses should be reported whenever there is a decrease in value or when there is no apparent benefit or value to be received in the future arising from the use of goods or services. The concept of income that emphasizes cash flows leads to the conclusion that expenses should be reported as close to the actual cash expenditure as is reasonable. Traditional accrual accounting is somewhat between these two extremes, but it leans toward the value concepts somewhat in that it suggests that input (cost) prices should be retained until an increase in value is reported by the substitution of the exit (sales) prices. That is, expense should be recognized in the period in which the associated revenue is recognized. This is the matching process—the timing of revenue reporting comes first, followed by the reporting of related expenses in the same period. Only in unusual cases are revenues deferred until expenses can be measured or identified.

The matching concept. If income were reported gradually over the entire operating process of the firm, the measurement of the net assets of the firm would be increased as value was added by the firm. In this case, there would be no necessity for a matching concept. But because revenue and expense transactions are reported separately, and because the acquisition and payment for goods and services do not usually coincide with the sales and collection processes related to the same product of the enterprise, matching has come to be considered a necessity or at least desirable. The leads and lags in the acquisition and use of, and payment for, goods and services are assumed to be the reason for accruals or deferrals in order to match the expenses with associated revenue.

As defined by the 1964 AAA committee on the matching concept, matching is the process of reporting expenses on the basis of a cause-and-effect relationship with reported revenues. The committee advocated that costs (defined as product and service factors given up) should be related to revenues realized within a specific period on the basis of some discernible positive correlation of such costs with the recognized revenues.[24]

That is, the measurement of net income is assumed to represent the excess of revenues reported during a period over the expenses associated and reported during that same period. A proper matching is assumed to occur only when a reasonable association is found between the revenues and expenses. The timing of expenses, therefore, requires (1) association with revenue, and (2) reporting in the same period as the related revenue is reported.

The matching of expenses with revenues thus requires the finding of a proper association between the two. All expenses, by definition, are incurred as a necessary part of the revenue operation. This does not mean, however, that revenue will always result; expenses may be incurred without revenue resulting. Several calls by a salesman may be necessary before a sale is made; but all calls should be included in the expenses, as they are necessary in the revenue operations. In fact, even if no sales were made the calls would nevertheless be included in the operating expenses. As another example, normal breakage of merchandise should be classified as an expense even though no revenue can be associated with it. The display of merchandise that permits this breakage is necessary in the revenue process, and it is this fact that requires the classification as an expense.

The association of expenses with revenue is, therefore, a difficult step. In fact, in some cases, no association may be possible. This difficulty has led accountants to establish specific rules and procedures or to establish basic criteria for the timing of expenses. These basic criteria are established by drawing a distinction between direct expenses (product costs) and indirect or period expenses. Direct expenses are reported in the period in which the goods or services are used; or they are reported when a decline in economic value can be measured, or is assumed to occur because of an inability to relate the expenses to any future benefit.

Direct or product matching. By associating costs or other measurements of goods or services used with products, and by charging these as product costs to expenses at the time of reporting the associated revenue, a matching of expenses with revenues is obtained. That is, a transformation is assumed to take place; the measurement of the factor costs is assumed to be a proper measurement of the product prior to reporting any value added by the firm. The use of goods and services is associated with a specific product, and the product is then associated with the revenue at the time it is reported. If the revenue is reported at the time of sale, the product leaves the firm and the reporting of its cost or recorded value as an

---

[24] AAA 1964 Concepts and Standards Research Study Committee—The Matching Concept, p. 369.

expense is logical since a new asset (cash or a receivable) has taken its place. On the other hand, until the product leaves the firm, all associated costs can be assumed to represent a measurement of future benefits to the firm which can logically be carried forward as assets. But even under ideal conditions, the matching of product costs with revenues gives rise to several knotty problems. Among these will be discussed the following: (1) How can the use of goods and services be identified with the product of the firm? (2) When expenses can be associated directly with future revenue but do not increase the value of any specific product or products, how should they be reported while awaiting the reporting of these associated revenues? (3) When associated expenses are expected to be incurred subsequent to the reporting of the related revenues, how should they be recorded?

1. The identification of product costs. The various methods for valuing inventories and for charging these values to expenses will be discussed in Chapter 13. But the problem of identification of product costs is relevant at this point. According to the general view of the matching concept, all reasonable and necessary costs of production should be assigned to the product and reported as expenses at the time of reporting the associated revenue. Costs relating to the product on hand, either as unsold finished goods or as uncompleted goods, should be inventoried and carried forward as assets until the time of sale or revenue reporting. Some of these production costs can be associated directly with the production of specific products. Others can be associated only with production in general and are allocated to products by the use of specific rules or procedures.

Direct product costs include the costs of raw materials and labor incurred in the production of the specific product and the costs of other goods and services for which a direct association can be found with the product. It is also considered appropriate to include normal waste material and labor time required in setting up for production. Whenever labor and material costs are insignificant in relation to aggregate costs, they may be omitted from direct product costs for practical reasons. Thus, we see that even in the accounting for direct product costs, several methods of classification may be considered appropiate. And in some cases, no simple answer can be found. For example, when raw materials are used jointly in the production of two or more products, no meaningful allocation procedure may be possible. Allocations should not be attempted unless they result in meaningful measurements to the users of accounting reports.

Indirect product costs represent goods and services used in the process of production which cannot be identified with specific products. However, they are usually assigned to products on an assumed reasonable basis or by an expedient method. Accountants are not agreed, however, that all indirect production costs should be assigned to products. This disagreement rests on two separate controversies: (*a*) Costs that do not result in a salable product, such as idle capacity costs and abnormal spoilage costs, are claimed by some to represent losses or period expenses rather than product costs. (*b*) Under the concept of "direct costing," only variable production costs are said to be meaningful as inventoriable costs. Non-variable production costs are then charged off as period expenses.

2. *Expenses associated directly with future revenues, but not included in product costs.* In a few cases, costs that can be associated with future revenue cannot be assigned directly to the product of the enterprise because they do not represent value added to any specific products. In most cases, these are selling and administrative costs that can be associated clearly with future revenues. A common example is the carrying forward of organization costs that cannot be associated with a product, usually because there is no product at the time they are incurred. However, since they can be associated with the revenues of some future periods, they are usually capitalized and carried as intangible assets on the basis that they represent the value of the organization to the firm in its future operations.

Accountants are generally reluctant to carry forward other selling and administrative costs because of the uncertainty regarding their association with future revenues. But a case can be made for delaying expense recognition in a few instances. If an extensive market research program is carried out before placing a new product on the market, these costs may be associated directly with the revenues expected to be obtained from the new product. The classification and amortization of these costs will be discussed more fully in later chapters.

Other costs that may be carried forward are basically in the nature of prepaid expenses. Sales commissions, for example, may be paid at the time that a customer signs a contract for future delivery; but the revenue may not be recognized until the goods are delivered or, in some cases, until the goods are finally paid for. In these cases, it may be assumed that the services are not fully received until the transaction is completed, in which case the commission represents a prepayment for a service not yet received. However the commission cost should be carried forward, either because it is a prepaid expense or because of a deferral of revenue recognition and the necessity to match costs with related revenue.

One note of caution should be made at this point. Selling and administrative costs should not be carried forward to be matched with future revenue unless there is a reasonable assurance of future revenue with which it may be associated. The lack of current revenue or the possibility of recording an operating loss in the current period is not adequate reason for deferral. If no associated revenue is foreseeable, or if such revenue is highly uncertain, the expenses should be recognized in the current period even if they result in an operating loss.

The relevance of deferring the reporting of the use of goods and services as expenses when there is no direct association with any specific future product or service of the firm is questionable. The argument is that if the use of goods and services does not benefit the current period and does not represent a loss, it must benefit future periods; and therefore it should be allocated to future periods in order to match the expenses with the associated revenue. But, since there is no specific revenue associated with the expense, the matching process does not apply. The result is merely the smoothing of income by spreading the expense over several years. The information provided to users of financial statements is not improved by such allocations. An example would be the deferral and allocation of basic research and development expenditures which cannot be associated directly with any specific revenues. Even though these expenditures may benefit many periods, there may be no method of applying the matching concept in a meaningful and relevant way. Accordingly the FASB now requires the R&D expenses to be charged against income currently.

3. Direct expenses incurred subsequent to the reporting of related revenue. Occasionally, direct expenses will occur subsequent to the reporting of related revenue. For example, if a warranty is given at the time of sale of merchandise, a future related expense is quite probable. Proper matching requires that the expense be recorded at the time of sale (or other point of revenue reporting) and that a liability be recorded for the estimated cost of future repairs or replacements. Just the fact that this cost is uncertain is not an appropriate reason for delaying its recognition. If any reasonable estimation of the probable costs of future warranties can be found, they should be recorded at the time of revenue recognition. For a single sale transaction, an estimation may be impossible, but for a large number of sales during the year, a reasonable approximation can usually be found. If costs under express or implied warranties do occur in excess of all reasonable expectations, they should be recorded as losses rather than operating expenses. The proper criterion is the reasonableness or probability of their occurrence. This same reasoning can be applied to collection costs and other related administrative costs.

When revenue is reported prior to final delivery of merchandise, additional costs of completion and delivery are probable. In these cases it may be appropriate to record the revenue at the selling price less expected additional costs to complete and sell. The related receivable or inventory is then usually valued in the same way. This concept of net realizable value is discussed more fully later in Chapter 13.

In the case of installment sales, revenue may not be recognized until the cash is finally collected. The receivable is usually recorded at the full sales price, and a special account is set up for "deferred gross profit on installment sales." The recognition of both the revenue and the product costs are delayed by carrying forward the net amount. While this account is often called a deferred credit, it really represents an offsetting account to the receivable in order to be consistent with the reporting of revenue when cash is received. It is a measurement of the asset "installments receivable" rather than a liability in order to reflect the cash basis of accounting.

Occasionally, it is recommended that a portion of revenue be deferred until the final activity regarding the servicing of a product subsequent to sale has been accomplished; the amount of the revenue should be sufficient to equal the probable "after costs" and a portion of the income or value added by the firm.[25] However, the value added by the firm cannot be measured by separate activities. As indicated earlier, there is no logic in assigning an equal amount of revenue to each dollar of expenditure.

Indirect or period matching.   The reporting of expenses in the periods in which the goods and services are used is a process of matching the measurement of goods and services with the period in which they are used rather than reporting them in the period of acquisition or payment. Therefore, this is not matching in the sense of associating the expenses with the related revenues. However, it is frequently justified as either an approximation of the matching of expenses with revenues or as an exception to it; the following are frequently presented as justification for indirect matching: (1) Many period expenses are associated indirectly with the revenue of the current period, so that is no material deviation from the matching principle if the expenses are reported when the goods or services are used. For example, rent of a retail store can be associated with the sales during the period the store is rented. (2) In many cases there is an inability to find any direct association with revenue, but if the expenses are necessary for overall operations, they should be charged to the current period. For example, in the expense of maintaining a parking lot for employess in all activities of the firm, there is no direct association with any specific revenue. (3) A corollary to (2) is that if there is no measurable association with future revenue or no measurable benefit to future periods, there is no justification for carrying the expense forward to later periods. While the parking lot example might be appropriate in this case also, another example might be the expense of maintaining recreational facilities for employees of all departments. (4) If the expenses are regular and recurring, there may be no material effect on the net income of any period other than the first and last periods of the business life, even if perfect matching is not obtained. For example, reporting research and development expenses currently may result in reported expenses similar to those reported under the allocation procedure for most periods if such expenses are recurring and fairly constant in amount. (5) Many costs are joint costs, necessitating somewhat arbitrary allocations to different activities. An arbitrary allocation to different periods may be more misleading than no allocation because allocation implies a preciseness that may not be present. An example is property taxes on land and buildings which cannot be allocated to areas of activity within the plant except on an arbitrary basis.

The first step in the process of assigning expenses to periods is the determination of when the expiration of the goods or services occurs. The second step is the classification of the expenses by major activity. If the activity is the selling function of the enterprise, it may be assumed that

---

[25] See, for example, Norton M. Bedford, *Income Determination Theory: An Accounting Framework* (Reading, Mass.: Addison-Wesley, 1965), pp. 103–4.

the related revenue is recognized currently. Much of sales activity relates to providing goods and services during the current period. To some extent, however, there is a lag in the reporting of sales revenue following the selling activity. But if the selling expenses are regular and recurring, there will be little effect on the amount of net income of most periods. Arbitrary allocations of selling expenses to future periods may result in less meaningful statements than those in which the selling expenses are classified as period charges.

The joint-cost problem also presents a problem of allocation not only to different periods but also to different classifications. In reality, all enterprise activity can be classified as either relating to production or to the selling function of business. That activity that aids jointly both production and selling is classified as administrative. The top executives of the firm must direct their energies to the direction of all functions of the enterprise. Likewise, many service and staff departments, such as accounting and personnel, incur costs that are difficult to allocate to the selling and producing functions. Because this difficulty is often insurmountable, these expenses are usually classified as period charges.

Other costs of general operations and selling operations obviously relate in part to the production of future revenues. But if there is no reasonable means of associating these costs with future revenue, or if the benefit to future operations is highly uncertain, the only practical solution is to charge them to current operations. Advertising is a good example. Most advertising has a carry-over or cumulative effect with respect to revenue. Repeated advertising of a product, firm name, or trade name is more effective than a single advertisement. But the effect is always uncertain, and there is no possible method of determining, even in retrospect, which advertisement caused which revenue. Thus, period matching is most appropriate under normal circumstances.

Frequently in the past it was suggested that in special circumstances it may be appropriate to carry forward all costs of operations to be matched against the revenues of future periods. For example, it was considered appropriate to capitalize the costs of organizing a firm in order to charge these costs against the revenues of future periods. Other production and selling costs were carried forward to future periods during this period of organization if they were necessary in the preparation for future production and sales. Thus, if one year is required to organize and prepare for the production and sale of a product, all normal costs are capitalized and carried forward to be allocated to future periods. But if, in the second year, production bottlenecks prevent the manufacture of the expected quantity, or if the demand for the product fails to materialize, the costs of the second year should not be carried forward except to the extent that reasonable costs can be included in the inventories. Costs should not be carried forward merely because a loss would result by charging them to the current period. In 1975, the FASB in *Statement No. 7* required that start-up costs of development state enterprises be presented in the same way as for established enterprises. However, costs are still frequently carried forward to be matched with future revenues on the ground that they are assumed to benefit some future periods. This type of matching appears to the author to be of little relevance to users of financial statements because the allocation process is not based on any direct association with revenues reported in any period or periods. The result is merely a spreading of the effect of the expense so that no single period discloses the true effect of the activity.

THE ALLOCATION CONCEPT

Allocation in accounting is the process of partitioning a set or valuation amount and the assignment of the resulting subsets to separate classifications or periods of time. Allocations include both the assignment of assets to expenses and the assignment of liabilities or contra assets to revenues of different periods. Depreciation is an example of the former and the percentage-of-completion method for long-term contracts is an example of the latter.

In accordance with the traditional structural approach to accounting, allocations result from the application of specific rules for the assignment of costs to products or period expenses and the assignment of the value of the product of the enterprise to specific periods as revenues. Although an attempt has been made to reduce the number of acceptable allocation alternatives, most if not all accounting allocations are not defensible on the basis of real-world observations.

Thomas has suggested that for allocations to be theoretically justified, they should meet three criteria: additivity, unambiguity, and defensibility.[26] To be additive, the allocation must divide the total amount so that the sum of the parts is equal to the whole. To be unambigous, the allocation procedure should result in only one set of parts. Defensibility, the most important of the three criteria, implies that the allocation method selected must be demonstrated to be superior to all other allocation methods.[27]

Most attempts to support allocations are based on an assumption that there is a one-to-one relationship between cost or other value and physical units or uniform time periods. As will be discussed in the following chapters, these assumptions cannot be verified, with the result that such allocations are just as arbitrary as any other allocation method. No real-world observations have supported these assertions.

An alternative to the above is to defend allocations on the basis of their behavioral implications. One argument is that since allocations are used

---

[26] Arthur L. Thomas, "The Allocation Problem in Financial Accounting Theory," *Studies in Accounting Research No. 3* (AAA, 1969), pp. 6–15.

[27] See Arthur L. Thomas, "The Allocation Problem: Part Two," *Studies in Accounting Research No. 9* (AAA, 974), chap. 1, for an extended discussion of the criteria for allocations.

and accepted, they have purposeful utility. However, the fact that procedures *are* used and accepted in the measurement of accounting income does not mean that they *should* be used and accepted. Other arguments include the contention that allocations are either neutral with respect to investment decisions or that investors prefer or even demand allocations for their investment models. If the allocations are actually neutral in their effect, they are superfluous and reports would be better without them. If allocations that are misleading are requested by investors, some accountants suggest that they should be provided. However, information regarding investors' decision models is at present insufficient to use the preferences of any subgroup as a guide for all investors. Therefore, the lack of real-world correspondence is the overriding consideration to suggest that allocations are inappropriate for external financial reporting purposes.

It should be noted, however, that allocations may at times be necessary for the division of interrelated revenues or expenses among interested parties. For example, government contracts frequently require payment on the basis of costs allocated to the specific contract. In some cases, the allocation procedure is determined by bargaining among the interested parties. In the United States, the former Cost Accounting Standards Board was established to formulate uniform allocation methods that are at least acceptable to most of the interested parties, even though they cannot be verified by real-world observations.

GAINS AND LOSSES

Gains and losses represent favorable and unfavorable events not directly related to the normal revenue-producing activities of the enterprise. Deciding what is normal and what is not normal is difficult in many cases, and consistent treatment among firms and for different periods may be almost impossible. But the distinction is valid and useful in a proper interpretation of the several concepts of income.

The term *normal revenue-producing activities* refers to the intent of the enterprise regarding its major and related activities. These activities are usually regular and recurring. Nonrevenue-producing activities may be sporadic; however, they may also include ancillary activities of a recurring nature not related to the continuing objectives of the enterprise. The purpose of separate classification should be to disclose to the reader of the financial statements the results of the current activities of the firm that may be comparable with past and future activities and permit a basis for prediction of future results.

The definition of gains and losses presented in *FASB SFAC No. 3* is consistent with the above definition.[28] However, a distinction is made between gains and losses arising from customary business activities and

---

[28] *AICPA Professional Standards,* para. 1230.067.

extraordinary gains and losses. The latter are discussed at greater length
in Chapter 7.[29]

Gains

Gifts to the enterprise may be classified as either capital or income, depending on the intent of the donor and the circumstances surrounding the
gift. In a few cases the intent of a gratuity may be to increase the income
of the firm, as in the case of "conscience payments," or extra payments to
show gratitude for special services received. But in the case of contributions in aid of construction required before service can be supplied to some
public-utility customers, and in the case of special donations to attract a
firm into a community, the intent is to provide permanent capital.

Gifts should be measured like revenues—by the current value of the
assets received. Most other gains result from an exchange, so that a
matching of the favorable and unfavorable aspects is required. The measurement of the favorable aspect is similar to the measurement of
revenue—by the current value of the assets received or recognized or by
the current value of debt reduction.[30] The unfavorable aspects should be
measured similarly to expenses—by the value of the goods and services
used or exchanged in the transaction. Only those items directly associated
with the transaction, however, are matched against the favorable aspects
in computing the gain. In the sale of assets not usually traded by the firm,
these unfavorable aspects would include the value of the assets sold plus
the direct costs of sale. The allocation of income taxes to the transaction
will be discussed in Chapter 18.

Cost, book value, or other recorded value is usually used in computing
the gain, for several reasons. Probably the most significant of these reasons is that it is not important to make a distinction between a true
windfall gain and a correction or prior periods. Other reasons are that
costs are verifiable and are assumed to represent the exchange value of
the assets at the time they were acquired by the enterprise. But if the
increase in value is due in part to the changing value of the monetary unit,
cost is not appropriate; a part of the increase in value represents a restatement of the capital of the firm, rather than an increase in retained
earnings. This is discussed further in Chapter 9.

The timing of the recognition of gains is similar to the recognition of
revenues, except that accountants generally have held more closely to the
realization concept. That is, gains are not generally recognized until an
exchange or sale has taken place. However, an increase in the market
value of securities may, under some circumstances, be sufficient evidence
to recognize a gain. But most accountants require that the increase in

---

[29] See above, pp. 162–63.
[30] See above, pp. 175–76.

value be almost impossible of reversal before making recognition.[31] From a theory point of view, this is an extreme position. The most probable outcome in uncertain situations should be recorded, rather than limiting recognition to only those cases that are certain. Also, there is an inconsistency in using a double standard for the recognition of gains and losses; both should be recognized on the same basis of probability.

Basically, the reluctance of accountants to record appreciation stems from two sources: (1) the uncertain and possibly ephemeral nature of the increase in value, and (2) the fact that an increase in value does not give rise to liquid resources that can be used for the payment of dividends. This emphasis on liquid resources or cash flows may be relevant for some types of decisions, but not for the measurement of most concepts of income. For income determination, relative certainty and verifiable measurements are more relevant criteria. If a long-term investment in bonds is made at a cost less than the face value of the bonds, accountants usually consider it appropriate to write up the value of the investment to the face value at maturity. The total increase is definite, according to a contract, and verifiable, even though the amount of increase each year may be indeterminate. For investments in marketable securities, the recording of gains and losses arising from material changes in market prices is becoming more acceptable in accounting practice because both verifiability and liquidity are present, even though the change has not been validated by a sale or exchange in which the firm is a party. But if land increases in value, it is generally thought inappropriate to increase the recorded valuation above cost. However, to the extent that verifiable measurements can be obtained regarding the changes in the market price of land, changes in its price may be just as relevant in the determination of income as are changes in the value of bonds or investments in marketable securities. The economic gain or loss is not more real just because the securities or land are sold and the proceeds used to reacquire securities or land of the same type. The opportunity to do so, however, may be relevant information regarding the firm, even though the intent is not to sell.

Losses

The term *loss* is used by accountants to designate the excess of expenses over the revenues of a period—the opposite of net income. But the term is used here as the opposite of gains, relating to the net unfavorable events not arising from normal revenue-producing activities.

In the traditional structural approach to accounting, the term *loss* is used to mean the expiration or write-off of costs not related to revenues of any period. However, for a loss to have real-world interpretation, it should reflect a decline in market value or other observable measurement of

---

[31] See, for example, Floyd W. Windal, "The Accounting Concept of Realization," *Accounting Review*, April 1961, p. 256.

value at the time of the sale or abandonment of property or at the time of whole or partial destruction by casualty.

A basic part of the definition of losses is that they represent expirations of value not related to the normal operations of any period. That is, they result from extraneous and exogenous events that are not recurring or anticipated as necessary in the process of producing revenues. If they were anticipated, they possibly could have been avoided; if they were necessary in the production of revenues, they should be included among the expenses. To the extent that value expirations represent corrections of the expenses of prior periods, they should not be included among the losses, but separately classified as prior period corrections. But this distinction is usually very difficult to make. Unforeseen declines in value represent losses; but if they had been foreseen, would they have been included in the expenses? The answer to this question is not always clear. In some cases, if the decline in value had been foreseen, the asset would not have been acquired; in this case the recognition of the decline is clearly a loss.

The measurement of losses is similar to the measurement of expenses except that any proceeds are offset directly to reflect a net amount. As with expenses, it seems preferable to define losses as value expirations, rather than as cost allocations. With this definition, the question of measurement is left open for further discussion. As with expenses, cost represents a verifiable measurement and the exchange value of the assets at the time they were acquired. But in many cases current value may be more appropriate in the measurement of the loss. For example, a building destroyed by fire before the end of its useful life represents a loss to the firm (to the extent that it is uninsured), even though it may be fully depreciated in the accounts. Logically, depreciation for prior periods should be adjusted and a loss recorded. However, since these are offsetting items in their effect on total stockholders' equity, using the traditional structural approach accountants may prefer to refrain from attempting a measurement of the loss in favor of disclosure in some other way.

The criteria for the recognition of losses are similar to the criteria for the recognition of period expenses. Losses cannot be matched with revenue, so they should be recorded in the period in which it becomes fairly definite that a given asset will provide less benefit to the firm than indicated by the recorded valuation.

In the case of a sale of assets not traded normally, and in the case of a loss by fire or other catastrophe, the timing of the event is fairly definite. But, when the decline in value is gradual over several periods, it is difficult to determine exactly when the loss occurs. The asset may eventually be sold or abandoned; but if the asset has lost its usefulness it is unreasonable to withhold the recognition of the loss until the final disposition. Reporting should occur as soon as it appears quite probable that the asset has lost its usefulness and that this loss of usefulness is not likely to be reversed in the future.

In no case should a loss be deliberately carried forward to later periods.

If it is fairly definite and if the amount of the loss can be measured reasonably well, it should be recorded as soon as it is ascertainable. For example, when equipment is replaced, the undepreciated cost should not be added arbitrarily to the cost of the new asset. Also, when bonds are refunded, the unamortized discount and call premium represent a change in the value of the bonds and should be written off rather than carried forward and allocated over the life of the new bonds.[32]

SELECTED ADDITIONAL READING

The timing of revenue reporting

American Accounting Association 1964 Concepts and Standards Research Committee—The Realization Concept. "The Realization Concept," *Accounting Review,* April 1965, pp. 312–22.

American Accounting Association 1972–73 Committee on Concepts and Standards—External Reporting. *Accounting Review,* supplement to vol. 49 (1974), pp. 203–22.

Horngren, Charles T. "How Should We Interpret the Realization Concept?" *Accounting Review,* April 1965, pp. 323–33.

Thomas, Arthur L. "Revenue Recognition." Michigan Business Reports No. 49. Ann Arbor: Bureau of Business Research, Graduate School of Business Administration, University of Michigan, 1966.

Walker, Lauren M.; Gerhard G. Mueller; and Fauzi G. Dimian. "Significant Events in the Development of the Realization Concept in the U.S." *Accountants Magazine (Scotland),* August 1970, pp. 357–60.

Installment accounting

Cerf, Alan Robert. "Accounting for Retail Land Sales." *Accounting Review,* July, 1975, pp. 451–65.

Scott, Richard A., and **Rita K. Scott.** "Installment Accounting: Is It Inconsistent?" *Journal of Accountancy,* November 1979, pp. 52–58.

The matching of expenses and revenues

American Accounting Association 1964 Concepts and Standards Research Study Committee—The Matching Concept. "The Matching Concept." *Accounting Review,* April 1965, pp. 368–72.

Liao, Shu S. "The Matching Concept and Cost Allocation." *Accounting and Business Research,* Summer 1979, pp. 228–36.

Most, Kenneth. "The Rise and Fall of the Matching Principle." *Accounting and Business Research,* Autumn 1977, pp. 286–90.

Whittred, G. P. "Accounting for the Extractive Industries: Use or Abuse of the Matching Principle?" *Abacus,* December 1978, pp. 154–59.

---

[32] For an extended discussion of the treatment of unamortized bond discount at the time of refunding, see Chapter 17.

CHAPTER 9

REPORTING THE
EFFECTS OF
PRICE CHANGES

Inflation has become an important and constant fact of life in almost all countries of the world. The changing value of the monetary currency is now well recognized among accountants, but there is disagreement regarding the theoretical and practical means of adjusting for it. In the United States, *FASB Statement No. 33* requires special disclosures by certain large firms, but it does not specify the relationship of these disclosures to the basic financial statements.

An unstable monetary unit is a measurement constraint in the inductive-deductive approach to accounting theory. When financial measurements are based on historical prices or when comparisons are made of price aggregates among different years, the usual assumed relationships in financial statements are altered. Attempts to overcome this constraint have resulted in proposals to modify or restate traditional accounting measurements. Generally this approach is more acceptable to the accounting profession than a radical approach that would establish a new structure of accounting to avoid comparisons and aggregations of prices of different years.

The purpose of this chapter is to analyze the alternative methods of accounting for price changes. The first two sections discuss the nature of price changes and the importance of monetary and nonmonetary classifications. The third section discusses the purchasing-power approach. It should be emphasized that the purchasing-power approach includes both the restatement for general purchasing power changes and the restatement to reflect specific purchasing power as these are competing alternatives. The fourth section discusses current value accounting, including the use of both current costs and replacements costs as surrogates for current input values. Foreign currency translations are discussed in the final section because they represent restatements of the monetary unit and because exchange rates are related to the relative changes in prices in the separate countries.

The main objective of purchasing power accounting is to restate the unit of measure into a common denominator. That is, the restatement is a scale adjustment and not a substitution of one measurement for another.

For example, I could say that I traveled 1,000 miles in the United States and 1,000 kilometers in Europe, a total of 2,000 miles and kilometers. The latter, of course, is meaningless because it reflects the summing of two different scales of measurement. If I wished to restate this into a single scale of measurement, I could say that I traveled a total of 1,620 miles or 2,610 kilometers. Likewise, the summation of historical costs incurred at different periods of time represents the aggregation of different scales of measurement.[1] The restatement of historical costs for changes in purchasing power is assumed to result in figures measured in terms of the same scale of measurement.

An important observation regarding purchasing power accounting is that the major objective is to improve the measurement system in the structural framework of the accounting process. Although the behavioral impact of price-level adjusted accounting information is not fully understood at the present time, some studies have supported the hypothesis that price-level restated data do contain information not included in traditional financial reports.[2]

THE NATURE OF PRICE CHANGES

Prices reflect the exchange value of goods and services in the economy. These goods and services include the several factors of production and items at intermediate stages of production, items held for speculative purposes, and goods and services acquired for consumption purposes. In general, these prices can be classified as either input prices (prices of factors of production or of goods and services at intermediate stages, acquired for further production or resale) or output prices (prices of goods and services sold as the product of the enterprise).

Price changes occur only when the prices of goods or services are different from what they were previously in the same market. The fact that a firm buys a commodity in its input market at one price and sells it to its customers at a higher price does not mean that the price of the commodity has changed. A price change occurs only if a price increases or decreases either in an input market or in an output market or in both.

Price changes can be classified as one of three types, although these classifications are interdependent and not mutually exclusive. These are (1) general, (2) specific, and (3) relative price changes. General price changes reflect increases or decreases in the value of the monetary unit. They may be caused by changes in the supply or velocity of money that are greater or less than the changes in the total supply of goods and

---

[1] See Maurice Moonitz, "Changing Prices and Financial Reporting" (Champaign, Ill.: Stipes Publishing, 1974), esp. chap. 2, pp. 5–21.

[2] See, for example, Arie Baran, Josef Lakonishok, and Aharon R. Ofer, "The Information Content of General Price Level Adjusted Earnings: Some Empirical Evidence," *Accounting Review,* January 1980, pp. 22–35.

services in the economy, by an imbalance in the total supply and demand of goods and services in general, or by changes in world prices of basic commodities. Specific price changes occur for several reasons, including changes in tastes of consumers, technological improvements, speculation, and natural or artificial changes in the supply of particular products or as a result of changes in the value of money. Relative price changes reflect the change in the structure of prices or the change in the price of one commodity relative to the prices of all goods and services. General and relative price changes are both reflected in changes in the prices of specific goods. Although it is difficult, if not impossible, to separate the two effects on specific prices, they are different economic phenomena conceptually.

General price-level changes

A general price-level change occurs as a result of a change in the value of the monetary unit during periods of inflation and deflation. In the absence of structural or relative price movements, all prices would move together by the same percentage. However, if prices are moving at different rates, which is the usual case, a measure of general price changes can be obtained only by computing an average or index of prices to express the general level of current prices compared with some base period. The ratio of the current index of prices to the base-period index expresses the relative change in all prices included in the index. The reciprocal of this ratio expresses the change in the value of the dollar or the change in *purchasing power*. For example, if the price index should increase from 100 to 200, prices would have doubled, but the purchasing power of the dollar would have decreased to one half of its previous level.

The term *purchasing power* refers to the ability to buy goods and services with a given quantity of money (e.g., one dollar) compared with what the same quantity of money could have purchased at an earlier date. To obtain a good comparison of the purchasing power of money at two different dates, the goods and services available at the two dates must be the same or similar. Since the types and qualities of goods and services available change considerably over time, good comparisons of purchasing power cannot be obtained over several decades.

General purchasing power refers to the ability to buy all types of goods and services available in the economy, and it is measured by changes in the general price level. *Specific purchasing power* refers to the ability to buy specific goods and services at different dates. Thus, specific purchasing power can be measured by changes in specific prices. In between the concepts of general purchasing power and specific purchasing power are many concepts relating to the ability to buy certain goods and services that may be purchased by specific groups of individuals or that may be used for certain purposes. For example, the Consumer Price Index of the U.S. Bureau of Labor Statistics (CPI–U) measures the average change in prices of a specific "market basket" of goods and services bought by all urban consumers. Therefore, this index can be used to measure ability of these individuals to maintain their level of living by purchasing the "basket" of goods and services usually acquired by them. However, the CPI–U was selected by the FASB for use in complying with *Statement 33* because it is fairly well understood and it is broad enough to be considered a general index, rather than a specific one. In a like manner, it is also possible to measure the purchasing power of business enterprises to buy the goods and services usually acquired by them. These concepts of specific purchasing power (purchasing power for certain groups) are discussed at greater length below in the discussion of the choice of a proper index.

Specific price changes

In the absence of general price movements or changes in the value of the monetary unit, a change in the price of a specific commodity represents a change in its exchange value. Changes in prices in an input market result in increases or decreases in costs or expenses of the firm, and changes of prices in the output market result in a shift in revenues (assuming that the price change does not affect the quantity sold). In the traditional transactions approach to accounting, the original transaction price of goods or services acquired is matched with the revenue associated with the period or the goods sold. Changes in the specific input prices of goods sold are, therefore, included in the computation of the reported net income for the period. A more relevant matching is thought to be obtained by reporting as expenses the current prices of the goods used in the process of obtaining revenue. This matching of the current input prices with the current output (revenue) prices is thought to be more relevant as a measure of operating efficiency and as a better basis for the prediction of the results of future transactions.

Although there is no general agreement regarding the nature of the changes in specific prices of goods held by a firm, one view is that an increase in prices results in a holding gain, and a decrease results in a holding loss. According to this view, these should be included in the computation of the income of the firm, because they represent changes in the value of the stockholders' equity (the net assets of the firm). However, most authors would not include these holding gains and losses in the computation of operating income because it is thought that they do not result from the normal recurring activities of the firm. That is, profit from normal operations is assumed to be the excess of selling price (or other determined revenue) over the current input price (current cost) of the product of the enterprise less other operating expenses.

The cost convention in accounting reports no change in value of assets until revenue is reported, usually at the time of sale. If current costs are used, holding gains and losses may be reported as prices change, although these gains and losses may be classified as either realized or unrealized.[3] For example, if a commodity has been purchased for $100 and sold for $150 at a time when its current input price (replacement cost) is $120, the operating gross profit is $30 and the holding gain is $20. If the increase in the input price had occurred in a prior period, Edwards and Bell would consider the $20 to be realizable cost savings (unrealized) in the earlier period, but realized in the current period when the item is sold.[4]

Current costs represent current exchange prices, and thus their use results in a deviation from the historical cost basis. An objection is frequently made regarding the use of current costs, on the ground that a subjective value is substituted for a verifiable exchange price (historical cost). However, verifiability may still be present in those cases where the current exchange prices are obtained from well-organized markets. Furthermore, while some verifiability may be lost in the use of current costs rather than historical costs, the former are likely to be more relevant in meeting the objectives of the users of financial reports. However, current input prices can be assumed to represent current costs to the firm only if the firm generally purchases the same types of assets and is continuing to do so. If the firm is not purchasing the same type of asset, there is no evidence that it would acquire the asset in use at the current price, and therefore the current price of an asset acquired earlier at a lower price may not represent the relevant price, either in evaluating the firm's activities or in making predictions regarding the future.

Relative price changes

In the usual situation, prices of goods and services are moving at different rates, and some even in different directions. The extent to which specific prices move at a different rate or in a different direction from an index of all prices represents a relative price change. That is, if all prices increase by 20 percent and the price of product A increases by 32 percent, the relative price increase of product A is 10 percent (132/120—1.00).

In traditional accounting, with the use of historical costs, no price changes are isolated for separate reporting; all price changes are included in income as a result of transactions. The accounts and statements can be adjusted for general price-level changes without making adjustments for specific price changes, in which case costs and expenses would be adjusted for changes in the value of money and the price-level effect of these restatements would be excluded from the income calculation. But holding gains and losses resulting from relative price changes would not be measured or separated from reported net income.

If current prices are used instead of historical costs, net operating income can be computed without including any of the effects of price

---

[3] Edgar O. Edwards and Philip W. Bell, *The Theory and Measurement of Business Income* (Berkeley and Los Angeles: University of California Press, 1961), esp. pp. 111–15.

[4] Ibid.

changes. But holding gains and losses cannot be measured unless the accounts are adjusted for both specific price changes and changes in the general price level. That is, the full effect of relative price changes cannot be measured and disclosed unless the accounts are adjusted for changes in the value of money and for changes in specific prices.

THE MONETARY AND NONMONETARY CLASSIFICATIONS

Monetary assets are claims to a fixed quantity of the monetary unit (e.g., dollars) representing general purchasing power. Although prices of goods and services may change, claims expressed in a given number of dollars remain unchanged, but the purchasing power, or ability to convert these claims into goods and services, is altered. Monetary assets include cash; contractual claims to a specific amount of money in the future, such as accounts and notes receivable; and investments that pay a fixed amount of interest or dividends and will be repaid at a fixed amount in the future, although the date of repayment need not be specified—as in the case of preferred stock.

Convertible debt and convertible preferred stock are hybrid items that may be monetary or nonmonetary depending on the circumstances. If the market price of the common stock into which they may be converted has increased sufficiently, the market will value the convertible securities in terms of the common stock equivalents. Therefore, investments in convertible securities should be classified as monetary or nonmonetary depending on whether the market values them as debt or equity securities.

Monetary liabilities represent obligations to pay a fixed amount of dollars at some time in the future, regardless of what happens to the value of the monetary unit. They also include obligations to pay a fixed number of dollars, even though the exact amount is not known for certain. The important criterion is that the amount to be paid does not depend upon changes in the value of the monetary unit. These would include accounts and notes payable, accruals, such as wages and interest payable, and long-term obligations payable in a fixed sum. Such items as rents and royalties received in advance are nonmonetary because they represent amounts payable in goods and services whose prices may fluctuate. As with investments in convertible securities, convertible debt should not be classified as a monetary liability. In most cases, where there is a possibility of future conversion, convertible debt should be treated as equity because it is not likely to be retired by the payment of a fixed number of dollars. *FASB Statement No. 33* (Appendix D), however, suggests that convertible debt should be classified as monetary until it is converted.

Nonmonetary assets, on the other hand, include those items whose prices in terms of the monetary unit may change over time, or claims to a variable amount of the monetary unit representing a predetermined amount of purchasing power. These would include all rights to goods and services and all other rights to future benefits other than claims or rights expressed in terms of a fixed dollar value at some future time. Nonmonetary liabilities would include the obligation to provide given amounts of goods and services or an equivalent amount of purchasing power, even though the payment might be in the form of cash. For example, an obligation to pay cash equal to the price of a given quantity of goods or services would be nonmonetary in nature.

The difficulty in defining monetary and nonmonetary assets and liabilities arises basically because the distinction is arbitrary. Only in a very extreme case would the price of an asset change by exactly the same percentage as the change in the general price level. On the other hand, it is possible that the price of an asset or the number of dollars to be exchanged for a claim may increase or decrease by a very small percentage in the relationship to the change in general prices. For example, a contract could call for the repayment of x number of dollars plus one tenth of the percentage change in general prices. Thus, if a claim for $100 comes due after a period when general prices increased by 10 percent, the amount of the claim would be $101. Is this not more closely related to a monetary claim than one that is nonmonetary by the above definitions? For those who would say that this is not a realistic case, let us look at claims to foreign currency and claims payable in a foreign currency. *FASB Statement No. 33* classifies them as monetary, but suggests that claims to foreign currency are technically nonmonetary. It is true that a U.S. firm may not necessarily receive the same number of dollars when the claims are converted as when they were established; but, like claims to domestic currency, they may result in purchasing power gains and losses. Therefore, they may be monetary or nonmonetary; the choice is arbitrary.

Gains and losses on monetary items

Inflation is known to be beneficial to debtors and detrimental to creditors. Increased price levels usually mean increased dollar incomes, making repayment of debt easier in terms of the economic sacrifice involved. If A should borrow $1,000 from B and repay it after a period during which the price level has increased by 60 percent, A has an economic gain and B has an economic loss. Although A repays $1,000, this represents only five eighths (62.5 percent) of the purchasing power it had when borrowed. From the point of view of capital maintenance, if A has held the value of the borrowed money in the form of assets that have increased in monetary value with the price level, A will have realized a gain of $600 by selling the asset and repaying the loan. The creditor will have sustained a loss of $600 in purchasing power.

The gain or loss from the holding of net monetary assets by a firm is not so easily evaluated. Normally a firm will have cash and receivables in excess of monetary current liabilities. With a positive net monetary current position, an economic loss occurs as price levels increase and an economic gain occurs as price levels fall. During periods of inflation, the purchasing power of this working capital is not maintained. In fact, if the volume of business remains constant in real terms, working capital must usually be increased.

A gain or loss also occurs because of the holding of long-term monetary assets, such as long-term receivables and investments in government bonds and preferred stocks, and because of outstanding long-term debt. If the long-term debt exceeds the long-term monetary assets, an economic gain will occur when the price level rises, and vice versa when the price level falls.

The computation of the purchasing power gains or losses on monetary items involves two distinct steps: (1) The amount of the claim is first restated for the change in the purchasing power of the dollar during the accounting period, or during the period it was held or outstanding if for less than a year. (2) This restated amount is then compared with the current value of the asset or liability at the end of the period or at the time the item was reduced. The difference is the gain or loss in purchasing power. This computation is similar to the restatement of nonmonetary items for changes in the value of money and a subsequent revaluation for changes in specific prices. However, monetary items are already expressed in current terms, so the computation is necessary only to measure the gain or loss arising from changes in their value expressed in terms of purchasing power.

Writers on this subject are not in agreement on the nature of this gain or loss or on the method of disclosing it in financial reports. Because it is similar to the holding gain or loss on nonmonetary items, one view is that it should be included in the computation of net income but not in income from operations. This is in accord with the financial capital maintenance concept and was preferred by the Board in the Exposure Draft. In *Statement No. 33,* however, the Board expressed no preference in the hopes of encouraging experimentation.

The fact that these gains and losses have no counterpart in conventional accounting has been responsible for much of the disagreement on the subject. Traditional accounting concepts and principles emphasize the allocation of costs to expenses and the recognition of gains through realization only at the time of external transactions. The discussions regarding the use of current costs and the recognition of holding gains and losses are not entirely comparable to the gains and losses on monetary items; this is because the former refer primarily to nonmonetary assets, and the latter do not even appear unless adjustments are first made for changes in the value of money.

An alternative view suggested by Deupree is that the purchasing power gain from the holding of liabilities (during periods of general price-level increase) represents a reduction in the cost of the assets acquired with the debt financing.[5] As an adjustment of the cost of assets, these credits (or debits in the case of deflation) should be taken into income as the assets are allocated to expenses, by depreciation or otherwise, or when they are sold. This view holds that the cost of an asset should be measured by the amount of cash finally paid for the asset, rather than the amount intended to be paid at the time of acquisition. It also holds strictly to the realization rule that the difference between this cost and the revenue against which it is matched should not be recognized until the asset is allocated to expense or sold.

Another interpretation is that because of the rapid turnover of monetary working capital items, the purchasing power gains and losses on these items can be considered to be realized as they occur, but that the purchasing power gains and losses from the holding of long-term debt should not appear in the current operating statement until they are realized through the payment of the bonds.[6]

Another view is that from the point of view of the enterprise, the gains and losses on long-term debt are not a determinant of income, but rather an adjustment of the total equity of the firm—a shift from the bondholders' equity to the stockholders' equity. During periods of price-level increases, stockholders gain and bondholders lose, but the enterprise as a whole is not affected by the existence of the long-term debt. Therefore, if the income statement shows the income to the enterprise before interest on long-term debt, the purchasing power loss on the long-term debt should not be included. But in showing net income to stockholders, the gain or loss should be included. Since most income statements are prepared with the latter objective, the gain or loss on the long-term debt should be included. However, since the equity of the *enterprise* is relevant for some comparisons, a distinction should be made between the gains and losses on monetary working capital and the gains and losses on the long-term debt.

Some of the difficulties in reporting the purchasing power gains and losses on monetary items relate to the logic of the structural framework of accounting. First, the arbitrary distinction between monetary and nonmonetary items weakens a structure that is already weak in terms of precise definitions. Second, the basic objective of purchasing power restatements is to utilize a consistent scale of measurement, not to measure changes in values of specific items. Since nonmonetary items are not stated at current values, the valuation of monetary items at current values is inconsistent. That is, monetary items are restated for the change in purchasing power and then restated again back to the nominal value

---

[5] See also Arthur Andersen & Co., *Accounting and Reporting Problems of the Accounting Profession,* 2d ed. (Chicago, 1962), pp. 16–17. Russell Morrison holds a similar view, except he offsets current liabilities against the current monetary assets and considers only the gains and losses from the holding of long-term debt as adjustments of the cost of assets. See AICPA, "Reporting the Financial Effect of Price-Level Changes," *Accounting Research Study No. 6* (1963), pp. 250–51.

[6] See Perry Mason, *Price-Level Changes and Financial Statements—Basic Concept and Methods* (AAA, 1956), fn., pp. 23–24.

that may approach current value; nonmonetary items are restated only for the change in purchasing power. A partial explanation is that traditional accounting also recognizes changes in the value of some items that are measured in terms of exit prices.

From the point of view of real-world interpretation, the purchasing power gains and losses are also deficient. A significant deficiency in the interpretation of such gains and losses arises from the fact that many future monetary commitments are made with the expectation of continuing inflation. In this case, protection against inflation may be included in the price of the goods exchanged giving rise to the monetary claim, in the rate of interest, or in the final amount to be paid. For example, if a one-year note is received requiring the repayment by the creditor of $100 plus 16 percent (including an expected price-level increase of 10 percent), there may be no purchasing power loss if the actual increase in general price level turns out to be 10 percent. The reporting of a $10 purchasing power loss from holding the monetary asset may permit a wrong interpretation of the advantage or disadvantage of holding that asset. The situation becomes more complex when the firm is able to compensate for anticipated price changes by altering its costs and prices. Problems of interpretation also arise because the measurement of the purchasing power gains or losses depends to a large extent upon the timing of the increases or decreases of monetary assets or liabilities. With a large number of transactions during the year relating to monetary assets and liabilities, a considerable difference in the amount of the reported purchasing power gain or loss may result from shifting the dates at which the changes in the monetary items are assumed to occur.

As indicated in Chapter 9, the presentation of income as representing changes in the value of the firm to stockholders is subject to many theoretical and practical difficulties. Since the value of a firm is dependent upon expectations regarding future cash flows and the individual utility preferences of stockholders, accounting reports can only provide the bases for the making of predictions and the evaluation of risk. Changes in the value of the firm as a whole cannot be measured by summing the changes in exchange prices or purchasing power of specific assets and liabilities. Furthermore, since purchasing power gains and losses are measured by the use of general purchasing power indexes, this measurement may be relevant to neither the firm nor the stockholder, as both may be interested in the ability to purchase specific goods and services; although this possibility has not been verified by adequate research. This concept is discussed later.

Another objection to reporting purchasing power gains and losses in income is the assumption that they are not relevant to most decisions of investors and other users of external reports. For example, if prices were rising, a firm could borrow money in order to pay a cash dividend or purchase treasury stock and thus report a purchasing power gain arising from the existence of the liability. But such a gain may not be relevant to a description of the assumed basic activities of the firm, nor to predictions by investors of the firm's future. Likewise, the holding of cash acquired by the sale of preferred stock may permit the firm to acquire operational assets that may significantly improve the income of the firm in the future; the presentation of a purchasing power loss on the holding of this cash while awaiting the proper opportunity may be deceptive with respect to the advisability of such a transaction and the future expectations regarding the firm. Therefore, it is likely that a separate reporting of purchasing power gains and losses does not provide information, because of their interrelationship with all other activities of the firm.

THE RESTATEMENT OF NONMONETARY ITEMS

Nonmonetary assets acquired in one period and held for sale or use in a later period can be measured in terms of the exchange prices existing when the assets were acquired or in terms of the exchange price at the date of reporting or some other date. These measurements are called nominal dollars because they represent the number of dollars at the date of measurement, and they cannot logically be compared with similar measurements at other dates. Only if the measurements are stated in terms of prices at the same date or if they are restated for changes in the purchasing power of money are they expressed in constant units. When they are restated in terms of changes in the value of money, they are referred to as constant dollars. When historical costs are restated for changes in the value of money, the result is referred to as historical cost/constant dollar information. When current costs are restated for comparative purposes or to express the amounts at other than the measurement date, the result is current cost/constant dollar information.

A frequent argument for the use of the historical cost/constant dollar approach has been that it retains the objectivity of historical costs, whereas the use of current costs substitutes a less objective measurement base—a current value. However, objectivity is maintained if current market prices for similar assets are obtained. If estimates are made, the resulting values are less objective. In evaluating the two measurement systems—historical cost/constant dollar and current cost/constant dollar—consideration should be given to the relevance and verifiability of the resulting amounts and the information content for security markets.

The restatement for changes in the general purchasing power is an improvement in the structural framework only. It leads to real-world interpretations only if the general price level and the specific prices move together in such a way that the general price-level restatement can be considered a surrogate for the specific prices.[7]

---

[7] See Yuji Ijiri, "Theory of Accounting Measurement," *Studies in Accounting Research No. 10* (AAA, 1975), p. 115.

PRICE-LEVEL RESTATEMENT MODELS

The following examples are drawn from the discussions initiated by Chambers.[8] The models assume a basic classification of assets and liabilities as monetary and nonmonetary, a transactionless interval, and either a general price-level change or changes in the prices of specific items or both.

General price-level restatements

Let us assume a firm with net monetary assets M, total nonmonetary assets N, and residual equity R, all expressed in dollars at time t_0:[9]

$$M_0 + N_0 = R_0 \tag{1}$$

Assume also that restatements are to be made by the use of an index of changes in the general level of prices p, representing the change in the general price level such that $p = (P_1/P_0 - 1)$ where P_1 = the price index at t_1, and P_0 = the price index at t_0. Then the restatement of the financial condition of the firm in terms of prices at t_1 is as follows:[10]

$$M_0(1 + p) + N_0(1 + p) = R_0(1 + p) \tag{2}$$

By multiplication we have:

$$M_0 + M_0 p + N_0 + N_0 p = R_0 + R_0 p \tag{3}$$

and because the amount of net monetary assets (M) remains constant from t_0 to t_1, we subtract $M_0 p$ from both sides and change M_0 to M_1:

$$M_1 + (N_0 + N_0 p) = (R_0 + R_0 p) - M_0 p \tag{4}$$

$(N_0 + N_0 p)$ represents the original price of the nonmonetary assets expressed in terms of a common dollar at t_1; and $(R_0 + R_0 p)$ represents the stockholders' equity at t_0 restated in terms of the purchasing power of the dollar at t_1. It can be assumed that stockholders would be as well off at t_1 as at t_0 if $R_1 = R_0 + R_0 p$. Since the dollar amount of monetary assets (M) cannot increase merely because of the increase in the general price level, R_1 is less than $R_0 + R_0 p$ by the amount of $M_0 p$; thus $M_0 p$ represents the purchasing power loss from the holding of net monetary assets while prices in general are rising. ($M_0 p$ would represent a gain in $M < 0$ or if $p < 0$.)

We can expand upon the above example by separating the net monetary assets (M) into two parts, net monetary current assets C and net

---

[8] R. J. Chambers, *Towards a General Theory of Accounting* (Adelaide: University of Adelaide, 1961) and *Accounting, Evaluation and Economic Behavior* (Englewood Cliffs, N.J.: Prentice-Hall, 1965), pp. 223–27.

[9] Nonmonetary liabilities are assumed to be negligible.

[10] Note that for simplification, it is assumed that there are no changes in the net monetary assets (M) or in the nonmonetary assets (N) and that no depreciable assets are included.

monetary long-term debt L, such that $M = C - L$. By substitution in equation 1, we have at t_0:

$$C_0 - L_0 + N_0 = R_0 \tag{5}$$

and by multiplying all expressions by $(1 + p)$, we have at time t_1:

$$C_0(1 + p) + N_0(1 + p) - L_0(1 + p) = R_0(1 + p) \tag{6}$$

or:

$$C_0 + C_0 p + N_0 + N_0 p - L_0 - L_0 p = R_0 + R_0 p \tag{7}$$

Because both C and L remain constant from time t_0 to t_1 (that is, $C_0 = C_1$ and $L_0 = L_1$), we must subtract $C_0 p$ from both sides and add $L_0 p$ to both sides of the equation, and change C_0 to C_1 and L_0 to L_1:

$$C_1 + (N_0 + N_0 p) - L_1 = (R_0 + R_0 p) + L_0 p - C_0 p \tag{8}$$

If income is measured by the net change in the purchasing power of the residual equity, $L_0 p$ represents a gain from the outstanding debt during the period, and $C_0 p$ represents the loss from holding monetary current assets from time t_0 to t_1. The argument that $L_0 p$ and $C_0 p$ are not gains and losses from a structural point of view can be supported only on the basis of a different concept of income. From example, under the transactions concept of income these are not part of income because they do not represent the results of activity on the part of the firm.

Another argument that the gain on long-term debt ($L_0 p$) is not a part of the income for the period is based on the assumption that capital invested in the firm includes both debt and residual equity capital, $R + L$. Therefore, capital is maintained if $R_1 + L_1$ at time t_1 is equal to $(R_0 + R_0 p) + (L_0 + L_0 p)$. Any loss to bondholders is equal to the purchasing power gain to stockholders, but the effect on the firm as a whole is neutral.[11]

Restatements for specific price changes

If assets are restated for the price changes of individual assets rather than for changes in general purchasing power, each nonmonetary asset must be adjusted by the rate of change in its specific price, s_i; net monetary assets are not restated because their specific prices in dollars do not change. Since each nonmonetary asset or group of similar assets N_i must be adjusted separately, equation 1 should be restated as follows:

$$M + \sum_{i=1}^{k} N_i = R \tag{9}$$

where

$$\sum_{i=1}^{k} N_i = N_1 + N_2 \ldots N_k$$

---

[11] See, for example, R. S. Gynther, *Accounting for Price-Level Changes: Theory and Procedures* (Oxford: Pergamon Press, 1966), p. 140.

By adjusting the nonmonetary assets for the rate of specific price changes (s_i), we obtain the following equation:

$$\sum_{i=1}^{k} N_i(1 + s_i) = \sum_{i=1}^{k} N_i + \sum_{i=1}^{k} N_i s_i \qquad (10)$$

where

$$\sum_{i=1}^{k} N_i(1 + s_i) = N_1(1 + s_1) + N_2(1 + s_2) \ldots N_k(1 + s_k)$$

so that the exchange price at time t_0 of each nonmonetary asset in the total set owned by the firm from asset N_1 to asset N_k is adjusted by the specific price change (s_i) relating to each asset.

Therefore, by adding $\sum_{i=1}^{k} N_i s_i$ to each side of equation (9) and combining as indicated in equation (10), we obtain the following equation:

$$M_0 + \sum_{i=1}^{k} N_{0i}(1 + s_i) = R_0 + \sum_{i=1}^{k} N_{0i} s_i \qquad (11)$$

The effect of equation 11 is to show on the left-hand side all net assets at their current prices; and on the right-hand side the total residual equity at the time period t_0, plus the increase in the prices of specific nonmonetary assets. Mathews argues that this adjustment results in no gain or loss to the firm because the specific purchasing power of the net assets is the same as it was at the beginning of the period.[12]

Gynther proposes similar adjustments for changes in the prices of specific nonmonetary assets, but he suggests that the purchasing power loss from the holding of net monetary current assets should be reported.[13] However, he recommends that the gains or losses on monetary current items should be computed by using the price indexes of the goods generally acquired by these monetary assets. That is, the firm can maintain its capital only if it maintains its purchasing power in terms of the specific goods it generally purchases. This position has some merit, as discussed later.

Relative price changes

If there is no change in the general purchasing power of the dollar, the increase in residual equity indicated in equation 11 represents a holding gain, according to some proponents of general price-level adjustments. That is, the firm is assumed to be as well off at the end of the period as at the beginning if $R_1 = R_0 + R_0 p$, but if $p = 0, R_0 p = 0$; thus, the increase in the prices of specific nonmonetary assets permits the firm to be better off at the end of the period in terms of its ability to use its resources to

---

[12] R. L. Mathews, "Price-Level Changes and Useless Information," *Journal of Accounting Research* 3, Spring 1965, p. 143.

[13] Gynther, *Accounting for Price-Level Changes,* p. 156.

purchase goods and services in general. The entire specific price changes in this case are assumed to be relative price changes.

If the prices of the specific goods held by the firm change at a different rate from the rate of change of general prices, the differences between the two rates represent the relative price change. For example, if the specific price of asset N_i has increased by the rate s_i and if this rate is greater than p, the increase in the general level of prices is such that $(s_i > p)$ and the holding gain due to the relative price increase would be $N_i(s_i - p)$. This result is obtained by subtracting the price of the specific asset N_i at t_0 adjusted for changes in the general price level from the current price of the asset at t_1. Thus:

$$N_i(1 + s_i) - N_i(1 + p) = N_i + N_i s_i - N_i - N_i p = N_i s_i - N_i p = N_i(s_i - p)$$

The current price of the specific asset can then be approximated as the sum of the price of the asset N_i at time t_0 adjusted for the change in the general level of prices and the relative price change of this asset. Thus:

$$N_i(1 + p) + N_i(s_i - p) = N_i + N_i p + N_i s_i - N_i p = N_i + N_i s_i$$
$$= N_i(1 + s_i) \tag{12}$$

Therefore, for the entire firm, the nonmonetary assets can be expressed in terms of the current specific prices by adjusting first for changes in the general level of prices and then adding the relative price changes to both sides of the equation. This can be computed as follows, starting with equation 9:

$$M_0 + \sum_{i=1}^{k} N_{0i} = R_0 \tag{9}$$

and adjusting both sides by the change in the level of general prices, we obtain:

$$M_0(1 + p) + \sum_{i=1}^{k} N_{0i}(1 + p) = R_0(1 + p) \tag{13}$$

By multiplication, and subtracting $M_0 p$ from both sides, we have:

$$M_0 + \sum_{i=1}^{k} N_{0i}(1 + p) = R_0 + R_0 p - M_0 p \tag{14}$$

Then by adding the relative price changes to both sides, we reach the following equation:

$$M_0 + \sum_{i=1}^{k} N_{0i}(1 + p) + \sum_{i=1}^{k} N_{0i}(s_i - p)$$
$$= (R_0 + R_0 p) - M_0 p + \sum_{i=1}^{k} N_{0i}(s_i - p) \tag{15}$$

Since $(R_0 + R_0 p)$ is necessary at time t_1 to maintain the residual equity in terms of a constant general purchasing power, $M_0 p$ represents the loss in purchasing power from the holding of a constant amount of monetary items and $\Sigma_{i=1}^{k} N_{0i}(s_i - p)$ represents the gains arising from the increase in relative prices of nonmonetary assets.

Since the practical application of equation 15 leaves much to be desired, a simpler application suggested by Chambers has considerable merit, although it does not permit the separation of purchasing power gains and losses on monetary items and the gains and losses from the holding of nonmonetary assets.[14] Chambers' suggestion can be interpreted as follows:

By combining the general and relative price adjustments of nonmonetary assets on the left side of equation 15 and expanding the right hand side, we obtain:

$$M_0 + \sum_{i=1}^{k} N_{0i}(1 + s_i) = (R_0 + R_0 p) - M_0 p + \sum_{i=1}^{k} N_{0i} s_i - \sum_{i=1}^{k} N_{0i} p$$

(16)

and since $M_0 p + \Sigma_{i=1}^{k} N_{0i} p = R_0 p$, we can substitute $R_0 p$ in equation 16 and obtain the following:

$$M_0 + \sum_{i=1}^{k} N_{0i}(1 + s_i) = (R_0 + R_0 p) + \left[\sum_{i=1}^{k} N_{0i} s_i - R_0 p \right] \qquad (17)$$

Therefore, according to equation 17, nonmonetary assets need be adjusted only for specific price changes, and the income effect of the general and specific price changes is measured by adding the sum of the increases in the specific price changes of nonmonetary assets and subtracting a capital adjustment ($R_0 p$) so that the total adjustment is

$$\left[\sum_{i=1}^{k} N_{0i} s_i - R_0 p \right]$$

This net adjustment to income could, of course, be positive or negative, depending upon the relative rates of change of s_i and p.

Equation 17 is significant because it points out the major difference between those who propose adjustments for only specific price changes and those who propose adjustments for general and relative price changes. If the $+ R_0 p$ and the $- R_0 p$ on the right-hand side of equation 17 are canceled, we then have equation 11, which represents the adjustments necessary according to those who propose the adjustment only for specific price changes. However, the interpretation is different, because the adjustment for specific price changes in equation 11 is assumed to represent an adjustment of capital, whereas in equation 17 it is a part of the adjustment of income. Therefore, the differences between the proponents of specific price adjustments only and the proponents of adjustments for general and relative price changes is primarily based on the assumptions regarding the nature of the firm and the objectives of financial reporting.

---

[14] Chambers, *Accounting, Evaluation,* p. 246.

AN EVALUATION OF
PRICE-LEVEL RESTATEMENTS

Some of the main controversies regarding price-level restatements center around the following questions: (1) Are the procedures and measurement techniques feasible? (2) Are the resulting accounting structures logical and internally consistent? (3) Are the resulting statements subject to meaningful interpretations? In other words, do they have real-world significance? (4) What is the behavioral impact of price-level restatements? Are they relevant for the decision models of investors and creditors? (5) Do the benefits of the information provided by price-level restatements exceed the costs of computing and reporting the data? Alternative approaches to price-level restatements must be evaluated in terms of all of the above questions. The following evaluations are intended to place these questions in proper perspective, although final answers cannot be given at this time because of a lack of sufficient empirical research on this subject.

General purchasing power

Most of the proposals and studies for the restatement of financial statements by the use of a single price index have made explicit or assumed that the index should measure the changes in prices in general, reflecting changes in general purchasing power or changes in the general value of the dollar.

General purchasing power, as measured by a general index of prices, shows the general tendency of all prices of goods and services in the economy to rise or fall or remain constant on the average as appropriately weighted, and reflects changes in the value of money. No index of all prices in the economy has ever been computed, and none is likely to be computed, but several available indexes may be used as close approximations.

The Gross National Product Implicit Price Deflators produced by the U.S. Department of Commerce are probably the best currently compiled indexes of the general level of prices in the United States. They are computed by dividing the current-dollar series of Gross National Product by the corresponding constant-dollar series, and therefore reflect all exchange prices in the economy. However, because the index does not generally reflect secular quality improvements and the emergence of superior products, the index does not provide a good comparison for years not close to each other. The Consumer Price Index for All Urban Consumers was selected by the FASB in *Statement No. 33* because of its widespread use and because it is generally understood by most people as well as its broad base in the economy.

From a structural point of view, the general purchasing power system appears to be logical and consistent with two exceptions: (1) The distinction between monetary and nonmonetary items is arbitrary, and (2) monetary items are restated twice—once for the change in general purchasing power and again for the restatement back to a nominal or current value—but nonmonetary items are restated only for general purchasing power changes. It should be recognized, however, that only the scale of measurement is changed. The structure continues to have all of the deficiencies of historical cost accounting.

From an interpretational point of view, it is assumed that general purchasing power is generally understood as a standard resource that can be used to acquire any or all types of goods and services in the economy.[15] The interpretation, however, is not intended to represent current values, but merely the historical cost restated for changes in general purchasing power. However, interpretation remains difficult because historical cost represents the number of dollars paid for a specific item, but the restated amount does not represent the amount that would have been paid for the item if the current price level and the current price structure were then known. And since it is not intended to be a surrogate for current value, there is difficulty in attaching any current market or utility valuation interpretation to it.

One of the major criticisms of general purchasing power restatements is that the concept is too broad. Individuals and corporations think of purchasing power in terms of the items they usually buy or might be interested in buying or selling. With a general purchasing power concept, it is assumed that the investor had a free choice to spend money in the economy in any way at the time of the investment, and that when the capital is recovered through the sale of product or services the investor will again have the freedom to spend the money in any way. That is, the operating cycle of the business is assumed to flow from cash to nonmonetary assets and back to cash, and the cash is then available to the investor for general spending. This is a single-venture concept that is not relevant to large corporate enterprises. An alternative way of looking at it is to assume that the firm is continually making choices to invest and reinvest its capital in the economy for all types of goods and services. However, the intentions and technical resources generally limit the types of goods and services that it will purchase.

From a behavioral point of view, the evidence of relevance for investment decisions is not conclusive. As a result of an empirical study, Petersen suggested that " . . . if one accepts the notion that published financial information is an input to the investment decision, some impact on that choice is suggested."[16] In another study of securities price behavior, it was concluded that price-level restated data do contain information not avail-

[15] See, for example, Paul Rosenfield, "GPP Accounting—Relevance and Interpretability," *Journal of Accountancy,* August 1975, pp. 52–59.

[16] Russell J. Petersen, "A Portfolio Analysis of General Price-Level Restatement," *Accounting Review,* July 1975, p. 532.

able in traditional statements.[17] However, as a result of research in the United Kingdom, Morris concluded that there is very little indication that the market has responded to information provided by inflation-adjusted earnings figures.[18] This lack of strong supporting relevance of general price-level restatements may result from several factors including the following: (1) the inability to define investment decision models; (2) the impounding of information in market prices from other sources in accord with the efficient markets hypothesis; and (3) the lack of interpretability of the restated data. Further research may, of course, prove otherwise.

Purchasing power of stockholders

One of the earliest concepts of purchasing power is that capital is maintained only if the ability of the stockholders to purchase a given quantity and quality of consumers' goods and services is held constant. For example, Sweeney held the view that the cost-of-living index was the ideal, and this concept has been implied by many other writers. The adoption of the CPI–U by the FASB in *Statement No. 33* may have been influenced by this reasoning, but as indicated above, there are several other reasons for using the CPI–U as a measure of general purchasing power. It is generally claimed that investors buy production goods only because they hope to obtain, eventually, more consumption goods than they could have had by consuming rather than investing. However, this is unrealistic for two reasons: (1) Large corporations usually intend to continue in business indefinitely rather than liquidate so that stockholders can consume their investments. (2) Stockholders do not usually liquidate their holdings in order to consume the amount of the investment. Although investors are constantly liquidating their holdings, it is more common for stockholders to reinvest their savings and consume only the income from the investments than it is for them to consume the amounts invested in corporate stocks.

Investment purchasing power of the firm

The postulate of continuity assumes that the firm will continually reinvest its assets in order to maintain its *invested capital*. Thus, the operating cycle of the business is from nonmonetary assets to cash to nonmonetary assets. However, continuity of life does not imply that the firm must replace specific assets. But it does mean that the firm should maintain its purchasing power to acquire investment goods.

Investment purchasing power can be looked at from at least three

---

[17] Arie Baran, Josef Lakonishok, and Aharon R. Ofer, "The Information Content of General Price-Level Adjusted Earnings: Some Empirical Evidence," *Accounting Review,* January 1980, pp. 22–35.

[18] R. C. Morris, "Evidence of the Impact of Inflation Accounting on Share Prices," *Accounting and Business Research,* Spring 1975, p. 90.

different views: (1) the ability of the firm to reinvest in an equal quantity of investment goods in general, (2) the ability of the firm to reinvest in capital goods generally purchased by all firms in the industry, and (3) the ability to reinvest in investment goods similar to those it has acquired in the past. Each of these views is a relevant description of some parts of the economy. Some firms diversify their investment over time and actually move from one industry to another or branch out into different industries. Other firms remain in the same industry but change the composition of their investment to keep up with technological innovations and to produce new products. And many firms do reinvest in capital goods and inventories similar to those they have had in the past.

The first view—general investment purchasing power—may reflect a dynamic economy, such as in the United States. Although there are some institutional frictions to movement, many firms do branch out into different industries, and accounting data should indicate when this is desirable. Adjustments for price-level changes in this case would require the use of an overall investment price index. No such comprehensive index is now available, but an approximation could be obtained by combining the implicit price deflators for the "other new construction" and "producers' durable equipment" segments of GNP and adjusting for changes in the prices of inventories. A single-investment index for the economy has the advantage of uniformity among firms and ease of application once the index is determined.

The second view—industry investment purchasing power—is a logical interpretation because firms do generally reinvest in the same industry. However, it would require a different investment index for each industry. A major practical difficulty in applying this approach is the fact that many firms produce a wide variety of products, so it is impossible to determine exactly in which industries they operate.

The third view— purchasing power relating to the past behavior of a specific firm—may be a good approximation of firm investment purchasing power because firms do maintain continuity of operations over time. However, technological changes in methods of production and in products require firms to alter their investment mix constantly.

From an interpretational point of view, it appears that the greater the correspondence between the investment index and specific movement in prices, the greater will be the interpretability of the data. That is, the individual measurements will then reflect valuations closer to current values. However, the use of an investment index has the advantage over specific revaluations in that the resulting valuations are less subjective and are not as easily manipulated for personal or firm advantage. While considerable research would be necessary to determine its feasibility, interpretability, and relevance for investment decisions, the investment purchasing power concept is appealing as a method of capturing the best of both worlds—general purchasing power revaluations and specific replacement purchasing power revaluations.

ACCOUNTING FOR CURRENT COSTS

Current costs reflect the prices that would need to be paid for an asset or its use at the date of the balance sheet or the date of the use or sale if that asset were not already owned. For inventories, current cost is the current acquisition price of the merchandise or the current cost to produce it. For plant, equipment and other property, the best measure of current cost is the used asset price of a similar asset in the same condition and of the same age as the asset owned. If there is a competitive market for used plant and equipment with many buyers and sellers, the price in this market may reflect the current value of the asset to the firm if its expectations can be assumed to be similar to the expectations of other firms in the industry. If the market is not highly competitive or if the asset is used for different purposes, the used equipment price is not relevant except as an indication of what the firm could obtain for the asset in liquidation.

In the absence of used asset markets, the current cost may be approximated by using the acquisition cost of an identical new item purchased in current established markets less accumulated depreciation for a period equal to the age of the asset in use. If identical assets are not available, the cost of an asset that will provide the equivalent service capacity may be substituted. This price, however, must be adjusted for technological changes in either operating efficiency or in product quality. A reproduction cost may be substituted for a current replacement cost, but a reproduction cost is not relevant if the asset cannot be produced efficiently with current production tools and methods. The reproduction cost of early vintage automobiles, for example, is in excess of the cost of new automobiles that are greatly superior to the former models.

An alternative to the use of market prices is the application of specific cost indexes to the historical cost of the specific asset. Although this may provide an acceptable approximation of current cost, technological changes in production of the asset and obsolescence should be taken into consideration. If the asset could be reproduced currently with technologically superior methods, the current cost might be overstated if broad cost indices are applied to the historical costs. On the other hand, if the equivalent service is obtainable by using newer and more efficient equipment, the current value of the old equipment may be little more than its scrap value or its unallocated historical cost, even though replacement cost has increased considerably. Unless the accumulated depreciation is adjusted for this obsolescence, the recording of obsolete equipment at its replacement cost (estimated by using price indexes) less normal depreciation has the effect of delaying the recognition of the loss in value until the period of use, at which time depreciation would be excessive as a measurement of the value of the asset's service contribution to the product. *FASB Statement No. 33* requires that current costs should not exceed recoverable amounts measured by the net realizable value for items to be sold or the value in use for other assets. The value in use is the discounted value of future expected cash flows. Since the future cash flows cannot be measured for most assets, an indication that value in use is less than current cost would be evident if the firm would not replace an existing asset because of its high operating costs.

Capital maintenance concepts

As discussed in Chapter 7, one of the interpretations of accounting income is that it is based on the concept of capital maintenance. That is, *income* is defined as the amount a firm could distribute to its stockholders and be as well off at the end of the period as it was at the beginning. However, the term *well off* has several interpretations relevant for the accounting for price changes. These include financial capital maintenance, general purchasing power capital maintenance, and physical capital maintenance.

In the financial capital maintenance concept, income results from the increase in the number of nominal dollars representing capital. The traditional historical cost/nominal dollar approach is a financial capital maintenance concept because revenues must exceed historical costs before income can be reported. Likewise, the current cost/nominal dollar approach may be based on a financial capital maintenance concept. However, increases in the prices of assets held during a period result in holding gains, and decreases result in holding losses. The current cost at the beginning of the period is subtracted from the current cost of the same asset at the end of the period to arrive at the holding gain or loss as described above. In the financial capital maintenance concept, these holding gains and losses would be included in the determination of income for the period.

The historical cost/constant dollar approach is based on the general purchasing power capital maintenance concept. Income is the excess of the capital at the end of the period over the capital at the beginning, both expressed in terms of a constant general purchasing power of the dollar. Accordingly, restatements of nonmonetary assets and liabilities are not included in income, but the purchasing power gains and losses on monetary items are included. In the current cost/constant dollar approach, current costs at the beginning of the period are restated in terms of a constant purchasing power at the end of the period, and the difference between this and the current cost of the asset at the end of the period is a holding gain or loss. This is the relative price change discussed above (also referred to as the change in current costs net of inflation).[19] In the financial capital maintenance concept, these holding gains and losses should be included in the income computation.

In the physical capital maintenance approach, also referred to as the operating capability approach, the assumption is made that capital is maintained if the firm is able to replace its assets with assets of the same

---

[19] See above, p. 219–21.

type or if it is able to maintain the capacity to produce a constant supply of goods and services. Firms may not necessarily replace specific assets or even continue to produce the same goods and services, but the use of current costs (or restatements by the use of specific indexes) may in the aggregate be an acceptable surrogate for the physical capacity purchasing power of the firm. The major difference between the physical capital maintenance concept and the financial capital maintenance concept is that in the former the holding gains and losses are not included in income. Instead, they are considered to be adjustments to stockholders equity. An alternative is to consider the holding gains and losses to be restatements of equity with the thought that equity is restated for changes in the specific purchasing power of the firm. In the current cost/constant dollar approach, the holding gains and losses arising from the relative price changes are likewise excluded from the computation of income.

Although there are doubts regarding the logic of including purchasing power gains and losses on monetary items in the computation of income as discussed above, many writers would include them even under the physical capital maintenance concept. Gynther, for example, recommended that gains and losses on monetary items be computed by using specific indexes representing the price changes of the goods for which the monetary items are held. For example, gains and losses on accounts receivable might be computed by using an index of the prices of merchandise generally purchased by the firm. For cash items, an index of the prices of merchandise generally purchased by the firm, representing changes in the prices of supplies, wages, and operating expenses might be used.[20] This approach is consistent with the physical capital maintenance approach, but a broader index would probably be more appropriate because monetary assets are not generally held for specific purchases, and monetary liabilities do not generally finance specific items. Because of the similarity of purchasing power gains and losses on monetary items and holding gains and losses net of inflation for nonmonetary items, logic is on the side of excluding them from income and considering them to be adjustments of equity. However, *FASB Statement No. 33* specifies that both purchasing power gains and losses on monetary items and the changes in current costs net of inflation should not be included in income. But no disposition is suggested in order to permit greater experimentation.

An evaluation of accounting for current costs

Current costs are claimed to have several advantages over the historical cost concept. Among these are the following:

1. The current cost represents the amount the firm would have to pay currently to obtain the asset or its services; therefore, it represents

---

[20] Gynther, *Accounting for Price-Level Changes*, pp. 252–53.

the best measure of the value of the inputs being matched against current revenues for predictive purposes.

2. It permits the identification of holding gains and losses, thus reflecting the results of asset management decisions and the impact of the environment on the firm not reflected in transactions.

3. The current cost represents the value of the asset to the firm if the firm is continuing to acquire such assets and if value has not been added by the enterprise to the asset.

4. The summation of assets expressed in current terms is more meaningful than the addition of historical costs incurred at different time periods.

5. It permits the reporting of current operating profit, which may be used to predict future cash flows.

With respect to the second objective, the emphasis is on the distinction between trading and price facets of business operations to provide better information for management decisions and to provide a better measure of managerial efficiency. However, it can be argued that this separation of income into holding gains and losses and current operating profit is artificial because since efficient buying is a part of operations, it is impossible to separate the two effects that arise jointly from the same decision.

The fifth objective assumes on theoretical grounds that current operating profit of one year is a good indicator of the operating profit of the succeeding year, which, in turn, is a surrogate for that year's distributable operating flow.[21] The distributable operating cash flows, in turn, may permit the prediction of potential future dividend contributions.

One of the disadvantages of the current cost concept is that some objectivity has been lost; unless the assets currently sold in the market are identical in all respects to the assets held, some subjectivity must be applied in transferring current exchange prices to the owned assets. Also, current costs might not represent the current value to the enterprise. If the firm were required to pay the current costs, it might be economically advantageous to acquire other asset forms instead. The present value of the benefits to be provided by the asset may not be equal to the current or replacement cost of the asset. This is particularly true when technological changes have occurred in the demand for the product. For example, if the demand for a product has declined significantly, the specialized equipment required for its production will have declined in service value to the firm; the depreciated cost of acquiring similar equipment is not a good measure of the service value to the firm.

From an interpretational point of view, the current cost concept appears to be more relevant than the general purchasing power concept. That is, costs restated by the use of specific indexes or replaced by current cost

---

[21] Lawrence Revsine, *Replacement Cost Accounting* (Englewood Cliffs, N.J.: Prentice-Hall, 1973), p. 137.

measurements are probably closer to current values than are historical costs adjusted for general purchasing power changes. However, the use of conventional allocation and amortization procedures applied to the current costs of new items weakens the potential correspondence between the resulting figures and current values.

From a behavioral point of view, recent research has found little empirical evidence supporting the existence of information content for current cost information.[22] Additional research may prove otherwise as more empirical data become available.

FOREIGN CURRENCY TRANSLATIONS

In those cases in which it is desirable to aggregate assets or liabilities or transactions expressed in different currencies, a translation of the amounts expressed in the different currencies should be made in terms of the currency of the country in which most of the readers of the financial statements reside. The need for translation generally occurs when the statements of a branch or subsidiary are consolidated with a domestic parent corporation or when the statements of an independent foreign corporation are translated for use in a different country.

The translation of foreign currency measurements is not the same problem as the restatement of dollar amounts for changes in the price level. In the former an actual exchange rate does exist at a specific point in time, but it is impossible to exchange purchasing power at one time with purchasing power at another time. However, some of the concepts relating to restatements for price changes are also relevant in the translation of foreign currencies. For example, one of the purposes of foreign currency translation is to be able to obtain meaningful sums of amounts originally expressed in different currencies—similar to the objective of restating historical dollar amounts for the changes in the value of the dollar. The financial and physical capital maintenance concepts are also relevant for both foreign currency translations and price-level restatements in deciding whether the so-called gains and losses are elements of income or of stockholders' equity.

In making foreign currency translations, the two basic questions relate to the decision regarding which exchange rate to use and the decision regarding the nature of the gain or loss on the translation. Several approaches have been suggested including the following: (1) the monetary/nonmonetary approach, (2) the current/noncurrent approach, (3) the temporal approach, (4) the current approach, and (5) the net-investment approach.

The monetary/nonmonetary approach is similar to the historical cost/

[22] See, for example, A. Rashad Abdel-khalik and James C. McKeown, "Disclosure of Estimates of Holding Gains and the Assessment of Systematic Risk," *Journal of Accounting Research,* Supplement 1978, pp. 46–77.

constant dollar approach to price-level restatements. Monetary assets and monetary liabilities are expressed in current terms and therefore should be translated by using the exchange rate at the date of the balance sheet. When monetary assets are held or monetary liabilities are outstanding during the periods when the exchange rate changes, gains or losses from the translation arise. These gains and losses are assumed to be realized because the amounts are monetary and therefore they should be reported in the income statement. This is similar to the purchasing power gains and losses on monetary items resulting from general price-level restatements. The nonmonetary assets and liabilities are translated at the exchange rates prevalent at the dates of acquisition. That is, the assumption is made that the historical cost in dollars or other domestic currency of the parent firm is the equivalent number of dollars that would have been needed to purchase the foreign currency which, in turn, was used to acquire the asset. A decline in the exchange rate of the foreign currency subsequent to the date of acquisition does not result in a loss by this method because the historical cost in equivalent dollars has not changed. One of the difficulties with this approach is that the monetary, nonmonetary classification is arbitrary as discussed above.

A second approach is based on the current/noncurrent classification. Current items are translated at the current rate because they relate to the current operations of the firm. However, it is argued that by reporting the changes in exchange rates applied only to current items, the resulting gains and losses reflecting the exposure to foreign exchange risk is overstated. That is, the assets, current and noncurrent, operate as a hedge against the risk from having liabilities outstanding and vice versa.

The temporal method is a modification of both of the above approaches. Under the temporal method, the exchange rate for translation purposes is determined by the measurement basis employed in the accounting system. That is, items reported in terms of historical costs are translated at historical exchange rates; items reported in terms of current prices or future expected prices are translated at the current exchange rate. This method appears to be in accord with the structural procedures of the historical cost accounting system. However, it is not logical because foreign exchange gains and losses are related to the accounting procedures used and not to economic reality. Therefore, the readers of financial statements are not provided with any interpretation of existing economic relationships.

The net investment approach views the business of a foreign subsidiary or division as an investment with a return measured by the net income of the foreign operation, which accrues to the benefit of the parent. That is, in concept, the foreign operation is treated as a separate entity rather than as a part of the operations of the parent. Therefore, all assets and liabilities should be translated in terms of the exchange rate at the date of the balance sheet (the current approach). Income statement items would be translated at the exchange rates existing at the dates for which the operating transactions are reported, generally the average for the year. It is the net investment that is assumed to be exposed to the risks of the changes in exchange rates. Whether or not the effects of changes in exchange rates should be reported as gains or losses depends on the view of the net investment and the assumptions regarding the exposure to risk. If the investment is assumed to be relatively permanent in nature, the argument is that no gains or losses occur so long as the investment is not converted into the domestic currency; that is, no gain or loss occurs until the investment is liquidated, at which point the gains or losses are assumed to be realized.

Economic theory supports the view that, over relatively long periods, most assets and liabilities are not exposed to exchange gains and losses. Assuming perfect and complete markets, the Purchasing Power Parity theory states that changes in equilibrium exchange rates are proportional to changes in the ratio of prices of similar combinations of non-monetary assets in two countries. For monetary assets and monetary liabilities, the Fisher Effect refers to the proposition that changes in exchange rates are reflected in the relative differential in interest rates in the two countries. If these propositions are valid over long periods, a net investment would not be exposed to exchange risks and, therefore, exchange gains and losses should not be reported.[23] Transactions in a foreign currency that will be completed in a relatively short time, however, are subject to exchange risks, and the exchange gains and losses should be reported as income statement items.

Adjustments for current costs and for price-level changes in a foreign country are relevant in the reporting of foreign operations, particularly in those cases in which there is an intent to continue such foreign operations. That is, the purchasing power in the specific or general goods and services in the foreign country is relevant to external financial reporting if operations are expected to continue in that country. Changes in the prices of the specific or general goods and services of the country of the parent company are relevant only when cash is remitted to the parent company.

When foreign currency translations are made at the rates of the historical dates in the strict historical cost tradition, the amounts expressed in the foreign currency are first translated into U.S. dollars and then restated for changes in the general purchasing power of the dollar. However, when the translations are made using current rates, the assets and liabilities should be restated first for changes in the price level of the foreign country and then translated into the domestic currency. This latter procedure carries the weight of logic and also provides measurements that are more meaningful from an interpretational point of view.

---

[23] See, for example, Robert Z. Aliber and Clyde P. Stickney, "Accounting Measures of Foreign Exchange Exposure: The Long and Short of It," *Accounting Review,* January 1975, pp. 44–57.

SELECTED ADDITIONAL READING

General price-level restatements

Gill, Charles W., and S. Thomas Moser. "Inflation Accounting at the Crossroads." *Journal of Accountancy,* January 1979, pp. 70–78.

Devon, Philip C. "Price-Level Reporting and Its Value to Investors." *Accounting and Business Research,* Winter 1978, pp. 19–24.

Griffin, Paul, ed. *Financial Reporting and Changing Prices: The Conference.* FASB, 1979.

Ijiri, Yuji. "The Price-Level Restatement and Its Dual Interpretation." *Accounting Review,* April 1976, pp. 227–43.

Staubus, George J. "The Effects of Price-Level Restatements on Earnings." *Accounting Review,* July 1976, pp. 574–89.

Vickrey, Don W. "General Price-Level Adjusted Historical Cost Statements and the Ratio-Scale View." *Accounting Review,* January 1976, pp. 31–40.

The choice of an appropriate price index

Bromwich, Michael. "Individual Purchasing Power Indices and Accounting Reports." *Accounting and Business Research,* Spring 1975, pp. 118–122.

Ma, Ronald, and M. C. Miller. "Inflation and the Current Value Illusion." *Accounting and Business Research,* Autumn 1976, pp. 250–63.

Staubus, George J. "Price-Level Accounting: Some Unfinished Business." *Accounting and Business Research,* Winter 1975, pp. 42–47.

General versus specific price changes

AICPA Task Force. *The Accounting Responses to Changing Prices: Experimentation with Four Models.* AICPA, 1979.

Rosenfield, Paul. "Confusion between General Price-Level Restatement and Current Value Accounting." *Journal of Accountancy,* October 1972, pp. 63–8.

Sterling, Robert R. "Relevant Financial Reporting in an Age of Price Changes." *Journal of Accountancy,* February 1975, pp. 42–51.

Vancil, R. F. "Inflation Accounting—The Great Controversy." *Harvard Business Review,* March–April 1976.

Accounting for current costs

Arnold, Donald F., and Ronald J. Huefner. "Measuring and Evaluating Replacement Costs: An Application." *Journal of Accounting Research,* Autumn 1977, pp. 245–52.

Bromwich, Michael. "The General Validity of Certain 'Current' Value Asset Valuation Bases." *Accounting and Business Research,* Autumn 1977, pp. 242–49.

Lemke, Kenneth W. "The Achilles Heel of Sandilands." *CA Magazine,* September 1976, pp. 37–42.

McKeown, James C., ed. *Inflation and Current Value Accounting* Urbana: Board of Trustees of the University of Illinois, 1979.

Prakash, Prem, and **Shyam Sunder.** "The Case against Separation of Current Operating Profit and Holding Gains." *Accounting Review,* January 1979, pp. 1–22.

Revsine, Lawrence. *Replacement Cost Accounting.* Englewood Cliffs, N.J.: Prentice-Hall, 1973, esp. chap. 5.

————. "Technological Changes and Replacement Costs: A Beginning." *Accounting Review,* April 1979, pp. 306–22.

Samuelson, Richard A. "Should Replacement Cost Changes Be Included in Income?" *Accounting Review,* April 1980, pp. 254–87.

Monetary items

Bradford, William D. "Price-Level Restated Accounting and the Measurement of Inflation Gains and Losses." *Accounting Review,* April 1974, pp. 296–305.

Gringyer, John R. "Holding Gains on Long-Term Liabilities—An Alternative Analysis." *Accounting and Business Research,* Spring 1978, pp. 130–48.

Heath, Loyd C. "Distinguishing between Monetary and Nonmonetary Assets and Liabilities in General Price-Level Accounting." *Accounting Review,* July 1972, pp. 458–68.

Kaplan, Robert S. "Purchasing Power Gains on Debt: The Effect of Expected and Unexpected Inflation." *Accounting Review,* April 1977, pp. 369–78.

Behavioral and Empirical Studies

Abdel-khalik, A. Rashad, and **James C. McKeown.** "Disclosure of Estimates of Holding Gains and the Assessment of Systematic Risk." *Journal of Accounting Research,* supplement, 1978, pp. 46–77.

Baran, Arie; Josef Lakonishok; and **Aharon Ofer.** "The Information Content of General Price Level Adjusted Earnings: Some Empirical Evidence." *Accounting Review,* January 1980, pp. 22–35.

Hillison, William A. "Empirical Investigation of General Purchasing Power Adjustments on Earnings per Share and the Movement of Security Prices." *Journal of Accounting Research,* Spring 1979, pp. 60–73.

Ketz, J. Edward. "The Effect of General Price-Level Adjustments on the Predictive Ability of Financial Ratios." *Journal of Accounting Research,* supplement 1978, pp. 273–84.

————. "The Validation of Some General Price Level Estimation Models." *Accounting Review,* October 1978, pp. 952–60.

Parker, James E. "Impact of Price-Level Accounting." *Accounting Review,* January 1977, pp. 69–96.

Short, Daniel G. "The Impact of Price-Level Adjustment in the Context of Risk Assessment." *Journal of Accounting Research,* supplement 1978, pp. 259–72.

Foreign Currency Translation

Aliber, R. Z., and **C. P. Stickney.** "Accounting Measures of Foreign Exchange Exposure: The Long and Short of It." *Accounting Review,* January 1975, pp. 44–57.

Clarke, F. L. "A Note on Exchange Rates, Purchasing Power Parities, and Translation Procedures." *Abacus,* June 1977, pp. 60–66.

Dukes, Roland E. *An Empirical Investigation of the Effects of Financial Accounting Standard No. 8 on Security Return Behavior.* FASB, 1978.

Lorensen, Leonard. "Reporting Foreign Operations of U.S. Companies in U.S. Dollars." *Accounting Research Study No. 12.* AICPA, 1972.

Norris, D. "Improved Foreign Exchange Disclosure for the Investor." *Financial Analysts Journal,* March–April 1977, pp. 17–20.

Patz, Dennis H. "A Price Parity Theory of Translation." *Accounting and Business Research,* Winter 1977, pp. 14–24.

Shank, John K., and Gary S. Shamis. "Reporting Foreign Currency Adjustments: A Disclosure Perspective." *Journal of Accountancy,* April 1979, pp. 59–65.

Wyman, Harold E. "Analysis of Gains or Losses from Foreign Monetary Items: An Application of Purchasing Power Parity Concepts." *Accounting Review,* July 1976, pp. 545–58.

CHAPTER 10

CASH AND
FUNDS FLOWS

In the final analysis, cash flows into and out of a business enterprise are the most fundamental events upon which accounting measurements are based and upon which investors and creditors are assumed to base their decisions. Cash attains its significance because it represents generalized purchasing power that can be transferred readily in an exchange economy to any individuals or organizations for their own specific needs in acquiring goods and services desired by them and available in the economy. By far the most significant method of transferring cash (claims for generalized purchasing power) is the bank check or other means of instructing a bank to transfer bank credit from one individual or organization to another. Currency and coins represent only a small fraction of the total means of transferring cash to and from a business firm.

With only a very few exceptions, business firms acquire asset rights to goods and services in order to produce other goods and services for sale to customers, with the intent of distributing interest and dividends to long-term investors. Very seldom do stockholders receive benefits from the firm in a form other than cash.

Most accounting measurements are based upon past, present, or expected flows of cash. Revenues are generally measured in terms of the net cash expected to be received from the sale of goods or services. Expenses are generally measured in terms of the cash paid or expected to be paid for goods and services used by the firm. Accruals represent the allocation to the current period of expected future receipts or disbursements for services. Deferrals represent the allocation to current and future periods of past receipts and disbursements for goods and services.

The theoretical measurements of assets, liabilities, and income are also based heavily on actual and expected cash flows. As will be discussed in Chapter 11, the present value of an asset is frequently defined as the discounted expected net receipts to be derived from the asset. Liabilities can be measured in terms of the discounted amount to be paid in the future. One of the definitions of *income* discussed in Chapter 7 was that it represents the excess of the discounted expected net cash distributions to stockholders as measured at the end of the period over the same expectations at the beginning of the period plus actual dividend payments.

Income and balance sheet items measured on the accrual basis are usually proposed and accepted on the basis that they provide useful measurements of firm efficiency and relevant information for the prediction of future firm activity and dividend payments. Because of the deliberate and inherent biases created by the use of allocation procedures and historical transaction prices, there is some doubt that traditional accounting methods are adequate to report the complex economic activities of today. One way of avoiding some of these biases is to emphasize the reporting of cash flows, supplemented by other information and appropriate classifications to permit the users of financial statements to make their own predictions regarding the future.

Although very few writers advocate a complete elimination of income statement and balance sheet reporting, many suggest a preference for certain procedures on the basis of their approximation of cash flows and their avoidance of allocations to several periods that appear to be arbitrary in nature. For example, the use of direct costing of inventories, the flow-through method of treating interperiod tax differences (nonallocation), and the tax reduction method of handling the investment credit are all advocated at least in part because they are more closely related to the actual cash flows.

Historical cash flow information as well as budgeted cash flows may provide relevant information, either alone or as supplements to conventional financial reports for investors and creditors in their evaluation of the firm and in their predictions of expected dividend payments. A step in this direction is the use of funds flow statements, although the relevance of the information and the type of information communicated by these reports is dependent somewhat upon the concept of *funds* employed and the extent of the information presented.

Since not all cash flows are necessarily relevant for external reporting, and since many financial events and relationships do not result from cash flows, statements presenting different concepts of funds flows are frequently suggested or used for financial reporting. The several concepts and objectives of funds flows are discussed following the discussion of cash flow information.

THE OBJECTIVE OF CASH FLOW INFORMATION

One of the main objectives of presenting data regarding cash flows is to provide information that it is assumed will (1) help the investor or creditor predict the amount of cash likely to be distributed in the future in the form of dividends or interest and in the form of liquidation distributions or repayment of principal and (2) aid in the evaluation of risk. *Risk,* in this context, includes both the expected variability of future returns and the probability of insolvency or bankruptcy. Therefore, cash flow data are assumed to provide basic information in the evaluation of market prices of securities.

Using the decision usefulness approach to accounting, *FASB Statement of Financial Accounting Concepts No. 1* makes the assumption that the users of financial statements are interested in the ability of a firm to generate favorable cash flows. A further assumption is that investors and creditors are generally interested in the performance of the firm as measured by accrual accounting, rather than information directly about its cash flows. This assumption, however, does not flow logically from an analysis of the accounting process as discussed in Chapter 2, nor has it been verified empirically.

An alternative use of cash flow data is in the investor decision-model approach. (This approach was discussed in Chapter 5.) In one form of these models, the expectation of future dividends is assumed to be one of the most important factors in the evaluation of security market prices. Cash flow data are then assumed to be relevant in the prediction of future cash flows.

Cash flows and the prediction of dividends

Net income is frequently claimed to be an indication of the ability of the firm to pay dividends. However, the dividend decision must take into consideration many other factors, such as the availability of cash; the opportunities and objectives of the firm with respect to capital growth and expansion; and the policies of the firm regarding external financing, as well as ability of the firm to obtain outside funds. But one of the greater deficiencies of reported net income as a predictor of future dividends is that it may be considerably biased, because of the inability in many cases to obtain a proper matching of expenses with revenues, and because of the arbitrary nature of allocation procedures. The use of cash flows as a predictor of future dividends, therefore, avoids the biases of reported net income, except to the extent that the timing of certain cash receipts and disbursements can be altered by management.

One of the difficulties in using historical cash flows as a predictor of future cash dividends is that many cash flows including dividends are interdependent. For example, available cash or expected cash receipts may be used for capital expenditures or for the repayment of debt as well as for the payment of dividends. Therefore, plans and expectations of management, as well as other information, such as a statement of the resources and commitments of the firm, should supplement the cash flow information.

Although the dividend decision of the firm each period is based on many complex factors, investors may be able to obtain some assistance in the prediction of future dividends if they have information regarding the following types of flows:

1. Cash flows relating to the basic current operations of the enterprise.
2. Recurring or occasional cash flows unrelated to current operations, but arising from either unexpected events or the desire to maintain a good environment for the firm in the future.
3. Cash flows required to increase operating facilities and inventories or obtained from their sale when not needed for future operations.
4. Cash obtained from or repaid to bondholders and stockholders as a part of firm financing.
5. Payments of interest and dividends to investors with priority claims.

Dividends to common stockholders can be looked on as that amount available after the above expected flows are predicted. However, as indicated above, many of these flows are interrelated, and consideration should also be given to the needs of the firm for holding cash or increasing its cash holdings. In addition to the knowledge of past cash flows, the investor should have information regarding the philosophy or attitudes of the firm regarding the payment of dividends and regarding the investment or reinvestment of cash available or obtainable by additional financing.

In making predictions regarding future cash flows from operations, it is important to start with historical information classified according to the behavioral characteristics of the cash flow requirements. For example, the various types of cash flows relating to operations should be classified according to major product groups or product categories, so that predictions can be made regarding future demand for the products and regarding special cost relationships related to specific product groups. Geographic distribution of source and sales of products may also be significant, particularly where foreign countries are involved. Furthermore, classifications of cash flows should permit a prediction of changes in future flows that are related to other known or predictable variables. For example, cash flows that are committed should be classified separately from cash flows that are variably related to the quantity of sales or production.

One of the most difficult of cash requirements to predict is that needed for capital expenditures. Depreciation as generally computed for measuring income is not relevant for this purpose because replacements are not necessarily related to either the cost of items acquired in the past or to period allocations of this cost. Although capital expenditure patterns in the past may provide some guide to the future, expectations of management regarding its plans and opportunities would greatly assist this prediction.

The use of historical cash flow information in the making of predictions regarding future dividends is, therefore, a complex process. However, the reliability of the predictions that take cash flow information into account may be considerably greater than predictions made from historical income data alone. If this is true, and some empirical studies have already provided evidence that it is, the presentation of historical cash flow information in external financial reports should be encouraged. Furthermore, the disclosure of budgeted cash receipts and expenditures for the following period and plans for long-run capital outlays and long-run financing should be of aid to investors and investment analysts, particularly if past plans can be compared with the actual results of the same planning period.

THE PRESENTATION OF CASH FLOW INFORMATION

The presentation of historical cash flows should not be considered a part of the presentation or computation of net income. That is, revenues and expenses should not be computed according to specific procedures on the grounds that these procedures result in amounts that are more closely related to the actual cash flows. For example, the flow-through method of presenting interperiod tax differences and the direct costing of manufactured goods are occasionally proposed as valid because they reflect more closely the actual cash flows. These methods may be relevant for other reasons, as discussed elsewhere in this book, but they should not be included in the income statement merely because they reflect cash flows. Although the income statement and cash flow statement are related to the same information over time, they represent different information and different concepts.

Because of the leads and lags between cash receipts and disbursements on the one hand and the operational activities giving rise to these cash flows on the other, a cash flow statement for a single period has little significance. A comparison of cash flows over several periods is necessary to begin to observe the behavior of recurring flows and to predict the likelihood and frequency of nonrecurring flows. Receipts and disbursements relating to the recurring activities of the enterprise should be classified by product groups and according to whether they are committed or discretionary. Capital expenditures should be classified in such a way that the effect on future cash flows can be predicted. That is, major expenditures that are nonrecurring or discretionary should be classified in such a way that the reader can predict whether the effect will be a replacement or continuation of existing operations, an improvement in efficiency that will reduce future annual expenditures, or an addition to capacity that will permit an expansion of future receipts.

One of the major difficulties with a reliance on cash flow information is that, occasionally, significant transactions are carried out without a transfer of cash. For example, common or preferred stock may be exchanged for additional capacity or for new businesses, as in the acquisition of an operating firm to continue as a subsidiary. In these cases, supplementary information should be provided to indicate the extent to which the cash flows in the future are likely to be different from the cash flows in the past. Furthermore, supplementary information should be presented whenever new contracts or changes in contracts, such as pension commitments or long-term leases, will affect future cash flows.

FUNDS FLOW CONCEPTS

One of the main difficulties with the presentation of cash flow information for evaluative and predictive purposes is that many cash receipts and disbursements over short periods of time, or even over a year, do not behave in a predictive way or even in a way that describes the basic cash flows over time. For example, the receipt or payment of cash may frequently be advanced or deferred for short periods at the request of suppliers or customers, or to permit a better control of the firm's cash position. Furthermore, the firm may engage in many types of cash transactions, such as borrowing from the bank on short-term loans and transfers of cash to short-term securities and back again into cash, all of which are incidental to the basic operations of the enterprise. An additional problem arises in the definition of cash itself. Currency and bank deposits are the most common types of money claims considered to be cash; but many near-cash items, such as savings accounts and U.S. Treasury notes or short-term certificates, may be the equivalent of cash.

An alternative to the presentation of cash receipts and disbursements is the use of a concept of funds that may be interpreted narrowly or broadly. In the narrow sense, the term *funds* may be used to represent the short-term monetary assets, a concept that has the advantage of eliminating from the reports transactions that represent the conversion of monetary assets into cash, or transfers of cash into near-cash items. A second alternative is to define *funds* as net monetary assets, which has the advantage of eliminating the short-term borrowing and repayment of cash without affecting the basic availability of cash for other uses. A more traditional view of the concept of funds is that it represents the net current resources of the firm conventionally defined as net working capital. A much broader concept is to treat funds as representing all of the economic resources of the firm. Although this broad view has the advantage of disclosing changes in the structure of the firm's resources, it has the disadvantage of not disclosing the extent to which cash may be available for distribution to stockholders or for commitment to other uses.

Short-term monetary asset flows

Monetary assets that represent resources readily convertible into cash can be treated for practicable purposes as cash or near-cash items. In situations where the firm has excess cash for immediate needs, it may transfer these funds to interest-bearing notes or deposits or invest them in marketable securities. On the other hand, if additional cash is needed at the present, these marketable securities may be sold and receivables may generally be converted into cash upon short notice by factoring or discounting, with little cost to the firm, even though the amount is not collectible from the customers at the present time. Therefore, transfers into noncash monetary items or from these items into cash may be a part of cash management, but provide little information regarding the longer run sources and needs for cash.

A second advantage of the monetary asset concept is that it is consistent with the concept of constructive receipt. An increase in a monetary asset represents a constructive receipt of cash if such asset is readily convertible into cash. A rigid adherence to the cash concept results in the making of arbitrary distinctions between cash and near-cash items. Particularly from the point of view of making predictions and decisions based on cash and funds flow information, the presentation of inflows and outflows of monetary current assets may be more relevant than a presentation of cash flows only. However, although monetary asset flows may be more relevant than cash receipts and disbursements, care must be taken in both the definition and the classification of the specific items included in the concept. Securities that are marketable should be included only if they are held as temporary depositaries of funds. That is, if they are held as cash resources, their sale and subsequent use in the acquisition of plant and equipment or the repayment of long-term debt is essentially only one transaction. Thus, with a proper classification, a short-term monetary asset flow concept may be more interpretable than a strict cash flow concept.

Net monetary asset flows

A further refinement of the funds concept is obtained by subtracting short-term obligations requiring cash from the current monetary assets. The advantage of this definition is that many of the cash transactions relating to short-term borrowing or the repayment of short-term debt are irrelevant to the basic decisions of investors and creditors regarding the firm. That is, by netting many of these short-term cash movements, the more basic cash flows can be highlighted. This is close to what is frequently referred to as net quick assets or net monetary current assets. However, the inclusion of the current portion of long-term debt among the current liabilities leads to a distortion of current net monetary asset flows. The reclassification of long-term debt is not the equivalent of a cash or monetary asset outflow.

A further advantage of this concept is that short-term monetary obligations represent constructive outflows of cash. The timing of these payments can frequently be altered by agreements with creditors or by short-term bank financing. Therefore, the more basic cash movements can be disclosed by eliminating the transactions resulting from the management of net current monetary assets.

The effect of increases and decreases of short-term obligations on the availability of cash for different purposes is not apparent without further analysis. For example, how long is a short term? In answering this question, consideration should be given to the relevance of the information. The traditional concept of one year is not necessarily a relevant criterion. In many cases, obligations due after about six months are not neutral with respect to the availability of funds for other purposes. Cash obtained under a six- or nine-month loan should probably be reported as a funds inflow and the repayment of the loan as a funds outflow, since this may be relevant information for the predictions and decisions of investors. An arbitrary cut-off point is difficult to make without considerably more information regarding the relevance of the information. However, a disclosure of the terms of loans outstanding would be of assistance in predicting future cash outflows. Although intent is frequently difficult to determine, it may be relevant in making cash flow projections. For example, short-term loans that are intended to be repaid from the proceeds of the sale of bonds or stock should be considered to be long term from the start, as they are not neutral with respect to the availability or disposition of cash.

In summary, the definition of *funds* as net current monetary assets (excluding the current portion of long-term debt and other obligations that are intended to be converted into long-term obligations) has many advantages over a strict cash flow concept. Increases in receivables arising from the sale of goods and services can be considered a constructive receipt of cash, although some minor adjustments for cash discounts and uncollectible accounts may be necessary. Increases in accounts payable may be considered to represent the constructive payment for goods and services received. The collection of receivables and the actual payment of accounts payable, on the other hand, represent conversions from one monetary form into another, rather than actual funds flows. Short-term borrowings and their repayment represent cash flows, but their elimination from the reporting of funds flows can be supported on the ground that they do not represent relevant transactions that will affect the ability of the firm to pay dividends and interest and repay long-term obligations over the relevant time horizon.

Working capital concept of funds

The most traditional concept of funds is its definition as net working capital. In this definition *funds* represent the net current resources available to the firm or expected to become available for distribution or recommitment. Funds are increased whenever current assets are increased or current liabilities are decreased, when these changes are not offset by changes in other working capital items. Funds are decreased, on the other hand, when current assets are decreased or current liabilities are increased without affecting other current accounts.

Several advantages of the working capital concept of funds have been suggested from time to time. These include the following: (1) A funds statement constructed on the basis of the working capital concept is readily articulated with the income statement and the balance sheet. (2) It follows closely the traditional definitions used in financial reporting, and therefore it is more understandable to the users of financial statements who are acquainted with conventional accounting procedures. (3) It tends to concentrate the information presented on the infrequent interfirm transactions rather than the day-to-day transactions resulting from regular operations. (4) It has been proposed as a means of presenting the general liquidity of the firm.

The above propositions are only partially true, depending on the objectives of the funds statement. A funds statement based on the working capital concept is usually a brief presentation, and many significant interfirm transactions are not disclosed. For example, significant additions to inventories financed by short-term notes would not be shown because the two items are offset in the computation of the net change in working capital. Furthermore, transactions not affecting working capital, such as the acquisition of plant and equipment by the issuance of common stock, would not be included in the statement. Therefore, the funds statement in this presentation would not disclose structural changes in the financial relationships in the firm or major changes in policy regarding investments in current assets and short-term financing.

One of the major disadvantages of the working capital concept of funds is that nonmonetary assets, such as inventories and prepaid expenses, and a few nonmonetary liabilities, such as advance receipts for services to be performed by the firm in the future (frequently referred to as unearned income or deferred credits to income), are included.[1] The inclusion of inventories and prepaid expenses in the concept of funds is particularly disturbing if the information is to be relevant to investors and creditors in their predictions of future funds and cash flows. The main reason for this is that the dollars assigned to inventories and prepaid expenses are the result of allocations of cost or other measurement over several periods. An increase in the reported amount of these items, for example, could not be interpreted as an increase in general purchasing power available for other uses. An exception to this might be made in the case of such inventories as refined gold and other precious metals or work performed under cost-plus-fixed-fee contracts, in which cases the reported measurement may be expressed in terms of the cash expected to be received in the near future, thus making them similar to receivables.

---

[1] Advance receipts for services are classified as nonmonetary because the obligation is expected to be discharged by providing a given quantity of specified services, rather than a specified quantity of cash representing general purchasing power.

The all-financial-resources concept of funds

One of the basic objections to the working capital concept of funds is that many interfirm transactions are omitted from the funds statement merely because they do not directly affect working capital. Thus, important information regarding changes in the resources of the firm and in the financial structure of the firm are omitted. A suggested alternative to alleviate this omission is an all-resources concept of funds that would permit the inclusion of such transactions as the acquisition of property in exchange for stock or bonds, the receipt of property as a gift, and the exchange of noncurrent assets for other noncurrent items.

An advantage of the all-financial-resources concept is that some of the most significant transactions would otherwise be omitted from the funds statement, or acquisitions would be grossly understated by presenting only the cash exchanged in the transaction rather than the entire transaction. Although writers differ regarding the amount of detail that should be shown in the funds statement, working capital is frequently presented as a net item. Therefore, a decrease in working capital would be a source of funds, and an increase in working capital would be an application or use of funds. Since all resources are taken into consideration, sources of funds must by definition equal the applications of funds, rather than a single concept of funds, such as cash or working capital representing the net increase or decrease in funds.

A major disadvantage of the all-financial-resources concept of funds is that the concept of financial resources is vague and ill defined. The separate items included in the classifications of sources and applications of funds do not necessarily represent increases and decreases of resources. Therefore, there is no direct disclosure of the extent to which the total resources of the firm have changed during the period. A second disadvantage is that acquisitions of property in exchange for stock cannot be measured with the same degree of reliability as assets acquired for cash. Therefore, the summation of gross additions to plant and equipment, for example, may result in misleading interpretations of the amount of resources acquired.

The all-significant-financial-events approach

One of the interpretations of the all-resources concept is that the funds statement should disclose the effects of all significant interfirm transactions. In effect, the funds statement is prepared so that it reflects all material changes in balance sheet accounts from the end of one period to the end of the next, with the exception that all intrafirm transactions are omitted. This has the effect of treating current assets and current liabilities as separate items. Therefore, significant changes in the working capital section of the balance sheet would be disclosed, rather than treating working capital as a net item. For example, increases in receivables and inventories would be reported as separate changes, even though they are offset by increases in short-term liabilities.

By presenting the material changes in specific assets and liabilities, the major shifts in the resources of the firm and their financing can be highlighted. Many of these changes can be observed from a comparative balance sheet, but the balance sheet figures show only the net change in specific classifications. For example, expenditures for new plant and equipment may be difficult to compute from balance sheet figures if several types of transactions—such as sale, abandonment, trade-in, and acquisition by merger in addition to acquisition by purchase—all occur during the same period. Likewise, increases and decreases in capital stock accounts may be a result of a combination of transactions, including the purchase of treasury shares, the sale of new shares, and bond conversions. All of these types of transactions should be disclosed in a funds statement. Generally, however, current practice does not disclose in the funds statement the reclassifications of major items of long-term debt or stockholders' equity, such as the conversions of bonds and preferred stock into common stock. If the funds statement is to reflect structural changes in the financial relationships in the firm, these types of transactions should probably be included, even though they might be disclosed elsewhere in the financial statements or in notes thereto.

LIQUIDITY, SOLVENCY AND FINANCIAL FLEXIBILITY

An additional objective in the presentation of data regarding cash flows is to permit an evaluation of liquidity and firm solvency. *Liquidity* is the relative ability to convert assets into cash, sometimes referred to as the nearness of assets to cash. It also refers to the relationship between a firm's short-term liabilities and its cash and near cash items. *Solvency* is a broader term referring to the ability of a firm to obtain cash or have cash available for whatever purpose may be required by the business. More specifically, solvency is the ability of a firm to pay its debts when they become due. *Financial flexibility* is the ability of a firm to obtain cash on short notice in order to meet unforseen contingencies or to take advantage of favorable opportunities. All three concepts are related, but financial flexibility is a broader concept than solvency, and solvency is broader than liquidity.

The importance of solvency is that it is necessary for firm continuity. Insolvency may lead to bankruptcy, forced liquidation, and the loss of claims by both stockholders and creditors. However, even in the absence of bankruptcy, insolvency may lead to a restructuring of debt and equity claims, resulting in a loss to both stockholders and creditors.

But insolvency itself is not necessary to cause losses to stockholders and creditors. The mere threat of insolvency may cause the equity and credit markets to react by a reduction in the market price of shares and certificates of indebtedness and an increase in the costs of additional borrowing and new equity. The reason for the reaction of market prices to a threat of insolvency is that it creates an increase in risk—the risk of complete or partial loss of equity or credit claims.

Since liquidity refers to asset characteristics, a discussion of the presentation of liquidity information is deferred to Chapter 12. However, liquidity information is part of the information necessary to evaluate solvency and financial flexibility. These broader concepts require not only information regarding the ability to convert existing assets into cash, but also information regarding the commitments and expectations relating to future cash receipts and disbursements.

The discussion of cash and funds flow information presented earlier in this chapter emphasized the providing of information to help investors and creditors predict cash flows likely to be distributed in the form of dividends or interest and repayment of principal and evaluate probable risk. Information regarding solvency and financial flexibility would help in meeting these goals by permitting better predictions of the probabilities of future returns, rather than just predictions of expected values. The probabilities of insolvency and bankruptcy on the one hand and a very high return on the other are important in the evaluation of risk.

The funds statements are frequently thought to provide information regarding solvency and financial flexibility as well as information about the financing and investing operations of the firm. However, they are deficient because they lack appropriate interpretation and because they are unable to meet all of the objectives required of them.

From a semantic point of view, cash receipts and disbursements probably permit the greatest degree of interpretation. The current monetary asset concept and the net current monetary asset concept also have interpretive significance, although the distinction between monetary and nonmonetary items is not always clear. The working capital concept is inferior because it includes nonmonetary assets and occasionally nonmonetary liabilities. These nonmonetary items are generally measured in terms of amounts resulting from historical transactions and interperiod allocations; therefore, they do not represent homogeneous items. As a result, the reported changes in working capital do not reflect changes in a fund that can be interpreted conceptually in a uniform manner. Since nonmonetary assets, particularly inventories and prepaid expenses, are included in working capital, the net change and the source of funds from operations are likely to be subject to bias as a result of the many acceptable methods of computing these items.

In order to permit the presentation of information regarding solvency and financial flexibility, as well as to permit a prediction of cash flows, it is suggested that two statements be presented. One statement would provide information to permit the prediction of future cash flows, and another statement would permit a prediction of the basic changes in the resources of the firm and its financial structure. Loyd Heath has suggested that three statements are needed to replace the traditional statement of changes in financial position. These are (1) a statement of cash receipts and payments, (2) a statement of financing activities, and (3) a statement of investing activities.[2]

The need for a statement of cash receipts and disbursements arises because of the increased complexity of business activity. This complexity results in a greater disparity between the time when income and expense items are reported and the time when the related cash flows occur. It may also result in a greater variability of cash flows. Inflation and major changes in the structure of the economy may also create a need for cash flow statements because these external changes and influences affect cash flows more quickly than reported income.

A statement of financing activities would disclose changes in the capital structure of a firm and show increases and decreases in both debt and equity financing. Additional information might include schedules of committed and planned sources of financing and committed and planned repayments with indicated repayment dates. A statement of investing activities would include information regarding increases and decreases in operating properties and in property and security investments.

SELECTED ADDITIONAL READING

Cash flow concepts and reporting

Brennan, M. J. "Approach to the Valuation of Uncertain Income Streams," *Journal of Finance,* June 1973, pp. 661–74.

Jones, Colin J. "Accounting Standards—A Blind Alley?" *Accounting and Business Research,* Autumn 1975, pp. 273–79.

Lee, T. A. "A Case for Cash Flow Reporting." *Journal of Business Finance,* Summer 1972, pp. 27–36.

Sorter, George, et al. "Earning Power and Cash Generating Ability." Accounting Objectives Study Group, *Objectives of Financial Statements. Vol. 2, Selected Papers.* AICPA, 1974, pp. 110–16.

Funds concepts

Buzby, Stephen L., and **Haim Falk.** " A New Approach to the Funds Statement." *Journal of Accountancy,* January 1974, pp. 55–61.

Giese, J. W., and **T. P. Klammer.** "Achieving the Objectives of *APB Opinion No. 19." Journal of Accountancy,* March 1974, pp. 54–61.

Grinnell, D. Jacque, and **Corine T. Norgaard.** "Reporting Changes in Financial Position." *Management Accountant,* September 1972, pp. 15–22.

---

[2] Loyd C. Heath, *Financial Reporting and the Evaluation of Solvency* (AICPA, 1978), p. 109.

Heath, Loyd C. "Let's Scrap the 'Funds' Statement." *Journal of Accountancy,* October 1978, pp. 94–103. See also **James A. Largay III, Edward P. Swanson,** and **Max Block.** "The 'Funds' Statement: Should It Be Scrapped, Retained or Revitalized?" Replies by Loyd C. Heath. *Journal of Accountancy,* December 1979, pp. 88–97.

Nurnberg, Hugo. "*APB Opinion No. 19,* Pro and Con." *Financial Executive,* December 1972, pp. 58–71.

Liquidity, solvency, and financial flexibility

Backer, M., and **M. L. Gosman.** *Financial Reporting and Business Liquidity.* New York: National Association of Accountants, 1978.

Fadel, Hisham, and **John M. Parkinson.** "Liquidity Evaluation by Means of Ratio Analysis." *Accounting and Business Research,* Spring 1978, pp. 101–7.

Heath, Loyd C. *Accounting Research Monograph No. 3.* "Financial Reporting and the Evaluation of Solvency." AICPA, 1978.

Heath, Loyd C., and **Paul Rosenfield.** "Solvency: the Forgotten Half of Financial Reporting." *Journal of Accountancy,* January 1979, pp. 48–54.

Empirical research

Beams, Floyd A., and **Robert H. Strawser.** "Preferences for Alternative Presentations of the Statement of Changes in Financial Position." *Massachusetts CPA Review,* November–December 1973, pp. 14–18.

CHAPTER 11

ASSETS AND
THEIR MEASUREMENT

As discussed in Chapter 3, *measurement* refers to the assignment of numerical values to represent specific attributes of selected objects or events. The valuation of assets is the process of measuring financial attributes (past, present, or future) of assets or aggregations of assets. In the traditional accounting structure, the balance sheet has become a link between two income statements, and asset valuation has become a process of computing how much to carry forward to future periods. But the balance sheet is frequently referred to as a statement of financial position, and there is strong support for the development of a statement that will present clearly interpretive measurements of the resources and commitments of a firm at a specific time as well as permit interpretive measurements of changes in financial position over time.[1] Also, one of the objectives of financial reporting should be the presentation of information that will permit investors and creditors to make their own predictions regarding future cash flows from the firm. Thus, asset measurements should be evaluated on the basis of their behavioral characteristics as well as on their interpretive content and their ability to fit into a logical reporting structure. The purpose of this chapter is to appraise the various measurement concepts in light of the several objectives. Emphasis will be placed on assets and their valuation. Liabilities will be discussed in a later chapter.

THE NATURE OF ASSETS

If accounting theory is to provide the proper guidelines for the development of accounting thought and accounting principles, there is considerable merit in an explicit definition of *assets* and an analysis of the basic nature of all assets. A discussion of the classification and valuation of assets may be of help in this analysis, but the initial emphasis should be on the characteristics that are common to all assets. Several attempts have been made to tackle the problem in this way. One of the first to

---

[1] See, for example, *Statements of Financial Accounting Concepts Nos. 2* and *3, AICPA Professional Standards,* Sections 1220 and 1230.

attempt a fairly comprehensive definition was Canning, who defined an *asset* as follows:

> An asset is any future service in money or any future service convertible into money (except those services arising from contracts the two sides of which are proportionately unperformed) the beneficial interest in which is legally or equitably secured to some person or set of persons. Such a service is an asset only to that person or set of persons to whom it runs.[2]

Although Canning believed that this expressed what accountants meant by the term *assets*, he did believe that the definition would be improved if the parenthetical material were removed.

Because of the emphasis on the determination of income, many of the previous discussions of assets have stressed, either directly or indirectly, their nature as unallocated costs or as amounts to be carried forward to future periods. For example, *APB Statement No. 4* defined *assets* as " . . . economic resources of an enterprise that are recognized and measured in conformity with generally accepted accounting principles," including "certain deferred charges that are not resources."[3] The emphasis in this definition is clearly on the amount carried forward in a trial balance, with the main objective being the computation of periodic income. A basic change in this emphasis was made by *FASB Statement of Financial Accounting Concepts No. 3 (SFAC No. 3)*. *Assets* are there defined as "probable future economic benefits obtained or controlled by a particular entity as a result of past transactions or events."[4] This basic definition permits semantic interpretation as opposed to the definition in *APB Statement No. 4*, which required procedural (syntactical) interpretation. Notice that the three basic characteristics are (1) probable future economic benefits, (2) control by the entity and (3) the result of a past transaction or event.

As economic resources, assets represent service potentials or rights to prospective benefits. This emphasis provides for an all-inclusive definition and permits the problem of measurement to be treated separately. With this basic definition, the following characteristics are essential:

1. There must exist some specific right to future benefits or service potentials. Rights and services that have expired cannot be included. Also, the rights must have a positive benefit; rights with zero or negative potential benefits are not assets. If a building has lost its service value and if the cost of removal is exactly equal to the salvage value of the materials, the building is not an asset. In fact, if the cost of removal is greater than the salvage value, the valuation of the land will be reduced, but the building is not an asset or even a negative asset. However, the fact that the future value of a right or service potential may be uncertain does

---

[2] John B. Canning, *The Economics of Accountancy* (New York: Ronald Press, 1929), p. 22.

[3] *Accounting Principles Board Statement No. 4*, "Basic Concepts and Accounting Principles Underlying Financial Statements of Business Enterprises" (AICPA, 1970), p. 49.

[4] *AICPA Professional Accounting Standards*, para. 1230.019.

not remove it from the definition of assets. The uncertainty affects the valuation, but it changes the nature of the item only if the uncertainty is so great that the expected future benefit is zero or negative.

2.   The rights must accrue to a specific individual or firm. The right to benefit from driving on public highways does not result in an asset. The right must permit the exclusion of others, although in some cases the right may be shared with specific firms or individuals. Ijiri placed considerable emphasis on *control* criteria in his definition of assets.[5] That is, assets are resources under the control of the entity. However, control can be interpreted broadly enough to include the ability of the firm to exercise its rights. Chambers also defined assets as means under the control of an entity, but he stressed the severable nature of the assets.[6] However, the severance characteristic is necessary only in Chambers' model to fit his measurement scheme. Eventually, the asset rights must be able to be transformed or utilized in such a way that other assets are severable.

3.   There must be a legally enforceable claim to the rights or services or some other evidence that receipt of the future benefits is probable. Services that may be withdrawn at will by some other firm or individual or by the government without compensation should not be included as assets. This does not mean, of course, that the firm must have a formal legal title or even a formal contract. In most cases, the accountant must rely upon the apparent intent of those who may have an interest in the asset rather than on the strict legality of the right.

4.   The economic benefits must be the result of past transactions or events. Assets should not include benefits that will arise in the future but that do not exist or are not under the control of the entity at the present. However, it can be argued that this criterion is unnecessary because if economic benefits do exist and are under the control of the entity, they must have arisen from past transactions or events.

In addition to the above characteristics, it should be noted that all assets are fundamentally identical regardless of the conventional classification. Both cash and intangibles provide rights to future benefits. The classification does not change the nature of the items as assets.

THE OBJECTIVES OF
ASSET MEASUREMENT

Accounting places emphasis on the quantification of economic relationships and economic changes in terms of a monetary unit. The quantification of assets in terms of a monetary unit is the valuation process, although other measures, such as physical units, may be relevant in specific circumstances. And since some form of valuation is necessary in the ac-

---

[5] Yuji Ijiri, *The Foundations of Accounting Measurement* (Englewood Cliffs, N.J.: Prentice-Hall, 1967), p. 70.

[6] Raymond J. Chambers, *Accounting, Evaluation and Economic Behavior* (Englewood Cliffs, N.J.: Prentice-Hall, 1966), p. 103.

counting process, the objectives of valuation are in part the same as the objectives of accounting. The following will, therefore, summarize only briefly the objectives of valuation, with specific emphasis on the valuation of assets.

As with the income concept, we find that there is a definite advantage in the general acceptance of one all-pervasive concept. But a close analysis of valuation indicates that a single concept cannot serve all purposes equally well. The appropriate concept in each case requires the knowledge of who will use the information and for what purpose it will be used. We are primarily interested in the development of valuation concepts useful to investors and included in external financial reports; creditors and management may require different concepts.

Valuation as a method of measuring income

As discussed in Chapters 7 and 8, accounting income can be evaluated in terms of its structural form, its interpretive content, or its behavioral significance. In its structural traditional form, valuation is a step in the matching process. In the economic interpretation of income, the capital maintenance concepts require the valuation of assets in such a way that income can be computed from the increase in these valuations over time. From a behavioral point of view, valuations should permit the computation of income useful in predictions or as direct inputs into investment decision models.

Valuation as a step in the matching process. The conventional approach to valuation is to record monetary assets in terms of net realizable values and nonmonetary assets in terms of input values until they are allocated to expenses and either matched with product revenues or charged to a specific period. Therefore, the objective of valuation for nonmonetary assets is to obtain a basis for the computation of the gross operating margin and the income from all transactions. This computation is the difference between total revenues and the input value of all expenses associated with these revenues or with the period.

Total operating income results from the assumed matching of valuations in terms of historical costs with the related revenues. With changes in the value of the monetary unit, a better measure of income may be obtained by restating the historical costs in terms of dollars representing the same purchasing power as the current revenue. A separation of current operating income from holding gains and losses may also be obtained by valuing the inputs in terms of current replacement costs.

Two basic approaches to valuation for income determination purposes are: (1) The emphasis may be placed on the valuation of the inputs as they expire. For example, the cost of goods sold may be valued on a current basis, by the use of LIFO or current replacement costs, while the ending inventories are left in terms of residuals. (2) The nonmonetary assets may be restated at the balance sheet date or periodically during the year, permitting assumed matching as these assets expire. The application of these procedures, particularly to inventories and plant and equipment, will be discussed at greater length in the following chapters.

The main difficulty with using the matching process as a basis for determining asset valuations is that most enterprise activities do not lend themselves to accurate matching. As a result, many, if not most, of the allocations of asset valuations to products or expenses are arbitrary in nature. Therefore, the valuations carried forward have no particular relationship to any specific future benefits. This has led to the adoption of many procedures that cannot be supported on logical grounds. The use of the deferred charge classification and the allocation of the cost of intangibles are examples that cast considerable doubt on the usefulness of the matching concept to provide relevant information to investors and other interested parties.

Valuation as a measure of accretion.   According to the accretion concept, income accrues to a firm as asset valuations increase (or as liability valuations decrease) in the absence of capital transactions. Thus, income results from increasing valuations from input values to output values or from increasing discounted net realizable values to cash values. For example, inventory valuations, initially recorded at cost, may be increased to discounted net realizable values when the revenues have been earned—at the completion of production or at the time of sale. The discounted net realizable values may then be increased to cash values when the receivables are collectible or converted into cash. Other types of assets are increased in value by the accrual of interest receivable, rent receivable, and other claims to cash.

Note that the objective of valuation in this concept is to approach the output values and cash values as soon as the basic services have been performed by the firm and as soon as verifiable measurements can be obtained. By so doing, income is recorded on an accretion basis. The income may be separated into realized and unrealized elements, but this is not necessary to meet the objectives of this approach. The accretion approach results in an all-inclusive concept of income, but the extraordinary gains and losses can be separately reported by combining this with the transactions approach.

The importance of this approach to valuation is that the emphasis is on recognizing and recording all changes in value based on the best evidence of the final output value or the amount of cash finally to be received. Thus, net realizable value should take precedence over input values; current replacement cost may be closer to net value to the firm than historical cost; and historical cost may be relevant if it represents the current value to the firm. The type of valuation selected depends on whether or not the basic services have been performed by the firm, the verifiability and relative freedom from bias of the valuation procedure, the relative certainty of the expected conversion to cash, and the ability to measure related expenses. The objective of the valuation, however, remains: to measure the increment in specific asset valuations, rather than to present the value of the firm as a whole to the investors or to any other group.

The presentation of financial position
to investors

The summarization of information regarding the resources, commitments, and equities of a firm is generally presented to stockholders and other investors at periodic intervals as one of the objectives of accounting. But accountants are not agreed on the valuation concepts that should be used. The term *financial position* is often used to mean the balance sheet as it is drawn from accounting ledgers and based on current accounting conventions and accounting practice. As a result, the statement of financial position is a residual statement—a step between two income statements. As such, it provides little information because it lacks interpretability. An alternative view is that the statement of financial position presented to investors should be restored to a more useful status by including valuation concepts and other information that would be more meaningful for investment decisions.

The balance sheet as a step between two income statements. With the emphasis on the income statement, the balance sheet has become a statement of residual amounts to be carried forward to future periods. It is said to be a point of arrival and departure in the accounting process, but it is related more closely to the past than to the future. Monetary accounts, such as cash and receivables, may represent current purchasing power or expectations of future funds flows, but the nonmonetary accounts reflect only past costs and residuals resulting from past amortization and expensing procedures.

In spite of these deficiencies, there are several positive claims for the residual type of balance sheet. First, it is claimed that the conventional balance sheet provides for the accountability of the dollars invested by the owners. Actual dollars invested can be traced either through enterprise operations or to residual valuations at the end of the period. Thus, fraud and embezzlement can be detected more readily than if other valuation concepts had been substituted. Second, one of the functions of the position statement is to summarize the nature of the operations of the enterprise and the nature of the monetary assets and unused services of the firm. It is claimed that the process of determining value is too subjective and that the best that can be accomplished is a fairly complete disclosure of the economic relationships by the use of adequate terminology and descriptions. It is also claimed that the nature of operations of the firm can be disclosed by the use of supplementary statements, such as the funds statement. Third, it is claimed that history has shown that when subjective valuations are permitted in the balance sheet not only does the balance sheet become less informative, but the income statement also becomes distorted. Thus, it is better to have one statement—the income statement—objectively determined and understandable than to have both statements misleading and failing in comparability. In the view of the author, these claims are completely inadequate in supporting the residual balance sheet.

The position statement as a means of prediction. As discussed in the previous chapter and in Chapter 7, investors are clearly interested in predicting the future flows to stockholders in the form of dividends and other distributions, in order to make decisions regarding the purchase or sale of shares of the enterprise. A series of income statements and cash and funds flow statements are relevant for this purpose, and a position statement should also provide relevant information for the making of these predictions. In discussing the ideal meaning of *financial position,* Canning stated:

> Beyond doubt the accountants would like to mean by "financial position"
> a position declared by direct positive measures of funds to be provided by
> enterprise operations.[7]

In order for a statement of financial position to provide information relevant to a prediction of future cash flows, it should include quantitative measurements of resources and commitments for comparisons with other periods or with other firms. The quantities of resources available to the firm, however, are relevant to predictions only if they are related to the cash flows likely to be generated by the firm. That is, valuations of assets held by the firm can provide relevant information only if the investor can detect some relationship between such measurements and expected cash flows. In some cases, the relevant attribute of available resources may be measured in terms of current replacement costs. In other cases, the best measure may be the current output values or some other available measurement.

The presentation of the claims of the several equity holders. According to traditional accounting concepts, the invested capital of a firm is equal to the valuation of the net assets of the enterprise. This figure cannot represent the value of the firm as a whole to the equity holders, but it is possible that the accounting statements may be able to give the equity holders some information regarding their relative rights and risks. Commonly, several classes of equity holders are represented in the capital structure of a firm, including some whose rights may change through the conversion of bonds into stock, or of one class into another, or by the exercise of warrants. Many of these relationships cannot be described by single measurements or even in quantitative terms, but certain valuation

---

[7] Canning, *Economics of Accountancy,* p. 191.

procedures may provide at least partial information, such as the relative amount of buffer that may exist for the protection of equity holders with priority rights.

Valuation for use by creditors

In the early part of the 20th century and before, one of the major objectives of the balance sheet was the presentation of financial information to creditors. Because of the lack of reliable information, creditors had to rely heavily on any indication of the security of the loan. Liquidation values were thus considered more important than other valuation concepts, and the doctrine of conservatism gained a strong influence in reporting. But if the probability of enterprise continuity is good, current output values are probably more important than liquidation values for an evaluation of the enterprise by creditors. Current debt will generally be paid from funds becoming available to the firm in the future rather than from the forced sale of assets now held. However, if it should become apparent that a firm will not have continuity of existence, the expected conversion values may be at or close to forced liquidation levels.

Valuation for use by management

For managerial purposes, the valuation process should provide information relevant to the making of operating decisions. But the information required by management is not necessarily the same as that required by investors and creditors. Investors and creditors are interested primarily in predicting the future course of the business from an evaluation of the past and from other information, but management must continually make decisions that determine the future course of action. Therefore, management has greater need for information regarding valuations arising from different courses of action. For example, managements must occasionally compare the benefits of using assets in the firm with their liquidation values. Also, opportunity costs, marginal or differential costs, and present values from expected differential cash flows are relevant for many types of management decisions. But just because they are relevant to managerial decisions does not necessarily mean that they are also relevant to the decisions of investors and creditors. Therefore, these valuations do not need to be reported in the position statement; they can be made readily available to management in supplementary reports. These uses for valuation concepts will be treated only briefly in the following discussion.

VALUATION CONCEPTS

Valuation in accounting is the process of assigning meaningful quantitative monetary amounts to assets. Since the business enterprise is not a consuming unit, economic values based on subjective utility are not relevant in accounting. Therefore, the relevant valuation concepts should be based on exchange or conversion values. There are, however, two markets in which the firm operates, and therefore two types of exchange values—output values and input values. Output values reflect the expected funds to be received by the firm in the future, based particularly on the exchange price for the firm's product or output. This term is used broadly, however, in order to include fund items and receivables. Input values reflect some measure of the consideration given up in obtaining the assets used by the firm in its operations—the inputs.

Canning drew a distinction between direct and indirect valuation that is similar in some respects to the distinction between the concepts of output and input values.[8] Direct valuation applies to those assets for which the conversion to future cash flows is capable of being measured with some reliability. Indirect valuation must be applied when there is no means of estimating directly the funds to be provided. Canning stated that it would be desirable, ideally, to have direct measures of all assets.[9]

A direct measure of the valuation of all assets is, however, impossible because most of the resources of a firm contribute jointly to the net cash flows of the firm. However, in a few cases the best concept of valuation is one that is related to the expected future net receipt of funds directly associated with the asset. In those cases where there is no direct association with future cash flows, one or more alternative valuation concepts may provide better information regarding the quantity of resources available to the firm. Output values (exit prices) measured in current markets may be substituted for expectations of future net receipts in many cases, and it may be argued that they are more relevant or more verifiable than valuations based on expectations. On the other hand, many assets are held by a firm for use without any direct relationship to future cash receipts. In such cases, input values or entry prices are more relevant for describing the resources of the firm and for providing information that may permit rational decisions by investors and creditors.

It should be emphasized that assets do have several attributes that can be measured by the use of different valuation concepts. Although investment decision models have not been well defined, it is apparent that the measurement and publication of more than one attribute may be relevant to investors and other users of financial statements. Therefore, the several valuation concepts should be considered to be complementary to each other as well as competing in some cases.

Exchange output values

Output values are based on the amount of cash or the value of other consideration to be received when an asset or its service finally leaves the

---

[8] Ibid., pp. 182–83.
[9] Ibid., p. 184.

firm by an exchange or conversion. Those assets that represent money or claims to money should be expressed in terms of their current values. What can or will be done with the money is not relevant at this point. Nonmonetary assets that have fairly certain exchange prices likely to be received at specific future periods can be treated similarly to receivables. When the future exchange price is less certain, a current exchange output price may be substituted. And in those cases where the normal exchange market has disappeared or where circumstances require disposition in a different market, forced liquidation values may be relevant.

Discounted future cash receipts or service potentials. When expected cash receipts require a waiting period, the present value of these receipts is less than the actual amount expected to be received. And the longer the waiting period, the smaller is the present value. Conceptually, the present value is determined by the process of discounting. But discounting involves not only an estimate of the opportunity cost of the money, but also an estimate of the probability of receiving the expected amount. The longer the waiting period, the greater is the uncertainty that the amount will be received.

This valuation concept requires the knowledge or estimation of three basic factors—the amount or amounts to be received, the discount factor, and the time period or periods involved. The following examples demonstrate the technical process of valuation when these factors can be quantified. In the first example, assume that $1,000 is to be received at the end of three years. If the appropriate discount factor is 12 percent, the present value of the asset is $711.78. Using v for the present value of the asset, a for the monetary value to be received, i for the discount factor, and n for the number of years of waiting, the formula for the computation of the present value is

$$v = a(1 + i)^{-n}, \text{ or } v = \frac{a}{(1 + i)^n}$$

This can be expressed graphically as follows:

Present value	Amount to be received and period		
$711.78			$1,000
	1	2	3

If the amounts to be received are at different time periods, each amount must be discounted at the appropriate discount rate for the specific waiting period. For example, suppose that $500 is to be received at the end of the first period, $400 at the end of the second, and $300 at the end of the third.[10] The present value of this series can be expressed graphically as follows:

Present value	Years and amounts to be received		
	1	2	3
$446.43	$500		
318.88		$400	
213.53			$300
$978.84	$500	$400	$300

This type of computation can be expressed by the following formula, where P_0 is the present discounted value of the expected cash flow at the time t_0, R_j represents the expected cash to be received at the end of year j (representing each of the years from t_1 through t_n), and i is the opportunity rate of interest.

$$P_0 = \sum_{j=1}^{n} \frac{R_j}{(1 + i)^j}$$

The interest rate in the above formula is assumed to be a constant, and the formula can easily be changed to include the case where different opportunity rates are expected for each of the periods.

The above formula is similar to the one presented in Chapter 5, which expressed the present value of a firm to an investor as the discounted value of expected future distributions to stockholders.[11] However, two basic differences in the above formula are that the individual income tax adjustment and the utility preference for risk factors are omitted. The omission of the risk factor makes the formula less complete, although we can assume that the expected cash flows are certainty equivalents—that is, single-valued amounts treated as the equivalent of cash flows that are certain.

Although the discounted cash flow concept has validity in the valuation by an investor of an entire firm, or in the valuation by owners of single ventures, it is of doubtful validity when applied to separate assets of a firm, for the following reasons:

1. The expected cash receipts generally depend upon subjective probability distributions that are not verifiable by their nature.
2. Even though opportunity discount rates might be obtainable, the adjustment for risk preference must be evaluated by management or the

---

[10] It should be recognized that these receipts are net amounts. For example, the gross receipts at the end of the first year might be $1,100, and additional outlays might be $600. If the additional outlays are required at time periods different from the gross receipts, each must be discounted separately; the present value of the asset would then be the excess of the discounted gross receipts over the discounted additional outlays.

[11] See Chapter 5, fn. 7.

accountants, and it might be difficult to convey the meaning of the resultant valuation to the readers of financial statements.

3. When two or more factors, including human resources as well as physical assets, contribute to the product or service of the firm and the subsequent cash flows, a logical allocation to the separate service factors is generally impossible. It has been suggested that the marginal net receipts associated with the asset can be used, but the sum of the individual marginal net receipts is not likely to add to the total net receipts from the product or services.

4. The discounted value of the differential cash flows of all of the separate assets of the firm cannot be added together to obtain the value of the firm. This is partly due to the jointness of the contributions of the separate assets, but it is also due to the fact that some assets, such as intangibles, cannot be separately identified.

In spite of the above difficulties, the discounted cash flow concept has some merit as a valuation concept for single ventures where there are no joint factors requiring separate accounting or where the aggregation of assets can be carried far enough to include all of the joint factors. But it is also relevant for monetary assets where waiting is the primary factor determining the net benefit to be received in cash by the firm. For example, if a note receivable is fairly certain of being collected and if the timing of the payments is specified by contract, the discounted value of the note represents the amount of cash that the firm would be indifferent to holding as compared to holding the note. The minimum amount, however, would be the amount of cash that could be obtained by discounting or selling the note to a bank or other financial institution. The longer the waiting period, however, the greater the uncertainties will usually be, making the discounted cash receipts concept less applicable. On the other hand, when the waiting period is short, the discounting process can usually be ignored for monetary assets because the amount of the discount is usually not material. For example, if a receivable of $1,000 is due in 30 days, the discounted present value of this at 12 percent would be $990.09. Since the discount of $9.91 is probably not material, it can usually be ignored, and the receivable is not significantly overstated if it is valued at $1,000.

Current output prices. When the product of the enterprise is generally sold in an organized market, the current market price may be a reasonable estimate of the actual selling price in the near future. Therefore, the current output price may be a close substitute for the discounted expected cash receipt value of merchandise inventories, and products or by-products at or close to the completed stage. If, however, the product is not expected to be sold within a short period, the current market price (used as a substitute for the expected sales price) should be appropriately discounted. If additional costs of production or expenses of selling are anticipated, these costs as a minimum should be subtracted from the current sales price to obtain an approximation of the current valuation. This current valuation is referred to as the net realizable value.

A current output (exit) price has some serious limitations as a generalized valuation concept. First, it applies only to assets that are held for sale, such as merchandise, special manufactured products, investments, and plant and equipment or land no longer of use to the firm in its operations. Second, since it is a surrogate for a future sales price, the relevance of the transformation is open to question. The current sales price represents the amount that is being paid by the marginal buyer and does not necessarily represent the amount that will be paid in the future except under conditions of *ceteris paribus*. Third, because all assets of the firm cannot be valued on the basis of a current sales price, different valuation methods must be applied as surrogates, and the aggregation of assets measured by different valuation concepts can be interpreted only if all methods used represent current sales prices or valid surrogates.

The use of a current output price results in the reporting of income or loss prior to the final exchange of the product or service. In Chapter 8, it was pointed out that this valuation results in the reporting of revenue during production or at the completion of production and that this reporting is appropriate when the current output price is a good estimate of the future sales price and when there is good evidence that the product will be sold at this price in the near future. If the expected future sales price is discounted for a possible waiting period, only the operating income is reported currently, and the income representing interest will be reported at the completion of the exchange.

Current cash equivalents.   The term *current cash equivalent* has been proposed by Chambers as a single measurement concept for all assets, representing their present realizable prices.[12] It represents the amount of cash or generalized purchasing power that could be obtained by selling each asset under conditions of orderly liquidation, which may be measured by quoted market prices for goods of a similar kind and condition. This current cash equivalent is assumed to be relevant because it represents the position of the firm in relation to its adaptive behavior to the environment. That is, it is assumed to be the contemporary property of all assets, which is relevant for all actions in markets and thus uniformly relevant at a point in time. Past prices are irrelevant to future actions, and future prices can be nothing more than speculation. Therefore, the current cash equivalent concept avoids the necessity to aggregate past, present, and future prices.

One of the major difficulties with the current cash equivalent concept is that it provides justification for excluding from the position statement all items that do not have a contemporary market price. For example, non-

---

[12] Chambers, *Accounting Evaluation*, p. 92.

vendible specialized equipment, as well as most intangible assets, would be written off at the time of acquisition because of an inability to obtain a current market price. However, Chambers would modify the procedures somewhat to provide approximations of the current cash equivalents by the use of specific price indexes and by making subjective depreciation computations. From the author's point of view, the main deficiency in using the current cash equivalent concept for all assets is that it does not take into consideration the relevancy of the information to the prediction and decision needs of the users of financial statements, although it does provide the investor with contemporary information regarding the financial position of the firm and some alternatives available to it.

The concept has been criticized because it has a nonadditive property, the summation of the current cash equivalents of the individual assets is not equal to the cash equivalent of the assets as a group; and the sale of assets in combination or the sale of the firm as a whole may be just as relevant or more relevant than the sale of individual assets in the adaptive behavior of the firm. These criticisms, however, do not deny the current cash equivalent concept as having semantic interpretation as an accounting measurement.

Liquidation values.   Liquidation values are similar to current output prices and to current cash equivalents, except that they are obtained from different market conditions. Current output prices assume normal selling operations and usually a normal profit, and current cash equivalents assume at least orderly liquidation. But liquidation values assume a forced sale, either to regular customers at greatly reduced prices or to other firms or dealers usually at prices considerably below cost. The application of liquidation values usually results in the writing down of asset valuations and the recognition of losses. Because they are not realistic under normal circumstances, liquidation values should be used only under two main situations—(1) when merchandise or other assets have lost their normal usefulness, have become obsolete, or have otherwise lost their normal market and (2) when the firm expects to discontinue business in the near future, so that it will not be able to sell in its normal market.

Exchange input values

Input values are often assumed to be more appropriate than output values because they are possibly more verifiable or because they do not permit the reporting of revenue before it is "realized." Actually, however, accounting is eclectic in nature, choosing output values in some cases and input values in others. Although output values may be better conceptually for the presentation of the financial statements, as discussed above, in many situations input values are more appropriate because they may represent the maximum value to the firm or because an output market does not exist, so that it is impossible to obtain exchange output values.

Input values may be expressed in terms of actual historical costs, current costs, future costs, or costs imputed from expected output values.

Historical costs.   Cost has been the most common valuation concept in the traditional accounting structure. Assets are generally recorded initially on the basis of the exchange prices at which the acquisition transactions take place. They are then presented in financial statements at this acquisition cost or some unamortized portion of it. Therefore, cost is the exchange price of goods and services at the time they are acquired. When the consideration given in the exchange consists of nonmonetary assets, the exchange price is determined by the current fair value of the assets given up in the exchange. Cost is thus the economic sacrifice expressed in monetary terms required to obtain a specific asset or a group of assets. Very often cost is not represented by a single exchange price, but it includes many sacrifices of economic resources necessary to obtain the asset in the form, location, and time in which it can be useful to the operations of the firm. Thus, all of these sacrifices should be included in the concept of cost valuation. But it should be recognized that the term *cost* is used in many senses and for various purposes. In many cases, it includes only a part of the total sacrifices, and in other cases, it includes too much. This problem is discussed later in this chapter and throughout much of the discussion of the following chapters.

Cost as a valuation concept for nonmonetary assets has its main advantage in the fact that it is verifiable. Cost represents the exchange price agreed upon by the buyer and seller in a relatively free economy. It is possible that the firm may occasionally pay more than it should for an asset, but it is usually assumed that prudent judgment was used and that the firm could not have obtained the same asset or service elsewhere for a lower total cost. It is also assumed that cost represents the value of the asset to the firm at the time of acquisition, but this cannot be proved, since all factors of the enterprise are used jointly in providing the cash available for distribution to investors. One of the strongest reasons for adhering to historical cost, however, has been its close relationship to the realization concept in the measurement of income.

One of the main disadvantages of historical cost valuation is that the value of the asset to the firm may change over time; after long periods of time it may have no significance whatever as a measure of the quantity of resources available to the enterprise. Historical cost valuation is also disadvantageous because it fails to permit the recognition of gains and losses in the periods in which they may actually occur. Also, because of changes over time, costs of assets acquired in different time periods cannot be added together in the balance sheet to provide interpretable sums. The historical cost valuation concept has the added practical disadvantage of blocking out other possibly more useful valuation concepts.

Current input costs.   Current costs and historical costs are the same only on the date of acquisition of an asset. After that date the same asset or its equivalent may be obtainable for a larger or smaller exchange price. Thus current costs represent the exchange price that would be required today to obtain the same asset or its equivalent. If a good market exists in which similar assets are bought and sold, an exchange price can be obtained and associated with the asset owned; this price represents the maximum value to the firm (unless net realizable value is greater), except for very short periods until a replacement can be obtained. It should be noted, however, that this current exchange price is a cost price only if it is obtained from quotations in a market in which the firm would acquire its assets or services; it cannot be obtained from quotations in the market in which the firm usually sells its assets or services in the normal course of its operations, unless the two markets are coincident.

Current cost has become an important valuation basis in accounting, particularly as a means of presenting information regarding the effect of inflation on an enterprise. In a number of other situations, current cost is an appropriate measure of fair value, either in establishing an initial acquisition price (as in certain exchanges of nonmonetary assets) or in establishing a maximum value (as in determining the present value of a capital lease for the lessee). Because of the potential increase in relevance of current costs as compared with historical costs, its use is likely to increase in the future. Some of the advantages and disadvantages of current costs and certain problems of measurement are discussed in Chapter 9.[13]

Discounted future costs.　Most nonmonetary assets represent goods or services acquired in advance. These goods or services are usually acquired in advance because (1) it is less costly to acquire them in large quantities; (2) some assets (e.g., a building or equipment) by their nature represent a stream of future services that cannot be acquired separately; (3) it is often desirable to purchase future services (e.g., leasehold) in order to be sure that they will be available when they are needed; and (4) it is often desirable to obtain rights to property to protect other investments, such as leasehold improvements. In these cases, the equivalent cost of the service at the time of *use* may be the most relevant valuation concept. In this context, the present value of these services (the asset) is the discounted value of the future costs.

In those cases where the services will be available in the near future, the process of discounting will not have a material effect on the valuation of the asset. For example, many prepaid expenses would cost the same if they were acquired when needed rather than in advance; thus the recording of these assets at acquisition cost may be very close to the valuation based on the future expected costs or the discounted future costs.

In other cases, however, the cost price may be less than the amount that would have been required if the services had been acquired when needed. For example, a leasehold purchased in advance for 10 years would

---

[13] See Chapter 9, pp. 226–30.

probably be less than the sum of 10 payments paid annually during the same period. In part, this difference is due to the interest factor, and in part to other causes. In either case, the present valuation of the leasehold should not exceed the discounted value of the 10 rents if the other terms of the contract are the same. This same concept can be applied to the valuation of plant and equipment and other assets, but usually on a less precise basis. Nevertheless, the concept is useful in valuation problems. The present value of an asset is assumed to be equal to the discounted value of the future expected service costs. It should be noted that this is a cost concept; the discounted amounts are input exchange prices, not output service values.

Although the discounted future cost concept may be relevant in the acquisition decision in those cases in which the firm has the alternative of purchasing the services as required rather than in a lump sum, after the asset has been acquired, the discounted future cost concept has serious limitations. Even if the current input price of the services acquired separately can be obtained, the firm no longer has the alternative of purchasing the services separately once the advance commitment has been made. Also, even if the total cost could be assumed to be equal to the value of the asset at the date of acquisition, this identity of discounted future expected costs of equivalent services and the current value of the asset to the firm is not likely to persist in subsequent periods. Therefore, the discounted future cost concept has all of the disadvantages of historical cost plus the limitations applicable to the discounted service potential concept.

Standard costs

Although standard costs have their primary significance as a managerial tool of cost control, they also provide a useful concept of valuation for produced assets. Standard costs can be defined as a valuation on the basis of what costs should be under certain assumptions regarding the desired level of productive efficiency and capacity utilization. Valuation on the basis of standard costs is an input valuation concept based on the appropriate exchange prices of the proper quantities of goods and services necessary for the production of the product.

A major advantage of the standard cost concept is that the costs of inefficiencies are omitted. A product is not worth more because it is produced under inefficient conditions. Nor is it worth more because of the existence of idle capacity. The costs of inefficiency and idle capacity are losses incurred by the firm in the current or past periods. They should not be carried forward to future periods to be matched against future revenues, and they cannot be converted into future funds flows.

From a valuation point of view, however, standard costs are not necessarily superior to actual costs. An efficiently produced product is not necessarily worth less than one that is produced under less efficient methods. The value of a product to the firm depends more on its future service potential or expected sales price than upon either what it did cost or what it should cost. Thus, since the standard cost concept is an input exchange value, it has many of the disadvantages of other input valuations.

The appropriateness of the standard cost concept as a good measure of input exchange values depends in large part on the type of standard cost chosen and the way it is applied. Ideal standards may be useful for managerial purposes, but they tend to understate asset valuations because they tend to exclude some of the normal costs of inefficiency and idle capacity. Current standards that take these normal inefficiencies into account may be more appropriate; but there is always a difficulty in keeping them current by incorporating changes in prices and production methods.

The lower-of-cost-or-market valuation

The lower-of-cost-or-market valuation procedure is neither an output nor an input valuation concept, but a mixture of the two concepts. The term *market* may refer to either an output or an input price. When the concept is applied to inventories, the term *market* usually refers to replacement cost (an input concept), but it may refer to selling price or net realizable value (output concepts) under certain conditions. When it is applied to the valuation of investments in securities, *market* usually refers to the selling price, although in this case, the costs and selling prices are obtained from the same market; the difference between the two is represented primarily by the costs of buying and selling. However, since securities are not usually purchased with the purpose of selling in a different market at a higher price, both the cost and selling price of securities can be considered output prices. The application of the lower-of-cost-or-market rule to securities and inventories will be discussed in later chapters. The following discussion emphasizes the evaluation of the basic concept itself.

The lower-of-cost-or-market concept has a long history in accounting, going back to the 19th century and before. One of the reasons for its early prominence is the early emphasis on the balance sheet as a report to creditors. Without a reliable report on which to base expectations regarding future operations, creditors emphasized the lowest probable conversion value of assets. Thus, a policy of conservatism was adopted with regard to balance sheet valuations. The valuations presented in the statements could be assumed to be worth at least as much as stated.

With the change in emphasis to the income statement, the cost-or-market rule took on new meaning. It was now the income that would be conservatively stated. By reducing asset valuations at the end of a period because of a fall in prices, the net income for the period would be smaller. All possible losses would be included in the current income determination, but all probable gains would be deferred until the usual recognition at the time of sale or later. The recognition of gains is based on different criteria than the recognition of losses. Gains are not recognized until there is little or no possibility of their being reversed, but losses are recognized whenever there is some available evidence that they might occur.

There is some question whether the cost-or-market rule is a basic accounting concept or merely an accepted accounting procedure. It does not use any valuation concept different from the concepts discussed above, but because it does not apply any one of the valuation concepts consistently, it can be considered a different concept at least in its application, or it can be considered an eclectic application of various valuation concepts. Regardless of the level of dignity ascribed to the method, it has been vigorously criticized for many years in discussions of accounting theory. Its most amazing attribute is that it has found so many followers for so many years. It has even maintained formal recognition by the American Institute of Certified Public Accountants, the American Accounting Association, the Securities and Exchange Commission, the Institute of Chartered Accountants in England and Wales, and other associations and agencies.

The acceptance of the cost-or-market concept by the FASB is stated in *AICPA Professional Standards* as follows:

> A departure from the cost basis of pricing the inventory is required when the utility of the goods is no longer as great as its cost. Where there is evidence that the utility of goods, in their disposal in the ordinary course of business, will be less than cost, whether due to physical deterioration, obsolescence, changes in price levels, or other causes, the difference should be recognized as a loss of the current period. This is generally accomplished by stating such goods at a lower level commonly designated as *market*. [14]

In this context, the term *market* is used to mean replacement cost, with net realizable value as an upper limit and net realizable value less a normal profit margin as a lower limit.

The lower-of-cost-or-market concept is unacceptable in accounting theory for the following reasons:

1. As a method of conservatism, it tends to understate total asset valuations. Individual asset valuations may also be understated, but because valuations are not increased above acquisition cost in those cases where future service or sales values have increased, the total valuations would tend to be understated whenever the cost-or-market concept is applied. This understatement may not harm creditors, but it is deceiving to stockholders and potential investors, and management is kidding itself if it believes its own statements.

2. The conservatism in asset valuations is offset by an unconservative statement of net income in a future period. A lower asset valuation in the current period will result in a larger reported profit or smaller loss in some future period when the asset valuation is charged off as an expense. Because gains are not reported currently, the resulting net income will be less useful as a predictive device or as a measure of efficiency.

---

[14] *AICPA Professional Standards,* para. 5121.07.

3. While the cost-or-market concept can be applied consistently from year to year, it is internally inconsistent. No single valuation concept is used consistently; one valuation concept may be applied one year and another concept the next year. Also, there is no consistent application of valuation concepts to a single asset classification in the same year.

4. A less convincing argument is that the cost-or-market rule applies to decreases in costs as well as to diminished utility due to deterioration, obsolescence, or decreased earning capacity. There may not be any changes in net realizable value just because costs have changed.

EVALUATION OF
MEASUREMENT CONCEPTS

In the valuation of assets, there is no single concept or procedure that is ideal in the presentation of the statement of financial position, in the determination of income, or in the presentation of other information relevant to the decisions of investors, creditors, and other users of financial statements. From a structural point of view, historical cost valuation is frequently assumed to be the ideal insofar as it is based on double-entry bookkeeping, which requires the recording of all resource changes and permits their subsequent identification.[15] However, formal structures can also be devised for other valuation concepts.

An objective of asset valuation from an interpretational point of view is to provide a relative measurement of the resources available to the firm in the generation of future cash receipts. Historical cost valuation lacks interpretation (unless specific costs are associated with specific dates), and current replacement costs permit greater interpretation if the measurements are taken from used-asset markets rather than restating historical costs by the use of specific price indexes. Net realizable value and current cash equivalents permit interpretations if the valuations are taken from prices existing in markets. McKeown has demonstrated that current cash equivalents and current replacement costs differ from each other and from historical costs by material amounts, suggesting that none of these concepts can be used as a good surrogate for one of the others.[16]

Using normative investment models, it may be assumed that an objective of asset valuation is to provide information that will permit the prediction of future cash outflows necessary to acquire similar resources in the future in the continuation of business operations and to permit the prediction of future cash receipts. Current replacement costs obtained from existing markets may reflect the cash outflows required to duplicate

---

[15] See, for example, Yuji Ijiri, "A Defense for Historical Cost Accounting," in *Asset Valuation and Income Determination,* ed. Robert R. Sterling (Lawrence, Kans.: Scholars Book, 1971), p. 13.

[16] James C. McKeown, "Comparative Application of Market and Cost Based Accounting Models," *Journal of Accounting Research,* Spring 1973, p. 99.

the existing facilities.[17] Thus, as a prediction of future cash outflows, current input costs, and expected future input prices are more significant than past input valuations. A separation of fixed and variable costs may also permit a better prediction of future cash flows. In the prediction of future cash receipts, output concepts are generally superior to input valuation concepts. Thus, net realizable values and current cash equivalents may be relevant for many predictions. But when the expected future benefits are highly uncertain, the use of input valuations may offer a reasonable substitute in some situations. The following tabulation summarizes the various asset valuation concepts and the general conditions under which they may be applicable:

Valuation concept	*Conditions where applicable**
Exchange output values:	When reliable evidence of output values is available as an indication of future cash receipts.
1. Discounted future expected cash receipts or service potentials.	1. When expected cash receipts or the equivalent are known or can be estimated with a high degree of certainty and when the waiting period is relatively long.
2. Current output values.	2. When current sales prices represent the future output price.
3. Current cash equivalents.	3. When the best alternative is orderly liquidation.
4. Liquidation values.	4. When the firm is not likely to be able to sell its product in the usual marketing channels or it is not likely to be able to utilize normal expected service values.
Exchange input values:	When reliable evidence of output values is not available or as an indication of future cash requirements:
5. Historical cost.	5. As a measure of current input value when acquired recently.
6. Current input costs.	6. When verifiable evidence of current input values can be obtained.
7. Discounted future costs.	7. When future services of known or estimated cost are purchased in advance instead of being acquired when needed.
8. Standard costs.	8. When they represent current costs under normal conditions of efficiency and capacity utilization.

* Assuming an objective of the prediction of future cash receipts or future cash requirements.

SELECTED ADDITIONAL READING

Asset measurement and valuation

American Accounting Association Committee on Accounting Valuation Bases. "Report of the Committee on Accounting Valuation Bases." *Accounting Review,* supplement to vol. 47 (1972), pp. 535–73.

[17] See Lawrence Revsine, *Replacement Cost Accounting* (Englewood Cliffs, N.J.: Prentice-Hall, 1973), p. 84.

Barret, M. Edgar. "Proposed Bases for Asset Valuations." *Financial Executive,* January 1973, pp. 12–17.

Penman, Stephen H. "What Net Asset Value? An Extension of a Familiar Debate." *Accounting Review,* April 1970, pp. 333–46.

Sprouse, Robert T. "Balance Sheet—Embodiment of the Most Fundamental Elements of Accounting Theory." *Foundations of Accounting Theory.* Gainesville: University of Florida Press, 1971, pp. 90–104.

Staubus, George J. "Measurement of Assets and Liabilities." *Accounting and Business Research,* Autumn 1973, pp. 243–62.

Sunder, Shyam. "Accuracy of Exchange Valuation Rules." *Journal of Accounting Research,* Autumn 1978, pp. 241–67.

Walker, R. G. "Asset Classification and Asset Valuation." *Accounting and Business Research,* Autumn 1974, pp. 286–96.

Value to the enterprise

Brief, Richard P., and **Joel Owen.** "Present Value Models and the Multi-Asset Problem." *Accounting Review,* October 1973, pp. 690–95.

Bromwich, Michael. "The Use of Present Value Valuation Models in Published Accounting Reports." *Accounting Review,* July 1977, pp. 587–96.

Chambers, Raymond J. "Asset Measurement and Valuation." *Cost and Management,* March–April 1971, pp. 30–35.

Peasnell, K. V. "A Note on the Discounted Present Value Concept." *Accounting Review,* January 1977, pp. 186–89.

Warrell, C. J. "The Enterprise Value Concept of Asset Valuation." *Accounting and Business Research,* Summer 1974, pp. 220–26.

Wright, F. K. "Relationship between Present Value and Value to the Owner." *Journal of Business Finance,* Summer 1973, pp. 19–25.

Market values

Backer, Morton, assisted by Richard Simpson. *Current Value Accounting.* New York: Financial Executive Research Foundation, 1973. For a review, see Morton Backer, "Model for Current Value Reporting." *CPA Journal,* February 1974, pp. 27–33.

Beidleman, Carl R. "Valuation of Used Capital Assets." *Accounting Research Study No. 7.* AAA, 1973. For a review, see Carl R. Beidleman, "Determinants of Second-Hand Asset Values." *Accounting and Business Research,* Spring 1974, pp. 102–15.

Bromwich, Michael, "Asset Valuation with Imperfect Markets." *Accounting and Business Research,* Autumn 1975, pp. 242–53.

Chambers, Raymond J. "Evidence for a Market-Selling Price Accounting System." In *Asset Valuation and Income Determination,* Edited by Robert R. Sterling. Lawrence, Kans.: Scholars Book, 1971, pp. 74–96.

Edwards, Edgar O. "The State of Current Value Accounting." *Accounting Review,* April 1975, pp. 235–45.

King, Alfred M. "Fair Value Reporting." *Management Accounting,* March 1975, pp. 25–30.

Parker, James E. "Testing Comparability and Objectivity of Exit Value Accounting." *Accounting Review,* July 1975, pp. 512–24.

Historical costs

Ijiri, Yuji. "A Defense for Historical Cost Accounting." In *Asset Valuation and Income Determination,* edited by Robert R. Sterling. Lawrence, Kans.: Scholars Book, 1971, pp. 1–14.

———— . "The Significance of Historical Cost Valuation." *The Foundation of Accounting Measurement.* Englewood Cliffs, N.J.: Prentice-Hall, 1967, pp. 64–67.

Mautz, Robert K. "A Few Words for Historical Cost." *Financial Executive,* January 1973, pp. 23–27, 64.

Current costs

See Chapter 9, Suggested Additional Reading.

Comparative valuation studies

Bedford, Norton M., and **James C. McKeown.** "Comparative Analysis of Net Realizable Value and Replacement Costing." *Accounting Review,* April 1972, pp. 333–38.

McKeown, James C. "Comparative Application of Market and Cost Based Accounting Models." *Journal of Accounting Research,* Spring 1973, pp. 62–99.

Lower-of-cost-or-market rule

See Chapter 13, Suggested Additional Reading.

CHAPTER 12

CURRENT ASSETS AND
CURRENT LIABILITIES

Classification is necessary for the study and communication of relevant information in all of the physical and social sciences. Accounting is no exception. The classification of the resources and commitments of a firm into appropriate categories is needed in order to present interpretable summaries of accounting information that can be understood and analyzed by investors and other users of financial statements in their decision processes. Historically, the main categories and subclassifications of assets and liabilities have been carried forward into the present on the basis of traditional practices, devised originally to meet specific assumed needs that in many cases no longer exist. For example, assets and liabilities are usually presented in published financial statements in some order of solvency or liquidity to meet the assumed special needs of creditors. In the first part of this chapter, the objectives of the current asset and current liability classifications are evaluated.[1] Alternative methods of classification and their objectives are also discussed and related to various aspects of accounting theory.

Following this discussion of the objectives and definitions, attention is given to an examination of the valuation concepts and procedures related to specific categories of current assets and current liabilities. However, the subject of inventories is deferred to the following chapter.

In this and the following chapters, keep in mind the fundamental relationships between the problems of valuation, income determination, and cash flows; but we should not be bound by the limits of the double-entry accounting structure when we discuss the development of theoretical accounting concepts and their application to the communication of relevant accounting information. In the traditional accounting structure, some of the concepts discussed in Chapter 8 relating to the reporting of revenues and gains and losses may dictate the valuation concept applied. At other times, however, the guidelines for valuation applied in practice seem to dictate the timing and classification of revenues, gains, and losses. The following discussion attempts to evaluate the objectives and keep the

---

[1] For a discussion of the nature of assets, see Chapter 11, and for a discussion of the nature of liabilities, see Chapter 17.

process of valuation, income determination, and the presentation of cash flows in proper balance.

THE OBJECTIVES OF ASSET AND
LIABILITY CLASSIFICATIONS

The main purpose of asset and liability classifications is to provide meaningful summaries of financial data. The grouping of like items is necessary to permit the readers of financial statements to (1) obtain a reasonable understanding of the financial position and operations of a firm, (2) make meaningful comparisons with past periods and with other firms, and (3) make predictions regarding future cash flows. If unclassified data were presented to those interested in the firm, they would be forced to make their own summarization; the mind can cope with only a reasonable amount of data at one time. But if the summarization and classification are performed for them, a choice is made for them regarding what information is important and what is not important and what items should be emphasized more than others. When the readers of external reports have different objectives or different backgrounds regarding their knowledge of the firm, this summarization and classification necessarily omits some information and relationships that may be of value to specific readers or groups of readers. Thus, the principal guidelines for summarization and classification are an important part of accounting theory. But an evaluation of these guidelines depends upon who the intended readers are and what information they need.

The presentation of solvency to creditors

The earliest objective of the current asset and current liability classifications was the presentation to creditors of information showing the relative security of their debts. The primary test of this security was the liquidity of specific assets and their availability for the payment of debts, particularly those debts falling due within the following year. This emphasis on the liquidity of assets and on the order in which debts would become payable stemmed from the lack of other reliable operating data and from the fact that creditors (particularly short-term creditors) represented the major group demanding financial information.

Today, the objectives of financial reporting have broadened considerably, and the statement of financial position has become only one of several financial reports. But current accounting practice and thought still carry many of the earlier ideas and practices. Assets and liabilities are still generally classified according to their relative liquidity; the lower-of-cost-or-market rule still finds many ardent supporters; and the time period of a year is still the general rule in the classification of many assets and liabilities as current.

The classification of assets and liabilities as *current* and *noncurrent* as a method of presenting the solvency of the firm is less important today than earlier for several reasons:

1. Other statements, particularly the income statement and the statement of changes in financial position, may provide better information regarding expectations of solvency.
2. External financial reports are used more by investors and other groups than by creditors.
3. Corporations are generally considered to be more permanent in nature and more stable than were most of the 19th century firms.
4. The widespread use of some valuation procedures, such as LIFO, has made the working capital ratio less meaningful than it once was.
5. The demand by creditors and others for a "favorable" working capital ratio forces managements to take certain actions, such as the payment of current liabilities immediately preceding the balance sheet date, and places pressure on accountants to permit reclassifications to make the working capital appear favorable, even though in so doing the operations and solvency of the firm are not affected.
6. Business enterprises are becoming highly complex, so that no predetermined working capital ratio can be deemed to be necessary for adequate solvency.
7. The increased entry of many firms into the service industries has made the solvency of firms less dependent upon resources classified as current.

An alternative to the current-noncurrent classification is (1) present a classification of the liabilities based on the type of credit source available to the firm, and (2) disclose supplemental information regarding the amount and timing of expected cash receipts and cash disbursements related to specific assets and obligations.[2] Liabilities would be classified as either spontaneous or negotiated; that is, as either originating from the normal operations of the firm, such as normal trade credit and accruals, or from the specific negotiations of the firm with banks and other financial lending institutions for either short- or long-term loans. This classification is relevant because the former sources are fairly automatic, and the latter require negotiation and the lender's evaluation of the financial position of the firm. Information regarding the amount and timing of cash receipts and disbursements would include schedules classifying receivables and payables by due dates and schedules showing the amount and timing of interest, lease, and other periodic receipts or disbursements related to the financing contracts.

---

[2] Loyd C. Heath, "Is Working Capital Really Working?," *Journal of Accountancy,* August, 1980, pp. 55–62; and Loyd C. Heath, *Financial Reporting and the Evaluation of Solvency,* Accounting Research Monograph No. 3 (AICPA, 1978).

The description of enterprise operations

One of the objectives of financial statements is to describe the operations of the enterprise. This can be achieved partially by an appropriate classification of items in the statements according to (1) the frequency of opportunity to decide about the continued commitment or recommitment of enterprise resources to specific forms of investment and (2) the frequency of the necessity to obtain commitment for specific forms of capital sources. Thus, if the current assets and current liabilities are classified according to the operating activities of the specific firm, the reader of the statements should be able to obtain a better interpretation of the information and find it more useful in decision models than if the classification were based on some other objective.

As we shall see in the following discussion, the description of the operating activities of the firm is currently one of the objectives of balance sheet classification. The contemporary definitions of current assets and current liabilities are expressed in terms of the operating cycle of the business, and many published balance sheets show working capital (current assets less current liabilities) as a separate item. Thus the groupings are in terms of their function in the operations of the enterprise rather than in terms of the timing of their conversion into cash.

In proposing this operational objective of classification, it is generally assumed that working capital items are closely related to current operations and that long-term assets and liabilities are related to the long-term planning functions of the organization. This distinction is also reflected in the classifications in the income statement; expenses related to the use of current resources are often classified separately from the amortization and depreciation of long-term assets. And it is also clearly reflected in the funds statement; funds (often defined as working capital) provided from operations are usually classified separately from the funds obtained from other sources.

One of the main difficulties in applying the operational objective of classification is that in most firms there is little relationship between working capital and current operations. Cash flows becoming available for the payment of liabilities may be as closely related to the use of long-term resources as to the sale of inventories. This is particularly true in the service industries, where inventories may be relatively small or nonexistent and current obligations will be paid from the revenues derived from the use or leasing of depreciable assets.

Classification according to the accounting structure

Accounting classifications have often been established because of their convenience in the bookkeeping process. The deferred charge classification, for example, has often been used as a resting place for unallocated debits. As a result, such items as unamortized discount on bonds payable, discount on preferred stock, and losses carried forward have found a place among the assets of published balance sheets.

Classification according to the accounting process, however, is not necessarily irrelevant to the readers of published financial statements. It may be meaningful to draw a distinction between those items that will be disposed of through charges and credits to income and those items that will result directly or indirectly in cash flows. Gilman called the former items "deferred charges and credits to revenue" and the latter items "deferred charges and credits to cash."[3] Deferred charges to cash would include receivables, marketable securities, and long-term investments; deferred charges to revenue would include prepaid expenses, plant and equipment, and inventories. Most liabilities are deferred credits to cash, but obligations to provide specific goods or services are considered deferred credits to revenue.

The main difficulty with this objective is that it is an attempt to explain the results of technical accounting procedures and it is, therefore, nontheoretical in nature. Because of its lack of logical orientation, the use of deferred charges and deferred credits permits the application of procedures that have no logical basis, or at least do not permit an explanation of the meaning of the deferral. Therefore, the classifications of deferred charges to revenue and deferred credits to revenue are highly objectionable.[4]

Classification according to valuation methods

Most of the valuation concepts discussed in the previous chapter are used in published financial statements, and very often many of the concepts are used in the same balance sheet. From a theory point of view, an eclectic procedure is not necessarily objectionable, as the valuation concept chosen should depend upon the available evidence and the degree of uncertainty in each case and an attempt to approach the relevant concept of income. But groupings of assets and liabilities that include different valuation concepts may be misleading to even informed readers of published statements.

A grouping of assets according to valuation concepts would include the following classifications: (1) cash and expected cash receipts (properly discounted when appropriate); (2) assets valued in terms of current or expected sales prices (output prices); (3) assets valued in terms of current costs (input prices); and (4) assets valued in terms of historical costs or

---

[3] Stephen Gilman, "Accounting Principles and the Current Classification," *Accounting Review* 19 (April 1944): p.114.

[4] See Chapter 17 for a discussion of the meaning of the term *deferred credits to revenue* and Chapter 16 for a discussion of *deferred charges* and the objections to this terminology and classification.

costs restated to adjust for changes in the general level of prices. Other classifications may be used when appropriate. The main advantage of classification according to valuation concepts would be to provide better interpretation of the balance sheet and its relationship to the income statement and funds flow statement. In the author's opinion, however, adequate disclosure of valuation procedures can be obtained by parenthetical notations and in other ways, rather than through the grouping of assets.

The prediction of cash flows

As indicated in Chapter 10, the presentation of information that will permit the prediction of the future cash flows of the firm should be one of the objectives of financial reporting. No classification of resources and commitments alone can permit predictions of future cash flows, but a classification may be relevant when it is associated with historical and budgeted cash flow information. Such a classification should provide information regarding the likely timing of conversions of resources into cash, or their availability for conversion and the timing of the payment of obligations.

WORKING CAPITAL

The concept of working capital refers to the net investment required in a business enterprise to maintain the day-to-day operations, as opposed to that investment that is committed for a longer period. This has sometimes been called circulating capital. The investment in assets committed for long periods includes land, plant, and equipment that provide the facilities for enterprise operations; generally, these assets provide services and wear out gradually, but some assets represent indefinite commitments. The investment in working capital, on the other hand, is in a continual process of change through daily transactions. Because the short-term liabilities are not generally thought of as providing permanent invested capital but are closely related to the financing of the working assets, the term *working capital* is used to mean the excess of current assets over current liabilities.

The conventional classification of assets and liabilities as current and noncurrent is not based on either the accounting process or similarities in valuation. But the classification may serve at least partially the objectives of presenting information to short-term creditors regarding the solvency of the firm, and of presenting a partial description of enterprise operations.

The objective of presenting information regarding solvency was probably the most important objective in early balance sheet presentations, although many of the early writers did not state specifically their objectives. Sprague, for example, emphasized the importance of liquidity and debt-paying ability, but he also implied the importance of the description of enterprise operations. He stated:

> The arrangement of the items in the balance sheet is of some importance especially if the list is voluminous. . . . In our example the order of availability has been followed, or, as it might be termed, the order of liquidation. . . . In an industrial enterprise where it was thought that productivity or earning power was more important than readiness in debt-paying, it might be that the fixed plant was entitled to the first place among the assets and that the cash on hand would be placed at the end as the least productive of assets. But, at any rate, *some* principle of arrangement is better than haphazard.[5]

The presentation of working capital does provide some valid information to the grantors of short-term credit because it indicates the degree of protection or the amount of buffer carried by long-term creditors and stockholders. But neither the amount of working capital nor the working capital ratio is necessarily a good indication of the ability of the firm to pay current liabilities as they come due. This is because working capital is a static concept, and debt-paying ability is dynamic. Cash becoming available for the paying of debt arises primarily from operations, not from the liquidation of particular assets. Cash and other liquid assets available at a particular balance sheet date are likely to be used in operations for the payment of liabilities not yet incurred at balance sheet date (e.g., current payroll), rather than being held for the payment of the balance sheet liabilities as they mature.

Furthermore, nonliquid current assets become liquid sequentially (that is, from raw material inventories to work in process to finished inventories to accounts receivable to cash), and current liabilities become due simultaneously or at dates that are unrelated to each other. Therefore, if revenues are contracting, the liquidation of assets through normal operations will be delayed, but the due dates for liabilities will not change.[6] This type of situation presents a good argument for the valuation of current assets in terms of current cash equivalents.

The current classification as a description of operations has long been established in governmental fund accounting. The current assets and current liabilities are often set up as a separate fund, either in the accounts or in the statements or in both. The term *fund* is used in this situation to refer to a segregation of assets and liabilities for a given purpose as a specific unit of operations or as a center of interest. Vatter has suggested that the current classification is also very appropriate in the application of fund theory to general financial accounting.[7]

---

[5] Charles E. Sprague, *The Philosophy of Accounts* (New York: 1907), p. 32.

[6] Robert D. Hunter, "Concept of Working Capital," *Journal of Commercial Bank Lending*," March 1972, pp. 24–30.

[7] William J. Vatter, *The Fund Theory of Accounting and Its Implications for Financial Reports* (Chicago: University of Chicago Press, 1947), p. 60.

The use of the concept of working capital as a partial description of enterprise operations is reflected in the practice of subtracting current liabilities from current assets in the balance sheet, a practice that gained considerable popularity in the 1940s and is commonly employed in the United States today. This objective is also implied in the section on "Current Assets and Current Liabilities—Working Capital" from *AICPA Professional Standards*. The implication comes from the change from the one-year rule for classification to the criterion of the operating cycle of the business. But this change did not reflect entirely a change in objective, as it was thought that it would also provide better information for creditors.

A major criticism of the working capital concept is that it is merely a net figure obtained by subtracting some of the liabilities from some of the assets, without a necessary relationship between the two classifications or their components. Furthermore, the net figure has little meaning as either a homogeneous grouping of net resources or as a margin or buffer available for the protection of creditors. The current classification includes both monetary and nonmonetary items, which should be measured with different objectives in mind or with different degrees of reliability, even if an attempt is made to make them homogeneous. The description of working capital as a buffer assumes that current liabilities will be paid from resources classified as current, and that the current assets will not be required for other purposes having priority over the payment of the current liabilities; since neither of these assumptions is realistic, the presentation of working capital as a net figure is of doubtful relevance in financial reporting.

The definition of *current assets*

According to *AICPA Professional Standards, current assets* is defined as "cash and other assets or resources commonly identified as those which are reasonably expected to be realized in cash or sold or consumed during the normal operating cycle of the business." This compares with the earlier, much narrower, definition presented by Sanders, Hatfield, and Moore: "those assets which in the regular course of business will be converted into cash and those assets acquired with a view to their availability for conversion into cash."[8] The one-year rule was common in the application of this earlier definition.

Three main changes can be noted in the currently accepted definition as compared with earlier ones: (1) a greater emphasis on expectations or intent to convert rather than the availability for conversion particularly with respect to marketable securities (However, because intent is difficult to determine, availability is still the major criterion in many cases.), (2) a broadening of the scope of current assets in order to include prepaid ex-

---

[8] Thomas Henry Sanders, Henry Rand Hatfield, and Underhill Moore, *A Statement of Accounting Principles* (New York: American Institute of Accountants, 1938), p. 70.

penses (items to be consumed), and (3) an emphasis on the normal operating cycle of the business, rather than on the one-year rule.

The above definition, however, does not place the main emphasis on the nature of the operations of a going concern. The emphasis should be on the frequency of the opportunity to decide whether or not to recommit the funds for use in current operations. Current assets in the aggregate may be just as permanent as the investment in noncurrent assets, but the opportunity for reinvestment in current operations occurs within the current operating cycle of the business. However, once assets are committed by management for investment in specific long-term forms, they should not be classified as current assets. For example, cash, securities, or other assets committed by management for the later acquisition of plant and equipment or for other noncurrent uses should not be included among the current assets. The commitment need not be legally binding on management, but it should be explicit. The investment is not intended to become available for the current operations of the business, nor for investment opportunities other than that for which it is allocated. It is necessary but not sufficient that the current assets be capable of being converted readily into cash or other monetary assets; they must also be free of commitment for long-term uses. The earlier reference to availability for conversion emphasized the liquidity of the assets, while the criteria of intent and commitment emphasize the operating aspects of the business.

A major criticism of the emphasis on intent, however, is that it is frequently difficult to determine and may be subject to change. As a result, investments are frequently classified as current because of the intent to convert them when and if needed for current operations, even though there may be very little expectation that they will ever be needed. Furthermore, there is also an inclination to classify investments as current because of the desire to make the working capital position appear more favorable.

Prepaid expenses were included in the definition because if they had not been acquired, they would require the use of current assets in the normal operations of the business. But, in this regard, they are the same as inventories; both would require the use of current funds if they had not been acquired previously. The main reason for their inclusion is that they represent resources committed for only a short period—the current operating cycle. Like inventories, they result in current funds becoming available for recommitment through the sale of the product or services and the collection of the proceeds. However, the reporting of prepaid expenses is a product of the traditional accounting structure. Little economic interpretation can be obtained from this information, and it is doubtful that it can be helpful to investors in their prediction and decision activities.

The *operating cycle* is defined as the time it takes to convert cash into the product of the enterprise and then to convert the product back into cash again. This concept permits an operational demarcation between short-term commitments and long-term commitments. Plant and equipment items are omitted from the current asset classification because their turnover period covers many product turnover periods. On the other hand, although some insurance policies may cover more than one operating cycle, little advantage would be gained by classifying these separately as long-term commitments.

One of the difficulties in the way the operating cycle concept is applied in practice is that if it is less than one year, the one-year rule still applies; the result is that the current asset classification does not disclose consistently the frequency of the circulation of assets. But even if the operating cycle criterion were applied consistently, there would still be some major difficulties because of the complexity of many business enterprises and the resultant inability to determine the length of the operating cycle. However, the frequency of circulation of assets is relevant to the prediction of cash flows, but the ability to tie this information to the income and cash flow information is difficult when all current assets are classified as if they had the same frequency of circulation. Classification on the basis of the operating cycle is also opposed on the grounds that it might obscure more significant relationships.[9] Because of these difficulties regarding the interpretation of the operating cycle and because of the lack of evidence regarding the relevance of the current asset classification to any specific user's needs, other methods of classifying assets should be investigated.

The definition of *current liabilities*

The term *current liabilities* is generally defined either in terms of the timing of their payment of in terms of the conditions under which they were incurred. The first view states that current liabilities include obligations *payable* within a year or before the end of the operating business cycle.[10] The second view states that current liabilities include obligations whose payment requires the use of current assets or those that are incurred in the *acquisition* of items to be used in the operating cycle.[11]

Both of these views lack adequate economic interpretation. The one-year rule is too arbitrary, and the operating cycle concept is too vague. The assumption that current liabilities will be paid from current assets is not realistic even under conditions of complete liquidation. Assets are converted sequentially into more liquid forms, and current liabilities have independent due dates. An alternative would be to classify liabilities

---

[9] See William Huizingh, *Working Capital Classification* (Ann Arbor: Bureau of Business Research, Graduate School of Business Administration, University of Michigan, 1967), p. 109.

[10] See, for example, Paul Grady, "Inventory of Generally Accepted Accounting Principles for Business Enterprises," *Accounting Research Study No. 7* (AICPA, 1965), p. 65.

[11] See *AICPA Professional Standards* (Chicago: Commerce Clearing House, Inc., 1975), paras. 1027.25 and 2031.07. See also *Accounting Research Bulletin No. 43*, pp. 21–23.

by due dates that would permit better interpretation and better information for use in the prediction of future cash flows.

Frequently, current assets are defined in terms of their availability for the payment of current liabilities. But generally, the relationship between current assets and current liabilities is not as direct as this. Current liabilities are more directly related to operating cash flows than to the assets existing at a specific date. They generally arise from the short-term financing of current operations, and they are usually paid from cash generated by current operations.

Current liabilities tend to be fairly permanent in the aggregate, but they differ from long-term liabilities in several ways. The main distinctive features are these: (1) they require frequent attention regarding the refinancing of specific liabilities; (2) they provide frequent opportunities to shift from one source of funds to another; and (3) they permit management to vary continually the total funds from short-term sources.

One of the major differences between the definition of current assets and the definition of current liabilities is that the current portion of long-term debt is reclassified each year as a current liability, and the current portion of fixed assets is not. The reason for this difference is found in the conventional emphasis on liquidity and the effect on cash and cash flows; the current portion of long-term debt will require current cash or cash becoming available, but the current depreciation is only indirectly related to any obligations or cash flows during the current period. From an operational point of view, however, the current portion of long-term debt is not a part of the short-term financing operations of the firm. Although the payment of the current portion of long-term debt does require the use of current funds, so do payments of dividends declared after the date of the balance sheet and requirements for capital expenditures. If the current portion of long-term debt were not reclassified as current, however, the cash or other current resources intended or committed to be used for the payment of this debt should be classified as noncurrent, just as cash and other resources committed for other nonoperating purposes.

Inadequacies of the current asset and current liability classifications

The conventional definitions of current assets and current liabilities are assumed to provide some information to users of financial statements, but they are far from adequate in meeting the desired objectives. These inadequacies can be summarized as follows:

1. One of the main objectives of the classification is to present information useful to creditors; however, it is far from adequate in serving this purpose. Creditors are primarily interested in the ability of the firm to meet its debts as they mature. This ability depends primarily on the outcome of projected operations; the pairing of current liabilities with

current assets assumes that the latter will be available for the payment of the former.

2.   Creditors are also interested in the solvency of the firm—the probability of obtaining repayment in case the firm is liquidated. Vatter suggests that special statements should be prepared for this purpose.[12] Such a statement should show the expected sources of cash in liquidation and the special restrictions regarding the use of particular assets or sources of cash. In the conventional balance sheet, the pairing of current assets with current liabilities leads to the false assumption that, in liquidation, the short-term creditors have necessarily some priority over the current assets and that only the excess is available to long-term creditors. A solvency statement should show the specific priorities that do exist and the rights of all general creditors, regardless of whether they are short term or long term in nature.

3.   As a device for describing the operations of the firm, the classification is also defective. Such assets as interest receivable do not arise from the same type of operations as accounts receivable and inventories, but they are all grouped together as current assets. Among the current liabilities, dividends payable does not arise from the same type of operations as accounts payable, and from an operational point of view, the current portion of long-term debt is not dissimilar to the remainder of the long-term debt.

4.   From the point of view of invested capital, it is sometimes argued that the distinction between working capital and the investment in noncurrent assets is superficial. The investment of the long-term equity holders is tied up in receivables and inventories just as much as in plant and equipment. For a going concern, they all represent permanent investments; there is no greater intent to liquidate receivables and inventories as a whole than there is to liquidate the plant and equipment. This argument is usually directed at the liquidation objective, however; it is not valid as a criticism of the objective to describe operations.

5.   The current asset and current liability classifications do not help in the description of the accounting process or in the description of valuation procedures. In the opinion of the author, the first is not necessary and the latter objective can be met by other means.

While the current asset and current liability concepts are deficient in meeting the main objectives of financial statements, the reason seems to be that conventional statements attempt to do too much. It would be better to concentrate on a classification that would permit a valid prediction of operating cash flows and then present specific information of interest to creditors in a separate statement. It may be better to restrict the objectives and present special statements for special purposes than to present a general-purpose statement without specific stated objectives.

---

[12] Vatter, *The Fund Theory,* p. 58.

MONETARY CURRENT ASSETS

Monetary current assets are claims to a fixed number of dollars of general purchasing power becoming available and intended to be used in current operations within the operating cycle of the business or one year, whichever is the longer. These include money in its various forms and claims to money. The claims generally are represented by formal or informal contracts specifying that a second party pay the firm a given sum of money at a specified date or within a specific time period (possibly implied from general business practice).

Money

Cash and the various other forms of money are expressed in terms of their current value, which is definite. Therefore, any gains or losses resulting from the exchange of other assets for the given amount of cash or money forms should have been recognized; no gain or loss should be recognized from the holding of cash and money forms except possibly in consideration of purchasing power gains and losses during periods of price-level change, as discussed in Chapter 9. Holdings of convertible foreign currency or moneys should be expressed in terms of the domestic equivalent at the balance sheet date.

Receivables

Receivables and monetary securities should be valued in terms of the discounted value of the cash to be received in the future. Since the cash is not available until after a waiting period, the receivable is not worth its maturity value (the amount finally due under the contract). Unless it is specifically stated, the rate of interest or discount that should be used is the market rate for credit of equal risk. However, there is some merit in using the firm's cost of capital rate or its internal rate of return, because these represent an approximation of the opportunity cost of the money to the firm. But, the actual differential cost of granting credit to customers may be very low or even negative because of the possible loss of product revenue if credit were not granted. Although the timing of income is still a factor for most short-term receivables, the amount of interest (discount) is usually small and therefore not material in the computation of the firm's net income for the year. However, material amounts representing specific finance charges and interest should be deducted from the related receivables.[13]

Another factor in the proper valuation of receivables is the treatment of the uncertainty of collection. As indicated in Chapter 8, revenue should

---

[13] See *AICPA Professional Standards,* Section 4111.

be measured by the expected amount to be collected. The receivables should be valued at the same amount, usually by deducting an allowance based on a large number of receivables. The amounts actually collected are likely to be closer to the expected values when a large number of receivables are involved in the estimate than when there are few receivables.

The estimate of the allowance for doubtful accounts is most accurate when it is based on the age and characteristics of the outstanding accounts at the balance sheet date and the probabilistic expectations of collectibility. On the other hand, the "bad debt loss" (reduction of revenue) associated with the revenue of the current period is more accurate when it is based on an estimated percentage of the revenue of the period. In the former procedure, the bad debt loss is residually determined, and in the latter procedure, the allowance for bad debts is the residual. Theory dictates that both should be placed in proper perspective. For income statement purposes, the percentage of revenue based on statistical analysis of past experience adjusted for current conditions should be used. The valuation of the receivables in the balance sheet, however, should be based on expectations regarding the specific composite of accounts existing at the balance sheet date.[14] Technically, any differences between the two methods would represent corrections of prior periods. The commonly accepted procedure of adjusting the current year's charge to bad debt losses for any errors of estimation in prior years is not consistent with the current operating concept of income, unless the amounts involved are clearly immaterial.

As discussed in Chapter 8, revenue should be reported whenever there is verifiable evidence of the value of the asset received in exchange for the product. Since a receivable is generally expressed in money terms, there is a verifiable measure of valuation, and the revenue should have been reported at the time of sale or before; after the period of sale, any effect on net income should arise only from interest (implicit or actual) during the waiting period or from corrections for errors in estimation of uncollectible amounts.

The installment basis.   The Accounting Principles Board, in *Opinion No. 10,* stated that the installment method of reporting revenue is not acceptable except when the collection of the sales price is not reasonably assured. As indicated in Chapter 8, this exception is not generally justified. Collection statistics are available for most types of loans if a firm has not obtained its own experience data. But if the installment basis is at all justified for other reasons, the deferred gross profit account should be treated as a valuation account to the receivables rather than as deferred income. The nature of installment sales is to defer the reporting of income until the cash has been received. Thus, at the time of the sales, the receiv-

---

[14] See *FASB Statement No. 5,* particularly paras. 22 and 23. *AICPA Professional Standards* (Chicago: Commerce Clearing House, Inc., 1975), p. 9189.

able takes the place of the product inventory, and the receivable should be valued in terms of the valuation of the product (the input value), rather than in terms of the present value of the receivable (the output value). Treating the deferred gross profit as a liability does not affect the computation of net income on the installment basis, but it does distort the asset and liability relationships.

When the revenue from installment sales is reported at the time of sale for accounting purposes but at the time of collection for income tax purposes, a deferred tax credit arises.[15] *APB Opinion No. 11* requires that the deferred tax credit relating to installment sales be classified as a current liability when the related installment receivable is classified as current, and as noncurrent when the related receivable is classified as noncurrent. This paired classification is based on the assumption that the collection of the receivable will result in a tax liability payable in the same year that the receivable is collected. Although there is a time lag for the payment of the tax after the collection of the receivable, the assumption that both relate to the same operating cycle is basically correct. However, there is theoretical support in this case for presenting the installment receivable at a valuation net of the expected tax, as the specific obligation to pay the tax arises only when the receivable is converted into cash.

Monetary investments

Monetary securities (such as bonds and notes) with known maturity dates and values should be treated similarly to receivables, with proper adjustment for the discount factor and for uncertainties of collection. The interest is usually included in the contract, however, and the uncertainties of collection are usually negligible. But the current values (market exchange values) of these securities often change because of changing market rates of interest. Under conventional accounting procedures, securities (when held for current working capital purposes) are generally recorded on the basis of the lower of cost or market. The argument for this method has been that cost is generally the most relevant basis for measuring the gains or losses realized when the securities are sold. If market price rises above cost, the increase in value is not generally recorded, because it is thought that this gain is unrealized in the technical sense of the word and because it is possibly ephemeral in nature and may disappear before the asset is sold. If the market value of the securities is less than cost, however, it is thought that the loss should be recorded and the securities should not be shown in the balance sheet in excess of their current realizable value.[16]

Since the FASB has not specified the procedures for reporting monetary investments classified as current, it is presumed that they may be

---

[15] See Chapter 18 for a more complete discussion of income tax allocation.

[16] See Chapter 11 for a more complete discussion of the lower-of-cost-or-market rule.

included in portfolios of marketable equity securities for which the port-folio lower-of-cost-or-market method (discussed in the following section) is followed. However, the use of current market prices for the valuation of all securities classified as current assets is common in special industries and as supplementary information for many other firms. There are many advantages for the use of current market prices for all marketable securi-ties including the following:

1.   Market values are as verifiable as cost in most cases (except where the market is "thin"), and they provide more useful information to inves-tors.

2.   They provide better information regarding the effects of holding securities. The gains and losses from holding securities are just as impor-tant as the gains and losses from selling them.

3.   When identical securities are acquired at different prices, it seems reasonable that they should be given identical values.

4.   Current assets are more homogeneous when all items are ex-pressed in terms of current values. Thus, the investment classification permits a better interpretation of these resources and is more likely to be meaningful in aiding the prediction of cash flows.

When long-term marketable corporate bonds are acquired at a pre-mium or discount and held as temporary investments, the maturity value does not reflect the amount that will be received when the bonds are sold. Therefore, the amortization of the premium or discount is not appropriate. Current market quotations are better not only because the bonds are expected to be sold in the near future, but also because the current market price reflects changes in the market rate of interest, while amortization assumes a constant rate.[17]

When corporate bonds or notes are held as long-term investments, the accepted procedure is to amortize the discount or premium over the re-maining life of the bonds. The current market price or the lower of cost or market is not generally considered applicable in this case because there is no intent to convert the bonds into cash until the maturity date. However, *APB Opinion No. 21* states that when bonds or notes are received in exchange for property or services that do not have an established ex-change price, the notes should be recorded initially at the discounted present value using current implicit interest rates. This is assumed to be equivalent to a market rate at the date of acquisition, but the valuation is not changed when interest rates change. This is based on the traditional historical cost accounting structure and the assumption that gains and losses resulting from temporary fluctuations in bond prices and interest rates tend to offset each other over the life of the bond or note because of the fixed-dollar maturity value. But, since amortization procedures as-sume a constant rate of interest, the reporting of current market prices or present values would provide a better base for the interpretation of the

---

[17] However, premiums may be amortized because of the favorable tax effect of so doing.

economic resources of the firm. Long-term and short-term investments should not be valued on different bases. Consistency of reporting within the firm and uniformity among firms should permit a better interpretation of a firm's resources and an improvement in the evaluation of investment decisions.

NONMONETARY CURRENT ASSETS

Nonmonetary current assets are rights or claims that cannot be converted into a currently known quantity of dollars at a specific future date. The most common examples are investments in common stock of other corporations, product inventories, and prepaid expenses. These items have a common characteristic different from monetary assets in that their current value cannot be estimated by discounting a future maturity value and adjusting for the uncertainties of collection. But they do not have homogeneous characteristics among themselves. Marketable investments in common stocks are similar to monetary investments in that they may be converted directly into cash when such funds are needed for current operations. The conversion of inventories into cash requires the sale through the marketing operations of the business and through the final collection of receivables. Prepaid expenses are not converted directly into cash; the benefits are received by the firm through their use in current operations. From a procedural point of view, however, inventories and prepaid expenses are usually treated alike as amounts to be allocated to expense in the future. Marketable equity securities and prepaid expenses will be discussed more fully in the following paragraphs; inventories will be discussed at length in the following chapter.

Marketable equity securities

FASB Statement No. 12[18] requires that marketable equity securities be reported on a portfolio lower-of-cost-or-market basis. The application of the lower-of-cost-or-market rule to a portfolio, rather than to each security, is consistent with portfolio theory. That is, the relevant return to the firm is the return on the portfolio, since an investor is not rewarded for the failure to diversify.

Declines in the market price of the portfolio are reported as unrealized holding losses; increases in market prices of the portfolio are reported as recoveries of losses, rather than as gains resulting from the reduction or elimination of a valuation allowance. This reversal represents a change in the accounting estimate of the unrealized loss reported previously.

The reporting of the reversal of the unrealized holding loss is an improvement over the conventional lower-of-cost-or-market rule, but its general application to the valuation of the portfolio is still objectionable

---

[18] *AICPA Professional Standards,* Section 5132.

for the same reasons as indicated earlier. However, this objection is reduced by the requirement that the aggregate cost and market value of each portfolio be disclosed in the body of financial statements or in notes and that information regarding the gross unrealized gains and the gross unrealized losses also be presented. But a case similar to that presented above for monetary investments can be made for the reporting of marketable equity securities at current market prices and the reporting of the holding gains and losses.

Temporary investments are generally held as secondary cash reserves. Therefore, dividend and interest income on these investments and gains and losses from holding and selling them are incidental to the main operations of the business. While interest income is accrued and recorded in the period in which it is earned, dividend income is not. Dividend income is generally recognized when it is declared, because the stockholder has no legal claim before that time and because of the uncertainty of the amount that will be declared, if any. However, if expectations regarding payment of dividends are good, there is no theoretical reason why dividends could not be estimated and accrued. The validity of recording the accrued dividend asset and the resulting income depends more on the validity of the estimate than on the legal right to receive the dividend.

When the cost basis is used for several identical lots of marketable securities acquired at different prices, a question arises regarding the measurement of the gains or losses when some of the securities are sold. The realized gains and losses are computed by taking the difference between original cost and the current net selling price. But how should we select the relevant costs? Is it the specific cost of the certificates sold, or should the cost be computed on the basis of a FIFO or LIFO flow concept or on the basis of an average cost? Since this problem is similar to that faced in the valuation and expensing of inventories, it will be deferred until the next chapter, where it will be discussed at length. It should be noted at this point, however, that if the securities are all valued at current market prices, the problem does not exist; all lots are then valued in terms of the same prices.

The above discussion has related specifically to current marketable equity investments, but much of the discussion is also relevant for long-term investments in common stocks. Such investments may be held for a variety of reasons, such as providing permanent financing to suppliers or customers, maintaining partial or complete control of subsidiaries, or obtaining diversification of the firm's investment.

FASB Statement No. 12 requires the noncurrent investments in equity securities be classified separately and valued on the basis of the lower-of-cost-or-market rule applied to the portfolio in the same way that it is applied to the current portfolio, with the exception that the accumulated changes in the valuation allowance are included in the equity section of the balance sheet instead of showing the current changes in the income statement. If the decline in market value is considered to be other than temporary, the write-down is to be reported as a realized loss. These reporting requirements are inconsistent and appear to be illogical as discussed in Chapter 16.[19]

Prepaid expenses

Prepaid expenses are benefits to be received by the firm in the future in the form of services. They include such items as office and factory supplies, prepaid rent, unexpired insurance, prepaid interest, and prepaid taxes.

Although the various prepaid expenses have some common characteristics for classification purposes, they also have some major differences. Some represent specific tangible assets (e.g., supplies), others represent the right to use assets owned by others (e.g., prepaid rent), and still others are related quite closely to other assets or liabilities. Canning, for example, asserted that prepaid taxes and prepaid insurance are really valuation accounts relating to the specific assets for which they are incurred.[20] A building for which taxes and insurance have been prepaid is worth more than a building for which no taxes or insurance have been prepaid. There is some merit in this argument, but the presentation of these items as additions to plant and equipment would not necessarily provide better information to investors. Taxes and insurance must be paid at current intervals unrelated to the life span of the plant and equipment.

The procedures for allocating the prepaid expenses to periods depend primarily on the type of asset to be amortized. Tangible assets, such as supplies, are normally transferred to expenses as they are consumed or used. Prepayments that relate to a specific period—such as prepaid rent, unexpired insurance, and prepaid taxes—are normally charged off to costs or expenses on the basis of the passing of time, similar to the straight-line method of depreciation. In both cases, the objective is to allocate the cost or other basis of valuation to the periods in which the goods or services are used or when the benefits are received by the firm.

As indicated in Chapter 8, under the matching rule, expenses should be recorded in the period in which the related revenue is reported. Thus, when prepaid expenses are associated with the production process, the amounts are transferred to product costs. In most other cases, however, prepaid expenses cannot be associated directly with revenue. Therefore, indirect or period matching must be used; they must be charged to expenses in the period in which they are used or in which the services are received by the firm.

In the case of supplies, costs are usually identified with specific items, and these are then charged to expense when the items are used. The methods for cost identification are similar to the problem of inventories

---

[19] For a more complete discussion of noncurrent investments, see Chapter 16.

[20] John B. Canning, *The Economics of Accountancy* (New York: Ronald Press, 1929), p. 37.

treated in the following chapter. Current values may provide useful information for some purposes, but costs are generally adequate as a measurement of supplies used because (1) the costs are generally recent exchange prices and therefore they will usually represent close approximations of current values, and (2) the differences between costs and current values are usually not material in relationship to net income. When price levels are changing rapidly, however, restatements should be made, as suggested in Chapter 9.

As indicated above, for prepayments of services to be received on a time basis, the straight-line method of amortization is the method most commonly found in practice. The assumption is that the services are to be received continually over a specific period and that the final benefits are received in these same periods. While this assumption may not necessarily be true, the short period over which the prepayments are to be allocated and the immaterial effect of different allocation methods are convincing pragmatic reasons for the use of a simple allocation procedure. The theory involved in evaluating amortization procedures is similar to the theory for the evaluation of depreciation procedures, to be discussed in Chapter 15. One observation should be made at this point. The argument for straight-line depreciation on the basis of a similarity of plant and equipment to prepaid expenses is not valid. Straight-line amortization may not be appropriate for either, but its use in the amortization of prepaid expenses is of less concern in meeting the basic objectives of financial reporting.

THE MEASUREMENT OF CURRENT LIABILITIES

The problem of defining liabilities and many of the problems connected with measuring and recording them will be deferred to Chapter 17. The objective at this point is to focus on the measurement of current liabilities and its effect on the presentation of working capital and on the computation of net income.

Monetary current liabilities

Most current liabilities are monetary in nature; they require the payment of a fixed sum of money at some time in the near future. The amount of the liability is therefore generally thought to be a definite amount fixed by the terms of a formal or informal contract. If the contract requires the payment of a specific amount at a later date without interest, the present value of the liability is the discounted amount. When the liability is an open account to be paid after a short time, the discount can be ignored because it is not material. But when the amount of discount or interest is material, the present value of the liability should be recorded.

APB Opinion No. 21 does not require the discounting of notes due within one year, but logic dictates that they should also be recorded at their present discounted value if the discount is material (e.g., rates above 15 or 20 percent). What is frequently referred to as prepaid interest should be deducted from the face value of the note to present the current discounted value. For practically all current liabilities, there is little or no uncertainty regarding the amount of dollars to be paid under the contract. Uncertainties and contingencies will be discussed in a later chapter.

The point at which a liability should be recognized is generally thought to be quite definite; the obligation arises as a result of a transaction. But the point in time when the transaction takes place is not always clear. As indicated in Chapter 8 under the matching rule, an expense should be recognized when the goods or services are consumed or used in the process of obtaining revenue. If the obligation to pay for these goods and services has not already been recorded, it must be done no later than the time the expenses are recognized. In many cases, however, the goods or services are received before they are used. In this case the asset and the liability should be recorded, unless, of course, payment is made immediately. The obligation arises when the right to use the goods and services is obtained.

Accrued liabilities are not basically different from other payables. The liability arises from the use of services by the firm and the obligation to pay for them under the terms of a formal or informal contract. Because the services are usually received continuously, the recording of the expense and the accrual is usually made at the end of the accounting period. Failure to record the accrual would misstate current income and the amount of current liabilities in the balance sheet. However, unless a contract or market price is available, an accrual is the result of an allocation and as such is arbitrary in nature.

In the above cases, the recognition of the current liability is dependent upon the simultaneous recognition of an asset or expense. In fact, the necessity to recognize the asset or expense is often the impelling reason for the recognition of the liability. But in the case of a loss arising from a claim against the firm without current or future benefit to the firm, the focus of recognition must come from the liability itself. The amount of the obligation and the timing of its recognition determine the amount and timing of the loss recognition. As soon as the obligation becomes definite and capable of being estimated, it should therefore, be recognized and the loss recorded.

Accountants have usually been careful to avoid the offsetting of current assets against current liabilities in balance sheet presentations. Even though specific funds are available for the payment of specific liabilities, both should be shown on the balance sheet as separate items. The intent to use specific resources does not justify the offsetting. But in a few cases, the offsetting may be justified. The conditions for justification may be summarized as follows: (1) There must exist a legal right of offset or an agreed unconditional setoff. A receivable and a payable to the same firm would be a good example. But a negotiable note payable to Firm A cannot be offset against a receivable from Firm A without an unconditional agreement to that effect, because otherwise the right of offset would not be legally binding on the holder in due course. (2) There must be an intent to apply the right of offset. If the items will be treated as other assets and liabilities, the offsetting would not be descriptive of the circumstances. (3) The amount offset against a liability cannot be greater than the amount of the liability and vice-versa.

As a general principle, assets and liabilities should not be offset except where a specific right of setoff exists.[21] Cash and other assets, for example, should not be offset against taxes payable. The only exception is when the purchase of certain securities is in substance an advance payment of taxes and the securities are specifically designated by the relevant governments as being acceptable for the payment of taxes owing to them.

Nonmonetary current liabilities

Nonmonetary current liabilities are those obligations to provide goods or services of specified quantity and quality. They usually arise from the advance payment for services by customers. Subscriptions to periodicals and season tickets are good examples. Other obligations arise from advances by customers for special merchandise. It should be noted, however, that not all advances are nonmonetary in nature. Some advances represent a given number of dollars that may be applied against a future purchase or purchases at the prices existing when the advance is liquidated. These are monetary advances because they represent the obligation to repay a given number of dollars or the equivalent in goods or services at a future date. The nonmonetary obligations are expressed in terms of predetermined or agreed prices for specific goods or services. Thus, the monetary value of the goods and services might change, but the quantity and quality would not.

These nonmonetary obligations have frequently been classified as deferred income or deferred credits. Technically, deferred income represents income items received by the firm, but not yet reported as income. However, it is also used to refer to revenue that would normally have been included in income but where the recognition is deferred until later expenses can be matched with it—frequently referred to as deferred revenue. The term *deferred credit* is frequently used synonymously with deferred income and deferred revenue, but it is also used in a broader sense including monetary advances by customers.

These terms do not have clear meanings because they include a heterogeneous group of items and they are not consistently classified in the balance sheet. Some of the deferred income and deferred credit items found in published annual reports are classified as current liabilities; others are classified as noncurrent liabilities; a few are reported as un-

---

[21] *AICPA Professional Standards,* para. 1027.25.

earned revenue in the stockholders' equity section; and a majority are found listed as an unclassified item between the liabilities and the stockholders' equity section of the balance sheet. The latter presentation is partly a carry-over from a former classification in a reserve category. However, it is frequently rationalized on the ground that it represents amounts that will be added to income in a subsequent period but excluded in the current period, for one of several reasons. The deferred income concept apparently arose from the idea that the "realization" of income is closely related to the receipt of cash, but that when the services have not yet been performed or when the amount is likely to be reduced because of subsequent related expenses or losses, the income reporting should be deferred. However, the separate classification of deferred income does not indicate the nature of the items included in the classification and it is subject to abuse, just as was the former reserve classification.

Frequently, the advance payments for goods or services by customers have been considered to represent a mixture of liabilities and profit. If cost is the predominant element, the entire amount could be considered a liability; but if cost is only a small part of the total, it is argued that the whole may be considered a deferred credit to income (gross income) rather than a current liability, presumably classified as unearned income in the stockholders' equity section of the balance sheet. If the advance payment represents both costs and income, it is argued that it may be divided between the amount of prospective cost that should be included among the current liabilities and the amount representing prospective income, which should be classified as unearned income.

This separation of the advance payment into the cost element and the part representing prospective profit stems from the traditional reliance upon the cost concept and the reporting of revenue only after all services have been performed and when all expenses can be measured and matched with the associated revenues. However, it may be more relevant to report the obligation to perform services or provide goods in terms of the output (sales price) of such goods or services. The important consideration is that unless the funds are returned to the customer, the advance payment does not represent an outflow of cash in the future. Regardless of how it is measured, it cannot be identified with specific goods or services to be acquired in the future and used in operations. Some of the services will have been acquired in the past in the form of plant and equipment and thus will be classified as noncurrent assets; others will represent inventories and prepaid expenses classified as current assets; and many of the associated expenses will represent goods and services not yet acquired at the time of the receipt of the advance. Therefore, the advance cannot be associated with costs incurred or to be incurred.

AICPA Professional Standards (par. 2031.07) specifically includes among the current liabilities advances for the delivery of goods or the performance of services in the normal course of operations. This treatment of the advance as a current liability is correct for two reasons: (1) The advance is a current financing transaction rather than a revenue-producing one.[22] Although other reasons may give rise to the advance, such as an attempt to avoid bad debt losses, the result is an aid in the financing of the operations of the enterprise. (2) The obligation to provide goods or services is generally a part of current operations. Only in the case of incidental transactions would the advance generally represent an obligation extending beyond the normal operating cycle of the business.

Value is added to the firm during the entire process of production, selling, and collection, but revenue is generally reported at a single point in time, as discussed in Chapter 8 above. If the critical event in the operations is the providing of the goods or services, rather than the collection of the cash, no profit, deferred or current, should be reported at the time of the receipt of the advance. The entire amount is a liability, regardless of whether it is to be repaid in cash or in goods or services. Accounting terminology would therefore be improved if the term *advances from customers* were substituted for the term *deferred income*.

There are a few cases, however, where the reporting of deferred income arises for reasons other than advance from a customer. In these cases, the services have been provided and the revenue-producing operations have been completed, but the reporting of the income is deferred because of uncertainties in the collection of the receivables or because of uncertainties regarding additional expenses. These so-called deferred credits are not liabilities, as there is no obligation to the customers. They should be included in the income of the current period, less the estimated additional expenses and uncollectible receivables. But, as indicated above in the discussion of installment sales, if the deferral of income is at all justified, the deferral can be accomplished by carrying the receivables at the input (cost) values. That is, the "deferred gross profit" can be used as a valuation or offset account deducted from the receivables in the balance sheet. However, in almost all cases, the uncertainties are not so great that estimates are impossible. Therefore, the income should be reported on the basis of the best estimates, with an indication of the probabilities of expected values, and the expected future related costs should be reported as liabilities. In all too many cases, the existence of uncertainties is used as an excuse for the deferral of income reporting, with the goal or result being the smoothing of income artificially. For these many reasons, the deferred income concept should be ousted from the kit of tools for financial reporting.

SELECTED ADDITIONAL READING

Working capital

Dun, L. C. "Working Capital—A Logical Concept." *Australian Accountant,* October 1969, pp. 461–64.

[22] See William A. Paton, " 'Deferred Income'—A Misnomer," *Journal of Accountancy* 112 (September 1961): p. 38; and for a criticism, see Robert W. Hirschman, "A Look at 'Current' Classifications," *Journal of Accountancy* 124 (November 1967): 55.

Heath, Loyd C. "Is Working Capital Really Working?" *Journal of Accountancy,* August 1980, pp. 55–62.

Hunter, Robert D. "Concept of Working Capital." *Journal of Commercial Bank Lending,* March 1972, pp. 24–30.

Lemke, Kenneth W. "The Evaluation of Liquidity: An Analytical Study." *Journal of Accounting Research,* Spring 1970, pp. 47–77.

Current assets and current liabilities

Cramer, Joe J. "Incompatibility of Bad Debt 'Expense' with Contemporary Accounting Theory." *Accounting Review,* July 1972, pp. 596–98.

Heath, Loyd, "Financial Reporting and the Evaluation of Solvency." *Accounting Research Monograph No. 3.* AICPA, 1978.

————— and Paul Rosenfield. "Solvency: The Forgotten Half of Financial Reporting." *Journal of Accountancy,* January 1979, pp. 48–54.

Huizingh, William. *Working Capital Classification.* Ann Arbor: Bureau of Business Research, Graduate School of Business Administration, University of Michigan, 1967.

CHAPTER 13
INVENTORIES

The separate classification and measurement of inventories are necessary because of their significance as a basic resource of many firms and because the basis of valuation of inventories has a direct effect on the reported income and the funds flow presentations. An evaluation of current and suggested measurement procedures should take into consideration the basic nature of inventories in relationship to the firm's operations, and the objectives and basic concepts of accounting as discussed in the earlier sections of this book. In recent years, emphasis has been placed on the computation of the cost or other input values to be matched against revenues at the time of revenue reporting (usually the point of sale). While an emphasis on net income is not necessarily misdirected, it has led to inventory valuation practices that result in inventory amounts in the balance sheet that have no economic interpretation. One of the objectives of accounting theory should be to provide useful guides in the search for evaluation procedures that will provide better measurements of the inventory resources and better information regarding the potential cash flows of the firm. The objective of this chapter is to evaluate the several bases of the measurement of inventories in terms of their interpretive content and their possible relevance for investment decisions. The several procedures for the matching of input values against related revenues are derived primarily from the traditional accounting structure and are evaluated in terms of that structure, but they are also evaluated in terms of their economic interpretation and their potential relevance for the prediction of future cash flows as well as their information content for capital markets.

THE NATURE OF INVENTORIES

The term *inventories* includes merchandise destined for sale in the normal course of business and materials and supplies to be used in the process of production for sale. Excluded from this category are supplies that will be consumed in nonproducing operations, securities held for resale, but incidental to the operations of the firm, and plant and equipment in use or awaiting final disposition upon termination of use. In the traditional definition, inventories are current assets, because they will normally be converted into cash or other assets within the operating cycle of the business. Obsolete and unsalable merchandise, however, if material in

298

amount, should be excluded from this classification unless it can be disposed of in available markets within normal selling periods.

Inventories are usually thought of as *stocks* of merchandise, although the accounting for the *flow* of the merchandise is usually considered more important. In the traditional accounting structure the stocks at the end of one period are interrelated with the flows of that period, even though they may be residually determined. The valuation of the stocks, therefore, is affected by the matching of the input values with revenues for the period preceding the balance sheet date, and it may also be affected by the matching process of prior periods.

In the valuation process, inventories are different from both monetary assets and prepaid expenses. Monetary assets represent amounts of purchasing power available or to become available at some time in the future. The current value of monetary assets can, therefore, be computed by discounting the expected cash receipts or conversions. Prepaid expenses, on the other hand, represent services to be received by the firm in the process of obtaining its revenue. Generally, there is no possible way of determining the value of these services in terms of the additional revenue to be generated by them. They can be valued only in terms of their acquisition value—a current or past cost. Inventories, however, are between the two extremes. They are not monetary assets, because the amount of cash or the liquid resources to be generated by their sale is usually dependent upon expectations regarding future price changes; but even when prices can be predicted accurately, the timing of the future cash receipts may also be uncertain, making estimates of present values difficult. The validity of output prices for inventories also depends on the amount of additional direct expenses and the use of joint resources and joint activities of the firm required in selling the goods and collecting the proceeds. In this regard, they are similar to prepaid expenses. But generally speaking, the present value of merchandise can be estimated more readily from expected future cash flows than can prepaid expenses.

THE OBJECTIVES OF INVENTORY MEASUREMENT

The most common objective of inventory measurement is the attempt to match costs with related revenues in order to compute net income within the traditional accounting structure. This emphasis on the computation of income based on the reporting of revenues at the time of sale requires an allocation of cost or other basis to the period of sale of merchandise. Thus, the relationship of inventories to the process of income measurement is similar to the common characteristics of prepaid expenses and plant and equipment. This requires the valuation of inventories on the basis of an input price, and the assignment of this valuation to cost of goods sold on some explicit or implicit pricing and flow assumptions. However, the use of output values (sales prices) may also meet the objective of income measurement under certain conditions.

A second objective of the measurement of inventories is frequently stated to be the presentation of the value of the goods to the firm.[1] This value is generally assumed to be the net difference in the value of the firm with a specific asset compared to the value of the firm without it. For assets that are readily replaced, the value of the asset is close to the replacement cost; but the loss of some inventory items would result in a reduction of production or sales, so their value may be greater than their replacement cost. For other items of inventory, their value may be less than replacement cost. The important objective is that the measurement be subject to interpretation and that the intended interpretation be made clear. For example, the current cash equivalent can be interpreted as the amount that the firm can receive in the liquidation of its inventories in the ordinary course of business. The current replacement cost permits the interpretation as the amount of cash the firm would have to hold if it did not possess the goods but had to acquire them.

A third objective is to present information regarding the inventories that will help permit investors and other users to predict the future cash flows of the firm. This can be accomplished from two points of view. First, the amount of inventory resources available will support the inflow of cash through their sale in the ordinary course of business. Second, the amount of inventory resources available will, under normal circumstances, have an effect on the amount of cash required during the subsequent period to acquire the merchandise that will be sold during the period. The inventory should be measured in ways that will aid in the prediction of both the inflows of cash from sales and the outflows required for the acquisition of the merchandise.

THE DETERMINATION OF INVENTORY QUANTITIES

The computation of inventory valuation and the calculation of the cost or other value to be matched with current revenues requires both a determination of physical quantities and an assignment of a price to each item. A large number of homogeneous articles and the continual flow to customers or into production is a common characteristic of inventories. Thus, the quantity determinations are just as important as the assignment of unit values. The most common methods of determining quantity are: (1) the use of a periodic count of inventory on hand, (2) a perpetual record of each item, (3) a combination of periodic and perpetual methods, and (4)

---

[1] See for example, F. K. Wright, "A Theory of Inventory Measurement," *Abacus* 1 (December 1965): 152–53.

methods of determining total value amounts by aggregative relationships.

A count of merchandise on hand is usually considered a necessary prerequisite to the audit and presentation of unqualified published financial statements. If beginning and ending inventory quantities are accurate, it is generally assumed that net income is properly determined. But it should be kept in mind that the quantity sold is a residual computed by subtracting the amount remaining at the end of the period from the total available during the period. This residual may include quantities lost by theft, evaporation, spoilage, or other causes. With the all-inclusive concept of income, the separation of the quantity sold from the quantity lost is not important; but if the loss is to be reported separately as an expense or as an extraordinary item, the periodic inventory method alone is not sufficient.

A perpetual inventory procedure has the opposite effect. The quantities sold or used are determined from the records, and all items not sold are assumed to be on hand at the end of the period. Thus, any losses are included in the ending inventory. The result is that if there are losses, the inventory valuation in the balance sheet is overvalued and the all-inclusive net income is overstated. Thus, the best procedure is obtained when a perpetual system is maintained but verified by a count at the end of each accounting period. Although this procedure may not disclose the cause of losses, at least the quantities sold and the quantities lost would be known separately.

The aggregative methods, particularly the gross profit method and the retail inventory method, will be discussed under the topic of pricing. It should be noted at this point, however, that these procedures have some of the same difficulties as the perpetual inventory methods unless they are supplemented by periodic inventory counts.

THE BASES FOR VALUATION
OF INVENTORIES

As indicated in Chapter 11, one of the more important objectives of valuation is to present information that will permit investors and other users to predict the future cash flows to the firm. Inventory valuations that reflect the expected future net receipt of funds should be relevant for this objective. Output values may also be relevant in permitting an interpretation of inventory measurements as representing the value to the firm, particularly under conditions where the firm can sell its entire stock without altering its prices (that is, where the demand for the products is elastic). But when selling prices or other conversion values are highly uncertain, some measure of cost or other input value may permit a better interpretation of inventory valuation and also permit better information for the prediction of future cash requirements for the acquisition of merchandise for sale.

Output values

Inventories appear at various stages in the operating process of a business. In some cases they appear at the beginning of the process, as raw material or as a semifinished product with considerable economic activity still required before they can be transferred to customers. In other cases, very little additional economic activity is required. While in the former case input values may be appropriate, in the latter case the crucial events have occurred, so that inventories should be valued in terms of their current or expected output values in order to meet the income reporting objectives and to present a description of resources related to the expected future receipt of cash. The types of output values appropriate in this case would include (1) discounted money receipts, (2) current selling prices, and (3) net realizable values.

Discounted money receipts. Two important facts must be known before inventories can be valued in terms of the discounted future money flows. First, the amount to be received by the future sale or exchange of the merchandise must be definite or determinable with a reasonable degree of certainty. Second, the timing of the expected cash receipts must be fixed or fairly definite. Very seldom are these facts known with reasonable certainty, except when merchandise is produced and sold under specific contracts. But if merchandise is held for future delivery under a contract with specific terms regarding price and payment, the inventory should be treated as a receivable and valued accordingly.

Current selling prices. An exception to the usual realization rule is permissible in the valuation of commodities at selling prices when there is an effective government-controlled market at a fixed price.[2] The two necessary characteristics are: (1) the existence of a controlled market with a fixed price applicable to all quantities brought to the market and (2) no material costs of selling. A further requirement would be that there is little expected delay in receiving the sale price in cash, so that any interest (discount) is not a material factor in the measurement of income.

A similar situation may exist where there is a delivery contract with little delay in collection. In these cases, the firm's product is completed and any additional effort is negligible. The revenue should be reported, and the selling price is the best measure not only of the revenue but also of the funds to be received in exchange for the goods.

---

[2] *AICPA Professional Standards—Accounting* (Chicago: Commerce Clearing House, 1981), para. 5121.15.

Net realizable values. One of the most important aspects of income determination in the traditional accounting structure is the proper matching of revenues with costs or other input values. Therefore, whenever output values are used in the measurement of inventories, additional costs of completion or sale and collection should be estimated and recorded in the period in which the revenue is reported. An alternative is to deduct these estimated future costs and expenses directly from the output value in arriving at a *net realizable value* of the inventory. *Net realizable value* is, therefore, defined as the current output price less the current value of all additional anticipated incremental costs and expenses (exclusive of tax effects) relating to the completion, sale, and delivery of the merchandise. Additional expenses of collection should also be deducted, if material.

Sprouse and Moonitz stated that " . . . inventories which are readily salable at known prices with negligible costs of disposal, or with known or readily predictable costs of disposal, should be measured at net realizable value."[3] They suggested further that this should not be an exception to usual acceptable valuation procedures, but rather, it should be considered " . . . in keeping with the major objectives of accounting."[4] *Bulletin No. 43*, on the other hand, stated that "only in exceptional cases may inventories properly be stated above cost."[5] According to this source, cost is the primary basis for inventory valuation.

Because of this difference in approach to the concept of net realizable value, the two above sources present different conditions required for its use. As to be expected, the conditions prescribed by *Bulletin No. 43* are more restrictive than those prescribed by Sprouse and Moonitz. In *Accounting Research Study No. 3,* Sprouse and Moonitz stated two basic conditions, both of which are necessary: (1) inventories must be "readily salable at known prices," and (2) additional costs must be known or readily predictable. These conditions are consistent with the objective of recognizing revenue whenever it has been earned as a result of the firm's activities and whenever it can be measured objectively. The term *known prices,* however, should not be interpreted as known with certainty. Even government-controlled prices may be subject to change. But the amount of the anticipated revenue (based on current sales prices) should be readily determinable with a reasonable degree of certainty.

The conditions required by *Bulletin No. 43* for stating inventories above cost are as follows: (1) immediate marketability at quoted prices; (2) interchangeability of units; (3) deduction of additional expenditures to be incurred in disposal; and (4) difficulty or inability to estimate appropriate costs. This last condition is not required for "precious metals hav-

---

[3] Robert T. Sprouse and Maurice Moonitz, "A Tentative Set of Broad Accounting Principles for Business Enterprises," *Accounting Research Study No. 3* (AICPA, 1962), p. 27.

[4] Ibid., p. 28.

[5] *AICPA Professional Standards,* para. 5121.15.

ing a fixed monetary value and no substantial cost of marketing." The first condition, immediate marketability, implies that the product must be completed so that substantially all of the value has been added; external quoted prices are required because of the desirability of objective evidence. The condition of interchangeability of units is stated in order to assure that the quoted market prices are applicable to the merchandise in question. But actually, if the first condition holds, the second condition is either true by definition or it is unnecessary. That is, marketability implies that the specific goods can be sold at the quoted prices, regardless of whether the quoted prices refer to the specific goods only or to interchangeable goods.

The condition that exceptions to cost must be justified by an inability to measure costs stems from rigid adherence to the cost basis in *Bulletin No. 43*. Except in the case of precious metals, it is assumed that revenue should not be reported until realization at the time of sale, but it is permitted earlier as a necessary expedient. Thus, the main reason why selling prices are used in practice for some products is the inability to measure costs. However, the author's opinion, consistent with that of Sprouse and Moonitz, is that the inability to compute costs is not a logical basis for using net realizable value. If the net realizable value can be measured objectively, it should be used regardless of whether costs can or cannot be computed.

One of the major difficulties with the net realizable value concept is that it is usually quite difficult to estimate the additional out-of-pocket costs necessary to complete, sell, and deliver the product. As an alternative, a normal *gross* margin is frequently deducted from selling price to be sure that all possible additional costs are taken into account; but this may approximate an input value if the additional expected costs are not large.[6]

Another difficulty with the net realizable value concept is that the net income from the transaction is reported before all of the activities of the firm relating to the sale have been accomplished. If it can be assumed that value is added by the firm throughout the entire period during which activities relating to the sale are performed by the firm, some of the income will have been reported before it has been "earned." An alternative is to deduct from net realizable value the normal profit on activities yet to be performed. Thus, income would be accrued as the several activities are performed by the firm for the production, storing, selling, shipping, and possibly servicing of the merchandise. The main difficulty with this alternative is in making the allocation of the normal operating income to the various activities. Ideally this could be accomplished by making the allocation on the basis of the value added by the firm in the several activities, but an allocation on the basis of total costs incurred and expected might be a reasonable alternative in many cases. Because of these difficulties of measurement, the arbitrariness of the allocations and

---

[6] See below, p. 308.

the little advantage of the extra refinement, this approach should probably remain a theoretical ideal rather than a practical goal.

Input values

As applied to inventories, input values may be defined as some measurement of the resources used to obtain the inventory in its present condition and location. When the consideration given for the inventory is cash or its equivalent, the interpretation of the input value is fairly clear. However, when merchandise is manufactured, the input value of the inventory represents a summation of the valuations of resources used in production and other resources assignable to the product. Because of the necessity for allocations of resource valuations to periods and the reallocation to departments and products, the interpretation of the final input valuation of the product is difficult. Furthermore, the use of allocation procedures diminishes the possibility that the inventory valuations will be relevant in the prediction of cash flows or directly in investment decision models.

In the traditional accounting structure, the difference between the input values and the output values of the product sold, generally referred to as the gross profit or gross margin, should represent the nonproduct input values of the firm plus the profit or minus the net loss to the firm. The effect of all input valuation methods is to defer the recognition of revenue and net income until a later period. This delay in the recognition of revenue is justified whenever considerable services are yet to be performed by the firm or whenever verifiable output values cannot be obtained.

Input values are generally expressed in terms of historical costs, but they can also be expressed in terms of current costs or standard costs. Current costs can often be estimated by starting with net realizable value and subtracting a normal gross margin (normal markup). The lower-of-cost-or-market rule has its own peculiarities, but it is classified here as an input valuation method because the term *market* as used in this context is basically an input concept.

Historical cost. The validity of historical costs rests on the assumption that they represent the input value of the resources obtained at the time of acquisition or use in the process of production. They are measured by the net monetary payment made in the past or to be made in the future in the acquisition of the goods or services. If payment is to be made in the distant future, the amount should be discounted to obtain the present cost. When nonmonetary assets are exchanged for current goods or services, the current value of the nonmonetary assets represents the cost of the goods or services acquired; but accountants generally go back to the original monetary payment for the asset given up in the exchange. Thus, historical cost generally means the monetary consideration paid or to be paid in the acquisition or production of merchandise, including all of those services necessary in obtaining the merchandise in a salable state.

Care must be taken, however, to exclude from historical cost payments not intended or anticipated by the buyer at the time of the purchase decision. Costs should include only that amount which the purchaser considered the item to be worth to him at the time of purchase. The mere fact that a cost is incurred does not justify including it in the initial asset value.

According to the traditional historical cost model, costs of production should include the normal direct costs of material and labor and the normal indirect costs that can be allocated to the product on the basis of logical association. Normal wasted material and normal idle labor time are logical costs of production, but excessive material waste and abnormal amounts of idle time are not costs of production but losses to the firm. What are normal and what are abnormal uses of resources depends, of course, on the production standards of the firm. But, within given limits, necessary production costs can be determined from existing engineering and institutional standards of performance.

Similar concepts of cost can be applied to the acquisition of retail merchandise. Normal costs of transportation, storage, and handling should be included as a part of total inventoriable costs. But excessive costs of shipping because of the acquisition of inefficient lot sizes, or excessive costs due to reshipping or rehandling, should be excluded from inventory valuations.

The advantages of historical cost for the valuation of inventories can be summarized as follows:

1. For inventories of raw material and newly acquired merchandise, little value has been added by the firm's activities, so that cost represents a measure of the quantity of resources available.
2. When selling prices are highly uncertain or when additional costs cannot be predicted with reasonable accuracy, a net output value cannot be estimated. Cost thus serves as a reasonable alternative to net realizable value.
3. Cost is based on a past exchange transaction; therefore, it is considered verifiable and not subject to the biases of management or the accountants.
4. Because cost is measured by the value of the consideration given at the time of acquisition of the merchandise, there should be evidence that the purchaser considered the cost to represent the value to the firm at that time; with prudent management, it can generally be assumed that the willingness or intent to pay the specific amount is evidence of what management considered to be its value.
5. Valuation in terms of cost permits the accountability for cash and other resources used in acquiring the products and accountability for the inventory.

Some of the major disadvantages of historical cost are as follows:

1. While cost may represent value to the firm at the time of acquisition, it soon becomes outdated; not only do input prices change over time but also the value to the firm changes as value is added by the firm.
2. When two or more items in the inventory are acquired at different times, the costs are not comparable because they do not necessarily relate to the same value of money; their addition may not result in a meaningful sum.
3. Many cost computations require the allocation of joint costs, and even the best allocation methods are inadequate in reflecting causal relationships.
4. Because costs are historical, the matching of costs with revenues does not provide a meaningful measure of the results of current operations.

The authority for cost as the basis for inventory valuation is deep-rooted in current accounting principles. In fact, for many years, it has been considered the only acceptable basis for most inventories, exept when the lower-of-cost-or-market rule is applicable. For example, *Bulletin No. 43* states that historical cost is the primary basis of measurement for inventories in financial accounting.[7]

Current costs.   In an attempt to avoid many of the disadvantages of historical costs, current costs for inventory valuation have been suggested by several writers and committees for the following reasons:[8] (1) It permits a matching of current input values with current revenues to measure the result of current operations. (2) It permits the identification of holding gains and losses, thus reflecting the results of inventory management decisions and the impact of the environment on the firm not reflected in transactions. (3) It represents the current value of the inventories at the end of the period if the firm is still acquiring such merchandise and if net realizable values are not applicable. (4) It permits the reporting of current operating profit which may be used to predict future cash flows.

The general objectives of current costs as well as its advantages and disadvantages are discussed in Chapter 9. A specific advantage of the application of current costs to inventories is that it eliminates the need for an assumption regarding the actual or artificial flow of merchandise or

---

[7] *AICPA Professional Standards,* para. 5121.04.

[8] See, for example, Edgar O. Edwards and Philip W. Bell, *The Theory and Measurement of Business Income* (Berkeley and Los Angeles: University of California Press, 1961); Committee on Concepts and Standards—Inventory Measurement, AAA, "A Discussion of Various Approaches to Inventory Measurement," supplementary statement no. 2, *Accounting Review* (July 1966), pp. 700–14; and Lawrence Revsine, *Replacement Cost Accounting* (Englewood Cliffs, N.J.: Prentice-Hall, 1973).

costs. Thus, the application of FIFO, LIFO, or weighted average methods is unnecessary.[9]

Some of the disadvantages of current replacement costs are as follows: (1) Current costs or quotations are not available for seasonal and style items and for goods produced by obsolete methods. Estimates of the current input values of these items may, therefore, be subjective in nature. (2) Changes in current costs do not always reflect changes in current selling prices. Values do not necessarily change because of changes in costs. (3) Increases in costs would result in gains recorded in the current period (through the holding of inventories) even though they have not been realized through sale.[10] For example, an increase in labor costs would appear to be profitable in the current period even though sales prices have remained stable. (4) Gains and losses caused from changes in specific input prices would be included in the net income from operations unless the cost of sales, as well as the ending inventory, is valued in terms of costs current at the time of sale.

A major qualification with respect to the usefulness of current replacement costs is that they may be irrelevant in those cases where the firm would not have acquired the items if it had to do so at current prices. For example, if merchandise is acquired at a low price because of a liquidation of a supplier's stock or for other special reasons, the current replacement cost in the regular markets may be irrelevant. The net realizable value of the merchandise, in this case, is dependent on the expected sales prices, and this is more relevant than the current cost when the firm would not acquire the goods at this price. Also, the trading margin representing the difference between the expected sales price and the current cost has no significance either to the firm or to readers of financial statements.

Net realizable value less a normal markup. When replacement costs are not available, they can sometimes be estimated by subtracting a normal gross profit margin from the net realizable value (estimated selling price less additional expected incremental costs). Before this procedure can result in a good approximation of current cost, however, there must be a direct relationship between costs and selling prices. If these do not move together, the result will not be an approximation of current costs. The normal markup assumed, of course, must also apply to the specific items in question as well as to the original items from which they were derived.

Net realizable value less a normal markup is also occasionally suggested as a measure of the net value of the inventory to the firm when this value is below historical cost and current cost. The assumption is that a loss should be recorded currently and the normal profit should be per-

---

[9] This is not necessarily true if holding gains and losses are to be classified as "realized" or "unrealized," as some writers propose.

[10] Except when the increase is considered to be a capital adjustment resulting from inflation. See Chapter 9.

mitted when the goods are sold. However, this is an incorrect usage of the concept. While this method is often used in the valuation of used equipment received by an equipment dealer as trade-ins on new equipment, it must be recognized that the trade-in allowance does not necessarily represent cost. In most cases, valuation at net realizable value alone would be more appropriate.

In the application of the lower-of-cost-or-market rule, replacement cost does not represent the current utility to the firm when it is below net realizable value less a normal markup. The application of the concept in this context is discussed further below.

The lower of cost or market. As discussed earlier, the lower-of-cost-or-market rule is internally inconsistent and is not a logical basis for the valuation of inventories.[11] But since it has received such widespread support over the years, it is important to understand the logic or rationalization of the rule. The following discussion pertains primarily to the concepts applied in *AICPA Bulletin No. 43* in the valuation of inventories. Because *market* is initially defined as replacement cost, we have chosen to classify it here as an input valuation method, although in some cases it is an eclectic method, reflecting output values at some times and input values at others.

While federal income tax regulations have consistently defined *market* as the current bid price for the specific item as generally purchased by the taxpayer, accountants have looked more at the utility value of the merchandise. Sanders, Hatfield, and Moore, for example, defined *market* as "the cost of reproduction or replacement, unless the realization prices are lower, in which case they would govern."[12]

AICPA Bulletin No. 43 extended the concept of utility by stating that ". . . in accounting for inventories, a loss should be recognized whenever the utility of goods is impaired by damage, deterioration, obsolescence, changes in price levels, or other causes."[13] In measuring utility, however, it defines market as replacement cost, but with both an upper and a lower limit. The upper limit (ceiling) is net realizable value; utility to the firm cannot exceed the expected sales price less additional costs of completion and disposal. The lower limit (floor) is net realizable value less a normal profit margin. No loss should be recognized if the fall in replacement cost does not reflect a similar fall in expected sales price. That is, a loss should not be recognized in the current period if it will result in the recognition of an abnormal profit in a later period. The existence of the potential abnormal profit is evidence that the loss was overstated. Note, however, that any write-down below net realizable value results in the creation of profit

---

[11] See Chapter 11.

[12] Thomas Henry Sanders, Henry Rand Hatfield, and Underhill Moore, *A Statement of Accounting Principles* (American Institute of Accountants, 1938). Reprinted in 1959 by American Accounting Association, p. 73.

[13] *AICPA Professional Standards,* para. 5121.08.

in the following period equal to the amount of the reported loss in the current period.

The following example describes this procedure:

| | | Market | | |
Case	Cost	Replacement cost	Net realizable value (ceiling)	Net realizable value less normal profit margin (20 percent) (floor)
A	*$1.00*	$1.04	$1.20	$0.96
B	1.00	*0.96*	1.10	0.88
C	1.00	0.80	1.05	*0.84*
D	1.00	0.92	*0.90*	0.72

In case A, cost is below replacement cost and net realizable value, so there would be no adjustment of cost. Note that the gross profit to be recognized in the period of sale (assuming no additional changes in prices) will be less than normal. But it would be incorrect to show a loss in one period just so that a normal profit could be reported in a later period. As Moonitz and Jordan so aptly phrased it, "to write down assets in order to be able to book a subsequent 'profit' appears to be dangerously close to manipulation of the accounts."[14]

In case B, replacement cost would be chosen because it is below cost and between the upper and lower limits of market. There is some question whether the net utility to the firm has really fallen when net realizable value is still above cost, however. But if net realizable value is quite uncertain, replacement cost may be the best measure of utility to the firm.

In case C, replacement cost is below historical cost, but if it is used in the valuation of the inventory, the resulting expected profit in the subsequent period would be greater than normal. Therefore, the net utility to the firm is assumed to be not less than the net realizable value less a normal markup. This, however, results in a normal reported profit in the subsequent period as a result of the current write-down.

In case D, replacement cost is below cost but above net realizable value. Since the utility to the firm cannot exceed net realizable value, this should be used as the market valuation. However, the valuation should not be reduced below net realizable value just so that a profit can be recorded in the period of sale.

Bulletin No. 43 recognized that these concepts cannot generally be precisely determined but that they should be used as a basis for judgment. However, if all of the valuation concepts can be measured with equal certainty, the rule is internally inconsistent. The best measure of utility

---

[14] Maurice Moonitz and Louis H. Jordan, *Accounting, an Analysis of Its Problems,* rev. ed. (New York: Holt, Rinehart & Winston, 1963), vol. 1, p. 250.

to the firm is net realizable value in all cases where this can be measured with a reasonable degree of certainty. Cost is relevant when no value has been added by the firm or when the sales price is highly uncertain. As a measure of current input value, however, replacement cost is more significant, both as a measure of current utility valuation and as a means of matching current costs with current revenues. This leaves "net realizable value less a normal profit margin" with very little support. Its reliability is based on the certainty of net realizable value; but as indicated above, if net realizable value can be measured with reasonable certainty, it should be used as the inventory valuation. The only possible case for "net realizable value less a normal profit margin" is where the sales price is fixed by contract or a stable market but most of the services relating to the sale are still to be performed by the firm. However, the concept and measurement of "normal profit margin" are generally nebulous and imprecise, with the result that replacement cost is probably more accurate in these cases.

The cost-or-market concept when applied to inventories is tied closely to the concept of realization of revenue at the time of sale, but with the recognition of loss as soon as evidence of the loss appears. But even in this context, it has been criticized severely by many writers. The major objections can be summarized as follows: (1) It violates the concept of consistency because it permits a change in valuation base from one period to another and even within the inventory itself. (2) It has been said to be a major cause of distortion of profit and loss.[15] (3) Although it may be considered conservative with respect to the current period, it is unconservative with respect to the income of future periods. (4) The current period may be charged with the results of inefficient purchasing and management, which should be included in the measurement of operating performance at the time of sale.[16] However, it may also be argued that these should be recorded in the current period rather than in the period of sale. (5) An increase in the market price in a subsequent period may result in an unrealized gain if the original cost is always used as the basis for comparison with the current market price (assuming, of course, that market in both periods is below the original cost). This would not be the case if the inventory valuation at the beginning of the period is considered "cost" for subsequent accounting purposes regardless of the computation in arriving at this valuation, as recommended by *AICPA Bulletin No. 43*.[17] (6) The cost-or-market rule is said to permit excessive subjectivity in the accounts. This is based on the assumption that market is always more subjective than cost.

---

[15] Stephen Gilman, *Accounting Concepts of Profit* (New York: Ronald Press, 1939), pp. 459–60.

[16] Carl Thomas Devine, *Inventory Valuation and Periodic Income* (New York: Ronald Press, 1942), p. 79.

[17] *AICPA Professional Standards,* para. 5121.05, n2.

Standard costs.   Current standards reflect what a product should cost to produce under current conditions of prices and technology and with a desired standard of efficiency. Current standard costs, therefore, resemble replacement costs, with the exception that costs of inefficiency and idle capacity are excluded. However, replacement costs may also exclude some of these costs that are unnecessary in the production process. The main difference is that standard costs are determined independently of past production techniques, on a scientific basis, while current replacement costs may be computed by applying current factor prices to past production techniques.

There is always a danger that when standard costs are used for inventory valuation purposes they may not reflect current conditions unless they are revised frequently. Thus, they are often considered undesirable for inventory valuation purposes because they tend to represent neither current costs nor historical costs. They are admittedly useful for control purposes and for other managerial uses, but they are considered undesirable for valuation purposes because they are thought to be more subjective than either historical costs or replacement costs. An additional objection is that if actual costs are less than standard costs, the valuation at standard results in the recognition of increases in value before the point of sale.[18]

AICPA Bulletin No. 43 states that "standard costs are acceptable if adjusted at reasonable intervals to reflect current conditions so that at the balance sheet date standard costs reasonably approximate costs computed under one of the recognized bases." Such recognized bases would include average cost and first-in, first-out. The implication is, however, that standard cost should not be used to reflect current replacement cost. It is the author's opinion that one of the major advantages of standard costs in the valuation of inventories may be that they can be used to reflect current production costs under efficient and normal conditions.

Normal-stock valuation.   The base stock and last-in, first-out inventory methods are frequently classified as normal-stock methods. The main common attribute of these methods is that the inventory valuation represents an arbitrary amount or a residual of previously incurred costs. There is no pretense that they represent either the utility of the inventory to the firm or costs that should be matched against some future revenue. As a result, they cannot be said to represent true input *valuation* methods.

The main objectives of the normal-stock methods are to match current costs with current revenues and to remove "paper" profits and losses arising from the changes in inventory prices. The original base stock method was founded on the assumption that a normal quantity of inventory was necessary as a part of the permanent investment of the firm, and therefore it should be treated as a noncurrent asset. As a noncurrent asset,

---

[18] Devine, *Inventory Valuation*, p. 59.

no profit or loss arising from changes in prices should be recognized until the base stock is finally sold, presumably when the firm is liquidated. Current operating profit is assumed to arise from purchases and sales in excess of the normal base inventory.

In the original base stock method, the base inventory was to be written down at the time of acquisition to an amount below that to which any future replacement cost could be expected to fall.[19] The amount of the write-down was considered to be a capital adjustment charged to retained earnings. Modifications of the base stock method place a valuation on the normal inventory in terms of the historical cost when it was first acquired. Amounts held in excess of the normal are recorded on the basis of an average cost, first-in, first-out, or last-in, first-out. When the last-in, first-out method is used, it becomes very similar to the current application of LIFO.

The inventory valuation is, therefore, a residual amount set at some arbitrary low level or determined by the costs occurring at the time the method happened to have been started. The result is that net assets are understated and the recognition of gains from price increases relating to the normal inventory or the LIFO base is deferred almost indefinitely.[20] Since the normal inventory quantities are not intended to be sold, it was thought that gains from price increases were not "realized." This reasoning is related to two other objectives: (1) Under the replacement theory, income is assumed to arise only if the revenues from sale exceed the replacement cost of the goods sold. The replacement goods are assumed to carry the same valuation as the goods they replace. (2) The relevant income is assumed to be the disposable income arising from the excess of revenues over replacement costs. Cash is available for dividends only after inventories have been replaced. Unrealized gains and losses arising from the holding of a normal-stock inventory do not affect the amount of cash available for the payment of dividends. Note that the objective is to report net income based on the replacement cost concept of capital maintenance rather than a money investment concept.

As a basic concept of inventory valuation, the normal-stock methods are objectionable for the following reasons: (1) The inventory valuation does not begin to approximate the utility value to the firm. (2) Inventories acquired at different times and inventories of different firms are not expressed in comparable terms. (3) Because the inventory amounts represent residual valuations, they do not represent either input or output valuations and therefore they are not comparable with other items in the balance sheet. (4) In the computation of net income, they do not permit the inclusion of all gains and losses.

Although the base stock method has never gained widespread acceptance, it has been given some formal recognition. In the 1930s, recognition

---

[19] Ibid., p. 92.

[20] Unless the LIFO method was started during a period of higher costs than currently prevailing.

was given by the American Institute of Accountants (AICPA)[21] and by Sanders, Hatfield, and Moore; the latter accepted the base-stock methods for specific industries as a proper basis for arriving at cost,[22] but they also recognized that it "frankly abandon(s) the usual basis of keeping inventories within the cost or market area."[23] *Bulletin No. 43* does not include the base stock methods among the acceptable cost methods, but it does include last-in, first-out.[24] Because of this, and its acceptance for federal income tax purposes, LIFO has become a commonly accepted method in the United States. Its appropriateness in matching costs against revenues is discussed at greater length later in this chapter.

WHAT SHOULD BE INCLUDED IN COST?

Cost is a measure of the value of the inputs necessary in the acquisition of material or merchandise in its present condition and location. The value of the inputs, in turn, is measured by the value of the consideration given up in acquiring them. The questions still to be answered, however, are these: What costs can be considered necessary? What costs can be associated with merchandise and therefore with future revenue? What costs should be considered period expenses?

What costs are necessary is a matter of judgment. The accountant must use either an engineering standard or some other basis for comparison in making this judgment. *Bulletin No. 43* suggests that the concept of normality can be used as an acceptable basis: ". . . under some circumstances, items such as idle facility expense, excessive spoilage, double freight, and rehandling costs may be so *abnormal* as to require treatment as current period charges rather than as a portion of the inventory cost."[25] The American Accounting Association committee, on the other hand, suggested that only costs *reasonably traceable* to the product should be included in acquisition costs.[26]

There is some similarity between the concepts of normality and traceability. Many of the abnormal costs cannot be traced to specific products. For example, the costs of idle capacity and excessive spoilage of raw materials or finished product cannot be traced to the production of specific products. They are not costs of producing anything. But presumably, costs of inefficiency in production can be traced to the product even though they are abnormal in nature. Thus, the AAA Committee concept of cost is somewhat broader than that of the AICPA. Although the concept of

[21] American Institute of Accountants, *Examination of Financial Statements by Independent Public Accountants* (New York: January 1936).

[22] Sanders, Hatfield, and Moore, *Statement of Accounting Principles,* p. 73.

[23] Ibid., p. 15.

[24] *AICPA Professional Standards,* para. 5121.05.

[25] Ibid., para. 5121.05. Italics added.

[26] Committee on Concepts and Standards—Inventory Measurement, p. 4.

Summary of valuation bases

Base	Extent of revenue and income reported	When applicable*
I. Output values:		
A. Discounted money receipts.	All revenue reported except interest.	1. Sale price known. 2. Timing of cash receipts known.
B. Current selling prices.	All revenue and gains and losses included.	1. Sale price known. 2. Collection period short.
C. Net realizable value.	All net revenue reported.	1. Same as B. 2. Costs of disposal are known or predictable.
II. Input values:		
A. Historical cost.	No recognition of operating revenue or gains and losses from changes in specific prices until time of sale.	1. When historical costs are close to current costs. 2. When selling prices are highly uncertain.
B. Current replacement costs.	Gains and losses from changes in specific prices included in income. Operating revenue not included.	When current costs can be measured objectively.
C. Net realizable value less a normal profit margin.	All value changes included in income but with deferral of normal gross profit.	As an approximation of replacement cost or as a minimum valuation when it is above replacement cost. Not recommended as a standard.
D. Lower of cost or market.	Income includes losses but not gains from specific price changes. Operating revenue reported only at time of sale.	Although currently acceptable, it has little justification in current accounting theory.
E. Standard cost.	Income includes abnormal gains and losses arising from inefficiency or idle capacity. Operating revenue reported only at time of sale.	To reflect current production cost under efficient and normal conditions.
F. Normal-stock valuation.	The effect on income is similar to the use of replacement costs except that there is no recognition of gains or losses from specific price changes relating to the base of normal-stock inventory.	Although LIFO is currently acceptable for income determination, it results in a distortion of inventory valuation.

* Assuming an objective of the prediction of future cash receipts or future cash requirements.

traceability is an important aspect of cost assignment, abnormal costs are not really input values, but rather losses to the firm.

The substitution of current replacement costs for historical costs does not avoid the problem of determining what costs are necessary. Costs expressed in current terms must still be classified as normal or abnormal and as traceable or not traceable to specific products. Current costs, however, require a closer focus on the necessary costs of production or acquisition. The substitution of current costs of inefficient production for historical costs of efficient production is not an improvement in valuation procedures.

The second basic question—what costs should be associated with the inventory valuation and thus be matched with future revenues—is an even more difficult problem. *AICPA Bulletin No. 43* is not explicit on this point. It states that general and administrative expenses should not be included in product costs unless they are clearly related to production. It also states that ". . . the exclusion of all overheads from inventory costs does not constitute an accepted accounting procedure."[27] But this does not define what overhead costs should be included. The ambiguous nature of this statement has resulted in the proponents of both full absorption costing and direct costing claiming formal acceptance by the AICPA. Certainly full costing is acceptable, as there is no requirement that any normal manufacturing overhead be excluded from cost. On the other hand, the proponents of direct costing claim that since it includes variable overhead costs, direct costing is an acceptable method.

The question of which costs should be included in the measurement of inventories has generally been answered within the historical cost accounting structure on the basis of the matching concept. That is, costs are allocated to the inventory if there is an assumed association between such costs and the revenues of future periods. This allocation, however, is necessarily arbitrary and is generally resolved by the use of allocation rules applied consistently. Thus, the accounting structure can be designed to be consistent with either variable costing or full costing. The choice must be made on other than structural logic.

In an attempt to attain economic interpretation of product costs, it can be assumed that as long as costs are current, they represent value to the firm because the inventory could not be obtained without incurring the costs. While generalizations are always subject to exceptions and modifications, it is probably safe to state that costs should be added to inventory valuations to the point at which the merchandise is in the proper condition and location for sale or transfer to customers. In addition to specific manufacturing costs, this would include necessary costs of shipping, storage, and handling in bringing the merchandise to the store, display room, or warehouse. The inability to trace some of these costs, however, may necessitate their treatment as period expenses. If the turnover period is

---

[27] *AICPA Professional Standards,* para. 5121.05.

short and if these costs are not a substantial part of acquisition costs, inventory valuation and income determination will not be materially affected by the treatment of these costs as period expenses. Costs incurred in selling the product and in shipping the merchandise to customers, in many cases, can also be considered as increasing the inventory valuation. But since the selling prices should be available at this time, a better economic interpretation could be obtained by using the net realizable value.

From the point of view of using the inventory valuations as predictive indicators and as inputs into decision models, it would appear that variable costs might be more appropriate because they are more closely associated with cash flows and because they avoid the use of most arbitrary allocations required for full costing. Little is known about decision models, but under certain assumptions it appears that the classification of costs by their behavior and predictive ability might be more relevant than classification by product association.

THE ASSOCIATION OF COSTS WITH INVENTORIES AND COST OF SALES

In spite of the theoretical difficulties with historical costs, they continue to be used widely (almost universally in the United States and many other countries) for the measurement of goods sold in the computation of net income. Therefore, we should evaluate carefully and critically the several methods used to allocate the identified product costs with the specific quantities of merchandise sold and the specific quantities on hand. Note that all methods of allocation rely upon certain basic assumptions which may or may not be valid. The most universal assumption is that when homogeneous units are acquired in a single lot or in different lots at the same quoted price per unit, the amount allocated to cost of goods sold must be the same for each unit of product. That is, it is assumed that when the unit prices of a product do not change, all cost methods would result in the same valuation for inventories and net income. However, it may be argued—on the basis of a diminishing utility value of goods, for example—that some units actually cost more than others even though the quoted price is the same for all. This is particularly true where, for example, the goods must be acquired in lots of 100 and only 60 are required for the main objective, but the other 40 can be used as a substitute for other goods of varying lower quality and cost. Therefore, all cost methods are arbitrary to some extent in the allocation of costs between goods sold and those not sold.

Even if we can assume that each unit in a lot of homogeneous goods should be assigned the same cost, the usual pattern is that homogeneous units are frequently acquired at different prices, so that the problem of associating these costs with goods sold and goods not sold is difficult not only on pragmatic grounds but also because of the different theoretical objectives of association. Accountants have attempted to solve this problem by setting up specific rules of association based on certain assumptions of product flows, cost flows, and inventory valuation. The most common methods of association include (1) specific identification, (2) average cost methods, (3) first-in, first-out, (4) normal-stock methods, (5) retail inventory methods, and (6) gross profit method. The accountant must choose among these methods on the basis of existing conditions and specific objectives. The following discussion will evaluate these several methods in terms of their effects and specific objectives.

The objectives of cost association

The main objectives of cost identification for inventories have been the matching of costs with revenues and the association of costs with inventories for balance sheet valuation purposes. When costs are changing over time, however, these objectives are imprecise, because they do not specify which costs should be associated with the goods sold and which should be associated with the inventory. Therefore, accountants have looked to more basic objectives, which place emphasis on either the costs of goods sold or the ending inventory, or attempt to give equal attention to both. These objectives can be summarized as follows:

1.   Costs should be identified as closely as possible with each unit of merchandise. This accomplishes the result of providing for a matching of the specific costs of each unit with its revenue and also the identification of specific costs of the merchandise in the inventory. This objective is based on the assumption that each unit of product represents a specific venture; the income of the venture should be measured by the difference between the specific costs and revenue, and therefore the specific costs of the venture should be carried forward in the inventory until the revenue is reported.

2.   The operations of the firm may be viewed as a continual series of transactions rather than as a series of separate ventures. The emphasis is, therefore, on considerations other than the physical flow of goods. If the determination of current income is considered more important than the valuation of the inventory, emphasis is placed on the matching of current costs with current revenues; the inventory is considered to be a residual of historical costs. The inventory is not valued in terms of current costs, but it is argued that this is unimportant and will not affect the computation of current income of any period so long as the firm continues to maintain its inventory at the same level in the future. Another argument is that an emphasis on this objective permits the computation of current operating income and the exclusion of "unrealized" gains and losses from price changes relating to the basic inventory.

3.   A third objective places the emphasis on the need for a current valuation for the ending inventory which is then assumed to permit better

economic interpretation. The inventory is assumed to be continually replaced, and the best valuation method is assumed to be one that is based
on the most recent acquisition costs. The resulting net income for each
period, therefore, includes all gains and losses from price changes relating
to the goods assumed to have been sold.

4. Another objective is to identify the gains and losses from price
changes and measure separately the income arising from the buying and
selling operations. A strict adherence to cost, however, cannot accomplish
this completely. A replacement cost or some other measure of current
prices must be introduced. Operating income results from the matching of
current costs with current revenues, and the gains and losses from price
changes can be measured by comparing current costs with historical
costs.

Supplementary Statement No. 6 of the AAA Committee on Accounting
Concepts and Standards proposed that the first objective listed above is
the ideal. It stated: "Ideally, the measurement of accounting profit involves the matching precisely of the identified costs of specific units of
product with the sales revenue derived therefrom."[28] In preparing *Supplementary Statement No. 6,* the committee recognized that where specific
identification was not possible, an assumed flow of costs could be used to
approximate the matching of identified costs with revenues. However, the
assumed flow of costs should be realistic and reflect the actual movement
of goods. Artificial flow assumptions were, therefore, considered inappropriate. The 1964 AAA committee on the matching concept endorsed
this concept in its recommendation of the first-in, first-out method as one
that most nearly reflects the buying and selling relationship.[29]

The AICPA appears to have endorsed the second major objective listed
above. *Bulletin No. 43* states that "the major objective in selecting a
method should be to choose the one which, under the circumstances, most
clearly reflects periodic income."[30] In the discussion that follows this
statement, it is clear that identified cost is not the objective in inventory
valuation, particularly where the identity of specific lots is lost before the
time of sale. It is not entirely clear, however, what is meant by periodic
income.

The third objective—stating the inventory as close as possible to current prices—has been frequently suggested, but only as one of several
objectives.[31] Since the change in emphasis from the balance sheet to the
income statement in the early 1930s, the objective of showing current costs
in the balance sheet has been subservient to the income measurement
objective. The Study Group on the Objectives of Financial Statements,

---

[28] Committee on Concepts and Standards—Inventory Measurement, p. 36.

[29] 1964 Committee on Accounting Concepts and Standards—The Matching Concept,
AAA, "The Matching Concept," *Accounting Review* 40 (April 1965): 369.

[30] AICPA, *Professional Standards,* p. 9343.

[31] Committee on Accounting Concepts and Standards, p. 6.

however, recommended that financial statements should include current values as well as historical costs in order to permit their use as indicators of prospective benefits and for the prediction of prospective cash flows.[32]

The fourth objective, disclosing gains and losses from price changes, cannot be achieved completely by a strict adherence to the cost basis of valuation. The suggestion that replacement cost be substituted for historical cost would, however, provide the basis for meeting this objective. Some of the cost methods do achieve this objective in part; the extent to which this is accomplished is discussed in the following paragraphs.

Specific identification of cost

The first objective of matching specific costs with specific revenues is achieved most precisely by the specific identification of costs. Each unit is tagged with its cost at the time of acquisition, and this is then compared with the sales price when it is transferred to a customer; the difference is assumed to be the gross profit on this specific transaction. On the surface, this method seems ideal; what better method of matching could possibly be found? For unique items and items of high cost value, it is particularly appealing because of the ease of determining and identifying specific costs of specific units. In a small retail store, it is often convenient to record the cost of each item in code on the box or sales tag, so that the cost can be identified when an inventory is taken. When there is a high turnover of a large number of homogeneous items purchased at different lot prices, the bookkeeping is more difficult, or sometimes impossible except with the aid of high-speed computers. But in these cases, the specific identification is the standard, and other methods are used as approximations of specific identification.

A closer scrutiny, however, causes specific identification to lose some of its halo. One of its basic assumptions is that greater precision results from breaking down the operations of the firm into the smallest units possible and computing profits or losses from each of these units. However, the firm is in reality an integrated whole rather than a series of disconnected ventures. As a result, many costs are joint costs, in the sense that they relate to the firm as a whole or to major divisions of the firm. Other costs relate to many lots of heterogeneous products; any attempt to allocate these joint costs to specific units results in an appearance of precision that is not, in fact, present. For example, costs of shipping, storage, and handling may apply to groups of items, and any allocation to specific units may be abitrary. Even discounts and other cost-determining mechanisms may relate to large lots of purchases rather than to specific units.

Another argument against specific identification as a costing procedure is that it permits the manipulation of profits by the business firm. When

---

[32] Report of the Study Group on the Objectives of Financial Statements, "Objectives of Financial Statements" (AICPA, October 1973), p. 35.

homogeneous units have different costs, the manager can increase profit by choosing a unit with a low cost or decrease profit by choosing a unit with a high cost. A good example is the buying and selling of corporate stock. One share is just as good as another share of the same class of stock of the same corporation. If several lots are acquired at different prices, the owner may select which lot to sell in order to liquidate only a part of the holdings. The proponents of specific identification as the ideal, however, draw attention to the fact that the business manager is continually making decisions to alter the profit position by selecting which of different items to sell or attempt to sell in certain periods. Note also that if specific identification is used only as a standard for the choice of other methods, the possibility of manipulation is minimized.

In spite of some of the difficulties associated with specific identification, it is a useful goal to provide good matching when alternatives to historical cost are not acceptable as a measure of input value. It should be recognized, however, that the specific identification method results in an income concept that includes operating income and gains and losses from specific price changes. Also, when specific identification is applied to homogeneous units, a flow of goods assumption is made even if the manager does not attempt to direct which items are sold in what order. If the customer is permitted free choice of which item to buy, the result may be that the choice is random; or the customer may choose the most convenient item in front, which may be the oldest item, thus effecting a first-in, first-out flow; or the customer may choose the item with the least dust on it, thus effecting a last-in, first-out flow.

Average cost methods

The use of averages permits each purchase price to influence the inventory valuation and the cost of goods sold. The assumption is that the buying and selling operation results in the aggregation of costs and the assignment of these costs to goods sold and goods unsold on the basis of a single price. This single price is assumed to be a representative unit cost of all goods handled during a specific period. No specific flow of goods is assumed, unless it can be said that it represents a random selection of goods by customers so that any item handled during the period has an equal chance of appearing in the inventory at the end of the period. Usually, however, it is not thought to be in agreement with the physical flow of goods but in conflict with it.

Average costs do not reflect either the matching of current costs with current revenues or balance sheet valuations in terms of current costs. In this respect they are somewhat neutral with regard to income determination and balance sheet valuation. But the extent to which they are neutral depends, in part, on how the average is computed. An unweighted average of prices could lead to inconsistent and capricious results, depending on the rapidity of price changes and the timing of acquisitions. A weighted average is generally thought to be more representative than an unweighted average, and a moving weighted average even more appropriate where perpetual inventory records can be maintained. A moving weighted average or a simple weighted average computed for short periods of time may approximate a first-in, first-out flow of goods if the turnover is high and specific lots are purchased frequently. In these cases, it is not entirely neutral in its effects.

First-in, first-out

The first-in, first-out rule is based primarily on the assumption that it is a good approximation of specific identification for most types of goods in most industries. It is thought to be good inventory management to sell or use the oldest units first and maintain a current inventory representing the most recent purchases. Thus, FIFO represents an approximation of the specific flow of goods. As an approximation of the specific identification of unit costs, it has the advantage that management has little or no control over the selection of units in order to influence recorded profits. It also has the advantage of not being influenced by the arbitrary or whimsical choices of customers. As a result, it provides a more consistent and systematic determination of inventory and cost of goods sold, permitting better comparisons among different firms in the same industry and among several years.

A second objective of FIFO is the combining of all elements of profit reported at the time of sale. As with specific identification, it is assumed that no separation can be made of gains and losses arising from price changes and income resulting from managerial decisions in the course of normal operations. It is also sometimes assumed that FIFO does not permit the recognition of unrealized gains and losses (except as possibly modified by the lower-of-cost-or-market rule). But this assumption is based on the proposition that the operating cycle is from cash to merchandise and back to cash again. Others propose that the cycle should be viewed as being from merchandise to cash and back to merchandise, in which case unrealized appreciation is included in income if the ending inventory is recorded at prices higher than those at the beginning of the period.

A third objective of FIFO is the presentation of the ending inventory for balance sheet purposes in terms of the most recent costs, which can be assumed to approximate replacement costs. The closeness of approximation to replacement costs depends on the frequency of price changes and on the stock turnover. When the stock turns over rapidly, the inventory valuations will reflect current prices unless prices change considerably after the recent purchases. But seldom will the inventory valuations under FIFO be identical with replacement costs except accidentally, or under unusual conditions of stable prices from the dates of acquisition of the ending inventory to the date of the balance sheet.

The objectives of matching current costs with current revenues and the separate reporting of gains and losses from price changes are not generally met with the first-in, first-out inventory procedure. Thus, the major objections to the method are expressed in terms of its failure to meet these objectives. There are also serious practical disadvantages to the FIFO method when many lots are purchased during the period at different prices or when goods are returned to stock after subsequent lots have been sold.

Last-in, first-out methods

The normal-stock methods of inventory valuation have as their objectives the matching of current costs with current revenues and the elimination of the reporting of gains and losses from the holding of inventories. Early in the 20th century, the base-stock and reserve methods gained in popularity, largely because they presented a conservative valuation of the inventory for balance sheet purposes. However, they failed to gain widespread acceptance, largely because they were rejected in the United States for income tax purposes. But when the Internal Revenue Codes of 1938 and 1939 gave formal recognition to the acceptability of the last-in, first-out method, LIFO gained rapidly in popularity as a means of attaining the above objectives.

Last-in, first-out. In a few situations, LIFO has been assumed to reflect the specific identification of goods or the normally expected flow of goods. For example, certain nonperishable raw materials such as coal and ores may be stored in such a way that new acquisitions are placed on top of the pile and amounts transferred to production or use are taken off the top, leaving a semipermanent base inventory that may be used only in emergencies. When goods do not flow in this specific order, the last-in, first-out method is generally referred to as *artificial* LIFO.

Most proponents of LIFO, however, do not consider it to be an approximation of the flow of goods, but rather a logical procedure for other reasons. The main objective is the matching of current costs against current revenues, resulting in an operational concept of income which excludes gains and losses from the holding of inventories. Although the LIFO method stems from the idea that the base inventory is similar to a fixed asset in that it must be maintained continually throughout the life of the firm, it is not necessary that the inventory be classified as a fixed asset. The basic assumption is that the operations of the firm require an investment in inventories that must be maintained throughout the life of the enterprise. The flow of transactions is assumed to be from inventories to cash to inventories rather than from cash to merchandise to cash; income, therefore, cannot be measured until the inventories have been replaced.

LIFO is claimed to be useful for the following reasons: (1) A matching of current costs against current revenues is facilitated. (2) If prices are rising, the inventory valuation is conservatively stated. (3) Price changes over the business cycle do not result in the reporting of unrealized gains and losses arising from the holding of the initial and increasing amounts of inventory. (4) It permits the smoothing of income over the business cycle if prices are rising and falling. (5) Income is reported only when it is available for distribution as dividends or for other purposes. Holding gains do not represent disposable income. (6) Probably the most impelling reason for the adoption of LIFO in the United States has been its acceptance for income tax purposes. Since prices have generally moved upward in recent years, the adoption of LIFO by corporations has permitted a permanent deferral of taxes compared with what would have been paid if other inventory methods had been used.

In the early discussions of LIFO, it was thought to be useful in obtaining results similar to hedging operations where actual hedging was not possible. Therefore, it was thought to be applicable only in those industries where the conditions were similar to those in the flour milling industry and other industries where hedging is possible. Thus, the last-in, first-out method was considered to be appropriate when (1) the inventory consists of basic or homogeneous goods; (2) these goods form a substantial part of the cost of the final product sold; (3) the inventory is large in relationship to the total assets of the firm; (4) the inventory turnover is slow, generally because of the time required for processing; (5) changes in raw material prices tend to be reflected quickly in the prices of the finished product. Note, however, that LIFO only gives the illusion of a hedging transaction. The reported net income approximates that which would result if hedging had been used, but the gains and losses from the holding of inventories are not transferred to others; they are merely buried in the under- or overstatement of the inventories.

With the change in the Internal Revenue Code in 1939 and the decision of the Tax Court in 1947, the door was opened for the use of LIFO by all taxpayers required to compute inventories.[33] Therefore, the specific industry and firm characteristics were no longer considered necessary. The main consideration now is that LIFO should be used where it "more clearly reflects current income." Some argue that LIFO rightfully omits unrealized gains and losses arising from specific price changes, but others argue that LIFO is a good method of meeting the price-level problem, particularly if it is used in conjunction with replacement cost depreciation.

The main arguments against LIFO can be summarized as follows:

1.   One of the principal objections to LIFO is that the valuation of the inventory for balance sheet purposes is continually out of date, reflecting prices of some past period completely meaningless in the context of current conditions. And since the inventory valuation is dependent on the level of prices in the year the LIFO method was adopted, comparisons among firms, even in the same industry, are invalid even if all of the firms

---

[33] *Hutzler Bros.*, 8 T.C. 14 (1947).

are using LIFO. The computation of the working capital ratio and other financial ratios is, therefore, useless, and the balance sheet is meaningless as a report of financial conditions. The parenthetical reporting of current inventory valuations would alleviate this difficulty in part, but this has seldom been done in published financial statements.

2. As a method of solving the price-level problem, LIFO is erroneous and incomplete. It adjusts income only for specific price changes of merchandise and only for price changes since the last purchase. Asset valuations in the balance sheet are not restated and cannot be interpreted in terms of current dollars.

3. A corollary to the above objection to LIFO is that it permits a deferral in the recognition of gains and losses from the holding of inventories while specific prices are changing at a rate different from that of prices in general. It is generally claimed that these gains are not realized and therefore are not available for dividends, but they are an important part of the operations of any firm where actual hedging is not possible. On the other side of the coin, losses are also omitted from reported income, but this implies that the reported net income is available for dividends without consideration for the decrease in the invested capital resulting from the loss. These unrealized gains and losses may also arise from the efficient or inefficient buying practices of the firm. To the extent that this is true, they are very relevant in the measurement of the overall performance of management.

4. LIFO is occasionally rejected on the ground that it is diametrically opposed to the usual physical flow of goods and, therefore, does not permit a good matching of specific costs and revenues. But even as a procedure for matching current costs and revenues, it is not perfect. The most recent purchase costs are matched against the revenues of the current period. However, unless both purchases and sales occur regularly in even quantities, the revenues will not be matched with the costs current at the time of sale. When purchases are irregular and unrelated to the timing of sales, the matching is haphazard, particularly if prices and costs are changing rapidly.

5. When it becomes necessary to reduce the inventory below the normal quantity, either voluntarily or involuntarily, the matching of ancient costs against current revenues produces absurd results. Income of a single year may include the accumulated gains and losses since the start of LIFO, resulting in a major distortion. Some accountants have suggested that this problem can be remedied by setting up a reserve for the excess of replacement cost over the recorded LIFO cost of the inventory liquidated. This method (sometimes referred to as NIFO—next-in, first-out) has been accepted for tax purposes in special cases of involuntary liquidation. But as a general practice, it may lead to absurdities. When the composition of the inventory is changing over time, or when the product itself changes, it may be impossible and at least unrealistic to obtain replacement or reproduction costs for items that are no longer produced. This procedure may also lead to the absurd position of a reserve that exceeds the inven-

tory cost, thus resulting in a negative inventory in the balance sheet. Thus, the reserve is a meaningless figure that represents neither a contra to the inventory valuation nor a liability to replace the inventory. It is merely a device to keep from including in income the gains due to price increases since the LIFO prices were first recorded.

6. The fear of liquidation of the LIFO inventory and the tax consequences has led some firms to pursue irrational buying policies, particularly at the end of the tax year. Not only is this practice close to manipulation of the firm's income, but also it may result in unhealthy economic consequences. If many firms in the same industry attempt to replace their inventories at the end of the year, the pressure on the market may result in increased prices, at least temporarily, and a false indication of the real demand for the raw material or finished product.

7. Many of the proponents of LIFO claim that one of the benefits is a smoothing of net income. Smoothing occurs only if prices move down as well as up, but even if this is the case, smoothing is not a desirable attribute of financial accounting, particularly if it is artificial. The goal of smoothing confuses an operational goal of the firm with an accounting goal. If the results of operations are not smooth, accounting should not make them appear as if they were.

8. Even though LIFO does not generally reflect the flow of goods, it is argued that the objective is to present a flow of costs. However, costs do not flow; they move only to the extent that accountants move them. Therefore, LIFO is artificial and thus invalid as a logical method of associating costs with goods sold and goods on hand.

9. Empirical studies suggest that FIFO is superior to LIFO as a method of reporting to common stock investment decision makers.[34] However, another study has demonstrated that FIFO has a high propensity to overstate accounting income during periods of high inflation rates when compared with the use of current replacement costs.[35]

LIFO or market. Lower of cost or market is incompatible with LIFO because of some basic incongruities that seemed to be partly responsible for the requirements of the Internal Revenue Code and Regulations that when LIFO is used for tax purposes, the inventory must be taken at cost regardless of market value. LIFO must be used for annual reporting purposes when it is used for tax purposes, hence, "LIFO or market" is unacceptable for reporting annual income when LIFO is used for tax purposes.[36]

---

[34] See, for example, George J. Staubus, "Testing Inventory Accounting," *Accounting Review,* July 1968, pp. 413–24.

[35] C. W. Bastable and Jacob D. Merriwether. "FIFO in an Inflationary Environment," *Journal of Accountancy,* March 1975, pp. 49–55.

[36] 1954 Code, Sec. 472 (c), Regs. 1.472–2 (b), and Regs. 1.472–2 (e). For a discussion of different interpretations of these regulations, see Sidney Davidson, "LIFO Cost or Market and Compulsory Tax Reporting Requirements," *Journal of Accounting Research* 3, no. 1 (Spring 1965): 156–58. To the author's knowledge, this point has not been interpreted by the courts.

In spite of the opposition to LIFO or market, it has been proposed particularly for tax purposes for several reasons: (1) One of the early reasons for the proposal was to provide relief for those firms that were not permitted to use LIFO under the 1939 code because of an inability to identify specific units. On the basis of the decision of the Hutzler Brothers Company case in 1947, the door was opened for the use of dollar-value LIFO, but these firms were not permitted to apply LIFO retroactively if they had not elected formally to change to LIFO in the previous period.[37,38] LIFO or market would have been a very haphazard way of providing for this relief, however. (2) A second argument for LIFO or market was to encourage firms to adopt LIFO immediately rather than wait until price levels should reach a lower point. Since many firms had failed to adopt LIFO when prices were still low, they became reluctant to adopt LIFO in the face of possible falling prices and the consequent tax disadvantage. Thus, it was thought that LIFO or market would create greater uniformity in the use of inventory procedures in many industries. (3) A third argument is that LIFO could result in inventory valuations that exceed replacement cost and that this is not in accordance with generally accepted accounting principles based on conservative valuations.

The arguments against LIFO or market can be summarized as follows: (1) The general objections to the lower-of-cost-or-market rule also apply to LIFO or market. (2) It permits an inconsistent valuation of inventories, based on LIFO in some periods and on FIFO in others. If prices are rising, the inventory will be valued on the basis of the older costs and the cost of goods sold will reflect the recent costs; but if prices are falling, the ending inventory would reflect current costs and the cost of goods sold would represent older costs. Thus, LIFO would be used when prices are rising, and FIFO would be approximated when prices are falling. But when prices again rise, there would be a shift back to LIFO with an even lower base valuation. This effect is sometimes known as HIFO (highest-in, first-out). The inventory will always be recorded at the lowest valuation experienced since the start of the LIFO method. (3) One of the main advantages of LIFO is the matching of current costs against current revenues. But, if LIFO or market were permitted, unrealized losses would be included in the computation of income when replacement costs fall below the LIFO base, although they are excluded at all other times.

Dollar value LIFO. The dollar value LIFO method was established as an expedient to avoid the necessity of maintaining records of the original LIFO prices and the prices of increments for each of the many items included in the inventories of a manufacturer. The ending inventory quantities are measured at base year prices; if this amount exceeds the dollar value of the beginning-of-the-year inventory in base year prices, the excess is the increment for the year. This increment is then restated in

---

[37] *Hutzler Bros.*, 8 T.C. 14 (1947).
[38] See *R. H. Macy & Co.*, I AFTR 2d 1733 (1958).

terms of current year prices by multiplying the increment in base year prices by the ratio of the ending inventory at end-of-year prices to the same quantities priced at base year prices. Occasionally, the ratio is determined by using a sample of the inventory rather than the entire goods on hand. Thus, the base year dollar is assumed to be a proper measure to determine the change in inventory quantities.

If the dollar value LIFO method is to approximate the individual LIFO computations, the items in the inventory should be grouped into homogeneous "cost pools." Their homogeneity should be in terms of their similarity of price movements, however, rather than in terms of their physical nature or use. However, the tendency in practice has been to use groups that are much too broad and that include items whose prices do not move in a similar fashion.

The result of the dollar value LIFO method is that the inventory can be stated at prices lower than would otherwise be stated if LIFO were applied to the individual items because, with the use of the "cost pools," increases in the quantities of some items may offset decreases in other items. In addition to all of the disadvantages of LIFO, dollar value LIFO suffers from the inaccuracies arising from the use of dollar amounts to represent quantities and the measurement of price changes on the basis of indexes or averages. Therefore, the dollar value method meets none of the objectives of inventory valuation and should be one of the first methods in the accountants' kit of tools to be abandoned.

Retail inventory methods

In small retail stores owned and operated by a single proprietor, it is often convenient to mark the cost in code on each box of merchandise as it is placed on the shelf. When an inventory is taken at the end of the year, the cost of each item can be recorded at the same time as the taking of the count. Thus, a specific identification method of costing is effected. In larger department stores, this procedure is too cumbersome and is not desirable from the point of view of inventory control. Perpetual records are also cumbersome because of the large number of items and styles that must be carried by such stores. High-speed computers permit specific identification and perpetual records, but until they are widely adopted, large retail stores have turned to the use of departmental averages to obtain estimates of inventory costs and to aid in setting up inventory control procedures.

In the retail inventory methods, the inventory quantity is determined by actual count and priced initially at current retail prices. For interim statements, the inventory at retail prices can be estimated by subtracting the net sales for the period to date from the total goods available at retail prices. In this procedure, the inventory is a residual similar to that obtained by using the perpetual inventory method. The main difficulty is that losses are buried in the inventory amount, resulting in an overstatement of the inventory and of net income. But if a count is also taken, the losses from theft or other causes can be estimated and recorded separately for accounting and control purposes.

After the inventory is computed or estimated at retail prices, it is converted to an input valuation by multiplying the inventory at retail by an average ratio of cost to retail pices for the current period. The computation of this average ratio is demonstrated as follows:

	Cost	Retail	Ratio of cost to retail
Inventory, January 1	$12,000	$ 16,000	
Purchases during the year (net)	72,000	100,000	
Markups (less cancellations)		4,000	
Total	84,000	120,000	(A) 70%
Deduct markdowns (less cancellations)		8,000	
Goods available for sale	$84,000	112,000	(B) 75%
Deduct sales (less returns and allowances)		90,000	
Inventory (residual) at Dec. 31, at retail		22,000	
Physical inventory at Dec. 31, at retail		$ 20,000	

The inventory at retail is reduced to an input valuation by multiplying this amount by the ratio of cost to retail for the goods available for sale in the current period. A more current ratio may be obtained by using only the purchases for the current year, but a practical difficulty arises in allocating the markups and markdowns to the beginning inventory and to the purchases. In either case, there is an assumption that the resulting average ratio is representative of the ratio of cost to retail prices in the ending inventory. To increase the probability of this, a separate ratio should be computed for each department or type of goods that carries a relatively uniform mark-on. If mark-on percentages are not uniform, the proportion of each type of merchandise in the ending inventory should be similar to the proportion of each type in the total goods available for sale during the year.

In the above example, the use of ratio B is assumed to result in an estimate of cost. Markups and markdowns are determinants of selling prices and independent of the original costs. Thus, the ending inventory at cost would be $15,000 ($20,000 × 75 percent). But this assumes that the markups and markdowns are proportionately distributed between goods sold and goods not sold. If we assume two extreme possibilities, we see that the ending inventory may be grossly understated or grossly overstated. Assume first that the markups are all made at the end of the year and are reflected in the inventory at retail; the markdowns are assumed to relate uniformly to the goods sold and the goods not sold. If the inventory had not been written up at the end of the year, it would have amounted to $16,000 at retail and $12,480 ($16,000 × 84,000/108,000) at cost. On the other hand, if we assume that the markdowns were all made at the end of the year and relate to the ending inventory and that the markups relate uniformly to all goods, the inventory expressed at $15,000 (at cost) would be understated. If these markdowns at the end of the year had not been made, the ending inventory at retail would have been $28,000 ($20,000 + $8,000) and the inventory at cost would have been $19,600 ($28,000 × 70 percent). Thus, the inventory at assumed cost could range from $12,480 to $19,600, depending on the assumptions made. If the markups and markdowns are included only in the ending inventory and reflect current selling prices, the best that can be said for the method is that it states the valuation of the inventory at net realizable value less a "normal" net markup.

It has occasionally been assumed that the retail cost method results in an approximation of the weighted average method because the cost-retail percentage is computed as a weighted average of the cost-retail relationship of all goods available for sale during the period.[39] However, the averaging results primarily from the use of the same cost-retail percentage for all goods in the departmental inventory regardless of individual mark-on percentages. Only if selling prices are relatively stable, or at least unrelated to the changes in cost prices during the period, will the ending inventory valuation approximate a weighted average cost. If selling prices are moving in the same direction as costs and in approximately the same percentages, a first-in, first-out inventory method may be approximated. For example, if both costs and selling prices have increased by 20 percent during the period, the mark-on percentage will have remained constant; and since the ending inventory will be priced initially at the selling prices existing at the end of the period, the conversion to cost will result in an approximation of the most recent purchase costs, reflecting a first-in, first-out flow.

Retail lower of cost or market. The customary practice in the department store and apparel businesses is to use percentage A in the above example, computed from the cost-retail relationship after adding markups, but before subtracting markdowns.[40] This practice has become common because it is assumed to reflect the lower of cost or market. There is little question that percentage A represents the lowest cost-retail ratio that can be computed from the current cost-retail relationships and, therefore, the most conservative. But there is considerable doubt that it does reflect *market* defined as replacement cost.

As indicated above, ratio B is an estimate of cost only if the markups and markdowns apply proportionately to the ending inventory and to the

[39] See, for example, Devine, *Inventory Valuation,* pp. 170–71.

[40] Malcolm P. McNair and Anita C. Hersum, *The Retail Inventory Method and LIFO* (New York: McGraw-Hill, 1952), p. 42.

goods sold; that is, it must be assumed that the goods sold and the goods unsold are marked up or down by the same percentage. If this assumption is valid, we could estimate current replacement cost by using the cost-retail percentage computed before markups and markdowns. But one further assumption must be made—the markups and markdowns must have been made as a direct result of changes in replacement costs. The most likely situation, however, is that markups do reflect increases in costs, but that markdowns do not reflect decreases in cost. Additional markups, unless they are merely corrections of errors, reflect decreases in cost. Additional markups, unless they are merely corrections of errors, reflect enhanced salability connected primarily with a rising wholesale market.[41] On the other hand, markdowns are made for a large number of reasons other than changes in costs.[42]

We see, therefore, that using a ratio computed *before* markups would result in an approximation of replacement cost (although above cost) if the markups are reflected proportionately in the ending inventory. But because markdowns do not reflect decreases in costs, the cost-retail ratio computed before markdowns cannot be used to approximate replacement costs. Therefore, we must search further for some justification for using the cost-retail percentage computed *after* markups but *before* markdowns. This justification is in the assumption that markdowns reflect declines in the utility of the merchandise to the firm. That is, a markdown is assumed to result in a current loss because it represents a decline in the expected revenue to be obtained from the sale of the merchandise on hand. The merit of this argument rests in the fact that merchandise that must be marked down is not worth as much to the firm as merchandise that need not be marked down. Thus, if the latter is worth no more than cost, the former must be worth less. Note, however, that this argument is based on the assumption that revenue is realized only at the time of sale and that any impairment of this potential realization results in a current loss. The concept of market is, therefore, that of net realizable value less a normal net markup.

But the word *normal* has a different meaning in this context than it does when the so-called cost retail method is used. Ratio A is here considered to be normal, implying that markups are normal or rare but that markdowns are not. In the cost approach, the average net mark-on for the period is considered to be normal. Two other concepts of normality could also be considered: (1) the ratio of cost to retail *before* markups and markdowns and (2) the ratio of cost to retail *before* markups but *after* markdowns. The former should probably be considered the minimum ratio (the maximum anticipated mark-on).[43] The complement of this ratio

---

[41] Ibid., p. 37.

[42] Ibid., p. 40.

[43] In the above example, this ratio would be 72.4 percent ($84,000 ÷ $116,000). But the ratio for the current year's purchases may be considered more appropriate. This would amount to 72 percent ($72,000 ÷ $100,000).

represents the anticipated gross profit margin at the time the merchandise was originally priced. It does not seem reasonable that a loss should be recorded in the current period so that a larger gross margin could be realized in the following period. The second ratio (2 above) of cost to retail before markups but after markdowns is not now generally accepted because it might possibly permit the recording of unrealized gains if markups are made in response to increases in replacement costs, but it would not reflect losses arising from decreases in replacement costs. However, markups are not generally considered normal, at least not unless inflation rates are predictable. But markdowns are a normal part of the pricing process of retail stores. Therefore, markdowns can be anticipated and markups cannot. Normality should refer to that which is recurring in the absence of extraneous events. If some of the markdowns are caused by unusual and nonrecurring events, they should be omitted in the computation of the cost-retail ratio. Since the cost-retail ratio is multiplied by the inventory expressed in terms of the retail prices at the end of the year, the input valuation of the inventory would be the net realizable value less a normal net markup.

LIFO applied to the retail method.   When LIFO was generally accepted for income tax purposes in 1939, it was still thought to be inapplicable to department stores, primarily because of the lack of homogeneity of the merchandise and the inability to identify specific quantities of inventory at the beginning of the year with specific quantities of similar merchandise at the end of the year. Department stores, therefore, turned to the use of index numbers to identify changes in inventory volume, and procedures for the application of LIFO to the retail method became acceptable for tax purposes in 1947. The reasons for the adoption of LIFO by retail firms are similar to the basic arguments discussed earlier in this chapter. The following is a brief evaluation of some of the basic characteristics of the LIFO retail method.

The first characteristic is that the LIFO base is measured in terms of a specific dollar value of inventory at the time the LIFO method was started plus the dollar value increments since that date. Since the types of merchandise handled change over time, specific quantities of merchandise cannot be used as the base stock. Instead, the dollar retail value of the ending inventory is converted into the dollars of the base year by the use of price indexes. Therefore, it permits the maintenance of investment in specific categories of merchandise. Gains and losses from the holding of inventories are excluded from income only if the indexes are representative of the specific types of merchandise in the inventories.

A second characteristic is that the "lower of cost or market" is not considered applicable because it is assumed to result in "LIFO or market." But because the use of the cost-retail percentage after markups and before markdowns does not necessarily approximate replacement cost, this argument is not sound. However, since the use of the ratio computed after both markups and markdowns reflects a better concept of normality and is possibly a closer approximation of cost, there is some merit in its use.

A third characteristic is that the increments to the inventory are computed on the basis of prices at the end of the year, so that they reflect the FIFO method for the current year rather than a strict adherence to LIFO throughout.

The gross profit method

The gross profit method differs from the retail method in two main computations: (1) The cost-sales ratio is computed by taking an average of the ratios of cost of sales to sales for several prior years, whereas in the retail method, the cost-retail percentage relates to the ratio of goods available for sale in the current year at cost to the same goods priced at retail. In the gross profit method, the ratio is less current, but it is computed from costs that are more comprehensive and include such items as normal losses. (2) The inventory is computed by subtracting the estimated cost of sales from the cost of goods available for sale. In the retail method, the goods available for sale are priced at retail, and by subtracting the sales for the period, an estimate of the ending inventory at retail is obtained. These two methods are similar, but the gross profit method is less accurate because the cost of goods sold is a rough estimate resulting in an approximation of both the volume and cost of the goods on hand.

The main uses of the gross profit method are as a means of estimating an inventory when a count of the inventory is not possible or practicable and as a test of the ending inventory computed by other means. Because of the inaccuracies in the method, it should not be relied on in the computation of the ending inventory except as a last resort. For example, when the inventory has been destroyed by fire or when a part has been stolen, and the retail method cannot be used, the gross profit method may provide a reasonable approximation. As an auditing test, the gross profit method cannot prove the accuracy of the physical inventory or inaccuracies in the inventory computation, but it can indicate whether or not the computed inventory is reasonable. If the difference between the actual inventory and that computed by the gross profit method cannot be accounted for by the inaccuracies of the gross profit estimate, further investigation is required.

The gross profit method is not generally considered to be acceptable for financial reporting purposes for two principal reasons: (1) A physical inventory is not taken, so the inventory valuation is a residual with all of the limitations of the perpetual inventory method. (2) The gross profit percentage is computed as an average of prior years. The relationship between costs and selling prices is not generally uniform over time, so that an average of the gross profit percentage of prior years is not a reliable estimate of the relationship in the current period.

Comparison of the various cost methods
during periods of price changes

When specific prices are changing in the same direction during the accounting period, the several methods of inventory valuation based on cost provide different effects on the net income for the period and on the balance sheet valuation at the end of the period. In all of the cost methods, however, the dollar value of the goods available for sale is equal to the sum of the ending inventory and the cost of goods sold. The effect of price changes is reflected in either the inventory or the cost of sales. It can be isolated and reported separately only if a current cost valuation or some other valuation basis is substituted for cost. Note that none of the cost methods can provide a substitute for the adjustment for price-level changes as discussed in Chapter 9.

The specific effect of price changes on current income and on balance sheet valuation depends on several factors, including the degree of price fluctuations, inventory turnover, the level of prices existing at the time the current procedure was adopted, and the relationship of inventory costs to other costs. The following generalizations, however, can be made: (1) FIFO will generally result in the highest inventory valuation and the highest net income if the specific prices are rising steadily throughout the period. The reverse is true when prices are falling steadily. (2) LIFO results in the lowest income for the current period when prices are rising steadily and when there is no liquidation of the beginning inventory. The valuation of the ending inventory may be above or below that under FIFO, depending on the level of prices when LIFO was started. (3) The weighted average method is neutral with respect to inventory and cost of sales. Generally, cost of sales and net income will fall between the extremes of FIFO and LIFO. When a moving weighted average is used, the result is closer to that obtained by the use of FIFO because the recent purchases receive greater weight. (4) The retail method approximates net realizable value less a "normal" net mark-on for the ending inventory. Because the ending inventory is priced initially at the selling prices existing at the end of the period, the result is closer to FIFO than to average costs.

When prices move upward and downward with equal amplitude over the business cycle, LIFO tends to result in a smoothing of income as compared with other methods. That is, LIFO results in the lowest income when prices are rising and in the highest income when prices are falling, while FIFO results in the opposite. The more rapid the turnover rate, the smaller will be the difference between the several methods. Also, the smaller the change in prices, the smaller will be the difference between the methods. In fact, if prices are perfectly stable and all lots of merchandise are purchased at the same prices, all of the various cost methods will result in the same net income and asset valuation.

A summary comparison of cost association methods

Method	Objective	Effect on income and balance sheet	Special conditions
Specific identification	Specific matching.	Depends on actual flow of merchandise.	For valuable or unique items or items easily identifiable.
Weighted average	Permits a single representative price	Neutral.	Periodic inventory only.
Moving weighted average	Single price with greater weight to recent purchases.	Similar to FIFO, particularly if turnover is high.	Perpetual inventory only.
First-in, first-out	Approximation of specific matching.	Balance sheet expressed in recent costs. Reflects highest income when prices are rising.	Goods assumed to be sold on FIFO basis.
Last-in, first-out	Matching of current costs with current revenues.	Balance sheet valuation based on old costs. Cost of sales in terms of recent purchases. Results in lowest income when prices are rising.	Valid only if base inventory is not liquidated. Useful when holding gains and losses are not relevant.
Retail method	Approximation of specific costs or lower of cost or market.	Similar to FIFO under certain conditions.	For a large variety of items with similar mark-on percentages. May be used for perpetual or periodic inventories.
Gross profit method	Estimation of inventory when count is not taken or as a test of other methods	Similar to FIFO under certain conditions.	Perpetual inventory procedure only. Assumes stability of gross profit percentage over time.

Summary of cost association methods

The several methods of associating costs with inventories and goods sold are compared briefly with respect to their objectives, their effect on income and the balance sheet, and the special conditions relating to each method in the table entitled "A summary comparison of cost association methods."

BEHAVIORAL EFFECTS OF INVENTORY METHODS

One justification for different valuation methods for inventories is that each method should reflect different economic circumstances. However, in a questionnaire study, Chasteen found this not to be the case. His study suggested that firms in the United States make a choice on the basis of the effects on reported income and the tax effects to a much greater extent than they do on the basis of economic circumstances.[44] But the direct effect on reported income is cosmetic only and does not reflect any real change in the resources of the firm. The income tax effect, on the other hand, does reflect a real change in future cash payments for taxes. Therefore, there does not appear to be any justification for the many alternative pricing methods except possibly to reveal the tax effect.

A second possible justification might be the effect of different pricing methods on stock prices in an efficient securities market. The traditional view is that methods resulting in lower reported earnings would result in lower stock prices and vice versa. However, studies have shown that the market is not fooled by changes in accounting methods that manipulate reported income but do not reflect real economic changes in the firm.[45] This is consistent with the efficient market hypothesis, which states that (in the semistrong form) all publicly available information is immediately impounded in the market price of stock and, conversely, irrelevant information or data are ignored.

A more recent study suggests that a change to LIFO results, at least in the short run, in a downward movement in stock prices.[46] In another study, individuals were influenced negatively by lower reported earnings resulting from a switch to LIFO, even though they were shown the posi-

---

[44] Lanny G. Chasteen, "Economic Circumstances and Inventory Method Selection," *Abacus,* June 1973, pp. 22–27.

[45] S. Sunder, "Relationship between Accounting Changes and Stock Prices: Problems of Measurement and Some Empirical Evidence," *Empirical Research in Accounting: Selected Studies, 1973,* supplement to *Journal of Accounting Research,* pp. 1–45; and R. Ball, "Changes in Accounting Techniques and Stock Prices," *Empirical Research in Accounting: Selected Studies, 1972.*

[46] Robert Moren Brown, "Short-Range Market Reaction to Changes to LIFO Accounting using Preliminary Earnings Announcement Dates," *Journal of Accounting Research,* Spring 1980, pp. 38–63.

tive impact of the switch on net cash inflows.[47] These studies suggest the presence of market inefficiencies at least in the short run and the existence of functional fixation on reported earnings.

It is not logical to draw conclusion regarding accounting policy from the limited studies to date. However, there is at least a suggestion that the existence of a number of alternative pricing methods for inventories may cause more harm than benefit and that the methods of reporting information regarding inventories should be improved.

SELECTED ADDITIONAL READING

Valuation of inventory

Barden, Horace G. *Accounting Research Study No. 13.* "The Accounting Basis of Inventories." AICPA, 1973.

Buckley, John W., and **James R. Goode.** "Inventory Valuation and Income Measurement: An Improved System." *Abacus,* June 1976, pp. 34–48.

Chasteen, Lanny Gordon. "Empirical Study of Differences in Economic Circumstances as a Justification for Alternative Inventory Pricing Methods." *Accounting Review,* July 1971, pp. 504–8.

————. "Economic Circumstances and Inventory Method Selection." *Abacus,* June 1973, pp. 22–27.

Hoffman, Raymond A., and **Henry Gunders.** *Inventories: Control, Costing and Effect upon Income and Taxes.* 2d ed. New York: Ronald Press, 1970.

Net realizable values and replacement costs

Benjamin, James. "Accuracy of the Period-End Method for Computing the Current Cost of Materials Used." *Abacus,* June 1973, pp. 73–80.

Cadenhead, Gary M. "Net Realizable Value Redefined." *Journal of Accounting Research,* Spring 1970, pp. 138–40.

Petri, Enrico. "Holding Gains and Losses as Cost Savings: A Comment on *Supplementary Statement No. 2* on Inventory Valuation." *Accounting Review,* July 1973, pp. 483–88.

Revsine, Lawrence. *Replacement Cost Accounting.* Englewood Cliffs, N.J. Prentice-Hall, 1973.

————. "A Test of the Feasibility of Preparing Replacement Cost Accounting Statements." *Objectives of Financial Statements, Vol. 2, Selected Papers.* AICPA, 1974, pp. 229–44.

The lower-of-cost-or-market rule

Holmes, William. "Market Value of Inventories—Perils and Pitfalls." *Journal of Commerical Bank Lending,* April 1973, pp. 30–35.

Parker, R. H. "Lower of Cost and Market in Britain and the United States: An Historical Survey." *Abacus,* December 1965, pp. 156–72.

---

[47] Rashad Abdel-Khalik, "Earnings or Cash Flows: An Experiment on Functional Fixation and the Valuation of the Firm, *Studies in Accounting Research No. 16.* (AAA, 1979).

LIFO versus FIFO

Bastable, C. W., and **Jacob D. Merriwether.** "FIFO in an Inflationary Environment." *Journal of Accountancy,* March 1975, pp. 49–55.

Copeland, Ronald M.; Joseph F. Wojdak and **John K. Shank,** "Use LIFO to Offset Inflation." *Harvard Business Review,* May-June 1971, pp. 91–100.

Sunder, Shyam. "Optimal Choice between FIFO and LIFO." *Journal of Accounting Research,* Autumn 1976, pp. 277–300.

Behavioral effects

Brown, Robert Moren. "Short-Range Market Reaction to Changes to LIFO Accounting using Preliminary Earnings Announcement Dates." *Journal of Accounting Research,* Spring 1980, pp. 38–63.

Halperin, Robert. "The Effect of LIFO Inventory Costing on Resource Allocation: A Public Policy Perspective." *Accounting Review,* January 1979, pp. 58–71.

CHAPTER 14

PLANT AND EQUIPMENT: PURCHASED AND LEASED

In many respects, the measurement of plant and equipment should be the same as the measurement of other assets. Classification alone should not be the determinant factor in the measurement process. However, there are some basic differences between inventories and plant and equipment that require a separate discussion of the latter. Nevertheless, much of the discussion in the previous chapter on inventories is also relevant here. As with inventories, one of the important aspects of accounting for plant and equipment within the traditional structural form is the computation of the amount to be charged to expense in the determination of the net income of each period. This computation of the current depreciation charge is often considered to be the main objective in the accounting for plant and equipment; but the measurement process should have as one of its goals the economic description of the capital resources available to the firm. This economic interpretation of plant and equipment (a second objective) is not generally possible in traditional financial statements because the conventional depreciation methods and balance sheet valuations are inadequate as measurements of plant and equipment services used during a period and measurements of the service potentials remaining at the end of the period. This is partly the result of an inability to identify specific items or services used during the accounting period and the quantity of services remaining unused at the end of the period as well as the inadequacy of their measurement.

The third objective of measuring plant and equipment is to present information that will permit the prediction of future cash inflows and outflows. For purchased long-term plant and equipment, this is a difficult assignment under the best of circumstances. However, information that indicates either implicitly or explicitly the productive capacity, estimated lives, operating efficiency, and cash requirements for replacement should be relevant. When plant and equipment are leased, at least some of these requirements are specified in the lease contract so that better information regarding some of the expected cash flows can be presented. The objectives of this chapter are to discuss the nature of the plant and equipment classification under both purchased and leased situations and to evaluate the several measurement bases available in terms of the accounting structure, the economic interpretation of the valuation, and the predictive ability of the information for use by investors. The nature and evaluation of methods of depreciation will be discussed in the following chapter.

THE NATURE OF PLANT AND EQUIPMENT

Although all assets have some basic common characteristics, as indicated in Chapter 11, the additional characteristics of plant and equipment are summarized as follows: (1) The assets represent physical goods held to facilitate the production of other goods or to provide services to the firm or its customers in the normal course of operations. (2) They all have a limited life, at the end of which they must be abandoned or replaced. This life may be an estimated number of years determined by wear and tear caused by the elements, or it may be variable, depending on the amount of use and maintenance. (3) The value of the assets stems from the ability to enforce the exclusion of others in obtaining the legal property rights to their use rather than from the enforcement of contracts. (4) They are all nonmonetary in nature; the benefits are received from the use or sale of services rather than from their conversion into known quantities of money. (5) In general, the services are to be received over a period longer than a year or the operating cycle of the business. However, there are some exceptions. For example, a building or a piece of equipment is not reclassified as current when it has less than a year of remaining life. In a few cases, such as tools, some items may have an original life less than the operating cycle of the business.

Plant and equipment items have some common characteristics; they also have some similar financial reporting objectives. One of these objectives is based on their similarity in the accounting process. Plant and equipment are held for their future services; therefore, they are charged to expense during their useful lives in a manner similar to prepaid expenses. The main difference between prepaid expenses and plant and equipment is in the life of the asset. Prepaid expenses are usually charged to expense during the current operating cycle of the business or one year, whichever is the longer, and plant and equipment are charged to expense over a longer period. But if similarity in the accounting process is the main objective of classification, those intangibles with a limited life should probably be included. However, in the author's opinion, classification according to the accounting process is not a relevant objective for financial reporting.

A second objective in the description and measurement of plant and equipment items is to provide an indication of the amount of physical quantities or productive capacities held by the firm as well as some indication of their relative ages and expected future lives. It is unlikely that aggregate dollar figures can provide this information. However, for specific assets or groups of assets, an input valuation basis is likely to be more relevant than a liquidation value; and a valuation based on the expected value of future goods or services or cash flows is not possible of measurement either on theoretical or practical grounds. For reasons discussed in the next chapter, an accumulated depreciation amount subtracted from an input valuation cannot provide an adequate description of the relative age or condition of the physical plant and equipment.

A third, and probably the most important, objective of the plant and equipment classification and valuation is to present a description of the operations of the firm. Just as a grouping of monetary assets and current assets presents information about the operations of the firm, so does a grouping of the investment in capital items. The relative amount of capital invested in plant and equipment is relevant information for investors and creditors because it can possibly add information to aid in the prediction of future cash flows and give an indication of the period of time before the firm will have the opportunity to recommit its resources to the same or other uses without a forced liquidation. In public-utility firms and in many other service corporations, the amount invested in long-term capital items is the most important category as a source of future revenues. For this reason, most public utilities present the plant and equipment items first in the balance sheet, ahead of current assets.

Nonoperating plant and equipment items are usually presented in the balance sheet in a separate classification, but the valuation and depreciation problems are similar to those relating to operating plant and equipment. Accordingly, most of the following discussion relates to both operating and nonoperating plant and equipment items.

THE BASES OF VALUATION

Except in certain cases where property is leased to others under a long-term contract (used as a financing device), plant and equipment cannot be valued in terms of discounted, expected receipts. The main reason for the inability to use discounted expected receipts is that the revenues of a firm result from the use of many goods and services. In some cases it may be possible to estimate the future stream of revenues and costs to the firm and, by discounting appropriately the expected stream of net cash distributions to investors, an estimate of the current valuation of the entire firm may be obtained. But it is not possible to assign this stream of net cash flows to specific assets. All operating assets contribute to the revenue stream, but it is a joint contribution; there is no way to determine how much each asset contributes. The uncertainty regarding the amount and timing of the revenue stream alone may be considerable, but the further uncertainty of determining the contribution of the specific goods and services used in the operating process makes the use of output valuation bases too imprecise for application to plant and equipment. Arbitrary allocation methods could be used, but the result would not be meaningful for financial reporting.

A more important objection to the use of an output valuation for non-current assets is that very little value is added to the firm from the acquisition and holding of them. As indicated in Chapter 8, value is added in an economic sense throughout the entire production process. That is, income results from the entire operations of the firm, from the initial organization of the firm through the acquisition of producing facilities and other factors of production to the final sale of the product and the collection of the sales price. But the acquisition of the facilities generally comes early in this process, so that very little revenue-producing activity has occurred by that time. Accountants are correct in holding to the general rule that reported income should not result from the recording of acquisitions.[1]

When plant and equipment are no longer of value to the firm in its normal operations, or when they are to be sold in a secondhand market, the sale price of the fixed asset itself may become the best valuation basis. This is not an output value in the normal sense, however, since it is determined by the sales price of the asset itself rather than from the sales price of the product of the asset. The price is the liquidation or scrap value obtained from an entirely different market than that from which the input or output value of the product is obtained.

However, if there are many buyers and sellers in the used asset market, the price quoted in this market may reflect the market's expectations regarding the discounted input value of the remaining services to be obtained from the use of the asset. For example, the market for second-hand trucks and trailers used by public carriers is well organized and is made up of many buyers and sellers. The sales prices are, therefore, fairly uniform for equipment of similar age and mileage operated. Thus, the prices of similar units in the used market reflect expectations of the input value of the remaining service life because they represent the opportunity cost of the asset held by the firm and the amount that many other users are willing to pay for the future services of similar assets to be used under similar conditions.

According to the current cash equivalent concept proposed by Chambers, durable items that have an active secondhand market should be priced at the amount that could be obtained for the items by selling them in an orderly process. For nonvendible durables, Chambers suggests, consistently with his other recommendations, that the items should be written off immediately upon acquisition, just as development costs are writ-

---

[1] This does not preclude the theoretical propriety of showing gains and losses arising from favorable acquisition prices or from changes in input values, however, even though it is not in accordance with generally accepted realization rules.

ten off in many cases because they do not have a current cash equivalent.[2] However, Chambers also suggests that the current cash equivalent can be approximated, as an expediency, by the application of specific price indexes to the purchase price.[3] But this alternative does not provide a valuation basis consistent with his general theory. An input price adjusted by specific indexes must be reduced by subjective depreciation allocations, so that the net result cannot be assumed to represent the current cash equivalent or the ability of the firm to make appropriate adaptation.

McKeown has suggested the use of linear regression techniques to estimate the market price of plant and equipment because they permit the use of a larger number of relevant factors than with either a market price or the application of specific price indexes to the purchase price.[4]

Since output values are difficult or impossible to assign to plant and equipment, and liquidation values represent the present value of future services for only a few interchangeable assets, accountants must turn to input values for the valuation of fixed assets. But because the services of plant and equipment for any particular year can usually be obtained only by the acquisition of whole assets with many years of service, only the initial input value can be measured objectively. The valuation of the asset at any subsequent date is dependent on the depreciation process. However, the initial input value for the asset as a whole may be restated whenever changes occur in the general price level or in the specific markets in which they are generally acquired.

Input values

Probably the area of greatest agreement in the traditional literature of accounting theory is that plant and equipment should be valued initially on the basis of their acquisition cost.[5] Lower amounts are suggested or required in the government regulation of public utilities when the acquisition cost exceeds the original cost new less depreciation or the "prudent" cost. Subsequent to the date of acquisition, the net valuation is generally cost less accumulated depreciation, but the depreciation charge is based on the acquisition cost. The allocation of these acquisition costs—the depreciation process—is the main subject of most discussions of the accounting for plant and equipment. The emphasis on the computation of the depreciation charge is correct because of its importance in the determination of periodic net income, but the choice of a proper valuation base is

---

[2] Raymond J. Chambers, *Accounting, Evaluation, and Economic Behavior* (Englewood Cliffs, N.J.: Prentice-Hall, 1966), pp. 238–45.

[3] Ibid., pp. 245–49.

[4] James C. McKeown, "Comparative Application of Market and Cost Based Accounting Models," *Journal of Accounting Research,* Spring 1973, p. 63.

[5] See, for example, W. A. Paton and A. C. Littleton, *An Introduction to Accounting Standards* (American Accounting Association, 1955), p. 81; and Robert T. Sprouse and Maurice Moonitz, "A Tentative Set of Broad Accounting Principles for Business Enterprises," *Accounting Research Study No. 3* (AICPA, 1962), p. 32.

equally important in the presentation of meaningful amounts in the balance sheet.

The main reason that input values are the most relevant for the valuation of plant and equipment is that they may be assumed to represent the minimum value to the firm, at the date of acquisition, of the future services of the asset. The subjective output value of the asset should exceed the total input price if it is worth acquiring. However, there are several concepts and methods for computing the total input valuation of an asset. Although the historical acquisition cost is the most common method, it represents only one of several input valuation concepts.

Other input valuation concepts have been suggested and used from time to time to attain specific objectives or to obtain more meaningful measurements of current depreciation or more meaningful balance sheet valuations. The most important alternative to acquisition cost is replacement cost because it represents a *current* input valuation concept. Other current input values include appraisal value and fair value.

Historical input values

One of the main advantages of historical input values is that since they represent transaction prices paid by the firm, they are verifiable. It is also argued that they provide a consistent basis for the valuation of plant and equipment for each firm and among all firms. Whereas historical cost is generally agreed to be the most acceptable basis for the valuation of plant and equipment, we shall see in the following main section that accountants are not agreed on what should be included in cost. Variations of the historical input valuation method may be considered to be modifications of cost content, however, original cost (sometimes known as aboriginal cost) and prudent cost are so different in their application that they require separate discussion in this section.

Historical cost to the firm.[6]   Historical cost is defined as the aggregate price paid by the firm to acquire ownership and use of an asset, including all payments necessary to obtain the asset in the location and condition required for it to provide services in the production or other operations of the firm. If the price is to be paid at a later date under the terms of the contract, the cost of the asset should be the present discounted value of the contractual obligation. However, short delays in payment may be ignored because the discount is usually immaterial. When assets other than cash are given in exchange, the cost is the current value of the assets given up. However, the relevant current value of the asset exchanged is its current selling price, rather than its book value or other input value, because the asset is no longer being held for the value of its future services, if any.

The main advantage of historical cost is that it can be assumed to

---

[6] See also the discussion of historical cost in Chapter 13.

represent the value of the asset to the enterprise at the time of acquisition. But it must be noted that the term *value* is used here in a special sense. It is determined by market forces, or at least by a bargained arm's-length transaction; thus, it represents the market price of the asset at the time of acquisition. That is, cost represents the market value of the inputs at the time they are acquired.

Frequently, cost is rationalized as being the value to the going concern.[7] The firm is assumed to have a life long enough to be able to receive the service benefits to be provided by the asset. Thus, a liquidation value is assumed to be not relevant. But cost is a minimum value to the firm. It can be assumed that the firm would not have acquired the asset at its cost price if it did not feel that its future benefits would be equal to or greater than its cost. In the absence of changes in the expectations of the firm, the unallocated cost at the end of each successive period should continue to represent the minimum expected value to the firm.

The main disadvantage of historical cost is that it does not continue to reflect either the value of its future services or its current market price if economic conditions or prices change in subsequent periods. Even if prices remained constant, it is unlikely that the expectations regarding future services would remain constant. Expectations may change because of greater certainty as the remaining life of the asset becomes shorter or because of changes in technology or in economic conditions. Price changes affect the relevancy and comparability of historical costs applied to noncurrent assets to a greater extent than costs applied to current assets, because of the longer period from the date of acquisition to the average period of use. The longer this period is, the greater is the cumulative effect of price changes since the date of acquisition.

Prudent cost. Only those costs that would normally be paid for property by reasonably prudent management should be included in prudent costs. This concept has been used by public-utility regulators as a method of placing the public interest ahead of the interests of promoters, management, and stockholders. But the prudent cost concept is also applicable to the general valuation of plant and equipment. The costs to be allocated to the services of future periods should not include excessive costs representing costs of inefficiency and other losses incurred in the period of acquisition. However, the concept is difficult to apply because it requires the use of value judgments in determining what costs are excessive and what costs are required. In general, the costs intended to be incurred by management at the time of the initial commitment can be assumed to be based on prudent judgment unless evidence is clearly to the contrary. Unanticipated additional costs should be excluded because evidence is lacking that management would have agreed to incur these costs initially.

---

[7] See the discussion of *continuity* above, pp. 64–66.

Original cost. As used in public utility regulation, the term *original cost* refers to the cost of property to the firm first devoting it to public service. Any amounts paid in excess of the original cost less accumulated depreciation in the purchase by a second firm must be classified separately and disposed of by methods approved by the utility commission. But they cannot be charged to operating expenses, which may be used in the rate-making process. The logic behind this concept is that customers should not be required to pay rates that permit a utility to earn excessive profits by selling its property, whereas it could earn only a reasonable return by holding it. Because of the absence of competition in the selling of utility property, a buying firm would not be encouraged to pay the lowest price possible if it were permitted to pass whatever it paid along to its customers. There is considerable truth in this position during periods of stable prices; however, the equity involved becomes clouded when prices are rising rapidly.

While the original cost concept has some merit in the process of utility rate making, there is little merit to its application in the competitive sector of the economy. If the revenue of the firm is not related directly to the amount of its investment and the amount of operating expenses, there is an incentive to pay as little as possible for plant and equipment. The cost of secondhand equipment can be assumed to represent a bargained price and therefore the current market price of the asset. The cost paid by the original purchaser is no longer relevant. Exceptions are made, and the original cost is relevant, however, in cases where there is not an arm's-length transaction or where there is deemed to be a pooling of interest, rather than a purchase.

Current input values

Frequently, current input valuations have been suggested as a means of obtaining a better measurement of capital resources than can be obtained by using historical costs, particularly when the difference between the two is caused by relatively permanent changes in the structure of prices or changes in the price level, rather than by ephemeral changes caused by temporary shortages in supply. Current values are generally suggested as a means of obtaining current measurements of depreciation. However, it should be noted that the allocation of current costs is just as arbitrary as the allocation of historical costs. Therefore, current cost less accumulated depreciation to date may not permit better economic interpretation than historical costs. If the current costs are obtained from the used asset markets, however, economic interpretation is obtained. Under certain circumstances, an appraisal value may be an alternative. In the public-utility field, the concept of fair value has a special meaning, but basically it is an attempt to obtain current input values.

Current cost. The best measure of the current-cost of plant and equipment is the current market price of a similar used asset in the same condition and of the same age as the asset owned. It is, therefore, the price that would have to be paid for the asset if it were not already owned by the firm. Alternative methods of estimating current costs include (1) the acquisition cost of an identical new item purchased in current markets adjusted for depreciation to date, (2) the current price or reproduction cost of a new improved asset adjusted for technological differences and depreciation, and (3) historical cost restated by specific price-level indexes. These methods of estimating current cost and special problems relating to plant and equipment are discussed in Chapter 9 in addition to a discussion of the relative merits of the current-cost concept.

Appraisal value. The appraisal process is a method of estimating current costs or current values by systematic procedures. Whether an input or an output value is obtained depends on the objective of obtaining the appraisal. If an appraisal is obtained for the fixed assets of a going concern, it should represent an estimate of the current replacement or reproduction cost less depreciation to the date of the appraisal. Therefore, if the objective is properly stated, an appraisal value should represent the current input value of the asset to the firm. The main advantage of obtaining an appraisal value is that, since it is usually computed by someone outside of the firm, it is considered to be more objective than replacement costs computed by the firm itself. The main disadvantage of appraisals is that they can be obtained only at periodic intervals, and therefore they become out of date, just as do historical costs.

Fair value. The term *fair value* has been used primarily in the public-utility field to refer to the total amount on which the investors are entitled to earn a fair return. The courts have held that the computation of fair value should include all relevant facts, including the prudent past costs and reproduction costs.[8] Public-utility firms have claimed that it should include primarily replacement costs. Fair value, therefore, is not a specific valuation basis that can be applied to financial statements generally. It is, rather, a combination of valuation bases determined by the commissions and courts for a specific purpose.

DEFINITION AND CONTENT OF COST

Regardless of whether historical costs or current costs are used, the problem of what should be included in costs is present. When plant and equipment are acquired initially by purchase or when they are produced under contract, the initial cost is the total value of the resources given up to acquire the asset, install it at the proper location, and place it in the condition necessary for its intended service. Questions arise, however, regarding the measurement of the value of what is given up, the treat-

[8] J. Rhoads Foster and Bernard S. Rodey, *Public Utility Accounting* (Englewood Cliffs, N.J.: Prentice-Hall, 1951), pp. 27–29.

ment of expenditures made subsequent to the initial installation, and the computation of costs of assets constructed by the firm intending to use them. These problems affect not only the input value of the plant and equipment, but also the periodic depreciation and the amounts charged directly to current expense.

The content of initial cost

The initial cost of plant and equipment is definite only when a single asset is acquired for a cash price at the time that it becomes available for use. In a "basket" purchase, the total price may be definite, but the allocation to specific assets is a matter of judgment. The solution generally suggested is to allocate the total cost among the specific assets in the ratio of the appraised values of each or in the ratio of the book values carried by the previous owner. The former assumes that any saving or excess payment should apply proportionately to all of the assets acquired. The latter assumes that the excess (or deficiency) over the previous owner's book value should apply proportionately. Both are arbitrary allocations, but they have the advantage of at least providing an answer to an extremely difficult problem. There is no reason to believe that the initial value to the firm is necessarily in the ratio of the appraised values. But this method is preferred to the second method because the allocation on the basis of the book values to the previous owner results in a perpetuation of errors and differences arising from price changes during the period that the assets were held by the previous owner.

When nonmonetary assets must be destroyed and removal costs must be incurred to make space for the new asset being constructed, the costs of the new asset should include the liquidation selling price of the old asset plus the removal costs. These both represent costs that could have been avoided by not constructing the new asset; and it can be assumed that the value of the new asset is at least as great as its total cost—including the liquidation price and removal cost of the old asset net of the tax effect—or the new asset would not have been constructed.

In general, the initial cost should include the cash price plus freight and installation costs. Trade discounts and cash discounts should be deducted. When a cash discount is allowed but not taken, there is a question whether the invoice price represents the cost or whether the net price allowed should be recorded and the allowed cash discount shown as a loss. Some argue that the invoice price is the correct cost because it represents the amount actually paid. Others prefer to record the net price that could have been paid because it represents the prudent cost to the firm. Although the latter is logical, it leads to the conclusion that the lowest cost available should always be recorded because it is the prudent cost to the firm. In many cases, this is a reasonable conclusion, but there are frequently valid reasons why the lowest initial cost is not the most favorable price to the firm in the longer run.

Nonmonetary exchanges. *APB Opinion No. 29* states that, in general, a nonmonetary asset obtained by exchanging a nonmonetary asset for it should be recorded at the fair value of the asset given up.[9] This same concept applies to the acquisition of a nonmonetary asset in exchange for equity securities of the enterprise; that is, the asset should be recorded at the fair value of the stock given in exchange. However, in a nonreciprocal transfer[10] or when the fair value of the assets given up is not determinable within reasonable limits, the fair value of the nonmonetary asset received should be used as the basis of the acquired asset. In most cases it can be assumed that the exchange is the result of arm's-length negotiation, so that the fair value of the asset received is equal to the fair value of the asset surrendered. This use of fair value is consistent with the concept that nonmonetary assets should be recorded at their cost to the enterprise, which in this case is the fair value of the asset exchanged. Fair value is the amount that could be obtained for an asset in orderly liquidation; that is, it is the price that could be obtained for a similar asset of the same age and condition. It is also assumed that the exchange is equivalent to the sale of the one asset and the purchase of the other.

Two exceptions to the above rule are made by *APB Opinion No. 29*. One exception is that when neither the fair value of the asset surrendered nor the fair value of the asset received are determinable within reasonable limits, the transaction should not be recorded at fair value. Presumably, the asset received would be recorded in the amount of the carrying value of the asset given up. However, the carrying value is not likely to be a reasonable estimate of fair value either. It merely perpetuates an error in the valuation of one asset into the valuation of another. Although no measurement estimate may be ideal, an estimate of fair value based on the evidence available is better than no estimate.

A second exception is an exchange transaction that does not result in the culmination of the earning process. One type of exchange transaction is the exchange of assets held for sale in the same line of business. Another type is the exchange of nonmonetary productive assets of the same general type and that perform the same function. For these exchanges, if the fair value of the asset given up is less than the carrying value, the asset received should be recorded at fair value and a loss should be recorded. However, if the fair value is greater than the carrying value, *APB Opinion No. 29* states that the asset received should be recorded at the carrying amount of the asset transferred or the sum of the monetary consideration and the carrying amount of the asset given up. No gain should be recorded. In the case of monetary consideration received in addition to the nonmonetary asset, a pro rata share of the gain should be recorded and the asset received would be recorded at the carrying value of

---

[9] *AICPA Professional Standards*, para. 1041.18.

[10] A *nonreciprocal transfer* is defined as a transfer of assets in one direction, such as a contribution to the firm or a transfer of assets to stockholders.

the asset given up plus the gain recognized minus the monetary consideration received.

This second exception is also of doubtful validity. The purpose of the rule was to prevent firms from reporting gains when there was, in substance, no real change in the quantity or type of assets held. A lack of culmination of the earnings process is not a sufficient guide in this case because, as discussed in Chapter 8, earnings are reported at many different times before the final collection of cash from the sale of products. Furthermore, if the fair value is interpreted to mean the price in a market in which the nonmonetary asset can be bought and sold, the gain or loss resulting from the use of fair value represents a holding gain or loss, and not operating income. Since current costs are assumed to be relevant to users of accounting information, it would appear that fair value would be relevant in all exchanges and that all holding gains and losses should be recorded at the time of the transaction if not on a continuing basis.

Interest on construction. Assets constructed for a firm's own use present the problem of whether or not to capitalize interest on the funds invested during the time required to get them ready for their intended use. Four general proposals are these: (1) Capitalize no interest. (2) Capitalize only interest actually paid for funds borrowed for the specific purpose. (3) Capitalize interest on borrowed capital, but not exceeding the total interest paid by the firm. (4) Capitalize interest on all funds invested regardless of whether the funds are obtained from borrowing or from equity sources.

The first proposal, that no interest should be capitalized is based on the interpretation that it is not a cost of construction, but rather a financial charge. Since financial charges are generally debited to expense in the period that they are incurred, a deferral is assumed to result in the overstatement of current income during the period of construction or, if there are no sources of income during this period, the deferral would result in the failure to show a loss that is assumed to be real. Another basic argument is that interest could be avoided by financing the construction with stockholders' equity rather than with debt equity. But this does not eliminate the cost of using money; it merely shifts the burden to the stockholders and permits a deferral of actual payment since undeclared dividends are not contractual obligations of the firm.

The second proposal, to capitalize only the actual interest paid, is based on the assumption that interest is a cost of construction, but that only amounts actually paid represent costs. Charging interest on funds provided by the owners is assumed to result in unrealized income and the valuation of assets in excess of cost. Interest on ownership funds is rejected also because it is subjectively determined and its final realization is uncertain. But the uncertainty of the present value of the asset is the same, regardless of how it is financed. Thus, there is little justification for adding interest in one case and not in the other. It is difficult to argue that a building is more valuable simply because it was constructed with borrowed funds, rather than funds acquired by the sale of stock. Furthermore, since funds are generally commingled, there is no way of determining what proportion of the asset is financed by debt equity and what proportion by stockholders' equity, except in a new firm.

The third proposal avoids the problem of deciding how much of the investment was financed by debt and how much by equity. The entire investment is assumed to arise from debt, but with the limitation that the total interest capitalized should not exceed the total interest cost incurred during the period. The interest therefore represents an opportunity cost—the amount that could have been avoided by not borrowing or by using the funds to reduce outstanding debt. This is the approach selected by the FASB in *Statement No. 34*.[11] One of the advantages of this approach is that the interest capitalized represents a cost to the firm consistent with basic historical cost accounting methods. However, it does not lead to comparable results by different firms producing similar assets but with different capital structures. Also, there is an opportunity cost for using funds obtained from equity sources; the different treatment of debt and equity sources leads to inconsistent and noncomparable valuations.

The fourth proposal, that interest should be charged for all funds used is based primarily on the assumption that it represents an economic cost. From a logical point of view, this is the best procedure, although it is generally not acceptable in the United States. The total cost of the asset is the value of goods and services given up in order to acquire it. Interest represents the service value of the money invested in the acquisition of the asset before its use. Since this money is not used for current operations, but rather for future operations, a deferral of the implicit interest is appropriate. The argument that it should not be recorded because it represents unrealized income is tied more closely to the realization rules than to the basic principle that income should be reported during the entire period of production.

The main application of the third proposal is in the area of public utilities. The primary reason for its use in this situation arises from the fact that the income of a utility firm is regulated on the basis of its total capitalization. If a normal rate of return is permitted only on revenue-producing assets in use, there would be no opportunity for the firm to earn any income on investments necessary during the construction period before assets are placed in operation. The common practice of crediting the interest to interest expense, however, implies that the construction was financed with debt equity. As indicated above, generally no specific allocation can be made.

Overhead on self-constructed assets. When plant and equipment are constructed by the firm that will use the asset, the accumulation of costs is

---

[11] *AICPA Professional Standards,* Section 5155.

little different from the costing of manufactured products. Labor and material costs can usually be assigned directly to the fixed asset being constructed. The main difficulty comes in the allocation of joint overhead costs to the asset and to the normal production. At least four proposals are frequently made to handle this problem: (1) Assign no overhead to the fixed asset. (2) Assign only variable overhead. (3) Assign overhead equal to the amount that would have been assigned to the production that is curtailed because of the construction. (4) Assign a proportionate share of overhead to the construction on the basis of the procedure that is used for the assignment to normal production.

The first proposal, the assignment of no overhead to the asset constructed, is based on the assumption that overhead is primarily a fixed expense, that it is chargeable only to the normal operations of the current period, and that an allocation of overhead to the plant and equipment results in an overstatement of the net income for the current period. In general, the assumption that all overhead is fixed is false; the construction of fixed assets practically always results in some increase in total overhead costs. To the extent that this is true, the second proposal (to assign variable overhead costs to the constructed asset) is far superior to the first proposal. The variable or incremental costs are the minimum that should be assigned to the constructed asset. All of the variable costs are incurred to benefit future periods rather than current operations. However, if there is evidence that such costs result from errors or inefficiencies, they represent a loss to be recognized in the current period.

The arguments for charging only variable costs to the constructed asset are similar to the arguments for direct costing of inventories. The main argument is that the allocation of fixed overhead results in additional income in the current period because of the construction. That is, the net income would have been smaller if the overhead had been charged to current operations. This capitalization of fixed overhead appears to be inconsistent to those who advocate that income should reflect sales effort only and not production or construction effort. The second argument for direct costing—that there is no benefit to future periods if there is likely to be excess capacity in later years—is less convincing in this situation. Plant and equipment, unlike inventories, must be constructed in anticipation of many years' use. They cannot be constructed piecemeal only as the services are needed. Therefore, the failure to construct a needed fixed asset in the current year may result in a lower total income in the following year.

One of the strongest arguments for charging only variable costs to the construction is that if normal production and sales are not curtailed by the construction (the most likely situation), there is no evidence that management would have been willing to incur additional costs. Thus, there is no evidence that management considered the constructed asset to have a value greater than the variable costs incurred. But this is only the minimum value; the subjective value to the firm based on expectations of future benefits is probably much greater than the variable costs. Should accountants take the conservative position and include only those costs that represent clear evidence of future value, or should they exclude costs only when there is good evidence that they do not represent the value of future benefits?

The third proposal, to assign overhead equal to that which would have been allocated to curtailed production, seems plausible on the surface. The remaining overhead allocated to current production is no different than it would have been if the construction had not been undertaken, and it appears to represent service capacity that would have been utilized under normal conditions. But it is a cost based on what would have been allocated if an alternative course of action had been chosen. This is not a true opportunity cost because it is not based on a service value given up to obtain the construction.

The proposal to allocate a full share of all overhead to the constructed asset is an appropriate full-costing procedure. If the amount of overhead allocated to the constructed asset represents the input value of services actually used, the capitalization is logical on the basis that it represents the input value of future service benefits. If there is an expectation of future benefits in the form of either larger revenues or smaller costs, capitalization is assumed to provide a better matching of revenues and expenses in future periods and a better measurement of the net income from operations during the construction period. Whether there is excess capacity to handle the construction is not the determining factor in the capitalization decision, although the argument for capitalization is weaker if facilities are used that would otherwise have been idle. The important consideration is the expectation of future benefits.

Capital and revenue expenditures

Once plant and equipment are installed ready for use, the costs (historical or current) should be capitalized. All maintenance expenditures and anticipated or normal replacements of parts of the asset should also be charged to operations during the normal life of the asset. The total cost of obtaining a given amount of service from the asset during its expected life should, therefore, include the initial acquisition costs and all maintenance and normal replacement expenditures. How these costs should be allocated to the individual years or periods is a separate problem, which will be treated in the following chapter on depreciation; repairs, normal replacements, and depreciation are interrelated. The repairs and normal replacements should be charged to the expenses or operations of one or more years, depending on the depreciation method used and the distribution of the expected benefits to be received from the asset or other bases of allocation.

Certain types of expenditures, however, are incurred to obtain greater future benefits, rather than to maintain a given quantity of services.

Since these expenditures affect only future periods, they should be capitalized and allocated to only those future periods benefiting from them. This increase in future benefits can arise in one of three ways: (1) an increase in the life of the asset—that is, an increase in the number of years over which services will be obtained, (2) an increase in the quantity of services to be obtained in each year during the remaining life of the asset, and (3) an increase in the quality of the service to be obtained in each year during the remaining life of the asset. These increases in future benefits may arise from expenditures that may be classified as either additions, improvements and betterments, or major replacements.

There is little doubt that additions should be capitalized. By definition, additions increase the productive or service capacity of the plant and equipment. But, what about costs of tearing out parts of an old building to make room for the new facilities or to integrate the new with the old facilities? The answer depends upon the circumstances. Usually, if the need for the addition could not have been anticipated or if it was not practical to include it in the original construction, all costs of tearing out should be included in the cost of the addition; and none of the costs of the old facilities should be removed from the accounts except to the extent that these costs exceed the service value of the old asset before adding the new facilities. The additional services cannot be obtained without incurring these costs, and the construction of the addition at an earlier date, before the services were needed, would probably have added more to the total costs of the firm. But this does not mean that such costs should be capitalized in every case. It is possible that the necessity for tearing out and reconstruction is due to inefficiencies in planning or in construction. In these cases, such costs represent losses, rather than costs chargeable to operations.

Improvements and betterments are more difficult to define than additions, but the treatment is very similar. If the result is an increase in the quantity of service provided by the assets, it may, in fact, be difficult to distinguish improvements from additions. A truck may be improved by adding overload springs and a larger bed, thus permitting heavier payloads. The result may be little different from the acquisition of a trailer, which would be considered an addition. On the other hand, many improvements may result in an increase in the quality of the service provided by the asset. The installation of an improved lighting system in a factory building improves the services provided by the building. One of the greatest difficulties in the accounting for improvements arises when they are made as a part of a normal repair and replacement program. An attempt should be made to capitalize only those costs resulting in an increase in the future services of the asset, as opposed to the expenditures necessary to maintain a given level of services. To the extent that an improvement involves the replacement of major components, the discussion in the following paragraph is also relevant.

Major replacements are the most difficult to define and treat properly because the effect is similar to that of minor replacements and normal repairs. If an asset is made up of a single unit, a replacement involves the entire asset; in this case, the solution is simple—the old asset is retired and the replacement asset is recorded as a new asset. But in most cases, plant and equipment items are made up of several units that wear out at different rates. Recurring replacements of parts of the asset can be charged to operations in the years in which they occur because they are necessary to obtain the expected service life of the composite asset. No advantage would be obtained by capitalizing these items, because it is not possible to associate the outlays directly with the benefits to be received from them; and since all periods are charged with some replacement costs, an allocation to each period by a depreciation method would not necessarily improve the computation or meaning of net income. However, as we shall see in the next chapter, if the amount of repairs varies in a predictable manner, it can be taken into consideration in the selection of a depreciation method for allocating the initial cost of the asset in order to obtain desired results.

Major replacements that occur infrequently, however, need to be capitalized so that all periods will be charged with a portion of the replacement costs. This can be accomplished by including the costs of major replacements in the depreciation charge in one of two ways: (1) If the life of the asset is determined by the maximum life of the most durable major component, replacements should be charged to the asset or set up as a separate account and allocated over its separate life. (2) The depreciation can be computed on the basis of the average composite life of all of the components of the asset, in which case the replacements should be charged to the accumulated depreciation.

By using the maximum life of the most durable component, the replacements are not included in the depreciation based on the original life alone. Since they occur infrequently, it would not be correct to charge the entire amount of the replacement to operations in the year that it is made. The best solution in this case would be to set the amount up as a separate account (or debited to the main asset account) and allocate it over the period from the date of the replacement to the next replacement of the same component. For example, if major redecorating is necessary every three years, the redecorating costs can be capitalized and allocated over a three-year period. Care must be taken, however, to be sure that the original decorating costs are charged through depreciation to the first three years; if they are not, subsequent years will be charged twice with decorating costs, once through the depreciation based on the original total costs and a second time through the allocation of the redecorating costs.

The second treatment of major replacements bases the depreciation on the average composite life of all of the components. For example, if the maximum life of a building is 50 years, the average composite life could be 30 years. The original cost of the building would then be allocated on the basis of a 30-year life, but by carrying the depreciation over 50 years, the total depreciation for the 50 years would be equal to the original cost of the building plus the cost of all major repairs minus the ending scrap value. When replacements occur, they are then charged to the accumulated depreciation account. The effect is to increase the net carrying value at the time of the replacement without increasing the original cost basis. This procedure has the same effect as writing off the replaced asset and debiting the asset account with the replacement cost if two basic conditions exist: (1) the cost of the replacement must be the same amount as the original cost of the component that it replaces, and (2) the total cost of all replacements must have been anticipated with some fair degree of accuracy, so that the depreciation charge will be adequate to include all replacements.

Because of the extreme difficulty of finding allocation procedures with economic significance, the procedure of capitalizing costs and allocating them to subsequent periods is of dubious value from either a semantic point of view or from the point of view of relevance to the users. An alternative might be to classify and report the capital expenditures according to their recurring or nonrecurring behavior and the approximate remaining useful lives as well as the current market prices of the assets in used capital asset markets.

LEASES OF PLANT AND EQUIPMENT

Plant and equipment are occasionally rented or leased to other firms or individuals for short periods extending from a day to a year or more. In these cases, the lessor usually takes care of the maintenance of the property and pays the recurring expenses related to the property, such as taxes and insurance; and he must continually enter into new lease contracts during the life of the property. Therefore, the rental revenues are part of the operating revenues of the firm and the maintenance, tax, and insurance expenses, as well as depreciation on the leased property, should be included in the operating expenses. The reporting of the leased plant and equipment in financial statements is thus no different than the reporting of plant and equipment used in manufacturing or in providing services to customers. From the lessee's point of view, the lease results in rental expense, which is recorded as the services are received or when payment is made.

When the lease contract covers a long period and is noncancelable, the conditions are different, and alternative reporting methods may be desirable. Some leases may be in substance an installment sale and purchase of property, but most leases are more complex. Their basic characteristics include the transfer by the lessor to the lessee of the use of property for a period of time subject to certain restrictions, such as the withholding of specific tax advantages, and including certain special rights, such as the right of the lessee to purchase the property under favorable arrangements.

Because of the complex nature of most leases, it is not sufficient to assume that they represent in substance sale/purchase contracts and normal debt instruments. They should be reported in a way that describes their nature and characteristics as completely as possible, rather than attempting to incorporate all of the information in the traditional form of assets and liabilities. This is not to say that the measurement of the resources and obligations is not meaningful; it is if it captures only some of the relevant characteristics. Other characteristics, such as the patterns and terms of cash flows and purchase rights, should be described by other methods.

Leases having sale or financing and purchase characteristics

Among the many different types of leases that have basic financing and purchase characteristics is the obvious case in which a financing company finances the acquisition of equipment by a manufacturer's customer. The finance company (the equity holder) pays the manufacturer for the equipment in exchange for title to it and receives an installment note from the customer, who receives the right to use the property for what may be almost the entire life of the asset. If the manufacturer finances the lease, sale characteristics are also present in the lease transaction.

The characteristics of ownership of plant and equipment present in the lease include the right of the lessee to use the property during the life of the lease with the obligation to pay generally a fixed price in the form of installments. Thus, the lessee has a nonmonetary asset in the form of a right to receive benefits from the use of the plant and equipment. The lessor, even though it holds the equity in the property, has a receivable that is a monetary asset representing the right to receive a specified number of dollars over the life of the contract. However, the rights held by the lessee and the receivable of the lessor differ from those arising from usual sale/purchase transactions in several respects. Either the lessor or the lessee may be required to provide for the maintenance of the equipment and pay for the expenses, such as taxes and insurance, relating to the property leased. The residual equity is held by the lessor rather than by the lessee who receives the benefits, although it may be transferred to the lessee at the end of the contract or during the lease period under option terms. In addition, special tax benefits may accrue to the lessor, rather than to the lessee who holds the property.

Although it is difficult to determine when sufficient purchase characteristics exist to require capitalization of the lease by the lessee, the FASB has suggested some criteria for determining when the lease should be classified as a capital lease from the point of view of the lessee.[12] At least one of the following should be present: (1) The property title will be transferred to the lessee by the end of the lease term or under a bargain

---

[12] *AICPA Professional Standards,* para. 4053.007.

purchase option. (2) The term of the lease is at least 75 percent of the economic life of the property, unless the lease term begins within the last 25 percent of this life. (3) At the inception of the lease, the present value of the minimum lease payments (excluding executory costs) equals or exceeds 90 percent of the fair value of the leased property to the lessor (reduced by any related investment credit to be used by the lessor). As with the second criterion, this criterion is not relevant if the lease term begins within the last 25 percent of the life of the property. These three criteria are applied under the assumption that the basic characteristics of a purchase include the transfer to the purchaser by the seller of the risks and benefits to be obtained from owning and using the property during its expected life, including the obligation to pay for the benefits. The only basic criterion inherent in the above cases is that if the unguaranteed residual value is relatively small, the risks and benefits of ownership are transferred and, therefore, the lease should be capitalized. Thus, the determination of when a lease transfers a sufficient amount of the risks and benefits to classify it as a capital lease can only be based on an arbitrary decision.

From the point of view of the lessor, the FASB used the same criteria described above in determining when a lease should be classified as a sales-type lease or a direct financing lease. However, two additional criteria are required: (1) The collection of the minimum lease payments should be reasonably predictable. (2) The unreimbursable costs to be incurred by the lessor under the lease other than for insurance, maintenance, and taxes should be measurable and not be surrounded by important uncertainties. Therefore, in addition to classifying the lease according to whether or not it transfers risks and benefits of ownership, the classification is also determined by the measurability of the net receivable to the lessor.

The above criteria for the classification of a lease (from the viewpoint of the lessee) emphasize the characteristics of the transference of risks and benefits of owning property, rather than the transfer of property rights (which is a legal question) or whether or not the lease is essentially equivalent to an installment purchase of property. The basic criticism of these criteria is that they still emphasize the similarities to purchased property, rather than recognizing that a lease has characteristics of its own. It is not necessary that all new forms of economic relationships be molded to fit the traditional accounting classifications. A similar criticism applies to the additional criteria that apply to the classification of the lease as a sales-type lease or a direct financing lease by the lessor. It is not uncommon to defer the reporting of a sale (and the presentation of the receivable) until there is a relative degree of certainty regarding the collectibility of the receivable. However, the existence of uncertainty should not determine the classification of the lease and whether or not a receivable exists. Instead, the degree of uncertainty should be reported by presenting a range of measurements or by the use of probabilities.

Leases reported by the lessee. The classification of the lease as a capital lease requires that the lessee report in the financial statements both and asset and a liability. The FASB states that the amount capitalized at the inception of the lease should be the sum of the present value of the minimum lease payments after deducting the amounts that represent expenses, such as maintenance, insurance, and taxes (executory costs); the present value of the amount to be paid in a bargain purchase option, if any,[13] should be included in the minimum lease payments. Thus the amount to be capitalized represents the present value of the property rights in the lease.[14]

The distinction between that portion of the lease payments that represents the acquisition of property rights and that portion that represents the purchase of periodic services is taken from an analogy with the ownership of property. The ownership rights generally include the rights to hold, use, and dispose of property within certain restrictions of the law and the rights of others. A long-term noncancelable lease has most of these rights of ownership with the exception of disposal; but, in many cases, the lessee can purchase ownership rights for a nominal sum at the termination of the lease. When property is owned, the value of the property rights is capitalized by setting up an asset equal to its cost when acquired. However, the cost of maintenance and periodic payments for insurance and taxes are charged to expense only as they are incurred or accrued. No asset or obligation is generally shown in the balance sheet for the cost of services and other expenditures necessary to provide proper use of the property during its lifetime. Similarly, only the property rights being acquired under the terms of a lease should be capitalized. That is, where the terms of the lease require the lessor to provide necessary repairs and to pay taxes, insurance, and other costs of making the property available and useful to the lessee, that portion of the periodic lease payments representing the payment for these services should be excluded from the amount capitalized in the balance sheet. The payments for these items should be recorded as expenses in each period of payment, as with owned property.

One of the advantages of capitalization of the property rights inherent in lease contracts is that it presents a clearer picture in the financial statements of the rights and obligations of the firm. It also permits comparability with firms that own their property and with other firms with long-term leases. The capitalization, however, does not eliminate the necessity for additional disclosure, by footnote or otherwise, of the annual payment and other material terms of the lease contract. Finally, a major advantage of capitalization is that it permits a separation of the property rights and the lease obligations. Thus, the value of the property can be

---

[13] Ibid., para. 4053.005.

[14] See John H. Myers, "Reporting of Leases in Financial Statements," *Accounting Research Study No.* 4 (AICPA, 1962), p. 38.

amortized independently of the timing of the contractual payments, in a manner similar to the depreciation of owned plant and equipment.

Two of the major problems of capitalization of the property rights are (1) the difficulty in separating that portion of the rentals considered to be payment for property rights and that considered to be payment for services yet to be performed and (2) the selection of a proper rate of interest for capitalization. The value of the property rights can be estimated either by estimating the value of the property without the additional services provided and subtracting the discounted value of the property at the termination of the lease, or by estimating the value or cost of the services to be provided by the lessor annually. In the latter method, the annual payment for the property rights can be estimated by subtracting the value of the annual services from the total annual lease payment. The FASB states that the discount rate should be the incremental borrowing rate available to the firm currently for long-term credit with similar risks and terms.[15] This rate places an emphasis on the measurement of the liability, which in turn determines the amount that represents the historical cost of the asset.

This capitalization procedure can be criticized for two basic reasons: (1) The capitalization of only the minimum lease payments for the benefits from ownership of property assumes that the lease is directly comparable to the owning of property. As stated above, instead of trying to mold the reporting of the lease into the traditional property classification, it would be better to recognize that the lease has individual characteristics. These characteristics might be captured better by capitalizing all expected payments, not just the amounts that represent property rights. (2) The use of the incremental borrowing rate at the inception of the lease is based on the historical cost tradition. This is one situation in which the current value can be computed quite easily each year by using the current incremental rate and the expected remaining payments.

Leases reported by lessors. From the point of view of the lessor, a lease may be either a direct financing lease or a sales-type lease. In the direct financing lease, the finance or leasing company holds a secured installment note receivable. The FASB states that this receivable should be computed initially in the same way that the amount of the capital lease is computed for the lessee, with the exception that the amounts of minimum lease payments are not discounted and the residual value is included. However, this receivable is reduced by what is called unearned income so that the net amount represents the cost or carrying value of the asset plus any initial direct costs associated with the lease. A problem arises with the inclusion of the residual value because, if it is not guaran-

---

[15] The implicit rate used by the lessor should be used if it is known and is less than the incremental borrowing rate.

teed by the lessee, it is more in the nature of a nonmonetary asset than a receivable.[16]

In the above situation, the effective rate of discount is the earning rate or internal rate of return, which is the rate that would equate the cash flows to be received under the contract with the cost of the asset.[17] The total income to the finance company over the life of the lease is the excess of the aggregate rentals over the cost of the asset less the residual value. According to the direct financing method, this income is reported by the lessor over the life of the lease in proportion to the amounts of unrecovered investment in each period. Thus, reported income from the contract would be decreasing over the life of the lease; and if the cash receipts are constant in amount, a decreasing amount of each installment would be reported as income and an increasing amount would be reported as reduction of the receivable. Note that the total gross income from the lease agreement is assumed to represent interest on the investment; none is associated with the precontract arrangements, the signing of the contract, or the supervision and accounting for the collections, which may be constant over the life of the lease. However, since the investment of the funds may be a crucial function of the finance company, an allocation of the gross income to other functions would not improve the reporting of income, particularly since such allocations would need to be arbitrary.

Sales-type leases reported by the lessor.   When manufacturers use the leasing method to report the financing of their own products transferred to customers under long-term lease contracts, income should be reported separately for the two basic functions: (1) the manufacture and sale of the product and (2) the investment in the lease contract during the life of the lease. The manufacturing revenues can be reported at the time of signing the lease by reporting the value of the lease contract receivable equal to the normal selling price of the product. The FASB states that the manufacturing revenues should be equal to the discounted amount of the future minimum lease payments (net of executory expenses) using the rate implicit in the lease. However, the implicit rate cannot be known without estimating the sales price. If a normal sales price is not well established or readily available, the lessor has considerable discretion regarding the amount to be reported as gross profit from sales and the amount to be reported as interest income. But it does not necessarily result in poor information because any procedure would represent an arbitrary allocation of the gross rental income between the manufacturing and investment functions.

---

[16] The FASB does not require that reductions in the estimated residual value be reported currently during the term of the lease.

[17] This is so because the "unearned income" is amortized to income over the lease term in proportion to the remaining balance of the receivable.

The FASB does not specifically forbid the use of the installment method of reporting the income from manufacturing and selling, but the denial of such a procedure is implied. For, if the conditions that would normally support the use of the installment method do exist, it is recommended that the lease be classified as an operating lease. These conditions would include (1) unpredictable credit risks and (2) material uncertainties regarding the amount of additional costs relating to the lease.

The operating lease. For the lessee, a long-term lease is classified as an operating lease if it does not meet the criteria for a capital lease. For the lessor, the lease is an operating lease if it does not meet the criteria for direct financing leases or sales-type leases. That is, if the lease does not have the basic characteristics of a purchase or a sale/financing transaction, it is assumed that the lease is a long-term executory rental contract. Thus, the rental payments would normally represent rent expense to the lessee. However, the FASB states that if the payments are not constant, the rental expense should be recognized on a straight-line basis unless some other method can be justified. But, like depreciation, no allocation method can be defended on economic grounds alone, and information is lacking to justify any allocation method on the basis of behavioral effects.

For the lessor, the FASB has recommended that the asset be classified as plant and equipment, that it be valued at cost or cost less accumulated depreciation, and that the rental receipts be reported as the gross revenues unless they depart radically from a straight-line basis or from the economic usefulness of the property in each period. The result is that the cash basis of reporting is used for the rental receipts and most operating expenses except depreciation and initial indirect costs, which should be allocated over the life of the lease if material.

Leveraged leases

In some respects many two-party leases are leveraged leases. That is, if the lessor is entitled to the investment tax credit and accelerated depreciation on the property being leased, the net cash flows (including the effects on tax payments) will be larger in the early years of the lease and less in later years, giving the lessor an effective leverage in increasing the rate of return on investment. When a substantial part of the financing is provided by a long-term creditor in the form of nonrecourse debt, the leverage to the lessor is increased substantially. The net effect is that the net cash flows and net investment value each have three phases. The cash flows are positive and decreasing during the initial period and then become negative and increasing until end of the lease life, at which time a positive amount is received from the sale of the residual asset value. The net investment is positive and decreasing during an initial period, then becomes negative, and again turns positive and increasing until it reaches the residual value of the asset at the end of the lease.

The FASB states that the income from the lease should be recognized on the basis of the net investment and the implicit rate of return during the years when the net investment is positive. Although secondary earnings from the investment of funds held temporarily are also a part of the economic advantages of a leveraged lease to the lessor, the FASB stated that these earnings should be reported as they occur. The Board supported this position on the basis of a lack of support for the anticipation of future interest on temporarily held funds in present generally accepted accounting principles.

Ignoring the secondary earnings, the effect of the above procedures is to report a constant rate of return on the book value of the net investment during the years when it is positive and no return when it is negative. Because a constant implicit rate is used instead of an opportunity rate, the net investment in any year represents the unallocated portion of the original computed value of the investment. A current value of the investment is not presented except at the inception of the lease. An exception is made when a revision of the basic assumptions results in a reduction of the net investment balance; in this case, the net investment balance is reduced and a loss is reported. This is similar to the lower-of-cost-or-market rule. Therefore, it is not likely that the reported book value of the lease investment can necessarily be interpreted as a market value or as a value to the firm.

Capitalization of all long-term noncancelable commitments

An alternative approach to the above methods of handling long-term leases is to consider them a part of the broader problem of long-term noncancelable commitments. Whenever a firm enters into a long-term contract to acquire goods or services and to make appropriate payment, certain specific rights and obligations arise. If these goods and services are acquired on a year-to-year basis or under contracts that are cancelable on short notice, the rights and obligations are generally not material regarding their effect on the balance sheet, and it is appropriate to record the transactions when the goods and services are received or accrued or when payment is made. No capitalization is necessary. But, if the contract is noncancelable by either party and if each has a valid and material claim against the other, the contract should be capitalized, and the discounted value of both the rights and obligations should be disclosed.

While this position does not have the support of currently accepted accounting practice, it does have considerable merit in its favor. A contract to purchase a given quantity of goods gives rise to a liability just as much as an obligation to pay for goods already acquired. The main difference is that in the first case the firm has an obligation to pay for goods when they are received, but in the latter case the obligation is to pay for goods that have already been received. In the case of the noncancelable contract to purchase, there is not an unconditional right of offset. The purchasing firm has an obligation to pay for the merchandise to be acquired under the contract, even though it should decide later that the goods are not wanted. The going-concern postulate assumes that the firm intends to carry out its commitments, and it also assumes that other firms will normally carry out theirs. The nature of the obligation is not different simply because of a possible default on the part of the seller. Of course, if the seller does default, a right of unconditional offset does arise and the obligation to pay for the unperformed part of the contract may be canceled. But default is not the normal pattern, and the best expectation is that both sides of the contract will be carried out.

The asset arising from the long-term commitment is the right to receive goods or services, and this claim should be recorded on the basis of the discounted amount of its expected values. As with receivables, the value of the claim depends on the expectations that they will materialize. The possibility of default is the exceptional case rather than the rule, and this possibility should be taken into consideration only in the determination of the valuation of the rights and obligations.

The distinction between long-term and short-term obligations is not important in the decision whether or not to capitalize the rights and obligations. The important criterion is the materiality of the discounted value. But there are many other considerations that must be studied thoroughly before a definite broad principle of capitalization can be established. Employment contracts probably should not be capitalized because they are usually cancelable by the employee. Other types of contracts may also be cancelable with a penalty. Capitalization should be necessary only if the penalty is sufficient to act as a deterrent to unilateral default.

In general, the arguments for capitalization of long-term commitments other than leases are not as compelling as the arguments for capitalization of long-term leases. The similarity to property rights is not generally present. The obligation is not generally an alternative to other forms of financing. And the asset or right received is not generally amortized over its useful life. But one advantage of capitalization of long-term commitments in general is that the valuation of the rights can then be treated separately from the valuation of the obligations. A contract to purchase a given quantity of merchandise over a long period of time at a predetermined price results in an obligation that is monetary in nature but rights or claims that are nonmonetary. If the value of the goods to be acquired should change materially, capitalization would permit showing the valuation of the asset differently from the valuation of the liability. Therefore, holding gains and losses could be recorded conveniently. The current practice of recording losses on long-term commitments requires setting up a partial liability or a reserve. Capitalization permits the valuation of the asset and the valuation of the liability to be treated separately.

The application of this general principle to long-term leases has the effect of extending the amount to be capitalized. The principle does not limit the amount to the property rights. If the lease requires a fixed payment that is noncancelable, the entire amount should be capitalized regardless of whether it represents payment for property rights or for additional services, including repairs, maintenance, and taxes, and other services related to the use of the property. On the other hand, if the lessee is required to take care of the maintenance and repairs and pay the property taxes and insurance, these amounts should also be capitalized as long-term commitments if they require unconditional payments regardless of whether or not the property is used. But payments for utilities and other related costs should not be capitalized if they can be avoided by not using the property.

One of the main arguments against the capitalization of long-term commitments other than long-term leases is that since capitalization is not a common practice in this case, there is no lack of comparability among firms. But, in the case of long-term leases, there is a lack of comparability, because those firms that own property do show the assets and related obligations, and those that lease the property traditionally have failed to show either the asset or the liability in the balance sheet. Thus, many financial ratios computed from the statements of property owners cannot be compared with similar ratios computed from the statements of firms that lease property. It is also claimed that, generally, the payments under long-term commitments other than leases are more related to the associated expenses than is generally the case with long-term leases. It may also be argued that the reporting of current payments better discloses the actual cash flows of the firm. However, the capitalization of noncancelable commitments should not preclude the disclosure in financial statements of current cash payments and the amount and timing of future cash requirements under the contracts.

Disclosure of leases

It is frequently argued that the capitalization of leases, particularly operating leases, by lessees presents misleading information because the lease obligation is different from other debt instruments and because the reporting of the obligation in the balance sheet would distort the traditional debt ratios and take away the advantages of "off balance sheet financing." However, it can equally be argued that the omission of the lease obligation also results in misleading information. In order to avoid misleading information, the FASB stated that the minimum lease rental payments for operating leases should be disclosed in notes to financial statements in the aggregate and for each of the succeeding five years. Additional lease payments contingent on the amount of use or total revenue or other activity should be presented for the current past year with a disclosure of the basic characteristics relating to contingent lease rentals.

This disclosure of information relating to cash flows is at least an attempt to meet the assumed needs of investors and creditors. How well these needs are met should await the results of empirical research.[18]

SELECTED ADDITIONAL READING

Bases of valuation of plant and equipment

Beidelman, Carl R. "Valuation of Used Capital Assets." *Studies in Accounting Research No. 7.* AAA, 1973.

McKeown, James C. "Comparative Application of Market and Cost Based Accounting Models." *Journal of Accounting Research,* Spring 1973, particularly pp. 65–78.

NAA Committee on Management Accounting Practices. "Fixed Asset Accounting: The Capitalization of Costs." *CPA Journal,* March 1973, pp. 193–207.

Snavely, Howard J. "Current Cost for Long-Lived Assets: A Critical View," *Accounting Review,* April 1969, pp. 344–53.

Nonmonetary exchanges

Capettini, Robert, and **Thomas E. King.** "Exchange of Nonmonetary Assets: Some Changes." *Accounting Review,* January 1976, pp. 142–47.

Interest on construction

Anthony, Robert N. *Accounting for the Cost of Interest,* Lexington, Mass.: Lexington Books, 1975.

Bierman, Harold, Jr., and **Thomas R. Dyckman,** "Accounting for Interest During Construction." *Accounting and Business Research,* Autumn 1979, pp. 267–72.

Frazer, Robert E., and **Richard C. Ransom.** "Is Interest During Construction Funny Money?" *Public Utilities Fortnightly,* December 21, 1972, pp. 20–27.

Long-term leases

Abdel-khalik, A. Rashad; Robert B. Thompson; and **Robert E. Taylor.** "The Impact of Reporting Leases off the Balance Sheet on Bond Risk Premiums: Two Exploratory Studies." *Economic Consequences of Financial Accounting Standards.* FASB, 1978, pp. 103–55.

Bowman, Robert G. "The Debt Equivalence of Leases: An Empirical Investigation." *Accounting Review,* April 1980, pp. 237–53.

Coughlan, John W. "Regulation, Rents and Residuals." *Journal of Accountancy,* February 1980, pp. 58–66.

---

[18] In a recent research project, Elam concluded that his research did not support the hypothesis that capitalization of leases will increase the predictability of firm bankruptcy. Rick Elam, "The Effect of Lease Data on the Predictive Ability of Financial Ratios," *Accounting Review,* January 1975, pp. 25–43.

DeFliese, Philip L. "Accounting for Leases: A Broader Perspective." *Financial Executive,* July 1974, pp. 14–23.

Elam, Rick. "Effect of Lease Data on the Predictive Ability of Financial Ratios." *Accounting Review,* January 1975, pp. 25–43.

Financial Accounting Standards Board. "Accounting for Leases," *Statement No. 13. AICPA Professional Standards,* Section 405. See also *Statements Nos. 17* and *23* (Sections 4054 and 4056).

Finnerty, Joseph F.; Rick N. Fitzsimmons; and **Thomas W. Oliver.** "Lease Capitalization and Systematic Risk." *Accounting Review,* October 1980, pp. 631–39.

Hawkins, David, and **Mary M. Wehle.** *Accounting for Leases.* New York: Financial Executives Research Foundation, 1973.

Myers, John H. "Reporting of Leases in Financial Statements." *Accounting Research Study No. 4.* AICPA, 1962, pp. 63–67.

Ro, Byung T. "The Disclosure of Capitalized Lease Information and Stock Prices." *Journal of Accounting Research,* Autumn 1978, pp. 315–40.

Wyatt, Arthur R. "Leases *Should* Be Capitalized." *CPA Journal,* September 1974, pp. 35–38.

Leveraged leases

Anton, Hector R. "Leveraged Leases—A Marriage of Economics, Taxation and Accounting." In *D. R. Scott Memorial Lectures in Accountancy,* vol. 6. Edited by Alfred R. Roberts. Columbia: University of Missouri, 1974, pp. 81–113.

Bullock, Clayton L. "Accounting Conventions and Economic Reality." *CPA Journal,* July 1974, pp. 19–24.

Shanno, David F., and **Roman L. Weil.** "The Separate Phases Method of Accounting for Leveraged Leases: Properties of the Allocating Rate and an Algorithm for Finding it." *Journal of Accounting Research,* Autumn 1976, pp. 348–56.

CHAPTER 15

DEPRECIATION

In the traditional accounting structure, depreciation refers to the process of allocating the initial (or restated) input valuation (cost or other basis) of plant and equipment to the several periods expected to benefit from their acquisition and use. As stated in Chapter 8, allocation in accounting is the process of partitioning a set or valuation amount and the assignment of the resulting subsets to separate classifications or periods of time. The main emphasis of the depreciation process is generally on the computation of the periodic charge to be allocated to expense or to the cost of the product to be "matched" with the revenues reported in each period. Seldom is the balance sheet valuation given much attention, except in consideration of the total amount to be allocated to future periods.

The most serious difficulty with depreciation is that no allocation method is fully defensible.[1] That is, it is not possible to defend one allocation method as being superior to all others. An additional difficulty is that before a pattern or formula for allocating the original or restated valuation (less scrap value) to expense or production costs can be applied, certain estimates must be made, including the following: (1) the valuation (cost or other basis) of the asset when acquired or a restatement of this at a subsequent date, (2) the expected service life of the asset, and (3) the scrap value or liquidation value at the end of the service life. The last two (and in some cases the first) of these are *ex ante* measurements of uncertain future values. Although the estimates may be based on multiple probabilities, their reduction to single values is at best a difficult problem. The conventional application of depreciation methods, however, is static because it generally assumes that these estimates remain constant over time. Therefore, because of the difficulties involved in making these estimates (particularly where the uncertainties are high) and because of the failure to make adjustments over time, it is possible that no allocation procedure, even if it could be logically defended, would be relevant for income reporting.

Regardless of the above difficulties, researchers and writers on the subject of depreciation frequently attempt to defend depreciation procedures on the basis of economic interpretation or on behavioral grounds primarily relating to the relevance of the depreciation figures for decision

---

[1] See Arthur L. Thomas, "The Allocation Problem: Part Two," *Studies in Accounting Research No. 9* (AAA, 1974), p. 2.

making. Real-world interpretation is frequently assumed to be derived from the following general concepts: (1) a measurement of the decline in the value of the asset (restated for general or specific price changes) is assumed to represent depreciation, and (2) depreciation is assumed to be an allocation of the cost or other basis according to the benefits expected to be received in each period. Attempts to defend depreciation on behavioral grounds include estimation theory and purpose utility. This chapter evaluates the assumed logic of alternative depreciation methods and determines to what extent, if at all, the alternative methods are defensible. If, all allocation methods are arbitrary and do not result in measurements that can be defended within reasonable limits, depreciation should be abandoned, and alternative reporting methods should be substituted.

DEFINITIONS OF *DEPRECIATION*

The most commonly accepted definition of *depreciation* is that it is a systematic and rational method of allocating costs to periods in which benefits are received. Notice that this definition is a static concept. The initial cost or other value is not changed during the life of the asset; the sum of all depreciation charges is equal to the initial value less any salvage value. The definition does not suggest how the cost or other value should be distributed; it is sufficient that the allocation procedure be systematic and rational. The requirement that it be rational probably means that it should be reasonably related to the expected benefits in each case.

Statement of Financial Accounting Concepts No. 3 attempts to give semantic interpretation to the term *depreciation* by stating that wear and tear from use is a major cause of depreciation.[2] It states further, however, that wear and tear cannot normally be measured and that usually there is no traceable relationship between the allocations and specific revenues or the periods to which they are charged. *Depreciation* is, therefore, defined as the systematic and rational allocation of costs to periods in which the assets are assumed to be used. However, the causal relationship cannot be specifically identified and the relationship to benefits is only indirect. The possible semantic interpretation of *depreciation* and the possible relationships to benefits are discussed in the following paragraphs.

Decline in service potential

The American Accounting Association Committee on Concepts and Standards definition of *depreciation* leads to the same conclusions as the FASB definition, but it is based on a measure of asset valuation (the service potential), rather than on an allocation of cost. The Committee asserted that depreciation represents the decline in service potential of long-term

---

[2] *AICPA Professional Standards,* para. 1230.89.

assets and that the decline in service potential may be the result of physical deterioration, consumption through use, or loss in economic value because of obsolescence or change in demand.[3] Under this definition, the initial cost of an asset is assumed to represent the value of a storehouse of services that can be released over the life of the asset. Whenever a portion of these services expires through use or other *cause,* the quantity of service potential declines; and a portion of the cost of the asset should be transferred to an expense, another asset, or a loss account. This definition is also a static concept because it is based on an allocation of cost to each quantity of potential service of the asset. But it is less static than the FASB definition because it recognizes that the loss in service potential may be irregular and may be subject to many factors that cannot be foreseen when the asset is acquired. The FASB definition assumes that the conditions anticipated at the time of acquisition will continue without material change over the expected life of the asset. However, both definitions are based on single-valued expectations regarding the total expected quantity of potential service or the expected life of the asset.

The AAA Committee on Concepts and Standards—Long-Lived Assets also defined the term as an expiration of service potential of the asset. But the committee stated further that "depreciation must be based on the current cost of restoring the service potential consumed during the period."[4] This definition is based on a decline in the value (the service potential) of the asset, but it is also related to the capital maintenance concept.

The maintenance of capital

A broader concept of depreciation is that income emerges only if the invested capital at the end of a period exceeds the invested capital at the beginning (assuming no capital transactions or dividend payments during the period). The definitions of the FASB, the AAA statement, and the AAA committee all apply the maintenance concept, but the concept of capital to be maintained is slightly different in each case. Under the FASB definition, it is the original monetary investment that should be maintained (financial capital maintenance) at least by the end of the asset's life; recovery of original cost may be assumed to occur gradually over the life of the asset in any rational manner. The AAA definition assumes that it is the service potential or its equivalent in terms of the original cost of services used that should be maintained. The AAA committee definition emphasizes the maintenance of operating capacity or physical capital maintenance. In none of the cases, however, is it necessary that actual

---

[3] AAA Committee on Accounting Concepts and Standards, *Accounting and Reporting Standards for Corporate Financial Statements and Preceding Statements and Supplements* (AAA, 1957), pp. 4, 6.

[4] Committee on Concepts and Standards—Long-Lived Assets, AAA, "Accounting for Land, Buildings, and Equipment," supplementary statement No. 1, *Accounting Review* 39 (July 1964): 696.

replacement or equivalent replacement be made; the failure to maintain physical capital or dollar capital because of a loss or for other reasons does not deny the existence of the depreciation.

The advantage of the capital maintenance concept is that it permits the recognition of changes in the value of the dollar and changes in specific replacement values. The capital to be maintained can be interpreted to be the original investment expressed in terms of a common dollar, or it can be expressed in terms of the current replacement values at the beginning or end of the accounting period.

The main disadvantage of the capital maintenance concept is that it results in a failure to permit a separation of operating income from extraordinary gains and losses. Unless other criteria are introduced, it does not provide a basis for determining the normal operating depreciation separately from the abnormal losses of service potential. Also, it requires a further definition of what is meant by capital maintenance. Therefore, it is not a precise definition that can be used as a specific guide; rather, it is only a broad guide subject to further interpretation.

The current cost of services consumed

The FASB definition of depreciation is similar to the definition suggested by Sprouse and Moonitz in *AICPA Accounting Research Study No. 3*, but the latter suggested that current replacement costs are more significant than historical costs, particularly when some significant event occurs in the organization of the firm. Depreciation is assumed to represent an allocation of current costs, and the depreciation charge for a specific period is the current cost of the services consumed in that period.

The advantages and disadvantages of current costs are discussed in Chapter 9. However, it should be kept in mind that nonmonetary assets by their very nature represent large blocks of potential services. The use of current costs does not alleviate the problem of making allocations to specific periods.

CONCEPTS OF DEPRECIATION

The definition of *depreciation* as a systematic and rational allocation of costs is a syntactical definition only. Attempts to give semantic interpretation to the word have either attempted to explain it in terms of its *cause* or in terms of the *benefits*. The cause is usually specified as decline in asset value resulting from wear and tear and obsolescence of an asset on its "irresistible march to the junk heap."[5] The benefit is usually discussed in terms of the association of the use of the asset with cash flows or net

---

[5] Henry Rand Hatfield, *Modern Accounting* (New York: Appleton-Century-Crofts, 1919), p. 121.

revenue contributions. A behavioral approach has also been suggested, which stresses the usefulness of the reported allocations.

By far the most common basis used in attempts to defend alternative depreciation concepts under all three approaches is the distribution of benefits expected to be received by using an asset over time (its net revenue contribution each period). However, the determination of net revenue contributions is the result of two allocation processes. First, the total revenues of the firm must be allocated to specific periods of time. Second, the total revenues of each period must be allocated to specific assets or asset classes. But it is rarely possible to measure either the *ex ante* or *ex post* net revenue contributions in the several periods during the use of an asset because of the many interactions of the production functions or inputs in the production and other operating processes of a firm. Most defenses of depreciation methods merely assume the plausibility of certain patterns and amounts of net revenue contributions. The association of these net revenue contributions to real-world observations has been made only in very general terms or indirectly by observing market prices of used assets.

The support for depreciation methods based upon the net revenue contribution concept is usually couched in terms of the capital budgeting solution for the evaluation and selection of investment projects. The capital budgeting solution, however, generally requires the estimation of marginal cash flows to be received each period from making the investment compared with the alternative of not investing. If several investments in different assets or asset groups are to be made simultaneously, the marginal contributions must be made sequentially, although the amount and distribution of the contributions may depend upon the order in which they are selected. The expected cash flow contributions may result from expected increases in total revenues of the firm or from expected cost savings, such as decreases in labor or fuel costs, or they may represent a combination of expected revenue increases and cost savings. When allocations are proposed on the basis of matching cost or other valuations of the assets with expected benefits, the expected effect on cash flows must be adjusted to the accrual basis, so that depreciation will be allocated on the basis of the periods in which the expected increased revenues or cost savings will be reported in the income statement.[6] Thus, in these cases, the term *net revenue contribution* is more appropriate than the cash flow concepts applied in capital budgeting solutions.

Although most of the depreciation concepts proposed are based in some way upon the expected net revenue contribution of the specific items of plant and equipment, they can be classified generally as concepts that either (1) measure depreciation as the decline in the value of the asset or (2) measure the amount of cost (or other basis) to be allocated to each

---

[6] See, for example, Harold Bierman, Jr., "A Further Study of Depreciation," *Accounting Review* 41 (April 1966): 271–74.

period on the assumption that there is a matching of the input values with the expected revenues or net revenue contribution. The decline in the value of the asset may be measured in terms of the discounted value of the expected benefits or in terms of the liquidation value (exchange price) at the end of each period. The matching process may be obtained by assuming a constant internal rate of return on the investment or by assuming a constant ratio of the input value of the services assumed to be used to the expected net revenue contribution in each period. However, the matching may also be attained indirectly by associating the cost with the services of the asset or with some other intermediate stage rather than directly with the net revenue contribution.

Decline in asset value—a cause of depreciation

The AAA committee on concepts and standards referred to depreciation as the decline in service potential, and the AAA committee on long-lived assets referred to it as the expiration of service potential. Since a measure of service potential is a measurement of the value of an asset, both of these definitions can be classified as measuring depreciation in each period by computing the decline in the value of the asset during the period.

Decline in discounted net revenue contribution. The service potential of a durable asset at any time can be measured by discounting the expected cash flows (or expected cash savings) to be obtained from acquiring and using the asset. Assume, for example, that an asset is expected to generate cash savings over a five-year period in the amounts of $500, $600, $1,000, $400, and $500, respectively, with the scrap value included in the final amount. The formula for computing the present vaue at time t_0 is as follows:

$$V_0 = \sum_{t=1}^{n} \frac{R_t}{(1 + r)^t} \tag{1}$$

where:

V_0 = The present value at time 0.
R_t = The cash flow in each period (t).
t = The opportunity rate of return or the cost of capital.

As indicated in Chapter 5, if r is assumed to be the opportunity rate of return for a riskless investment, the discounted cash flow for each period should be adjusted by a risk preference factor. However, in much of the literature, r is assumed to represent the cost of capital. The limitations of these assumptions are also discussed in Chapter 5.

The present value at time t_1 is computed by the following formula:

$$V_1 = \sum_{t=2}^{n} \frac{R_t}{(1 + r)^{t-1}} \tag{2}$$

Depreciation (D_1) for the first year is computed as follows:

$$D_1 = V_0 - V_1 \tag{3}$$

The depreciation for the above example would then be computed as indicated in Table 1.

TABLE 1:   Computation of depreciation based on the decrease in the discounted value of the expected cash flows (cost of capital is assumed to be 8 percent)

Year	(1) Expected net cash flow benefit	(2) Present value at beginning of year	(3) Present value at end of year	(4) Depreciation (col. 2 − col. 3)
1	$ 500	$2,406*	$2,099	$307
2	600	2,099	1,667	432
3	1,000	1,667	800	867
4	400	800	464	336
5	500	464	—0—	464

* The present value for the beginning of year 1 is computed as follows:

$$
\begin{array}{rl}
500 \times 0.9259 = & \$ \ \ 463 \\
600 \times 0.8573 = & 515 \\
1{,}000 \times 0.7938 = & 794 \\
400 \times 0.7350 = & 294 \\
500 \times 0.6806 = & \underline{340} \\
 & \$2{,}406
\end{array}
$$

If, in the above example, the cost of the asset was $2,025, an initial gain of $381 would need to be recorded in order to depreciate the beginning value of $2,406 over the life of the asset. An alternative would be to allocate the $381 gain over the life of the asset in proportion to the expected cash flow benefits or according to some other method; however, such an allocation would be purely arbitrary and would find acceptance only because it appears to be in accordance with the conventional realization rules. If the cash benefit of $500 in the fifth year includes a final scrap value of, say, $100, this $100 should be subtracted from the depreciation in the fifth year, making that amount $364.

One of the disadvantages of computing the depreciation on the basis of the decline in the discounted service potential or the discounted expected cash flows is that it is static in nature. The cost of capital at the date of acquisition and the expectations regarding the amount and timing of cash benefits are assumed to be constant over the life of the asset. Although it is possible to compute a new value for the asset each period on the basis of the current cost of capital and new expectations regarding expected benefits, such revaluations would be of doubtful validity, primarily because once the asset is acquired it becomes a part of the total operating facilities and its marginal benefits can no longer be measured because of the interaction of all of the factors of production in generating the net revenue of the firm. Therefore, a separate value for each asset cannot be obtained after the date of acquisition. In addition, reporting the gain at the date of acquisition is of doubtful relevance in the decision processes of investors and creditors, because it is subjective in nature and bears little relationship to the valuation of the enterprise as a whole.

Decrease in resale price of used asset. An alternative to the measurement of depreciation in terms of the decline in the discounted expected values of an asset is the use of current market prices. In this proposal, depreciation is the decline in the current market price of the asset measured by the resale price in a secondhand market. The main advantage of this procedure is that it avoids the need to make allocations and to rely on subjective expectations. However, it too has some major disadvantages. In the case of nonvendible durables, the entire asset must be written off at the date of acquisition or some amortization procedure must be used as a substitute. In this case allocation is not avoided, since the charge of the entire amount to one period is still an allocation. Another disadvantage of the use of current market prices for durable assets is that there is no evidence that the current resale prices are relevant to any of the prediction or decision models of investors and creditors or other external users of financial statements. The resale price does not necessarily represent what the firm would pay for the asset if it did not own it since the policy of the firm may be to acquire assets only in larger lots—that is, new.

The current exit-value models of Chambers and Sterling suggest the use of current exit values that are allocation free.[7,8] However, the decline in these values over time should not be interpreted as depreciation in the usual sense. The objective of using current exit values is to report the firm's present position and the consequences of its past actions as reflected in purchasing power.

Depreciation as a process of matching costs with expected benefits

In most discussions of depreciation allocations, there is an assumption, explicit or implicit, that the amount of the cost or other basis of the asset allocated to each period should represent the amount that is being matched with the expected revenues or net revenue contribution of the period. This matching of the input valuation with the expected benefits can take the form of (1) time-adjusted depreciation, which uses an average internal rate of return during the entire life of the asset, (2) depreciation allocations that are proportional to the net revenue contributions of each period, and (3) depreciation allocations that are in the same relative pro-

---

[7] Raymond J. Chambers, *Accounting, Evaluation and Economic Behavior* (Englewood Cliffs, N.J.: Prentice-Hall, 1966), pp. 208–9.

[8] Robert R. Sterling, *Theory of the Measurement of Enterprise Income* (Lawrence: University Press of Kansas, 1970).

portion as a surrogate for net revenue contributions, such as a measure of the service provided by the asset.

Time-adjusted depreciation.   By equating the historical cost (or other input valuation) with the present value of the asset in equation (1) above, and by substituting the internal rate of return for the opportunity rate or the cost of capital, we obtain the following equation:

$$C = \sum_{t=1}^{n} \frac{R_t}{(1 + s)^t} \tag{4}$$

where:

C = The cost of the asset.
s = The internal rate of return.

By subtracting C from each side of the equation, we obtain:

$$\sum_{t=1}^{n} \frac{R_t}{(1 + s)^t} - C = 0 \tag{5}$$

or, by summing the individual terms:

$$\left[\frac{R_1}{(1 + s)} + \frac{R_2}{(1 + s)^2} \cdots + \frac{R_n}{(1 + s)^n} \right] - C = 0 \tag{6}$$

If we use the above example, the cost (C) is \$2,025, and the net revenue contributions $(R_1, R_2,$ etc.) for each of the five years are \$500, \$600, \$1,000, \$400, and \$500, respectively. By substituting these values in equation 6, we can solve for the internal rate of return (s). In this example, the internal rate of return is 15 percent. By assuming that this is a constant rate during the life of the asset, the depreciation for each year can be computed as indicated in Table 2.

An advantage of this concept of depreciation is that depreciation represents an allocation of the total input cost, although the input value may

TABLE 2:   **Computation of depreciation based on the net revenue contribution less the associated earnings on the investment at a 15 percent earning rate**

Year	(1) Investment – book value at beginning of year	(2) Associated earnings at 15%	(3) Net revenue contribution	(4) Depreciation (col. 3 – col. 2)
1	\$2,025	\$304	\$ 500	\$ 196
2	1,829	274	600	326
3	1,503	225	1,000	775
4	727	109	400	291
5	435	63*	500	437
				\$2,025

* Adjusted for rounding error.

be expressed in terms of historical cost, cost adjusted for changes in the price level, or current costs. It also may have an advantage in permitting a prediction of future incomes, because it uses a constant average rate of return; however, predictability depends upon the relationship between expected net revenue contributions and actual contributions and upon whether or not the firm is able to reinvest continually in new projects at the same internal rate of earnings.

Disadvantages of the time-adjusted rate of return concept are these: (1) it assumes that the rate of return is constant over the life of the asset; (2) like the decrease in value concept, it is static in nature; (3) when the net revenue contribution is less than the associated earnings in any year, the depreciation would be negative; (4) if the expected net revenue contribution is negative in any one or more years, the solution of the discounting equation may result in multiple rates of return; and (5) like other concepts relying on expected net revenue contribution values, its validity is questionable because of the interactions of the separate assets and other factors contributing to the total revenues of the firm.

Depreciation based on a constant cost to net revenue contribution ratio. Depreciation, in this concept, is assumed to represent an allocation of the original cost (or other basis) to each year in such a way that it is matched with the associated net revenue contribution of each year on the basis of a constant ratio. The ratio is computed by dividing the historical cost of the asset (less scrap value if any) by the total expected net revenue contribution during the life of the asset. The depreciation for each year is, therefore, the expected net revenue contribution for that year multiplied by this ratio.[9] The ratio can be computed by the following formula:

$$m = \frac{C}{\sum_{t=1}^{n} R_t} \tag{7}$$

where:

m = The ratio of historical cost to the total expected net revenue contribution.

C = The cost or other basis (less scrap value) of the asset.

R_t = The expected net revenue contribution in each year (t) during the life of the asset.

Depreciation in each year can be computed as follows:

$$D_t = mR_t$$

where D_t is the depreciation allocated to year t.

---

[9] See, for example, Orace Johnson, "Two Concepts of Depreciation," *Journal of Accounting Research* 6 (Spring 1968): pp. 29–37.

Using the same figures as in the previous example, the cost of the asset is assumed to be $2,025, and the net revenue contributions are expected to be $500, $600, $1,000, $400, and $500, respectively, for each of the five years. Assuming no scrap value, the ratio would be 0.675 (computed by dividing $2,025 by $3,000). The depreciation for each of the five years would be as shown in Table 3.

TABLE 3: **Computation of depreciation based on a constant ratio of cost to expected net revenue contribution**

Year	(1) Expected net revenue contribution	(2) Ratio	(3) Depreciation
1	$ 500	0.675	$ 338
2	600	0.675	405
3	1,000	0.675	675
4	400	0.675	270
5	500	0.675	337
	$3,000		$2,025

An advantage of this depreciation concept is that it avoids the difficulties of computing an average internal rate of return when there are possible multiple rates, and it avoids the possibility of negative depreciation figures (unless the expected net revenue contribution in any year is negative). An additional advantage is that it may avoid many of the interactions among factor inputs by using a ratio computed from the net contribution (total expected revenues less variable costs) and total costs for aggregations of assets such as an entire plant, although this may be only a rough guide and the logic of applying a single ratio to all assets may be very indirect indeed. But for an asset such as a hotel, for example, the revenues may be greater when it is new and has prestige status than when it is old. It may eventually be converted into an office building and provide an entirely different type of service with lower revenues. If variable costs can also be estimated, the net revenue contributions from the entire hotel may be used as a rough guide for the allocation of all specific assets associated with the net revenues from operating the hotel. It is also possible to recompute the net revenue contribution pattern expected for the remaining life of the asset at any time during its life, so that the actual ratios used in computing the depreciation may come close to the final *ex post* ratio. To this extent, it may be possible for external users of financial statements to predict future relationships, but this is so only if the ratio of cost to net revenue contributions is relatively constant for additional investments by the firm.

One of the disadvantages of this concept is that it may cause the rates of return on invested assets to vary widely because it does not adjust for the timing of the net revenue contributions. Interactions among the several assets and other factors used by the firm are not eliminated even if the ratios are computed from groups of assets. Other disadvantages of this concept are similar to the disadvantages of other concepts discussed previously that are also based on expectations of net revenue contributions.

Depreciation as an allocation of cost to physical service units. As an alternative to basing depreciation allocations on the pattern of expected net revenue contributions, it is possible to substitute a physical measure of the expected services to be obtained by using the assets. A nonmonetary measure of the benefits expected to be received is substituted for the dollar measurement of the net revenue contribution. Examples of such surrogates would include the number of units produced, number of hours, days or months of operation, kilowatt hours of electric power produced, or some other intermediate unit of production input or output. The pattern can be either an expected distribution determined in advance or the allocation of a predetermined cost per unit to the actual number of service units used in any accounting period.

A major question that arises, therefore, is whether the total costs should be allocated over all potential services or over just the services that the firm anticipates using in operations. An asset is usually acquired with certain services in mind, and it is logical to allocate the initial input cost less salvage, if any, over the period of anticipated use. For example, a crane could be acquired for use on a specific contract. Its total cost less salvage should be assigned to the specific contract, even though it is used for only a few days and remains idle for long periods of time. If this is the most economical way of getting the job done, there is no reason why the total cost should not be assigned to the anticipated use. But this is not inconsistent with the net-revenue-contribution concept. In other cases, an asset may be acquired with an anticipation of using it only 3 or 4 years out of 10. If it is not feasible to utilize the services in all years, there is logic in charging depreciation only in the years of anticipated use. It was for this purpose that the asset was acquired, and to insist on depreciation in every year is not consistent with the pattern of expected benefits. On the other hand, however, if an asset is acquired for use and forced to remain idle for one of many reasons, depreciation should be recorded if the service units expected to be obtained during the period of idleness cannot be obtained in a later period. A charge for the services expired should be made even though they serve no benefit to the firm; however, they may be shown as a loss rather than as a charge to current operations.

An advantage of using this indirect measure of the net revenue contribution is that the allocation can be adapted to unanticipated changes in the pattern of use, particularly in those cases where the decline in the expected future benefits is more closely related to use than to obsolescence and the passage of time.

A disadvantage of the physical services method of allocating asset costs is that there may not be any necessary relationship between the physical services produced or consumed and the net revenue contributions from the asset. Therefore, the allocations may result in capricious charges to income, which are not likely to be relevant to the predictions and decisions of investors and other external users of financial reports. Furthermore, both the choice of a measure of the physical service of the asset and the allocation of cost to each service unit are likely to be based upon expediency rather than logic. The service unit is likely to be some measure that is readily available, such as direct labor hours or units of production, and each unit of such service is usually assumed to provide an equal benefit value or net revenue contribution. Different costs can be assigned to different service units, but it is seldom possible to do so in a logical manner except by resorting to an alternative cost of obtaining the same services or by making expectations regarding changes in total revenues. It is generally difficult to take into account changes in variable costs or cost savings.

Depreciation allocations based on the usefulness of the reported figures

Because of the theoretical and practical limitations of all of the allocation concepts discussed above, a possible alternative might be to evaluate the results, rather than the allocation concepts. If allocation procedures can be found that permit good predictions or otherwise provide information useful to investors and creditors, they would appear to be acceptable regardless of how arbitrary they might seem to be from a theoretical point of view. Such solutions, however, cannot be evaluated by deductive reasoning alone; they must meet the tests of rigorous empirical research. As a starting point, the solutions to the above example using three of the concepts discussed above are presented in Table 4, which also compares the rates of return on invested book value of the asset in each case with the ratio of depreciation to net revenue contributions.

As Table 4 indicates, the rates of return for the decline in value concept and the time-adjusted concept are both constant and would be useful in making predictions of future rates if the firm is likely to continue to earn these rates. The 8 percent rate, however, is a minimum rate, because it can be assumed that the firm would not invest in assets that yielded less than this. But the 15 percent may not be typical of investment opportunities available to the firm. The third concept results in rates of return for each year that vary from 8 percent to 48 percent. Therefore, this example suggests that none of these three methods is necessarily valid in permitting prediction of future rates of return; but empirical studies could prove otherwise, particularly under different conditions or assumptions.

An attempt to develop a complete theory relating to the prediction of cash flows but using the traditional accounting framework is estimation

TABLE 4: Comparison of depreciation, rate of return on book investment, and ratio of depreciation to net revenue contribution for three depreciation concepts

Year	Net revenue contribution	Decrease in value depreciation				Time-adjusted depreciation				Depreciation proportionate to net revenue contributions			
		Depreciation	Book value beginning of year	Rate of return (percent)	Ratio to contribution	Depreciation	Book value beginning of year	Rate of return (percent)	Ratio to contribution	Depreciation	Book value beginning of year	Rate of return (percent)	Ratio to contribution
1	$ 500	$ 307	$2,406	8	0.614	$ 196	$2,025	15	0.392	$ 338	$2,025	8	0.675
2	600	432	2,099	8	0.720	326	1,829	15	0.543	405	1,687	12	0.675
3	1,000	867	1,667	8	0.867	775	1,503	15	0.775	675	1,282	25	0.675
4	400	336	800	8	0.840	291	728	15	0.728	270	607	21	0.675
5	500	464	464	8	0.928	437	437	15	0.874	337	337	48	0.675
		$2,406				$2,025				$2,025			

theory.[10] In this theory, either the total future cash flows of the firm or the long-run internal rate of return are assumed to be capable of estimation from annual reports of income designed for this purpose. The current ratio of the contribution less depreciation to the contribution is computed in such a way that it permits an estimation of the ratio of the total cash flows less cost to the total cash flows. Since the presentation of a probability distribution of future cash flows is not acceptable in current accounting practice, this information is presented indirectly by computing depreciation in such a way that the *ex post* ratios used approximate the *ex ante* long-run ratios. In a similar fashion, the depreciation can be computed on the basis of an estimated rate of return that approximates the *ex ante* long-run rate of return. One difficulty with this theory is that it is based on an assumption regarding what parameters the investor or creditor wishes to use in the decision models. Furthermore, as can be seen from Table 4, rates of return and ratios of depreciation to contribution may vary depending on the method used. An investor who is not told what rates of return or ratios are being used may be deceived into attempting to estimate one of these when, in fact, the other is the parameter assumed to be constant.

Only the third concept results in a constant ratio of depreciation to the expected net contributions, and thus a constant ratio of the contribution less the depreciation to the contribution, because one is the complement of the other. In the third concept of Table 4, the former ratio is 0.675 and the latter is 0.325. The other two concepts result in widely varying ratios. Therefore, only the third concept is likely to permit any prediction, but such a prediction depends on the likelihood of this ratio being relatively constant for all investments in the future. Although this is subject to empirical verification, an a priori answer would be that this is not likely to be the case because it would assume constant production functions and relatively constant capital intensity, neither of which is likely to be true because they would exist only under static conditions.

The net service contribution

In the above example, it was assumed that the net contribution of the asset could be estimated at the time of acquisition and that the pattern of contributions over the life of the asset would serve as a basis for the depreciation allocation. As in a capital budgeting decision, the expected net contribution of the asset should take into consideration its effect on the additional costs or cost savings as well as its effect on revenues. However, once the asset has been installed, it becomes a part of the entire operation, and the additional revenues and net cost savings can no longer be attributed to the one asset alone. All of the assets and other factors of

---

[10] Richard P. Brief and Joel Owen, "A Reformulation of the Estimation Problem," *Journal of Accounting Research,* Spring 1973, pp. 1–15.

production interact in producing the revenue of the firm. Therefore, it would be necessary to make a simultaneous allocation of the revenues of the firm to all of the assets. But simultaneous allocations of revenue or net revenue contributions cannot be supported on theoretical grounds unless the firm's inputs do not interact, a condition that is highly unlikely.[11]

Even when able to predict the net revenue contributions using the capital budgeting techniques, the accountant is plagued by other problems.[12] The total cost of obtaining the net benefits from an asset includes not only the initial cost of acquiring the plant or equipment, but also the costs of repairs and maintenance over the life of the asset. But the policy of the firm with respect to repairs and maintenance and improvements will affect the associated labor and power costs as well as the operating efficiency. Therefore, the initial cost is only one of the input factors that should be considered in the basic allocation problem.

The main disadvantage of attempting to allocate total expected operating costs is that new uncertainties are introduced into a problem that is already complex. When a new asset is acquired, it may be almost impossible to estimate the total repair, maintenance, and operating costs and their interrelationships. In some cases, operating costs may decline over a lengthy break-in period. Repair and maintenance costs may increase over the entire life of the asset, or over only a part of the life to prevent other operating costs from increasing even more rapidly. These interrelationships and their influence on decisions regarding the choice of a depreciation method are discussed in the following section.

DEPRECIATION, REPAIRS, AND REPLACEMENTS

The objective of considering all expected operating costs as well as operating revenues in the computation of depreciation allocations stems from the fact that repairs, maintenance, and other operating costs are interrelated. This interrelationship was referred to in the previous chapter in the discussion of capital and revenue expenditures. But the extent of the interrelationship and the effect on depreciation allocations require closer scrutiny. First, the expected life of an asset is directly associated with the extent of the anticipated repairs and maintenance. Second, because most assets include many components with different lives, many so-called repairs are really replacements. Third, the efficiency of an asset frequently declines as an asset ages, and this decline in efficiency accelerates when repairs and maintenance are curtailed or delayed.

---

[11] Committee on External Reporting, AAA, "An Evaluation of Current Accounting Practices," *Accounting Review*, supplement to vol. 44 (1969), pp. 107–8.

[12] See, for example, the AAA Committee on Managerial Decision Models Report, *Accounting Review*, supplement to vol. 44 (1969), pp. 72–76.

Repairs, maintenance, and asset life

The life of an asset can be extended or shortened by varying the amount of repairs and maintenance. In some cases, assets can be preserved almost indefinitely for historical or cultural reasons. But the cost of doing so is generally greater than the cost of replacement with a new asset. Furthermore, obsolescence usually makes such continued maintenance uneconomical. On the other hand, repair and maintenance costs can be reduced to a minimum whenever the economic life of an asset is expected to be quite short. For example, if specialized equipment is to be used for the completion of a specific contract and abandoned upon the termination of the contract, the most economical level of repair and maintenance expenditures would be that minimum necessary to keep the equipment operating only until the completion of the contract. Usually, the life of an asset is determined by what may be considered an optimum level of repair and maintenance expenditures or by economic obsolescence, whichever is the shorter. If repair or maintenance expenditures are delayed or curtailed for any reason below that required to obtain the expected economic life of the asset, the current depreciation allocation should be increased accordingly.

Repairs and replacements. The term *maintenance* generally refers to the normal upkeep of property in an efficient operating condition. Maintenance is frequently considered to include normal recurring repairs, and the term *repair* refers to the restoration of an asset without increasing its expected service life or capacity. However, repairs may be of two general types: (1) the adjustment of a machine or working parts and the labor necessary to restore a damaged or worn component to its original condition and (2) the replacement of one or more parts of an asset with new parts without replacing the entire asset.

Maintenance expenses and repairs of the first type may increase over the life of an asset because of the increasing need for adjustment and care when items of plant and equipment become worn through use or age. If the revenue contribution of the asset remains the same throughout its life while the repair and maintenance expenses increase, the net contribution of the asset itself must be decreasing. This factor, by itself, calls for a declining depreciation charge.

The replacement of specific parts, however, is a function of the unit or composite selected for depreciation, and the distinction between replacements and maintenance is dependent upon the amount of the aggregation and the selected composite life. If each component is depreciated separately on the basis of its own expected life, the replacement requires the retirement of the component and the setting up of a new component in its place. For example, if the tires on an automobile are depreciated separately, they would be depreciated over their individual expected lives and written off when they are replaced; the new tires would then be capitalized and depreciated over their expected lives. Truck tires are occasionally treated in this fashion, but it is not common to identify and depreciate other parts of a truck or automobile separately. Usually, an item of equipment or a building is treated as a single asset and assigned a life based on the expected life of the major components. If the original cost of the asset is allocated over the life of the major components, some consideration must be made for the fact that minor components will be replaced before the anticipated retirement of the entire asset. If some of the parts are replaced every year or two and if others are replaced at longer intervals, there will be a bunching of replacements in the later years of the asset's life. This results in increasing repair expenses as the asset ages. The charging of the cost of all parts over the entire life, with the charging of the costs of replacements to expense in the year that they occur, results in double charges in later years and inadequate charges in the early years. Therefore, the allocation procedure should be adjusted so that this double charging can be avoided.

Accountants have occasionally recommended that repair costs should be equalized over the life of an asset by setting up a budgetary reserve. The need for this allocation or equalization of repair costs is based on the assumption that the annual depreciation charge represents an allocation of only the original cost of the asset, without regard to the timing of repairs. The recommendation usually requires an estimation of the total repair costs during the life of the asset and an allocation to each period by setting up an allowance or reserve for repairs. This allowance account is usually classified as a liability reserve. However, it does not have the usual characteristics of a liability because it is based on the occurrence of a future event. A better alternative would be to treat it as a contra to the related asset account, similar to the treatment of accumulated depreciation. This treatment is more logical because it represents an additional allocation of costs of the parts with lives shorter than that of the major components. Therefore, it is depreciation and could just as well be credited to the accumulated depreciation account. When repairs are actually incurred, they would be debited to the allowance for repairs account or the accumulated depreciation account. This procedure is therefore similar to the treatment of major repairs. Although it would be more precise to write off an asset and capitalize the repair costs, it is usually too difficult to determine the cost of the item being replaced. But this procedure also has the same limitations as the similar method suggested for handling major repairs.

Repairs and efficiency. Repairs and maintenance can frequently be delayed or minimized, with the result that other operating expenses, such as fuel and labor costs, may increase. Thus, if the value of the output of the asset remains constant, the net contribution of the asset declines. This decline in net contribution also occurs as a result of frequent repairs as the asset grows older; the frequent repairs curtail the time available for production or use and thus diminish the output of the equipment. The several concepts of depreciation based on the net revenue contribution require that this decline in output potential be taken into consideration in the allocation process.

EVALUATION OF VARIOUS DEPRECIATION METHODS

Accountants have long recognized that plant and equipment have limited lives and that some consideration must be made in the accounts for the inevitable necessity to junk productive assets. During the 19th century and the early part of the 20th century, many of the firms that treated the problem at all did so by a periodic revaluation of the assets or by charging either replacements or retirements to current expense. More recently, depreciation has become recognized as a systematic allocation of cost or other value over the life of the asset. Many methods of allocation have been proposed and used, but practically all of the methods can be classified according to which of the following patterns they resemble: (1) allocations varying according to activity or use, (2) straight-line or constant charge methods, (3) increasing charge methods, and (4) decreasing charge methods.

Methods preceding the use of cost allocation

Although the methods preceding the use of cost allocation are not based on good accounting theory, a brief review is helpful in placing them in proper perspective and in recognizing them when they appear in current discussions of accounting theory and practice.

Inventory method. Probably the earliest method of recognizing depreciation was to revalue the assets periodically or at the termination of a venture. The inventory valuation was based on either the valuation of the asset to the new venture or on the cost of the asset adjusted for any loss in productive efficiency. The first basis may be determined by a liquidation value or by a current market price. The second valuation basis results in what is called observed depreciation, which is based on the change in engineering efficiency of the asset rather than on the decline in service potential.

The use of a liquidation value or current market price is advantageous because it permits a real-world interpretation and avoids the necessity for arbitrary allocations. However, the decline in these prices does not represent what is normally thought of as depreciation because it includes gains and losses due to market factors. The use of observed depreciation is usually thought to be inadequate because it does not take into consideration such economic factors as obscolescence.

Although the inventory method is obsolete, it is occasionally applied in one of several forms as an expedient. For example, an inventory of small tools is occasionally taken at the end of each period and valued on the basis of its physical condition; the depreciation expense is computed by subtracting this inventory valuation from the sum of the beginning inventory and the cost of tools acquired during the period.

The replacement method. When a firm had a large number of similar assets, it was thought that the current cost of using plant and equipment could be approximated best by charging to depreciation expense the cost of current replacements. In a large mature firm, replacements were thought to occur regularly and provide a good substitute for depreciation charges. The cost of the original asset was retained as the book value of the asset in use regardless of the change in costs at the time of replacement. A modification of this method required the use of a reserve account and a periodic charge to depreciation during the early years of the life of the enterprise until replacements reached a relatively constant level.

The replacement method is generally considered obsolete, but it is still used by railroads for ties, rails, tie plates, and ballast. Its current counterpart in general financial accounting is the charging of ordinary repairs to expense as they occur, while continuing to carry the original cost of the replaced parts in the total cost of the main asset.

Cost allocation methods

In accordance with the various objectives of depreciation, the cost or other value of an asset should be allocated over the service life in a systematic and rational pattern. The method selected for any specific asset or group of assets should reflect the specific expectations regarding the following factors: (1) the relationship between decline in market value and use, (2) the effect of obsolescence, (3) the expected pattern of repairs and maintenances, (4) the anticipated decline in operating efficiency, (5) expected changes in revenues, (6) the long life of assets and the necessity for waiting—the interest factor, and (7) the degree of the uncertainty regarding the later periods of the asset's life.

Theoretically, the selection of a depreciation pattern should be based on all of the above listed factors. However, in many cases, one or a few of the factors will dominate and the minor effects of the others may be ignored. Usually, one of several established depreciation methods is selected if the general pattern appears reasonable or if income tax effects are permitted to influence the selection of the method chosen for accounting purposes. Although there is some merit in using standardized methods, it would be possible to combine the expectations of the several determining factors and derive a mathematical equation for each asset or group of assets. Such equations derived from past experience and from specific expectations might provide more useful information under estimation theory than the common practice of fitting a standard model to each situation.

Variable charge methods.　　The activity or use methods of depreciation are based on the assumption that depreciation is a variable rather than a fixed cost. That is, it is assumed that the value of the asset declines as a function of use rather than because of the passing of time. For example, a truck may be expected to operate for 100,000 miles during its lifetime, or a machine may be expected to operate for a given number of hours or turn out a given number of units of product.

For many types of assets, the assumption of a variable depreciation is reasonable, particularly if the physical wear and tear are more important than economic obsolescence or if the expected services can normally be expected to be obtained before obsolescence sets in. Accordingly, if an asset's services are not used in one year, no depreciation should be recorded because there is no decline in service value. This is similar to a coal pile; if no coal is used while the plant is shut down temporarily, no charge is made for coal during that period. Even though obsolescence may be a significant factor in determining the expected life of an asset, the activity method of depreciation may be appropriate if the obsolescence can be anticipated and if an estimate can be made of the approximate usage to be obtained from the asset. Under these conditions, the cost of the asset can be assumed to represent the purchase of a given number of service units, and the allocation of the cost to these units is then reasonable. The main objective of depreciation applied in this case is the allocation of input value to each service unit; the measurement of the decline in service value may be of secondary importance.

The production method of depreciation appears to be ideal for those situations where the service value of the asset declines with use, but there are some serious disadvantages to the method as it is usually applied: (1) Although a variable charge to each year is accepted, the production method is similar to the straight-line method in the sense that it assigns an *equal* amount to each unit of service, but there is no basis for assuming equal costs per unit of service. Furthermore, because of the necessity of waiting for the later units of service, the total service value does not, in fact, decline uniformly unless interest is assumed to be zero. (2) No consideration is usually given to increasing repair and maintenance costs, decreasing operating efficiencies, or declining revenues. (3) Uncertainties regarding the quantity of services that the asset is capable of producing can be taken into consideration by using the expected value based on engineering probability estimates, but the probability of early obsolescence is more difficult to anticipate.

A modification of the production method is allocation on the basis of revenue. For major components, this may be a good approximation of use, and it has the added advantage of taking into consideration changes in revenue per unit. But is has all of the other disadvantages of the production method. Furthermore, it is inapplicable in those cases in which goods are produced for stock and where overall revenue cannot be reasonably attributed to specific assets. Notice that an allocation on the basis of revenue does not justify an allocation on the basis of net income; none of the objectives of depreciation is met by using income as a basis for allocation.

Straight-line allocation. The straight-line method of allocation is based on the assumption that depreciation is a function of time rather than of use; obsolescence and deterioration over time are considered to be determining factors in the decline in service potential, as opposed to physical wear and tear caused by use. Thus the service potential of the asset is assumed to decline by an equal amount each period. And the total cost of the services used in any period is assumed to be the same regardless of the extent of use.

How well does the straight-line method fit the usual situation? Because of the simplicity of the model, the results are correct only if the following assumptions are true or reasonably accurate: (1) The interest factor can be ignored or the cost of capital can be assumed to be zero. (2) Repairs and maintenance expenses are constant over the life of the asset. (3) The operating efficiency of the asset is just as good in the last year as in the first year. (4) The revenues (or net cash flows) made possible by the use of the asset are constant for all years of asset life. (5) All necessary estimates, including the anticipated useful life, can be predicted with a reasonable degree of certainty.

Because of the uncertainties connected with most of the above factors, it is difficult to find any depreciation method that is likely to take all of the various factors into consideration. Therefore, the straight-line method is often assumed to be as accurate as any other method. It is also frequently claimed that the straight-line method may be the most appropriate because the several factors tend to be offsetting. For example, it may be possible that declining operating efficiencies and increasing repair and maintenance expenses are exactly offset by increasing revenues and decreasing insurance and property tax expenses. In addition, the straight-line method has the advantage of ease of operation and understanding.

A major disadvantage of the straight-line method is that it ignores the discount factor; and even if the other assumptions are correct, the reported net income gives the appearance of a rising rate of return on total invested capital. For example, assume that a machine is acquired at a cost of $5,000 and is expected to have a life of five years with no scrap value at the end of this period. Also assume that the investment provides a constant net revenue stream (total revenues less all operating costs other than depreciation) of $1,252. The total reported income is assumed to be withdrawn each year, but an amount equal to the accumulated depreciation is invested in securities at an average rate of return of 8 percent. The result is shown in Table 5.

The effect demonstrated in Table 5 indicates the error of ignoring the discount factor. The rate of return would drop back to 5 percent in the sixth year if the asset is replaced at the same cost, but erroneous conclu-

TABLE 5: Rate of return earned on a five-year asset using straight-line depreciation (revenues and operating costs are assumed to be constant)

	Year				
	(1)	*(2)*	*(3)*	*(4)*	*(5)*
Total capital invested at beginning of year	$5,000	$5,000	$5,000	$5,000	$5,000
Carrying value of machine at beginning of year	5,000	4,000	3,000	2,000	1,000
Investment in securities at beginning of year	—0—	1,000	2,000	3,000	4,000
Operating revenues less operating expenses other than depreciation	1,252	1,252	1,252	1,252	1,252
Depreciation	1,000	1,000	1,000	1,000	1,000
Net operating income	252	252	252	252	252
Interest on securities	—0—	80	160	240	320
Total income	$ 252	$ 332	$ 412	$ 492	$ 572
Reported rate of return on total investment (percent)	5	6.6	8.2	9.8	11.4

sions may be drawn during each five-year period. An upward trend in income is apparent but not real. Projections based on this trend would be erroneous. Furthermore, it leads to the observation that a technologically improved machine must have considerable operating superiority to challenge the existing asset before the end of its physical life. Like the "one-hoss shay," the existing machine would be used until it finally fell apart. If additional operating equipment is obtained each year, instead of purchasing securities as in the above example, it can be demonstrated that the rate of return will oscillate with a decreasing amplitude until an average 8 percent rate of return is finally reached. If the compound-interest method of depreciation is used under the above assumptions, a constant rate of return results. This is demonstrated below in the discussion of the increasing-charge methods.

The assumption of a positive rate of return, however, does not discard the straight-line method entirely. Under specific conditions, the decline in operating efficiency may offset the decline in associated earnings so that the computed depreciation may be constant each year. For example, in Table 6, the net revenue contribution is assumed to decline by a constant amount of $80 each year. If the rate of return is 8 percent, the excess of the contribution over the associated earnings would be constant each year, thus supporting a straight-line depreciation charge.

Increasing-charge methods. In the direct financing method of treating long-term leases in the reports of the lessor discussed in the previous chapter, the cost of a product purchased and leased under a long-term contract is reclassified as the net investment in the lease. Income is reported by multiplying the internal rate of return by the book value at the

TABLE 6: Computation of depreciation assuming an 8 percent rate of return and a constant decline in service contribution of $80

Year	(1) Book value of asset at beginning of year	(2) Associated earnings 8 percent of col. 1	(3) Net Revenue Contri- bution	(4) Depreciation (col. 3 – col. 2)
1	$5,000	$400	$1,400	$1,000
2	4,000	320	1,320	1,000
3	3,000	240	1,240	1,000
4	2,000	160	1,160	1,000
5	1,000	80	1,080	1,000

beginning of each year. The amount of cash received each period less this reported income is assumed to represent a return of the amount invested in the lease (equal to the cost of the product). Therefore, if an equal cash rental is received each year, an increasing amount would be reported as a return of the investment. Although this return of the investment is not generally referred to as depreciation, the effect is the same and an allocation procedure is required. The effect of this method is demonstrated in Table 7.

TABLE 7: Computation of the return of investment for direct financing leases reported by lessors (assuming an 8 percent rate of return)

Year	(1) Book value of lease at beginning of year	(2) Associated earnings 8 percent of col. 1	(3) Annual cash receipt	(4) Net decline in book value
1	$5,000	$400	$1,252	$ 852
2	4,148	332	1,252	920
3	3,228	258	1,252	994
4	2,234	178	1,252	1,074
5	1,160	92	1,252	1,160

The use of the cash flow as a basis for amortizing the investment in this case is assumed to be justified because the maintenance and operating costs are paid by the lessee and because there are few interactions with other assets. But it may be criticized on the basis of its assumption of a constant rate of return and on the basis of its failure to distinguish between a true interest income and the income from the operations of obtaining and servicing the lease contracts.

The annuity and sinking-fund methods of depreciation also result in increasing amortization amounts, similar to the computations in Table 7.

The sinking-fund method has been used occasionally by public-utility firms that have charged depreciation with the annuity portion only and charged interest expense with the increasing interest computed on the increasing accumulated depreciation (equal to a hypothetical sinking fund). This method is particularly relevant when the utility's rates are computed by using an undepreciated cost as the rate base. One of the most relevant arguments for the sinking-fund method is that it permits a public utility to earn a constant rate of return on its total investment when its revenue is held constant through regulation.

The increasing-charge methods are also relevant for those situations in which insurance and property tax expenses decline over the asset's life while operating efficiency, revenues, and repairs and maintenance remain fairly constant. Some public-utility properties meet these conditions. In other cases, expectations of increasing revenues may support the use of increasing-charge depreciation methods. For example, toll roads and toll bridges may be built to handle peak traffic loads anticipated after 10 or more years. Thus, the revenues may be expected to increase as demand increases over the asset's life.

The main arguments against the interest methods of depreciation are that (1) very few assets can be expected to provide services with a constant or increasing value; (2) repair and maintenance costs usually increase; and (3) operating efficiency usually declines over the asset's life. The interest methods are not necessarily more dynamic than the straight-line method just because they take into consideration one additional factor—the rate of return; they still omit more factors than they include.

Decreasing-charge methods of depreciation. Several methods of depreciation have been suggested and used from time to time that result in a decreasing depreciation charge over the expected life of an asset (also known as accelerated depreciation). The most common methods are the sum-of-the-years'-digits method and the constant-percentage-of-declining-book-value method. In the latter method, a precise formula can be used to determine the constant rate of decline when the scrap value is positive,[13] but an approximation of this rate (acceptable for tax purposes) is obtained by taking twice the straight-line percentage (known generally as the double-declining-balance method). However, other allo-

---

[13] $\left(r = 1 - \sqrt[n]{\dfrac{s}{c}} \right)$

where

r = the constant rate.
s = scrap value.
c = cost.
n = years of expected life.

cation distributions can be obtained by using smaller percentages or by applying one of many algebraic formulas resulting in declining charges.

The main impetus for the increased interest in the declining charge methods in recent years has come from the liberalization in the choice of depreciation methods permitted by the Internal Revenue Code. However, the theoretical justification for declining-charge methods is based on non-tax considerations. The conditions frequently claimed as justifications for the declining-charge methods are as follows: (1) declining annual service contributions without consideration for interest or the cost of capital; (2) declining operating efficiency or operating performance, resulting in increases in other operating costs; (3) asset values (represented by the discounted value of remaining service values) declining more in early years and less during the later years of asset life; (4) the expiration of the cost of equal service contributions discounted back to the date of acquisition—thus, more is paid for the service values becoming available in the early years than the service values of the later years even though all service values are equal when used; (5) increasing repair and maintenance costs; (6) declining cash proceeds or revenues; (7) the uncertainty of revenues of later years because of possible obsolescence. These conditions are discussed more fully in the following paragraphs.

Declining revenue contributions and declining operating efficiency are interrelated and have the same consequences with respect to the depreciation that should be charged to operations in each period. The decline in the annual net revenue contribution may result because of a decline in use in the later years of life, because more time is required for repairs, or because of the greater danger of breakdowns with heavy use. Net revenue contribution may also decline because of decreased efficiency and thus less output, as for a power generator. On the other hand, declining operating efficiency may result in larger fuel costs, higher labor costs, or greater waste in the use of materials. All of these mean that the net contribution of the asset is less than when it was new. Thus, if interest costs are ignored, this decline in the net service contribution of the asset provides a justification for a decreasing-charge depreciation method. For example, if interest were ignored in Table 6, the depreciation each year would be the net revenue contribution (column 3) divided by $6,200 (the total of column 3) and multiplied by $5,000 (the original cost of the asset). That is, a constant relationship is assumed between the net revenue contribution each year and the depreciation charge based on cost.

A declining pattern of annual net revenue contributions appears logical on a priori grounds. For most classes of equipment and buildings, one would expect a decrease in operating efficiency over the life of the asset, increasing repair and maintenance costs, and possibly declining net revenues because of increasing obsolescence and competition. Terborgh demonstrated that when using a 10 percent discount rate, the loss in total service value during the first half of the asset's life ranges from 71 percent for a 10-year asset to 56 percent for a 100-year asset.[14] On empirical grounds, Terborgh concluded that for equipment, the decline in total service value is about one half during the first third of the asset's life and about two thirds for the first half of the asset's life.[15]

Another proposed justification for the declining-charge depreciation methods is based on the assumption that the original cost represents the discounted value of the expected annual contributions to be obtained by using the asset. The cost of the earlier annual contribution is therefore greater than the cost of the more remote values.[16] Thus even if the annual net revenue contributions can be expected to be equal in all years of service life, the depreciation charge based on cost would be greater in the early years and smaller in the later years.

From a theoretical point of view, this proposal for a logical explanation of the declining-charge methods is quite weak. First, it represents a very rigid application of the cost rule—each unit of service value is charged to expense in the amount of its original discounted cost. The longer the waiting period, the lower this cost will be. Second, it applies a very rigid form of the realization rule. The difference between the original cost and the value of the services is assumed to be realized only when the asset is used or when its product is sold. Third, depreciation is assumed to represent the expiration of the original cost of each year's contribution, rather than the net revenue contribution less the earnings associated with a declining investment. Under the static conditions assumed in this proposal, the result would be a rapidly increasing rate of return based on the reported net income. Not only would greater amounts of interest be realized in later years, but also the income from reinvested capital would tend to increase the net incomes of the later years. This proposal is also subject to the same criticisms as the interest methods—it omits more factors than it includes in the logic. Declining depreciation methods have some support, however, for other reasons.

The argument that a declining depreciation charge should be used to offset increasing repair and maintenance expenses is not without merit. As indicated earlier in this chapter, repair and maintenance expenses are related to the depreciation process and should be included in the total cost of the services or in the computation of the net revenue contribution. One word of caution, however—only normal repair and maintenance expenses should be included in the process of equalizing the total of repair expenses and depreciation. Expenses resulting from inefficiencies should appear in the years in which they occur for managerial control purposes and as information to investors.

---

[14] George Terborgh, *Realistic Depreciation Policy* (Washington, D.C.: Machinery and Allied Products Institute, 1954), pp. 37–38.

[15] Ibid., pp. 44–45.

[16] For an excellent presentation of this case, see Robert L. Dixon, "Decreasing Charge Depreciation—A Search for Logic," *Accounting Review* 35 (October 1960): 590–97.

Decreasing expected cash proceeds or revenues also provide support for decreasing-charge depreciation methods for all assets used in operations. If revenues are expected to decline over the life of an asset, it may be assumed that a larger part of the original cost of the asset was incurred to obtain the revenues of the early years. Therefore, the revenues provide a good indication of the net contribution of the asset each year. Here again, standard depreciation methods should not be assumed to take care of the decreasing revenue factor automatically. Estimates should be made for specific assets, and appropriate depreciation schedules could then be devised. A question may be raised as to whether or not anticipated declines in the prices of products should be taken into consideration in the computation of the depreciation allocation. The answer is in the affirmative if the decline in price can be attributed to anticipated increases in competition or decreases in demand. Unanticipated changes in product prices would be reflected in the incomes of each period affected.

Uncertainty is the most difficult factor to treat in the allocation of depreciation charges. The uncertain values include the expected life, anticipated net revenue contributions, and future repair and maintenance charges. In most cases, the uncertain values can be converted into single-valued certainty equivalents by using the expected values adjusted for risk preference. Therefore, uncertainty in the life of the asset is not proper justification for the use of decreasing-charge methods of depreciation. Uncertainty regarding repair and maintenance expenses also provides little justification for declining depreciation charges because this uncertainty is primarily a result of inadequate experience and data rather than a result of uncertainty regarding unpredictable events. Uncertainty regarding future revenue contributions, however, does provide some support for declining-charge depreciation methods. The argument is that since early revenues are more certain than more distant revenues, the latter are discounted more heavily in the initial investment decision, and therefore a larger part of the cost of the asset should be allocated to the earlier years. The main defect of this argument is that it is difficult, if not impossible, to justify any specific depreciation schedule on the basis of uncertainty alone.

Summary of conditions under which each pattern is applicable. One or more of the conditions listed below may provide support for the general allocation pattern indicated. The specific depreciation method to be used should be selected on the basis of as many relevant factors as possible.

1. *Variable charge methods*

    The value of the asset declines as a function of use rather than because of the passing time.

    Obsolescence is not an important factor in determining the life of the asset.

Repairs, maintenance expenses, and revenues are proportional to use.

2. *Straight-line method*

Discounted value of future benefits declines as a function of time rather than use.

The interest factor can be ignored or assumed to be offset by other factors.

Repairs, maintenance expenses, operating efficiency, and revenues are relatively constant over the life of the asset.

3. *Increasing-charge method*

The cash flow or net revenue contribution of each year is constant, but the asset value each year represents the discounted value of remaining contributions.

Repair and maintenance expenses are constant or decreasing over the life of the asset.

Revenues and operating efficiency are constant or increasing over the life of the asset.

4. *Decreasing-charge methods*

Increasing repair and maintenance charges.

Decreasing operating efficiency and revenues.

Interest factor recognized only when "realized" through use of the asset.

Uncertainty of revenues of the later years.

Note that the above criteria are based primarily on an assumed relationship between depreciation and net revenue contributions. Except for estimation theory, there is no logical reason that has been proposed to support allocation on these grounds. The matching rule by itself is insufficient. However, it may be argued that by allocating on the basis of net revenue contributions, the depreciation charge becomes neutral or sterilized. That is, the allocation is neutral if the decision made on the basis of the information would have been the same if no depreciation had been reported. If this is the case, however, it appears that it would be better to omit allocations entirely than to take the chance that they might not be neutral.

It appears from the above discussion of depreciation that the allocation of cost or other bases of long-term assets is either arbitrary or it is based on unmeasurable variables such as net revenue contributions or cash flows. Four possible alternatives to this dilemma are (1) avoid allocations by measuring residual asset valuations in terms of market prices at the end of each period; (2) attempt no allocations and present cash flow and funds flow statements instead of income statements; (3) select uniform methods of allocation on the basis of their ability to permit predictions, regardless of their inherent logic; or (4) present only neutral or sterilized allocations.

SELECTED ADDITIONAL READING

Concepts of depreciation

Bennett, Anthony H. M. "Depreciation and Business Decision Making." *Accounting and Business Research,* Winter 1972, pp. 3–28.

Burt, Oscar R. "Unified Theory of Depreciation." *Journal of Accounting Research,* Spring 1970, pp. 28–57.

Johnson, Orace. "Two General Concepts of Depreciation." *Journal of Accounting Research,* Spring 1968, pp. 29–37.

Lamden, Charles W.; Dale L. Gerboth; and Thomas W. McRae. *Accounting for Depreciable Assets.* AICPA Accounting Research Monograph No. 1. AICPA, 1975.

Lev, Baruch, and Henri Theil. "A Maximum Entropy Approach to the Choice of Asset Depreciation." *Journal of Accounting Research,* Autumn 1978, pp. 286–93.

McIntyre, Edward V. "Present Value Depreciation and the Disaggregation Problem." *Accounting Review,* January 1977, pp. 162–71.

NAA Management Accounting Practices Committee. "Fixed Asset Accounting: The Allocation of Costs." *Management Acccounting,* January 1974, pp. 43–49.

Peasnell, K. V. "The CCA Depreciation Problem— An Analysis and Proposal." *Abacus,* December 1977, pp. 123–40.

Wright, F. K. "Towards a General Theory of Depreciation." *Journal of Accounting Research,* Spring 1964, pp. 80–90.

Depreciation methods, economic life, and salvage values

Coughlan, Joseph D., and William K. Strand. *Depreciation: Accounting, Taxes, and Business Decisions.* New York: Ronald Press, 1969.

Ijiri, Yuji, and Robert S. Kaplan. "Probabilistic Depreciation and Its Implications for Group Depreciation." *Accounting Review,* October 1969, pp. 743–56.

Mullen Louis E. "Spotlight on Estimated Economic Life of Depreciable Assets." *CPA Journal,* August 1973, pp. 662–66.

Depreciation and allocation

Callen, Jeffrey L. "Financial Cost Allocations: A Game Theoretic Approach." *Accounting Review,* April 1978, pp. 303–8.

Eckel, Leonard G. "Arbitrary and Incorrigible Allocations." *Accounting Review,* October 1976, pp. 764–77.

Meyers, S. L. "A Proposal for Coping with the Allocation Problem." *Journal of Accountancy,* April 1976, pp. 52–56.

Thomas, Arthur L. *Studies in Accounting Research No. 9.* "The Allocation Problem: Part Two." AAA, 1974.

———. "Useful Arbitrary Allocations." *Accounting Review,* July 1971, pp. 472–79.

———. "Arbitrary and Incorrigible Allocations: A Comment." *Accounting Review,* January 1978, pp. 263–69.

Empirical Research

Archibald, T. Ross. "Stock Market Reaction to the Depreciation Switchback." *Accounting Review,* January 1972, pp. 22–30.

Barefield, Russell M., and **Eugene E. Comiskey.** "Depreciation Policy and the Behavior of Corporate Profits." *Journal of Accounting Research,* Autumn 1971, pp. 351–58.

Comiskey, Eugene E. "Market Response to Changes in Depreciation Accounting." *Accounting Review,* April 1971, pp. 279–85.

Staubus, George J. "Statistical Evidence of the Value of Depreciation Accounting." *Abacus,* August 1967, pp. 3–22.

CHAPTER 16

INTANGIBLES AND NONCURRENT INVESTMENTS

The accounting for intangible assets is one of the more difficult areas in accounting theory, partly because of difficulties of definition, but mainly because of the uncertainties regarding the measurement of their value and the estimation of useful life. The main approaches to accounting for intangibles can be classified according to the three basic levels of theory—syntactical, semantic, and behavioral. At the structural level, two views are generally presented. One view is that resource outlays for intangibles should be matched with associated revenues whenever possible and that allocations based upon assumed associations are better than no allocations. A second view is that nonmonetary assets should be carried forward to be matched with revenues only when there is a direct association between the two; since only rarely can intangibles be associated directly with specific revenue contributions, they should be reported as expenses in the year acquired (also a form of allocation).

At the semantic level of theory, intangibles should be reported in such a way as to permit real-world interpretation. A common view is that intangibles, like other assets, represent rights to future benefits, and conversely, if expenditures of resources result in potential future benefits, they should be carried as assets until such time as the benefits can no longer be expected to be received in the future. Because intangibles usually lack current market prices, however, a description of intangibles in monetary measurements is usually inadequate; written descriptions will most likely permit better interpretations. At the behavioral level, it is frequently suggested that emphasis should be on the reporting of possible inputs into decision models of investors and creditors, such as cash or net monetary flows or on information for securities markets. The objective of this chapter is to discuss the nature of intangibles and evaluate the alternative methods of reporting them in terms of the above three levels of theory.

THE NATURE OF INTANGIBLES

An *intangible* is usually defined as "a capital asset having no physical existence, its value being dependent on the rights that possession confers upon the owner."[1] Webster's dictionary defines it as an asset that is not corporeal.[2] The defining of intangible assets as capital assets merely implies that they are noncurrent; otherwise, such items as prepaid insurance, prepaid rent, and franchise taxes paid in advance would also be intangibles. Therefore, one common characteristic is that they are expected to benefit the firm beyond the current operating cycle of the business; and the invested capital represented by the asset will be available for reinvestment only gradually over several or many years. The characteristic of a lack of physical existence, however, is not clear-cut. Other noncurrent assets, such as long-term receivables and long-term investments also lack corporeal existence.

The most important single characteristic of intangibles is the high degree of uncertainty regarding the value of the future benefits to be received. In most cases, the possible values may range from zero to very large amounts. Some intangibles relate to the development and manufacture of a product, and others relate to the creation and maintenance of the demand for the product. Patents and copyrights reflect primarily the former; trademarks and trade names reflect primarily the latter. Goodwill may represent either or both. All, however, represent benefits that are highly uncertain and difficult to associate with specific revenues or specific periods.

Both tangible and intangible nonmonetary assets derive their economic value from the expectations of future earning power. However, many tangible assets have value in alternative uses, and their value to the firm can, at least in part, be compared with their physical condition, their replacement cost, the market value for used assets, and the market for the product of the enterprise. But, most intangible assets represent the development of exclusive processes or products or the protection of marketing superiority, none of which can be transferred to alternative uses. Although their value is derived from expected future revenues, it is impossible in most cases to determine what part of the revenue results from the intangibles and what part from other assets and services.

An alternative view of intangible assets is that they arise only from conditions of imperfect competition.[3] Patents, copyrights, and franchises grant the firm special partial monopolistic powers or rights to limit direct competition. Therefore, these rights do not add directly to the wealth of the economy and are differentiated from plant and equipment, which are productive assets. However, this distinction is not clear because the rights associated with the owning of productive property may also be at least in part the result of imperfect competition.

---

[1] Eric L. Kohler, *A Dictionary for Accountants,* 3d ed. (Englewood Cliffs, N.J.: Prentice-Hall, 1963), p. 269.

[2] *Webster's Third New International Dictionary* (Springfield, Mass.: G. & C. Merriam Co., 1961), p. 1173.

[3] See, for example, J. E. Sands, *Wealth, Income, and Intangibles* (Toronto: University of Toronto Press, 1963), p. 28.

One common characteristic of most intangibles is that they cannot be separated from the firm or the physical property of the firm. They exist and have value only in combination with the tangible assets of the firm. Because of this, they are frequently considered to represent residual benefits after all tangible assets are specifically identified. However, this concept has very little merit for accountants in their attempts to identify and measure intangibles individually or as a group.

THE VALUATION OF INTANGIBLES

The valuation of intangibles for reporting purposes depends upon the reporting objectives and concepts applied. If the objective is to measure and report each period the individual assets of the firm, the only alternative is to measure the value of the firm as a whole and subtract from this value the valuation of other specific net assets. But as indicated in Chapter 11, the only meaningful valuation of the firm as a whole is that determined subjectively by the investor except for the value of the firm derived from the market price of the shares. The accountant should not attempt to determine this value for the investor because of the subjective expectations required and the necessity of adjusting these expectations for personal preferences or aversions for risk.

If the objective, however, is to measure and report specific assets in order to provide the users of financial reports with an indication of the resources available to the firm, an independent measurement of the intangibles might be desirable. But there are some major differences between the measurement concepts that can be applied to intangible as opposed to tangible assets. Valuation on the basis of output values and earning power is difficult to apply in any situation and, except in rare cases, impossible to apply even roughly to intangible assets. Replacement cost, a measure of current input value, is likewise generally impossible of calculation. Each intangible is usually unique and cannot be compared with other similar items. And because of this uniqueness, meaningful and relevant price indexes cannot be found to compute specific replacement costs. The only practical valuation is, therefore, the actual input value—historical cost—or cost adjusted for changes in general purchasing power, although neither of these has sufficient interpretive significance.

When intangibles are acquired by purchase, individually or as a part of a basket purchase, the determination of cost is similar to the computation of the cost of plant and equipment under like circumstances. When intangibles are acquired by self-development, however, the computation of their cost involves all of the difficulties of self-constructed assets plus some additional problems of its own. Most of the costs of patents, trademarks, and trade names are joint costs. Many patents may emerge from joint research and development expenditures, and several trademarks and trade names may be advertised jointly. These problems can be solved by the use of known costing methods, but the results are likely to be arbitrary if they include allocated joint costs. To the extent that they do, the valuations are likely to be meaningless.

The basic characteristics of high uncertainty and uniqueness have led most accountants and accounting associations to recommend that intangibles should not be valued in excess of cost.[4]

Although cost is also generally recommended for tangible assets, other valuations may be acceptable and are occasionally recommended. But for intangibles, there must be compelling evidence that some other valuation is more appropriate. Even when intangible assets are donated to the firm, there is a general reluctance to record any value in the accounts because of the high degree of uncertainty regarding whatever valuation may be chosen.

When intangibles are acquired through the issuance of capital stock, the determination of cost is a difficult, if not almost impossible, problem. In this case, cost may be considered to be either the fair value of the stock given or the fair value of the rights acquired, whichever is the more evident. If the stock does not have a current market price, the determination of the cost of the intangibles is extremely difficult because the intangibles generally have no market value either. It is inappropriate to assume that cost is equal to the par value or stated value of the shares issued in exchange.

Because most intangibles are not severable from the firm and cannot be measured in terms of a current cash equivalent, Chambers suggested that they are not assets and should not be included in the statements of the firm.[5] Current practice does not permit the charging of purchased identifiable intangibles to expenses immediately upon acquisition.

THE AMORTIZATION OF INTANGIBLE ASSETS

Most intangibles that are generated gradually by the firm through annual expenditures are charged immediately to expense. However, intangibles that are acquired through a lump-sum purchase or that are developed through extraordinary identifiable expenditures are frequently capitalized and amortized similarly to the depreciation allocations of plant and equipment. Once the initial valuation to be amortized is determined, the major factors to be estimated are (1) the useful life of the asset and (2) the pattern of allocation to the several periods of the life of the asset. The residual or scrap value is generally nonexistent or immaterial.

Intangibles can be classified on the basis of how they are acquired, whether they can be specifically identified, or whether their lives are

---

[4] *AICPA Professional Standards,* para. 5141.25.

[5] Raymond J. Chambers, *Accounting, Evaluation and Economic Behavior* (Englewood Cliffs, N.J.: Prentice-Hall, 1966), p. 209.

limited and can be estimated or are indeterminate. According to the traditional accounting structure, if resource outlays are incurred in order to benefit future periods, the cost should be capitalized and allocated to the future periods. It does not matter how the intangible asset was acquired. However, from the point of view of semantic interpretation, the intangible asset acquired must be identifiable. An intangible asset is assumed to be identifiable if it is acquired from other enterprises or individuals. For intangible assets that are developed by the firm, the costs should be charged to expense unless the asset is specifically identifiable, has a determinable limited life, and is not inherent in the continuation of the business. Although one of several methods of classification can be used, the classification according to whether the asset has a limited life or an indeterminate life does provide a useful breakdown in studying the alternative allocation procedures and their effects.

Intangibles with limited life

Patents, copyrights, and some franchises have a maximum legal life, and only rarely will the economic life exceed this legal life. If circumstances permit the value to extend beyond the legal life, the cost or other value should be amortized over this economic life; but without the legal protection, the value beyond the legal life is too uncertain to include in the amortization schedule. More commonly, the economic life is shorter than the legal life because of market demand conditions or because of obsolescence. When this is the case, the economic life should definitely be the controlling factor. It is very unusual for copyrights to provide benefit to the firm for the entire period of the copyright. Textbooks, for example, frequently become obsolete in five years or less. But if the book is revised, some of the initial value carries into the second and third editions.

Like depreciation, the pattern of amortization of intangibles is generally thought to be appropriate if it is related to the expected associated revenue contributions. However, since such an association is not likely to be apparent with most intangibles, *APB Opinion No. 17* suggests that the straight-line method be used unless other systematic methods can be demonstrated to be more appropriate. As a definition of *appropriate* is not given, it can only be assumed that an association with expected future benefits would be an appropriate criterion. In the case of copyrights, the benefits frequently increase during the first few years and then drop off substantially. If frequent revisions are expected, some of the initial acquisition costs should be amortized over the lives of subsequent editions. The benefit pattern for patents may depend on many economic considerations, including the effect of subsequent supporting or competing developments. Each case must be judged on its own circumstances and expectations.

Because of the high degree of uncertainty regarding the periods to be benefited, it is more likely that changes in expectations will occur for intangibles than for plant and equipment. Therefore, *APB Opinion No. 17* recommends that when changes in expectations of useful lives occur, the unamortized cost should be allocated to the remaining periods in the revised useful life, but not to exceed 40 years. However, if the value is reduced significantly, a partial write-down should be made by reporting an extraordinary loss in the income statement. Note that a write-up of an intangible is not permitted. If excessive amortization has occurred, the amortization to subsequent periods is generally reduced by an amount large enough to offset the earlier overamortization, even if this does result in a material reduction in the reported expense. This is a major inconsistency in the traditional accounting structure.

Amortization of intangibles is considered by many to represent the matching of expenses with associated revenues, but there are many difficulties with this procedure. The major difficulty is that the expected benefits are the result of the interactions of all of the resources of the firm. Since these difficulties were discussed in Chapter 15, they will not be repeated here. However, further difficulties occur because of the inability to measure even expected life. Each intangible is more or less unique, so that experience is of little help. Also, the capital expenditure decision is generally not so precisely formulated. As a result, the amortization procedure results in a method of smoothing income to prevent fluctuations of income due to the irregular acquisition of intangibles unrelated to current operating activities. If the net income figure is used as the major item for prediction purposes, the smoothing process may be of some assistance; however, it seems highly unlikely that arbitrary allocations can provide relevant information for investors and creditors.

Intangibles with indefinite lives

Trademarks, trade names, organization costs, and goodwill are examples of intangibles generally considered to have no limited term of existence and no natural limited life. However, the economic life of each of these is definitely limited unless expenditures are continually made for maintenance and replacement. Even initial organization costs require periodic reorganization expenditures, most of which are interrelated with goodwill and current operations. But the time when the original asset value is completely replaced by additional expenditures cannot be determined even in retrospect. Therefore, one position is that the original cost should remain on the books and the costs of maintenance or replacement should be charged against current income. No amortization is required because the value of the original asset is thought to continue if proper maintenance expenditures are made.

The procedure of carrying the intangible asset at its original cost and charging maintenance and replacement expenditures to current income accounts is similar to the replacement method of depreciation. However, its application to intangibles is more appropriate than its use for the depreciation of plant and equipment, because replacement is a continual process with some intangibles and it is sporadic and infrequent for plant and equipment. Thus, the replacement expenditures are charged against the incomes of all periods fairly evenly. This method is also advantageous because it provides for an income charge based on current costs, like LIFO. But there are some major disadvantages: (1) If the value of the intangible is being increased through current expenditures, the charge against current income is excessive, and the reverse is true if the value of the intangible is not maintained. (2) As with LIFO, the value of the intangible soon becomes out of date and not representative of the value to be charged to future periods. (3) The current charge against income is subject to manipulation by management. (4) It does not result in a systematic matching of expenses with benefits received or with current revenues.

The position of *APB Opinion No. 17,* however, is that all intangibles eventually lose their value and therefore should be amortized over the period estimated to be benefited but not exceeding 40 years. This 40-year period is arbitrary and can be defended only on the basis that it is long enough so that the income of no period is significantly affected. Therefore, it can be assumed that this type of allocation is really neutral or sterilized with respect to the information presented to investors and creditors. It does not provide useful information, but neither does it harm or distort other information being presented.

A major difficulty with the amortization of intangibles with indefinite lives is that allocation is required despite the fact that current expenditures are being made and charged against income for the maintenance of their value. This results in a double charge against income during the amortization period. It is similar to charging the cost of replacement equipment against income while at the same time depreciating the cost of the original equipment. If the replacement method is acceptable, the amortization of the original cost is not also appropriate; if amortization is proper, the cost of replacements should be capitalized. This capitalization of replacements and the continual amortization of the total cost of intangibles would provide a practical method for charging the cost of benefits received to expenses. Difficulties in the measurement of replacements, however, indicate that the replacement method without amortization of the original cost may be the most appropriate, or at least the most expedient, method.

APB Opinion No. 17 does permit a lump-sum write-off of intangibles when there is reasonable evidence that they have become worthless, but it is very clear in prohibiting write-offs immediately after acquisition. The assumption is that if the intangible has been acquired at a cost, it must be worth this price, at least at that time. The main purpose of this restriction was to prevent undue conservatism in asset valuation and overstatement of the incomes of subsequent periods; however, it does not recognize that an error can be made in the acquisition of the intangible. If this error is recognized immediately, the loss should be recorded; there is no justification of carrying forward the loss to future periods. Immediate recognition

of an overstatement of an intangible should also be permitted when there
has been an error in the valuation of a nonmonetary asset exchanged for
the intangible.

RESEARCH AND DEVELOPMENT COSTS

To the extent that research and development activities are carried out to
develop new products, improve old ones, or reduce future operating costs,
they are expected to benefit future periods, rather than only the current
period. Because future periods are expected to be benefited, the knowledge
gained is either an asset of the firm or an increase in the value of existing
assets or of the firm as a whole. Therefore, according to the matching
concept, the research and development costs should be capitalized and
amortized over the period benefited. Even though the period and the timing of the benefits are highly uncertain, proponents of the matching concept claim that an appropriate allocation is better than an immediate
write-off because a subjective estimate of the value is better than an
arbitrary valuation of zero.[6] Allocation is also assumed to be better because an immediate write-off may result in lower net earnings, thus indicating an adverse situation while the reverse may be true. A firm that
sponsors a large amount of research may have a very favorable future,
and one that carries out no research may be doomed to failure. Thus, if it
is all expensed, there may be an incentive to cut back research just at the
time it is needed to maintain market position or efficiency.

An alternative to full capitalization and amortization is the common
practice of expensing general research and development costs and
capitalizing only research costs that relate to specific projects with expected net revenue contribution streams.[7] These special projects are
treated like investments in plant and equipment, and the amortization
would be similar to the depreciation concepts related to net revenue contributions discussed in Chapter 15.

The position of the FASB in *Statement No. 2* is that all research and
development costs should be charged to expense when incurred, except
when R&D are conducted for others under contract. This recommendation
appears to be a major step in relying on criteria other than that established by the traditional historical cost accounting structure. Insofar as
this recommendation is based on the observation that there is no causal
relationship between R&D expenditures and future benefits, it is consistent with the traditional accounting structure. However, it is also based
on the lack of interpretation of the asset (arising from capitalization of
expenditures) because it does not reflect the value of any specific future

---

[6] See, for example, Allan R. Drebin, "Accounting for Proprietary Research," *Accounting
Review* 41 (July 1966): 425.

[7] See, for example, J. A. Milburn, "A Look at Problems in Research and Development
Accounting," *Canadian Chartered Accountant* 72 (June 1968): 404–8.

benefits, and if they do exist, their value is not measurable. The conclusion of the FASB was also based on the lack of usefulness of the information arising from capitalization. The Board was influenced by the fact that security analysts and investors suggested that capitalization was not useful in assessing the earnings potential of the enterprise. Further, there was no evidence that capitalization would improve the ability to predict either the amount or variability of future rates of return. In addition, the expensing of R&D is consistent with the efficient market thesis so long as there is full disclosure of the amount and types of expenditures.

GOODWILL

The nature of financial goodwill has been the subject of debate since before the end of the 19th century. However, the early discussions centered primarily on the legal recognition and definition of the concept. From an accounting point of view, three major conceptions of goodwill appear frequently in the literature: (1) the valuation of intangible attitudes toward the firm, (2) the present discounted value of the excess of expected future profits over that considered a normal return on the total investment not including the goodwill, and (3) a master valuation account—the excess of the value of the business as a whole over the valuations attaching to its individual tangible and intangible net assets. In the first and second definitions, goodwill is usually considered to be a separate asset with specific characteristics. In the third definition—as a master valuation account—it is not generally considered to be a separate distinct asset.

It should be emphasized at this point that the problem of goodwill arises as a result of peculiarities of the traditional accounting structure. The attempts discussed below to provide goodwill with semantic interpretation have basically failed. Furthermore, little or no evidence has been found to indicate that the reporting of goodwill provides relevant information for investors or creditors in their decision making. Because goodwill lacks real-world interpretation and cannot be measured independently, it should be omitted from financial statements. This does not mean, however, that aggregations of resources should not be reported separately from measurements of individual assets. Aggregations of resources may have valuations greater or less than the summation of identifiable parts because of synergism among the resources acquired or with resources already owned. The following is an evaluation of goodwill as currently reported within the accounting structure.

The valuation of favorable attitudes toward the firm

Goodwill is frequently thought to arise from advantageous business relationships, good relations with employees, and favorable attitudes of customers. These favorable attitudes may be due to an advantageous location, an excellent reputation and name, monopolistic privileges, good business management, and other factors. When the purchase price of a going business exceeds the sum of the valuations of all individual assets other than goodwill, the excess may be assumed to represent the payment for these specific intangible attributes. However, specific values cannot be assigned to each of these characteristics individually. Therefore, because a total valuation for goodwill cannot be computed by adding the sum of the parts, the mere listing of these characteristics does not provide any meaningful insight into their valuation, either individually or collectively.

A fallacy of this specific attribute approach is that most of these characteristics attach to specific assets including other intangible assets. A favorable location, for example, means that the land and buildings are worth more than similar property elsewhere. The value of excellent reputation and name attach to the valuation of trade names and brand names. Good business management and monopolistic privileges, however, do not necessarily attach to specific assets, but represent attributes of the firm as a whole. But the listing of specific attitudes and attributes does not provide a meaningful approach to the definition and valuation of goodwill. Certain favorable attributes should be included in the valuation of tangible assets; others should be classified separately as specific types of intangibles; and the remainder (that which can now be called goodwill) represents the residual benefits that cannot be associated with specific attributes.

The present value of superior earnings

A common approach to the nature of goodwill is to assume that it represents the present discounted value of expected future earnings (or cash payments to equity holders) in excess of that which may be considered a normal return. However, this is a measurement of goodwill, not a description of its nature. Furthermore, there is doubt that it is valid conceptually even as a measurement concept.

As indicated in Chapter 11, the value of the firm as a whole to individual investors can only be determined subjectively by the investors, because it depends upon their expectations of future cash flows, the expected opportunity rates of return, and personal utility risk functions. As Chambers stated, "the goodwill of a going concern runs to the constituents, not to the firm."[8] Therefore, neither management nor the accountants can place a correct valuation on goodwill. But neither can the investor allocate this total value of the firm logically to specific tangible and intangible assets and to goodwill. The assumption that the tangible assets can earn only a "normal" rate while other factors are responsible for the excess is fiction.

---

[8] Chambers, *Accounting, Evaluation,* p. 211.

Tangible assets may have value in their specific use because of imperfect competition and changes in demand for the products as well as efficient utilization. All factors interact in the production of the final service or product and in permitting cash distributions to stockholders. Any attempt to allocate a portion of the total value of a firm on the basis of the capitalization of superior earnings is, therefore, artificial.

Goodwill as a master valuation account

Canning was one of the early writers who questioned whether goodwill is an asset at all in the usual sense, and he preferred to view goodwill as a master valuation account.[9] All assets obtain their value to the firm because of their expected contribution to the stream of future earnings and cash flows. Therefore the entire value of the firm should be associated with the specific assets giving rise to this stream of cash flows. If expectations of cash flows should increase (after making payment for superior management skills), the values of all assets or of specific assets contributing to this increase are now worth more than before.

Generally, however, it is not possible to allocate the total value of the firm over the specific assets. Receivables can be valued in terms of the discounted expected cash receipts; inventories can be valued in terms of net realizable value; but land, plant and equipment, and patent rights cannot usually be associated with specific expected money flows. The unallocated value is, therefore, recorded as goodwill—a master valuation account.

Frequently, however, no attempt is made to allocate to specific assets the excess of the price paid for a business over the carrying value of the specific assets. Even though this residual may be called goodwill, it has even fewer of the attributes of an intangible asset. Instead, it represents unallocated costs of tangible assets and some specific intangibles. Goodwill is not an adequate substitute for the careful determination of the cost of specific assets, based as closely as possible on their value to the firm at the date of acquisition. However, in the opinion of the author, since goodwill is not a severable asset, it should not be reported separately. An alternative would be to report the current values of measurable assets and the total price of the basket purchase. The summation of the separate values of the measurable assets should not be forced to equal the purchase price. The allocation of the purchase price to individual assets including goodwill is necessarily arbitrary and serves no useful purpose.

As a master valuation account, can goodwill be negative as well as positive? Logically, the answer is no. If the total price paid for a business is less than the replacement cost of the assets, this is evidence that the specific assets are not worth their replacement cost; the deficiency should be allocated to the individual assets. In general, accountants are less

---

[9] John B. Canning, *The Economics of Accountancy* (New York: Ronald Press, 1929), p. 42.

reluctant to record assets at less than their current replacement value than they are to record them at a value greater than this. But if the assets are recorded at their carrying value to the old firm and no allocation is made, the deficiency is a negative valuation account. It would be inappropriate to call this overvaluation in the specific accounts a negative goodwill.

THE RECORDING OF GOODWILL

Costs incurred by a firm to improve its future earning power are generally charged immediately to expense unless they can be directly associated with specific tangible or intangible assets. Since goodwill represents advantages not specifically identifiable when acquired in the normal course of business, it is not recorded as an asset, even though future periods will be benefited. The main reasons supporting this practice are the inability to identify and measure the goodwill created each period and the absence of any logical method of associating these costs with any specific revenue in future periods. This is in accord with *APB Opinion No. 17,* which states that expenditures for "nonpurchased" goodwill should be deducted from income when incurred. The author agrees with this practice because no apparent advantage would be obtained by attempting to capitalize goodwill acquired in this fashion. A disclosure of such expenditures may be relevant for a valuation of the firm by investors, but capitalization would not determine the value of the firm because many changes in the value of the firm occur for other reasons, such as exogenous changes in the demand for the product and fortuitous discoveries of previously unknown resources. Since there is little controversy regarding the treatment of the nonpurchased goodwill, the following discussion relates primarily to goodwill acquired by a lump-sum purchase—the total cost of operating property in excess of the amounts that can be associated with specific tangible or intangible classifications.

Purchased goodwill

When a business as a whole is acquired by another firm, the excess of the price paid in stock or other assets over the fair value of the separable tangible and intangible assets acquired, less obligations assumed, represents the amount paid for goodwill. It is, therefore, a master valuation amount.

In the pooling method of accounting for acquisitions, goodwill would not be reported in the financial statements, but there is some merit in the proposition that the total amount of consideration paid for the acquired firm or properties is relevant information for the evaluation and decisions of investors and other interested parties. However, once the amount of the goodwill is reported, there is no agreement regarding its disposition. In accordance with *APB Opinion No. 17,* goodwill is considered to be an asset with indeterminate life and, therefore, should be amortized over a maximum life of 40 years unless it is deemed to have a shorter life. This recommendation is based on the assumption that the life of goodwill is generally neither specifically limited nor finite. The life of 40 years for amortization purposes is at least long enough so that the income of no period is likely to be materially affected.

The systematic amortization is supported on the ground that goodwill represents benefits to be matched with future revenues over a reasonable period of time. It is also frequently argued that if it represents a payment for superior earnings, the purchase price was based on expectations regarding a limited period during which the superior earnings would be received. If goodwill does continue beyond this reasonable period, it is assumed that it then represents benefits accumulated, since the acquisition of the property, and therefore it should be accounted for consistently with other nonpurchased goodwill as current expense. Thus, the amortization of goodwill is supported on the ground that the value of the purchased goodwill declines over time.

The argument for nonallocation is based in part on the fact that if nonpurchased goodwill is charged to expense, the allocation of purchased goodwill results in a double charge. Catlett and Olson also present the argument that purchased and nonpurchased goodwill should be treated alike; neither should be reported as an asset in the financial statements.[10] One of the more valid arguments against allocation, however, is that both the life and the pattern of allocation must by necessity be arbitrary, and thus without a logical basis. Without a logical basis, it is highly unlikely that the resulting reported net income figures would be more meaningful than if the allocation had not been made.

A major difference between the requirements of *Opinion No. 17* and *ARS No. 10,* however, is that the former prohibits the immediate write-off of an intangible, and the latter suggests that goodwill should be accounted for as a reduction of stockholders' equity. The reasoning for this reduction (suggested by *ARS No. 10*) is that the amount paid for the goodwill represents a reduction of the firm's resources in anticipation of future earnings. The remaining equity would then represent the values of the separate resources and property rights consistent with the reporting for a continuing enterprise. A fallacy of this argument, however, is that the entire purchase price is a payment for future cash flows and earnings; the amount paid for the acquired enterprise represents invested capital just as much as does an amount paid to acquire an addition to existing plant.

The author is sympathetic with the recommendations of *ARS No. 10* for other reasons, however. After the date of acquisition, there appears to be little evidence that the continual presentation of the goodwill as an

---

[10] George R. Catlett and Norman O. Olson "Accounting for Goodwill," *Accounting Research Study No. 10* (AICPA, 1968) p. 89.

asset will provide useful information to investors or other interested readers of financial statements because it lacks semantic interpretation. Furthermore, the amortization of the goodwill to income by the use of arbitrary procedures seems of doubtful validity because of the homogeneity problem and interactions mentioned in the previous chapter.

"Negative" goodwill

If goodwill is defined as representing a group of unidentifiable favorable attributes of the firm that are separable from the values of the identifiable assets, it is difficult to conceive of this being negative. For if the firm is worth less than the values of the separable assets, the previous owners would have sold them separately, rather than as a whole. Therefore, negative goodwill could not exist; the amount paid for the firm would represent the values of the separable assets only and the total should be so allocated. This seems to be the position of *APB Opinion No. 16* in its recommendation that when a combination is deemed to be a purchase, the assets acquired should be recorded at their fair value or the fair value of the consideration given in the exchange.[11] This view is consistent with the cost concept because the assets are recorded at their current value only if the consideration given is not as clearly measurable as the assets received.

APB Opinion No. 17, however, does suggest that when the cost of an acquired company is less than the sum of the market or appraised values of identifiable assets less liabilities, the difference should be allocated to reduce the values of the noncurrent assets. If a difference remains that cannot be allocated (after the noncurrent assets are reduced to zero), it is suggested that it be shown as a deferred credit and taken into income in future periods by systematic amortization. However, since the excess of the amount assignable to net assets over the cost to the parent represents either an advantageous purchase or an overvaluation of all net assets as a whole, there is no logic in any allocation of this amount to income on a "reasonable and systematic" basis. Without a knowledge of the meaning of the credit, no allocation can be reasonable. Furthermore, since most firms report this deferred credit as neither a liability nor stockholders' equity, it is a meaningless item in the balance sheet; thus, it appears to be only a method of smoothing the effect of the acquisition. Since both the classification of the deferred credit and its amortization are uninformative to users of financial statements, they create more questions than answers.

Accounting Research Study No. 10 suggested that when negative goodwill appears to exist, a careful evaluation of the separate assets and liabilities should be made. It suggests, however, that negative amounts that cannot be assigned to specific items may indicate the necessity for future expenditures to improve the organization and efficiency of the firm;

---

[11] *AICPA Professional Standards,* para. 1091.67.

in this case, *ARS No. 10* suggests that the difference should be reported as a liability to be charged with these costs in the future. However, the need to improve the efficiency of a firm does not fall into the usual definition of a liability. Since any costs could be charged against this "liability," the result could be just as capricious and arbitrary as that suggested in *APB Opinion No. 16*. An alternative suggested by *ARS No. 10,* however, is to credit the amount immediately to retained earnings or capital surplus. Although there is little theoretical justification for this method, it probably creates less misinformation than other methods, so long as the net purchase price is disclosed at the date of acquisition. If the reason for the difference cannot be identified, it should not be taken into income merely to stay within the double-entry reporting system.

NONCURRENT INVESTMENTS

Investments in securities of other firms held for other than current purposes are generally classified and accounted for on the basis of the intent of holding the securities and the relationship with the investee firm. Investments that represent a controlling interest in the voting stock of a firm (generally in excess of 50 percent) should be included in the consolidated financial statements. When less than a controlling interest is present but the investor is able to exercise significant influence over the operating and financial policies of the investee (generally representing from 20 to 50 percent of outstanding shares), the investment should be accounted for on the equity basis. Noncurrent marketable securities should be reported at the lower of cost or market for the noncurrent portfolio. Noncurrent investments not included in the above classifications would normally be reported at cost.

Noncurrent marketable equity securities

As discussed in Chapter 12, *FASB Statement No. 12* requires that a separate portfolio be set up for noncurrent marketable equity securities and that the portfolio should be valued on the lower-of-cost-or-market basis. The reduction to market, however, results in a valuation allowance as an offset to the portfolio and accumulated changes reported as an offset to stockholders' equity.

The apparent purpose of this procedure is to report the portfolio on the lower-of-cost-or-market basis without including the reduction in income until it is considered to be realized. Realization is assumed to occur when securities are either transferred to the current portfolio or are sold or when the decline in market price is considered to be other than temporary. The result is that all gains and losses on the investments are included in income at or before the sale of the investment; the procedure results in only changing the timing of the reporting of losses and recoveries.

The main difficulty with this procedure is that it is inconsistent with the comprehensive concept of income, which would include all changes in asset valuations other than those arising from equity transactions. In addition, it uses an offset to stockholders' equity as a means of deferring the reporting of losses. Thus it has all of the deficiencies of the use of deferred charges when used for the same purpose. Also, these procedures have all of the disadvantages of the lower-of-cost-or-market method discussed in Chapter 11.

The equity method for unconsolidated subsidiaries

APB Opinion No. 18 requires the use of the equity method for investments where consolidation is not considered appropriate and for investments of about 20 to 50 percent of the voting stock when the investor can be assumed to be able to exercise considerable influence over the investee. Under the equity method, the initial cost of the investment is adjusted each period to include the investor's share of the earnings or losses of the subsidiary. Dividends received reduce the amount of the investment. The excess of cost over the investor's equity in the book value of the investee at the date of acquisition should be allocated to specific assets and goodwill, and depreciable assets and goodwill should be allocated systematically to expenses. Intercompany profits and losses are eliminated and other adjustments are made as in consolidation. The result is that the investment and income each year are accounted for as if the investment had been reported as a consolidated subsidiary.

A major advantage of the equity method is that at the structural level it provides some consistency between the reporting of consolidated subsidiaries and investments that are not included in the consolidation, but which have some of the characteristics of subsidiaries. However, it also has all of the limitations of consolidations discussed in Chapter 19. In addition, there is inadequate information regarding what the investment valuation means, as it does not represent either the investor's equity in the book value of the investee or the market price of the stock. Also, the specification of a minimum of 20 percent of voting stock is arbitrary and the criterion of significant influence is vague.

On a priori grounds, it appears that the market value method would serve the needs of investors and creditors better than the equity method, in addition to permitting better real-world interpretation. Financial information would be improved if there were a disclosure of the dividends received over several periods as well as the firm's share of the investee's reported income. Such information would likely be helpful to investors in evaluating the firm as a whole and in predicting future cash flows. In an empirical study, Lloyd and Weygandt concluded that market value information would provide useful information for investors.[12] In another

---

[12] Michl Lloyd and Jerry J. Weygandt, "Market Information for Nonsubsidiary Investments," *Accounting Review,* October 1971, pp. 764.

study, Copeland, Strawser, and Binns suggested that the equity method does not provide an adequate surrogate for market value.[13]

SELECTED ADDITIONAL READING

Accounting for intangibles

Abdel-khalik, A. Rashad. "Advertising Effectiveness and Accounting Policy." *Accounting Review,* October 1975, pp. 657–70.

Falk, Haim, and **Joseph C. Miller.** "Amortization of Advertising Expenditures." *Journal of Accounting Research,* Spring 1977, pp. 12–22.

Picconi, Mario J. "A Reconsideration of the Recognition of Advertising Assets on Financial Statements." *Journal of Accounting Research,* Autumn 1977, pp. 317–26.

Goodwill

Catlett, George R., and **Norman O. Olson.** "Accounting for Goodwill." *Accounting Research Study No. 10.* AICPA, 1968.

Gynther, Reg. S. "Some Conceptualizing on Goodwill." *Accounting Review,* April 1969, pp. 247–55.

Lee, T. A. "Goodwill: An Example of Will-O'-the-Wisp Accounting." *Accounting Business Research,* Autumn 1971, pp. 318–28.

Miller, Malcolm C. "Goodwill—An Aggregation Issue." *Accounting Review,* April 1973, pp. 280–91.

Tearney, Michael G. "Accounting for Goodwill: A Realistic Approach." *Journal of Accountancy,* July 1973, pp. 41–45.

Weinwurm, Earnest H. "Modernizing the Goodwill Concept." *Management Accounting,* December 1971, pp. 31–34.

Research and development

Dukes, Roland E. "An Investigation of the Effects of Expensing Research and Development Costs on Security Prices." In *Proceedings in the Conference on Topical Research in Accounting,* Michael Schiff and George Sorter, eds. New York: New York University, 1976, pp. 147–93.

Gellein, Oscar S., and **Maurice S. Newman.** *Accounting Research Study No. 14.* Accounting for Research and Development Expenditures." AICPA 1973.

Gridley, F. W. "Accounting for R&D Costs." *Financial Executive,* April 1974, pp. 18–22.

Johnson, Orace. "Contra-Equity Accounting for R&D." *Accounting Review,* October 1976, pp. 808–22.

Noncurrent investments

Barrett, M. Edgar. "Accounting for Intercorporate Investments: A Behavioral Field Experiment." *Journal of Accounting Research,* Empirical Research in Accounting, 1971, pp. 50–65.

---

[13] Ronald M. Copeland, Robert Strawser, and John G. Binns, "Accounting for Investments in Common Stock," *Financial Executive,* February 1972, p. 46.

————. *"APB Opinion No. 18:* 'A Move toward Preferences of Users.'" *Financial Analysts Journal,* July–August 1972, pp. 47–50, 52–55.

Copeland, Ronald M.; Robert Strawser; and **John G. Binns.** "Accounting for Investments in Common Stock." *Financial Executive,* February 1972, pp. 36–38ff.

Lynch, Thomas Edward. "Accounting for Investments in Equity Securities by the Equity and Market Value Methods." *Financial Analysts Journal,* January–February 1975, pp. 62–69.

Lloyd, Michl, and **Jerry Weygandt.** "Market Value Information for Nonsubsidiary Investments." *Accounting Review,* October 1971, pp. 756–64.

O'Connor, Melvin C., and **James C. Hamre.** "Alternative Methods of Accounting for Long-Term Nonsubsidiary Intercorporate Investments in Common Stock." *Accounting Review,* April 1972, pp. 308–19.

Storey, Reed K. and **Maurice Moonitz.** *AICPA Accounting Research Monograph No. 1,* "Market Value Methods for Intercorporate Investments in Stock." AICPA, 1976.

CHAPTER 17

LIABILITIES AND
THEIR MEASUREMENT

The *Statement of Financial Accounting Concepts No. 3* defines *liabilities* as ". . . probable future sacrifices of economic benefits arising from present obligations of a particular entity to transfer assets or provide services to other entities in the future as a result of past transactions or events."[1] This definition stresses the importance of uncertainty regarding liabilities. However, a number of questions are raised regarding the nature and measurement of liabilities to permit economic and financial interpretations and to permit the use of the information in investment decisions, such as in the prediction of future cash flows and the measurement of risk. The identification of liabilities and their measurement are discussed in this chapter. Problems of measurement in specific areas are discussed in the following and other chapters.

THE NATURE OF LIABILITIES

In an attempt to provide specific real-world interpretation of liabilities, the following questions must be answered: (1) What circumstances give rise to a liability? (2) Should liabilities include equitable as well as legal obligations? (3) If there is an unconditional right of offset, should the obligation be included among the liabilities? (4) Should there be a relatively determinable amount to be paid and a reasonably determinable maturity date? (5) Should the payee be known or ascertainable?

Circumstances for liabilities to exist

In the traditional accounting structure, the reporting of a liability is dependent upon the importance of recognizing the other side of the transaction or event—the accrual of an expense, the recognition of a loss, or the receipt by the firm of specific assets. The first of these, the accrual of an expense, is generally thought to be the most important because it affects directly the computation of current income. If services have been received by the firm and used in current operations, it is necessary that the liabil-

---

[1] *AICPA Professional Standards,* para. 1230.028.

ity be accrued in order to include the expense in the determination of net income. Likewise, the reporting of an extraordinary loss is required in order to disclose the effect of the event on nonoperating income; a related liability must then be recorded to complete the transaction. When specific assets are received by the firm and recorded, a related liability must also be recorded in order to present a balanced statement of financial position.

The *SFAC No. 3* definition of liabilities is an attempt to give semantic interpretation to the term. Two of the basic characteristics are that the obligation must exist in the present and that it must be the result of past transactions or events. Thus, the existence of a liability by this definition is dependent upon the occurrence of an external transaction—a financial event arising as a result of a business deal with an outside firm or person—or a nonfinancial event, such as an accident resulting in an obligation to pay for damages. Acquisitions of goods or services are clearly transactions that may give rise to obligations to pay for them. On the other hand, obligations to pay for goods or services to be acquired in the future are not generally considered to be liabilities. Whether or not they are included in the definition depends upon the interpretation of transactions or events giving rise to them.

However, the conditions giving rise to the obligation are less important than a semantic interpretation of the obligation itself. If an obligation does in fact exist, it may be important to record it as a liability regardless of how it arose. Furthermore, from the point of view of the users of financial statements, the effect of the obligation on future cash requirements is more important than the past transactions or events which gave rise to it.

Equitable and legal obligations

A second major difference of opinion regarding liabilities involves whether liabilities should include equitable as well as legal obligations. Equitable obligations are not necessarily enforceable by legal means, but may nevertheless be regarded as obligations by both parties. The narrowest position is that only legal obligations or debts should be included. Kohler appears to imply the legal characteristics by stating that a liability is

> An amount . . . payable in money, or in goods or services . . . particularly, any debt (*a*) due or past due (current liability), (*b*) due at a specified time in the future (e.g., funded debt, accrued liability), or (*c*) due only on failure to perform a future act (deferred income; contingent liability).[2]

The last example, however, can hardly be called a legal obligation at the present time. A contingent liability is not a legal debt until and if a future event occurs.

---

[2] Eric L. Kohler, *A Dictionary For Accountants,* 4th ed. (Englewood Cliffs, N.J.: Prentice-Hall, 1970), p. 263.

Canning, however, included equitable obligations in his definition which stated that

a liability is a service, valuable in money, which a proprietor is under an existing legal (or equitable) duty to render a second person (or set of persons) and which is not unconditionally an agreed set-off to its full amount against specific services of equal or greater money value due from this second person to the proprietor.[3]

Although Canning did not present examples of equitable duties that should be included, presumably he would include amounts intended to be paid for damages sustained or services received when there is no legal obligation to make such payment. He would also probably include amounts to be paid to maintain goodwill and business confidence, such as refunds for damaged or returned merchandise when there is no legal obligation to make such refunds.

SFAC No. 3 includes both equitable and constructive obligations in the definition of *liabilities*. The equitable obligations arise from social or moral sanctions or custom. The legality of obligations is difficult to determine in many cases and may require a court decision. Therefore, it is more appropriate to follow custom and business practices. Social and moral obligations are probably just as difficult to determine as the legality of obligations. The accountant should not be required to make either purely moral or legal judgments.

Unconditional right of offset

What about obligations arising out of current contracts for the future acquisition of goods and services? In a sense these are transactions, and in another sense they are not. They are financial events arising from business dealings and giving rise to obligations to make payment in the future when the goods or services have been received. Traditionally, accountants have refrained from recording these contracts where neither party has performed. The reasoning is that until the goods are made available, the obligation of the buyer is offset by the buyer's rights to receive the goods. Until the goods are brought into existence and committed to the contract, there is an unconditional right of setoff. But when goods or services are committed under the contract, the buyer may not be able to cancel the contract without paying for the goods and services committed, even though they have not as yet been received. An example would be an obligation under a long-term construction project. Another example would be the long-term lease of property that is made available exclusively for the lessee, even though the lessee has not received the use of the property to be provided under the lease contract.

---

[3] John B. Canning, *The Economics of Accountancy* (New York: Ronald Press, 1929), pp. 55–56.

Traditionally, an exception to the practice of not reporting executory contracts for the purchase of goods and services is made when the obligation of the purchase commitment exceeds the value of the goods to be acquired. For example, if a material decline in the price of the goods occurs subsequent to the signing of a long-term purchase contract, the obligation exceeds the value of the rights under the contract and a loss has occurred. The recording of a liability equal only to the amount of the loss results from the reporting of net income and the need to record a credit equal to the loss debit under the double-entry system. This practice is deficient because it assumes that the total amount of the rights and obligations are not relevant to the predictions and decisions of investors and creditors. However, the total amounts are relevant, because the users of the statements may place different expectations on the values of the rights under the contract or on the effect of the committed cash disbursements.

The definition of liabilities in *SFAC No. 3* appears to exclude obligations that are subject to an unconditional right of offset. However, they could be included in the definition because they do arise from a past transaction or event and in many cases there is little uncertainty regarding the existence of the obligation. Since executory contracts usually do affect future cash flows, their disclosure should be relevant to investors and creditors.

Measurability of liabilities

In most cases, an obligation arises from a contract where the amount and time of payment of the obligation are specified or determinable from the conditions of the contract. However, in some cases, the amount to be paid is dependent upon future events, such as future gross sales from the use of leased property. In these cases, the liability does exist, even though the amount must be expressed in terms of certainty equivalents or as a range of probable amounts. In the case of loss contingencies, *FASB Statement No. 5* implies that a liability exists and should be recorded if the amount of the loss can be reasonably estimated.[4] Therefore, from a semantic point of view and from the point of view of the users of financial statements, an obligation should be classified as a liability if it can be reasonably measured or if a meaningful range of values or probabilities can be assigned to it.

Should the payee be known or ascertainable?

Another important question regarding the nature and timing of liabilities is whether or not a liability to a second party can arise out of a transaction with a third party. Examples are (1) royalties payable to a second party because of a sale of merchandise to a third party and (2) deferred income

---

[4] *AICPA Professional Standards*, p. 9184.

taxes payable to the government arising out of an installment sale to a third party. The first case clearly results in a liability, but the second case leaves some doubt.

One reason for the doubt in the case of the deferred tax liability is that the amount is not considered at the present time by the government to be an obligation of the firm. In similar situations, however, accountants do recognize obligations, even though they are not recognized specifically by the obligee. For example, obligations to make repairs under warranties may be based on the probability that a certain amount of repairs will become necessary, even though it may not be known to whom the obligation will accrue and none of the individual customers will regard the obligation as necessarily accruing to them.

SFAC No. 3 correctly states that the identity of the payee need not be known before the time of settlement if the future payment or transfer of assets is probable.

Basic characteristics of liabilities

In summary, from an interpretive point of view, liabilities may be defined as obligations or duties of the enterprise to provide money, goods, or services to a person, firm, or other organization outside of the enterprise at some time in the future. Specific characteristics would include the following:

1. The obligation must, of course, exist at the present time. That is, it must arise out of some past transaction or event. It may arise from the acquisition of goods or services, from losses already sustained for which the firm is liable, or from the expectation of losses for which the firm has obligated itself. Obligations contingent upon future events should not be included unless there is a reasonable probability that these events will occur.

2. Equitable obligations or duties should be included if they are based on the necessity of making future payments to maintain good business relationships or if they are in accordance with normal business practice.

3. There should be little or no discretion to avoid the future sacrifice. It is not necessary that the amount of the obligation be known with certainty so long as a future sacrifice is probable.

4. Normally there should be a determinable maturity value or the expectation that payment of an amount determined by reasonable estimation will be required at some specific time in the future, even though the exact timing is not known at the present. The time of payment may be extended by the substitution of new liabilities, or the obligations may be terminated by their conversion into stockholder equities. The repeated extension or conversion of the debt does not deny its classification as a liability.

5. Normally, the payee would be known or be identifiable either specifically or as a group. However, so long as the payee will become

identifiable by the settlement date, it is not necessary that the payer know the identity of the payee or that the creditor profess the claim or have knowledge of it at the present time.

THE VALUATION OF LIABILITIES AND
THE COMPUTATION OF INTEREST

The objectives of liability valuation are similar to the objectives of asset valuation discussed in Chapter 11. Probably the most important of these objectives is the desire to record expenses and losses in the determination of current income. However, the measurement of liabilities should also permit the presentation to investors and creditors of information useful as a means of prediction of cash flows as a base for interperiod and intercompany comparisons of income, and as a comparison of the claims of the several equity holders.

Liabilities cannot be included in the balance sheet as separate items unless they can be quantified. However, an inability to quantify an obligation does not imply that it is not a liability; but if it is not reasonably measurable, it must be disclosed by footnote or other means, rather than by listing among the liabilities in the balance sheet. If an actual obligation exists but has a range of probable values, the expected value should be listed as the estimated amount of the liability on the balance sheet. Only if the range is broad and if an estimated single value would be misleading is it preferable to omit the obligation from the list of liabilities and present a description, in a footnote or otherwise, indicating the range of probable values.

Contingent liabilities

According to *FASB Statement No. 5,* a contingency is defined as

> an existing condition, situation, or set of circumstances involving uncertainty as to possible . . . loss . . . to an enterprise that will ultimately be resolved when one or more future events occur or fail to occur. Resolution of the uncertainty may confirm the . . . incurrence of a liability.[5]

Although the emphasis in this definition is on the effect on income in the traditional accounting structure, similar characteristics can be used to place emphasis on the semantic definition of a contingent liability. Thus, *Statement No. 5* implies that a liability should be reported if it is likely that an obligation will have to be paid in the future and if the

---

[5] *FASB Statement No. 5,* "Accounting for Contingencies," *AICPA Professional Standards,* para. 4311.01.

amount of the liability can be reasonably estimated. The contingent obligation should be disclosed in a footnote if the probability that payment will be necessary is less than likely but more than remote.

A contingent liability, therefore, may be defined as an obligation that may arise dependent upon one or more future events that have some probability of occurrence. They should be included among liabilities if the probability of the occurrence of the future event is relatively high (e.g., warranties, contested income tax obligations, and refundable damage deposits). It should be disclosed in a footnote if the probability of occurrence of the future event is relatively low. The distinction should be based on whether or not an expected value would be meaningful to readers of the financial reports as a representation of the approximate most probable (modal) value and the extent to which the expectations must be subjective. If an obligation has a 90 percent chance of being $100,000 and a 10 percent chance of being zero, the expected value would be $90,000, and this would be a meaningful representation of the liability, particularly if the probabilities are based on past experience. On the other hand, if the obligation has a 90 percent chance of being zero and a 10 percent chance of being $100,000, the expected value would be $10,000; but this would not be as meaningful as a description of the probable amount to be paid. That is, if the most probable (modal) value of the obligation is positive, a liability exists and the amount should be estimated. If the obligation has a high probability of being zero, it should be disclosed in a footnote.

Obligations under warranties are definite liabilities because it is highly probable that some payments will be required even though the total amount must be estimated. A legal suit against the company for damages, however, is a contingent liability if it appears most likely that the firm will win the case. If it is almost certain that the case will be lost, a liability exists, and the main problem is in estimating the expected value of the damages to be awarded. In the case of legal suits, however, accountants may not be able to estimate the most probable amount of damages, and the best disclosure may be provided by a full description in a footnote or elsewhere.

Current valuation of liabilities

In the case of most monetary liabilities, the amount payable is determined by contract or agreement. Therefore, the current valuation of the debt is the present discounted amount payable in the future. Since current liabilities are generally payable within a short period of time, the amount of discount is usually immaterial and the amount of the liability can be presented at its face value (amount payable in the future). However, if the debt can be satisfied by two or more alternatives, the discounted value of the lowest of these is the current value of the liability. For example, if the credit terms permit a discount of 2 percent if payment is made within 20 days and require a penalty if payment is made after 60 days, the correct value of the liability is the invoice price less the 2 percent discount. The other alternatives require an excess payment that need not be made and should not be made under good business practice. If the higher price is paid, the excess should be recorded as purchase discounts not taken and treated as a loss arising from inefficiency.

LONG-TERM LIABILITIES

In the case of long-term liabilities, the amount of discount is generally significant and, therefore, the current valuation should be the discounted value of all future payments to be made under the contract. In the case of bonds, the contractual interest payments, the amount to be paid at maturity, and any serial payments of principal should all be discounted to the present. The appropriate discount rate is the current yield rate determined by the market for bonds of similar risk and term. Using a current yield rate produces a current value, whereas the use of the yield rate at the date of issue produces a value similar to historical cost. That is, the yield rate at the date of issue can be assumed to be the effective rate for which the firm is committed. The advantages of its use are that (1) the resulting value at the date of issue was the current value at that time and (2) it is objectively determined. By continuing to use the original yield rate, the holding gains and losses are not recorded, and the interest expense for each period is determined by the debt at the beginning of the period multiplied by the original yield rate. If the debt is held until maturity, changes in the yield rate can usually be ignored on the grounds that they are not material and that the total interest expense by this method will always be equal to the sum of the interest expense and the holding gains and losses if current yield rates are continually used.

When bonds are sold initially at a premium or discount, the interest expense in any specific period is the contractual (nominal) interest payment less the current amortization of the premium or plus the amortization of the discount. The carrying value of the debt at any date is then the maturity value plus the unamortized premium or less the unamortized discount. The true interest expense (the "true" interest method) in any period is the value of the debt at the beginning of that period times the original yield rate. The excess of this interest expense over the contractual cash interest payment during the year is the amount of the current discount amortization. If the bonds were sold at a premium, the premium amortization is the excess of the cash payment over the interest expense. The unamortized discount or premium represents a valuation of the bond liability. The effect of the interest method is to report a periodic interest expense that represents a level effective rate on the book value of the debt. *APB Opinion No. 12* considered this method as acceptable as the straight-line method, but the difference is usually not material if the contractual (nominal) rate for computing the interest payment is not significantly different from the original yield rate.

Early extinguishment of debt

If bonds are callable at a premium, it is generally worthwhile for the firm to call the bonds when the current value of the bonds, as determined by the current yield rate, is greater than the call price. When the bonds are repaid out of the available resources of the firm, the sum of the call premium and any unamortized discount represents the amount of the loss realized by repaying the bonds at a current value, which is in excess of the original "cost" or amortized carrying value. That is, the current value of the debt has increased as the market rate of interest has fallen. If current values are not recorded when the market rate changes, however, the entire accumulated holding loss is recorded when the bonds are called. If current values had been recorded each period, the holding losses would have been recorded gradually as the market rate of interest changed, and the value of the bonds would have reached or exceeded the call price. The current value would exceed the call price only by an amount equal to the cost of obtaining the necessary funds or only when the firm fails to take advantage of the opportunity. But, in the statements, the bond liability should not exceed the call price because this is the lowest amount for which the bonds could be repaid.

When an old issue of bonds is called by the process of refunding, the situation is very similar to the above. The new issue should be recorded at its issue price, since this is the current value of the debt at that time and it reflects the existing market rate of interest. The entire unamortized discount and call premium should be recorded as a realized holding loss in the period of repayment and reported as an extraordinary loss in the income statement.

The direct write-off of the unamortized discount and call premium to income as a loss is logical from the point of view of economic interpretation because the value of the debt has changed over time, and paying the call price is the most favorable method of liquidating the debt. If this change in value of the debt caused by a change in the market rate of interest (the yield rate) has not been reflected in the accounts, the entire holding loss should be recorded no later than the time the specific contract is terminated. It is also argued that the acceptance of this method is based on the view that the unamortized discount and call premium represent the cost of terminating a disadvantageous contract and thus relate to past transactions. *APB Opinion No. 26* states that this method should be used in all extinguishments of debt, including a call or purchase, refunding, and exchange for common stock (except when the bonds are convertible). The resulting loss should be reported in the same period as an extraordinary item in accordance with *FASB Statement No. 4*. A gain resulting from the termination of advantageous, low interest bond contracts would also be reported in the same period.

Convertible debt

Debt securities are frequently issued with a convertible feature, which permits the holder to convert the bond certificates into a determinable number of shares of common stock at any time before the conversion privilege expires. The convertible feature generally permits the issuer to sell the bonds initially at a price considerably above what could be obtained for nonconvertible bonds with the same contractual interest rate. Although many possible alternative features and relationships may be found in connection with convertible bonds, generally the contractual interest rate is considerably below the market rate for nonconvertible bonds; the initial conversion price is greater than the market price of the common stock; and the conversion price does not decrease over time except to the extent necessary to protect the bondholder from the dilution of the common stock rights (such as a stock split or a stock dividend).

Two views have been proposed for the accounting treatment of convertible debt at the date of issuance and for the subsequent reporting of interest expense. One view is that convertible debt possesses the characteristics of both debt and equity and that a portion of the proceeds from the sale of the securities should be allocated to the conversion privilege and credited to paid-in capital while the remainder should be allocated to the debt, resulting in the presentation of debt discount or a reduction of debt premium. The amount assigned to paid-in capital can be measured as the excess of the amount received for the securities over the estimated price that could have been obtained for similar securities without the conversion feature. A second view is that the convertible debt should be treated solely as debt with no portion of the proceeds being allocated to the conversion feature. This was the recommendation of *APB Opinion No. 14*.

The main arguments for the allocation of the proceeds between the debt and the equity characteristics are that the economic value of the conversion feature exists as a distinct element of the contract, as opposed to the debt, and that the measurement of interest expense should be based on the debt characteristics only. Although these two arguments are related in the accounting treatment, they are discussed separately. The argument for a separate reporting of the debt and equity portions is based on the premise that the classification of the proceeds from the sale of the securities should be comparable with the traditional debt and equity classifications. If an amount is actually paid for the right to become a holder of common stock at some time in the future, this is similar to the sale of an option or warrant for the purchase of common stock in the future at a fixed price. Therefore, the amount paid for the conversion privilege should be accounted for consistently with the treatment of stock options or warrants. Likewise, valuation of the portion classified as debt should reflect the market yield for similar debt at the time of issuing the securities, which would then be consistent with the reporting of nonconvertible bonds. The disclosure of a material discount on bonds would be relevant to make the presentation similar to other securities classified as long-term debt. Note, however, that in this case an adjustment should be made for the fact that the discount arising from the allocation to the conversion feature may not be deductible in arriving at taxable income.

A major difficulty with the allocation of the issue price between the debt and equity portions is that valuation and classification similar to nonconvertible issues gives the reader of the financial statements the impression that the face amount is expected to be paid at maturity. However, if the market price of common stock increases above the conversion price, the normal expectation is that the bonds will not be paid at maturity. Until the bonds are converted, the face value is a protection for the holders of the securities against loss through bankruptcy or reorganization; it is therefore similar to the liquidation value of preferred stock, although with a different degree of priority. Another difficulty is that the interest expense reported by this method is not related to the contractual cash outflows, whether conversion takes place or not. If the bonds are not converted but paid at maturity, the cash outlays include the contractual annual payment and the face value at maturity. If the bonds are converted, the cash outlay for interest also turns out to be the amount specified in the contract until the period of conversion. It may be argued that treating the convertible bonds as if they were nonconvertible does not disclose the cash flow attributes of the bonds under either potential alternative.

The arguments for the treatment of the bond issue only as debt are that the debt and conversion privilege are inseparable and that the practical problems of computing valuations for the conversion feature and the debt portion are too subjective to be meaningful. The valuation of debt that is nonconvertible but similar in other regards is difficult because of the many different features possible in the bond contract and because the valuation in the market may be unique to the special risks of the specific firm. However, the Accounting Principles Board, in *Opinion No. 14,* placed greater weight on the inseparability of the debt and the conversion option. The convertible bond is a hybrid form of security because under one set of conditions the conversion feature may be the more relevant attribute, but under another set of conditions the debt form may become the more important.

The treatment of the convertible bonds solely as debt, however, has some major weaknesses. Including the proceeds of the securities in the long-term debt classification may be misleading because generally, in a viable concern, it is not anticipated that they will ever be repaid as debt. In many cases, it may be the intent of the firm to force conversion at some time in the future by calling the bonds when the market price is above the conversion price. In most other cases, the attractiveness of the security rests primarily on the expectation that the market price of the common stock will increase significantly above the conversion price. The debt feature is regarded more as a protection under adverse conditions. Accordingly, the convertible debt security is more in the form of stockholders' equity than long-term debt. Therefore, the recommendation of *APB Opinion No. 14* to treat the securities solely as debt is inconsistent with the recommendation made in *APB Opinion No. 15* that they should be treated as common stock in the computation of primary earnings per share. It is also inconsistent with the additional recommendation in *APB Opinion No. 14* that if convertible debt is issued at a substantial premium, there is a presumption that the premium represents the value of the conversion feature and should be allocated to paid-in capital.

The recommendation of *APB Opinion No. 14* regarding convertible debt is also inconsistent with its recommendation regarding accounting for debt with detachable warrants to purchase stock. In the latter case, it recommends that the proceeds of the debt securities issued with detachable warrants should be allocated to the debt and to the warrants separately and that the amount allocated to the warrants should be treated as paid-in capital. However, convertible debt and debt issued with detachable warrants are in substance the same. The holder of convertible bonds may sell securities and buy similar nonconvertible bonds, just as the holder of the debt with the detachable warrants may sell the warrants and continue to hold the bonds. Likewise, if the investor wishes to hold stock, the convertible bonds may be converted, or if bonds with detachable warrants are held, the proceeds from the sale of the bonds may be used to purchase stock with the warrants. From the firm's point of view, they are also similar in substance because, if the detachable warrants are exercised, it may use the proceeds to call or repurchase the bonds. Therefore, the two types of securities should be treated alike. It is inconsistent to treat one solely as debt while treating the other as both debt and equity.

An alternative to the two solutions discussed above is to create a new classification between the long-term debt and the stockholders' equity for both convertible bonds and debt with detachable warrants. A major difficulty in accounting is the continual attempt to fit new circumstances into the same old molds. A new classification, however, would also require a new type of disclosure of the interest expense in the income statement. But a clear disclosure of the several attributes of convertible debt securities and debt with detachable warrants would present a more informative picture of the possible outcomes and permit investors and creditors to predict the future cash disbursements likely to be required and the potential relationship of the securities to existing and new securities of the firm, as well as the potential dilution of earnings per share.

SELECTED ADDITIONAL READING

The nature of liabilities

Carpenter, Charles G., and **Joseph F. Wojdak,** "Capitalizing Executory Contracts: A Perspective." *New York CPA,* January 1971, pp. 40–47.

Henderson, M. S. "Nature of Liabilities." *Australian Accountant,* July 1974, pp. 328–30, 333–34.

Hughes, John S. "Toward a Contract Basis of Valuation in Accounting." *Accounting Review,* October 1978, pp. 882–94.

Kulkarni, Deepak. "The Valuation of Liabilities." *Accounting and Business Research,* Summer 1980, pp. 291–97.

Ma, Ronald, and **Malcolm Miller.** "Conceptualizing the Liability." *Accounting and Business Research,* Autumn 1978, pp. 258–65.

Long-term debt

Clancy, Donald K. "What is a Convertible Debenture? A Review of the Literature in the U.S.A." *Abacus,* December 1978, pp. 171–79.

Falk, Haim, and **Stephen L. Buzby.** "What's Missing in Accounting for Convertible Bonds?" *CA Magazine,* July 1978, pp. 40–45.

Miller, Jerry D. "Accounting for Warrants and Convertible Bonds." *Management Accounting,* January 1973, pp. 26–28.

Stephens, Matthew J. "Inseparability of the Valuation of Convertible Bonds." *Journal of Accountancy,* August 1971, pp. 54–62.

CHAPTER 18

INCOME TAXES AND PENSION COSTS

The methods of accounting for taxes, for long-term leases by the lessee, and for pension costs involve some similar problems, although each has created new problems and challenges for the accounting profession and for accounting theory.[1] The common problems include the nature and reporting of the related assets and liabilities and the timing of expenses or other income effects. In each case, questions arise regarding the nature of liabilities. Does a liability exist when the creditor does not acknowledge the debt? Should obligations be reported if it is unlikely that they will be paid in the aggregate? Regarding the timing of expenses, questions arise regarding whether emphasis should be placed on cash flows, assumed or arbitrary associations with revenues, or on changes in the valuations of assets and liabilities. These questions are explored in the following discussions of income tax allocation and pension costs.

INCOME TAX ALLOCATION

The question of allocating corporate income tax expense has arisen because taxable net income is computed differently from accounting net income. The major differences between taxable and accounting net income can be classified as (1) permanent differences arising from special legislative allowances or restrictions permitted or required for economic, political, or administrative reasons not related to the computation of accounting net income; (2) differences arising from the direct charging or crediting to retained earnings or extraordinary gains or losses of items included in the computation of taxable net income; and (3) differences in timing of charges and credits to income. The permanent differences reflect the computation of the total tax to be paid by the corporation during its lifetime and, therefore, do not give rise to tax allocation. The second type—differences arising from direct charges and credits to retained earnings or extraordinary gains or losses—requires intraperiod allocation of taxes. The third type—differences in timing—is the subject of interperiod allocations.

---

[1] See Chapter 14 for a discussion of obligations arising under long-term leases.

The main controversy regarding tax allocation is centered on the interperiod type; but both intraperiod and interperiod allocations stem from the desire to record the "proper" amount and classification of tax expense in each period. Little opposition is found to intraperiod allocations because only the income and retained earnings statements of the same period are affected; the balance sheet and income statements of other periods are unaffected. Interperiod allocation, however, raises several basic questions of accounting theory.

Intraperiod allocation

If the all-inclusive concept of income were fully accepted, allocations of the tax between the income statement and the retained earnings statement would not be necessary. However, according to *APB Opinion No. 30* and *FASB Statement No. 16*, extraordinary gains and losses should be reported separately in the income statement, and some adjustments of prior periods should be reported as adjustments of retained earnings. In these cases, allocation within the income statement or between the income statement and the retained earnings statement may make the reported operating net income before extraordinary items more meaningful.

When certain material charges and credits are recorded as extraordinary items in the income statement, as recommended by the APB, or when an adjustment of retained earnings is made to correct earnings of prior years, allocation is necessary if the material charges or credits affect the amount of the income tax payable for the year. For example, if the net operating income before tax is $1,000, a 30 percent income tax rate would result in a tax of $300 and a net income before extraordinary items of $700. But if, in addition, a nonrecurring taxable gain of $600 is reported during the year, the total tax payable becomes $480 (30 percent × $1,600). Without allocation, the net operating income would be $520, and the $600 gain would be reported as an extraordinary gain. With allocation, the tax assignable to current operations would be $300, and that assignable to the extraordinary gain would be $180. Thus, the operating net income before extraordinary items would not be disturbed by the recording of the gain and the gain (net of the associated tax)—$420— would be reported separately.

The argument for allocation in the above example rests primarily on the usefulness of the reported figure of net income before extraordinary items. For financial reporting purposes, an operating net income figure should be useful to investors in making predictions regarding future income and making comparisons of the net incomes of several periods. Without allocation, the net income figure before extraordinary items is subject to misinterpretation. If operating revenues and expenses are the same in a second year and following years but the nonoperating gains or losses do not recur, the failure to allocate the tax in the first year would result in an erroneous prediction and a poor comparison of the efficiency of management in conducting normal operations. It also leads to a misinterpretation of the net effect on the firm of the nonrecurring gains or losses reported as extraordinary items.

A question is frequently raised regarding the rate that should be used in making the tax allocation. Should it be the marginal rate, the average rate, or some other rate? If the special capital gains tax rate applies to the item in the tax return, this rate should also be used in the allocation. But, if it is regular taxable income, the highest rate applicable should be used, on the theory that the special gain or loss is marginal, and because one objective is to show the tax on operating income and the net operating profit under normal conditions as if the special gains and losses had not occurred. There is little justification for using an average rate in this case, but it would be better to make an allocation by using an average rate than to make no allocation at all.

Interperiod allocation

When the difference between taxable net income and accounting net income is due to differences in the timing of the recognition of revenues and expenses, the recording of a tax expense (or equivalent effect on income) based on pretax reported income requires interperiod allocation. As in the case of intraperiod allocation, the basic principle of interperiod allocation is to let the tax follow the income on which it is based. Income taxable in the current period but recognized for accounting purposes in a later period requires a *deferral* of tax expense; income recognized for accounting purposes in the current period but taxable in a later period requires an *accrual* of tax expense.

Four types of cases are generally suggested as requiring interperiod allocation of taxes:

1. A deduction taken for tax purposes but deferred in the accounting statements. Common examples are the additional first-year depreciation on equipment and the use of accelerated depreciation for tax purposes while using the straight-line method in the accounts.
2. Revenue recorded currently in the accounts but reported for tax purposes at a later date. The use of the installment basis for tax purposes and the sales basis for accounting purposes is a common example.
3. Income included in the tax calculation but deferred in the accounting statements. An example is rent received in advance and taxable when received but reported as income for accounting purposes when the services are provided.
4. Expenses deducted in the income statement but deductible for tax purposes only in a later period. An example is the setting up in the accounts of estimated warranty expenses deductible for tax purposes only in the period of payment.

Cases 1 and 2 require the setting up of an income tax liability or other credit account because the tax expense related to the current accounting income is greater than the tax to be paid currently. Cases 3 and 4 require the setting up of a prepaid tax or other debit account because the amount of the tax paid currently is greater than the reported tax expense allocated to the income of the current period.

Controversy regarding interperiod tax allocation centers around the following questions: (1) Is tax allocation an appropriate accounting device? (2) If it is appropriate, should it be carried out on a partial or a comprehensive basis? (3) How should tax allocation be presented in financial statements? (4) What tax rate should be used in making the allocation? The discussions have, at times, been carried out on an emotional level, but there are some basic premises that are assumed to support the several positions. Since these same premises are at the root of much of the conflict in accounting literature, it is not surprising to find that they influence thinking regarding the reporting of income taxes, even though taxes based on income are unique in many ways. Some of the basic premises stated or implicit in the controversy are these: (1) The matching concept is assumed to be relevant to the reporting of income taxes, and the emphasis on the reporting of net income overrides any effect on balance sheet items in accordance with the traditional accounting structure. (2) Tax allocation must result in asset and liability valuations that permit economic interpretation both as to the item and its measurement. (3) Predictions of future cash flows are more important than predictions of reported net income. Accordingly, financial statements should reflect cash flows or effective cash flows as closely as possible in order to permit predictions of future cash flows.

The matching concept applied to income taxes. As indicated in Chapter 8, matching is the process of reporting expenses on the basis of a cause-and-effect relationship with reported revenues. Direct matching requires the reporting of expenses in the same period as the associated revenues. The application of the matching concept to the accounting for income taxes is found in *APB Opinion No. 11,* since the Board recommended that the reported income tax expense for a period should include the tax effects of all revenue and expense transactions included in the measurement of pretax income.[2] Three separate problems related to this recommendation should be discussed independently: (1) Is the corporate income tax an expense? (2) Is the matching concept relevant in the case of taxes? (3) Is the recommended method of matching logical?

Regarding the nature of income taxes as an expense, current practice defines it as an expense of doing business, and managements generally make decisions on the basis of an aftertax expected net income. The tax must also be taken into consideration in investment decisions. An addi-

---

[2] *AICPA Professional Standards* (Chicago: Commerce Clearing House, 1980), para. 4091.11.

tional impelling reason is that the FASB, as well as official bodies in other countries, has recognized income taxes as expenses. Practice, however, does not determine the logic of the classification. But since the expense classification does not have a clear definition other than what accountants choose it to be, the argument that tax allocation is inappropriate because the tax is not an expense is difficult to support. Note, however, that expenses are not homogeneous in nature; some are variable with output or sales, and others are fixed. Most expenses are incurred deliberately, with the objective of increasing revenues or decreasing costs, but some result from expected or unexpected outside influences beyond the control of the firm. Income taxes have their own characteristics, since they are functionally related to periodic taxable income, which may differ in many respects from reported pretax income. Since they are not directly related to revenues or revenue-seeking functions, some writers deny that income taxes are expenses; but, on the other hand, since they must be taken into consideration in determining the amount to be distributed as dividends, including the taxes in the expense classification has some merit.

However, many accountants consider the tax to represent a distribution of income similar to the payment of dividends. In support of this position, the proponents claim that since the tax is paid only if income is earned, it is more similar to dividends than to payments for wages and supplies used in the business. They also claim that the impact on the stockholder is similar to the impact of the personal income tax.

The government, however, is a beneficiary of the corporation only in a broad sense, in the same way that employees and suppliers are beneficiaries and receive payment for the services they render. The main difference is that the federal government does not provide services to the corporation in direct proportion to the amount of the tax. But there is no question that services are provided. The payment of the corporate income tax (like a franchise tax) is associated with the right to conduct a profitable corporation in a favorable economic climate provided by the government. And the classification of this payment is independent of its calculation. Whether the final incidence of the tax is on the stockholders, employees, or customers does not necessarily change the nature of the tax as an expense, but it may be pointed out that evidence does not support the supposition that the impact of the tax has been on the stockholder in the long run.

Regardless of whether or not the income tax is classified as an expense, if the income tax is reported as a separate item in the income statement, the question of allocation is still present. Therefore, we should turn to the question of whether or not matching is relevant. The first question regarding matching is whether or not the reported net income with tax allocation is more relevant to external users than a reported net income without allocation. This question cannot be answered satisfactorily without deciding which concept and objective of net income are most relevant. If reported net income is intended to represent an indicator for the prediction of future reported net incomes, tax allocation may have some relevance. Through allocation, the tax expense is made to appear functionally related to the reported pretax net income, except for the permanent differences between taxable net income and reported pretax net income. Therefore, it is assumed that if the investor can predict the reported pretax net income, the investor can also predict the tax expense and thus the reported aftertax net income. Generally, however, the information presented in financial statements regarding the computation of the tax is inadequate to make this prediction. Too great a reliance must be placed on the final reported net income figure and too little information is available to determine the functional relationships of the items determining this net figure.

A case for matching in the case of income taxes can be made on the basis of individual transactions, particularly in those cases in which cash flows affect reported net income in a period different from the effect on taxable income. For example, in the case of a single large installment sale, without allocation the financial statements indicate that the resources of the firm are increased by the amount of the sale price of the goods sold. However, the investor may discover only later that these resources (the installment receivable) can be converted to cash only by incurring a significant tax liability. Tax allocation prevents this type of misleading information. However, in the case of differences arising from the allocation of nonmonetary assets or nonmonetary liabilities, the relevance of matching even for individual items becomes suspect. The difficulty is that such allocations as the depreciation of plant and equipment and the amortization of research and development expenses are not based on logical matching concepts, as discussed previously in Chapters 15 and 16. Therefore, an attempt to match tax expense with these pretax income allocations is of doubtful validity. That is, it is doubtful that reported net income would be improved by the allocation of taxes to expense or income items that are the result of allocations unsupported by the matching concept.

The matching procedure recommended by *APB Opinion No. 11* is that the tax expense of any period should include the tax effects of *all* revenues and expenses reported in the determination of reported pretax income (comprehensive tax allocation). That is, the tax effects should be reported in the period during which the timing differences arise and also in the period during which the differences reverse. Between these two dates, the Board recommended that the differences should be reported as deferred charges or deferred credits. The tax effect is based on the tax rate at the time of reporting the initial difference, and no adjustment is made for changes in tax rates in accordance with the historical cost tradition.

The main difficulty with the recommendation of *APB Opinion No. 11* is that the deferred method is not supported by logic. The deferred charges and deferred credits are intended to represent neither assets and liabilities nor stockholders' equity. Therefore, they represent merely a method of shifting the tax effect from one period to another. Even if the method could be supported on the basis of the matching concept alone, the amounts carried forward should represent measurements of resources or obligations if the double-entry system is to be maintained. The use of undefined debits and credits makes the entire method suspect.

Tax allocation as a process of valuation.   Two alternative methods for treating the allocation of income taxes—the liability method and the net of tax method—are supported by valuation concepts. In the liability method, the reporting of tax expense in the current period in excess of the amount payable currently is assumed to give rise to an obligation to pay a higher tax in the future. Likewise, the payment of taxes in excess of the amount reported as tax expense is assumed to result in an asset representing a tax benefit available in the future. These concepts, however, are challenged on the ground that the items carried forward do not have the usual characteristics of assets or liabilities. The "prepaid tax" arising from the allocation of income taxes is not an unconditional right for future benefits, and it is not a claim that would be recognized by the Internal Revenue Service. Thus, it does not have the usual characteristics of assets. However, under normal expectations of future corporate income and the continuation of current income tax regulations, the item may have many of the normal characteristics of an asset. For example, the tax paid on rent received in advance gives the firm the right to provide services in the future without incurring a tax obligation in so doing. However, the benefit is less real when it results from differences in methods of depreciation or other allocations, rather than from the timing of cash flows. This is particularly true when the tax allocation is looked at from the point of view of the entire firm, rather than looking at each item separately, because of the many interactions even in the computation of the income tax payable.

The item "income taxes payable in the future" arising from tax allocation likewise has few of the normal characteristics of liabilities. An obligation to the government does not really exist, since the Internal Revenue Service would not recognize the obligation even for future payment. The future obligation will arise, in part, from a past transaction—the earning of the income not reported for tax purposes or the deduction for tax purposes of an expenditure carried forward in the accounts. But the main transaction—the levying of the tax—is a future transaction. In some circumstances, however, there will be an obligation to pay a tax in the future based on past or current activities. For example, income reported on the basis of the percentage-of-completion method for long-term contracts should take into consideration the fact that a tax obligation will arise when the contract is completed. But the "liability" arising from the use of the accelerated method of depreciation for tax purposes while using the straight-line method for reporting purposes is an obligation only under very limited assumptions regarding the validity of the depreciation method used for accounting purposes; because of the lack of theoretical logic behind such methods, the tax liability is of doubtful validity.

An alternative to treating these items as assets and liabilities is to treat them in close relationship to the items giving rise to them—the net-of-tax method. Thus, the prepaid taxes may be considered valuation accounts to the related liabilities, and the taxes payable in the future may be considered contra asset accounts, or the assets and liabilities may be reduced directly. For example, if a capital asset in the amount of $10,000 is written off for tax purposes but carried forward in the accounts, the net valuation to the firm is only $6,000 (assuming a 40 percent tax rate) because the use of the asset in the future cannot reduce the tax a second time. This net-of-tax method, however, is based on the assumption that an adjustment of the historical cost of an asset for the tax effect results in a current valuation of the asset. The difficulty with this concept is that many other factors should also be considered in measuring the value of the asset, either to the firm or in presenting evidence of the value of the firm to investors. The net-of-tax method is usually rejected on the ground that it is not the objective of accounting to measure and report the value of each asset or liability. But it is a more logical concept than either the deferred method or the liability method.

Valuation concepts are also applied in support of partial tax allocation. Under this method, tax allocation would be applied only in those cases in which tax benefits or tax obligations are likely to be reversed in the aggregate within a reasonable time in the future. For example, if the accelerated method of depreciation is used for tax purposes while straight-line is used in the financial statements, the tax difference will not be paid so long as the firm continues to replace its assets; and in a growth firm, the aggregate difference will continue to increase indefinitely. Therefore, since in the aggregate the tax difference is not likely to be paid, the liability does not exist. The counter to this argument is that there is a continual roll-over of the liability, so that each year a part is paid and an additional amount is accrued. Like accounts payable, the liability cannot be denied just because the aggregate does not decrease over time. However, the roll-over concept is not as applicable to the tax liability as it is to the accounts payable; because if the firm ceased profitable operations, the tax would not have to be paid, but the creditors represented by the accounts payable would maintain their claims.

A further argument against showing the full amount of the tax liability or prepaid tax is that since the obligations will be paid and the tax benefit received only at some distant time in the future, they should be discounted at some positive rate of interest. If the time period is long or infinite, the present value would be close to zero. Therefore, for these several reasons, the valuation concepts are of little assistance in providing complete logic to tax allocation.

Tax allocation and cash flows. One of the basic arguments against income tax allocation is that the financial statements should reflect as clearly as possible the cash flows of the firm. Even though the accrual basis is proposed for many items, it is argued that the tax payable reflects the effect on the firm for the period. That is, the tax levied each year represents the impact on the firm that year. Taxes are assumed to affect cash flows by the amount of the tax obligation. Therefore, because the tax obligation is not necessarily functionally related to reported net income, the current tax obligation is more meaningful to investors and creditors than some artificially allocated tax expense. Predictions and evaluations should be made on the basis of pretax net income and expectations regarding changes in the amount of the tax, rather than upon a single aftertax net income.

Tax allocation is also opposed on the ground that the uncertainties in making estimates of future tax obligations and future tax effects are too great to make allocation meaningful. Since the tax is payable only when taxable income is earned, tax "savings" of one period may result in permanent savings if the corporation incurs losses for several years. Likewise, expenses deductible for tax purposes only in a later period may never reduce taxes if losses are incurred beyond the carry-back and carry-forward periods. Also, future tax rates and tax regulations are uncertain and subject to change by Congress, and the method of application of the regulations may be subject to change by administrative decisions.

However, there is considerable doubt that the uncertainties in tax allocations are greater than they are in other areas of financial reporting, since certain information may be relevant if the firm is expected to be profitable, just as other information may be relevant if it may be expected to be unprofitable. Furthermore, the corporate income tax is a major source of federal income, and it is not likely to be abolished in the near future. Tax rates may change from time to time, but in the absence of war or national distress, they are not likely to change by amounts so great as to nullify all estimates.

Empirical studies to date have not been strongly supportive of tax allocation. Beaver and Dukes, for example, concluded in a preliminary study that tax allocation is a correct decision if one accepts market efficiency.[3] However, in a later study, they concluded that the premise on which tax allocation is based is open to serious question and that tax allocation is not necessarily the correct decision.[4] The lack of basic supporting theory and the many complications involved in the tax allocation process, therefore, make it doubtful as a relevant accounting procedure. Part of the difficulty, however, is not with the tax allocation itself, but it is with the

---

[3] William H. Beaver and Roland E. Dukes, "Interperiod Tax Allocation, Earnings Expectations, and the Behavior of Security Prices," *Accounting Review,* April 1972, pp. 320–32.

[4] William H. Beaver and Roland E. Dukes, "Interperiod Tax Allocation and δ-Depreciation Methods: Some Empirical Results," *Accounting Review,* July, 1973, pp. 549–58.

entire accounting process, which stresses the reporting of a single net income figure, which is then used as a predictive indicator. Alternative theoretical structures should be investigated and empirical studies should be made to find better methods of communicating the effects of corporate income taxation.

Carry-back and carry-forward of tax losses

According to income tax allocation concepts, the total tax payable over a series of years should be allocated to the revenues and expenses entering into the computation of taxable income when such items are reported in the determination of accounting net income. In years of operating losses, the deductions exceed the revenues, and therefore a negative amount of tax should be allocated to that year to the extent that such loss can be carried backward or forward to reduce the total tax payable by the corporation. The principle of allocation is the same for both carry-backs and carry-forwards, but the degree of uncertainty regarding the tax benefit is much greater in the latter case.

When an operating loss can be carried back to reduce the taxes paid in prior years, a claim for refund arises immediately, even though it may be subject to approval by the Internal Revenue Service at a later date. In most cases, the claim for refund is sufficiently certain and can be estimated with reasonable accuracy. And since the refund arises from the operating loss of the current period, the amount of the refund should be reported in the income statement for the year in which the loss occurs. This is the position of *APB Opinion No. 11,* which suggests that the amount of tax expense for the year (for example, in cases of consolidation) can be shown in the income statement with the amount of the reduction indicated in a footnote or parenthetically, or the amount of the refund can be shown on the income statement before arriving at the net loss (or income in the case of consolidation) for the year.[5]

In the case of a loss carry-forward, however, *APB Opinion No. 11* concluded that the amount of the benefit should be reported only in the year to which the loss is carried.[6] This *Opinion* states further that the amount of the tax refund arising from the carry-forward of the loss should be reported in the income statement of the year realized as an extraordinary item, unless it has been reported in the year of the loss. This may be interpreted as a correction of the income or loss of the prior period, but it is not clear why the Board did not recommend that it be excluded from income of the carry-forward period, which would then be consistent with the recommendations of *APB Opinions No. 9* and *No. 30* regarding prior period adjustments. However, the inclusion of the tax refund in the income statement is consistent with the more recent *FASB Statement No.*

---

[5] *AICPA Professional Standards,* para. 4091.11

[6] Ibid., An exception is made when realization is assured beyond a reasonable doubt, in which case the tax effect is reported in the loss year.

16. But this treatment of carry-forwards is not consistent with the treatment of carry-backs. The benefit should be treated consistently as relating to the operations of the loss year in both cases, in accordance with income tax allocation procedures.

The position of the APB regarding loss carry-forwards differs from the position taken regarding carry-backs, apparently because of the greater uncertainty of the benefits under a loss carry-forward than under a loss carry-back. If income is not earned during the permitted period, the tax benefit may be lost. But this uncertainty is always present when the allocation of taxes depends on future taxable income. However, there is some merit in the argument that a firm that has incurred losses is more likely to incur additional losses than a firm that has a long record of profitable operation; each case should be treated on its own merits. If there is a good probability of future income within the carry-forward period, the anticipated tax benefit should be recorded in the period in which the loss is incurred. The qualification of "beyond a reasonable doubt" reflects a conservative attitude of the Board.

The asset resulting from the allocation of a tax reduction to the loss year, however, is not the same as the prepaid taxes arising from other allocation problems; and it is not exactly a true receivable, since there will seldom be a direct claim against the government. However, it does represent an anticipated future benefit to the firm in the form of a reduction in a future liability. Although this benefit does not have all of the characteristics of normal assets, it does reflect the possibility of greater after-tax income than would otherwise occur. Other things being equal, a firm with a carry-forward tax loss is worth more than a firm without it.

The above recommended procedure for treating the carry-back and carry-forward of tax losses, however, can be criticized for several reasons. Since it is an attempt to be consistent with tax allocation procedures discussed above, it can be criticized for many of the same reasons. The use of the deferred charge in carrying forward the expected benefit from a tax loss is particularly subject to criticism. However, there are some additional problems. One of the presumed advantages of tax allocation is that it permits a better matching of the tax payments with the associated pretax income items, and thus permits a better prediction of reported net income in the future. However, if a loss in one year gives rise to a refund arising from the carry-back provisions, but a subsequent loss does not, the failure to make a provision for a potential refund arising from the carry-forward provisions will result in reported net income or loss figures for the two years that are not indicative of the operations of the two periods. If the pretax reported income or loss amounts are the same for the two years, the failure to allocate any potential refund to the second year will give the impression that the outlook for the firm is rapidly becoming worse. A further criticism is that a loss by itself does not create a tax refund; the refund is associated with the taxable income as well as with the loss. The functional relationship is not clear-cut. As with tax allocation itself, the allocation of tax refunds does not necessarily improve the communication of information. Full disclosure of tax effects is necessary because income taxes do not behave in the same way as other expenses; the reliance on a reported aftertax net income is not adequate for the decision and predictions made by investors and creditors.

THE INVESTMENT TAX CREDIT

The U.S. Revenue Acts from time to time have provided for a credit against the tax equal to a specified percentage of the cost of the investment in certain depreciable property acquired during the taxable year. The investment tax credit has been alternately canceled and reinstated to help stabilize the economy although some of the provisions have changed. Because it presented entirely new problems for accountants, the topic continues to be relevant to discussions of accounting theory. The investment credit gives rise to a permanent reduction of taxes; but since it is a direct reduction of the tax rather than a reduction of taxable income, it requires an inquiry into the basic nature of the credit itself and into the basic tenets of accounting.

Two methods of reporting the investment credit are (1) the cost reduction method and (2) the tax reduction method. In the cost reduction method, the effect is to allocate the tax benefit over future periods, preferably over the productive life of the acquired property. In the tax reduction method, the credit is treated as a reduction of federal income taxes reported in the year in which the credit arises. A third method—a subsidy considered a contribution of capital—has been proposed but rejected by the APB as unacceptable, although some accountants continue to claim this alternative on the grounds that the income tax is not a "true" expense. Because of pronouncements by the Securities and Exchange Commission and the Internal Revenue Service and an Act of Congress in 1971, the FASB is required to continue to permit flexibility in the reporting of the investment credit.

Cost reduction

The original recommendation of the Accounting Principles Board (the preferred method in *Opinion No. 4*) held that the investment credit should be reflected in income over the life of the productive property by treating it as a reduction of the asset or as deferred income. This method is supportable under the traditional accounting structure for the following reasons: (1) Accountants generally hold that earnings do not arise from the acquisition of assets, but only from their use. Therefore, the spreading of the credit over future periods in a "rational" manner is consistent with the treatment of depreciation. (2) The recapture clause of the Internal Revenue Code provides that under certain conditions, particularly when the asset is sold prematurely, a part of the credit must be repaid. The uncertainty of the final realization of the investment credit, therefore, supports the delaying of its recognition. From the point of view of obtaining economic interpretation, the cost reduction method is supported on the grounds that the original value of the asset can be measured by its net cost to the firm—the invoice price less the tax credit. However, as inputs into investment decision models, empirical research does not as yet support a preference for the cost reduction method.

The cost reduction method is based, in part, on the fact that there are some major differences between the investment credit and other permanent reductions of the tax. Most permanent reductions are based on the special treatment of current or past revenues and expenses or the application of special rates (such as the capital gains rate) applicable to certain income; the investment credit, however, is based on the acquisition of property for *future* use. The position of the Accounting Principles Board is that this permanent reduction in the tax is not realized until the asset has been used in service. Realization is assumed to come only through the use of the facilities and the sale of the products of the enterprise. By itself, this is an ultraconservative position. If the tax does result in an immediate gain, the recognition of the gain should not be delayed just because there has not been a sale or use of the property.

The second reason for the cost reduction method—the uncertainty of final realization—is at best a weak argument. The recapture of the investment credit by the government occurs only if the firm does not use the asset for the declared life and purpose. In most cases, this declared intent will be carried out, and the assumption of this is supported by the postulate of continuity. The uncertainty of the tax benefit in this case is not materially different from the uncertainties regarding the recapture of tax benefits in other cases. For example, if depreciable property is sold at a price in excess of the carrying value of the asset, the firm loses some of the tax benefit of the depreciation taken. Also, the uncertainty in the case of the investment tax credit is not greater than the uncertainties in many other situations involving the determination of business income.

The treatment of the tax credit as a reduction of the cost of the property has its greatest support in the position that this net cost to the firm represents the original value of the asset. In most cases, there may be no evidence that the firm would have acquired the asset at its invoice price if it had not anticipated the investment credit. Thus, the net cost of the asset at the time of acquisition can be assumed to be the invoice price less the investment tax credit, even though the purchase price is paid to one party and the tax saving is obtained from another; both are taken into consideration in the decision to acquire the asset. One difficulty with this procedure, however, is that it permits two firms purchasing identical items at the same invoice price to record different costs if one met the conditions for the tax credit and the other did not. But, in this case, the net cost to the two firms is different and the similarity of the invoice price is not sufficient evidence to indicate that the value of the item is necessarily the same to the two firms.

Tax reduction

The alternative method of treating the investment tax credit found acceptable by the Accounting Principles Board in *Opinion No. 4* is as a reduction of the tax expense for the year in which the credit arises (frequently referred to as "flow-through"). This procedure was found acceptable largely because the Securities and Exchange Commission had established a position accepting both the cost reduction method and the tax reduction method and because of the failure of the recommendation of *Opinion No. 2* to find general acceptance in the accounting profession. But several members of the Board found the tax reduction method preferable or at least just as acceptable as the cost reduction method.

The logic in support of the tax reduction method is as follows: (1) The investment credit is regarded as a selective reduction in taxes available to those who meet certain conditions. (2) It is thought to represent a permanent reduction in the tax that should be treated like all other permanent differences between taxable and accounting income. (3) The anticipated tax reduction is assumed to have no effect on the value of the asset at the date of acquisition. (4) If the tax reduction is recorded by setting up a "deferred income tax" account, it is feared that this may be treated as a capital contribution or as a deferred credit to income without an indication of its specific balance sheet classification.

As indicated above, the tax credit is a permanent decrease in taxes, but it is different from other permanent decreases. Even though it is different, however, it can be treated as a selective reduction in taxes if it is assumed that the tax credit has no effect on the correct valuation of the asset at the time of acquisition. Therefore, the question of valuation is the key issue.

The position of those who oppose the deduction of the tax credit from the purchase price is based on the assumption that the initial value of an asset is based on many factors, including anticipated cash flows and the anticipated tax reduction. This is a plausible approach to the problem, as the tax credit is anticipated at the time of the purchase and helps to support the decision to pay the invoice price to the vendor. But there are some major differences between the tax reduction and other anticipated cash savings and cash flows. First, the tax credit reduces the income tax expense generally in the same year in which the acquisition is made, and it may be assumed to occur simultaneously even though the effect on cash flow will be delayed until the actual payment of the tax. Second, it is not an anticipated factor that is generally taken into consideration in the choice of the depreciation method to allocate the cost of the asset to the several periods of use. One of the objectives of a depreciation method is to allocate the original cost over the life of the asset on the basis of expected benefits. If the tax reduction is one of these anticipated benefits, a portion of the invoice cost of the asset should be allocated as depreciation to the first year of the asset's life to match the tax savings. Thus, the effect on net income would be the same as that resulting from deducting the tax credit from the cost of the asset at the time of acquisition. However, since the tax reduction would not generally be taken into consideration in computing the first year's depreciation, the direct deduction from the original cost is a more expedient method of assuring proper treatment of the tax credit. But we cannot be sure of this, because depreciation methods are not logically conceived (as discussed in Chapter 15).

In the opinion of the author, the most relevant issues in deciding between cost reduction and tax reduction are (1) the determination of the relevant valuation of the asset to be carried forward to future periods and (2) the presentation of information to permit predictions of future cash flows. Cost reduction accomplishes the better valuation of the asset at the time of acquisition. But because of an inability to allocate the initial value of the asset through depreciation on a logical basis, subsequent valuations are likely to be meaningless. In presenting the immediate effect on cash flows, the tax reduction method is superior. However, it is also deficient because of the emphasis on the final net income figure. Adequate information is not usually presented to permit a prediction of future tax payments. This is particularly important when the investment credit is canceled or temporarily removed. The investment credit points out a fundamental weakness in traditional accounting practice; unfortunately, accounting theory is unable to provide conclusive evidence for one method or the other. However, since the cost reduction method has many of the deficiencies of tax allocation as well as the deficiencies inherent in depreciation methods, the tax reduction method may be the better of the two if full disclosure is made of the tax effects, so that undue reliance is not placed on the final net income amount.

ACCOUNTING FOR PENSION COSTS AND OBLIGATIONS

Employee pension plans are a type of long-term commitment, but they possess some special characteristics not found in other types of commitments. Pension plans vary widely in the detailed requirements, but most plans contain a provision that each employee upon reaching a specified age can retire and receive a specified or determinable amount during each year of retirement. Most plans also require that the firm provide a pension trust fund which, with the income from the investment of the fund, will be adequate to assure continued payments under the terms of the plan. The firm itself may manage the trust fund, or the amounts funded may be transferred periodically to a trustee or agent who in turn manages the investments and makes the retirement payments. The basic accounting problems are (1) allocation of the pension costs to periods, (2) reporting appropriate amounts for the rights and obligations existing at different points in time, (3) disclosure of major terms of the plan, including the amount and timing of cash disbursements required or intended to be paid into the fund, and (4) the presentation of financial statements of the fund or plan.

The allocation of pension costs

The total costs of providing for retirement benefits to employees can be determined by estimating the total amount that must be in the fund which when invested will permit the payment of the agreed retirement benefits to eligible employees during their expected retirement periods. This total pension cost is uncertain because the amounts expected to be paid depend on several future events, including the longevity of the employees after retirement, death before retirement, employees leaving the firm or losing retirement benefits for other reasons, and future changes in pension commitments. The amount required to be placed in the fund also depends upon the income that can be earned by the fund. Generally, these uncertainties can be resolved by the use of actuarial methods, and the computation is usually made by an actuary.

Since this total pension cost is assumed to represent an expense of operating the business, a major problem of accounting for pension costs is the allocation of this total cost to periods. Note, first, that the problem of allocating the pension cost to periods is not related to the methods of financing the pension plan, just as the method of amortizing the cost of plant and equipment is not related to the method of paying for such assets. Therefore, the process of allocating pension costs to periods is similar to the depreciation of plant and equipment, except that the costs of plant and equipment are measured by current or past transactions and prices, and the costs of pension plans are measured in terms of expected cash outlays in the future. As with depreciation, the alleged objective of allocating pension costs is to match the expense with the net revenue contribution in each period. However, because of the interactions with other factors of production, it is impossible to measure the net revenue contribution of employees. An alternative suggested by Dewhirst is to allocate the total pension cost to years on the basis of the ratio of the services received in a year to the total services expected over the working lives of the employees of that year.[7] But this merely begs the question, since services received and net revenue contribution are not necessarily the same and since there is no necessary relationship between pension benefits and total employee services.

Other suggested methods have as their objective the prevention of widely varying charges from period to period within a firm. Such methods are claimed to have merit because they are systematic and prevent mate-

---

[7] John F. Dewhirst, "A Conceptual Approach to Pension Accounting," *Accounting Review,* April 1971, p. 366.

rial distortion of net income by the whim of management. However, since they are based on arbitrary assumed relationships, the suggested methods cannot be supported on theoretical grounds. The arbitrary smoothing of income is not supported by theoretical or empirical research. These allocation methods, however, are generally discussed separately for current (normal) costs, prior service costs, and actuarial gains and losses.

Current-service cost. The current-service cost, generally referred to as normal cost, is the annual pension cost assigned to each year subsequent to the inception of the pension plan or a change in the plan. Although an infinite number of systematic allocation procedures could be devised for the determination of the current annual pension cost, it is frequently suggested that the annual provision should be based on an accounting method that uses an acceptable actuarial cost method.[8] However, since the actuarial cost methods are methods of financing the pension fund, it is difficult to understand why they necessarily represent good matching concepts. But in the absence of a theoretical base, this at least limits the choice to several alternatives. However, the actuarial cost method selected for allocation purposes may differ from the method selected for funding purposes.

The several actuarial cost methods differ in that some result in decreasing pension costs until the plan reaches maturity, and other methods result in level normal costs, and others in increasing costs. The basic similarity is that all methods include an interest factor equal to the assumed earning rate on pension fund investments. The accrued-benefit cost method assumes that each employee receives each year a pension benefit equal to the present discounted value of a given amount to be added to his or her pension fund at retirement or a specified number of units to be credited to the account at retirement (the unit-credit method). Therefore, the pension cost is the accrual of the benefit assumed to be earned by the employee. As the employee approaches the retirement age, the accrued benefit each year will increase because it is discounted for a shorter period of time. The total pension cost for all employees, however, will depend upon several factors, and it may become fairly level when the plan matures and the average age and number of employees become relatively constant. An increase in the normal cost allocated to each period for an employee may be supported on the grounds that the pension cost is a means of compensation and that it should be related to the employee's other compensation, which is likely to increase during his or her employment period. However, the use of the investment earning rate is a crude method of adjustment for this factor, and some plans take care of it by relating the retirement benefits accrued to the salary levels.

The projected benefit cost methods result in a level normal cost, equal to a constant sum for each individual, which when invested at the earning

---

[8] See, for example, *APB Opinion No. 8, AICPA Professional Standards,* para. 4063.17.

rate will reach the projected benefit cost at retirement. The level amount will vary for different individuals, however, depending upon the age of the employee when hired or when the plan is started. The total cost will stay level after the plan matures, regardless of salary levels, so long as the projected benefit cost is correctly anticipated. Therefore, the result is similar to the straight-line method of depreciation. Since the net income contribution cannot be measured, a level pension cost is as logical as any other, and it has the advantage of permitting greater predictability of its effect on income.

Since cash payments into the pension fund need not be paid according to the same actuarial cost method as that used to determine the pension expense, the pension fund may not accrue interest as rapidly as that assumed in the allocation method. If this is the case, an equivalent amount for interest expense should be accrued, but there is good argument for charging this to a separate financial expense, rather than to the employment expenses.

Some arguments have been made in favor of accruing only pension costs that become legal liabilities of the firm, but the general view is that expenses should be accrued even though the pension plan is subject to cancellation or has a terminal date established by a union contract. The most likely situation is that the pension plan will be continued indefinitely. This is supported by the Pension Reform Act of 1974 (ERISA), which requires minimum vesting, minimum funding, and termination insurance. Since vested benefits represent the amounts accruing to the employee even if the employee's services with the firm are discontinued, such vested benefits represent a legal liability of the firm and determine the minimum pension cost to be accrued. However, equitable considerations present a strong argument for the accrual of full pension costs. But if only vested benefits are accrued, significant increases in the accrual may be necessary in particular years.

Past-service costs.[9]   When a pension plan is initiated or when the benefits are increased significantly, they are frequently made retroactive to apply to service performed before the inception of the plan or the alteration in the benefits. At least five alternatives have been suggested for treatment of these past-service costs: (1) an immediate charge to income as an extraordinary item representing a correction of prior years, (2) an immediate charge to the income of the current period, (3) nonrecognition, (4) allocation over the remaining period of employment of the employee, and (5) allocation as an intangible over a period during which the benefits from the adoption of the plan or change are assumed to be received.

The immediate charge to retained earnings or to current income as either an operating charge or an extraordinary item has not been generally accepted because it is assumed that these costs will benefit only

---

[9] Referred to as Supplemental Actuarial Value in *FASB Statement No. 35.*

current and future periods. The concept of prior-service costs, however, is a misnomer, because it reflects the way the pension benefits of an employee are computed. It is not a cost of the past period; but according to some actuarial cost methods, the pension benefit is computed by assuming that the accrual started when the employee would have been eligible to accrue benefits if the plan had been in effect at that time. Therefore, if such actuarial cost method is used for the allocation method, a lump sum that would have been allocated to the prior period remains unallocated. But since there was no benefit received by the firm in the prior periods, it cannot be a correction of prior years' income. And since the firm hopes to enjoy better employee relations in the future, there is no loss or gift to be recognized at the time of the adoption of the plan.

The argument that there should be no recognition of the prior-service costs is based on the assumption that if the plan is to continue indefinitely into the future, the accrual of normal costs plus interest on unfunded past service costs will be adequate at all times to provide for current retirement benefits. This is the minimum provision for annual pension costs recommended by *APB Opinion No. 8* except for the provision for vested benefits. But this is a confusion of the costs of a retirement plan and the funds necessary to carry out the plan. The costs do exist even though full funding may not be necessary from a financial point of view.

Several of the actuarial cost methods are based on the assumption that the projected benefit represents the amount that accrues with interest only from the inception of the plan or change until retirement. Therefore, no prior-service cost arises; the entire projected cost less the assumed interest on the pension fund is allocated over the period after the inception of the plan. The result is that total normal pension costs will be greater for several years after starting the plan than after the plan matures because the costs per year for employees who have been with the firm for many years will be greater than the costs allocated to new or younger employees. The disadvantage with this procedure is that it is difficult for an investor or analyst to determine when the pension costs will start to decline.

Other actuarial cost methods assume that the benefits to the employees started accruing when the employee would have been eligible if the plan had been in effect. Therefore the total amount that would have been allocated to this period plus the interest that would have been earned if it had been funded represents the past-service cost. *APB Opinion No. 8* recommends that as an alternative to the minimum annual provision discussed above, the annual charge can include, in addition to the normal cost and interest equivalents, a portion of the past-service cost amortized on a 40-year basis. The maximum provision should be an allocation of the prior-service cost or increase in benefits over a 10-year period in addition to the normal cost and equivalent interest. The allocation of the prior-service cost over such arbitrary periods appears to have as its sole objective the smoothing of net income. Although it is consistent with recommendations regarding the amortization of intangibles, no logical matching is obtained. Without a logical matching concept there appears to be no reason for permitting such wide deviations in the amount of pension costs that can be reported, particularly considering that some of the actuarial methods result in normal costs that may be twice the amount resulting from the use of other methods.

Actuarial gains and losses. Since actuarial assumptions are based upon expectations of future events, it may be necessary to revise the pension cost estimates as conditions change. These actuarial gains and losses represent the difference between the actuarial assumptions and the actual conditions affecting the final pension cost. They may arise from investment gains and losses or changes in interest rates or other actuarial assumptions. Although many firms have recognized these gains and losses by adjusting the pension costs of the current period, *APB Opinion No. 8* recommended that either they should be spread over several years (10 to 20 years being suggested), or an averaging method should be used. Under averaging, the net gains and losses that occurred in the past and those expected to occur are averaged, and such average annual net gain or loss is included in the normal cost. Either spreading or averaging results in a smoothing of net income and cannot be justified unless it can be assumed that the normal cost is adjusted to what it should have been if correct actuarial assumptions had been made.

Disclosure of pension information

Since the pension plan is a form of long-term commitment, there is some merit in the capitalization of the discounted amount of the entire retirement benefits to employees. But the rights under the pension plan are not unconditional, and furthermore, they represent only a part of the benefits to be received from employees during their remaining years of service. The obligation under the pension plan is only a small part of the total obligation to employees for services to be performed. Therefore, since there is little justification for the capitalization of future wage commitments, there is also little justification for the capitalization of all future pension benefits and obligations.

There is a need, however, to disclose sufficient information regarding a defined benefit plan so that investors and other users of financial statements will be able to evaluate the possible future cash consequences of the plan as well as its benefits in attracting competent employees. These disclosures should include information regarding the present value of the actuarially determined pension obligation and the current value of the pension assets. Separate disclosure of the obligation for vested benefits and for nonvested benefits would be apropriate; however, there should not be an inference that only the vested benefits represent the liability of the firm. As discussed in Chapter 17, obligations should be reported whether or not they are legally binding. The vesting of pension rights should not be the determining factor for the presentation of pension obligations.

Because the pension cost allocation is not based on logic or upon actual accrued benefits to employees, a liability or prepaid pension cost reflecting the difference between the amount funded and the amount allocated to pension cost has no real meaning except to permit the firm to stay within the double-entry accounting system. But there should be a disclosure of the extent to which the pension plan is being funded with respect to the actuarially determined pension obligation. Because of the limitations of the asset and liability concepts, this disclosure cannot be made adequately in the body of the balance sheet alone. More extensive descriptions should be included in the footnotes or other presentations to disclose the extent to which the pension plan is being funded, including an amount for prior-service costs if the actuarial method used treats them separately. Furthermore, the annual cash disbursements required or expected to be made into the pension fund should be disclosed in cash flow or funds flow statements or in footnotes to the financial statements.

Financial statements of the fund or plan

The objectives of the financial statements of the fund or plan should be to provide the beneficiaries of the plan with sufficient information to evaluate the adequacy of the plan and to provide investors with information regarding future cash requirements of the plan. The timing and amounts of cash requirements are important to permit predictions of future dividend payments. Therefore, the financial statements of the pension plan should be incorporated into the basic financial statements of the firm or reported in notes or schedules of these financial statements.

SELECTED ADDITIONAL READING

Income tax allocation

Bevis, Donald J., and **Raymond E. Perry.** *Accounting for Income Taxes.* AICPA, 1969.

Bierman, Harold, and **Thomas R. Dyckman,** "New Look at Deferred Taxes." *Financial Executive,* January 1974, pp. 40ff.

Black, Homer A. "Interperiod Allocation of Corporate Income Taxes." *Accounting Research Study No. 9.* AICPA, 1966.

Hawkins, David F. "Controversial Accounting Changes." *Harvard Business Review,* March–April 1968, pp. 20–41.

Moore, Carl L. "Deferred Income Tax—Is It a Liability?" *New York CPA,* February 1970, pp. 130–38.

Nurnberg, Hugo. "Discounting Deferred Tax Liabilities." *Accounting Review,* October 1972, pp. 655–65.

Revsine, Lawrence. "Some Controversy Concerning Controversial Accounting Changes." *Accounting Review,* April 1969, pp. 354–58.

Watson, Peter L. "Accounting for Deferred Tax on Depreciable Assets." *Accounting and Business Research,* Autumn 1979, pp. 338–47.

Weber, Richard P. "'Misleading Tax Figures: A Problem for Accountants." *Accounting Review,* January 1977, pp. 172–85.

Williams, Edward E., and M. Chapman Findlay. "Discounting Deferred Tax Liabilities: Some Clarifying Comments." *Journal of Business Finance and Accounting,* Spring 1975, pp. 121–33.

Tax allocation—empirical studies

Beaver, William, and Ronald E. Dukes, "Interperiod Tax Allocation; Earnings Expectations and the Behavior of Security Prices." *Accounting Review,* April 1972, pp. 320–22.

————. "Interperiod Tax Allocation and Delta-Depreciation Methods: Some Empirical Results." *Accounting Review,* July 1973, pp. 549–59.

Allocation of carry-backs and carry-forwards

Laibstain, Samuel. "New Look at Accounting for Operating Loss Carry-Forwards." *Accounting Review,* April 1971, pp. 342–51.

Wolk, Harry I., and Michael G. Tearney. "Income Tax Allocation and Loss Carry-Forwards: Exploring Unchartered Ground." *Accounting Review,* April 1973, pp. 292–99.

Investment tax credit

Moonitz, Maurice. "Some Reflections on the Investment Credit Experience." *Journal of Accounting Research,* Spring 1966, pp. 47–61.

Stamp, Edward. "Some Further Reflections On the Investment Credit." *Journal of Accounting Research,* Spring 1967, pp. 124–28.

Throckmorton, Jerry J. "'Theoretical Concepts for Interpreting the Investment Credit." *Journal of Accountancy,* April 1970, pp. 45–52.

Accounting for pension costs

Deaton, William C., and Jerry J. Weygandt. "Disclosures Related to Pension Plans." *Journal of Accountancy,* January 1975, pp. 44–51.

Dewhirst, John F. "A Conceptual Approach to Pension Accounting." *Accounting Review,* April 1971, pp. 365–73.

Hicks, Ernest L. "Accounting for the Cost of Pension Plans." *Accounting Research Study No. 8.* AICPA, 1965.

Langenderfer, Harold Q. "Accrued Past-Service Pension Costs Should Be Capitalized." *New York CPA,* February 1971, pp. 137–43.

Schuchart, J. A., and W. L. Sanders, Jr. "Pension Fund Considerations." *Management Accounting,* March 1972, pp. 49–52.

CHAPTER 19

OWNERSHIP EQUITIES

The rights of owners of business firms are many and varied, but those rights of greatest interest to accountants are the rights to share in the cash or property distributions of the firms, the residual rights to assets in the case of final liquidation, and the equity (proprietary) rights in a going concern—the right to sell or transfer all equity rights in the enterprise. The disclosure of these economic rights and any abridgment of them is an important objective in the presentation of financial statements.

In this chapter, the nature of ownership equities is explored and viewed from the perspective of several equity theories—the proprietary theory, the entity theory, the residual equity concept, the enterprise theory, and the funds theory. The objectives and logic of the classification of partnership and stockholder equities are then discussed in the general framework of the various equity theories. The classification of equities in consolidated statements is treated separately. The following chapter is concerned with changes in the composition of stockholder equities, those changes arising from business combinations, and the potential dilution effect of convertible securities and warrants.

THE NATURE OF OWNERSHIP EQUITIES

Individual assets and liabilities of a business enterprise can be defined and measured independently of other elements in the accounting equation. This is not so with ownership equities (also commonly known as proprietorship or stockholder equities in a corporation). Generally, there is no pretense that these equities as presented in the balance sheet represent either the current market value or the subjective value of the enterprise to the owners. The total amount presented in the statements is a result of the methods employed in measuring the specific assets and liabilities and from traditional structural accounting procedures. Since the total value of the firm to its owners cannot be measured from the valuation of specific assets and liabilities, the reported amount of proprietorship cannot represent the current value of the rights of the owners. Instead of looking at specific rights to future benefits, as with assets, or at specific obligations of the enterprise, as with liabilities, the proprietorship or stockholders' equity looks at the aggregate resources from the view of ownership rights, equities, or restrictions, depending upon the equity concept employed.

Although the rights and priorities of some classes of corporate stock may be similar to those of some types of long-term debt, in general the differences between stockholder equities and liabilities are (1) the extent to which other equity holders have priority rights, (2) the degree of certainty in the determination of amounts to be received by the equity holders, and (3) the maturity dates of the payments of final rights. In normal circumstances, creditors have priority over stockholders for the payment of periodic interest and in the repayment of principal. Preferred stockholders may have priorities over common stockholders, but both are residual claimants in relationship to the claims of creditors. In a viable concern, the amounts payable to creditors are usually determinable in advance, the amount to be paid at maturity is usually a fixed number of dollars, and the interest payments are usually expressed as a percentage of a face value. Dividend payments to stockholders are generally dependent on reported income or retained earnings, the availability of cash, and a formal declaration by the board of directors. The maturity date of creditors' claims is generally fixed or determinable, but stockholders' equities do not represent legal obligations of the enterprise. Dividends become liabilities only upon declaration by the board of directors and, with few exceptions, stockholders cannot expect repayment of capital at definite or determinable dates.

The proprietary theory

The notion of proprietorship originated with an attempt to place logic into the exposition of double-entry bookkeeping. In the accounting equation $\Sigma A - \Sigma L = P$, the proprietor is the center of interest. The assets are assumed to be owned by the proprietor, and the liabilities are the proprietor's obligations. Hatfield, however, in his discussion of the proprietary concept, treated liabilities as negative assets and stated that capital, ". . . in the initial bookkeeping equation, represents the net wealth of the proprietor."[1] Regardless of the treatment of liabilities, the proprietorship is considered to be the net value of the business to the owners. When the business is organized, this value is equal to the investment of the owners. During the life of the enterprise, it is equal to the original investment and additional investments plus the accumulated net income in excess of that withdrawn by the proprietors (or minus net losses and withdrawals). It is, therefore, a wealth concept.

Under the proprietary theory, revenues are increases in proprietorship and expenses are decreases. Thus, net income, the excess of revenues over expenses, accrues directly to the owners; it represents an increase in the wealth of the proprietors. And since income is an increase in wealth, it is

[1] Henry Rand Hatfield, *Accounting, Its Principles and Problems* (New York: Appleton-Century-Crofts, 1927), pp. 171, 221.

immediately added to the owner's capital or proprietorship. Cash dividends represent withdrawals of capital, and retained earnings are a part of total proprietorship. Stock dividends represent merely a transfer from one section of proprietorship to another; they do not represent income to the stockholders. Interest on debt, however, represents an expense of the proprietors and should be deducted before arriving at net income to the owners. Corporate income taxes are likewise expenses in the proprietorship theory; however, some argue that the corporation is acting as an agent of the stockholders in paying the tax that is really a tax on the income of the stockholders.

The comprehensive income concept is based on the proprietary theory, because net income includes all items affecting proprietorship during the period except dividend withdrawals and capital transactions. But the classification of the sources of net income is independent of the equity theory employed. The proprietary concept does not dictate how the net income shall be computed; it emphasizes only the nature of the change in proprietorship and its classification in the balance sheet.

The proprietary theory is adapted best to the single proprietorship form of organization because in this form there is generally a personal relationship between the management of the business and the ownership. The proprietary theory is also a logical framework for the partnership form of organization, particularly when it is organized under common law. In accounting for both the single proprietorship and the partnership forms, the proprietary theory appears to dominate, particularly because net income is added each period to the personal capital accounts of the owners, although the traditional computation of income does not measure a net increase in wealth.

The proprietary theory is not so readily applicable to the corporate form of organization as it is to the single proprietorship and the partnership. However, many writers have chosen to look through the veil of the corporate form and describe the total of the capital stock, paid-in surplus, and retained earnings as the net wealth of the stockholders, implying the proprietary theory.[2] The proprietary theory is also implied in many accounting practices and in accounting terminology relating to corporations. For example, the net income of the firm is often referred to as net income to the stockholders. Furthermore, financial statements must make reference to earnings per share and occasionally refer to book value per share. But these computations are not necessarily meaningless without the proprietary concept. "Net income to stockholders" can be interpreted to be the residual net income allocable to the stockholders' equity, and "book value per share" can be interpreted to be the book equity per share under the entity approach.

The equity method for accounting for nonconsolidated investments in subsidiaries also implies a proprietary concept. The parent's propor-

---

[2] See, for example, ibid., p. 172.

tionate share of each year's income is added to the investment account on the theory that the income of the subsidiary accrues to the stockholders, including the parent corporation as the major stockholder. It may be argued, however, that this accrual is merely a reflection of an increase in the value of the stock held by the parent and is, thus, in accord with the entity view. However, there is little merit in this view, since the proportionate share of the recorded income of the subsidiary is at best a poor indicator of an increase in the value of the stock to the parent.

The entity theory

The existence of a business entity separate from the personal affairs and other interests of the owners and other equity holders is recognized in all concepts of ownership and equities. In the entity theory, however, the business firm is considered to have a separate existence, even personality, of its own. The founders and owners are not necessarily identified with the existence of the firm. This relationship finds legal and institutional support in the form of the corporation, but it is also found in other forms of business enterprises, and the entity theory is said to have actually preceded the corporate concept. This separate existence is not unique to business enterprises; universities, hospitals, governments, and other organizations have a continuity of existence separate from the lives of the organizers and even separate from the individuals directly associated with the organization.

The entity theory is based on the equation: $\Sigma A = \Sigma L + SE$, or Assets = Equities (Liabilities plus Stockholders' Equity). The items on the right-hand side of the equation are occasionally called liabilities, but they are really equities with different rights in the enterprise. The main difference between the liabilities and the stockholder equities is that the valuation of the rights of the creditors can be determined independently of other valuations if the firm is solvent, while the rights of the stockholders are measured by the valuation of assets originally invested plus the valuation of reinvested earnings and subsequent revaluations. But the rights of the stockholders to receive dividends and share in net assets upon liquidation are rights as equity holders, rather than as owners of the specific assets.

The liabilities, therefore, are the specific obligations of the *firm,* and the assets represent the rights of the *firm* to receive specific goods and services or other benefits. The valuation of assets, therefore, should reflect a measurement of the benefits to be received by the enterprise.

The net income of the enterprise is generally expressed in terms of the net change in the stockholders' equity, not including changes arising from dividend declarations and capital transactions. This is not the same as saying that the net income is the income to the stockholders, as is implied in the proprietary theory. It represents the residual change in equity position after deducting all other claims, including interest on long-term debt and income taxes. It is personal income to the stockholder only if the value of the investment has increased or to the extent of a dividend declaration.

A much narrower view of the entity theory was expressed by Husband in his proposal of the proprietary or agency viewpoint as a logical alternative to the entity theory. In his strict interpretation of the entity theory, the "income earned by the corporate endeavor is the property of the corporation, per se."[3] Only the dividends declared represent income to the stockholders. The retained earnings represent the *"corporation's proprietary equity in itself."*[4] It also follows logically from this view that, since the corporate income is not added to the stockholders' equity, a stock dividend represents income to the stockholders. This interpretation does have some merit, but the generally accepted view is that although corporate income accrues to the corporation rather than directly to the stockholders, the retained earnings represents an allocation of the undistributed income to the stockholders' equity. That is, the entity theory is based on the equation Assets = Equities; no portion of the total equities remains unallocated. Therefore, a stock dividend is not income to the stockholders, but rather a reclassification of the stockholders' equity.

Although an allocation of corporate income to specific equities is possible under the entity theory, a strict adherence to the concept requires that interest on debt should be considered a distribution of income rather than an expense. That is, all distributions or allocations to equity holders are considered to be allocations of corporate income. The 1957 AAA statement, for example, stated that "interest charges, income taxes, and true profit-sharing distributions are not determinants of *enterprise* net income."[5] Income taxes, in the opinion of the author, however, are not a distribution of income, but rather an expense of the business, as discussed in Chapter 7.

Since corporate net income is not considered to be directly the net income of the stockholders, revenues and expenses are not increases and decreases in the stockholders' equity. Revenue is the product of the enterprise, and the expenses are the goods and services consumed in obtaining the revenue. Therefore, expenses are deductions from revenue, and the difference represents the corporate income to be distributed to stockholders in the form of dividends or reinvested in the business.

The entity theory has its main application in the corporate form of business enterprise, but it is also relevant to unincorporated firms that have a continuity of existence separate from the lives of individual owners. The entity theory is also relevant to the preparation of consolidated financial statements. However, in this case, the economic entity, rather

---

[3] George R. Husband, "The Entity Concept in Accounting," *Accounting Review* 29 (October 1954): p. 554.

[4] Ibid.

[5] AAA Committee on Accounting Concepts and Standards, *Accounting and Reporting Standards for Corporate Financial Statements and Preceding Statements and Supplements* (AAA, 1957), p. 5.

than the legal entity, is the relevant accounting unit. The classes of equity holders are increased to include the minority stockholders as a separate class in addition to the stockholders of the parent corporation and all creditors of the parent and its subsidiaries.

Several authors have proposed or implied that the proprietary and equity theories lead to different bases for asset valuation. Under the proprietary theory, it is claimed that the assets should be valued in terms of current values because the owners' equity is considered to be their net worth or net wealth. Under the entity theory, the firm is not concerned with current values because the emphasis is on the accountability of cost to the owners and other equity holders.[6] However, recent discussions of valuation have stressed the importance of current values as relevant in the determination of the income of the enterprise, as a measure of the future services to the firm, and as a basis for future decisions of management. Even in meeting the objective of accountability to equity holders, it may be argued that current values are just as important as costs. Therefore, in the author's opinion, the proprietary and entity theories do not necessarily dictate different valuation bases.

The residual equity theory

Paton referred to the residual equity as one of several types of equity under the entity theory. In the entity theory, the stockholder has an equity in the firm like other equity holders, but is not the owner. Paton emphasized, however, the special relationship of the residual equity holder to the work of the accountant.[7] Changes in asset valuation, changes in income and in retained earnings, and changes in the interests of other equity holders are all reflected in the residual equity of the common stockholders. But even though the equities of creditors, preferred stockholders, and common stockholders should be classified separately, they are all equities under the entity theory.

The residual equity point of view is a concept somewhere between the proprietary theory and the entity theory. In this view, the equation becomes: Assets − Specific equities = Residual equity. The specific equities include the claims of creditors and the equities of preferred stockholders. However, in certain cases where losses have been large or in bankruptcy proceedings, the equity of the common stockholders may disappear and the preferred stockholders or the bondholders may become the residual equity holders.

The objective of the residual equity approach is to provide better information to common stockholders for making investment decisions. In a corporation with indefinite continuity, the current value of common stock is dependent primarily upon the expectation of future dividends. Future

---

[6] See, for example, Stephen Gilman, *Accounting Concepts of Profit* (New York: Ronald Press, 1939), p. 74.

[7] William Andrew Paton, *Accounting Theory* (New York: Ronald Press, 1922), pp. 84–89.

dividends, in turn, are dependent upon the expectations of total receipts less specific contractual obligations, payments to specific equity holders, and requirements for reinvestment. Trends in investment values can also be measured, in part, by looking at trends in the value of the residual equity measured on the basis of current values.

Common stockholders are generally thought to have a residual equity in the income of the firm and in the net assets upon final liquidation. Since financial statements are not generally prepared on the basis of possible liquidation, the information provided regarding the residual equity should be useful in predicting possible future dividends to common stockholders including liquidation dividends. The income statement or combined income statement and statement of retained earnings should show the income available to the residual equity holders after all prior claims are met, including the dividends to preferred stockholders. The equity of the common stockholders in the balance sheet should be presented separately from the equities of preferred stockholders and other specific equity holders. The funds statement should also show the funds available to the firm for the payment of common dividends and other purposes.

An alternative approach to the residual equity concept is that, since under the usual assumption of enterprise continuity the common stockholders' only claim against the corporation is to receive dividends when and if declared, the residual equity in capital is not assigned to the residual equity holders. Both the initial capital supplied by the common stockholders and the retained earnings are, therefore, the equity of the corporation in itself. Note that this is similar to the strict entity approach proposed by Husband.

The residual concept has a different meaning in the context of the earnings per share computations; however, it can be considered an extension of the residual equity theory. A *residual security* is defined as a common stock equivalent, which would include debt or preferred stock convertible into common stock, and warrants for the purchase of common stock. Under certain conditions, holders of these securities may obtain the rights of common stockholders, thus giving them residual rights. The disclosure of these potential residual rights and the potential dilution effect is discussed in Chapter 20 in a section on earnings per share.

The enterprise theory

The enterprise theory of the firm is a broader concept than the entity theory, but less well defined in its scope and application. In the entity theory the firm is considered to be a separate economic unit operated primarily for the benefit of the equity holders, whereas in the enterprise theory the corporation is a social institution operated for the benefit of many interested groups. In the broadest form these groups include, in addition to the stockholders and creditors, the employees, customers, the government as a taxing authority and as a regulatory agency, and the general public. Thus, the broad form of the enterprise theory may be thought of as a social theory of accounting.

This concept of the firm is most applicable to the large modern corporation that has been obliged to consider the effect of its actions on various groups and on society as a whole. From an accounting point of view, this means that the responsibility of proper reporting extends not only to stockholders and creditors, but also to many other groups and to the general public. The large corporation can no longer operate solely in the interests of the stockholders, and it cannot be assumed that the forces of competition will necessarily protect the interest of other groups. Employees, particularly through labor unions, utilize accounting data in presenting their claims for wage increases or increases in other benefits. Customers and regulatory agencies have been interested in the fairness of price changes, and the government has been interested in the effect of price changes on the general state of the economy.

The most relevant concept of income in this broad social responsibility concept of the enterprise is the value-added concept discussed in Chapter 7. The total value added by the enterprise is the market value of the goods and services produced by the firm less the value of the goods and services acquired by transfer from other firms. Thus, value-added income includes all payments to stockholders in the form of dividends, interest to creditors, wages and salaries to employees, taxes to governmental units, and earnings retained in the business. The total value-added concept also includes depreciation, but this is a gross product concept rather than a net income concept.

The term *enterprise net income* as used by the 1957 AAA statement is a narrower concept than the value-added concept. In addition to the traditional net income to stockholders, this concept of enterprise net income includes interest charges and income taxes. Therefore, it is closer to the entity concept. The inclusion of income taxes in enterprise net income apparently stems from the idea that this is paid to the government on behalf of the stockholders. If income taxes are an expense under the entity theory as proposed earlier, they should not be included in enterprise net income. If a broader concept of income is intended, the enterprise net income should also include payments to other beneficiaries of the corporation.

The position of retained earnings in the enterprise theory is similar to its position in the entity concept. It either represents part of the equity of the residual equity holders, or it represents undistributed equity—the equity of the corporation in itself. In the entity theory there is considerable merit in the former position; but in the enterprise theory the earnings reinvested in the business do not necessarily benefit only the residual stockholders. Capital employed to maintain market position, to improve productivity, or to promote general expansion may not necessarily benefit only the stockholders. In fact, it is possible that the stockholders may not be benefited at all if future dividends are not increased.

The fund theory

The fund theory abandons the personal relationship assumed in the proprietary theory and the personalization of the firm as an artificial economic and legal unit under the entity theory. Instead, the fund theory substitutes an operational, or activity-oriented, unit as the basis for accounting. This area of interest, called the fund, includes a group of assets and related obligations and restrictions representing specific economic functions or activities.

The fund theory is based on the equation: Assets = Restrictions of assets. Assets represent prospective services to the fund or operational unit. Liabilities represent restrictions against specific or general assets of the fund. The invested capital represents either legal or financial restrictions on the use of assets; that is, the invested capital must be maintained intact unless specific authority has been obtained (with few exceptions) for partial or complete liquidation. Even partial liquidation of invested capital, however, requires full disclosure. Appropriations of retained earnings represent restrictions imposed by management, by creditors, or by legal requirements. Unappropriated retained earnings also represent restrictions—a residual overall restriction that the assets be used for the purposes for which they are devoted. Thus, all equities represent restrictions imposed by legal, contractual, managerial, financial, or equitable considerations.

The fund concept has found its greatest usefulness in governmental and nonprofit institutions. In a university, for example, the most commonly used funds are the special funds for endowments, student loan funds, plant funds, auxiliary enterprises, and current educational activities. Each of these funds has its specific assets restricted for particular purposes. But the fund concept is also relevant to specific areas of interest within the corporation, or even for areas of interest greater than the single legal form of enterprise. Examples of direct applicability are the sinking fund in financial reporting, branch or divisional accounting, and accounting for estates and trusts. The preparation of consolidated statements is also an application of the fund theory just as much as it is an extension of the theory of the economic entity. The fund theory can also be applied in other areas of financial accounting; for example, the fund theory can find usefulness in the distinction between current and fixed assets and equities.

Although the income concept can be retained under the fund theory, it is not the central concept in financial reporting. Instead, the description of the operation of the fund is presented more clearly in the funds statements. The major financial statements are statistical summaries of the sources and dispositions of funds. An income statement, if it appears at all, is an adjunct of the funds statement—a description of the funds provided from operations. Although the funds theory is not oriented toward the interests of any specific equity holder, all interested parties should be able to find the information they want in the financial statements. Like the enterprise theory, it is neutral with respect to the interests of any specific group.

Summary of the equity theories

The several theories or approaches to the nature of an enterprise and the relationships or activities to be reported are all relevant under different circumstances of organization, economic relationships, and accounting objectives. Therefore, accounting theory and practice should take an eclectic approach to these theories. All help to explain and understand accounting theory and to develop logical patterns for the extension of theory. However, care must be taken to apply the most logical equity theory in each case and to use a single theory consistently in the same circumstances. For example, it is inconsistent to argue that a pro rata share of a subsidiary's income should be added to the investment in the parent company's assets (a proprietary concept) and also to argue that a stock dividend of the subsidiary should require the capitalization of an amount equal to the market value of the shares capitalized (a narrow entity concept). It is not inconsistent, however, to apply the proprietary concept to a small single proprietorship, the entity concept to a medium-size corporation, and the enterprise theory to a very large corporation.

Each of the several equity theories interprets the economic position of the enterprise in a different way and thus presents a different emphasis on the method of disclosure of the interests of the several equity holders or interested groups. They also lead to different concepts of income or different methods of disclosing the equity interests in the income of the enterprise. There is also some evidence that the proprietary concept requires an emphasis on current valuations of assets, the entity and funds theories are neutral with respect to asset valuation, and the enterprise theory emphasizes the need for a market output valuation concept. However, the associated valuation method and the associated concept of income are primarily the result of the way the several concepts have been developed. The problem of valuation and the most relevant concept of income are basically independent of the equity theory selected. The main questions raised by the several equity concepts are related to these questions: (1) Who are the beneficiaries of net income? (2) How should the equity relationships be shown in the financial statements? These questions are closely related to the objectives of accounting.

THE CLASSIFICATION OF SINGLE PROPRIETORSHIP AND PARTNERSHIP EQUITIES

In the single proprietorship, the entire ownership equity is generally presented in one amount. In accordance with the proprietary theory, this equity represents the ownership of the business by the proprietor. There is no need to present subclassifications of this equity because the owner is not restricted regarding how much to invest or take out of the business, and there are no superior claims other than those held by the creditors of the business. In case of liquidation or insolvency, the creditors can reach the personal assets of the owner, making the distinction between permanent invested capital and reinvested earnings of little importance for this purpose. This does not mean, however, that a distinction is not made between capital and income. Income is computed periodically and added to the capital account at the end of each period; capital transactions (withdrawals and additional investments) are recorded directly in the capital account; and all changes are generally summarized in a separate statement of the proprietorship.

The ownership equity of the partnership is similar to the equity of a single proprietor, except that it is classified according to the interests of each of the partners. Separate drawing accounts may be used to establish control over withdrawals or to force compliance with a withdrawal agreement. But even these accounts are generally closed into the capital accounting at the end of each period, so that no classification according to source of the equities is maintained.

What, then, is the value of the classification according to the several partners' interests? First, it should be recognized that this classification shows only the interest in the net assets of the business; each partner's interest in the income of the enterprise may be entirely different according to the terms of the partnership agreement. But the capital accounts do not show the specific rights of the partners in liquidation (except in the unusual case where there are no gains or losses in the liquidation process). If the gains and losses are allocated to the partners' capital accounts in a ratio other than the ratio of the capital balances, the final distribution to partners may be entirely different from the apparent interests in the business before starting liquidation. Therefore, the capital accounts serve primarily as a starting point in determining the distribution of assets in final liquidation and dissolution unless all or a part of the income is allocated on the basis of capital balances. Creditors are not as interested in the capital balances of the partners as they are in the total ownership equity and the personal assets of the partners because any partner may become personally liable for any or all of the debts of the partnership.

THE CLASSIFICATION OF STOCKHOLDER EQUITIES

The relationships between a corporation, the stockholders, and the creditors are much more involved than the relationships in a single proprietorship or in a partnership. Therefore, the financial statements should present more information regarding these relationships than is expected in the financial statements of the less formal types of organization. But the information that is traditionally presented is an outgrowth of certain assumed legal and economic relationships, rather than being a result of a complete analysis of the needs of the various users of financial statements. Therefore, traditional stockholders equity classifications attempt to meet several objectives and, as a result, meet none of the objectives adequately.

What are the objectives of stockholder equity classifications? The basic objectives should be to provide information to stockholders, investors, creditors, and other interested groups regarding the efficiency and stewardship of management and regarding the historical and prospective economic interests of the groups holding specific equities and the groups (such as employees, customers, and the government) that have a general economic interest in the corporation. In meeting these objectives, the information in the financial statements should disclose some or all of the following: (1) the sources of capital supplied to the corporation; (2) the legal restrictions on the distribution of invested capital to stockholders; (3) the legal, contractual, managerial, and financial restrictions on the distribution of dividends to current and potential stockholders; and (4) the priorities of the several classes of stockholders in partial or final liquidation. Each of these specific objectives of classification will be discussed and evaluated in the following paragraphs.

Classification by source of capital

Classification of stockholders' equity by some source is generally considered to be the major classification objective in balance sheet presentation in the traditional accounting structure. This emphasis is not entirely misplaced, because a description of the sources of capital provides information regarding the historical development of the corporation. Corporate growth provided through internal sources of funds is relevant information when compared with a firm that has grown entirely through the sale of preferred and common stocks or through the sale of debentures. However, the amounts can be interpreted only in a relative sense because of the limitations of the historical cost accounting measurement system.

The main sources of corporate stockholder equity are: (1) amounts paid in by stockholders, (2) amounts arising from the restatement of assets for changes in the purchasing power of the dollar, (3) the excess of net income over dividends paid to stockholders (earnings retained in the business), and (4) donations from other than stockholders. The traditional fourfold classification of stockholder equities—capital stock, paid-in capital in excess of par or stated value, revaluation capital, and retained earnings—does not entirely meet the objective of classification by source, although it appears to meet it partially. The capital stock and additional paid-in capital categories generally represent the amounts paid in by stockholders, except that donations are generally included in the additional paid-in capital classification. Revaluation capital generally includes the write-up of assets prior to realization. If the write-ups represent increases in specific values rather than increases in prices in general, the revaluation capital should be included in the retained earnings classification as an income source. Technically, the amounts arising from the restatement of assets for changes in purchasing power do not represent a separate source of capital. They should be allocated to paid-in capital and retained earnings if such an allocation is possible. As indicated in Chapter 9, the amounts paid in by stockholders should be restated, and the remainder of the restatement should then be allocated to the retained earnings classification.

A main disadvantage of the conventional classification is that the classification by source is lost whenever transfers are made from retained earnings to capital stock and additional paid-in capital by issuing stock dividends or other means. The original classification by source is also lost in a recapitalization and in some treasury stock transactions.

The disclosure of legal capital

In a corporation, stockholders generally have no personal liability for the debts of the business; creditors must look only to the assets of the enterprise. Without this provision, corporate stock would not be so readily transferable as it is today. In order to obtain this provision, however, the legislatures felt a need to provide some protection to creditors from unscrupulous promoters, stockholders, or directors. To provide this protection to creditors, the courts and legislatures established the trust-fund theory. This title is a misnomer, however, because there is no actual fund established and there is no real "trust" in any legal sense of the word. The basic principle is that a restriction is placed on the amount of assets that can be distributed legally to the stockholders under normal circumstances prior to final liquidation.

Most states define *legal capital* or *stated capital* as the aggregate par value of all par value shares issued (not subsequently canceled) and the aggregate consideration received for all shares issued without par value. In the case of no-par value shares, however, many states permit the directors or stockholders to designate how much of the consideration received shall be classified as stated capital and how much shall be classified as additional paid-in capital. A few states also require the excess of the amount paid in over the par value of par value shares to be included in stated capital. As a result, it is difficult to determine the exact amount of legal capital in specific situations. In general, it may be assumed that the legal capital is at least equal to the par value of par value shares plus the stated value of no-par value shares. But there are exceptions to this (e.g., in the case of wasting asset corporations).

Current financial statements do not disclose the amount of legal capital, although there are usually separate classifications for capital stock and additional paid-in capital, a practice that apparently stems from the trust-fund theory. But even a disclosure of the number of shares issued and outstanding of each class and the par value or stated value per share of each class is not adequate in many cases to permit the informed reader to compute the total legal capital. In some states subscribed shares become a part of legal capital, and in other states they are included only after they have been paid for and issued. In some states legal capital can be increased by a declaration of the board of directors without the issuance of additional shares. Differences in the treatment of treasury shares makes it difficult to know how they should be treated in the computation of legal capital.

As a result of the differences between legal capital and invested capital for accounting and financial purposes, the separation of invested capital into the two classifications (capital stock and additional paid-in capital) is probably more misleading than helpful. An alternative would be to disclose in a footnote what the accountants consider to be the legal or stated capital, making it clear that a final determination of stated capital is a legal decision subject to court interpretation and not basically an accounting problem. Some state codes describe specifically what should be included in a paid-in capital in excess of par account or what accounts should be credited or charged in certain circumstances, but none of the codes appears to dictate how the financial statements shall be classified or what disclosure is necessary in the statements.

In the author's opinion, the disclosure of legal capital is probably unnecessary in all cases except in small or incipient corporations. In large and profitable concerns, the legal capital is generally a small part of the total stockholders' equity. In these cases, it is generally apparent that the amount of current and future dividends is not dependent on the amount of legal capital. Therefore, the entire stockholders' equity acts as a buffer for the protection of creditors, and the creditors rely more on the total resources, profitability, and financial policies of the firm than on the status of legal capital.

The disclosure of restrictions on the disposition of income

A disclosure of the *intended* distribution or disposition of the income of a corporation is not the same as a disclosure of the *restrictions* on the disposition of income. Frequently, the former is assumed from the latter, but generally this is unwarranted. Therefore, the classification of stockholder equities and footnotes to the financial statements should make a clear distinction between these two.

A first general assumption is that cash dividends should not be paid if the result will be to reduce net assets below the total paid-in capital of the firm, even though a part or all of the paid-in capital in excess of par value may be distributed legally. This is a self-imposed restriction influenced by the accounting distinction between invested capital and income. If a divi-

dend should be paid "out of" additional paid-in capital, accounting principles would require that this be disclosed as a liquidating dividend—a
return *of* capital rather than the usual assumption that a dividend is a
return *on* capital. This disclosure is also required by the model corporation act adopted by many states.

It cannot be assumed, however, that any or all of the retained earnings
will be made available for distribution to stockholders as cash dividends.
In fact, the current titles for this amount of accumulated earnings deny
this. "Earnings retained for use in the business" or simply "retained
earnings" implies that the income not already distributed as dividends
has been invested permanently in the business. This implication is supported by two general observations: (1) The dividend distributions of most
large firms are correlated highly with the current year's income, the prior
year's income, and the prior year's dividends. With a short lag and with
minor deviations, there appears to be an attempt to limit dividends to
income of the firm for the current year, rather than pay dividends out of
the earnings retained in prior years. (2) In most mature firms, the amount
of retained earnings is either larger than the capital invested directly by
stockholders or it is at least a large percentage of total stockholders'
equity. Therefore, corporate financial policy would not permit the payment of dividends equal to retained earnings; to do so would be tan-
tamount to a distribution of the capital of the corporation. What, then, is
the logic behind the capitalization of stock dividends in excess of the legal
or stated capital?

Since the classification of a part of stockholders' equity as retained
earnings does not indicate the amount that is likely to be paid out as
dividends in the future nor even the intent of the firm, an alternative is to
show the legal, contractual, or financial restrictions on the payment of
dividends. Care must be taken, however, not to leave the impression that
unrestricted retained earnings will be or are likely to be distributed as
dividends. The appropriation of retained earnings and the labeling of the
residual as "unappropriated" or "free" is, therefore, possibly misleading.
It may still be restricted by managerial or financial policy. A footnote
disclosure may be less misleading. But even here, the restriction may be
meaningless from the point of view of possible dividend distributions,
particularly if only a small part of the total retained earnings is restricted. Therefore, classification of stockholders' equity according to the
probable distribution of income or retained earnings should not be an
objective, and it should not be permitted to influence or distort the
classification according to source. When amounts are transferred from
retained earnings to permanently invested capital, there is a declaration
that these amounts are henceforth not available for dividends. But the
source should not be lost sight of. A separate classification entitled "retained earnings transferred to paid-in capital" would aid in maintaining
the classification according to source and still disclose the restriction on
dividend payments.

Dividend payments to common stockholders are also restricted by contractual preferences granted to preferred stockholders or other stockholder groups given priority rights above those of the residual stockholders. The traditional classification of stockholders' equity does not provide for disclosing these restrictions. Cumulative preferred dividends in arrears are not generally shown as appropriated retained earnings because under the entity theory all stockholders are treated as a group. Under the residual equity theory, an appropriation would be acceptable to disclose the restriction on the payment of dividends to common stockholders. But, as indicated above, all restrictions can be disclosed more fully by parenthetical explanations or by footnotes.

The disclosure of restrictions on liquidation distributions

Creditors always have priority in liquidation over stockholders, and certain classes of stockholders have priority over other classes by the terms of the corporate charter or by contractual arrangements. This liquidation preference of preferred stock may be equal to the par value or stated value per share or it may include a premium. Usually the preferred dividends in arrears are included if the preferred dividends are cumulative.

Liquidation preferences, therefore, are not the same as legal or stated capital, and an entirely different classification than that used to disclose legal capital would be needed to disclose them. But how important is it that they be disclosed? If a profitable corporation has no intent to liquidate, the liquidation preference may be relatively unimportant. And even if the corporation has incurred losses for one or several years, the liquidation preference may still be unimportant if the net assets of the firm exceed the amount of the liquidation preference by a wide margin. In these cases, the shareholders can determine their rights by reading the fine print on the back of their share certificates or by other means. But if the total liquidation preferences become large in proportion to total net assets or if partial or final liquidation appears likely, disclosure in the financial statements should be made clear.

Even the necessity for full disclosure of liquidation priority rights does not mean that classification is the best method of achieving this disclosure. Parenthetical and footnote disclosure will usually be adequate. However, if the firm is in final liquidation or liquidation is being planned, the original source of the capital is unimportant and the final disposition is most relevant. Thus, since the objective of reporting has changed in this case, the classification objectives should also be changed. The residual equity theory should dominate the reporting of stockholder equities.

In the author's opinion, it is not possible to maintain consistent classification of stockholders' equity according to source, legal restriction, disposition or restrictions of earnings, and the partial or final distribution of invested capital. The classification of invested capital and retained earnings on the basis of committed and uncommitted capital appears logical from an accounting point of view alone; but in reality, in most large corporations, retained earnings have become a very significant part of invested capital without formal action by the board of directors. Therefore, it is the author's recommendation that the primary basis for classification should be source, to maintain logic within the traditional accounting structure. And this source should not be disturbed by transfers of retained earnings to invested capital. The amounts so transferred should be designated as retained earnings formally capitalized.

Legal capital may be shown if it does not thereby disturb the classification according to source. Restrictions regarding the distribution of earnings and the priorities of assets in liquidation can generally be disclosed properly by parenthetical notes or in footnotes. This major emphasis on classification according to source would permit a disclosure of the source of all distributions to stockholders. That is, payments should be designated as either (1) distributions of current income, (2) reductions of uncommitted retained earnings, (3) reductions of retained earnings capitalized, or (4) distributions of capital invested by stockholders or from other sources.

The sources of invested capital, however, can be disclosed more clearly in a cash flow or funds statement. As suggested by the Committee on External Reporting of the American Accounting Association, the stockholders' equity section of the balance sheet is fairly sterile with respect to its relevance to the needs of investors and creditors.[8] A major difficulty with this classification is that it is a residual, its amount being determined by the measurements of assets and liabilities. However, information regarding the current and potential relationships of the several classes of long-term equity holders is relevant for an evaluation of the current and prospective rights of each of the creditors and stockholders.

CONSOLIDATED FINANCIAL STATEMENTS

When one corporation has a majority ownership and control in one or more related subsidiary firms, valuable information can be obtained and presented by combining the financial data and preparing consolidated financial statements for the entire group. Although the consolidated group is generally thought of as a single economic unit, the accounting procedures of consolidation frequently deny this. Therefore, there does not appear to be a reliance on a single theory, such as the proprietary theory, the entity theory, or the funds theory to serve as a guide in the establishment of consistent logical procedures of consolidation. Furthermore, the classification of stockholders' equity has not developed into a logical, con-

---

[8] Committee on External Reporting, "An Evaluation of External Reporting Practices," *Accounting Review,* supplement to vol. 44 (1969), pp. 103–4.

sistent pattern. In fact, accounting practice is far from being uniform in this area, reflecting either a lack of a logical basis for classification or a failure to agree on the basic objectives of classification. These areas are discussed at greater length in the following paragraphs.

The purpose and nature of consolidated financial statements

Accounting Research Bulletin No. 51 states that

> the purpose of consolidated statements is to present, primarily for the benefit of the shareholders and creditors of the parent company, the results of operations and the financial position of a parent company and its subsidiaries essentially as if the group were a single company with one or more branches or divisions.[9]

This objective implies that we should look through the legal relationships of the corporations and view the enterprise as a single economic unit. But the emphasis on the interests of the shareholders and creditors of the parent company is inconsistent with this major objective. If the entire enterprise is really one economic unit, all interested parties should be given equal consideration, as in the enterprise theory; or the entity theory should be expanded to include the entire economic entity rather than merely the legal entity of the parent corporation.

Consolidated balance sheet. In the balance sheet, the common practice of adding together the separate classifications of assets and liabilities of the parent corporation and the subsidiaries is in keeping with the idea of presenting a financial statement of the entire enterprise as a whole. By eliminating all intercompany obligations and adding together all other assets and liabilities, a picture of the group as a single enterprise is obtained. However, when the cost to the parent company of a subsidiary's shares exceeds the proportionate book value of those shares, the conventional pattern (the parent company concept) is to show this excess value in the consolidated statements as consolidated goodwill unless it can be allocated to the specific assets of the subsidiary. To be consistent with the entity approach to consolidated statements, the revision of the asset valuation of the subsidiary should include not only the excess amount paid by the parent company but also the minority interest's share in this increased valuation.[10] Cost is relevant at the time of acquisition only because it is the best evidence of value. But when only a fractional interest is obtained, the cost of the partial interest should be used as evidence of the value of the whole. For example, if a 60 percent interest in a subsidiary (holding only one asset, a building with a book value of $50,000) is

---

[9] *AICPA Professional Standards,* p. 8181.

[10] Maurice Moonitz, *The Entity Theory of Consolidated Statements* (Brooklyn: Foundation Press, 1951), pp. 58–59.

obtained by a parent company for $60,000, the value to the consolidated enterprise is $100,000, as evidenced by the payment of the parent. The recording of the building in the consolidated statements at $80,000 (representing the cost to the parent plus $20,000—the minority interest in the original cost) is not consistent with the general policy of including the full value of all other assets in the consolidated statements. This same reasoning cannot be applied to the valuation of consolidated goodwill.

Consolidated income statements. The enterprise theory is also followed in the preparation of consolidated income statements. Intercompany sales and intercompany profits are eliminated in their entirety, and other sales and expenses are combined to show the activities of the enterprise as a whole. However, the occasional practice of allocating the entire intercompany profit or loss to the majority interest alone is not consistent with this position. An alternative is to allocate these intercompany profits or losses proportionately between the majority and minority interests when reported by the subsidiary, although this also is arbitrary.

The consistent application of the enterprise theory again breaks down in conventional practice because most firms subtract the minority interest in the total income to arrive at consolidated net income. Thus, the net income is not the income of the enterprise as a whole, but only that portion allocated to the majority interest. But it is difficult to interpret just what this final income really represents, particularly if the minority interest is a negative figure arising from a net loss of the subsidiary. It is not in the nature of a residual equity in net income because there is no consideration for the preferred equities in either the majority or minority groups. And it does not provide useful information regarding the amount available for dividends to the majority interest because the parent firm may be able to pay dividends even though the subsidiaries are operated at a loss and vice versa. Therefore, the implication is that the consolidated net income represents the proprietary equity of the stockholders of the parent company in the income of the entire enterprise. But this is inconsistent with the entity or enterprise theories. It would be better to show the net income of the enterprise as a whole and then disclose separately the relative interests of the majority and minority interests.

The classification of consolidated equities

In the classification of consolidated equities in published statements, there is not only a lack of uniformity, but also a lack of understanding of the specific objectives. Is the objective to disclose the legal stated capital, the sources of capital, or the possible disposition of either income or invested capital?

There is little doubt that the position of legal capital and the extent of the legal protection to creditors can be presented more clearly in the separate financial statements of each corporation than in the consolidated statements. The creditors of a subsidiary firm must look at the individual statements of the subsidiary to determine the relevant legal capital (if indeed, it can be found even there) and their relationships to other creditors. For, they, of course, have no claim against the assets of the parent corporation. But the creditors of the parent must also look at the separate statements of the parent firm to establish their specific relationship to stockholders and other creditors because they have only a secondary claim against the assets of the subsidiary, but a primary claim against the assets of the parent. Therefore, the presentation of legal capital and the rights of creditors cannot and should not be a major objective in the classification of the equities of a consolidated enterprise. However, many firms, through tradition, show on the consolidated balance sheet the par value of shares issued separately from the capital received in excess of par value.

Probably the most common objective in the classification of consolidated equities is to disclose the sources of capital. It is not uncommon to find captions designating the stockholder's equity section of the consolidated balance sheet as "sources from which capital was obtained" or "derived from." In practically all of these cases, however, the classification is not strictly according to source. The limitations of this method of classification are similar to the limitations of attempting to maintain a classification by source in unconsolidated corporations. But there are several additional limitations in consolidated statements. The capital obtained from the majority stockholders is represented by the capital stock and additional paid-in capital of the parent firm in most cases. However, the minority interest is generally included among the liabilities or as a separate item between the liabilities and the stockholders' equity. This item generally represents the minority stockholders' interest in the total equities of the subsidiaries; but it is just as much a source of capital for the entire enterprise as is the capital contributed by the stockholders of the parent firm.

Another basic limitation of the conventional practice of classification by source is that the amount of capital derived from retained earnings is not clearly presented. In the first place, the minority interest is not generally classified according to the separate sources of capital invested by stockholders and earnings retained by the subsidiary. Also, of course, there is no distinction between the minority stockholders' interest in the retained earnings at the date of consolidation and the minority interest in the earnings retained since consolidation. In the second place, the consolidated retained earnings amount represents the earnings of the parent firm retained since its incorporation (except for transfers to capital stock and additional paid-in capital) and the majority interest in the earnings of the subsidiaries retained since the date of consolidation. Thus, the consolidated retained earnings does not represent a homogeneous source of invested capital.

A suggested remedy to give the source objective a better role in the

classification of consolidated equity is to include in the consolidated invested capital the minority interest in the total stockholders' equity at the
date of consolidation, and to classify the retained earnings as either (1)
that obtained from the earnings retained by the parent company since its
organization or (2) that retained by the subsidiary firms since the date of
consolidation (without consideration of the majority's and minority's
separate interests in the subsidiaries' retained earnings).[11]

By stating that consolidated statements are presented primarily for
the benefit of the shareholders and creditors of the parent company, *Accounting Research Bulletin No. 51* implies that the objective is to show the
possible distribution of income and capital or the relative equities of the
beneficiaries in the consolidated enterprise. But information regarding
ownership equities is relevant only if it provides some information about
the possible distribution of income and capital. That is, it should show
some information regarding the relative rights of the several classes of
equity holders in any distributions that may be made. However, the conventional classification of equities of consolidated enterprises fails to disclose the possible distribution of income to majority and minority stockholders. If the subsidiaries are operating at a loss, the consolidated income
may be distributed entirely to the majority stockholders without paying
any dividends to the minority group. On the other hand, if the consolidated net income is obtained entirely from the operations of subsidiaries,
substantial dividends may be required to be paid to the minority stockholders before the stockholders of the parent may be able to receive any
dividends.

The conventional classification also fails to disclose the rights of the
various classes of equity holders in the possible distribution of capital.
Creditors, in general, have preference in liquidation over stockholders.
The creditors of the subsidiaries, however, have no claim to the separate
assets of the parent and, therefore, the bonded indebtedness of subsidiaries and of the parent should not be combined if the objective is to
disclose this priority. The creditors of the parent have only a secondary
claim against the assets of a subsidiary, on the same level as the claim of
the minority interest. This fact is probably the strongest justification for
classifying the minority interest among the liabilities or as a separate
item between the liabilities and capital on the consolidated balance sheet.

We see, therefore, that the disclosure of the possible distribution of
income and capital appears to be the major objective in the conventional
classification of the equities of a consolidated enterprise. In the income
statement, the consolidated net income is assumed to represent the
amount that could be distributed as income to the stockholders of the
parent company. In the balance sheet, the separate interests of the creditors, minority stockholders, and stockholders of the parent company are

---

[11] See S. R. Sapienza, "The Divided House of Consolidations," *Accounting Review,* July
1960, pp. 503–10.

presumably disclosed. But the failure to show just what these interests represent and what are the interrelationships of the several groups places severe limitations on the usefulness of this classification. Except when dissolution or reorganization seems probable or imminent, a strict classification by source would seem to be more consistent with the traditional accounting structure, although even this classification is of doubtful value because of the problems of measurement.

SELECTED ADDITIONAL READING

Equity theories

Committee on Tax and Financial Entity Theory. "Report of the Committee on Tax and Financial Entity Theory." *Accounting Review,* supplement to vol. 48 (1973), pp. 187–92.

Bird, Francis A.; Lewis F. Davidson; and Charles H. Smith. "Perceptions of External Accounting Transfers under Entity and Proprietary Theory." *Accounting Review,* April 1975, pp. 233–44.

Goldberg, Louis. *An Inquiry into the Nature of Accounting. American Accounting Association Monograph No. 7.* AAA, 1965, pp. 162–74.

1964 Concepts and Standards Research Committee—The Business Entity. "The Entity Concept." *Accounting Review,* April 1965, pp. 358–67.

Classification of stockholder equities

Melcher, Beatrice. "Stockholders' Equity." *Accounting Research Study No. 15.* AICPA, 1973.

Scott, Richard A. "Owners' Equity, The Anachronistic Element." *Accounting Review,* October 1979, pp. 750–63.

Consolidated financial statements

Accountants International Study Group. "Consolidated Financial Statements," 1973.

Baxter, George C., and James C. Spinney. "A Closer Look at Consolidated Financial Statement Theory." *CA Magazine,* Jan. 1975, pp. 31–36.

Chen, Raymond S. "A Comment." *Accounting Review,* April 1975, pp. 359–64. And Enrico Petri and Roland Minch. "A Reply." *Accounting Review,* April 1975, pp. 365–69.

Petri, Enrico, and Roland Minch. "The Treasury Stock Method and Conventional Method in Reciprocal Stockholdings—An Amalgamation." *Accounting Review,* April 1974, pp. 330–41.

Walker, R. G. "An Evaluation of the Information Conveyed by Consolidated Statements." *Abacus,* December 1976, pp. 116–24.

CHAPTER 20

CHANGES IN STOCKHOLDERS' EQUITIES

The original classification of stockholders' equity is generally considered to be descriptive of its source; however, changes and reclassifications of equities make it difficult to retain this information. For example, in the case of stock dividends or other transfers to invested capital, the identity of the original source is lost.

The main reason for the loss of the source information is that the conventional procedures to record changes and reclassifications of stockholders' equity are based primarily on other objectives. Generally, these procedures attempt to maintain a distinction between invested capital and retained earnings, disclose legal capital, and indicate the amount available for distribution as dividends. As a result, none of the objectives is met adequately. In this chapter, the procedures for recording changes and reclassifications of stockholders' equity, the problems of business combinations, and the reporting of earnings per share are analyzed critically in terms of the relevant objectives and on the basis of consistent equity theories.

INCREASES IN INVESTED CAPITAL

What accountants call invested capital in a corporation may be increased by the subscription or sale of additional shares of stock, by the acquisition and resale of treasury shares, by the conversion of indebtedness into stockholder equities, and by the transfer of retained earnings into invested capital. However, a basic principle widely held at least since the early 1930s is that retained earnings should include no credits from transactions in the company's own stock or transfers from paid-in capital or other capital account.[1] Therefore, the apparent basic objective in the

---

[1] Executive Committee of the American Accounting Association, "A Tentative Statement of Accounting Principles Underlying Corporate Financial Statements," *Accounting Review* 11 (June 1936): 191. Reprinted in AAA Committee on Accounting Concepts and Standards, *Accounting and Reporting Standards for Corporate Financial Statements and Preceding Statements and Supplements* (AAA, 1957), p. 63. *APB Opinion No. 9, AICPA Professional Standards* (Chicago: Commerce Clearing House, 1976), p. 7929.

classification of these increases in capital is to prevent the showing of equity arising from capital transactions as income or retained earnings and to prevent the implication that these amounts are available for ordinary dividends.

Capital stock subscriptions

When shares of previously unissued stock are sold for cash or other consideration, the total increase in equity represents invested capital. Although it is still common practice to separate this amount into two parts—par value or stated value and the excess over par or stated value—the entire amount represents capital invested by stockholders for an indefinite period. But when subscriptions for shares are received by the corporation, has the invested capital of the firm actually been increased or is there merely a promise to increase the capital?

In some states, the codes regulating corporations treat stock subscribed but not issued as a part of legal capital. However, the Model Business Corporation Act includes in stated capital only shares that have been issued.[2] But whether or not the subscribed shares are legal capital, they should be included in invested capital if (1) the subscriptions represent legal claims against the subscribers, and (2) the corporation intends to collect the subscriptions within a reasonable and definite period of time. If the subscriptions are not intended to be called or if the time of call is indefinite, the subscriptions do not really represent invested capital. But a valid commitment to invest and a reasonable expectation that the amounts will be paid in to the corporation in due course should be sufficient to consider the subscriptions to be permanent investments.

Conversions of debt and preferred stock

When convertible bonds are exchanged for stock, two methods have been suggested for treating the conversion:

1. The book equity of the long-term debt (the face value of the bonds plus unamortized premium or minus unamortized discount) is reclassified as capital stock and additional paid-in capital when the new shares are issued. No gain or loss is recognized on the transaction; the book value of the indebtedness is merely converted into stockholder equity.

2. The current market price of the bonds or the current market price of the stock is capitalized as stockholder equity, and the excess of the current price over the book value of the bonds is shown as a loss on conversion. If the book value of the bonds exceeds the current market price of the bonds or stock, a gain on conversion would result.

A preference for method 1 is implied in *APB Opinion No. 14,* which recommends that the entire proceeds from the sale of convertible debt be

---

[2] Model Business Corporation Act, Committee on Corporate Laws of the American Bar Association, 1962, Sec. 2 (j).

classified as debt.[3] Since none of the initial proceeds is allocated to the conversion privilege, a gain or loss cannot be measured by comparing the book value of the securities with their market value or the market value of nonconvertible debt (with similar characteristics) at the time of the conversion. But this method is also assumed to follow the entity theory because all long-term equities are treated as interests in the enterprise, and a transfer from one type of equity to another does not change the capital invested in the enterprise nor should it result in enterprise income.

Method 2 was preferred by the American Accounting Association Committee on Accounting Concepts and Standards in 1957.[4] It is assumed to follow the proprietary theory because changes in the valuation of liabilities are considered from the point of view of their effect on the stockholders. However, to follow this concept through clearly, the gain or loss should be measured from the change in the investment value of the debt only. Since the investment value represents the value of nonconvertible debt with characteristics similar to the convertible securities except for the conversion feature, an allocation of the proceeds should be made to the conversion privilege and the portion allocated to debt (adjusted for discount or premium amortization) should be compared with the investment value at the time of conversion. The market value of the convertible securities is not relevant at either date because the securities derive a part of their value from the conversion feature.

The conventional procedure for the conversion of preferred stock into common stock is to follow method 1. That is, the par value of the preferred plus the pro rata share of paid-in surplus on preferred shares is transferred to common stock and paid-in surplus on common. No gain or loss should be shown on this transaction because both are included in the stockholders' equity classification.

The sum of the par value of the preferred stock and the pro rata portion of the additional paid-in capital from the original sale of the preferred stock represents the source of the original invested capital. Note that it does not represent the amount of book equity of the preferred stock since, in the case of dissolution, preferred stockholders are entitled to the par value or liquidation value of the preferred stock. But there is some merit in reclassifying the additional paid-in capital, because if all of the preferred stock is finally converted, it may be misleading to show paid-in capital from the sale of preferred stock when there is no preferred stock outstanding. The transfer of these amounts from a preferred stock to a common stock classification does not violate the source objective because it all represents capital invested by stockholders. The reclassification represents mainly a change in the rights of the several classes of stockholders. The original source classification is lost only if a transfer from re-

---

[3] See Chapter 17 for a discussion of the recording of convertible debt.

[4] AAA Committee on Accounting Concepts and Standards, *Accounting and Reporting Standards,* p. 7.

tained earnings is required; and in this case, the reclassification of retained earnings is similar to a stock dividend, discussed below.

An alternative is to transfer to common stock an amount equal to the current market value of either the preferred shares retired or the new common shares issued although these amounts should be fairly close. If this amount is in excess of the paid-in capital of the retired preferred stock, the excess must be transferred from retained earnings. The result is that the original source classification is lost. Also, this implies a strict entity theory interpreting the retained earnings as the firm's equity in itself. That is, it implies that the current market price of the common stock does not reflect an interest in the retained earnings; if it did, there would be double counting. However, it also implies that there are two transactions, a retirement of preferred shares resulting in a partial distribution of retained earnings and the sale of new shares of common stock at the current market value. Since the convertible preferred shares are generally issued originally with the convertible feature, the treatment of the conversion as a single transaction seems more logical.

Stock dividends and stock splits

Both stock dividends and stock splits are basically financial maneuvers that have nothing to do with the accounting principles of income determination and balance sheet valuation. In fact, if accountants held strictly to the classification of equities by original source, there would be no need for equity reclassifications as a result of these types of transactions. The only requirement would be to disclose the change in the number of shares outstanding and any change in par value or stated value and recompute the reported earnings per share for the current and prior periods. This is the case with a pure stock split. Since there is no change in either the legal or stated capital, no reclassification of equity is necessary. The number of shares outstanding is increased in inverse proportion to the decrease in par value or stated value per share; if the increase in the number of shares is accompanied by an increase in the total capital stock (total par value or stated value of shares outstanding), a partial stock dividend is also present. On the other hand, a 100 percent (or other large percentage) increase in the number of shares held by the same stockholders without an increase in total stockholders' equity or a decrease in par value per share is considered to be a stock split effected in the form of a stock dividend.

When accountants recognize classification objectives other than by the original source of capital, stock dividends present a problem in the treatment and disclosure of the transaction. Basic questions arise regarding the nature of the transaction and the amount to be capitalized. The nature of the transaction depends, in large part, on the equity theory selected as the most relevant. The amount to be capitalized depends on the objectives of classification and the assumed nature of the transaction. The amounts most commonly suggested for capitalization are (1) the par value or stated value (or other legal capital amount) of the shares issued as a dividend, (2) the current market value of the shares issued, and (3) the paid-in capital per share prior to the dividend times the number of shares issued.

The nature of stock dividends. Most accountants agree that stock dividends are not income to the recipients, but they differ in the reasoning leading to this conclusion. The AICPA Committee on Accounting Procedure based its belief that stock dividends are not income to the recipients on the entity theory.[5] It argued that the corporation is a separate entity and that there can be no income to the stockholders until there is a severance of corporate assets. The income of the corporation is corporate income, not income to the stockholders. Cash dividends represent a transfer of assets to stockholders and, therefore, represent income to the recipients; stock dividends may result in unrealized appreciation, but it is not income to the stockholders until it is realized by them as a result of a division, distribution, or severance of corporate assets. Note that a rigid adherence to the realization concept rather than the entity theory is the controlling feature of this argument.

Another interpretation of the entity theory that leads to different conclusions is that retained earnings represent a part of the total equity of the stockholders. Therefore, corporate income resulting in an increase in retained earnings is also an increase in stockholders' equity. Income is earned by stockholders when the value of their equity has increased either because of the reinvestment of corporate income, because of unrecorded increases in the value of the firm, or because of the transfer of equity from other equity holders as a result of price-level changes or other reasons. In this interpretation, neither cash dividends nor ordinary stock dividends are income to the common stockholders, since they do not result in an increase in the value of the stockholders' assets, including their equity in the firm.

Still another interpretation of the entity theory is that retained earnings represent the equity of the corporation in itself. The stockholders' equity includes only the invested capital reflected in capital stock and additional paid-in capital. Therefore, both cash dividends and stock dividends should be considered income to the stockholders, since they give them something they did not have before. A stock dividend increases the stockholders' equity by transferring to the stockholders a portion of the undivided corporate equity in itself.

The proprietary theory leads to the same conclusion as the first two interpretations—that stock dividends are not income to the recipients—but for different reasons. The income of the corporation is also income to the owners. Therefore, cash dividends represent withdrawals by the own-

---

[5] *AICPA Professional Standards* (Chicago: Commerce Clearing House, 1987), para. 5561.06.

ers of what already belongs to them. Stock dividends represent a reclassification of equity, but they are not income to the owners, since there is no increase in total proprietorship.

The capitalization of par or stated value. Under the prevalent interpretation of the entity theory, that stock dividends are not income to the recipients, the question becomes that of determining how much, if any, of corporate equity should be reclassified. If the objective of equity classification is to show the source of capital, the answer is that no reclassification should be made, since the original source has not changed. All that would be required is that proper disclosure should be made of the change in the number of shares outstanding. However, if we also wish to show the total amount of legal capital, it is necessary to transfer from retained earnings or additional paid-in capital to capital stock an amount equal to the stated value of the shares issued as required by the state of incorporation. In most states and in the Model Business Corporation Act, this amount is the par value of par value shares or the stated value of no-par shares.

Most writers agree that the par or stated value is the minimum amount that should be capitalized because of the legal considerations involved. While the AICPA Committee on Accounting Procedure recommended the capitalization of fair value in certain circumstances, as indicated below, it clearly recognized the showing of legal capital as one of the objectives of classification. This is reflected in its statement to the effect that the minimum amount capitalized should be, in all cases, that necessary to meet legal requirements, but this does not prevent the capitalization of a larger amount per share.[6] It also recommended that there is no need to capitalize more than that necessary to meet legal requirements in two special cases (1) when the number of additional shares issued is so great that it may reasonably be expected that the market price per share will be reduced materially and (2) in the case of closely held companies where it may be expected that intimate knowledge of the corporation's affairs would preclude any implication by the stockholders that the stock dividends represent a distribution of corporate earnings.

If the objective of classification is to show the legal capital, it should be recognized that the classification by source is destroyed. It is possible to meet both objectives only by a dual classification, by showing the legal capital in a footnote, or by maintaining a separate item in the balance sheet for the retained earnings capitalized equal to the par value (or stated value) of the shares issued as a stock) dividend.

The capitalization of market price. Only in the very strict interpretation of the entity theory can a stock dividend be considered to be income to the stockholders. But in this interpretation the amount of the dividend is

_____

[6] Ibid., para. 5561.11.

considered to be the current market price of the shares. For, it is held, the stockholders could sell these additional shares at this price and be as well off as they were before, since their relative equity (interpreted as representing their individual shares of paid-in capital) is increased because of the stock dividend but remains the same if these shares are sold. Thus it is interpreted as a distribution of undivided retained earnings by an allocation to the stockholders' permanent equity.[7]

Although the AICPA Committee on Accounting Procedure recognized that a stock dividend is not income to the recipient, it recommended that the amount to be capitalized (transferred to capital stock and additional paid-in capital) should be an amount equal to the fair value (market value) of the shares issued in all cases where the amount of stock issued is so small in comparison with the total shares outstanding that it has no apparent effect on the market price per share.[8] The reasoning for this recommendation is that, because of general representations, the recipients look on the stock dividends as distributions of corporate earnings equal to the market price of the shares issued. Therefore, if less than the market price were capitalized, an amount of the retained earnings thought to have been distributed to the stockholders would be available for additional stock dividends or cash distributions.

In those cases where the number of additional shares issued is large enough to materially influence the market price per share of the stock, *AICPA Professional Standards* recommends that there is no need to capitalize more than that necessary to meet legal requirements (usually par or stated value).[9] Although the situations where this condition is met are assumed to arise for varying percentages of new shares, depending upon differing market conditions for individual firms, an arbitrary rate of 20 to 25 percent of shares previously outstanding was suggested as the dividing line between a small and a large stock dividend. Subsequently, the SEC adopted an arbitrary rate of 25 percent as the upper percentage requiring a transfer from retained earnings to paid-in capital accounts.[10]

As noted above, the capitalization of retained earnings results in an abandonment of the objective of classification by source of stockholders' equity. In its place is substituted the objective of showing the possible disposition of equity. Retained earnings is presumed to show the amount available for distribution in the future as either stock dividends or cash dividends. However, since most states permit at least stock dividends, and in many cases both cash and stock dividend distributions, out of paid-in capital in excess of par value, this restriction on future distributions is purely a financial and accounting restriction. The main argument against this line of reasoning is that most firms do not intend to make cash

---

[7] See, for example, George R. Husband, "The Entity Concept in Accounting," *Accounting Review,* October 1954, particularly p. 555.

[8] *AICPA Professional Standards,* para. 5561.10.

[9] Ibid., para. 5561.11.

[10] *SEC Accounting Series Release No. 124.*

distributions out of earnings retained in prior years except in emergency situations. Retained earnings generally represent earnings reinvested in the business without formal action, but it is erroneous to assume that just because there has not been a formal transfer to permanent invested capital, they are then intended to be used for future distributions.

Two other arguments for the use of market value in the capitalization of stock dividends are the following: (1) The stock dividend can be thought of as two transactions—a cash dividend to stockholders and a subsequent sale to them of stock at the current market price. Therefore, the cash dividend would reduce retained earnings by the market value of the shares and the subsequent sale of stock would increase invested capital by this same amount. (2) The cost to the corporation of the stock dividend is assumed to be the opportunity cost of giving the shares to stockholders rather than selling them in the market. That is, since the corporation could have sold the shares at market price, this is the best evidence of the amount of the dividend and the amount that should be capitalized. Both of these arguments are weak in that they assume situations that do not really exist. The corporation has a right to sell shares to its common stockholders at amounts less than the market price (with some exceptions), and this action does not generally injure any class of equity holder.

The main argument in opposition to the use of market values is that if the stock dividend is not income to the stockholders, it is misleading to act as if it were, even if some people may believe that it is so. The capitalization of the market value of the stock issued only helps to continue the illusion that the stockholders are receiving something comparable to a cash dividend or that they are receiving something they did not have already. This illusion is generally strengthened by the fact that most firms continue the same cash dividend per share after the stock dividend as before, resulting in an increase in the total dividends declared.

Another argument in opposition to the use of fair value is that market value represents the total equity of the stock in the firm, including both invested capital and retained earnings. Therefore, it is illogical to transfer from retained earnings to invested capital that which represents both of these. It is better to present the transaction as a partial *stock split* with an accompanying increase in legal capital. In other words, the original source of capital should not be disturbed; disclosure of the increase in legal capital can be made in footnotes or by other means. This procedure would have the additional advantage of presenting a proper interpretation of retained earnings—as income reinvested permanently in the business.

It may appear that the widespread use of automatic dividend investment plans provides credence in the market value method. However, in these plans, the stockholders have the option to receive cash dividends or an equivalent number of shares computed on the basis of the current market price of the stock. Since stockholders are not required to receive shares, this represents two transactions—the issue of a cash dividend and a simultaneous reinvestment by the stockholder in exchange for additional shares. The effect is merely a convenient method of issuing additional shares in small lots at a low cost to the stockholders and to the issuing firm.

The distinction between a stock dividend and a stock split based on market reaction to the new shares is not supported by empirical research. Several studies of market behavior suggest that the requirement of the capitalization of market value in specific cases is based on a spurious premise.[11] This distinction also fails to find support in the efficient market thesis. If the market is efficient, any dilution of shares by either stock dividends or stock splits should be reflected immediately in share prices.

Stock options and stock warrants

Stock rights are frequently granted to current stockholders permitting them to purchase shares of stock (in proportion to the shares held) at a price less than the market price or less than the price at which the shares are offered to others. Generally, the granting of these stock rights does not result in an increase in invested capital because no new capital is brought into the enterprise until the stock is sold. According to the objective of classification by source, this solution is correct. But it is inconsistent with the procedure recommended by the AICPA for the handling of stock dividends discussed above. A stock dividend is an extreme form of a stock right—a right to acquire shares with no additional cost. Therefore, the main difference between a stock dividend and a stock right is the amount to be paid by the stockholders for the additional shares received by them. Turning the analogy around, a stock right is a stock dividend in the amount of the value of the right—the excess of the market value of the shares over the purchase price to the stockholders. To be consistent with the recommendations for the treatment of stock dividends, this amount should be capitalized by a transfer from retained earnings to invested capital, usually "contributed capital in excess of par or stated value." But, in the opinion of the author, the capitalization of market value is illogical in both situations because neither is a source of invested capital.

When stock warrants are sold by the firm, however, the proceeds represent invested capital whether or not the warrants are exercised. If the warrants are exercised, the original proceeds plus the additional amount paid by the holders to acquire the shares represent the total amount invested by the new stockholders, and that amount should be classified accordingly as contributed capital. Before the warrants are exercised, however, a potential dilution of dividends and earnings per share exists. The effect of this dilution is discussed below in the section on earnings per share.[12]

---

[11] See, for example, Taylor W. Foster III and Don Vickrey, "The Information Content of Stock Dividend Announcements," *Accounting Review,* April 1978, pp. 360–70.

[12] See pp. 497–501.

Rights granted to the purchasers of other securities. Detachable warrants are frequently granted to purchasers of bonds giving them the right to purchase common stock at a fixed price (frequently less than the market price of the stock when the rights are granted). As discussed in Chapter 17, *APB Opinion No. 14* recommended that the market prices of the bonds and the warrants be used to allocate the proceeds from the sale of the securities to debt and to stockholders' equity.[13] When the warrants are exercised, the amount allocated to the warrants plus the additional amount paid for the shares is treated the same as proceeds from the sale of new stock issued. However, since bonds with detachable warrants are not different in substance from convertible debt, both should be accounted for alike, as discussed previously.

An allocation is even less important when common stock options are granted to purchasers of preferred stock (or vice versa). In this case, the entire amount paid in by the stockholders represents invested capital. There is little advantage in showing the source from preferred stockholders separately from that obtained from common stockholders, particularly when the two sources are not independent of each other. A separation of the invested capital into the two classes does not change the rights of the two classes of stockholders nor does it aid in disclosing these rights. However, if legal capital is also to be shown, an allocation may become necessary if the option price is below legal or stated capital.

Noncompensatory employee stock purchase plans. Stock options are granted frequently to employees as a means of raising capital and as a means of gaining widespread ownership among the officers and other employees of the enterprise. In these cases, no compensation need be presumed, and therefore only the amounts paid in by the employees should be included in stockholder's equity. Four characteristics are considered essential in a noncompensatory plan: (1) Substantially all full-time employees meeting limited employment qualifications may participate. (2) The stock offer applies equally to all eligible employees or in the ratio of their salaries or wages. (3) The option period is short or reasonable in length. (4) The purchase price should not be lower than would be reasonable if the stock were offered to others. It is also assumed that the granting of the option does not generally impose additional obligations on the employees.

Compensatory stock option plans. The granting of stock options to executives has been a popular method of providing compensation because of the potential tax advantage to the recipient. When the stock option meets certain restrictions imposed by the Internal Revenue Service, no personal income tax is paid by the recipient when the option is received or exercised, and the gain on the sale of the stock acquired with the options

---

[13] See Chapter 17.

is taxed at the capital gains rate when certain technical conditions are met. But in qualifying for a restricted stock option, the corporation loses its right to reduce the corporate income tax by the amount of the compensation. Therefore, an option that is equivalent in amount to the aftertax cost of compensation paid in cash would be of greater value to the executive than the cash salary only if the executive is in a relatively high income tax bracket. Nevertheless, if compensation is involved, the amount of the compensation should be recorded as an expense of the corporation, and the amount of the invested capital should be increased by this amount or the aftertax cash salary equivalent. However, accountants are not agreed as to when compensation, if any, should be recorded and as to the method of determining the amount of compensation.

One view, applying the strict entity approach to accounting, is that the services received for which the stock options are granted do not cost the corporation anything, and therefore should not be recorded at all. However, this argument is weak because it is based on the assumption that cost to the entity must result in a decrease in its net assets. If this were true, there would be no reason to record nonmonetary assets acquired by the issuance of stock. But it is possible to invest services in the business just as it is possible to invest nonmonetary assets. The main difference is that the services benefit the current period while the nonmonetary assets may benefit a future period or periods.

APB Opinion No. 25 clearly recognizes the possibility of compensation arising out of stock option contracts. Under compensatory stock option plans, the consideration ". . . consists of cash or other assets, if any, plus services received from the employee."[14] Those accountants who recognize the existence of compensation generally agree that the amount of the compensation should be apportioned over the period that the services are received by the enterprise. The main area of disagreement is in the valuation of the services and the determination of the resulting increase in invested capital arising from the stock option grant. The most commonly proposed valuation methods are: (1) the excess of the fair value of the stock over the option price at the date of the option grant, (2) the excess on the date the option becomes the property of the employee, (3) the excess of the fair value over the option price at the date the option is first exercisable, (4) the excess on the date that the option is actually exercised, (5) the cost to the corporation at the date of exercise adjusted for the income tax effect to the firm, and (6) the probable value of the option to the recipient at the date of grant.

1. The excess value at date of grant. APB Opinion No. 25 recommends that the value of the compensation should be the excess of the quoted market price of the stock over the option price at the date that the option is granted. An exception to measurement at the date of grant is necessary when a plan may contain variable terms contingent on events

---

[14] *AICPA Professional Standards,* para. 4062.09.

after the date of grant. In this case, the measurement date is the first date that both the number of shares and the option price are known. The main reasons for the choice of the date of grant or the above alternative are summarized as follows: (a) The value at this date is assumed to be measurable and meaningful to both the employee and the employer. Although an option would have some value even if the option price were the same as or greater than the market value of the shares, the Board considered it impracticable to measure this value. (b) The value at the date of grant is assumed to be the value that both parties had in mind when the option was granted. Any additional value of the option to the employee is assumed to be offset by the restrictions imposed. From the point of view of the corporation, the value of the options at the date of grant must be estimated in order to determine the number of options to grant as just compensation for the services received. (c) The excess value at the date of grant represents the costs of restricting such shares to this purpose, because the principal alternative use of the shares is to sell them in the currently prevailing market. (d) Once an option is granted to an employee, the decision when to exercise the option, if at all, rests largely with the employee. Thus, changes in the market value of the shares are assumed to represent changes in the value of the option to the employee but not in the cost to the corporation.

The most important of these reasons is the inability to measure the true value of the option to the employee or the real cost to the corporation except for that portion of the value represented by the excess of the value at the date of grant over the option price.

2. Excess value on date the option right becomes the property of the grantee. The main argument for this alternative is that only at this date does the corporation have an unqualified obligation under the agreement. The employee can exercise the option only after fulfilling certain conditions; but when these conditions are met, the option belongs to the employee, and even though he or she must wait to exercise the option, the employee holds the property rights. This situation is compared with the granting of bonus shares to be issued at the end of the period of service, at which time the compensation is determined by the value of the bonus shares.

3. Excess value on date the options are first exercisable. Although the options may be exercisable as soon as the employee obtains the property right, a waiting period is frequently required before the options may be exercised. From this date on, the grantee may speculate on the option by either exercising it or holding it as long as possible before it expires. Therefore, it is argued that changes in the market value of the shares after this date are irrelevant to the corporation. It is also argued that the value of the option cannot be known before it can be exercised.

4. Excess value on the date the options are exercised. The argument that the amount of compensation is the excess of the market value over the option price at the date the option is exercised is based on the fact that only at this time does the grantee become a stockholder. Upon purchasing the shares, the employee acquires an interest in the enterprise that is worth more than the current cash outlay. This excess value is compensation because only as a stockholder could the employee obtain a capital gain due to the increase in the value of the shares. It is also assumed that this is the cost of the option to the corporation because before this date the option is only a contingency. Any valuation before this date is only an estimate of the final cost to the corporation, and any valuation subsequent to this date is irrelevant because the grantee has then become a stockholder.

5.   *Cost adjusted for income tax effect.*   A modification of the above method is to include in the cost of the compensation the amount of the income tax foregone by the corporation because of issuing the restricted stock option, which is not deductible as an expense by the issuing corporation. For example, if the value of the stock exceeds the option price by $60,000 at the time the options are exercised and if we assume a corporate tax rate of 40 percent, this would be equivalent to a cash salary of $100,000, which would represent the actual cost of the stock options to the corporation.

6.   *The cash value of the services at the time of option grant.*   When property is received by a corporation in exchange for stock, the amount of the invested capital is generally measured by the current value of the property received. If it is not possible to obtain a current value for the property, it may be assumed that the property value is equal to the current market value of the stock given in exchange. In a stock option contract, the employee makes an investment in the firm in an amount equal to the value of his services being compensated. However, since it is not generally possible to determine the value of the services received, it may be assumed that the compensation is equal to the current value of the stock options. But since the restricted stock options are not transferable, they have no market price and their current value is difficult to estimate. Nevertheless, a current value does exist, and some writers propose that a bargained price for the services can be obtained.

By accepting stock options rather than cash compensation, the executive is making an investment in the firm of an amount equal to the excess of the bargained value of his or her services over the cash salary received. Between the date of option grant and either the date that the option is exercised or the date it expires, the market price of the stock may increase substantially, or moderately, or it may decline. Therefore, the final value of the option to the grantee may possibly be very large, or it may be zero. At the date of the option grant, the expected value is between these two extremes. But note that it is always positive if there is some possibility of the market price rising above the option price; it would never be negative, and would be zero only if the option price were equal to or greater than the market price of the stock at the date of grant and if there were no expectation of an increase in the market price above the option price. This value can be estimated by projecting the likely trend in the market price of the firm's stock as indicated by all available evidence. The net aftertax value of the option to the executive should then be converted into the equivalent of a cash salary before consideration of the personal income tax effect.

An appraisal of valuation methods. In the opinion of the author, the most logical method of valuation is the cash value of the services as measured by the value of the option at the date of grant. However, most accountants shy away from this solution because it is highly subjective and depends upon speculation regarding the future. But in this case, there is no bargained price nor any marketable value, so that there is no alternative to the use of estimates. The position of the APB in *Opinion No. 25* was that only the obvious value at the date of grant—the excess of the market value at date of grant over the option price—should be recorded as the compensation. It did not deny that additional value exists; rather, it claimed only that it cannot be measured.

All other methods are attempts to find some objective measure of the value of the compensation based on either the benefit received by the employee or the final cost to the corporation. The excess of market price over option price at any specific date is based on a cost concept, rather than on a concept of service value invested by the employee. In the cost concept, we forget that invested capital is measured by the value of the consideration received by the firm and not the reverse. Even though the value of the option should be used in estimating the value of the services received, the value of the services is invested by the employee and this value should be determined by taking into consideration all possible outcomes and the risk taken by the grantee in receiving the option. The result is that the excess value of the market price over the option price at the time of property right or the date the option becomes exercisable is an incomplete valuation and probably understates the value of the option, particularly if it may be held by the grantee for several additional years before expiring. Even if the market price were equal to the option price at this date, the option would have a value to the grantee because of the possible increase in the market price before the option expires.

The excess of the market price over the option price at the date the option is exercised does represent the final gain to the employee, but this total gain is made up of two basic parts—the compensation to the employee and the gain or loss on the investment of the employee's services. The value of the compensation should be measured by the most probable change in market price; if the increase in market price exceeds this expectation, the grantee has a gain on the investment, and if it falls short of this expectation, there is a loss.

Regardless of which method is used in valuing the stock options, full disclosure should be made of the terms of the stock option contracts, the situation at the date of the balance sheet, and the method of valuation.

DECREASES IN INVESTED CAPITAL

Normally, the invested capital of a firm (the capital stock and contributed capital in excess of par or stated value) is thought to represent the permanent capital of an enterprise. Deliberate reductions in invested capital should not be made by payments to stockholders unless these payments are specifically disclosed as liquidating dividends. But partial liquidation also occurs when a specific class of stock is called and redeemed. The purchase of treasury shares is similar to the redemption of preferred stock, with the exception that few stockholders of any class may be involved and the purchase price is not usually prearranged. If the treasury stock is reissued, the net result may be either an increase, a decrease, or no change in stockholders' equity. Invested capital may also be reduced by a recapitalization recognition of the fact that accumulated losses have caused an effective reduction in capital without any distributions to shareholders.

Treasury stock

When stockholders' equity is increased as a result of transactions with shareholders, accountants are generally agreed that no gain results and no part of the increase should be added to income or retained earnings; it all represents invested capital. But when stockholders' equity is reduced as a result of the acquisition of the corporation's own shares, accountants are not in agreement regarding the effect on invested capital and retained earnings. Two basic questions relating to this controversy are these: (1) How much of the payment to stockholders should be treated as a return of invested capital, and how much should be considered a distribution of retained earnings? (2) How should the effect on legal capital be shown?

When a firm acquires its own shares and holds them for reissuing or subsequent cancellation, the acquisition and disposition can be treated as (1) a single transaction, or (2) two separate and distinct transactions. The former is commonly referred to as the cost method, and the latter is generally referred to as the par value method; however, it is possible to record the treasury stock at either cost or par value and still treat the purchase and sale as either a single transaction or as two separate transactions.

The single-transaction concept. If a firm acquires its own shares and then sells them to other stockholders at a price equal to cost, it does not seem logical that the classification of stockholders' equity should be disturbed merely because the corporation handled the shares. If the shares are purchased and sold merely for the convenience of the stockholders, the transaction is equivalent to the sale of shares by one stockholder to another. If the stock is sold by the corporation in excess of its cost, the excess represents an increase in invested capital in excess of par value. Therefore, the classification by source is maintained and the legal capital is not disturbed.

When treasury stock is sold at less than its cost to the firm, the excess of cost over sale price represents either a repayment of invested capital or a distribution of retained earnings. Although accountants are not in general agreement as to the accounts to be charged for this excess, three proposals are frequently made: (1) Following the suggestion in *APB Opinion No. 6,* many writers maintain that the excess represents a return of invested capital and should be charged to capital surplus arising from other treasury stock transactions or to contributed capital in excess of par value related to the same class of stock.[15] Only if the excess is greater than the total of these capital surplus accounts do these writers recommend that retained earnings should be reduced. (2) An alternative is to reduce contributed capital in excess of par from the original sale of this class of stock by a pro rata amount and treat the remainder as a distribution of retained earnings. The capital stock account is not disturbed because of a desire to show the amount of legal capital, which has not been reduced (in most cases) by the transaction. (3) A third solution is to treat the entire excess as a distribution of retained earnings. This alternative is popular because of its simplicity and conservatism. It is also frequently recommended for use in those states that include contributed capital in excess of par value as a part of legal capital, with the result that the presentation of legal capital is not disturbed by the transaction. However, in the opinion of the author it has considerable merit from a theoretical point of view. If the purchase and sale of treasury stock are treated as a single transaction, the net effect is a selective distribution of the firm's assets to one or more stockholders. Any distribution to stockholders that does not reduce the number of shares outstanding should be treated as a distribution of retained earnings if such is available. Invested capital should not be disturbed.

A major difficulty of the single-transaction concept and the application of the cost basis occurs when the treasury stock is not sold immediately or when it is subsequently canceled. While the stock is held in the treasury, the cost represents an unallocated reduction of stockholders' equity held in suspense until the completion of the transaction. Therefore, both invested capital and retained earnings are overstated and this may result in a misleading interpretation, particularly if the shares are later canceled or sold substantially below cost.

The two-transactions concept. In the two-transactions approach to treasury stock, the acquisition of a corporation's own shares is assumed to represent a contraction in its capital structure. If the shares are subse-

---

[15] *AICPA Professional Standards,* para. 5542.13.

quently reissued, the issuance of the reacquired shares is accounted for in the same way as the issuance of previously unissued shares.

When the outlay for the reacquired stock exceeds the prorata portion of contributed capital, the excess is considered a distribution of retained earnings. This is the view of *APB Opinion No. 6* for those cases in which the stock was purchased for constructive retirement. However, the Board recognized that alternatively, the excess of purchase price over par or stated value may be charged entirely to retained earnings as a capitalization of retained earnings. But the excess of par or stated value over the purchase price should be credited to contributed capital in excess of par value, according to *Opinion No. 6*.[16]

If the treasury shares are acquired at a cost in excess of the pro rata amount of invested capital, the effect of this recommendation would be to transfer a portion of retained earnings to additional paid-in capital as a result of the acquisition and resale of a firm's own shares. Retained earnings is reduced when the shares are purchased, and additional paid-in capital is increased when the shares are sold, even though the purchase and sale prices may be the same. On the other hand, if the stock is acquired and resold at a price less than the par or stated value, additional paid-in capital would be increased at the time of purchase, and a discount on stock or similar account would be established when the stock is resold.

Evaluation of the single-transaction and two-transactions concepts. Both the single-transaction and two-transactions concepts have some logic in their favor. The former is based on the premise that substance is more important than form and that a corporation should not transfer amounts from retained earnings to invested capital merely because it happens to handle the transfer of shares from one stockholder to another. The two-transactions concept is based on the idea that there is little difference between the purchase and sale of treasury shares and the acquisition and retirement of shares with a subsequent sale of new shares. In the opinion of the author, each concept is appropriate for different circumstances. If shares are acquired by purchase with the express purpose of reselling to employees, executives, or other special groups, the single-transaction concept is relevant. On the other hand, if the objective of the acquisition is to purchase the shares of dissident stockholders or to effect the eventual retirement of certain classes of stock, the two-transactions concept should apply, even though these shares might be resold at a later date. Of course, if eventual cancellation is the objective, the two-transactions approach is clearly appropriate.

This suggested solution has the disadvantage that it is not always possible to determine the intent of the corporation. Therefore, accountants are not likely to treat similar situations uniformly. If the objective is not clear, a suggested solution is to apply the two-transactions concept.

---

[16] Ibid., para. 5542.13.

BUSINESS COMBINATIONS

When the assets of one firm are acquired by a second firm as a result of a purchase transaction involving the payment of cash or the exchange of other assets, the purchased assets are generally recorded in the accounts of the acquiring firm at their cost (the value of assets given in exchange), which may be assumed to represent their current value. The historical cost to the selling firm is no longer relevant. And the stockholders' equity of the acquiring firm is not increased or reclassified because of the transaction.

If the acquisition is carried out by the purchase (for cash or other assets) of the entire capital stock of a second firm, the situation is similar to the above purchase. In fact, if the acquired firm is dissolved, the net result of the transaction may be the same as a purchase of the assets, with the possible exception that the acquiring firm may assume the liabilities of the purchased firm. Even if the acquired firm is not dissolved, the consolidated statement should show the acquired assets at their current cost, including the cost of intangibles; and no change in stockholders' equity occurs as a result of the acquisition of the shares or the consolidation of the parent and subsidiary firms. Only if a minority interest remains is there an increase in the total equity of the consolidated enterprise. As indicated in the previous chapter, however, the minority interest is not always shown as a part of the total equity in the consolidated balance sheet.

In the above cases, the acquisition of additional nonmonetary assets or stock of another firm for cash leads to a clear-cut treatment of the transaction as a purchase, even though several problems of consolidation remain unresolved. But when two or more firms combine by the exchange of the stock of one for the assets or stock of others or when a new corporation is formed for this purpose, a question arises as to whether the transaction is a purchase or, in fact, only a "pooling of interests" of the two or more firms. The nature of the transaction and the resulting enterprise rather than the legal form should dictate the accounting procedure to be followed.

Both the purchase and the pooling methods are consistent with different concepts of the traditional historical cost structure. However, neither method permits a good semantic interpretation of the economic situation and the resulting relationships. Therefore, the appearance of the financial statements resulting from the combination and the expected reaction of investors and creditors have usually been the determining factors in the choice of reporting method, and in many cases the determining factors in the decision whether or not to combine. Because of this emphasis on the accounting result rather than on providing interpretive information for investment decisions, the rule-making bodies both in the United States and in other countries have found it difficult to establish rules that cannot be circumvented in spite of their continual revision.

Combinations treated as purchases

Whenever assets are acquired by the exchange of capital stock, the valuation of the assets is assumed to be equal to the value of the stock given in exchange unless the current value of the assets can be obtained by other verifiable means. Similarly, when all of the assets of a firm or its stock are acquired by giving capital stock in exchange in a purchase transaction, the accounting treatment involves two parts: (1) The net assets are valued in terms of total market value of the stock issued in exchange. This total cost should be allocated to specific assets whenever possible, and any excess should be considered purchased goodwill or other intangibles. (2) The total value of the stock issued is credited to invested capital with a possible division between legal capital and capital in excess of par or stated value. The former classification of the stockholders' equity of the acquired corporation has no effect on the classification in the acquiring firm.

A purchase transaction is based on the traditional structural concept that the valuation of assets and liabilities received should be recorded in the amount of the valuations of the assets or equities given in the exchange. These values then become the historical costs reported in subsequent periods. However, there is strong support for the position that some combinations are not the result of purchase transactions, but rather the result of a mutual joining together where neither firm purchases the other. The distinction between a purchase transaction and a mutual joining together cannot be settled on either structural or semantic grounds. Therefore, the rule-making bodies have attempted to legislate this distinction but without success.

Because of this failure to establish workable criteria and because of the abuses of accounting for acquisitions permitted by this failure, the pooling method has come under severe criticism from many sides and the purchase method has been claimed to be appropriate in all cases. Wyatt, for example, in *Accounting Research Study No. 5* concluded that a business combination ". . . is basically an exchange event in which two economic interests bargain to the consummation of an exchange of assets and/or equities."[17] Therefore, it follows from this definition that almost all combinations are purchases and should be accounted for as such. This was also the conclusion of Catlett and Olson in *Accounting Research Study No. 10.*[18] Likewise, the AAA Committee to Prepare a Statement of Basic Accounting Principles recommended the adoption of the purchase method as opposed to the pooling concept because of greater relevance.[19]

---

[17] Arthur R. Wyatt, "A Critical Study of Accounting for Business Combinations," *Accounting Research Study No. 5* (AICPA, 1963), p. 104.

[18] George R. Catlett and Norman O. Olson, "Accounting for Goodwill," *Accounting Research Study No. 10* (AICPA, 1968), p. 110.

[19] Committee to Prepare a Statement of Basic Accounting Theory, *A Statement of Basic Accounting Theory* (AAA, 1966), p. 19.

One of the main advantages of the purchase method is that it permits a "fresh start" from an accounting point of view, at least for the acquired firm. If the assets of the acquired firm are overvalued, they can be adjusted to a fair value at the time of combination and a deficit in the acquired firm can be eliminated in the new combination. However, the purchase method is claimed to be disadvantageous if the fair value of the assets is greater than the previous book value, because the recording of these higher values will necessitate higher depreciation and amortization charges, resulting in lower reported net income for several years. This is compounded by the fact that if the combination is a tax-free combination, this extra depreciation and amortization is not deductible for income tax purposes. It is also assumed to be disadvantageous because it eliminates the retained earnings of the acquired corporation, thereby reducing the amount available for dividends out of accumulated income although the legal amount available may not be altered. These arguments are discussed more fully below.

Pooling of interests

A pooling of interests is assumed to occur when two or more firms combine to carry out their business functions as a single economic enterprise. The enterprise may take the form of one of the existing corporations, a new corporation organized for the purpose, or a continuance of the previous corporations with one being the parent and the others the subsidiaries. In the absence of general principles to determine when a pooling of interests occurs, rule-making bodies have chosen to define specific conditions where a pooling of interest accounting is permitted and have concluded that all other combinations should be treated as purchases. In spelling out the specific conditions, emphasis has been placed on the attendant circumstances surrounding the combination and the nature of the exchange transaction rather than the legal form. Among the attendant circumstances are the conditions that the firms being combined should be autonomous and without significant intercorporate investments. Earlier rules also emphasized the need for a continuity of management and business activities, although these conditions were difficult to define and control. An additional factor complicating the enforcement of rules is the ability of firms to manipulate stockholdings and other circumstances to give the appearance of meeting the rules at the time of the combination. As a result, the rule-making bodies were forced to establish rules relating to exchanges occurring both before and after the combination transaction.

The emphasis on the exchange has focused on the requirement that a pooling of interest accounting can be used only when common stock of the acquiring firm is exchanged for substantially all of the voting common stock of the acquired firm. The emphasis on this form of the transaction is assumed to provide evidence of a continuance of ownership interests assumed to be necessary in a pooling of interests. However, firms have manipulated stockholdings before and after the combination to give the appearance of a continuance of ownership interests at the time of the combination transaction. Thus, rules are necessary to prevent certain types of transactions both before and after the effective date of the combination.

In a pooling of interest, the accounting treatment involves two basic differences from the treatment as a purchase: (1) the assets and liabilities of the several combining enterprises are brought into the new enterprise at their book value in the accounts of the former separate organizations, with the exception that adjustments may be made to provide for uniform treatment; and (2) the retained earnings of the several corporations should be added together in the surviving corporation or in consolidation except for that amount that must be transferred to invested capital to present legal capital.

Pooling of interest accounting has been popular in business combinations for several reasons: (1) When the fair value of the assets combined is greater than the book value, the depreciation and amortization would be increased if the combination were treated as a purchase and the net income of the new combination would be less than the summation of the net incomes of the former enterprises. (2) The pooling of interest treatment avoids the dilution of earnings per share arising from the revaluation of assets. (3) It avoids the necessity of recording goodwill and other intangibles that present problems of amortization and interpretation. (4) The combining of the retained earnings of the several enterprises does not reduce the amount available for dividends as income distribution. These so-called advantages, however, are illusory and deceptive and should not be controlling factors in the decision to apply purchase or pooling of interest accounting.

An additional objective of the pooling of interest method is to present the effect of the combination for prior periods as if the firms had been combined at the earlier date. The apparent objective is to show meaningful trends of income and earnings per share data that can be used for predictive purposes. However, this is a misuse of comparative data, because a discontinuity has occurred. The combined firm is not the same as a group of separate firms and it is misleading to assume that nothing has happened. Furthermore, the combination generally results in a new capitalization and new relationships among the equity holders. It is misleading to assume that these new capitalization relationships existed in an earlier period, under entirely different circumstances. Comparative data should be prohibited in this case unless the nature of the discontinuity is clearly disclosed.

An evaluation of purchases and pooling of interests

The distinction between a purchase and a pooling of interests rests primarily on the selection and interpretation of the relevant surviving entity. In a purchase, only one combining enterprise survives; the others die both in form and in spirit. However, in a pooling of interests, the surviving corporation is really a combination of two or more viable economic enterprises. The fact that one of the legal organizations is chosen to house the new entity is not sufficient evidence that it has purchased the others. The evidence must rest in the attendant circumstances, rather than in the legal form of the combination.

Once a combination is decided to be either a purchase or a pooling of interests, the specific accounting treatment is then thought to be determined. The two major accounting problems are the valuation of the assets acquired or combined and the classification of the increased or combined equity of the stockholders. However, these two aspects of the combination should be analyzed and treated separately. There is no clear evidence in accounting theory that the classification of stockholders' equity in a combination is dictated by the method of asset valuation or vice versa.

The valuation of assets in a combination. When a combination is treated as a purchase, the net assets are acquired at their cost as measured by the market value of the stock given in exchange. This treatment is correct, not because it complies with the traditional cost basis of accounting, but because this cost represents the best measure of the current value of the assets to the combined enterprise. If the total cost cannot be allocated to specific assets as part of their current value, the difference represents the cost of unidentified goodwill or other intangibles to be reported, as discussed in Chapter 16.

The decision to treat a combination as a pooling of interests is generally assumed to dictate that the assets be carried forward at the book value in the accounts of the previous enterprise. This treatment is based upon the tradition that historical cost is the most objective and the most relevant valuation basis when there is continuity of ownership interests. However, current values are more relevant for most decisions to be made by external investors and for most decisions of management.

Even though a combination is considered to be a pooling of interests, it is a significant event in the history of the enterprise, and the assets should be recorded at their current value or current replacement cost, rather than the historical costs in the accounts of the former enterprises. Because the current value of the assets can be obtained by objective means if the stock given in exchange has a market value, the revaluation obtains greater reliability than an independent revaluation. However, a serious difficulty arises when one of the combining firms continues in its legal form and its assets cannot be revalued in terms of the market value of any stock given in exchange for it. A difficulty also arises when a new corporation is formed for the purpose of the combination, because the stock may not have a current market value. But in each of these cases, there is good reason to revalue all of the assets of the new combined enterprise by using available evidence, such as replacement costs and the market price of the stock of the combining corporations.

The classification of the stockholders' equity of the combination. When a new corporation is organized to purchase the assets or stock of two or more firms, a new enterprise is formed and the entire stockholders' equity at the inception of the new enterprise is invested capital. As indicated earlier, subclassifications may be made to disclose the interests of different classes of stockholders and to disclose the amount of legal capital. But since the firm is a new entity, none of the equity is derived from the retention of earnings. If an existing firm purchases the assets or stock of another firm, a situation similar to the acquisition by a new firm is encountered insofar as the acquired firm loses its identity; but the stockholders' equity of the acquiring firm is not affected because the transaction involves only an exchange of assets (or net assets).

When the acquiring firm issues common stock for the assets or stock of another firm, however, the classification of the stockholders' equity in the acquiring firm (or in a new firm organized for the purpose) depends upon the interpretation of the new enterprise as (1) an entirely new accounting entity, (2) an accounting entity comprised of the acquiring corporation only, or (3) a continuation of all combining enterprises as a single accounting entity. In the first interpretation, the new enterprise obtains a fresh start and all of the stockholders' equity is invested capital. The second case is assumed to represent a fresh start for the acquired firm, but not for the continuing corporation.

The idea of a fresh start is derived from the concept of a quasi reorganization. But this analogy is weak, because in a quasi reorganization there is continuity of interests, with a reclassification of stockholders' equity at the time of the fresh start; while in a combination treated as a purchase, the acquired firm or firms are assumed to disappear entirely. Therefore, rather than being a "fresh start," the entire net assets of the acquired firm or firms are *invested* in the new firm or the surviving firm. Therefore, all of the stockholders' equity arising from the exchange of shares for the net assets or stock of the acquired firms should be treated as invested capital.

What justification is there, then, for carrying forward the retained earnings of the combined firms when the combination is treated as a pooling of interests? If classification of stockholders' equity by source is considered to be the major objective of classification, the question is one of determining the relevant entity and the relevant sources of the equities of this entity. If several firms combine without changing the ownership interests, the source of the equity in the new firm is the summation of the sources in the predecessor corporations. However, if the ownership interests of the acquired firm changed from residual interests to preferred interests, the retained earnings of the corporation dissolving in form should not be carried forward into the combined enterprise because to do so would lead to a misinterpretation regarding the nature of this equity as being obtained from the retention of earnings that would otherwise have been distributed to the current residual equity holders.

If the ownership interests of the several firms are continued in the combined enterprise, however, a distinction between the capital originally invested by these stockholders and the capital obtained by the retention of earnings is relevant in the description of the combined firm. If the equities of the several firms are all material in relationship to the stockholders' equity of the combined enterprise, it would be misleading to carry forward the retained earnings of only one of the firms because this would distort the ratio between capital originally invested and that derived from the retention of earnings. There is considerable merit in disclosing the retained earnings of the several firms at the date of combination and making a separate disclosure of the earnings retained after the combination, unless the continuing firm is so large in relationship to the others that there is no material change in the total retained earnings resulting from the combination.

In summary, the continuation of the same classifications of stockholder equities in a combined enterprise as in the former firms is logical if the ownership interests continue with similar equity rights in the combined firms as in the predecessor corporation. Other criteria, such as relative size, continuity of management, and the basis of valuation of the assets of the combined enterprise, are not relevant in determining the classification of stockholders' equity. However, a major difficulty in a classification by sources originating in the former corporations is that a reclassification may be necessary if legal capital is increased by the combination and if the disclosure of legal capital is to be accomplished in the classification. The important point is that the rights in both liquidation and dividend distributions of all stockholders in the combined firm should be clearly disclosed.

EARNINGS PER SHARE

Earnings per share ratios are probably the most frequently published summaries of accounting data. One reason for their popularity is that they are thought to contain information useful in making predictions regarding future dividends per share and future share prices. They are also thought to be relevant in an evaluation of management effectiveness and dividend policy. The main difference of opinion, however, is whether earnings per share data should reflect historical information only or whether they should reflect pro forma and predictive information. The APB in *Opinion No. 15* chose an emphasis on the pro forma concept because it was thought to be more useful for investment decisions and for evaluating the potential of a firm for credit purposes. Accordingly, it requires the presentation of two earnings per share computations (when materially dilutive), both of which are pro forma in nature and are assumed to have predictive qualities.

As discussed in Chapter 10, cash flow data and other information relevant to a prediction of dividends may be more significant for investment decisions than net income and earnings per share data. If this is the case, more emphasis should be placed on the computation of dividends per share and total dividend requirements on a pro forma basis than on the computation and presentation of earnings per share.

Computation of number of shares

The computation of an earnings per share ratio requires a computation with net income to common stockholders as the numerator and the related number of common shares as the denominator. In a simple case in which there have been no significant changes in capitalization during the year and no obligations to issue additional shares, the relevant denominator is the number of shares outstanding at the end of the year. However, if additional shares have been issued during the year, an average of the number of shares weighted by the number of months outstanding is assumed to be more relevant because the capital invested through the sale of the additional shares was available to the firm to increase its earnings during the year. Therefore, the use of the weighted average of the shares outstanding during the year is assumed to reflect the historical conditions as well as to permit comparisons with other years.

When other securities that have some characteristics of common stock are outstanding, usefulness of earnings per share data may be increased if these securities are counted as common stock. For example, if preferred stock is fully participating with respect to dividends, the preferred stockholders have the same rights as common stockholders to share in dividend distributions in excess of the preferred rate. Therefore, if such securities have the right to share in future dividends on the same basis as common stock, they should be included in the computation of earnings per share. Convertible debt, convertible preferred stock, options, and warrants do not share in dividends on the same basis as common until they become common shares; but they have potential rights to share in future distributions. Therefore, from the point of view of using the earnings per share figure as a predictive indicator, they should be included in the computation if they are likely to gain the rights of common stockholders. For if these security holders exercise their rights, the earnings per share figure based on outstanding shares is likely to decrease.

Although there are many ways to compute earnings per share if these different types of securities are present, *APB Opinion No. 15* recommended two separate computations called "primary earnings per share" and "fully diluted earnings per share" respectively. But these two computations are based on neither the probability of conversion or exercise nor on their imminence. They are, rather, computations based on arbitrary rules and assumptions, without evidence that either computation is necessarily relevant for investment decisions.

Primary earnings per share. The primary earnings per share computation includes the weighted average number of shares outstanding during the year plus the number of shares represented by securities that are considered to be common stock equivalents and have a dilutive effect. A dilutive effect is assumed to occur if the earnings per share figure would be reduced by 3 percent or more if the common stock equivalents were included. Securities considered to be common stock equivalents include all stock options and warrants, participating securities, convertible securities that come within the limits of a specific formula at the time of issuance, and other securities having current or potential common stock rights. Convertible securities are considered to be common stock equivalents if the cash yield at the time of issuance is less than two thirds of the bank prime interest rate at that time.

The use of "primary earnings per share" can be criticized for the following reasons: (1) The use of the term *primary* implies that the computation is of greatest significance, whereas any one of a family of earnings per share computations may be the most relevant under different assumptions and expectations. (2) Convertible debt and convertible preferred stock are treated differently from debt and preferred stock with detachable warrants, since convertible securities are classified as common stock equivalents only at the date of issuance, warrants are included in the computation according to the conditions in each period, and the methods of adjusting income are different. However, they are in substance the same, since the proceeds from the exercise of the warrants can be used to purchase the bonds or preferred stock; so the firm would be in the same position as when convertible securities are converted. (3) Convertible securities are classified as common stock equivalents only at the time of issuance, rather than reflecting the conditions current in each year. (4) The use of the bank prime interest rate in the cash yield test does not differentiate among different types of securities nor among different investment standings of firms. (5) It is inconsistent to say that convertible debt should be classified solely as debt in the balance sheet (as required in *APB Opinion No. 14*) and to classify it entirely as a common stock equivalent in computing the earnings per share. (6) The primary earnings per share is a pro forma computation, but the title does not indicate its significance. Without full disclosure, the reader would not be able to determine which securities have been treated as common stock equivalents.

Fully diluted earnings per share. According to *APB Opinion No. 15,* the fully diluted earnings per share should be computed on the basis of the computation used for primary earnings per share plus the number of common shares represented by convertible securities that were not classified as common stock equivalents. The method of treating warrants and options may also be different if the closing market price of common exceeds the average price. Such securities should not be included, however, if the effect would be to increase the earnings per share or decrease the loss per share.

The alleged purpose of the fully diluted computation is to show the

maximum potential dilution of current earnings per share on a prospective basis.[20] However, this computation does not include the maximum
potential dilution, because the treatment of warrants is dependent upon
the market price at the end of the period while expected dilution may
depend upon expectations of *future* market prices. Thus, actual dilution
may be greater than that reported for two reasons: (1) Warrants are not
included if the market price of common stock at the end of the period does
not exceed the exercise price. This is similar to the assumption made with
executive stock options that no compensation is involved if the market
price does not exceed the exercise price at the date of the grant. However,
if the market price increases in a later period, dilution will occur when the
warrants are exercised. (2) The elimination of warrants from the computation on the basis of market price of the stock at the end of the period
assumes that the proceeds from the exercise of the warrants can be used to
purchase stock at that price. But when the warrants are exercised at a
later date, when the market price of the stock has increased, the proceeds
will not permit the acquisition of the same number of shares.

The fully diluted earnings per share computation can also be criticized
on the basis that it is likely to be interpreted as the most probable result.
However, experience is likely to indicate that not all conversion rights nor
warrants are exercised or are likely to be exercised. The computation,
therefore, may reflect a worse situation than is probable under any circumstances.

Computation of the earnings

The numerator in the computation of earnings per share must be adjusted, even on an historical basis, if there are senior stock equity issues
outstanding. Since the earnings relate only to common stock securities
with residual rights, dividends paid or payable on senior securities should
be deducted from the net income figures shown on the income statement.
If an addition is made to the common stock shares in the denominator to
represent convertible debt outstanding, the interest expense for the year
adjusted for the income tax effect should be added to the reported net
income. Convertible preferred stock included in the denominator, however, does not require an adjustment of reported net income because the
net income amount must be allocated to these shares as well as to common stock.

Stock options and warrants require, upon exercise, payment to the firm
of an amount referred to as "the exercise price." Since the equivalent
number of shares are included in the denominator on the assumption that
the options and warrants have been exercised since the beginning of the
period or date of grant, the net income should include an amount equal to

---

[20] *AICPA Professional Standards,* para. 2011.40.

the net income effect of utilizing the cash proceeds from the exercise of the warrants. Since this is a pro forma assumption, there is no way of knowing what the income effect would have been. One assumption is that the firm could have earned at least an amount equivalent to the interest on government securities or commercial paper adjusted for the income tax effect. An alternative assumption is that the firm could reacquire its long-term debt and thereby save interest expense. The assumption of *APB Opinion No. 15,* however, is that the proceeds could have been used by the firm to reacquire its own shares at the average market price during the year. Under this so-called treasury stock method, the number of shares added to the denominator would be reduced by the number of shares that could have been purchased with the proceeds from the exercise of the warrants, and the net income in the numerator is not increased. Thus, no dilution is assumed to occur if the average market price of the common stock is equal to or less than the exercise price. *Opinion No. 15,* however, suggested that if the number of shares obtainable upon exercise of the warrants exceeds 20 percent of the outstanding common shares, the proceeds from the shares in excess of 20 percent should be assumed to be used to repay debt or be invested in government securities or commercial paper. In this case, the net income should be increased by the net income effect of the interest that could have been saved or earned.

Criticisms of the recommendations of *Opinion No. 15* regarding the adjustment for the income effect of the proceeds from the exercise of warrants are: (1) The use of the treasury stock method does not reflect the best use of the funds or even the most likely use. (2) The use of a current market price to determine the number of shares that could be purchased does not reflect the potential of the firm to reacquire such shares in the future, particularly if the market price is increasing each year. (3) The 20 percent limitation is arbitrary and therefore does not necessarily lead to meaningful measurements. (4) The market price of the stock generally reflects expectations regarding future earnings and is not related to the current opportunities available to the firm for investment of the proceeds from the exercise of warrants.

SUMMARY

The earnings per share computations recommended by *APB Opinion No. 15* are pro forma ratios based on unsupported assumptions. Instead of presenting only two ratios that are assumed to be most relevant, the financial statements should present a full disclosure of all relevant information to permit investors to make their own evaluations of the potential of the firm. Furthermore, since future dividend distributions may be more significant than reported earnings per share computations, the information should be presented in such a way that alternative dividends per share computations can also be estimated under different assumptions.

SELECTED ADDITIONAL READING

Stock dividends and stock splits

Foster, Taylor W. III, and **Don Vickrey.** "The Information Content of Stock Dividend Announcements." *Accounting Review,* April 1978, pp. 360–70.

Millar, James A. "Split or Dividend: Do the Words Really Matter?" *Accounting Review,* January 1977, pp. 52–55.

Pusker, Henri C. "Accounting for Capital Stock Distributions (Stock Split-Ups and Dividends)." *New York CPA,* May 1971, pp 347–52.

Stock options

Alvin, Gerald. "Accounting for Investment and Stock Rights: The Market Value Method." *CPA Journal,* February 1973, pp. 126–31.

Boudreaux, Kenneth J., and **Stephen A. Zeff,** "A Note on the Measure of Compensation Implicit in Employee Stock Options." *Journal of Accounting Research,* Spring 1976, pp. 158–62.

Rogers, Donald R., and **R. W. Schattke.** "Buy-Outs of Stock Options: Compensation or Capital?" *Journal of Accountancy,* August 1972, pp. 55–59.

Smith, Clifford W., Jr., and **Jerold L. Zimmerman.** "Valuing Employer Stock Option Plans Using Option Pricing Models." *Journal of Accounting Research,* Autumn 1976, pp. 357–64.

Smith, Ralph E., and **Leroy F. Imdieke.** "Accounting for Stock Issued to Employees." *Journal of Accountancy,* November 1974, pp. 68–75.

Weygandt, Jerry J. "Valuation of Stock Option Contracts." *Accounting Review,* January 1977, pp. 40–51.

Business combinations

Anderson, John C., and **Joseph G. Louderback III.** "Income Manipulation and Purchase-Pooling: Some Additional Results." *Journal of Accounting Research,* Autumn 1975, pp. 338–43.

Brenner, Vincent C. "Empirical Study of Support for *APB Opinion No. 16.*" *Journal of Accounting Research,* Spring 1972, pp. 200–208.

Defliese, Philip L. "Business Combinations Revisited." *D. R. Scott Memorial Lectures in Accountancy, vol. 6.* Columbus: University of Missouri, 1974.

Emanuel, David M. "Accounting for Business Combinations." *Australian Accountant,* October 1973, pp. 518–22, 525–26.

Foster, William C. "Illogic of Pooling." *Financial Executive,* December 1974, pp. 16–21.

Gaertner, James F. "Proposed Alternatives for Accounting for Business Combinations: A Behavioural Study." *Abacus,* June 1979, pp. 35–47.

Gagnon, Jean-Marie. "Purchase-Pooling Choice: Some Empirical Evidence." *Journal of Accounting Research,* Spring 1971, pp. 52–72.

Hong, Hai; Robert S. Kaplan; and **Gershon Mandelker.** "Pooling vs. Purchase: The Effects of Accounting for Mergers on Stock Prices." *Accounting Review,* January 1978, pp. 31–47.

Earnings per share

Arnold, Donald F. "Earnings per Share: An Empirical Test of the Market Parity and the Investment Value Methods." *Accounting Review,* January 1973, pp. 23–33.

Ellon, Samuel. "Earnings per share Can Be Misleading." *Journal of Business Finance and Accounting,* Summer 1975, pp. 239–42.

Gibson, Charles H., and **John Daniel Williams.** "Should Common Stock Equivalents Be Considered in Earnings per Share?" *CPA Journal,* March 1973, pp. 209–13.

Parker, James E., and **Barry E. Cushing.** "Earnings per Share and Convertible Securities: A Utilitarian Approach." *Abacus,* June 1971, pp. 29–38.

Rice, Steven J. "The Information Content of Fully Diluted Earnings per Share." *Accounting Review,* April 1978, pp. 429–38.

Shank, John K. "Earnings Per Share, Stock Prices, and *APB Opinion No. 15.*" *Journal of Accounting Research,* Spring 1971, pp. 165–70.

Tritschler, Charles A. "Dilution and Counter-Dilution in Reporting for Deferred Equity." *Accounting and Business Research,* Autumn 1971, pp. 274–83.

CHAPTER 21

DISCLOSURE IN FINANCIAL REPORTING

The topic of disclosure is broad enough to encompass almost the entire area of financial reporting and, therefore, serves as an appropriate final chapter to a book on accounting theory. One of the major objectives of financial reporting is to supply information for decision making. This requires a proper disclosure of financial data and other relevant information. But the major questions are (1) For whom is the information to be disclosed? (2) What is the purpose of the information? and (3) How much information should be disclosed? The question of how and when the information should be disclosed is, of course, also important, as the method and timing of disclosure determine the usefulness of the information; but the question of method is less important than the question of the choice and timing of financial disclosure.

The question "For whom?" can be answered by stating that the financial reports are directed primarily to stockholders, other investors, and creditors; but employees, customers, governmental agencies, and the general public are also recipients of annual reports and other forms of disclosure. The decisions to be made by investors are primarily buy-sell-hold decisions, and the decisions of creditors are primarily related to the extension of credit to the enterprise. Stockholders may also make decisions regarding the hiring, firing, and compensation of management and the approval or disapproval of major changes in firm policy. The objectives of presenting information to employees, customers, and the general public have not been well formulated. However, it is generally assumed that the information useful to investors and creditors is also useful to others.

THE NATURE OF DISCLOSURE

Disclosure in financial reporting is the presentation of information necessary for the optimum operation of efficient capital markets. This implies that sufficient information should be presented to permit the prediction of future dividend trends and variability and the covariability of future returns with the market. Emphasis should be placed on the preferences of sophisticated investors and financial analysts. However, all investors need information to evaluate the relative risks of individual firms in order

504

to obtain diversified portfolios and combinations of investments that meet individual risk preferences. Creditors and governmental agencies generally have the power to obtain additional information for their needs.

How much information should be disclosed is dependent not only upon the expertness of the reader, but also upon the desirable standard. Three concepts of disclosure generally proposed are *adequate, fair,* and *full* disclosure. The most commonly used of these expressions is adequate disclosure. But this implies a minimum amount of disclosure congruous with the negative objective of making the statements not misleading. Fair and full are more positive concepts. Fair disclosure implies an ethical objective of providing equal treatment for all potential readers. Full disclosure implies the presentation of all relevant information. To some, full disclosure means the presentation of superfluous information and is therefore inappropriate. Too much information is harmful in that the presentation of unimportant details hides the significant information and makes the financial reports difficult to interpret. However, appropriate disclosure of information significant to investors and others should be adequate, fair, and full. There is no real difference among these concepts if they are used in the proper context. A positive objective is to provide the users of financial statements with significant and relevant information to aid them in the making of decisions in the best possible way with the limitation that the benefits should exceed the costs. This implies that information that is not material or relevant be omitted to make the presentations meaningful and understandable.

Empirical studies and a review of the literature provide evidence that corporations are reluctant to increase the extent of financial disclosure without pressure from the accounting profession or the government. However, disclosure is vital for the optimum decisions of investors and for a stable capital market. Timely disclosure of relevant information tends to prevent surprises that may completely alter the outlook for the future of the firm. It also tends to give investors greater confidence in the financial information available to them. However, the amount of data to be disclosed cannot be determined without more information regarding investors' decision models. But, at the present time, it is not likely that too much information will be presented for use by financial analysts.

Objections to increasing the amount of financial data to be disclosed include the following arguments: (1) Disclosure will aid competitors to the disadvantage of stockholders. This argument, however, has little merit, since competitors generally do obtain the information through other sources. (2) Unions are said to gain an advantage in wage bargaining by a complete disclosure of financial information. However, full disclosure will generally improve the general climate for bargaining. (3) It is frequently claimed that investors cannot understand accounting policies and procedures and that full disclosure will only mislead, rather than enlighten. This claim is also unsupported because financial analysts and investment managers are well educated in accounting and other investors either benefit from the use of financial information in an efficient market or they are able to learn through the study of reported financial information. (4) One argument that has some merit is that frequently other sources of financial information may be available to provide the information at a lower cost than if it were provided by the firm in its financial statements. (5) A lack of knowledge of the needs of investors is also given as a reason for limiting disclosure. But because of the possibility of many investment models and an increasing reliance on information intermediaries, this should not be a restricting factor.

WHAT SHOULD BE DISCLOSED?

The decision regarding what to disclose must be derived from the basic objectives of accounting discussed above in Chapter 3. If the specific and general preferences of sophisticated investors are emphasized, one of the objectives should be the presentation of sufficient information to permit comparisons of expected results. Comparability, however, can be applied in at least two different ways. One is to provide sufficient disclosure of how accounting numbers are measured and computed to permit investors to convert the amounts from different firms into measurements that are directly comparable. That is, it is assumed that adjusted accounting numbers for the several firms can be used by investors to determine the degrees of difference, for example, in the rates of growth of net income or dividends. A second way of applying comparability is to permit the investor to make ordinal rankings of the several inputs into the decision models. For example, an investor might compare the risks of two firms and conclude merely that one is more or less risky than the other.

Disclosure of quantitative data

In the selection of criteria for deciding what quantitative data are material and relevant for investors and creditors, emphasis should be placed on financial or other information that might be of use in decision models. However, in making comparisons over time and among different firms, investors cannot assume that all reported quantitative data have the same probability of accuracy. Therefore, research in accounting should focus on the method of measuring and reporting probabilistic data rather than deterministic amounts. But an informed reader generally places greater reliance on some items in the financial statements and should be able to expect full disclosure if this assumption is not justified. For example, it is generally thought that cash and related items can be measured relatively accurately; the current value of receivables is somewhat less accurate; and intangibles can be measured only within a relatively wide range of reliability. Therefore, a disclosure of uncertainties in cash items, such as deposits in closed banks or in foreign currencies, may be considered material and relevant, whereas an intangible item of the same magnitude may not be relevant.

In addition to the quantitative data usually presented in traditional financial statements, there is considerable merit in the presentation of greater detail regarding the several segments of a business enterprise representing product or geographical diversifications arising from normal growth or from mergers in the development of conglomerate firms. This will be discussed at greater length in a special section below. Considerable pressure has also arisen to require the reporting of forecast data.

The historical cost accounting structure has been thought to be a review of past events. Investors, on the other hand, are primarily interested in the future prospects of the firm. One view is that accountants should present only historical and current information that will permit investors to make their own predictions of the future. That is, the process of forecasting requires subjective evaluations in addition to an analysis of a large number of variables and assumptions; it is thought that the investor can understand the subjective evaluations and assumptions only by making the forecast. Another view is that management has far superior resources for making reliable forecasts and that the public availability of its forecasts increases the efficiency of the financial markets.

In a study on forecasting, Nickerson, Pointer, and Strawser concluded that forecasts are relevant to stockholders.[1] In another study, Gray concluded that forecasters tend to extrapolate current and past trends with the result that forecasting is less accurate at turning points in the economy. He also found some evidence that forecasters tend to be overly optimistic particularly for a period following a long expansion.[2] Although accurate forecasts at the turning points would be of the greatest assistance to investors, the regular publication of management's forecasts is likely to aid rather than hinder investment decisions although the basic questions that remain are what information should be forecast and how can the reliability be measured.

Although the most frequently mentioned forecast accounting numbers are probably net income and earnings per share, they are probably more difficult to predict and also the least reliable. This results from the fact that a projection of accounting income depends on many subjective variables and many assumptions regarding the firm and the economy. It is also of little significance for normative investment decision models because it has little if any real-world interpretation. Other items that have greater interpretive significance include expected sales, budgeted receipts

[1] Charles A. Nickerson, Larry G. Pointer, and Robert H. Strawser, "Published Forecasts: Choice or Obligation?" *Financial Executive,* February 1974, pp. 70–73.

[2] William S. Gray, "The Role of Forecast Information in Investment Decisions," in *Public Reporting of Corporate Financial Forecasts,* edited by Prem Prakash and Alfred Rappaport (Chicago: Commerce Clearing House, 1974), pp. 53–54.

and disbursements, and measurements relating to expected changes in the prices and demand for the product of the firm and expected changes in the costs of labor and goods generally acquired by the firm.

With a publication of the forecast of financial accounting information and other information relating to the firm, it is necessary that the basic assumptions relating to the economy and external factors be disclosed so that the users of the forecasts can better evaluate its reliability. Such assumptions should include expectations regarding the industry as well as assumptions regarding changes in economic conditions.

Nonquantitative information

Information that cannot be expressed in quantitative terms is more difficult to evaluate as to its materiality and relevance because it is given various weights by those using the information in decision making. In general, information that is given greater weight in decision making is more relevant than information given less weight. Therefore, the point should be sought where it can be said that the information is important enough in decision making that it should not be omitted.

The relevance of certain types of nonquantitative information can be determined by the relevance of the quantitative data to which they relate. For example, if certain assets are pledged as security to specific creditors, the pledging would be a relevant fact if the assets themselves are material in amount. If the assets are not material, the descriptive or qualifying information is not likely to be relevant. In a few cases, however, this may not be true; for example, the loss of an immaterial amount of inventory or cash may become a relevant fact if it is due to a fraudulent management.

Nonquantitative information is relevant and worthy of disclosure only if it is useful in the decision-making process. It is relevant only if it adds more to the total information than it detracts by making the statements overly detailed and difficult to analyze. The question should always be asked: Is the addition of the information likely to improve most decisions made on the basis of the financial reports?

Accounting policies. With the proliferation of accounting procedures in use by different firms and even within the same firm, direct comparability of financial statements has become more difficult. One suggested solution has been an attempt to reduce the number of alternatives in the hope that uniformity would automatically permit comparability. However, the selection of one procedure for all firms is not only a difficult choice but one that may not achieve its goal under conditions of differing circumstances. The argument for diversity on the grounds of differing circumstances has, however, been too often used as a rationalization for the prerogative of management to choose whatever methods it wishes, frequently those methods that present the firm in the best light.

An alternative solution to the reduction of available alternatives is to disclose in each case the specific methods used under the assumption that the reader will then be able to restate the accounting reports in order to gain comparability. Empirical evidence has shown that this is possible in some circumstances, such as when the investment credit is reported as a direct reduction of the tax, rather than being allocated to income over a period of time. But, in most cases, there is no evidence that investors can gain comparability by converting various statements into uniform methods. Abdel-khalik and Keller, for example, concluded from a research study that functional fixation on reported income prevented the decision makers participating in the study from adjusting for the effects of LIFO and FIFO inventory methods, even though they had the information and knew how to make the adjustment.[3]

Disclosure of accounting policies, nevertheless, may provide assistance in permitting better interpretation of the financial statements of any particular firm and therefore influence investment decisions. On the basis of this assumption, the Accounting Principles Board in *Opinion No. 22* concluded that information about accounting policies in use is necessary for a fair presentation of financial statements.[4] This assumption is also given support by the results of an empirical study by Falk and Ophir who found that investors did react to both the content and to the art of disclosure itself.[5]

Accounting changes. The consistent use of accounting principles and procedures has long been considered essential in the evaluation of a firm's activities and in the projection of future activities. *APB Opinion No. 20* supported this view, but stated that when justified such changes should be disclosed in the financial statements when the change is made along with a statement of the justification. Accounting changes include changes in accounting principles, in accounting estimates, and in the reporting entity. The disclosure of these changes, like the disclosure of accounting policies, is essential for optimum investment decisions.

Empirical evidence has supported the view that changes in reported net income resulting from changes in accounting methods have not materially affected the market price of stock when disclosure of the change has been made.[6] However, contrary to the opinion of the APB, there appears to be some logic in the restatement of financial statements of prior periods when these are included for comparative purposes. The efficient markets

---

[3] A. Rashad Abdel-khalik and Thomas F. Keller, "Earnings or Cash Flows: An Experiment on Functional Fixation and the Valuation of the Firm," American Accounting Association, *Studies in Accounting Research No. 16* (AAA, 1979).

[4] *AICPA Professional Standards* (Chicago: Commerce Clearing House, 1981), Section 2045.

[5] Haim Falk and T. Ophir, "Influence of Differences in Accounting Policies on Investment Decisions," *Journal of Accounting Research,* Spring 1973, pp. 108–16.

[6] See T. Ross Archibald, "Stock Market Reaction to the Depreciation Switch-Back," *Accounting Review,* January 1972, pp. 22–30.

hypothesis, on the other hand, would support the conclusion that disclosure itself would be sufficient if sophisticated investors or investment analysts can interpret the financial information correctly.

DISCLOSURE OF POSTSTATEMENT EVENTS

The income statement is a summary of certain types of changes during the period being reported on, and the balance sheet summarizes the resource measurements and financial relationships at the end of this period. However, almost all of the figures included in these statements are tentative in nature because of uncertainties regarding the future. As time passes and additional information is obtained, many of these uncertainties are resolved. Therefore, many of the events occurring after the statement date affect the validity of the statements or the interpretations of them and the resulting decisions based on the information presented in the statements. To the extent that material events occur or become known after the statement date and before the report is completed, the objective of disclosure requires that this information be properly revealed in the report.

Three types of relevant events that may occur after the statement date and before the completion of the report are (1) events that affect directly the amounts reported in the financial statements, (2) events that alter materially the continuing validity of balance sheet valuations or the relationships among equity holders or materially affect the usefulness of the prior year's reported activities as a prediction of the current period, and (3) events that might affect materially future operations or valuations.

Events of the first type arise from inadequate knowledge during the accounting period and result in changes in estimated valuations because of knowledge gained subsequent to the balance sheet date. For example, if a major customer goes into bankruptcy during this period, the receivables included in the balance sheet and not collected at the date of the bankruptcy are likely to be overvalued, and the related bad debt expense was probably understated. If knowledge of this type of information is obtained early enough, the financial statements should be adjusted appropriately before they are published. If knowledge is obtained too late to make a complete correction of the statements, the information can be disclosed by some other means unless the statements would be completely erroneous if direct correction is not made. The Auditing Standards Board recommended that this type of event should be recognized by an adjustment directly in the financial statements if the information would have been utilized had it been available at the balance sheet date.[7]

Events of the second type have no direct effect on the financial state-

---

[7] *Statement on Auditing Standards No. 1.*

ments of the prior year, but are likely to affect materially decisions based on these statements. These include (1) events that affect materially the financial structure of the firm or current or future relationships among equity holders and (2) events that affect the income or potential dividend distributions of the period following the period included in the report or in later periods. Thus, a relatively large sale of capital stock or bonds or the purchase or sale of assets representing a large part of the total assets of the firm is assumed to be relevant for investment or credit decisions regarding the firm. Events that may result in abnormal and nonrecurring gains or losses may also affect decisions by influencing predictions of the future economic health of the firm. The Auditing Standards Board stated that these events do not require adjustment, but it did say that disclosure is advisable.[8] In the opinion of the author, the recommendation should be much stronger than this. Appropriate disclosure is just as important for these events as for similar events occurring during the reporting period. For example, the disclosure of a new stock option plan or an agreement to negotiate a merger is just as important if the event occurs after the balance sheet date as it is if it occurred before. Partial recognition is given to this in *APB Opinion No. 16,* which recommends that in the case of a combination accounted for as a pooling, consummated after the close of the period but before the financial statements are issued, the financial statements should be restated to give effect to the pooling for the entire period.

Events of the third type have an unknown or uncertain effect on future incomes and valuations. Examples would include changes in specific market conditions or in prices affecting the firm; new management policies; the signing of major contracts; and such external events as wars, legislation, and economic conditions. The Auditing Standards Board stated that, although disclosure of these events may be required, "disclosure of such conditions or events frequently creates doubt as to the reason therefor, and inferences drawn could be misleading as often as they are informative."[9]

These recommendations, however, apply to disclosure in audited statements. Disclosure of the events of the third type, or of all types, may be made in the president's letter or in a separate section of the annual report without any implication that the auditors consider this information a qualification of the statements. A broader and more positive viewpoint is that events of all three types, including their effect on the expectations of management, should be disclosed directly in the financial report reviewed by the auditor. The author agrees with this position as a long-run goal to provide the best possible information for the making of investment decisions.

---

[8] Ibid.
[9] Ibid.

DISCLOSURE OF SEGMENTS OF A BUSINESS ENTERPRISE

The growth of diversified businesses and the expansion of firms into foreign markets has resulted in the aggregation of financial information that includes nonhomogeneous elements. This problem of aggregation has become more acute with the development of large conglomerate firms that obtain their diversification through mergers or acquisitions of a wide variety of unrelated businesses. With each combination, there is a loss of information to the investor community and to the general public, since firms previously reporting separately report only as a single firm after the combination. Also, because of the diversification of activities, an evaluation of these conglomerate firms and the prediction of their future activities and successes have become more difficult with only aggregated data available.

FASB Statement 14 requires the presentation (in specific cases) of information regarding a firm's operations in different industries, its foreign operations and export sales and its major customers.[10]

NEED FOR SEGMENT DISCLOSURES

The need for disclosure of the operations of the major segments of diversified firms and firms with geographical or customer segmented markets arises because growth trends, variability of operations, and risk cannot be evaluated adequately from aggregated data. Disaggregation of the financial data is necessary to permit the prediction of future cash flows and risk for use in investment decision models. In estimating the value of a firm and in evaluating the risk, investors need to make predictions regarding the future operations of the enterprise. Predictions that are based on or supported by extrapolations of historical data are likely to be more reliable if they are made from information regarding the various segments of a business that have different characteristics.

Whether the objective should be to permit comparability or to permit predictability has a bearing on the minimum size of a business segment that should be reported separately. In order to obtain *comparability* among firms for similar types of operations, the selection criterion should be the absolute size of the operations. If a criterion is based on a percentage of total revenues of the firm, one type of operation representing 50 percent or more of the revenues of a small firm would require disclosure; but if it represents less than, say, 10 percent of the total revenues of a large firm, it would not be reported, even though an operation of this type may be considerably larger than the similar operation of the smaller firm. For this reason, recommendations have been made that segments as small as 5 percent of the total operations of a diversified firm should be reported

---

[10] *AICPA Professional Standards,* Section 2081.

separately, with a minimum absolute dollar criterion. However, if *predictability* is the objective, a higher minimum percentage may be adequate in order to provide relevant information regarding the contribution of a segment to the firm's revenue and net income. The FASB has suggested that an industry segment is significant if it represents 10 percent or more of the firm's revenues, operating profit, or identifiable assets.

Information regarding segments of a business is also thought to be relevant in external reports to prevent management from hiding information that it does not want published. For example, managements may wish to hide the fact that certain segments of the business are being operated at a loss for fear that they will be criticized by the stockholders for their managerial inefficiency. If some segments are quite profitable, they can be used to cover up the fact that other segments are unprofitable. This ability to hide losses has also been used by large firms as a way to finance their entry into a new line and to compete with established firms without being accused of underpricing to gain monopolistic control in markets.

Accounting difficulties

One of the first problems in reporting on divisions or segments of a business is the decision regarding how logical breakdowns should be made for reporting purposes. Product lines may be relevant in some cases but not in others. Geographical divisions may be particularly relevant with respect to foreign operations, and in other cases, classification by type of customer may be relevant. Particularly those who look for comparability among firms have recommended that a uniform classification along industry lines, such as the Standard Industrial Code of the Bureau of Census, should be used. But from the point of view of the investor, the classification that permits the greatest degree of predictability would be the most relevant. That is, predictability would require the grouping of activities that have similar behavioral characteristics over time.

A second important problem in the reporting of profit for separate segments of a business is the allocation of joint costs. If the segments are autonomously operated divisions, the amount of joint costs may be small; but in relation to the net incomes of the segments, it may be significant. Since accountants make allocations in many areas of reporting (such as the computation of depreciation), it has been suggested that one more allocation might make little difference.[11] But since such allocations are arbitrary, it is unlikely that relevant information can be obtained by their use. An alternative is to report only the "defined profit" or contribution of each division, computed from only the revenues and expenses that

---

[11] See, for example, Sidney Davidson, "Implications of Conglomerate Reporting for the Independent CPA —Comments," in *Public Reporting by Conglomerates,* ed. Alfred Rappaport, Peter A. Firmin, and Stephen A. Zeff (Englewood Cliffs, N.J.: Prentice-Hall, 1968), p. 88.

can be directly associated with the reporting segment. However, some firms may fear that such contribution may be interpreted as the net income of the division and as being excessive.

Another accounting problem is the treatment of interdivisional transfer pricing. The final product of one division may be the raw material of another within the same firm, so that if transfers are made in excess of cost, income will appear at the time of the transfer rather than when the final product is sold to a customer outside the firm. Solomons suggested that the best procedure would seem to be to eliminate interdivisional sales from reports to stockholders and thus report all such transfers at cost.[12] From the point of view of the objective of attaining predictive ability, this seems to be the best solution because a prediction of the final cash to be received from customers is more important to investors than the amount of product transferred from one division to another. However, comparability among firms is not attained because in some cases the semifinished product may be the final product of the firm, whereas in other cases the output of the semifinished product would not be reported prior to the sale of the final product of which it becomes a part.

Since the profitability of a firm is frequently measured in terms of the net income in relationship to the amount of net assets invested in the firm, it seems logical that divisional reporting should also require the separate reporting of the net assets used by each segment of the business. This separate reporting of assets was included in the proposed rules of the SEC to the extent that it is practicable and in *FASB Statement No. 14.* However, the measurement of assets is a difficult problem even for an entire enterprise. The assignment of physical assets to segments of a business may be possible in some cases, but accounting has not yet devised a consistent method of measuring these assets in a meaningful way so they can be related to the revenue contribution derived from them. Even if physical assets could be assigned to segments and measured in a meaningful way, the intangible assets—which may be more important in many cases—are most likely to be omitted. Furthermore, the liabilities of the enterprise cannot usually be designated in a meaningful way to represent the financing of specific assets.

METHODS OF DISCLOSURE

Disclosure involves the entire process of financial reporting. However, several different methods of making disclosure are available. The selection of the best method of disclosure in each case depends on the nature of the information and its relative importance. The common methods of disclosure can be classified as follows: (1) form and arrangement of formal statements, (2) terminology and detailed presentations, (3) parenthetical

---

[12] David Solomons, "Accounting Problems and Some Proposed Solutions," ibid., p. 100.

information, (4) footnotes, (5) supplementary statements and schedules, (6) comments in the auditors' certificate, and (7) the letter of the president or chairman of the board.

Form and arrangement of formal statements

The most relevant and significant information should always appear in the main body of one or more of the financial statements if it is possible to include it there. Assets and liabilities and the resulting effect on net income, and stockholders' equity should be disclosed in the statements as soon as transactions and other changes can be measured reliably and with a fair degree of accuracy. But the form and arrangement of the statement can be altered effectively to bring out certain types of information not readily disclosed by traditional statements.

Position statement. In the position statement or balance sheet, relevant relationships can be disclosed by rearranging the basic classifications. For example, current liabilities are frequently subtracted directly from current assets to show working capital, although this procedure has some deficiencies (as discussed in Chapter 12). Alternative classifications may separate monetary from nonmonetary assets and liabilities, or group the firm's resources according to the several segments of the business in which they are used. The classification of assets and liabilities was discussed in Chapter 12, several alternative methods of classification and presentation of stockholders' equity were discussed in Chapter 19, and the problems of divisional reporting were discussed earlier in this chapter.

Income statement. In the income statement, different forms of presentation can emphasize different concepts of income or different interpretations of the data. The single-step income statement, for example, associates all items of expense with all items of revenue; gross profit and other preliminary net figures are considered to be more misleading than helpful to the readers of the statement. In a suggested alternative, expenses are classified as either fixed or variable in order to aid the reader in making predictions of future outcomes with changes in sales volume. The disclosure of other income concepts and relationships has been discussed in Chapter 7. The disclosure of earnings per share data in the income statement was discussed in Chapter 20.

Cash flow and funds statements. As discussed in Chapter 10, considerable relevant information can be presented in cash flow and funds statements, particularly if care is taken to provide relevant classifications. For example, classifications of cash disbursements should be more relevant for predictive purposes if the disbursements are grouped according to their functional behavior, such as fixed and variable characteristics. Additional groupings according to the major segments of the business are also likely to be relevant to the decisions of investors and other interested parties.

Terminology and detailed presentations

Just as important as the form of the statements in disclosure are the descriptions used in the statements and the amount of detail shown. Appropriate captions and descriptions of the items in the statements can be enlightening to the reader, but obscure terms can lead only to confusion or misunderstanding. Technical terms may be useful if they have precise meanings that are generally well known, but many technical terms in accounting lack this preciseness. In these cases, accountants should apply descriptive terms generally used by financial analysts and other informed readers. Uniformity of terms throughout all accounting reports would be helpful if the meanings are clear and if the items are similar in all cases where the term is applied.

Because of the limitations of human spans of attention and comprehension, accounting data must be summarized to be meaningful and useful. The choice of how much information to present and the selection of what items to list separately are dependent on the objectives of the reports and on the materiality of the items. Brevity is a desirable goal in financial reports, but appropriate disclosure of detailed information should take precedence if it is necessary to make the reports significant for decision making.

Parenthetical information

The most significant information should be presented in the body of a financial statement, rather than in footnotes or supplementary schedules. If the titles of items in the statements cannot be made fully descriptive without being overly long, additional explanations or definitions can be presented as parenthetical notes following the titles in the statements. These notes, however, must not be long or they will detract from the main data summarized in the statement.

Other nonquantitative data that can be presented in parenthetical notes include (1) an indication of the specific procedure or valuation method used, to give the reader a better understanding of the meaning of the data; (2) the special characteristics that give greater meaning regarding the relative importance of the item, such as the fact that certain assets are pledged or that certain liabilities have prior rights; (3) detail regarding the amount of one or more items included in the broader classification listed; (4) such alternative valuations as current market price; and (5) reference to related information in other statements or elsewhere in the report.

Footnotes

Current financial reports have been said to give rise to what is called the footnote era. On the one hand, this is an improvement in reporting because it has resulted in a fuller disclosure of financial events and relevant financial data. On the other hand, the extensive use of footnotes has hindered the proper development of the statements themselves because it has resulted in the substitution of footnotes for better information in the body of the statement. Footnotes have an appropriate place in financial reporting, but there is danger in placing too much reliance on footnotes as a method of disclosure or in using footnotes as an apology for inadequate formal statements. Although it is difficult to set forth clear principles of footnoting based on accounting theory, some basic rules of footnoting can be formulated to tie in with the basic postulates and principles of accounting.

Nature and purpose of footnotes.   The objective of footnotes to financial statements should be to disclose information that cannot be presented adequately in the body of a statement without detracting from the clarity of the statement. Footnotes should not be used as a substitute for proper classification or valuation and description in the statements, nor should they contradict or repeat the information in the statements.

The main advantages of footnotes are their uses (1) to present nonquantitative information as an integral part of the financial report, (2) to disclose qualifications and restrictions to items in the statements, (3) to disclose a greater amount of detail than can be presented in the statements, and (4) to present either quantitative or descriptive material of secondary importance.

The main disadvantages of footnotes are: (1) they tend to be difficult to read and understand without considerable study and thus they may be overlooked; (2) the textual descriptions are more difficult to use in decision making than the summarizations of quantitative data in the statements; and (3) because of the increasing complexity of business enterprises, there is danger of an overuse of footnotes rather than proper development of principles to incorporate new relationships and events into the statements themselves.

The most common types of footnotes can be classified as follows: (1) explanations of techniques or changes in methods, (2) explanations of rights of creditors to specific assets or priorities of rights, (3) disclosure of contingent assets or contingent liabilities, (4) disclosure of restrictions to dividend payments, (5) descriptions of transactions affecting capital stock and rights of equity holders, and (6) descriptions of executory contracts. Footnotes are also used to present detailed quantitative data that are not significant enough to include in the body of a statement, but these are in the form of supplementary schedules and therefore are discussed at greater length below as a separate form of disclosure.

Accounting policy and accounting changes. As discussed above a proper interpretation of the income statement, the balance sheet, and the funds statement requires an understanding of the accounting methods used and the effect of changes in methods. Because most valuation and allocation techniques affect the income statement, the balance sheet, and the funds statement, a footnote disclosure of the methods used may be better than parenthetical notes in each statement. And with a footnote the methods used can be given fuller treatment than if parenthetical notes are used. This fuller disclosure is important where the differences among the several accepted methods are material—that is, where an assumption of a different method would be a significant factor in the making of decisions. Where such an item as cost of goods sold is a summary of several items computed by different methods, the footnote disclosure should show the amount computed by each of the methods if material. In the case of LIFO, the year the method was started might also be relevant. Since depreciation is generally a major item in most income statements, the Accounting Principles Board, in *Opinion No. 12,* recommended that the methods used in computing depreciation should be presented for the major classes of depreciable assets.[13]

Changes in methods may be more significant than the methods themselves, particularly when comparative data are presented. The postulate of consistency requires that financial reports should be comparable from period to period and that, when changes are made, the effect of the change should be disclosed. In most cases, this disclosure can be made appropriately in footnotes. However, if the effect of the change is to make a comparison of the data completely misleading, a footnote would be inadequate. In this case, the data for prior years should be computed on the new basis to permit proper comparisons.

Prior rights of creditors. The usual types of priorities, such as those granted to mortgage bondholders, can generally be explained succinctly in the balance sheet by a brief reference to the mortgage or to the specific property granted as security. But when the prior claims are unusual or more complex than normal, a footnote disclosure is necessary. Such contract provisions are relevant and material if knowledge of them would affect the decisions of other creditors or investors. Generally, it can be assumed that knowledge of these provisions would affect credit or investment decisions if the provisions affect the risk of other creditors or stockholders. These contract provisions may also be relevant if they restrict the freedom of management and the board of directors in the general operations of the firm or in the financing of expansions or replacements.

Contingent assets and contingent liabilities. As indicated in Chapter 17, all assets and liabilities should be estimated if at all possible and

---

[13] *AICPA Professional Standards,* Sec. 2043.

included in the balance sheet; and the effect, if any, on net income should be reflected in the income statement. Only if the most probable value of the asset or liability is likely to be zero or if the best estimate of current or future value is very likely to be highly erroneous and misleading should the asset or liability be omitted from the statements. But if the probable occurrence of a gain or loss resulting from the failure to recognize the asset or liability would be a significant element in decision making, the relevant facts should be disclosed in a footnote.

In the case of a pending lawsuit, the amount of the claim and any other relevant information, such as the decisions of lower courts or decisions in other similar cases, should be disclosed to permit the reader to form some judgment regarding the possible effect of the case. Expectations regarding the outcome of the case and the probable damages to be awarded by the court are not generally meaningful unless the reason for the estimate is also given.

Restrictions to dividend payments.   From a legal point of view, dividends can usually be paid to the extent of total retained earnings and, in many states, additional paid-in capital. But, as explained in Chapter 19, the classification of stockholders' equity in the balance sheet does not disclose the extent of the legality of dividends, nor does it show the intent of the board of directors regarding future dividend payments. However, according to traditional textbook treatments, legal, contractual, and managerial restrictions on dividends may be shown by means of appropriations of retained earnings. Since the stockholders' equity section of the balance sheet is classified primarily by its source, rather than by intended distribution, this use of appropriations is more confusing than enlightening.

A positive statement of the policy of the board of directors regarding dividend distributions would be helpful to investors and other users of financial reports. Most dividend payments by large corporations are related to current earnings, past earnings, past dividends, and available cash resources. There is generally no intent to pay dividends to the full amount legally permitted or even to the extent of retained earnings. Therefore, a footnote explanation of dividend restrictions based on retained earnings may not be very relevant to investors who can expect that future dividends will not likely exceed future earnings. However, if current earnings are at all restricted for dividend payments, these restrictions should be disclosed. Because of the nature of the information, all relevant restrictions of either retained earnings or current earnings can be disclosed appropriately in footnotes. When there are several restrictions that are not cumulative, the most restrictive requirement or contract may provide appropriate disclosure.

Rights of equity holders.   Some of the rights of equity holders are apparent in the balance sheet classifications and descriptions, and others can be disclosed by appropriate parenthetical notes in the statements. Significant changes in these rights to share in income and the net assets of the firm arising from transactions or events during the period should be disclosed specifically in the balance sheet or in footnotes, even though the results of the transactions are reflected in the related items in the balance sheet. Several types of transactions, however, are not immediately reflected in the equity accounts, but affect the future rights of equity holders. It is particularly important that these types of transactions and events be disclosed appropriately in the footnotes to the statements. However, *APB Opinion No. 10* recommends that liquidation preferences of preferred stock be disclosed in the aggregate in the balance sheet either parenthetically or "in short," rather than in footnotes.[14]

One of the common types of transactions affecting the future rights of stockholders is the granting of executive stock options. As discussed in Chapter 20, the conventional method of disclosing these contracts does not show the true effect on income or the true effect on the rights of equity holders. Possibly, because of the uncertainties involved, the true effect cannot be anticipated, and therefore cannot appropriately be shown by merely recording the transaction in the formal accounts. Footnotes showing the nature of the options, the requirements of the contract, and the possible effects on income and stockholders' equity should supplement whatever information can be presented in the formal statements.

Other types of disclosure affecting the rights of stockholders include the potential rights of holders of stock warrants, convertible debt, or convertible preferred stock. Footnote disclosures should include information regarding the period of conversion or exercise of warrants, the conversion price or exercise price, and other relevant terms of the contracts relating to these securities.

Executory contracts. Traditional accounting does not recognize assets or liabilities arising from executory contracts.[15] One of the reasons for the failure to record these assets and liabilities is that their valuations are not easily estimated. Another reason is that the effect on income arises from later events rather than from the signing of the contract. However, in most cases, because the contracts represent commitments for the future, a disclosure of them is very relevant for investment and other decisions relying on some prediction of future cash flows. If this disclosure cannot be made appropriately in the formal statements, the information should be disclosed in footnotes.

Included in the executory type of contracts are long-term leases and purchase commitments. Although the capitalization of these commitments and the inclusion of them among the assets and liabilities of the balance sheet may improve the statements, the nature of these contracts

---

[14] Ibid., Sec. 5515.

[15] See the discussion of long-term commitments, Chapter 14.

usually requires supplementary information also. In addition to the capitalized valuation, the reader of the report would probably be interested in knowing the terminal date of the contract, the amount of annual payment, the annual charge of expense, and other features. Therefore, footnote disclosure may be desirable to provide supplementary information regarding the long-term contracts; it should not be viewed only as an alternative to capitalization.

Supplementary statements and schedules

In order that financial data may be summarized and presented in a statement brief enough to be understandable by reasonably informed readers, some of the significant detailed information must be taken out of the statements and presented in supplementary schedules. These schedules are sometimes included among the footnotes and sometimes in a section following the statements and footnotes. In many current annual reports, the supplementary schedules are included in a separate section of the report called financial highlights or some similar section preceding the formal financial statements. By using a separate section in the report, the information presented there is placed in a position secondary to the statements and footnotes and, therefore, it is assumed to be of less importance than the information in the statements and footnotes. But this separation of information by its relative importance is necessary to make the statements readable and understandable.

Supplementary statements perform a different function than supplementary schedules. Generally they present additional information or information arranged in a different fashion, rather than just more detailed information. Since they are not necessarily included in the statements covered in the report of the independent accountant, they can be used as methods of developing and experimenting with new exhibits and statements. An example of a supplementary statement frequently recommended for inclusion in the financial reports is a statement disclosing the effect of price-level changes or specific price changes on the financial condition and financial operations of the enterprise.

The auditor's certificate

The audit certificate is not the place to disclose significant financial information regarding the firm. But it does serve as a method of disclosure for the following types of information: (1) a material effect from using accounting methods different from those generally accepted, (2) a material effect from changing from one generally accepted accounting method to another, and (3) a difference of opinion between the auditor and the client regarding the acceptability of one or more accounting methods used in the reports. The first two types of information should also be disclosed in the reports themselves. The duplication of disclosure is required to be sure that the reader is not misled regarding the comparability of the reports with those of other firms or the consistency with other periods.

The financial statements are the report of management and not of the auditor. However, the auditor (AICPA member) cannot express an opinion that the financial statements are in conformity with generally accepted accounting principles if they contain any departures from the opinions of the FASB and former bodies. If a departure is made on the basis that the statements would otherwise have been misleading, the auditor must state in the auditor's certificate the reasons for the departure and its effects.[16] When accounting theory is further developed as an evaluation tool, the terms *logical* or *sound* should be substituted for "generally accepted." General acceptance does not make the methods logical or logically derived from accounting postulates and principles.

The president's letter

The formal financial statements with the footnotes and supplementary schedules and statements and the auditor's certificate complete the accountant's financial report. All relevant and significant financial data should appear in this report. However, certain types of information can be presented directly by management in the form of the letter of the president or chairman of the board or in other sections of the annual report. This additional information should include (1) nonfinancial events and changes during the year that affect the operations of the firm, (2) expectations regarding the future of the industry and the economy and the role of the firm in these expectations, (3) plans for growth and changes in operations in the following period or periods, and (4) the amount and expected effect of current and anticipated capital expenditures and research effort.

The nonfinancial events and changes would include shifts in top management and major policies; significant technological improvements in the firm or industry; shifts in the demand for the product of the firm or changes in prices of either major factors of production or of the product; and such events as strikes, wars, political actions, and natural disasters that may have a material effect on future operations of the firm. If any of these nonfinancial events is likely to have a material effect on the valuation of assets or liabilities at the end of the period or on the income of future periods, it should be reported in the financial statements, rather than being left for management to report. But the effect of many of these items is difficult to evaluate, and even though they are taken into consideration in the financial statements, a more complete disclosure by management is desirable.

Expectations are more difficult to disclose and evaluate than nonfinancial events. Management has a tendency to present only optimistic expec-

---

[16] Rule 203 of the Rules of Conduct of the AICPA. See also *AICPA Professional Standards,* Section 520.

tations and, therefore, make them somewhat meaningless. A common expression found in these letters of the president is "We are confident that the prospects for profitable operations will continue to improve." Expressions such as this are too vague to be useful in making predictions regarding the future of the enterprise.

Summary of disclosure methods

Disclosure is a relative term, but it should be the basic objective of financial statements after determining for whom and for what purpose financial information is to be presented. In accordance with the basic postulates of accounting, the most relevant financial data should be summarized in quantitative terms and be presented in the formal statements to the extent possible and desirable and then in footnotes, supplementary schedules, and supplementary statements. Descriptive information should appear in the body of statements only in brief form. More detailed descriptions should appear in footnotes or elsewhere in the financial reports.

SELECTED ADDITIONAL READING

Nature of disclosure

Bedford, Norton M. *Extension in Accounting Disclosure.* Englewood Cliffs, N.J.: Prentice-Hall, 1973.

Benjamin, James J., and **Keith G. Stanga.** "Differences in Disclosure Needs of Major Users of Financial Statements." *Accounting and Business Research,* Summer 1977, pp. 187–92.

Buzby, Stephen L. "Nature of Adequate Disclosure." *Journal of Accountancy,* April 1974, pp. 38–47.

—————. "Selected Items of Information and Their Disclosure in Annual Reports." *Accounting Review,* July 1974, pp. 423–35.

—————. "Company Size, Listed versus Unlisted Stocks, and the Extent of Financial Disclosure." *Journal of Accounting Research,* Spring 1976, pp. 16–37.

Chandra, Gyan. "Study of the Consensus on Disclosure among Public Accountants and Security Analysts." *Accounting Review,* October 1974, pp. 733–42.

Garrett, R. "Disclosure Rules and Annual Reports: Present Impact." *Financial Executive,* April 1975.

Nelson, Carl L. "Case for Accounting Disclosure." *CA Magazine,* March 1975, pp. 35–38.

Pastena, Victor, and **Joshua Ronen.** "Some Hypotheses on the Pattern of Management's Informal Disclosures." *Journal of Accounting Research,* Autumn 1979, pp. 550–64.

Pastena, Victor. "Some Evidence on the SEC's System of Continuous Disclosure." *Accounting Review,* October 1979, pp. 776–83.

Sommer, A. A., Jr. "The Limit of Disclosure." *Financial Executive,* October 1975.

Spicer, Barry H. "Investors, Corporate Social Performance and Information Disclosure: An Empirical Study." *Accounting Review,* January 1978, pp. 94–111.

Disclosure of company segments

Ajinkya, Bipin B. "An Empirical Evaluation of Line-of-Business Reporting." *Journal of Accounting Research,* Autumn 1980, pp. 343–61.

Barefield, Russell M., and **Eugene E. Comiskey.** "Segmental Financial Disclosure by Diversified Firms and Security Prices: A Comment." *Accounting Review,* October 1975, pp. 818–21; and "Reply," pp. 822–25.

Collins, Daniel W., and **Richard R. Simonds.** "SEC Line-of-Business Disclosure and Market Risk Adjustments." *Journal of Accounting Research,* Autumn 1979, pp. 353–83.

Emmanuel, C. R., and **S. J. Gray.** "Segmental Disclosures and the Segment Identification Problem." *Accounting and Business Research,* Winter 1977, pp. 37–50.

Kochanek, Richard Frank. "Segmental Financial Disclosure by Diversified Firms and Security Prices." *Accounting Review,* April 1974, pp. 245–58.

Ortman, Richard P. "The Effects on Investment Analysis of Alternative Reporting Procedures for Diversified Firms." *Accounting Review,* April 1975, pp. 298–304.

Disclosure of forecast data

Basi, Bart A.; Kenneth J. Carey; and **Richard D. Twark.** "A Comparison of the Accuracy of Corporate and Security Analysts' Forecasts of Earnings." *Accounting Review,* April 1976, pp. 244–54.

Beaver, William; Roger Clarke; and **William F. Wright.** "The Association between Unsystematic Security Returns and the Magnitude of Earnings Forecast Errors." *Journal of Accounting Research,* Autumn 1979, pp. 316–40.

Imhoff, Eugene A., Jr. "The Representativeness of Management Earnings Forecasts." *Accounting Review,* October 1978, pp. 836–50.

Jaggi, Bikki. "A Note on the Information Content of Corporate Annual Earnings Forecasts." *Accounting Review,* October 1978, pp. 961–67.

―――――. "Further Evidence on the Accuracy of Management Forecasts vis-à-vis Analysts' Forecasts." *Accounting Review,* January 1980, pp. 96–101.

Nichols, Donald R., and **S. Michael Groomer.** "A Study of the Relative Accuracy of Executives' Estimates of Earnings," *Abacus,* December 1979, pp. 113–27.

Nichols, Donald R.; Jeffrey J. Tsay; and **Paula D. Larkin,** "Investor Trading Responses to Differing Characteristics of Voluntarily Disclosed Earnings Forecasts." *Accounting Review,* April 1979, pp. 376–82.

Penman, Stephen H. "A Empirical Investigation of the Voluntary Disclosure of Corporate Earnings Forecasts." *Journal of Accounting Research,* Spring 1980, pp. 132–60.

Ruland, William. "The Accuracy of Forecasts by Management and by Financial Analysts." *Accounting Review,* April 1978, pp. 430–47.

APPENDIX

SELECTED CPA EXAMINATION QUESTIONS*

CHAPTER 1: INTRODUCTION AND METHODOLOGY OF ACCOUNTING THEORY

Deductive reasoning

Question 1–1

The following four statements have been taken directly or with some modification from the accounting literature. All of them either are taken out of context, involve circular reasoning and/or contain one or more fallacies, half-truths, erroneous comments, conclusions or inconsistencies (internally or with generally accepted principles or practices).

Statement 1

Accounting is a service activity. Its function is to provide quantitative financial information that is intended to be useful in making economic decisions about and for economic entities. Thus the accounting function might be viewed primarily as being a tool or device for providing quantitative financial information to management to facilitate decision making.

Statement 2

Financial statements that were developed in accordance with generally accepted accounting principles, which apply the conservatism convention, can be free from bias (or can give a presentation that is fair with respect to continuing and prospective stockholders as well as to retiring stockholders).

Statement 3

When a company changes from the LIFO to the FIFO method of determining the cost of ending inventories and this change results in a $1 million increase both in income after taxes and in income taxes for the year of change, the increase would stem from the elimination of LIFO reserves established in prior years.

* Material from the Uniform CPA Examinations, copyright © 1965, 1966, 1967, 1968, 1969, 1970, 1971, 1972, 1973, 1974, 1975, 1976, 1977, 1978, 1979, 1980, 1981 by the American Institute of Certified Public Accountants, Inc. is reprinted (or adapted) with permission.

Statement 4

If the value of an enterprise were to be determined by the method that computes the sum of the present values of the marginal (or incremental) expected net receipts of individual tangible and intangible assets, the resulting valuation would tend to be less than if the value of the entire enterprise had been determined in another way, such as by computing the present value of total expected net receipts for the entire enterprise (i.e., the resulting valuation of parts would sum to an amount that was less than that for the whole). This would be true even if the same pattern of interest or discount rates was used for both valuations.

Required:

Evaluate each of the above numbered statements on a separate appropriately numbered answer sheet (or sheets) as follows:

a. List the fallacies, half-truths, circular reasoning, erroneous comments, or conclusions and/or inconsistencies; and

b. Explain by what authority and/or on what basis each item listed in (*a*) above can be considered to be fallacious, circular, inconsistent, a half-truth or an erroneous comment or conclusion. If the statement or a portion of it is merely out of context, indicate the context(s) in which the statement would be correct.

Sociological approach

Question 1–2

Part a. Elmo Company operates several plants at which limestone is processed into quicklime and hydrated lime. The Bland Plant, where most of the equipment was installed many years ago, continually deposits a dusty white substance over the surrounding countryside. Citing the unsanitary condition of the neighboring community of Adeltown, the pollution of the Adel River, and the high incidence of lung disease among workers at Bland, the state's Pollution Control Agency has ordered the installation of air pollution control equipment. Also, the Agency has assessed a substantial penalty, which will be used to clean up Adeltown. After considering the costs involved (which could not have been reasonably estimated before the Agency's action), Elmo decides to comply with the Agency's orders, the alternative being to cease operations at Bland at the end of the current fiscal year. The officers of Elmo agree that the air pollution control equipment should be capitalized and depreciated over its useful life, but they disagree over the period(s) to which the penalty should be charged.

Required:

Discuss the conceptual merits and reporting requirements of accounting for the penalty as a
(1) Charge to the current period.
(2) Correction of prior periods.
(3) Capitalizable item to be amortized over future periods.

Part b. Elmo's Davis Plant causes approximately as much pollution as Bland. Davis, however, is located in another state, where there is little likelihood of governmental regulation, and Elmo has no plans for pollution control at this plant. One of Elmo's officers, Mr. Pearce, says that uncontrolled pollution at Davis constitutes a very real cost to society, which is not recorded anywhere under current practice. He suggests that this "social cost" of the Davis Plant be included annually in Elmo's income statement. Further, he suggests that measurement of this cost is easily obtainable by reference to the depreciation on Bland's pollution control equipment.

Required:

(1) Is Mr. Pearce necessarily correct in stating that costs associated with Davis' pollution are entirely unrecorded? Explain.
(2) Evaluate Mr. Pearce's proposed method of measuring the annual "social cost" of Davis' pollution.
(3) Discuss the merit of Mr. Pearce's suggestion that a "social cost" be recognized by a business enterprise.

CHAPTER 3: THE NORMATIVE-DEDUCTIVE APPROACH—CONCEPTS, MEASUREMENTS, AND STRUCTURE

Question 3–1

Three *independent, unrelated* statements follow regarding financial accounting. Each statement contains some unsound reasoning.

Statement 1

One function of financial accounting is to measure a company's net earnings for a given period of time. An earnings statement will measure a company's true net earnings if it is prepared in accordance with generally accepted accounting principles. Other financial statements are basically unrelated to the earnings statement. Net earnings would be measured as the difference between revenues and expenses. Revenues are an inflow of cash to the enterprise and should be realized when recognized. This may be accomplished by using the sales basis or the production basis. Expenses should be matched with revenues to measure net earnings. Usually, variable expenses are assigned to the product, and fixed expenses are assigned to the period.

Statement 2

One function of financial accounting is to accurately present a company's financial position at a given point in time. This is done with a statement of financial position, which is prepared using historical-cost valuations for all assets and liabilities except inventories. Inventories are stated at first-in, first-out (FIFO), last-in, first-out (LIFO), or average valuations. The statement of financial position must be prepared on a consistent basis with prior years' statements.

In addition to reflecting assets, liabilities, and stockholders' equity, a statement of financial position should, in a separate section, reflect a company's reserves. The section should include three different types of reserves: depreciation reserves, product warranty reserves, and retained earnings reserves. All three of these types of reserves are established by a credit to the reserve account.

Statement 3

Financial statement analysis involves using ratios to test past performance of a given company. Past performance is compared to a predetermined standard, and the company is evaluated accordingly. One such ratio is the current ratio, which is computed as current assets divided by current liabilities, or as monetary assets divided by monetary liabililities. A current ratio of 2 to 1 is considered good for companies, but the higher the ratio, the better the company's financial position is assumed to be. The current ratio is dynamic because it helps to measure fund flows.

Required:

Identify the areas that are not in accordance with generally accepted accounting principles or are untrue with respect to the financial statement analysis discussed in each of the statements and explain why the reasoning is incorrect. Complete your identification and explanation of each statement before proceeding to the next statement.

Question 3-2

Financial accounting usually emphasizes the economic substance of events even though the legal form may differ and suggest different treatment. For example, under accrual accounting, expenses are recognized when they are incurred (substance) rather than when cash is disbursed (form).

Although the feature of substance over form exists in most generally accepted accounting principles and practices, there are times when form prevails over substance.

Required:

For each of the following topics, discuss the underlying theory in terms of both substance and form, i.e., substance over form and possibly form over substance in some cases. Each topic should be discussed independently.

    a.   Consolidated financial statements.

    b.   Equity method of accounting for investments in common stock.

    c.   Leases (including sale and leaseback).

    d.   Earnings per share (complex capital structure).

CHAPTER 7: INCOME CONCEPTS FOR FINANCIAL REPORTING

Concepts and presentation of income

Question 7-1

The accounting profession, in the development and implementation of accounting principles, seeks to increase the usefulness of financial statements to their readers.

Required:

 a. The FASB requires including in net income all items of profit and loss recognized in the period except prior period adjustments and capital transactions involving equity accounts, and with extraordinary items shown separately as an element of net income of the period.

 (1) List the *advantages* of the recommendation.

 (2) List the *disadvantages* of the recommendation.

 b. The recommendation specified in requirement *a* above is based on the premise that capital transactions should be distinguished from income.

 (1) Why should capital transactions be distinguished from income?

 (2) In what way does the income expected to be generated by an asset relate to its acquisition cost and valuation in financial statements? Discuss.

Prior period adjustments

Question 7–2

The following characteristics relate to prior period adjustments:

 a. They can be specifically identified with business activity of a prior period.

 b. They depend primarily on determinations by persons other than management.

 c. They could not have been reasonably estimated in a prior period.

Required:

Discuss the significance of each of the above characteristics.

Question 7–3

Discuss briefly why each of the following would not be accounted for as a prior period adjustment.

 a. Change in the depreciable lives of fixed assets.

 b. Change in the method of computing depreciation of fixed assets.

 c. Change in inventory cost flow assumption from first-in, first-out to weighted average.

Extraordinary items

Question 7–4

In order to be classified as an extraordinary item in the income statement, an event or transaction should be unusual in nature, infrequent, and material.

Required:

 a. Discuss briefly how an unusual event not meeting the current criteria for an extraordinary item should be disclosed in the financial statements.

 b. Discuss briefly the conditions under which a flood damage would be considered to be an extraordinary item for financial reporting purposes.

   c. Explain briefly why each of the following would not normally be considered an extraordinary item for reporting results of operations:
      (1) Gains or losses on disposal of a segment of a business.
      (2) Adjustments of accruals on long-term contracts.
      (3) Gains or losses from a fire.

Net income to whom?

Question 7–5

   Income measurement can be divided into different income concepts classified by income recipients. The following income concepts are tailored to the listed categories of income recipients.

Income concepts	Income recipients
1. Net income to residual equity holders.	Common stockholders.
2. Net income to investors.	Stockholders and long-term debt holders.
3. Value-added income.	All employees, stockholders, governments, and some creditors.

Required:

   For each of the concepts listed above, explain in separately numbered paragraphs what major categories of revenue, expense, and other items would be included in the determination of income.

CHAPTER 8: REVENUES AND EXPENSES, GAINS, AND LOSSES

Revenue reporting

Question 8–1

   The earning of revenue by a business enterprise is recognized for accounting purposes when the transaction is recorded. In some situations, revenue is recognized approximately as it is earned in the economic sense. In other situations, however, accountants have developed guidelines for recognizing revenue by other criteria; such as, at the point of sale.

Required (ignore income taxes):

   a. Explain and justify why revenue is often recognized as earned at time of sale.

   b. Explain in what situations it would be appropriate to recognize revenue as the productive activity takes place.

c. At what times, other than those included in *a* and *b* above, may it be appropriate to recognize revenue? Explain.

Question 8–2

Bonanza Trading Stamps, Inc., was formed early this year to sell trading stamps throughout the Southwest to retailers who distribute the stamps gratuitously to their customers. Books for accumulating the stamps and catalogs illustrating the merchandise for which the stamps may be exchanged are given free to retailers for distribution to stamp recipients. Centers with inventories of merchandise premiums have been established for redemption of the stamps. Retailers may not return unused stamps to Bonanza.

The following schedule expresses Bonanza's expectations as to percentages of a normal month's activity which will be attained. For this purpose, a normal month's activity is defined as the level of operations expected when expansion of activities ceases or tapers off to a stable rate. The company expects that this level will be attained in the third year and that sales of stamps will average $2 million per month throughout the third year.

Month	Actual stamp sales (percent)	Merchandise premium purchases (percent)	Stamp redemptions (percent)
6th	30	40	10
12th	60	60	45
18th	80	80	70
24th	90	90	80
30th	100	100	95

Bonanza plans to adopt an annual closing date at the end of each 12 months of operations.

Required:

a. Discuss the factors to be considered in determining when revenue should be recognized in measuring the income of a business enterprise.

b. Discuss the accounting alternatives that should be considered by Bonanza Trading Stamps, Inc., for the recognition of its revenues and related expenses.

c. For each accounting alternative discussed in *b* above, give balance sheet accounts that should be used and indicate how each should be classified.

Question 8–3

Southern Fried Shrimp sells franchises to independent operators throughout the Southeastern part of the United States. The contract with the franchise includes the following provisions:

The franchisee is charged an initial fee of $25,000. Of this amount $5,000 is payable when the agreement is signed and a $4,000 noninterest bearing note is payable at the end of each of the five subsequent years.

All of the initial franchise fee collected by Southern Fried Shrimp is to be refunded and the remaining obligation canceled if, for any reason, the franchisee fails to open his franchise.

In return for the initial franchise fee Southern Fried Shrimp agrees to (1) assist the franchisee in selecting the location for her business, (2) negotiate the lease for the land, (3) obtain financing and assist with building design, (4) supervise construction, (5) establish accounting and tax records, and (6) provide expert advice over a five-year period relating to such matters as employee and management training, quality control, and promotion.

In addition to the initial franchise fee the franchisee is required to pay to Southern Fried Shrimp a monthly fee of 2 percent of sales for menu planning, recipe innovations, and the privilege of purchasing ingredients from Southern Fried Shrimp at or below prevailing prices.

Management of Southern Fried Shrimp estimates that the value of the services rendered to the franchisee at the time the contract is signed amounts to at least $5,000. All franchisees to date have opened their locations at the scheduled time, and none has defaulted on any of the notes receivable.

The credit ratings of all franchisees would entitle them to borrow at the current interest rate of 10 percent. The present value of an ordinary annuity of five annual receipts of $4,000 each discounted at 10 percent is $15,163.

Required:

a. Discuss the alternatives that Southern Fried Shrimp might use to account for the initial franchise fee, evaluate each by applying generally accepted accounting principles to this situation, and give illustrative entries for each alternative.

b. Given the nature of Southern Fried Shrimp's agreement with its franchisees, when should revenue be recognized? Discuss the question of revenue recognition for both the initial franchise fee and the additional monthly fee of 2 percent of sales and give illustrative entries for both types of revenue.

c. Assuming that Southern Fried Shrimp sells some franchises for $35,000 which includes a charge of $10,000 for the rental of equipment for its useful life of 10 years, that $15,000 of the fee is payable immediately and the balance on noninterest bearing notes at $4,000 per year, that no portion of the $10,000 rental payment is refundable in case the franchisee goes out of business, and that title to the equipment remains with the franchisor; what would be the preferable method of accounting for the rental portion of the initial franchise fee? Explain.

Question 8–4

Generally accepted accounting principles require the use of accruals and deferrals in the determination of income.

Required:

a. How does accrual accounting affect the determination of income? Include in your discussion what constitutes an accrual and a deferral, and give appropriate examples of each.

b. Contrast accrual accounting with cash accounting.

Question 8–5

Income determination for long-term construction contracts presents special problems because the construction work often extends over two or more accounting periods. The two methods commonly followed are the percentage-of-completion method and the completed-contract method.

Required:

Evaluate the use of the percentage-of-completion method for income determination purposes for long-term construction contracts. Discuss only theoretical arguments.

Question 8–6

In accounting for long-term contracts (those taking longer than one year to complete), the two methods commonly followed are the percentage-of-completion method and the completed-contract method.

Required:

a. Discuss how earnings on long-term contracts are recognized and computed under these two methods.

b. Under what circumstances is it preferable to use one method over the other?

c. Why is earnings recognition as measured by interim billings not generally accepted for long-term contracts?

d. How are job costs and interim billings reflected on the balance sheet under the percentage-of-completion method and the completed-contract method?

Expenses, costs, and losses

Question 8–7

An accountant must be familiar with the concepts involved in determining earnings of a business entity. The amount of earnings reported for a business entity is dependent on the proper recognition, in general, of revenue and expense for a given time period. In some situations, costs are recognized as expenses at the time of product sale; in other situations, guidelines have been developed for recognizing costs as expenses or losses by other criteria.

Required:

a. Explain the rationale for recognizing costs as expenses at the time of product sale.

b. What is the rationale underlying the appropriateness of treating costs as expenses of a period instead of assigning the costs to an asset? Explain.

c. In what general circumstances would it be appropriate to treat a cost as an asset instead of as an expense? Explain.

d. Some expenses are assigned to specific accounting periods on the basis of systematic and rational allocation of asset cost. Explain the underlying rationale for recognizing expenses on the basis of systematic and rational allocation of asset cost.

e. Identify the necessary conditions in which it would be appropriate to treat a cost as a loss.

Question 8–8

Kwik-Bild Corporation sells and erects shell houses. These are frame structures that are completely finished on the outside, but are unfinished on the inside except for flooring, partition studding, and ceiling joists. Shell houses are sold chiefly to customers who are handy with tools and who have time to do the interior wiring, plumbing, wall completion and finishing, and other work necessary to make the shell houses liveable dwellings.

Kwik-Bild buys shell houses from a manufacturer in unassembled packages consisting of all lumber, roofing, doors, windows, and similar materials necessary to complete a shell house. Upon commencing operations in a new area, Kwik-Bild buys or leases land as a site for its local warehouse, field office, and display houses. Sample display houses are erected at a total cost of from $3,000 to $7,000, including the cost of the unassembled packages. The chief element of cost of the display houses is the unassembled packages, since erection is a short, low-cost operation. Old sample models are torn down or altered into new models every three to seven years. Sample display houses have little salvage value because dismantling and moving costs amount to nearly as much as the cost of an unassembled package.

Required:

a. A choice must be made between (1) expensing the costs of sample display houses in the period in which the expenditure is made and (2) spreading the costs over more than one period. Discuss the advantages of each method.

b. Would it be preferable to amortize the cost of display houses on the basis of (1) the passage of time or (2) the number of shell houses sold? Explain.

CHAPTER 9: REPORTING THE EFFECTS OF PRICE CHANGES

Restatements for general price-level changes

Question 9–1

Barden Corp., a manufacturer with large investments in plant and equipment, began operations in 1938. The company's history has been one of expansion in sales, production, and physical facilities. Recently, some concern has been expressed that the conventional financial statements do not provide sufficient information for decisions by investors. After consideration of proposals for various types of supplementary financial statements to be included in the 1982 annual report, management has decided to present a balance sheet as of December 31, 1982 and a statement of income and retained earnings for 1982, both restated for changes in the general price level.

Required:

a. On what basis can it be contended that Barden's conventional statements should be restated for changes in the general price level?

b. Distinguish between financial statements restated for general price-level changes and current-value financial statements.

c. Distinguish between *monetary* and *nonmonetary assets and liabilities,* as the terms are used in general price-level accounting. Give examples of each.

d. Outline the procedures Barden should follow in preparing the proposed supplementary statements.

e. Indicate the major similarities and differences between the proposed supplementary statements and the corresponding conventional statements.

f. Assuming that in the future Barden will want to present comparative supplementary statements, can the 1982 supplementary statements be presented in 1983 without adjustment? Explain.

Question 9–2

Proponents of price-level restatement of financial statements state that a basic weakness of financial statements not adjusted for price-level changes is that they are made up of "mixed dollars."

Required:

a. What is meant by the term *mixed dollars,* and why is this a weakness of unadjusted financial statements?

b. Explain how financial statements restated for price-level changes eliminate this weakness. Use property, plant, and equipment as your example in this discussion.

Purchasing-power gains and losses

Question 9–3

Although cash generally is regarded as the simplest of all assets to account for, certain complexities can arise for both domestic and multinational companies.

Required:

a. Unrealized and/or realized gains or losses can arise in connection with cash. Excluding consideration of price-level changes, indicate the nature of such gains or losses and the context in which they can arise in relation to cash.

b. (1) How might it be maintained that a gain or a loss is incurred by holding a constant balance of cash through a period of price-level change?

(2) Identify and give a justification for the typical accounting treatment accorded these gains or losses.

Question 9–4

Asset measurement is a concept that involves the valuation or pricing of the future service of an asset. Receivables are particular assets that represent future claims to fixed amounts of monies.

Required:

a. Discuss how the asset measurement concept is applied to receivables (short term and long term).

b. Describe how a company that has a significant amount of receivables during an inflationary period sustains a "general price-level loss." Include in your answer an example of how such a "loss" would be computed when a $100,000 receivable exists at the beginning and end of a year that had an inflation rate of 10 percent.

Question 9–5

Price-level adjusted financial statements are prepared in an effort to eliminate the effects of inflation or deflation. An integral part of determining restated amounts and applicable gain or loss from restatement is the segregation of all assets and liabilities into monetary and nonmonetary classifications. One reason for this classification is that price-level gains and losses for monetary items are currently matched against earnings.

Required:

What are the factors that determine whether an asset or liability is classified as monetary or nonmonetary? Include in your response the justification for recognizing gains and losses from monetary items and not for nonmonetary items.

Current costs

Question 9–6

Advocates of current value accounting propose several methods for determining the valuation of assets to approximate current values. Two of the methods proposed are replacement cost and present value of future cash flows.

Required:

Describe each of the two methods cited above and discuss the pros and cons of the various procedures used to arrive at the valuation for each method.

Current costs and general price-level restatements

Question 9–7

The financial statements of a business entity could be prepared by using historical cost or current value as a basis. In addition, the basis could be stated in terms of unadjusted dollars or dollars restated for changes in purchasing power. The various permutations of these two separate and distinct areas are shown in the following matrix:

	Unadjusted dollars	Dollars restated for changes in purchasing power
Historical cost	1	2
Current value	3	4

Block number 1 of the matrix represents the traditional method of accounting for transactions in accounting today, wherein the absolute (unadjusted) amount of dollars given up or received is recorded for the asset or liability obtained *(relationship between resources)*. Amounts recorded in the method described in block number 1 reflect the original cost of the asset or liability and do not give effect to any change in value of the unit of measure *(standard of comparison)*. This method assumes the validity of the accounting concepts of going concern and stable monetary unit. Any gain or loss (including holding and purchasing power gains or losses) resulting from the sale or satisfaction of amounts recorded under this method is deferred in its entirety until sale or satisfaction.

Required:

For each of the remaining matrix blocks (2, 3, and 4) respond to the following questions. *Limit your discussion to nonmonetary assets only.*

Complete your discussion for *each matrix block* before proceeding to the discussion of the next matrix block.

a.   How will this method of recording assets affect the relationship between resources and the standard of comparison?

b.   What is the theoretic justification for using each method?

c.   How will each method of asset valuation affect the recognition of gain or loss during the life of the asset and ultimately from the sale or abandonment of the asset? Your response should include a discussion of the timing and magnitude of the gain or loss and conceptual reasons for any difference from the gain or loss computed using the traditional method.

Question 9–8

Financial reporting should provide information to help investors, creditors, and other users of financial statements. *Statement of Financial Accounting Standards No. 33* requires large public enterprises to disclose certain supplementary information.

Required:

a.   Describe the historical cost/constant dollar method of accounting. Include in your discussion how historical cost amounts are used to make historical cost/constant dollar measurements.

b.   Describe the principal advantage of the historical cost/constant dollar method of accounting over the historical-cost method of accounting.

c.   Describe the current-cost method of accounting.

   d. Why would depreciation expense for a given year differ using the current cost method of accounting instead of the historical cost method of accounting? Include in your discussion whether depreciation expense is likely to be higher or lower using the current-cost method of accounting instead of the historical-cost method of accounting in a period of rising prices, and why.

Foreign currency translations

Question 9–9

   The Financial Accounting Standards Board discusses certain terminology essential to both the translation of foreign currency transactions and foreign currency financial statements. Included in the discussion is a definition of and distinction between the terms *measure* and *denominate*.

Required:

   Define the terms *measure* and *denominate* as discussed by the Financial Accounting Standards Board, and give a brief example that demonstrates the distinction between accounts measured in a particular currency and accounts denominated in a particular currency.

Question 9–10

   There are several methods of translating foreign currency transactions or accounts reflected in foreign currency financial statements. Among these methods are current/noncurrent, monetary/nonmonetary, current rate, and the temporal method.

Required:

   a. Define the temporal method of translating foreign currency financial statements.

   b. Explain why the temporal method and the current rate method would result in significantly different amounts of translations gains and losses.

   c. Explain why translation gains and losses are deferred under the net investment approach.

CHAPTER 10: CASH AND FUNDS FLOWS

Funds statement and concepts

Question 10–1

   There have been considerable discussion and research in recent years concerning the reporting of changes in financial position (sources and applications of funds). *Accounting Principles Board Opinion No. 19* concluded

> . . . that the statement summarizing changes in financial position should be based on a broad concept embracing all changes in financial position and that the title of the statement should reflect this broad concept. The Board therefore recommends that the title be Statement of Changes in Financial Position.

Required:

a.   What are the two common meanings of *funds* as used when preparing the statement of changes in financial position? Explain.

b.   What is meant by ". . . a broad concept embracing all changes in financial position . . ." as used by the Accounting Principles Board in its *Opinion No. 19?* Explain.

Question 10–2

The following statement of source and application of funds was prepared by the controller of the Clovis Company. The controller indicated that this statement was prepared under the "all financial resources" concept of funds, which is the broadest concept of funds and includes all transactions providing or requiring funds.

Required:

a.   Why is it considered desirable to present a statement of source and application of funds in financial reports?

b.   Define and discuss the relative merits of the following three concepts used in funds flow analysis in terms of their measurement accuracy and freedom from manipulation (window dressing) in one accounting period:
(1)   Cash concept of funds.
(2)   Net monetary assets (quick assets) concept of funds.
(3)   Working capital concept of funds.

Question 10–3

The statement of changes in financial position is normally a required basic financial statement for each period for which an earnings statement is presented. The reporting entity has flexibility in form, content, and terminology of this statement to meet the objectives of differing circumstances. For example, the concept of funds may be interpreted to mean, among other things, cash or working capital. However, the statement should be prepared based on the "all financial resources" concept.

Required:

a.   What is the all-financial-resources concept?

b.   What are two types of financial transactions that would be disclosed under the all-financial-resources concept that would not be disclosed without this concept?

c.   What effect, if any, would each of the following seven items have upon the preparation of a statement of changes in financial position prepared in accordance with generally accepted accounting principles using the cash concept of funds?
(1)   Accounts receivable—trade.
(2)   Inventory.
(3)   Depreciation.
(4)   Deferred income tax credit from interperiod allocation.
(5)   Issuance of long-term debt in payment for a building.
(6)   Payoff of current portion of debt.
(7)   Sale of a fixed asset resulting in a loss.

Cash flows

Question 10–4

Mr. Erik, owner of Erik's Retail Hardware, states that he computes income on a cash basis. At the end of each year he takes a physical inventory and computes the cost of all merchandise on hand. To this he adds the ending balance of accounts receivable because he considers this to be a part of inventory on the cash basis. Using this logic he deducts from this total the ending balance of accounts payable for merchandise to arrive at what he calls inventory (net).

The following information has been taken from his cash basis income statements for the years indicated:

	1981	1980	1979
Cash received	$173,000	$164,000	$150,000
Cost of goods sold:			
Inventory (net),			
January 1	$ 8,000	11,000	3,000
Total purchases	109,000	102,000	95,000
Goods available			
for sale	117,000	113,000	98,000
Inventory (net),			
December 31	1,000	8,000	11,000
Cost of goods sold	116,000	105,000	87,000
Gross margin	$ 57,000	$ 59,000	$ 63,000

Additional information is as follows for the years indicated:

	1981	1980	1979
Cash sales	$151,000	$147,000	$141,000
Credit sales	24,000	18,000	14,000
Accounts receivable,			
December 31	8,000	6,000	5,000
Accounts payable for			
merchandise,			
December 31	33,000	20,000	13,000

Required:

a. Without reference to the specific situation described above, discuss the various cash basis concepts of revenue and income and indicate the conceptual merits of each.

b. (1) Is the gross margin for Erik's Retail Hardware being computed on a cash basis? Evaluate and explain the approach used with illustrative computations of the cash-basis gross margin for 1980.

(2) Explain why the gross margin for Erik's Retail Hardware shows a decrease while sales and cash receipts are increasing.

CHAPTER 11: ASSETS AND THEIR MEASUREMENT

Valuation bases

Question 11-1

You have been engaged to examine the financial statements of Custer Corporation for the year ending December 31, 1982. Custer Corporation was organized in January 1982 by Messrs. Moses and Price, original owners of options to acquire for $350,000 oil leases on 5,000 acres of land. They contemplated that first the oil leases would be acquired by the corporation, and subsequently 180,000 shares of the corporation's common stock would be sold to the public at $6 per share. In February 1982 they exchanged their options, $150,000 cash, and $50,000 of other assets for 75,000 shares of common stock of the corporation. The corporation's board of directors appraised the leases at $600,000, based on other acreage recently leased in the same area. The options were therefore recorded at $250,000 ($600,000—$350,000 option price).

The options were exercised by the corporation in March 1982 before the sale of common stock to the public in April 1982. Leases on approximately 500 acres of land were abandoned as worthless during the year.

Required:

   a.   Why is the valuation of assets acquired by a corporation in exchange for its own common stock sometimes difficult?

   b.   (1)   What reasoning might Custer Corporation use to support valuing the leases at $600,000, the amount of the appraisal by the board of directors?

   (2)   Assuming the board's appraisal was sincere, what steps might Custer Corporation have taken to strengthen its position on using the $600,000 value and to provide additional information if questions are raised about possible overvaluation of the leases?

   c.   Discuss the propriety of charging one tenth of the recorded value of the leases against income at December 31, 1968 because leases on 500 acres of land were abandoned during the year.

Question 11-2

A small but growing road building contractor would like to bid on a contract to rebuild and surface 10.6 miles of road. The job is considerably larger than any he has attempted in the past; and if he wins the contract, he estimates that he will need a $100,000 line of credit for working capital.

The contractor's most recent statement of financial position shows that he has a net worth of $170,000, of which $110,000 represents the book value of road building equipment. Most of the equipment was acquired a few years ago at a bankruptcy sale. The equipment has a current fair value several times as great at book value.

The contractor knows that his bank will not give him a $100,000 line of credit on the basis of a position statement that shows his net worth at $170,000. He wants to adjust his accounting records to show the current fair value of the equipment and to prepare a revised position statement.

Required:

a.   List the factors that, alone or in combination, may have caused the difference between the book value and the current fair value of the equipment.

b.   The current fair value of fixed assets may be estimated by using one of the following methods:
(1)   Reproduction cost.
(2)   Replacement cost.
(3)   Capitalization of earnings.
Describe each of the three methods of estimating the current fair value of fixed assets and discuss the possible limitations of each.

c.   Discuss the propriety of adjusting the accounting records to show the fair value of the equipment and preparing a revised position statement. Suggest a possible alternative approach. Your answer should take into consideration the factors that may have caused the difference between the book value and the current fair value of the equipment.

Historical cost and current cost

Question 11–3

Valuation of assets is an important topic in accounting theory. Suggested valuation methods include the following:

Historical cost (past purchase prices).
Historical cost adjusted to reflect general price-level changes.
Discounted cash flow (future exchange prices).
Market price (current selling prices).
Replacement cost (current purchase prices).

Required:

a.   Why is the valuation of assets a significant issue?

b.   Explain the basic theory underlying *each* of the valuation methods cited above. *Do not discuss advantages and disadvantages of each method.*

Question 11–4

When discussing asset valuation, the following valuation bases are sometimes mentioned: replacement cost, exit value, and discounted cash flow. Explain the advantages and disadvantages of each of these bases as a measure of current value.

Historical cost and current cost

Question 11–5

Financial statements are tools for the communication of quantifiable economic information to readers, who use them as one of the factors in making a variety of management and investment decisions and judgments. To fulfill this function accounting data should be quantifiable and should also be relevant to the kinds of judgments and decisions made. They should be verifiable and free from personal bias. There are many who believe that for some purposes current cost is a more useful measure than historical cost and recommend that dual statements be prepared showing both historical and current costs.

Required:

a. Discuss the ways in which historical costs and current costs conform to the standards of verifiability and freedom from bias.

b. Describe briefly how the current cost of the following assets might be determined.
(1) Inventory.
(2) Investments in marketable securities.
(3) Equipment and machinery.
(4) Natural resources.
(5) Goodwill.

CHAPTER 12: CURRENT ASSETS AND CURRENT LIABILITIES

Nature of current assets and current liabilities

Question 12–1

One of your corporate clients operates a full-line department store that is dominant in its market area, is easily accessible to public and private transportation, has adequate parking facilities, and is near a large permanent military base. The president of the company seeks your advice on a recently received proposal.

A local bank in which your client has an account recently affiliated with a popular national credit-card plan and has extended an invitation to your client to participate in the plan. Under the plan affiliated banks mail credit-card applications to persons in the community who have good credit ratings regardless of whether they are bank customers. A recipient who wishes to receive a credit card completes, signs, and returns the application and installment credit agreement. Holders of cards thus activated may charge merchandise or services at any participating establishment throughout the nation.

The bank guarantees payment to all participating merchants on all presented invoices that have been properly completed, signed, and validated with the impression of credit cards that have not expired or been reported stolen or otherwise canceled. Local merchants including your client may turn in all card-validated sales tickets or invoices to their affiliated local bank at any time and receive immediate credits to their checking accounts of 96.5 percent of the face value of the invoices. If card users pay the bank in full within 30 days for amounts billed, the bank levies no added charges against them. If they elect to make their payments under a deferred payment plan, the bank adds a service charge, which amounts to an effective interest rate of 18 percent per annum on unpaid balances.

Only the local affiliated banks and the franchiser of the credit-card plan share in these revenues.

The 18 percent service charge approximates what your client has been billing customers who pay their accounts over an extended period on a schedule similar to that offered under the credit-card plans. Participation in the plan does not prevent your client from continuing to carry on its credit business as in the past.

Required:

a. What are (1) the positive and (2) the negative financial—and accounting—related factors that your client should consider in deciding whether to participate in the described credit-card plan? Explain.

b. If your client does participate in the plan, which income statement and balance sheet accounts may change materially as the plan becomes fully operative? (Such factors as market position, sales mix, prices, markup, etc., are expected to remain about the same as in the past.) Explain.

Investments in marketable equity securities

Question 12–2

The Financial Accounting Standards Board issued its *Statement No. 12* to clarify accounting methods and procedures with respect to certain marketable securities. An important part of the statement concerns the distinction between noncurrent and current classification of marketable securities.

Required:

a. Why does a company maintain an investment portfolio of current and noncurrent securities?

b. What factors should be considered in determining whether investments in marketable equity securities should be classified as current or noncurrent, and how do these factors affect the accounting treatment for unrealized losses?

Question 12–3

Presented below are four *unrelated* situations involving marketable equity securities:

Situation 1

A noncurrent portfolio with an aggregate market value in excess of cost includes one particular security whose market value has declined to less than one half of the original cost. The decline in value is considered to be other than temporary.

Situation 2

The statement of financial position of a company does not classify assets and liabilities as current and noncurrent. The portfolio of marketable equity securities includes securities normally considered current that have a net cost in excess of market value of $2,000. The remainder of the portfolio has a net market value in excess of cost of $5,000.

Situation 3

A marketable equity security, whose market value is currently less than cost, is classified as noncurrent but is to be reclassified as current.

Situation 4

A company's noncurrent portfolio of marketable equity securities consists of the common stock of one company. At the end of the prior year the market value of the security was *50 percent* of original cost, and this effect was properly reflected in a valuation allowance account. However, at the end of the current year the market value of the security had appreciated to *twice* the original cost. The security is still considered noncurrent at year end.

Required:

What is the effect upon classification, carrying value, and earnings for each of the above situations? Complete your response to each situation before proceeding to the next situation.

Question 12-4

A marketable equity security that was classified as noncurrent in a prior period is reclassified as current in the current period.

Required:

a. What is the effect on the valuation allowance attendant to the above security assuming no change in its market value?

b. Discuss briefly the logic for making an adjustment in the valuation allowance because of the reclassification from noncurrent to current.

Accounts receivable

Question 12-5

When a company has a policy of making sales for which credit is extended, it is reasonable to expect a portion of those sales to be uncollectible. As a result of this, a company must recognize bad debt expense. There are basically two methods of recognizing bad debt expense: (1) direct write-off method and (2) allowance method.

Required:

a. Describe fully both the direct write-off method and the allowance method of recognizing bad debt expense.

b. Discuss the reasons one of the above methods is preferable to the other and the reasons the other method is not usually in accordance with generally accepted accounting principles.

Question 12-6

Due to calamitous earthquake losses the Morgan Company, one of your client's oldest and largest customers, suddenly and unexpectedly became bankrupt. Approximately 30 percent of your client's total sales have been made to the Morgan Company during each of the past several years.

The amount due from Morgan Company—none of which is collectible—equals 25 percent of total accounts receivable, an amount that is considerably in excess of what was determined to be an adequate provision for doubtful accounts at the close of the preceding year.

Required:

How would your client record the write-off of the Morgan Company receivable if it is using the allowance method of accounting for bad debts? Justify your suggested treatment.

Question 12–7

One of the methods of estimating bad debt expense is to estimate it on the basis of the percentage of past actual losses from bad debts to past net credit sales and adjust for anticipated conditions.

Required:

Explain the basic concepts supporting the above procedure for estimating bad debt expense.

CHAPTER 13: INVENTORIES

Current valuation

Question 13–1

The controller of the Robinson Company was discussing a comment you made in the course of presenting your audit report.

". . . and frankly," Ms. Fisher continued, "I agree that we, too, are responsible for finding ways to produce more relevant financial statements that are as reliable as the ones we now produce.

"For example, suppose the company acquired a finished item for inventory for $40 when the general price-level index was 110. And, later, the item was sold for $75 when the general price-level index was 121 and the current replacement cost was $54. We could calculate a holding gain."

Required:

a. Explain to what extent and how current replacement costs already are used *within* historical cost accounting principles to value inventories.

b. Calculate in good form the amount of the holding gain in Ms. Fisher's example.

c. Why is the use of current replacement cost for *both* inventories and cost of goods sold preferred by some accounting authorities to the generally accepted use of FIFO or LIFO?

d. Why do some authorities believe that the present market resale (exit or output) price is a conceptual improvement upon current replacement (entry or input) cost for inventory measurement?

Historical cost

Question 13–2

The Jonesville Company manufactures capacitors used in radios, television sets, and rockets. Some orders are filled from inventory; others are for capacitors that are specially made to customer specification as to size, lead wires, voltage, and tolerance.

When manufacturing a custom order, the Jonesville Company intentionally produces more capacitors than are ordered by the customer. These extra capacitors are carried at no value in the Jonesville Company inventory, since all costs of the job are charged to cost of goods sold at the time that the order is shipped. The extras are kept (1) to replace any capacitors that may be returned as rejects that currently constitute 20 percent of all units sold and (2) to fill any subsequent orders from the customer for additional units of the same item. Since there is no market for the unused custom manufactured capacitors, any that remain in inventory for two years are destroyed.

Jonesville warrants the replacement of defective capacitors returned by the purchaser. Often three to six months elapse between delivery of the order and receipt of the defectives.

Jonesville predicts that its production capacity is adequate so that no sales would be lost in future periods, even though it did not have the extras on hand to cover subsequent orders of custom manufactured capacitors.

Required:

a. What are the conceptual merits of Jonesville carrying the custom manufactured extras held for replacement of defectives at:

(1) No value? Explain.

(2) Marginal or incremental cost? Explain.

(3) Full cost? Explain.

b. What are the conceptual merits of Jonesville carrying the custom manufactured extras held for subsequent sale at:

(1) No value? Explain.

(2) Marginal or incremental cost? Explain.

(3) Full cost? Explain.

c. What disclosure, if any, should Jonesville make for its obligation to replace defective capacitors? Explain.

Question 13–3

Retail, Inc., sells normal brand name household products both from its own store and on consignment through The Mall Space Company.

Required:

a. Should Retail, Inc., include in its inventory normal brand name goods purchased from its suppliers but not yet received if the terms of purchase are FOB shipping point (manufacturer's plant)? Why?

b. Should Retail, Inc., include freight-in expenditures as an inventoriable cost? Why?

c. Retail, Inc., purchased cooking utensils for sale in the ordinary course of business three times during the current year, each time at a higher price than the previous purchase. What would have been the effect on ending inventory and cost of goods sold had Retail, Inc., used the weighted-average cost method instead of the FIFO method?

d. How and why will Retail, Inc., treat net markdowns when it calculates the estimated cost of ending inventory using the conventional (lower of cost or market) retail inventory method?

e. What are products on consignment and how should they be presented on the balance sheets of Retail, Inc., and The Mall Space Company?

Last-in, first-out

Question 13–4

In order to effect an approximate matching of current costs with related sales revenue, the last-in, first-out (LIFO) method of pricing inventories has been developed.

Required:

a. Describe the establishment of and subsequent pricing procedures for each of the following LIFO inventory methods:
   (1) LIFO applied to units of product when the periodic inventory system is used.
   (2) Application of the dollar-value method to a retail LIFO inventory or to LIFO units of product (these applications are similar).

b. Discuss the specific advantages and disadvantages of using the dollar-value-LIFO applications. *Ignore income tax considerations.*

c. Discuss the general advantages and disadvantages claimed for LIFO methods. *Ignore income tax considerations.*

Question 13–5

Part a. Inventory may be computed under one of various cost-flow assumptions. Among these assumptions are first-in, first-out (FIFO) and last-in, first-out (LIFO). In the past, some companies have changed from FIFO to LIFO for computing portions or all of their inventory.

Required:

   (1) Ignoring income tax, what effect does a change from FIFO to LIFO have on net earnings and working capital? Explain.
   (2) Explain the difference between the FIFO assumption of earnings and operating cycle and the LIFO assumption of earnings and operating cycle.

Part b. Companies using LIFO inventory sometimes establish a Reserve for the Replacement of LIFO Inventory account.

Required:

Explain why and how this reserve account is established and where it should be shown on the statement of financial position.

Standard costs

Question 13-6

Standard costs are being used increasingly by modern manufacturing companies. Many advocates of standard costing take the position that standard costs are a proper basis for inventory valuation for external reporting purposes. *Accounting Research Bulletin No. 43,* however, reflects the widespread view that standard costs are not acceptable unless "adjusted at reasonable intervals to reflect current conditions so that at the balance sheet date standard costs reasonably approximate costs computed under one of the recognized (actual cost) bases."

Required:

a. Discuss the conceptual merits of using standard costs as the basis for inventory valuation for external reporting purposes.

b. Prepare general-journal entries for three alternative dispositions of a $1,500 unfavorable variance where all goods manufactured during the period are included in the ending finished-goods inventory. Assume a formal standard-cost system is in operation, that $500 of the variance resulted from actual costs exceeding attainable standard cost, and that $1,000 of the variance resulted from the difference between the ideal standard and an attainable standard.

c. Discuss the conceptual merits of each of the three alternative methods of disposition requested in 2 above.

CHAPTER 14: PLANT AND EQUIPMENT—PURCHASED AND LEASED

Self-constructed assets

Question 14-1

Jay Manufacturing, Inc., began operations five years ago producing probos, a new type of instrument it hoped to sell to doctors, dentists, and hospitals. The demand for probos far exceeded initial expectations, and the company was unable to produce enough probos to meet demand.

The company was manufacturing its product on equipment that it built at the start of its operations. To meet demand, more efficient equipment was needed. The company decided to design and build the equipment, since that currently available on the market was unsuitable for producing probos.

In 1982 a section of the plant was devoted to development of the new equipment, and a special staff of personnel was hired. Within six months and at a cost of $170,000, a machine was developed that successfully increased production and reduced labor costs substantially. Sparked by the success of the new machine, the company built three more machines of the same type at a cost of $80,000 each.

Required:

   a. In addition to satisfying a need that outsiders cannot meet within the desired time, why might a firm construct fixed assets for its own use?

   b. In general, what costs should be capitalized for a self-constructed fixed asset?

   c. Discuss the propriety of including in the capitalized cost of self-constructed assets:
   (1)   The increase in overhead caused by the self-construction of fixed assets.
   (2)   A proportionate share of overhead on the same basis as that applied to goods manufactured for sale.

   d. Discuss the proper accounting treatment of the $90,000 ($170,000—$80,000) by which the cost of the first machine exceeded the cost of the subsequent machines.

Historical cost

Question 14–2

Among the principal topics related to the accounting for the property, plant, and equipment of a company are acquisition and retirement.

Required:

   a. What expenditures should be capitalized when equipment is acquired for cash?

   b. Assume that the market value of equipment acquired is not determinable by reference to a similar purchase for cash. Describe how the acquiring company should determine the capitalizable cost of equipment purchased by exchanging it for each of the following:
   (1)   Bonds having an established market price.
   (2)   Common stock not having an established market price.
   (3)   Similar equipment having a determinable market value.

   c. Describe the factors that determine whether expenditures relating to property, plant, and equipment already in use should be capitalized.
   d. Describe how to account for the gain or loss on the sale of property, plant, and equipment for cash.

Question 14–3

A company may acquire plant assets (among other ways) for cash, on a deferred-payment plan, by exchanging other assets, or by a combination of these ways.

Required:

   a. Identify six costs that should be capitalized as the cost of land. For your answer, assume that land with an existing building is acquired for cash and that the existing building is to be removed in the immediate future in order that a new building can be constructed on that site.

b. At what amount should a company record a plant asset acquired on a deferred-payment plan?

c. In general, at what amount should plant assets received in exchange for other nonmonetary assets be recorded? Specifically, at what amount should a company record a new machine acquired by exchanging an older, similar machine and paying cash?

Leases of plant and equipment

Question 14–4

Wright Aircraft Company manufactures small single and multiple-engine aircraft primarily for sale to individuals, flying clubs, and corporations. Wright is one of the pioneers in the industry and has developed a reputation as a leader in small-craft engineering and marketing innovations.

During the last few years Wright has profitably leased an increasing number of its aircraft to flying clubs. The leasing activity currently represents a significant portion of Wright's annual volume. Details of the leasing arrangements with flying clubs follow:

The flying club signs a long-term lease agreement with Wright for the aircraft.

The lease has a noncancelable term of 6 to 18 years, depending upon the aircraft's useful life. The lease term is set to be three fourths of the normal life of the aircraft leased.

The club is required to deposit with Wright an amount equal to 10 percent of the total lease rental for the term of the lease. The deposit is not refundable, but it is used in lieu of rent during the last one tenth of the lease term.

A bank loans Wright an amount equal to the remaining 90 precent of the total lease rental, after deducting a discount of 14 percent per year. The net discounted amount is immediately paid to Wright. The bank-loan agreement requires Wright to use the lease rental payments from the flying club to pay off the loan to the bank.

As a condition for the loan, the bank requires Wright to insure the leased aircraft for an amount equal to the loan.

The flying club signs Wright's bank-loan agreement as a surety, thus obligating itself if Wright should default on the loan.

When the bank loan is paid in full at the end of the lease term, the flying club can purchase the aircraft and receive title to it by paying Wright $100.

Required:

Discuss the criteria and other aspects of Wright's leasing activities that it should consider in determining whether to account for its flying club leases as operating leases or as sales-type leases. In your discussion, identify criteria that are clearly met in the facts presented in the question. For criteria that are *not* clearly met, indicate what additional information is needed to reach a conclusion with respect to each criterion.

Question 14–5

Cannon, Inc., was incorporated in 1980 to operate as a computer software service firm with an accounting fiscal year ending August 31. Cannon's primary product is a sophisticated on-line inventory-control system; its customers pay a fixed fee plus a usage charge for using the system.

Cannon has leased a large, BIG–I computer system from the manufacturer. The lease calls for a monthly rental of $30,000 for the 144 months (12 years) of the lease term. The estimated useful life of the computer is 15 years.

Each scheduled monthly rental payment includes $5,000 for full-service maintenance on the computer to be performed by the manufacturer. All rentals are payable on the first day of the month beginning with August 1, 1981, the date the computer was installed and the lease agreement was signed.

The lease is noncancelable for its 12-year term, and it is secured only by the manufacturer's chattel lien on the BIG–I system. On any anniversary date of the lease after August 1986, Cannon can purchase the BIG–I system from the manufacturer at 75 percent of the then current fair value of the computer.

This lease is to be accounted for as a capital lease by Cannon, and it will be amortized by the interest method. Borrowed funds for this type of transaction would cost Cannon 12 percent per year (1 percent per month). Following is a schedule of the present value of $1 for selected periods discounted at 1 percent per period when payments are made at the beginning of each period.

Periods (months)	Present value of $1 per period discounted at 1% per period
1	1.000
2	1.990
3	2.970
143	76.658
144	76.899

Required:

Prepare, in general journal form all entries Cannon should have made in its accounting records during August 1981 relating to this lease. Give full explanations and show supporting computations for each entry. Remember, August 31, 1981 is the end of Cannon's fiscal accounting period, and it will be preparing financial statements on that date. *Do not prepare closing entries.*

Question 14–6

Milton Corporation entered into a lease arrangement with James Leasing Corporation for a certain machine. James's primary business is leasing, and it is not a manufacturer or dealer. Milton will lease the machine for a period of three years which is 50 percent of the machine's economic life. James will take possession of the machine at the end of the initial three-year lease and lease it to another smaller company that does not need the most current version of the machine. Milton does not guarantee any residual value for the machine and will not purchase the machine at the end of the lease term.

Milton's incremental borrowing rate is 10 percent, and the implicit rate in the lease is 8½ percent. Milton has no way of knowing the implicit rate used by James. Using either rate, the present value of the minimum lease payments is between 90 percent and 100 percent of the fair value of the machine at the date of the lease agreement.

Milton has agreed to pay all executory costs directly, and no allowance for these costs is included in the lease payments.

James is reasonably certain that Milton will pay all lease payments, and because Milton has agreed to pay all executory costs, there are no important uncertainties regarding costs to be incurred by James.

Required:

a. With respect to Milton (the lessee) answer the following:
 (1) What type of lease has been entered into? Explain the reason for your answer.
 (2) How should Milton compute the appropriate amount to be recorded for the lease or asset acquired?
 (3) What accounts will be created or affected by this transaction and how will the lease or asset and other costs related to the transaction be matched with earnings?
 (4) What disclosure must Milton make regarding this lease or asset?

b. With respect to James (the lessor) answer the following:
 (1) What type of leasing arrangement has been entered into? Explain the reason for your answer.
 (2) How should this lease be recorded by James, and how are the appropriate amounts determined?
 (3) How should James determine the appropriate amount of earnings to be recognized from each lease payment?
 (4) What disclosures must James make regarding this lease?

Question 14–7

On the first day of its fiscal year Lessor, Inc., leased certain property at an annual rental of $100,000 receivable at the beginning of each year for 10 years. The first payment was received immediately. The leased property, which is new, had cost $650,000 and has an estimated useful life of 13 years and *no* salvage value. Lessor's borrowing rate is 8 percent. The present value of an annuity of $1 payable at the beginning of the period at 8 percent for 10 years is 7.247. Lessor had *no* other costs associated with this lease. Lessor should have accounted for this lease as a sale; but, it mistakenly treated the lease as an operating lease. What was the effect on net earnings during the first year of the lease by having treated this lease as an operating lease, rather than as a sale?

CHAPTER 15: DEPRECIATION

Nature of depreciation

Question 15–1

Depreciation continues to be one of the most controversial, difficult, and important problem areas in accounting.

Required:

    a. (1) Explain the conventional accounting concept of depreciation accounting; and

          (2) Discuss its conceptual merit with respect to (*a*) the value of the asset, (*b*) the charge(s) to expense, and (*c*) the discretion of management in selecting the method.

    b. (1) Explain the factors that should be considered when applying the conventional concept of depreciation to the determination of how the value of a newly acquired computer system should be assigned to expense for financial reporting purposes. (Income tax considerations should be ignored.)

          (2) What depreciation methods might be used for the computer system?

Question 15–2

Property, plant, and equipment (plant assets) generally represent a material portion of the total assets of most companies. Accounting for the acquisition and usage of such assets is, therefore, an important part of the financial reporting process.

Required:

    a. Distinguish between revenue and capital expenditures, and explain why this distinction is important.

    b. Briefly define depreciation as used in accounting.

    c. Identify the factors that are relevant in determining the annual depreciation, and explain whether these factors are determined objectively or whether they are based on judgment.

    d. Explain why depreciation is usually shown in the sources of funds section of the statement of changes in financial position.

Depreciation methods

Question 15–3

During the examination of the financial statements of the Fendo Company, your assistant calls attention to significant costs incurred in the development of EDP programs (i.e., software) for major segments of the sales and production scheduling systems (not R&D).

The EDP program development costs will benefit future periods to the extent that the systems change slowly and the program instructions are compatible with new equipment acquired at three- to six-year intervals. The service value of the EDP programs is affected almost entirely by changes in the technology of systems and EDP equipment and does not decline with the number of times the program is used. Since many system changes are minor, program instructions frequently can be modified with only minor losses in program efficiency. The frequency of such changes tends to increase with the passage of time.

Required:

    a. Discuss the propriety of classifying the unamortized EDP program development costs as

(1) A prepaid expense.

(2) An intangible fixed asset with limited life.

(3) A tangible fixed asset.

    b. Numerous methods are available for amortizing assets that benefit future periods. Each method (like a model) presumes that certain conditions exist and, hence, is most appropriate under those conditions.

Discuss the propriety of amortizing the EDP program development costs with

(1) The straight-line method.

(2) An increasing-charge method (e.g., the annuity method).

(3) A decreasing charge-method (e.g., the sum-of-the-years'-digits method).

(4) A variable-charge method (e.g., the units-of-production method).

Question 15–4

The Norvell Company manufactures electrical appliances, most of which are used in homes. Company engineers have designed a new type of blender which, through the use of a few attachments, will perform more functions than any blender currently on the market. Demand for the new blender can be projected with reasonable probability. In order to make the blenders, Norvell needs a specialized machine, which is not available from outside sources. It has been decided to make such a machine in Norvell's own plant.

Required:

    a. Norvell's plant may be operating at capacity or below capacity. Compare and contrast the problems in determining the cost to be assigned to the machine at these different levels of operations.

    b. (1) Discuss the effect of projected demand in units for the new blenders (which may be steady, decreasing, or increasing) on the determination of a depreciation method for the machine.

        (2) What other matters should be considered in determining the deprecial method? *Ignore income tax considerations.*

CHAPTER 16: INTANGIBLES AND NONCURRENT INVESTMENTS

Nature and measurement of intangibles

Question 16–1

On June 30, 1980 your client, The Vandiver Corporation, was granted two patents covering plastic cartons that it has been producing and marketing profitably for the past three years. One patent covers the manufacturing process, and the other covers the related products.

Vandiver executives tell you that these patents represent the most significant breakthrough in the industry in the past 30 years. The products have been marketed under the registered trademarks Safetainer, Duratainer, and Sealrite. Licenses under the patents have already been granted by your client to other manufacturers in the United States and abroad and are producing substantial royalties.

On July 1 Vandiver commenced patent infringement actions against several companies whose names you recognize as those of substantial and prominent competitors. Vandiver's management is optimistic that these suits will result in a permanent injunction against the manufacture and sale of the infringing products and collection of damages for loss of profits caused by the alleged infringement.

The financial vice president has suggested that the patents be recorded at the discounted value of expected net royalty receipts.

Required:

    a. What is an intangible asset? Explain.

    b. (1) What is the meaning of "discounted value of expected net receipts"? Explain.

        (2) How would such a value be calculated for net royalty receipts?

    c. What basis of valuation for Vandiver's patents would be generally accepted in accounting? Give supporting reasons for this basis.

    d. (1) Assuming no practical problems of implementation and ignoring generally accepted accounting principles, what is the preferable basis of evaluation for patents? Explain.

        (2) What would be the preferable theoretical basis of amortization? Explain.

    e. What recognition, if any, should be made of the infringement litigation in the financial statements for the year ending September 30, 1980? Discuss.

Research and development costs

Question 16–2

The Thomas Company is in the process of developing a revolutionary new product. A new division of the company was formed to develop, manufacture, and market this new product. As of year end (December 31, 1977) the new product has not been manufactured for resale; however, a prototype unit was built and is in operation.

Throughout 1977 the new division incurred certain costs. These costs include design and engineering studies, prototype manufacturing costs, administrative expenses (including salaries of administrative personnel), and market research costs. In addition, approximately $500,000 in equipment (estimated useful life—10 years) was purchased for use in developing and manufacturing the new product. Approximately $200,000 of this equipment was built specifically for the design development of the new product; the remaining $300,000 of equipment was used to manufacture the preproduction prototype and will be used to manufacture the new product once it is in commercial production.

Required:

    a. What is the definition of *research* and of *development* as defined in *Statement of Financial Accounting Standards No. 2?*

b. Briefly indicate the practical and conceptual reasons for the conclusion reached by the Financial Accounting Standards Board on accounting and reporting practices for research and development costs.

c. In accordance with *Statement of Financial Accounting Standards No. 2,* how should the various costs of Thomas described above be recorded on the financial statements for the year ended December 31, 1977?

Goodwill

Question 16–3

Accounting practitioners, accounting authors, and the courts have proposed various solutions to the problems of accounting in terms of historical cost for goodwill and similar intangibles.

Required:

a. In comparing the problems of accounting for goodwill and similar intangible assets to those for other plant assets,
(1) What problems are similar? Explain.
(2) What problems are different? Explain.

b. (1) What are the possible accounting treatments subsequent to the date of acquisition for the cost of goodwill and similar intangible assets? Explain.
(2) What is the logic in requiring a maximum life of 40 years for goodwill?

Question 16–4

After extended negotiations Beach Corporation bought from Cedar Company most of the latter's assets on June 30, 1980. At the time of the sale Cedar's accounts (adjusted to June 30, 1980) reflected the following descriptions and amounts for the assets transferred:

	Cost	Contra (valuation) account	Book value
Receivables	$ 83,600	$ 3,000	$ 80,600
Inventory	107,000	5,200	101,800
Land	20,000	—	20,000
Buildings	207,500	73,000	134,500
Fixtures and equipment	205,000	41,700	163,300
Goodwill	50,000	—	50,000
	$673,100	$122,900	$550,200

You ascertain that the contra (valuation) accounts were allowance for doubtful accounts, allowance to reduce inventory to market, and accumulated depreciation.

During the extended negotiations Cedar held out for a consideration of approximately $600,000 (depending upon the level of the receivables and inventory).

However, as of June 30, 1980, Cedar agreed to accept Beach's offer of $450,000 cash plus 1 percent of the net sales (as defined in the contract) of the next five years with payments at the end of each year. Cedar expects that Beach's total net sales during this period will exceed $15 million.

Required:

    a. The term *goodwill* often appears in connection with business combinations.

(1) What is goodwill? Explain.

(2) What is "negative" goodwill? Explain.

    b. (1) How should Beach Corporation record this transaction? Explain.

        (2) Discuss the propriety of recording goodwill in the accounts of Beach Corporation for this transaction.

Noncurrent investments

Question 16–5

Hawkes Systems, Inc., a chemical processing company, has been operating profitably for many years. On March 1, 1984 Hawkes purchased 50,000 shares of Diversified Insurance Company stock for $2 million. The 50,000 shares represented 25 percent of Diversified's outstanding stock. Both Hawkes and Diversified operate on a fiscal year ending August 31.

For the fiscal year ended August 31, 1984, Diversified reported net income of $800,000 earned ratably throughout the year. During November 1983, February, May, and August 1984, Diversified paid its regular quarterly cash dividend of $100,000.

Required:

    a. What criteria should Hawkes consider in determining whether its investment in Diversified should be classified as (1) a current asset (marketable security) or (2) a noncurrent asset (investment) in Hawkes' August 31, 1984 balance sheet? Confine your discussion to the decision criteria for determining the balance sheet classification of the investment.

    b. Assume that the investment should be classified as a long-term investment in the noncurrent-asset section of Hawkes' balance sheet. The cost of Hawkes' investment equaled its equity in the recorded values of Diversified's net assets; recorded values were not materially different from fair values (individually or collectively). For the fiscal year ended August 31, 1984, how did the net income reported and dividends paid by Diversified affect the accounts of Hawkes (including Hawkes' income tax accounts)? Indicate each account affected, whether it increased or decreased, and explain the reason for the change in the account balance (such as Cash, Investment in Diversified, etc.). Organize your answer in the following format.

Account name	Increase or decrease	Reason for change in account balance

Question 16-6

Part a. The most common method of accounting for unconsolidated subsidiaries is the equity method.

Required:

Answer the questions shown below with respect to the *equity* method.
(1) Under what circumstances should the equity method be applied?
(2) At what amount should the initial investment be recorded, and what events subsequent to the initial investment (if any) would change this amount?
(3) How are investment earnings recognized under the equity method, and how is the amount determined?

Part b. For the past five years Herbert has maintained an investment (properly accounted for and reported upon) in Broome amounting to a 10 percent interest in the voting common stock of Broome. The purchase price was $.7 million, and the underlying net equity in Broome at the date of purchase was $620,000. On January 2 of the current year, Herbert purchased an additional 15 percent of the voting common stock of Broome for $1.2 million; the underlying net equity of the additional investment at January 2 was $1 million. Broome has been profitable and has paid dividends annually since Herbert's initial acquisition.

Required:

Discuss how this increase in ownership affects the accounting for and reporting upon the investment in Broome. Include in your discussion adjustments, if any, to the amount shown before the increase in investment to bring the amount into conformity with generally accepted accounting principles. Also include how current and subsequent periods would be reported upon.

CHAPTER 17: LIABILITIES AND THEIR MEASUREMENT

Measurement of liabilities

Question 17-1

Business transactions often involve the exchange of property, goods, or services for notes or similar instruments that may stipulate no interest rate or an interest rate that varies from prevailing rates.

Required:

a. When a note is exchanged for property, goods, or services, what value should be placed upon the note
(1) If it bears interest at a reasonable rate and is issued in a bargained transaction entered into at arm's length? Explain.
(2) If it bears no interest and/or is not issued in a bargained transaction entered into at arm's length? Explain.

   b. If the recorded value of a note differs from the face value,

(1) How should the difference be accounted for? Explain.

(2) How should this difference be presented in the financial statements? Explain.

Long-term debt

Question 17–2

On January 1, 1971 Guadagno Corporation issued for $1,106,775 its 20-year, 8 percent bonds, which have a maturity value of $1 million and pay interest semiannually on January 1 and July 1. Bond issue costs were not material in amount. The following are three presentations of the long-term liability section of the balance sheet that might be used for these bonds at the issue date:

1.	Bonds payable (maturing January 1, 1991)	$1,000,000
	Unamortized premium on bonds payable	106,775
	Total bond liability	$1,106,775
2.	Bonds payable—principal (face value $1,000,000, maturing January 1, 1991)	$ 252,572*
	Bonds payable—interest (semiannual payment $40,000)	854,203**
	Total bond liability	$1,106,775
3.	Bonds payable—principal (maturing January 1, 1991)	$1,000,000
	Bonds payable—interest ($40,000 per period for 40 periods)	1,600,000
	Total bond liability	$2,600,000

    * The present value of $1,000,000 due at the end of 40 (six-month) periods at the yield rate of 3½ percent per period.

    ** The present value of $40,000 per period for 40 (six-month) periods at the yield rate of 3½ percent per period.

Required:

   a. Discuss the conceptual merit(s) of each of the date-of-issue balance sheet presentations shown above for these bonds.

   b. Explain why investors would pay $1,106,775 for bonds that have a maturity value of only $1 million.

   c. Assuming that a discount rate is needed to compute the carrying value of the obligations arising from a bond issue at any date during the life of the bonds, discuss the conceptual merit(s) of using for this purpose

(1) The coupon or nominal rate.

(2) The effective or yield rate at date of issue.

   d. If the obligations arising from these bonds are to be carried at their present value computed by means of the current market rate of interest, how would the bond valuation at dates subsequent to the date of issue be affected by an increase or a decrease in the market rate of interest?

Question 17-3

Gains or losses from the early extinguishment of debt that is refunded can theoretically be accounted for in three ways:

Amortized over remaining life of old debt.

Amortized over the life of the new debt issue.

Recognized in the period of extinguishment.

Required:

a. Discuss the supporting arguments for each of the three theoretic methods of accounting for gains and losses from the early extinguishment of debt.

b. Which of the above methods is generally accepted, and how should the appropriate amount of gain or loss be shown in a company's financial statements?

Convertible debt and debt with detachable warrants

Question 17-4

Incurring long-term debt with an arrangement whereby lenders receive an option to buy common stock during all or a portion of the time the debt is outstanding is a frequently used corporate financing practice. In some situations the result is achieved through the issuance of convertible bonds; in others the debt instruments and the warrants to buy stock are separate.

Required:

a. Describe the differences that exist in current accounting for original proceeds of the issuance of convertible bonds and of debt instruments with separate warrants to purchase common stock.

b. Discuss the underlying rationale for the differences described in a. above.

c. Summarize the arguments that have been presented for the alternative accounting treatment.

Question 17-5

The equityholders of a business entity usually are considered to include both creditors and owners. These two classes of equityholders have some characteristics in common, and sometimes it is difficult to make a clear-cut distinction between them. Examples of this problem include (1) convertible debt and (2) debt issued with stock purchase warrants. Both examples represent debts of a corporation, but there is a question as to whether there is an ownership interest in each case that requires accounting recognition.

Required:

a. Identify
  (1) Convertible debt.
  (2) Debt issued with stock purchase warrants.

b. With respect to convertible debt and debt issued with stock purchase warrants, discuss

(1) The similarities.

(2) The differences.

c. (1) What are the alternative accounting treatments for the proceeds from convertible debt? Explain.

(2) Which treatment is required by the FASB? Explain the logic of this method.

d. (1) What are the alternative accounting treatments for the proceeds from debt issued with stock purchase warrants? Explain.

(2) Which treatment is required by the FASB? Explain the logic of this method.

Question 17–6

One way for a corporation to accomplish long-term financing is through the issuance of long-term debt instruments in the form of bonds.

Required:

a. Describe how to account for the proceeds from bonds issued with detachable stock purchase warrants.

b. Contrast a serial bond with a term (straight) bond.

c. For a five-year term bond issued at a premium, why would the amortization in the first year of the life of the bond differ using the interest method of amortization instead of the straight-line method? Include in your discussion whether the amount of amortization in the first year of the life of the bond would be higher or lower using the interest method instead of the straight-line method.

d. When a bond issue is sold between interest dates at a discount, what journal entry is made and how is the subsequent amortization of bond discount affected? Include in your discussion an explanation of how the amounts of each debit and credit are determined.

e. Describe how to account for and classify the gain or loss from the reacquisition of a long-term bond before its maturity.

Loss contingencies

Question 17–7

Loss contingencies may exist for companies.

Required:

a. What conditions should be met for an estimated loss from a loss contingency to be accrued by a charge to income?

b. When is disclosure required, and what disclosure should be made for an estimated loss from a loss contingency that need not be accrued by a charge to income?

Question 17–8

The two basic requirements for the accrual of a loss contingency are supported by several basic concepts of accounting. Three of these concepts are: periodicity (time periods), measurement, and objectivity.

Required:

Discuss how the two basic requirements for the accrual of a loss contingency relate to the three concepts listed above.

Question 17–9

The following three *independent* sets of facts relate to (1) the possible accrual or (2) the possible disclosure by other means of a loss contingency.

Situation 1

A company offers a one-year warranty for the product that it manufactures. A history of warranty claims has been compiled, and the probable amount of claims related to sales for a given period can be determined.

Situation 2

Subsequent to the date of a set of financial statements, but prior to the issuance of the financial statements, a company enters into a contract that will probably result in a significant loss to the company. The amount of the loss can be reasonably estimated.

Situation 3

A company has adopted a policy of recording self-insurance for any possible losses resulting from injury to others by the company's vehicles. The premium for an insurance policy for the same risk from an independent insurance company would have an annual cost of $2,000. During the period covered by the financial statements, there were no accidents involving the company's vehicles and resulting in injury to others.

Required:

Discuss the accrual and/or type of disclosure necessary (if any) and the reason(s) such disclosure is appropriate for each of the three independent sets of facts above.

Complete your response to each situation before proceeding to the next situation.

CHAPTER 18: INCOME TAXES AND PENSION COSTS

Income tax allocation

Question 18–1

Part a. In preparing financial statements a corporation is expected to follow the practice of comprehensive income tax allocation. At various times three methods of allocation have been used: the deferred method, the liability method, and the net-of-tax method.

Required:

    (1) Discuss the theoretical justification for interperiod income tax allocation. (Do not discuss the theoretical aspects of intraperiod tax allocation.)

    (2) Describe briefly each of the above three methods of tax allocation and give reasons why each method is acceptable or unacceptable.

Part b. The following differences enter into the reconciliation of financial net income and taxable income of A. P. Baxter Corp. for the current year.

    (1) Tax depreciation exceeds book depreciation by $30,000.

    (2) Estimated warranty costs of $6,000 applicable to the current year's sales have not been paid.

    (3) Percentage depletion deducted on the tax return exceeds cost depletion by $45,000.

    (4) Unearned rent revenue of $25,000 was deferred on the books, but appropriately included in taxable income.

    (5) A book expense of $2,000 for life insurance premiums on officers' lives is not allowed as a deduction on the tax return.

    (6) A $7,000 tax deduction resulted from expensing interest during construction for tax purposes while such costs were capitalized for financial reporting.

    (7) Gross profit of $80,000 was excluded from taxable income because Baxter had appropriately elected the installment sale method for tax reporting while recognizing all gross profit from installment sales at the time of the sale for financial reporting.

Required:

Consider each reconciling item independently of all others, and explain whether each item would enter into the calculation of income taxes to be allocated. For any that are included in the income tax allocation calculation, explain the effect of the item on the current year's income tax expense and how the amount would be reported on the balance sheet. (Tax allocation calculations are not required.)

Question 18–2

Deferred income taxes are required under generally accepted accounting principles. *Accounting Principles Board Opinion No. 11* requires the use of the deferred method of comprehensive interperiod tax allocation. Two ways to account for timing differences under the deferred method are (1) gross change method and (2) net change method.

Required:

    (1) Describe the gross change method.

    (2) Describe the net change method.

Question 18–3

Part a. Income tax allocation is an integral part of generally accepted accounting principles. The applications of intraperiod tax allocation (within a period) and interperiod tax allocation (among periods) are both required.

Required:

(1) Explain the need for *intraperiod* tax allocation.
(2) Accountants who favor *interperiod* tax allocation argue that income taxes are an expense, rather than a distribution of earnings. Explain the significance of this argument. *Do not explain the definitions of expense or distribution of earnings.*
(3) Indicate and explain whether each of the following *independent* situations should be treated as a timing difference or a permanent difference.
    (a) Estimated warranty costs (covering a three-year warranty) are expensed for accounting purposes at the time of sale, but deducted for income tax purposes when incurred.
    (b) Depreciation for accounting and income tax purposes differs because of different bases of carrying the related property. The different bases are a result of a business combination treated as a purchase for accounting purposes and as a tax-free exchange for income tax purposes.
    (c) A company properly uses the equity method to account for its 30 percent investment in another company. The investee pays dividends that are about 10 percent of its annual earnings.
(4) Discuss the nature of the deferred income tax accounts and possible classifications in a company's statement of financial position.

Part b. The investment tax credit can be accounted for by one of two generally accepted methods for accounting purposes.

Required:

Identify and explain these two accounting methods for the investment tax credit. *Do not discuss income tax computations of the investment tax credit.*

Pension costs

Question 18–4

Part a. Generally accepted accounting principles require that pension costs be accounted for on the accrual basis. The various components of pension expense include (but are not limited to) (1) normal cost, (2) past service cost, (3) prior service cost, and (4) interest.

Required:

Define each of the four terms designated above, and discuss how each of the costs is accounted for under generally accepted accounting principles.

Part b. The accounting for past service cost has been a controversial issue. Some members of the profession advocate the accrual of past service cost only to the extent funded, and others advocate the accrual of past service cost regardless of the amount funded.

Required:

(1) What are the arguments in favor of accruing past service cost only to the extent funded?

(2)   What are the arguments in favor of accruing past service cost regardless of the amount funded?

Question 18–5

Part a.   Pension plans have developed in an environment characterized by a complex interaction of social concepts, legal considerations, actuarial techniques, income tax laws, and accounting practices. *APB Opinion No. 8* delineates acceptable accounting practices for the cost of pension plans.

Required:

(1)   The following terms are relevant to accounting for the cost of pension plans. Define or explain briefly each of the following:
   (a)   *Normal cost*
   (b)   *Past service cost*
   (c)   *Prior service cost*
   (d)   *Funded plan*
   (e)   *Vested benefits*
   (f)   *Actuarial gains and losses*
   (g)   *Interest*
(2)   Identify the disclosures required in financial statements regarding a company's pension plan.

Part b.   Liberty, Inc., a calendar-year corporation, adopted a company pension plan at the beginning of 1974. This plan is to be funded and noncontributory. Liberty used an appropriate actuarial cost method to determine its normal annual pension cost for 1974 and 1975 as $15,000 and $16,000, respectively, which was paid in the same year.

Liberty's actuarially determined past service costs were funded on December 31, 1974 at an amount properly computed as $106,000. These past service costs are to be amortized at the maximum amount permitted by generally accepted accounting principles. The interest factor assumed by the actuary is 6 percent.

Required:

Prepare journal entries to record the funding of past service costs on December 31, 1974 and the pension expenses for the years 1974 and 1975. Under each journal entry give the reasoning to support your entry. Round to the nearest dollar.

Question 18–6

Many companies have pension plans for their employees. Accounting for the cost of pension plans is a complex subject in which many technical terms are encountered.

Required:

   a.   Describe normal cost.

   b.   Describe vested benefits. Include in your discussion what the actuarially computed value of vested benefits represents.

   c.   How should actuarial gains and losses directly related to the operation of a pension plan be accounted for?

    d. What disclosures concerning pension plans should be made in the company's financial statements or notes?

CHAPTER 19: OWNERSHIP EQUITIES

Equity theories

Question 19–1

The concept of the accounting entity often is considered to be the most fundamental of accounting concepts, one that pervades all of accounting.

Required:

    a. (1) What is an accounting entity? Explain.
        (2) Explain why the accounting entity concept is so fundamental that it pervades all of accounting.

    b. For each of the following indicate whether the accounting concept of entity is applicable. Discuss and give illustrations.
    (1) A unit created by or under law.
    (2) The product-line segment of an enterprise.
    (3) A combination of legal units and/or product-line segments.
    (4) All of the activities of an owner or a group of owners.
    (5) An industry.
    (6) The economy of the United States.

Question 19–2

The Roz Corporation, a client, is considering the authorization of a 5 percent common stock dividend to common stockholders. The financial vice president of the corporation wishes to discuss the accounting implications of such an authorization with you before the next meeting of the board of directors.

Required:

    a. The first topic the vice president wishes to discuss is the nature of the stock dividend to the recipient.
    (1) Discuss the case *for* considering the stock dividend as income to the recipient.
    (2) Discuss the case *against* considering the stock dividend as income to the recipient.

    b. The other topic for discussion is the propriety of issuing the stock dividend to all "stockholders of record" or to "stockholders of record exclusive of shares held in the name of the corporation as treasury stock."
    (1) Discuss the case *for* issuing stock dividends on treasury shares.
    (2) Discuss the case *against* issuing stock dividends on treasury shares.

    c. These topics raise several issues about the nature of the accounting entity and the equities for which it is accountable. Of the theories that explain accounting equities, describe the
    (1) Proprietary theory.
    (2) Entity theory.

(3) Residual equity theory.

(4) Fund theory.

Equity classifications

Question 19–3

Problems may be encountered in accounting for transactions involving the stockholders' equity section of the balance sheet.

Required:

a. Describe the accounting for the subscription of common stock at a price in excess of the par value of the common stock.

b. Describe the accounting for the issuance for cash of no-par value common stock at a price in excess of the stated value of the common stock.

c. Explain the significance of the three dates that are important in accounting for cash dividends to stockholders. State the journal entry, if any, needed at each date.

d. Assume retained earnings can be used for stock dividends distributable in shares. What is the effect of an ordinary 10 percent common stock dividend on retained earnings and total stockholders' equity?

Question 19–4

Part a. A corporation's capital (stockholders' equity) is a very important part of its statement of financial position.

Required:

Identify and discuss the general categories of capital (stockholders' equity) for a corporation. Be sure to enumerate specific sources included in each general category.

Part b. Stock splits and stock dividends may be used by a corporation to change the number of shares of its stock outstanding.

Required:

(1) What is meant by "a stock split effected in the form of a dividend?"

(2) From an accounting viewpoint, explain how the stock split effected in the form of a dividend differs from an ordinary stock dividend.

(3) How should a stock dividend that has been declared but not yet issued be classified in a statement of financial position? Why?

Part c. Jones Company has adopted a traditional stock option plan for its officers and other employees. This plan is properly considered a compensatory plan.

Required:

Discuss how accounting for this plan will affect net earnings and earnings per share. *Ignore income tax considerations and accounting for income tax benefits.*

Consolidations

Question 19–5

Because of irreconcilable differences of opinion, a dissenting group within the management and board of directors of the Algo Company resigned and formed the Bevo Corporation to purchase a manufacturing division of the Algo Company. After negotiation of the agreement, but just before the closing and actual transfer of the property, a minority stockholder of Algo notified Bevo that a prior stockholders' agreement with Algo empowered him to prevent the sale. The minority stockholder's claim was acknowledged by Bevo's board of directors. Bevo's board then organized Casco, Inc., to acquire the minority stockholder's interest in Algo for $75,000, and Bevo advanced the cash to Casco. Bevo exercised control over Casco as a subsidiary corporation with common officers and directors. Casco paid the minority stockholder $75,000 (about twice the market value of the Algo stock) for his interest in Algo. Bevo then purchased the manufacturing division from Algo.

Required:

a. What expenditures are usually included in the cost of property, plant, and equipment acquired in a purchase?

b. (1) What are the criteria for determining whether to consolidate the financial statements of Bevo Corporation and Casco, Inc.?
   (2) Should the financial statements of Bevo Corporation and Casco, Inc., be consolidated? Discuss.

c. Assume that the unconsolidated financial statements are prepared. Discuss the propriety of treating the $75,000 expenditure in the financial statements of the Bevo Corporation as
(1) An account receivable from Casco, Inc.
(2) An investment in Casco, Inc.
(3) Part of the cost of the property, plant, and equipment.
(4) A loss.

CHAPTER 20: CHANGES IN STOCKHOLDERS' EQUITIES

Stock options

Question 20–1

Part a. Stock options are widely used as a form of compensation for corporate executives.

Required:

(1) Identify five methods that have been proposed for determining the value of executive stock options.
(2) Discuss the conceptual merits of each of these proposed methods.

Part b. On January 1, 1980 as an incentive to greater performance in their duties, Recycling Corporation adopted a qualified stock option plan to grant corporate executives nontransferable stock options to 500,000 shares of its unissued $1 par value common stock. The options were granted on May 1, 1980 at $25 per share, the market price on that date. All of the options were exercisable one year later and for four years thereafter providing that the grantee was employed by the Corporation at the date of exercise.

The market price of this stock was $40 per share on May 1, 1981. All options were exercised before December 31, 1981 at times when the market price varied between $40 and $50 per share.

Required:

What information on this option plan should be presented in the financial statements of Recycling Corporation at (1) December 31, 1980 and (2) December 31, 1981? Explain why this is acceptable.

Stock warrants

See Questions 17–4, 17–5, and 17–6.

Treasury stock

Question 20–2

For numerous reasons a corporation may reacquire shares of its own capital stock. When a company purchases treasury stock, it has two options as to how to account for the shares: (1) cost method and (2) par value method.

Required:

Compare and contrast the cost method with the par value method for each of the following:

   a. Purchase of shares at a price less than par value.

   b. Purchase of shares at a price greater than par value.

   c. Subsequent reseale of treasury shares at a price less than purchase price, but more than par value.

   d. Subsequent resale of treasury shares at a price greater than both purchase price and par value.

   e. Effect on net income.

Business combinations

Question 20–3

The boards of directors of Kessler Corporation, Bar Company, Cohen, Inc., and Mason Corporation are meeting jointly to discuss plans for a business combination. Each of the corporations has one class of common stock outstanding; Bar also has one class of preferred stock outstanding. Although terms have not as yet been settled, Kessler will be the acquiring or issuing corporation. Because the directors want to conform to generally accepted accounting principles, they have asked you to attend the meeting as an advisor.

Required:

Consider each of the following questions independently of the others, and answer each in accordance with generally accepted accounting principles. Explain your answers.

a. Assume that the combination will be consummated August 31, 1983. Explain the philosophy underlying the accounting and how the balance sheet accounts of each of the four corporations will appear on Kessler's consolidated balance sheet on September 1, 1983 if the combination is accounted for as a
(1) Pooling of interests.
(2) Purchase.

b. Assume that the combination will be consummated August 31, 1983. Explain how the income-statement accounts of each of the four corporations will be accounted for in preparing Kessler's consolidated income statement for the year ended December 31, 1983 if the combination is accounted for as a
(1) Pooling of interests.
(2) Purchase.

c. Some of the directors believe that the terms of the combination should be agreed upon immediately and that the method of accounting to be used (whether pooling-of-interests, purchase, or a mixture) may be chosen at some later date. Others believe that the terms of the combination and the method to be used are very closely related. Which position is correct?

d. Kessler and Mason are comparable in size; Cohen and Bar are much smaller. How do these facts affect the choice of accounting method?

e. Bar was formerly a subsidiary of Tucker Corporation, which has no other relationship to any of the four companies discussing combination. Eighteen months ago Tucker voluntarily spun off Bar. What effect, if any, do these facts have on the choice of accounting method?

f. Kessler holds 2,000 of Bar's 10,000 outstanding shares of preferred stock and 15,000 of Cohen's 100,000 outstanding shares of common stock. All of Kessler's holdings were acquired during the first three months of 1983. What effect, if any, do these facts have on the choice of accounting method?

g. It is almost certain that Mrs. Victor Mason, Sr., who holds 5 percent of Mason's common stock, will object to the combination. Assume that Kessler is able to acquire only 95 percent (rather than 100 percent) of Mason's stock, issuing Kessler common stock in exchange.
(1) Which accounting method is applicable?
(2) If Kessler is able to acquire the remaining 5 percent at some future time—in five years, for instance—in exchange for its own common stock, which accounting method will be applicable to this second acquisition?

h. Since the directors believe that one of Mason's major divisions will not be compatible with the operations of the combined company, they anticipate that it will be sold as soon as possible after the combination is consummated. They expect to have no trouble in finding a buyer. What effect, if any, do these facts have on the choice of accounting method?

Question 20–4

When a business combination is effected by an exchange of common stock, the transaction is accounted for as a purchase or as a pooling of interests, depending upon the circumstances. The methods are not optional, and each yields significantly different results as to financial position and results of operations.

Required:

Discuss the *supportive* arguments for each of the following:
a. Purchase method.

b. Pooling-of-interests method.

Do *not* discuss in your answer the rules for distinguishing between a purchase and a pooling of interests.

Question 20–5

Hanover Company and Case Company, both of whom have only voting common stock, are considering a merger whereby Hanover would be the surviving company. The terms of the combination provide that the transaction would be carried out by Hanover exchanging one share of its stock for two shares of Case's stock. Before the date of the contemplated exchange, Hanover had purchased 5 percent of Case's stock, which it holds as an investment. Case, at the same date, owns 2 percent of Hanover's stock. All of the remaining outstanding stock of Case will be acquired by Hanover in this contemplated exchange. Neither of the two companies has ever had any affiliation as a subsidiary or division of any other company.

Required:

a. Without enumerating specific criteria, how is a determination made as to whether a business combination is accounted for as a pooling of interests or as a purchase?

b. Based only on the facts above, discuss the specific criteria that would qualify or disqualify this business combination as being accounted for as a pooling of interests.

c. What additional requirements (other than those discussed in *b* above) must be met in order to account for this business combination as a pooling of interests?

Earnings per share

Question 20–6

The earnings per share data required of a company depend on the nature of its capital structure. A corporation may have a simple capital structure and only compute earnings per common share or may have a complex capital structure and have to compute primary earnings per share and fully diluted earnings per share.

Required:

   a. Define the term *common stock equivalent* and describe what securities would be considered common stock equivalents in the computation of earnings per share.

   b. Define the term *complex capital structure* and discuss the disclosures (both financial and explanatory) necessary for earnings per share when a corporation has a complex capital structure.

Question 20–7

   APB Opinion No. 15 discusses the concept of common stock equivalents and prescribes the reporting of primary earnings per share and fully diluted earnings per share.

Required:

   a. Discuss the reasons securities other than common stock may be considered common stock equivalents for the computation of primary earnings per share.

   b. Define the term *senior security,* and explain how senior securities that are not convertible enter into the determination of earnings per share data.

   c. Explain how convertible securities are determined to be common stock equivalents and how those convertible senior securities that are not considered to be common stock equivalents enter into the determination of earnings per share data.

   d. Explain the treasury-stock method as it applies to options and warrants in computing primary earnings per share data.

Question 20–8

   Earnings per share (EPS) is the most featured single financial statistic about modern corporations. Daily published quotations of stock prices have recently been expanded to include a times earnings figure for many securities, which is based on EPS. Often the focus of analysts' discussions will be on the EPS of the corporations receiving their attention.

Required:

   a. Explain how dividends or dividend requirements on any class of preferred stock that may be outstanding affect the computation of EPS.

   b. One of the technical procedures applicable in EPS computations is the treasury-stock method.
   (1) Briefly describe the circumstances under which it might be appropriate to apply the treasury-stock method.
   (2) There is a limit to the extent to which the treasury-stock method is applicable. Indicate what this limit is, and give a succinct indication of the procedures that should be followed beyond the treasury-stock limits.

   c. Under some circumstances convertible debentures would be considered common stock equivalents, and under other circumstances they would not be.

(1)   When is it proper to treat convertible debentures as common stock equivalents? What is the effect on computation of EPS in such cases?

(2)   In case convertible debentures are not considered as common stock equivalents, explain how they are handled for purposes of EPS computations.

CHAPTER 21: DISCLOSURE IN FINANCIAL REPORTING

Interim financial reporting

Question 21–1

Timely financial information is important to users of financial statements. As a result, many companies produce financial information more frequently than annually.

Required:

a.   How are revenues, costs and expenses recognized for interim reporting related to those recognized for year-end reporting?

b.   How are income taxes recognized at interim dates?

Question 21–2

Interim financial reporting has become an important topic in accounting. There has been considerable discussion as to the proper method of reflecting results of operations at interim dates. Accordingly, the Accounting Principles Board issued an opinion clarifying some aspects of interim financial reporting.

Required:

a.   Discuss generally how revenue should be recognized at interim dates and specifically how revenue should be recognized for industries subject to large seasonal fluctuations in revenue and for long-term contracts using the percentage-of-completion method at annual reporting dates.

b.   Discuss generally how product and period costs should be recognized at interim dates. Also discuss how inventory and cost of goods sold may be afforded special accounting treatment at interim dates.

c.   Discuss how the provision for income taxes is computed and reflected in interim financial statements.

Accounting changes

Question 21–3

Accounting Principles Board Opinion No. 20 is concerned with accounting changes.

Required:

a.   Define, discuss, and illustrate each of the following in such a way that one can be distinguished from the other:

(1) An accounting change.

(2) A correction of an error in previously issued financial statements.

b. Discuss the justification for a change in accounting principle.

c. Discuss the reporting (as required by *Accounting Principles Board Opinion No. 20*) of a change from the LIFO method to another method of inventory pricing.

Question 21–4

Sometimes a business entity may change its method of accounting for certain items. The change may be classified as a change in accounting principle, a change in accounting estimate, or a change in reporting entity.

Listed below are three independent, *unrelated* sets of facts relating to accounting changes.

Situation 1

A company determined that the depreciable lives of its fixed assets are presently too long to fairly match the cost of the fixed assets with the revenue produced. The company decided at the beginning of the current year to reduce the depreciable lives of all of its existing fixed assets by five years.

Situation 2

On December 31, 1976 Gary Company owned 51 percent of Allen Company, at which time Gary reported its investment using the cost method due to political uncertainties in the country in which Allen was located. On January 2, 1977 the management of Gary Company was satisfied that the political uncertainties were resolved and the assets of the company were in no danger of nationalization. Accordingly, Gary will prepare consolidated financial statements for Gary and Allen for the year ended December 31, 1977.

Situation 3

A company decides in January 1977 to adopt the straight-line method of depreciation for plant equipment. The straight-line method will be used for new acquisitions as well as for previously acquired plant equipment for which depreciation had been provided on an accelerated basis.

Required:

For each of the situations described above, provide the information indicated below. Complete your discussion of each situation before going on to the next situation.

a. Type of accounting change.

b. Manner of reporting the change under current generally accepted accounting principles including a discussion, where applicable, of how amounts are computed.

c. Effect of the change on the statement of financial position and earnings statement.

d. Footnote disclosures that would be necessary.

Segment reporting

Question 21-5

Part a. In order to properly understand current generally accepted accounting principles with respect to accounting for and reporting upon segments of a business enterprise, as stated by the Financial Accounting Standards Board in its *Statement 14,* it is necessary to be familiar with certain unique terminology.

Required:

With respect to segments of a business enterprise, explain the following terms:
(1) *Industry segment.*
(2) *Revenue.*
(3) *Operating profit and loss.*
(4) *Identifiable assets.*

Part b. A central issue in reporting on industry segments of a business enterprise is the determination of which segments are reportable.

Required:

(1) What are the tests to determine whether or not an industry segment is reportable?
(2) What is the test to determine if enough industry segments have been separately reported upon and what is the guideline on the maximum number of industry segments to be shown?

INDEX

A

This book has been set VIP, in 10 and 9 point Century Schoolbook, leaded 2 points. Chapter numbers and titles are 18 point Century Schoolbook. The size of the type page is 31 by 48 picas.